ARAB AND JEW, THEY SHARED A SINGLE PURPOSE
—TO POSSESS THE AMERICAN GUNS . . .

Somewhere on the other side of Roger Williams Park, a factory siren blew noon. Herschel saw Wilbur Burns walking toward the carousel. He had his hands in his pockets and his shoulders were hunched.

At the same moment, a slim Arab came around the corner. From his vantage point behind the tree, Herschel scrutinized the Arab's features—low, dark hairline, thin nose, wide mouth and weak chin.

Herschel squeezed his eyes shut and opened them again, expecting the hallucination to vanish.

It didn't. The Arab looked exactly as he had the day Herschel watched him enter the coffeehouse in Jerusalem.

The Arab shook hands with Wilbur. In faintly accented English, he said, "I'm so glad you have accepted our offer."

"Well, you know how it is," Burns stammered, obviously stalling. "Fifty thousand is a lot of money. You people must want my design something awful."

"Of course we value your work, Mr. Burns," the Arab replied, eyeing the gunsmith. "However, as I mentioned to you on the telephone, what is most important to us is your guarantee that the other interested party will *not* receive—"

The man froze as Herschel stepped from behind the tree.

Glancing sorrowfully at Wilbur, the Arab took several quick steps to separate himself from the gunsmith and then focused his attention on Herschel.

"It is you and I once again, my old friend," he muttered. "Always, I suppose, it shall be you and I. . ."

FRED LAWRENCE
ISRAEL

Miles Standish Press

Published by
Miles Standish Press, Inc.
353 West Lancaster Avenue
Wayne, Pennsylvania 19087

Dell ® TM 681510, Dell Publishing Co., Inc.

ISBN: 0-440-03842-1

First printing—December 1984

4 3 2 1

Printed in the United States of America

For my wife Marjorie and my friends and professional colleagues, Albert Zuckerman and Ed Claflin.

Thanks for believing in a dream begun, deferred, renewed.

Prologue

Israel, 1949

The silvery TWA Clipper banked like a hungry bird of prey over the sun-dappled Mediterranean. The big airliner's four prop-driven engines changed in pitch as the plane began its descent over the sandy dunes and pastel sprawl of Tel Aviv.

"We'll be landing at Lydda in just a few minutes," announced the haggard-looking stewardess as she lurched and swayed the length of the first-class cabin. "Please extinguish all cigarettes—"

"You've made a mistake," the stylishly dressed woman in her thirties said as the stewardess passed her.

"Pardon me?" the young stewardess asked, startled.

"It's not Lydda, it's Lod," Rebecca Pickman corrected her, stubbing out the remains of her Lucky Strike. "It's called Lod now that it's ours."

Rebecca, her large brown eyes steadfast, watched as the pink blush of confusion began at the stewardess' throat and rose to suffuse her ivory features. The stewardess, nodding, said, "Yes, of course—Lod," then continued down the aisle.

1

Rebecca chuckled, turning her attention back to the window to gaze at the dark green citrus groves and the patchwork of cultivated fields that rushed up at her as the Clipper lowered its landing gear and swooped down toward the airport. She was exhausted but exhilarated. Her journey had begun days ago in New York. The transatlantic leg of the trip was a nine-hour stomach-lurching battle between screaming headwinds and roaring, defiant engines; it ended in defeat when the plane was forced to make a detour to Ireland's Shannon Airport in order to take on fuel. The unscheduled stop before they could continue to Paris was to stretch into a delay of several hours due to inclement weather.

It was during this predawn hiatus that Rebecca, her courage already stretched to the breaking point by the long, bumpy flight, wondered if she wasn't being a fool by coming in the first place.

It's been so long since we've seen each other, she thought, watching the fog streak tears down the windows of Shannon's waiting lounge. So much has happened. What if we're not the same people?

The mist abruptly turned to a pelting rain that rattled the window panes. Rebecca, shivering against the damp, wrapped her cashmere coat around her shoulders. Her fingers nervously stroked the rich, soft fabric. Luxury had become her shield. It was luxury, won by her intelligence and determination, that had allowed her to blossom into an attractive, desirable woman. She was still young, but much had happened in her brief life. The immigrant shopkeeper's daughter had managed to transform herself from a poor drab creature into a radiant butterfly. She had risen to the top of her profession; she had been loved; and yet—

Rebecca Pickman, shivering like a waif in that Irish airport, listened to the rain, stared at the nicotine stains on her trembling fingers, brushed at her mahogany hair frizzing in the clammy weather and wondered if it hadn't all been a horrid joke on her. Tired, alone in a strange country and at a crossroads in her life, Rebecca was suddenly overwhelmed with the urge to give up this crazy pilgrimage to the newborn State of Israel and return to New York. If she didn't, in Israel she would become that drab shopkeeper's daughter all over again.

She didn't know what she might have done if that driving rain had continued, but it stopped, and then miraculously the mists began to lighten. In a matter of minutes Rebecca could see a bright morning sun. The boarding announcement was made and the flight went on to Paris, where a long hot soak in a tub and a good night's sleep in her favorite hotel restored her for the next leg of her journey, to Greece.

Rebecca started and then relaxed, realizing that what she'd just felt was the blessed bump of the Clipper's tires kissing the concrete of the runway. It seemed to her that the plane was going faster on the ground than it ever had in the air, but gradually it slowed and then began to taxi toward the low-slung barracks that housed arrivals and Customs.

At last the Clipper came to a halt, and one by one the propellers stopped spinning. The door swung open and Rebecca caught a glimpse of a flawlessly blue sky framed by the open portal. Then she was hurrying down the steep staircase to the ground.

The first thing to hit her was the warmth of the day, more than a little disconcerting after the still-raw spring in America and Europe. But then, she expected it to be warm. She thought of the last letter she had before she left.

No, it is not all like the desert you have seen in the movies. Come and I will show you pine trees on the slopes of Mount Carmel and snow on the peaks of Upper Galilee. I will show you forests of cypress and fragrant eucalyptus, acres of grapefruits hanging from leafy boughs like yellow balloons, olive groves like the ones in Greece, rivers winding through mighty rock formations like America's Grand Canyon, multi-colored carpets of wildflowers, and song birds like maybe in heaven itself.

There Rebecca noticed that his hand's bold blue stroke suddenly grew faint, the way his voice characteristically did when his own depth of feeling surprised him.

Come, Becky, and I will show you where our people began. Come home to Israel, Becky. Come home to me.

And here she was, tottering down the steps, her cashmere coat over her arm, an oddity in this land of khaki shirts and shorts. She had been drawn here not by one letter but by a chain of them, letters that came every day and left her hungry, yearning for word from him if ever one was delayed.

Now as she surveyed the airport and its Hebraic signposts, glistening like wet paint, as she stared out at the milling sea of khaki, she felt like a visitor to another planet. Now she wished she had his letters in her hands as a talisman against her insecurity the way her fine coat was a talisman. She was on the threshold of new experience. Rebecca knew this would be nothing like her posh life in New York, not even like her humble beginnings on the Lower East Side.

His letters were right on one count at least; Israel was like no other place on earth. But if it was to be her home—well, she would see.

"Mrs. Pickman?"

Rebecca turned, not easy in the midst of the crowd milling toward Baggage and Customs. The man hailing her—the boy, actually, for he looked too young to order a drink in New York City—bowed respectfully.

"I am in charge of Customs. There is no need for you to wait in line. Please follow me."

Rebecca did, feeling vaguely self-conscious at this special treatment. In New York she had come to expect it as her due, but here in the pioneer land of Israel she felt she was cheating at a new game.

"If you'll hand over your baggage check, I will see to your luggage." The customs official steered her toward a quiet gate. When they reached its desk, he stamped her passport. Smiling, he reached for her cashmere coat. "You won't be needing that. It'll be safe with your luggage."

Rebecca handed it over, feeling a faint twinge of panic. Suddenly she felt stripped of her past. Good-bye luxury. Here she was just another shopkeeper's daughter in a land spawned by shopkeepers.

The thought was fleeting, for Rebecca's attention was transfixed by the sight of a flag hoisted high and fluttering in the hot, dry breeze. It was a white banner with two horizontal blue bars, the ancient colors of the tallith, the prayer shawl. Between the two bars was the Mogen David, the six-pointed star, the symbol of Jewish life popular for over three hundred years in Central Europe.

The shield of David had no religious significance; it spoke for the physical reality of the Jews' existence on earth. The new Jewish nation could have chosen no other symbol.

"You look at it like you can't believe it is real, Mrs. Pickman," the young customs officer softly chided. "You of all people should know that it is real. You worked hard enough and gave enough money and speeches to make it so."

Rebecca felt her eyes grow wet. "Who knew I was telling the truth?" she laughed.

"Oh, you were telling the truth." He nodded, grinning.

"We have our own flag, our own passports, our own money, our own military, even our own language, Hebrew." He winked at her. "Which you must learn in order to fit in—"

"That'll be the day," she said. What she thought was, If I want to fit in. Who knows if I'm staying?

She was nervously reaching for her cigarettes when she heard a familiar voice call out, "Becky!" She was dimly aware of the Customs clerk beaming as she began to hurry toward the man who had summoned her to this strange land.

As Rebecca ran, she kept her eyes on the ground. To see him from a distance was useless; she would only know if everything was all right when she could touch him, when she could see herself reflected in his eyes. Only then would she know if she was truly home.

"Becky!"

She sensed him moving toward her. She wouldn't look at him, not until they embraced, and then she'd know.

As she ran, Rebecca Pickman could not help thinking about the pageant of history and all that she had personally won and lost to bring her to this moment.

PART I

DREAMS BEGUN

Chapter 1

New York, 1910

Abe Herodetzky woke to the sound of a squalling child.
He groped for his pocket watch and matches on the fruit
crate that served as his nightstand. Squinting against the
glare of the match, he saw that it was a quarter to five in
the morning.

No great shame, Abe thought in Russian. I'd have to
be up for work in a few minutes anyway. "No big deal,"
he yawned out loud in thickly accented English.

He used the last of the match to light a stub of candle
and took a moment to stare up at the cracked, blistered
ceiling plaster. He had been dreaming of the past, of his
arrival in America. Tattered fragments of his dream still
lingered. The oil-dark choppy waters of the bay, the scud-
ding clouds as grey as a Russian winter, the coppery
towers of Ellis Island—the remnants of the dream teased
him but refused to come quite clear.

Abe kicked away his tattered blanket. The dream
faded as he cursed the chill in the Montgomery Street
tenement. He climbed out of the rickety cot, stretching and
scratching his pale, spindly body beneath his nightshirt.

The baby was still crying in the kitchen. He wished the parents would do something to quiet it, but he dared not complain. A boarder had few rights.

Every day more and more newcomers were flooding into New York. All of them needed a place to stay until they got jobs and learned their way around a little. Abe knew Joseph and Sadie could throw him out and find a new boarder in a matter of minutes. He also knew that this room, tiny as it was, with its single window opening onto an airshaft, was a veritable blessing. A private room, even a closet in disguise, was a rarity.

Three short paces and he was at the airshaft window. On the sill was the jar of water filled at the kitchen sink the night before. He poured the lukewarm water into a tin basin and washed. Next he turned his attention to his one luxury, an expensive ivory-handled straight razor. He honed the gleaming blade and then carefully shaved. It was a bold thing to do, shaving. The sight of his smooth cheeks often provoked disapproving glares in the neighborhood. God's displeasure hung heavy on Abe's shoulders.

But this was not the old country, he reminded himself. He was in America and he would be clean-shaven like an American.

He dressed quickly in his baggy blue suit, stained white shirt buttoned to the neck with no tie. He smoothed down his thinning thatch of dark brown hair as best he could, dumped the basin of water out the window, extinguished the candle and left his room.

The Montgomery Street tenement was like all the others Abe had boarded in on the Lower East Side. There were four flats to a floor, with one hall toilet.

Abe's room opened onto the kitchen. Here illumination was provided by the ever-flickering gas mantle. There was a gas stove, cupboards for groceries and blue-curtained closets where clothing and the two sets of dishes and cookware were stored.

In addition to a table and chairs the kitchen had two tiers of bunkbeds for the children. Between the rusty sink and the stove was wedged a couch where Joseph and Sadie slept. More beds occupied the front parlor of the flat for Sadie's parents and her younger sister, an eighteen-year-old named Leah.

Area rugs covered the worn floorboards of the kitchen, which had tattered pink floral wallpaper. A yellow plucked chicken hung from a washboard across the sink, heavily salted to leach out the blood, which steadily dripped into the drain.

The kitchen was quiet except for the baby at the foot of the couch. The other children were still sleeping, oblivious to the noise. The curtain was still across the threshold that separated the parlor from the kitchen. Joseph sat at the kitchen table spooning oatmeal into his mouth between sips of tea. There was a place setting laid for Abe. His two dollars a week bought breakfast each morning and dinner with the family at night.

Sadie, stirring the pot of oatmeal on the stove, glared at Abe's clean-shaven features. She was a heavy-set sallow woman and a fiercely pious Jew. She took it as a personal affront that Abe defied the Book of Leviticus' ban against shaving. Late at night, when they thought Abe was asleep, Sadie and Joseph discussed their boarder's many shortcomings, or rather Sadie discussed and her husband listened.

Joseph was as big and strong as an ox and just as patient with his wife's constant nagging. Now his strong white teeth were startling against his glossy black beard as he grinned good morning to Abe, who seated himself at the table. Joseph's work clothes were stained with old blood. He worked, to Sadie's everlasting mortification, in a nonkosher slaughterhouse on the West Side, by the part of the Hudson known as the North River.

"It's Friday," Sadie announced in Yiddish. "Tonight starts Sabbath." She put a bowl of oatmeal before Abe and drew him a mug of tea from the steaming samovar on one corner of the stove. "Don't forget, if you want to eat, be home before sundown."

"He's not a goy that he has to be told it's the Sabbath," Joseph muttered.

"He should also know not to shave," Sadie replied.

"He wants to be a sport, let him."

"Let him . . ." Sadie echoed with infinite sadness. She went to the sink. There she took up a cleaver and began to hack away at the chicken with silent, furious eloquence.

Abe said nothing, but ate as quickly as he could. They were talking about him as if he were a child, but he could do little about it. He had to answer to these two the way they had to answer to their landlord.

Joseph stood up, ready to leave for work, but Sadie reminded him that he had to take the *tsholnt*. Down he sat as she took vegetables from the cupboard and set to work assembling the stew pot for her husband to carry to the nearby bakery. Many families would take similar pots so they could slowly cook in the baker's ovens for twenty-four hours. Tomorrow afternoon Joseph would bring it home for the Sabbath meal.

Abe took a deep breath to steel himself for a storm. "I must work tomorrow," he said.

"Shit," Joseph grumbled in his deep voice. Curse words made up the whole of his English vocabulary. The Kraviches had been in America twice as long as Abe, but the study of English—like so many things—was "not for them." Abe, on the other hand, had early on begun to frequent the university settlement on the corner of Eldridge and Rivington.

"In my house I don't need a boarder who doesn't go to shul, who shaves, who like a Polack desecrates the Sabbath." Sadie chopped at thin air with her cleaver. "Joseph, tell him this can't go on."

One of the children, disturbed his mother's fury, turned in his sleep. He was the oldest boy, who slept in the top bunk; it creaked and swayed with his movement like a willow in the wind. Sadie steadied the top-heavy tier, affectionately brushing back the comma of hair that had fallen across her slumbering child's forehead.

"If you won't throw this desecrator out for me, do it for your son," she demanded. "He'll be influenced by Abe's behavior—wait and see."

Abe felt sick to his stomach. The other day Joseph and his eldest son had quarreled over the boy's having skipped his Hebrew lessons in favor of playing stickball. It was not surprising. The street was filling up with immigrants of many backgrounds, and the children not having enough of their own kind to make friends with, freely mixed together, much to the displeasure of everyone's parents. This had nothing to do with Abe, but he knew that he would suffer if Sadie succeeded in convincing her husband that his son was under a bad influence from him.

Sadie, eyes gleaming with triumph, strutted from the kitchen into the parlor, where her parents and younger sister still snoozed.

"She's a *balebossteh*, eh?" Joseph chuckled shyly. His thick, callused thumbs drummed the tabletop.

Abe anxiously waited for his sentence to be passed. *Balebossteh* was literally "praiseworthy wife," but it implied bossiness. Abe had a sinking feeling he would be packing his cardboard suitcase by nightfall.

Joseph took papers and tobacco from his shirt pocket and rolled a cigarette. Sadie disapproved of smoking, but concerning some things Joseph put his foot down. Accordingly, Sadie restricted herself to silently pursing her lips in displeasure whenever he lit up.

Time passed as Joseph smoked. Occasionally he would tap the ash into the palm of his hand and then rub it onto the brown-stained green knees of his work pants. Finally

he took on a look of decision. "I don't need such aggrava-
tion in my home." He puffed on his cigarette.

Abe did not know how to respond. "More money?"
He cringed at the thought of paying more, but rooms were
hard to come by. "If a little more money might make
amends—"

Joseph shook his head. "You desecrate the Sabbath."

"I've got to work tomorrow," Abe insisted. "The
factory uses goyim as well as Jews. The Polacks and the
Italians don't mind working a Saturday—or a Sunday, for
that matter. If I refuse, I'd lose the work."

"What's better, to lose a shift or to lose the room?"

"Don't do this to me," Abe implored, furious at the
begging note he heard in his voice. That I should have to
crawl on my knees to this blood-smeared dolt, he thought,
but still he was careful to keep his tone and manner meek.
"Three months I've lived here, Joseph. You already know
why I work a double shift." He smiled encouragingly.

"To save money for a business of your own." Joseph
nodded impatiently. "Ambition is an admirable thing, but
why does it have to destroy the peace in my home?"

Abe tried to reply, but Joseph held up his hand to
silence him. "Listen to me a moment, if you please. Your
story I know by heart." He looked disgusted. "I also
happen to know that you are no closer to your dream than
you were when you landed two years ago."

"I've saved money," Abe replied, sullen.

"Yes, you have, but meanwhile the real estate has
grown dearer and you've grown older. When you landed
you were thirty-two. Now you're thirty-four."

"So?" Abe demanded.

"So when are you going to take for yourself a wife?
When do the children come?" He waited, smoking his
cigarette.

Abe's eyes were downcast. "After."

"After what?" Joseph scowled. "Your funeral maybe." He paused and his voice softened. "Listen to me. I'm talking to you like a friend. That sweatshop you slave in from dawn until dusk seven days a week manufactures suit coats; it manufactures pants and vests. Millionaires it doesn't manufacture."

"Others have done it—"

"In Russia you were a cobbler. You could take a nice job as a cobbler here," Joseph argued. "Then you could get married, have children, be a mensch."

"Joseph, please," Abe groaned.

Joseph glanced toward the curtain that separated the kitchen from the parlor. Behind it his wife was undoubtedly eavesdropping. "You make it so hard for yourself, Abe. If you make trouble with Sadie, I've got to throw you out, right? Every night she complains to me the same thing. You come home, you eat, you go into your room and you read your newspapers until you go to sleep. You never offer to watch the baby for her and you never so much as look at her sister Leah." He offered Abe a conspiratorial wink. "Leah is fond of you. Sadie told me so. Ask her to marry you. She'll accept, of that I can assure you."

"No doubt," Abe murmured.

"What?" Joseph sharply demanded.

"Oh, be reasonable," Abe complained. "If I married now, I'd have to support a family. It would be good-bye to my store." He leapt to his feet and dashed into his room for his overcoat. "I'm late for work. We'll talk more about this tonight," he called over his shoulder, heading for the door and beginning to think that he might make good his escape.

"Joseph?" Sadie stormed into the kitchen. Her voice was high and shrill. "Joseph!"

"Enough!" Joseph glowered at her. "Abe, tonight you will pack your bags and look for another room."

Abe slumped against the doorjamb. "Please," he

whispered. "Today I work a full day. Where can I find a room on Sabbath eve?"

"All of a sudden he's pious," Sadie sneered.

"Enough, I said." Joseph turned back to his boarder. "All right, you can stay until tomorrow night."

Abe nodded. "Thank you."

"That'll make a full week. I'll owe you no refund."

"Agreed."

"And what about the Sabbath?" Sadie asked pointedly.

"His last day here let him do what he wants."

"That's just dandy." Sadie frowned. "I see now that my wishes count for nothing."

"Tomorrow we will rent to a nice single young man, the sort who can appreciate the bride a girl like Leah would be."

"Talk a little louder, why don't you," Sadie reproached him. "Let the poor girl hear and be humiliated." But the anger had left Sadie. The deal had been struck.

She started as Abe let the apartment door slam shut behind him. "Good riddance," she muttered, returning to her cooking.

Abe stomped down the tenement's ill-lit, narrow stairs. He was ashamed and angry. The shame came from the way he'd allowed himself to beg; the rage sprang from the way he had been refused.

Be a cobbler, Joseph told him, a shoemaker—as if he'd journeyed to America and started a new life merely to ply the trade forced upon his family by the Russian nobleman who owned their village in the Ukraine. A sign of defeat it would be to go back to a cobbler's bench here in America. A cobbler could never be rich. A shoemaker could hand nothing to his son but his hammer and nails.

Despair threatened to engulf him as he stepped out onto the littered stoop and the cold predawn air bit into him. It would help if he could say the room was a sty fit only for pigs. But he knew the room was a prize, a blessing, even with Sadie's mouth. He'd be lucky if he was able to find something half as nice.

He buttoned his coat and turned up his collar against the cold. Abe's breath hung in front of his face, a cloud of white vapor like the puffs of steam that rose from his pressing machine at the factory loft on Allen Street.

The overcoat was too large. It flapped about his gaunt frame like a bathrobe. As he walked he pulled down his cuffs and shoved his hands into his coat pockets to hold it close to his body and keep the wind from whistling up his baggy sleeves.

He headed toward East Broadway, giving wide berth to the towering stands of garbage lining both sides of Montgomery Street. Now and then a rat, made bold by the darkness, streaked across his path.

The cold numbed his ears as he crossed Henry Street. He'd given up wearing hats. Going hatless, like shaving, was a gesture to honor his adopted country. Although Abe would be loath to admit it, he was trying to mold himself into the image of the wealthy Jewish philanthropists he'd learned about at the settlement house: Warburg, Schiff, Lewisjohn and the fabulous Straus brothers, benefactors of the Educational Alliance, sponsors of the milk stations where hungry children and expectant mothers could find nourishment—and most important to Abe, owners of magnificent stores: R.H. Macy on Fourteenth Street near Sixth Avenue and Abraham & Straus in Brooklyn.

"I should have mentioned the Straus brothers to Joseph," Abe muttered to himself. "Not that he wouldn't have laughed in my face." He savagely booted a tin can out of his path.

These great men were all German Jews, *Yekkes* to the Russian immigrants, who considered them as strange as the colored Jews who were said to live in the Orient. The Russians envied the Yekkes for their wealth and distrusted them for their Americanized ways. Abe himself often felt

uneasy about how much like the Goyim the Yekkes seemed
to act.

He, of course, would not act that way. When he was
rich, he would not pretend to be something he was not. He
would loudly proclaim his thanks to God. The rabbi would
shake his hand for donating the funds to make a proper
Hebrew school in the cellar of the synagogue. His shaving
and going without a hat would be waved away as the
trifling offenses they were. Abe considered himself a realist;
he knew that in America, as in Russia, money in a man's
pocket excused him from much obligation and condemnation.

A harsh, cutting wind along East Broadway brought
tears to his eyes and blew away his reveries. Here he
joined the press of other weary, hunched, coughing men
who trudged like slaves through the predawn twilight toward their sweatshop jobs.

I am growing old, Abe thought, just like Joseph said.
Two years of scrimping and saving and I am still far from
my goal.

Abe passed a synagogue and briefly thought about
stopping in that evening; the shul was a good place to find
out if anybody had a room to rent. He decided against it.
He went to shul only on the High Holy Days. Abe's
bargain with God specified that he would use the time that
might have been spent in shul working and studying to
better himself. Then when he was rich, he would make it
up to the Lord.

It was a covenant communicated more in thought than
in words. Still, it allowed Abe to sleep with a clear
conscience. Better to keep the deal by staying away from
the shul altogether than to insult God by going there for a
reason other than prayer.

Should I have agreed to court Leah? Abe wondered.
Perhaps he was being too stubborn in defying them—and
losing for himself such a nice room.

Abe paused at a newspaper stand, a collection of milk

crates with the periodicals held down by bricks, and bought the one Yiddish newspaper he allowed himself. He preferred to read the English papers to strengthen his grasp of the language, but every day Abe picked up a copy of the *Vorwärts*, the *Forward*. He did not pause to scan its front page but tucked the paper into his overcoat and hurried on across East Broadway onto Attorney Street.

His thoughts returned to Leah, Sadie's eighteen-year-old sister. She was a sweet girl, not at all like Sadie. Leah was slight of build and very docile and quiet. But maybe they were all like that before marriage. Abe mused. Who knew? He considered himself a moral man; he did not run with the tarts to be had at the red-lantern houses on Rivington Street. He knew very little about women and was by turns proud and wistful over that fact, depending on his mood. One thing he knew: a wife could help in the store—*if he ever got the store, that is*.

He reached Delancey Street, where the awnings of the dark locked shops drooped like sleepy eyelids and the pushcarts chained to the lamp posts awaited their peddler owners. The wind carried the aroma of *challah* bread baking for the Sabbath, then the breeze changed direction and the odor of spoiled fish discarded in an alley assaulted Abe.

Of course with a wife eventually came children. The appearance of the first-born a year after the marriage was an inevitability, else tongues in the neighborhood would start to wag. When Abe envisioned his offspring he saw a strapping boy as bright as the noon sun, a boy to make a father proud, a young man properly appreciative of the thriving business his father would one day hand over to him. Abe conceded the possibility of daughters. That was all right, for girls could bring much joy to a father, but it was the sons who counted.

Abe's musings about his children always began when they'd reached adolescence. He was aware that infancy

and childhood were stages in a person's life, and he could
be patient for his children to pass through these stages as
long as they didn't dawdle. But let their mother play with
them.

Frivolity was not in Abe's nature. He lived for the
day when he could present his son with all that he had
accomplished and see the light of admiration in his boy's
eyes. If there were daughters, they too could smile, for
their father's success would assure them of good matrimonial matches.

By now all along Delancey the horse-drawn ash carts
had appeared to haul away the previous day's rubbish. As
Abe walked toward Allen Street he carefully perused each
storefront, thinking about how he would rearrange this
window display of fabric or that one with its racks of suits
for men and boys. Every morning on his way to work he
lovingly inspected the closed shops on Delancey, Orchard and
Hester Streets and coveted the better ones. It inspired him
to do a good day's work. To see why he was slaving away
his last precious youth made the thought of the long day
ahead endurable.

Another year, perhaps, and it could be yours, he told
himself. Something good will happen, you will see. You
are working hard, and so God will see to it.

Still, without a miracle, Abe knew, it would more
likely be another two years before he had enough money
saved, and that was if the work remained steady and he
managed to find the strength to continue working a seven-
day double shift.

If only Leah's parents were not poor, Abe thought,
but a man in his circumstances could not expect a girl with
a dowry. If Leah's father were rich his last daughter would
have been married long ago, and Sadie, for that matter,
would have made a far better match than Joseph. At the
very least their father could have bought doctors for his

daughters by promising the price of a medical education in exchange for marriage.

No, Abe could not hope to find a girl with money. He was too old and if the truth be known too homely to attract the notice of a wealthy girl. Even the plain ones could pick and choose a man if their fathers had money.

Leah was not plain. She had big brown eyes, high cheekbones and a shy way of laughing, the memory of which often came back to distract Abe late at night, while he was trying to study his English.

It did not occur to Abe to think he might be fond of Leah. Abe could not be comfortable with the thought of conjugal love. If he gave in to feelings, how could he survive the misery ahead?

To Abe the world was God's emporium, all transactions retail. God stood behind the counter and on the shelves were all the goods a man on earth could hope to earn. Everything had a price, and hard work, faith and sacrifice were the currency God demanded. Not marrying was part of the price Abe had to pay.

Abe hurried up Allen Street to the factory loft behind the Greek and Arab clubs and restaurants, which were quiet now but would spring to gaudy, exotic life come evening. Tonight when Abe left work there would be wild Oriental music coming from these forbidden places, and in the upstairs windows would appear glimpses of gyrating belly dancers, half-naked savage women who had an exciting and disturbing effect on Abe.

But that would be tonight, and tonight was many hours of piecework away. The minimum he was allowed to work was twelve hours; the most he'd ever put in at one stretch was eighteen. Tonight he would turn his head away from Allen Street's distractions for God to see that he was not interested.

It is a different bargain I wish to conclude with God, Abe thought as he climbed the nine steep flights of stairs to the loft. Here the heat of the many steam pressing machines made it seem like summer. Abe at once stripped off his overcoat, suit jacket and white shirt. Over by the toilets were rows of lockers where the men could store their clothes. For the rest of the day Abe and the other men would work in sleeveless undershirts.

The walls were dull green. The windows had been painted black to shield the place from the notice of the factory licensing inspectors. The tin ceiling was criss-crossed with steam and water pipes and laced with electrical wiring from which dangled bare bulbs. The loft's sagging scrap-littered wooden floor was divided into cutting, sewing and pressing areas. Puffy-eyed boys wearing knickers, their small, thin bodies still stiff with sleep, carted the cloth, linings and finished garments from area to area and finally to the freight elevator. Downstairs horses and trucks would take the merchandise uptown.

A year ago the ILGWU, the International Ladies' Garment Workers Union, had found the loft and organized it. The ILGWU employed special trackers who did nothing but hunt down the sweatshops infesting New York. There was talk among the workers of a general strike to be called that summer. All of them, including Abe, were fatalistic about it, but they hoped the strike wouldn't happen. There were stronger union shops than the one on Allen Street, the ones that employed workers of only one nationality. Here on Allen Street, where mostly Jews and Italians worked together, basic mistrust was born of different languages, different customs, even different foods. The Jews rolled their eyes at the Italians' wine and pork. The Italians and Poles wrinkled their noses at the Jews' herring.

There was some communication between the different ethnic groups; Allen Street was not entirely a Tower of Babel. For that the workers could thank Abe Herodetzky.

*   *   *

The day of the breakthrough started, as usual, at six in the morning. By nine, Abe, working his presser, enveloped in a cloud of moist steam that kept him slick with sweat, found his thoughts wandering. He could easily do his job without concentrating on it. Perhaps the heat made him silly, but on that day it came to him that he and his fellow workers were lost in a maze. It was only the swearing, shouting foreman who could see the way out.

Abe was on the verge of letting the thought drift out of his mind when on impulse he confided it in halting English to the Italian who worked the presser next to his. For months Abe and this Italian had worked side by side, but they had never done more than nod silently. After overcoming his initial surprise the Italian, a short, barrel-chested man with a big belly and tousled black curls as shiny as patent leather, smiled at Abe. Then he said something, but it was lost to Abe against the clattering din of the machines all around them.

That was all for two weeks, until one day at lunch-time the Italian left his usual place on the Italian side to approach Abe, who was sitting by himself, reading his copy of the *Forward*. The Italian asked him why he never brought food and Abe explained that he was saving his money, even to the extent of skipping lunch.

The Italian looked skeptical, but as he stared at Abe, he evidently realized it was the truth.

"My name is Stefano de Fazio," he said in rhythmic, plodding English. "My wife, she gives me too much to eat." He patted his ample stomach. "In here I got plenty chicken, bread and wine." He presented a crumpled, oil-stained paper sack to Abe. "You take some, yes?"

Abe did not find it easy to believe this was happening. He just stared as the Italian sat down beside him.

Stefano de Fazio misunderstood Abe's hesitation. "Hey, I know you a Jew," he commiserated, clapping Abe on the shoulder. He wagged his finger at the paper sack. "Just chicken, bread and wine. No pork." With that he reached into the parcel and produced a quart milk bottle half-filled with red wine. It had a wad of paper stuffed into its mouth where the cork was supposed to be.

Wine from an Italian Abe was not about to drink, especially not from a bottle that had been who-knew-where. He did have the presence of mind, however, to know that something momentous was taking place. It was something very American, and that was what decided him.

"My name's Abe Herodetzky. Pleased to meet you." He'd smiled, doing his best to make the Italian think he was a Broadway sport. He held out his hand and Stefano shook it.

Next Abe made the ultimate gesture. He ate the chicken, wolfed it down without chewing. Stefano thought Abe was eating that way because he was famished, but Abe feared he'd get nauseated if he allowed himself to taste Italian poultry.

They began to talk a little each day, always careful to stay away from matters of religion and custom. They discussed not their differences, but what they had in common: tenement life and the sweatshop.

Eventually the other workers followed their lead. So it was that a few months later, when the union discovered them, the Allen Street workers knew enough about each other grudgingly to accept the union's gospel.

Today, as the hour when most of the men quit work for lunch approached, Abe paused to add up his tally. It had been a productive morning. Abe decided that he would reward himself with a few extra minutes with his newspaper. In a sweatshop there was no set time for eating. Each worker could take as little or as much time as he wished as long as he completed his quota for the day. A man could eat when he wanted or work right through, but it always seemed that as soon as one man took out his food, so did the rest.

One by one the loft's machines grew quiet. Abe settled himself into a corner with his paper and his tin can of drinking water. He sipped the water to quiet his rumbling stomach. He'd grown used to sharing Stefano's lunch, but today the Italian was busy talking to his fellow countrymen.

Just as well, Abe thought. Lately Stefano had been making him a little nervous. The man was full of crazy union talk. Stefano was the shop's union representative and he took his position very seriously. Late at night clandestine union meetings were being held by ILGWU organizers, and Stefano attended them all and reported to the men of Allen Street. The latest report made it sound as if support for a strike was building.

This was especially ominous to Abe. What he feared most was a repetition of last year's strike. On September 27, 1909, the union shut down the Triangle Waist Factory on nearby Greene Street. The owners called in the police to break up the picket lines and a battle ensued. The result was a lengthy general sympathy strike that spread as far as Philadelphia.

Abe could not find within himself the courage to confront the stony-faced, club-wielding police with a picket sign, but he stayed out of work. The temptation to scab at twice the normal rate was awful, but he resisted. It was agony to sit idle and be forced to dip into his precious savings.

Last payday Stefano had collected two dollars from each man, "for a strike fund, just in case." Abe paid and fervently prayed that it would turn out to be money he would never again see. Let the union keep it. Just let things stay calm; let the work remain steady.

The *Forward* was spread open on his knees. Eagerly he scanned the columns for news of Palestine. To read

Israel

about that faraway place was the only reason he bought the Yiddish newspaper. He was not a Zionist, but he had a personal interest in what was taking place in Palestine. His best friend had chosen to go to *Eretz Yisroel* instead of America.

Chapter 2

Russia, 1876–1903

In the Ukraine even the youngest, most vigorous Jew must live like someone who is very old and fragile. Even the youngest must tread carefully, avoiding all confrontation, giving daily thanks to God for not sending a calamity to snuff out tenuous life.

Abe Herodetzky was born in 1876 in a large village south of Kiev. It was a place of black muddy streets and whitewashed cottages with thatched roofs the color of tarnished copper. There were often bright blue skies and always crimson hens pecking in the yards but also brutal winter cold and in summer swarms of stinging gnats. It was a place where the rural peace and quiet were deceptive, for death could come to a Jew as fast as the crack of a Cossack's whip.

Years ago an overlord owned the village and the people who lived in it and decreed that Abe's great-grandfather must become a cobbler. The trade was handed down and by the time Abe was sixteen he was accomplished at the bootmaker's craft.

Abe's mother died of a fever when he was eleven.

When Abe was fifteen his father died of a beating during one of the pogroms that periodically swept through the region.

Abe lived in the rear of the little cobbler's shop. He paid his taxes and did not have to worry about being conscripted into the czar's army until he turned twenty-one. He had already begun to put away money toward the day when he would have to begin paying an annual bribe to the military recruiter to mark him unfit for duty. For a Jew to pay a bribe was nothing unusual. They had fewer rights than any Christian did; therefore they depended on bribes as defense against the corrupt officials who ruled their lives.

One day a boy appeared in the doorway of Abe's shop. Where the child came from he was never able to say, but Abe later came to view this occurrence as God's way of adding a little sweet to the sour of his solitary life. One moment Abe was at his cobbler's bench skiving leather; the next he was looking up into the large blue eyes of a silent child.

"Yes?" Abe called out. "What is it?" He knew all the families in his village, and this ragamuffin did not look familiar. Of course, since the May laws took effect and forced the Jews to congregate in the larger towns, the Ukraine had been in turmoil. These were the worst of bad times, when previously well-to-do Jewish families, banished from their homes and stripped of their property, wandered like beggars.

The boy, no more than ten years old, had a freckled face and dirty blond hair. He was wearing a filthy tunic, torn trousers and rags wrapped around his feet in lieu of shoes.

"I asked you what you wanted," Abe snapped. His own youth had faded away with the death of his father. His young back was bent and his face creased into a permanent scowl. In the last year, since sitting shiva for his father, Abe had grown increasingly taciturn, bitter and

full of scorn for his fellow man. In Abe the idealism of youth
was early aborted by misfortune. He grew up with a heart
that had become gnarled and twisted as a tree on a barren,
wind-swept plain.

From the boy's ragged condition Abe could tell that
nobody took care of him. The child stood in the shop's
open doorway as if waiting for something, and when Abe
rose from his bench, he tensed to flee.

"Wait. I won't hurt you," Abe promised, slowly
approaching. "Come in."

The boy moved like an animal, all his senses on the
alert. He took a tentative step into the shop and then
backed out.

"What's your name?" Abe asked.

"Haim."

Abe nodded approvingly. It meant "life" in Hebrew.
"You have a last name?"

The boy thought about it a minute, then shrugged.

"A family perhaps? Parents? A sister, a brother?"

More silence, another shrug.

"So you are an orphan, like me."

Try as he might, the boy was afraid to enter the shop.
He kept thrusting his rag-wrapped foot across the threshold
and then pulling it back, like a swimmer testing the chill of
a pond.

Sighing, Abe went over to the boy and picked him
up. Haim began to whimper, but Abe put him on his own
bed and covered him. Haim yawned, and a few seconds
later was asleep.

I can't be more than six years older than he is, Abe
sadly marveled. What kind of world is this where I have to
play the father?

Abe knew what he was going to do, but still he
pretended to brood about his decision, for that was his
way. The day wore on and Abe felt the boy's presence, as
warmly comforting as the stove.

Abe sewed and mended old shoes and his heart slowly

Israel

renewed itself. If he had been a few years older this chance at spiritual healing would have come too late, but he was still just a boy himself, barely an adolescent. His youthful resilience, combined with his own odd, precocious and paternal nature, settled the matter.

That night when Haim got into the bath, Abe was relieved to see that Haim was circumcised. Abe had not been sure he was Jewish due to his light coloring. The last thing Abe needed was to be accused of kidnapping a Christian child. Just such a rumor sparked the pogrom that cost Abe's own father his life.

Abe was about to throw the boy's filthy garments into the fire when he discovered a scrap of paper in one of Haim's pockets. Written in Yiddish was the name Haim Kolesnikoff. From the looks of the scrap it was torn from some larger document, now lost.

That night while Haim slept, the young cobbler walked the narrow lanes of the village to the synagogue, behind which lived the rabbi and his wife. The scrap of paper was presented, and over glasses of tea and a plate of honey cakes the matter was discussed. The rabbi was assured that Haim would attend the village heder and be taught the cobbler's trade. Still, the rabbi was doubtful.

"Abe, it is a great responsibility for one as young as you," he warned. "This child will depend on you for all things."

Responsibility, dependence, another's fortune linked to his—Abe finally realized that solitude and isolation had been slowly murdering his spirit. He needed Haim as much as Haim needed him.

"Think hard on whether you wish to take on a son before you take a wife," the rabbi advised him.

Abe had to grin. "God has seen fit to send the son before the wife."

The rabbi shrugged. One less orphan was to everybody's benefit. He summoned his wife to bring the schnapps.

Thimblefuls were poured and a toast was made to celebrate the adoption.

The next morning at breakfast Abe asked, "Haim, maybe you'll stay here awhile with me?"

Haim shrugged, nodded, shyly smiled—and that was that.

Haim turned out to be an excellent student and a hard worker. As he grew older he progressed from ward and apprentice to friend and partner. Haim grew to be a stocky, muscular youth, soon dwarfing the slender young man who had taken him in. The rabbi decreed that Haim was ten years old the day he wandered into Abe's shop. That day became his birthday. So it was that three years later, Abe, at nineteen, had the privilege of watching his foster son become a bar mitzvah, a responsible adult.

Several times Abe had been close to marriage, but each prospective bride balked at marrying a man with a stepson near his own age. For a girl still in her teens to take on an infant was one thing; it was quite another for her to be faced with a grown son.

Abe was not much bothered by remaining a bachelor. Even then marriage seemed to him to be more of an obligation than an advantage. He was most comfortable when he was working, and he took pleasure in watching Haim flirt with the village girls. Strong, handsome, always ready with a joke, Haim was the one people noticed. Abe, every inch the proud father, was content to let Haim have enough fun for both of them.

In 1897 Abe turned twenty-one and began the first annual payment to the recruiter to keep out of the czar's army. The rate would rise in the coming years, the recruiter warned. Abe understood. Since coming to power a few years previously, Nicholas II, intent on furthering Russia's involvement in international affairs, had begun to strengthen the army and navy.

The year before the czar had signed an alliance with war-torn China in which the two countries pledged to support each other by all land and sea forces should there be any further aggression against either by Japan. There were more than a million Jews living within the section of land along Russia's western border known as the Pale of Settlement. Abe had no doubt that should a war break out between Russia and Japan, the czar would not hesitate to use young Jewish men as cannon fodder.

That year also marked the founding of the World Zionist Organization. To go on a pilgrimage or to die in Jerusalem had always been a dream to Jews, but in 1881 a group of Russian students made the journey in order to till the soil of their forefathers, and the first Zionist settlement came into being.

Not only did these students begin to raise the house of Jacob in the Holy Land, but they also began to build in the minds of Jews everywhere the idea that a land of their own was possible. Young Zionist groups sprang up in villages throughout the pale. In curtained rooms and stuffy cellars young men and women met to drink tea and drill themselves in Hebrew even as the rabbis denounced Zionism for turning Jews away from religious ways.

In 1903 Haim turned twenty-one and the bribe to the army recruiter doubled. By now Haim was enamored with Zionism. To be dedicated to a cause was not Abe's way, but he appreciated the youth groups as a way to release frustrations. He said nothing when Haim impulsively donated some of their savings to the Jewish National Fund, which had begun to purchase land in Palestine.

The National Fund proposed that the land be in the hands of the nation, not individuals, and this idea was especially inviting to young Russian Jews, many of whom were Marxists.

Various socialist revolutionary parties had begun to call for the overthrow of the Russian autocracy and the socialization of the land. These groups meant to lure the peasantry to their cause by the call for reform, but the masses, knowing only that they were starving, preferred action to political talk. Violent uprisings occurred, during which peasants attacked estates and stripped them of food and livestock. The disturbances were especially violent in the Ukraine, where the Jews were held as scapegoats for the nation's misfortunes.

Half of Abe's village was sacked before the mobs grew weary and wandered off. Abe and Haim escaped without hurt, but the cobbler's shop was torn to pieces. Fortunately the rioters did not find the money Abe had cached beneath a floorboard.

For some time Abe had been thinking of emigrating to America. It was the czar's military recruiter who first put the idea in his head. This self-serving person came around with his hand out for a bribe on Haim's twenty-first birthday. He suggested that for a reasonable price he could get both Abe and Haim across the border into Austria and Germany. From there the danger would be past; all that would be needed was money to pay for steamship passage.

That was twenty-four months ago. Since then Abe had occasionally discussed the idea with Haim. Always Abe phrased it simply as "leaving Russia," naturally assuming that Haim understood where they'd be going. Haim was enthusiastic on the few occasions when the idea came up, but he respectfully made it clear that he would defer to Abe on the matter.

So Abe talked about it and then let the matter slide for months at a time. To begin a new life was difficult for a man of Abe Herodetzky's temperament. To go to America? To risk so many dangers? At least they knew what life had to offer them here in the village. There was the shop, the worn, familiar handles of their tools, the smell of leathers and polishes; there was food on the table each day, and tea from the samovar in the corner; and each evening before they went to sleep, a drink of schnapps. No, life wasn't so terrible after all, not when two who were at once father and son, brothers and friends, could make a living in a place where they had the respect and affection of their neighbors.

In Abe's mind just having the option of going to America was enough for the time being. Whenever life seemed unbearable, he would consider emigrating, and suddenly things didn't seem so bad. Maybe next month, next year. There was always time.

Now there was nothing left to hold them back. Abe stared at the wreckage of his shop, at his tools scattered and broken, while Haim quietly stood by. The ground beneath their feet was soggy with the blood of the injured and dead; the sky above was grey with smoke. All around them was ruination; the air was filled with the weeping of the adult and the wail of the children. So hellish was the scene that the only way to keep one's sanity was to shut it all out. A man had to numb himself if he was to keep control. There were things to be done: help the injured, the dead.

"They'll come again, won't they?" Haim whispered. "They'll rest and forget about this and drink some courage and be fired up by their priests, and they'll come back to wipe us off the earth."

"They won't come back," Abe said, but he believed it even less than Haim.

"We've got to escape while we can." Haim's red-rimmed blue eyes squeezed shut as the tears came.

Those who still had homes in the village opened their doors to those who did not, but Abe and Haim chose to sleep where they always had, wrecked or not. The night was mild and there was no threat of rain. They built a fire in their stove, spread their blankets and stared up at the starry sky through the wide chinks in the sagging roof of straw. They were too excited to sleep. Surrounded by the ruins of their old life, they began to make plans.

"We must get in touch with the recruiter," Abe began.

"What do we need the recruiter for?" Haim asked. "What can that corrupt bastard do for us?"

"I never told you this," Abe chuckled, "but he once offered to get us across the border. Once we are in Austria or Germany, we can—"

"Why do we need to go there?" Haim cut him off.

Now it was Abe's turn to be confused. "To sail across the Atlantic," he replied. "How else to get to America?"

The glow from the stove was far too feeble to see by, but Abe had known Haim too long not to be able to sense when he was troubled. "Little friend?" he softly called.

"How long ago you first called me that," Haim sighed. "I was so small and thin you could have fit me in one of the boots you were making."

Abe smiled in the darkness. "And now I could fit into one of your boots. But you are still 'little friend' to me, Haim, so please tell me what is troubling you."

"All this time you spoke of leaving Russia, I—well, I never thought to ask where you intended to go because for me the choice was always so obvious."

"Yes? Go on," Abe coaxed, feeding more wood into the stove and leaving the grate open for light.

"This is difficult for me," Haim said. "I owe you my very existence." He took a deep breath. "Abe, it never occurred to me that you did not intend to go to the Holy Land."

"Palestine?" Abe gasped. "You thought we were to go to Palestine? Of course not! We will go to America—"

"No." Haim spoke so firmly that Abe's heart broke at the sound. "You will go to America."

"Don't do this, Haim," Abe implored.

"For me there is no choice," he continued impassively. "I must go to Eretz Yisroel."

"Don't call it what it no longer is! Your so-called Promised Land now belongs to the Turks. My God, Haim, don't ruin your life—our lives—this way. The Zionist movement will come to nothing there. Even Hertzl, your movement's—"

"It is not just my movement, Abe," Haim sighed, his tone partly forgiving, partly condescending. "Zionism benefits all Jews."

Ungrateful upstart! Abe took a deep breath to calm himself. There was too much at stake to throw it away by letting his anger get the better of him. "Haim, I am sorry. Of course the Zionists mean well. But what I was trying to say was that even Hertzl, the movement's leader, has proposed that England's offer of Uganda as a refuge for Jews be accepted."

Haim shrugged. "Hertzl is entitled to his opinion."

"There is no such thing as a promised land—"

"And you are entitled to your opinion, Abe."

"At least in America if you work hard enough they promise success."

"Why not work as hard in Palestine?"

"America is the place for us."

"At the moment there is no place on earth for us. Nowhere on earth are Jews more than tolerated, including your precious America."

Abe stared at Haim's face in the flickering firelight, at his handsome features, animated by his passionate beliefs. He looks like one of God's angry angels, Abe thought, full of pride and love and the immeasurable pain of imminent loss.

"Since the Diaspora we have lived in ghettos," Haim was saying, his voice kept low but imbued with righteous thunder. "In Russia we live in a ghetto behind a wall that separates *us* from *them*. We live according to others' whims. We are tolerated, like poor distant relatives at an intimate family gathering that is the rest of the world. We have no place to call our own, and until we do, we shall be at the world's mercy. Do you understand, Abe? If the Jewish way of life is to survive it must develop roots in soil it can call its own. Only then will Jews be able to feel a measure of security and independence." Here Haim paused and smiled. "Even if they themselves don't choose to live in Palestine, at least they will know there is a homeland awaiting them if they need it."

"I don't believe I could survive in a desert like Palestine," Abe said.

Haim nodded. "Then you probably couldn't," he agreed. "As for me, I could not survive anywhere else."

"It'll be a hard life—"

"What else is new?" Haim's voice grew soft. "What is hardest is saying good-bye to the man who raised me like a father."

"Being your father helped me to overcome the loss of my own."

"So you will go to America and become a rich man. You will come visit me in Eretz Yisroel and all my neighbors will be impressed with your importance."

"Well, you will need money to go to Palestine," Abe said. "I don't know how to advise you, little friend." He frowned. "I don't know the procedure—"

"Don't worry," Haim reassured him. "There have been pioneers before me. The Zionists here and in Palestine will guide me."

"Did they say how much passage was?"

Haim gave him the figure. "Also something to live on until I know my way around a little, but all I'll take from you is the fare."

"Don't be foolish." Abe quieted him in a peremptory tone. "Maybe you do not need my guidance any longer, but for food and clothing you'd do best to rely on me and not your fellow *halutzum*."

"But you will need money for your own journey."

"In America a man can find work to make his own way. Who knows if there is any work in Palestine?"

"Of course there is work."

"The kind that pays? Right here I could plant a crop, and that's work, but it doesn't pay until the plants grow. What would I eat until then, without money in my pocket to buy food?"

"Perhaps you are right," Haim reluctantly admitted.

"Perhaps," Abe chuckled. From the leather pouch around his neck he extracted a sheaf of worn rubles. "Take this." He handed over the money.

"But this much?" Haim asked, astounded. "It must be all you have."

"In the first place it is not mine but ours," Abe said. "We earned it together. In the second place it is much less than half of our savings." He winked. "I am six years older than you, so I should get the lion's share, yes?"

Haim laughed and then grew quiet. Both men watched the fire for a while, until Abe broke the silence.

"When do you leave, little friend?"

"There's a train to Odessa at seven this morning," Haim began, then blushed, embarrassed at Abe's chortle.

"You are so anxious to leave?" Before Haim could say anything, Abe continued, "Do you know what I think? I think that probably I will not wake up until well after dawn. Before then you should go find your Zionist friends and begin your journey. What do you think?"

"I think that the thirteen years since I stood in your doorway, a ragged orphan boy, seems like only one day," Haim murmured. "You really will not come with me, Abe?" He filled his voice with hope.

"I won't." Abe wrapped himself in his blankets against the cool night air. There will be no way for us to write, he thought. After tonight it will be good-bye forever. He looked heavenward to pray for Haim's well-being. The stars against the velvety sky seemed more brilliant than usual.

"Good-bye, little friend."

"Good-bye, father."

Abe had to smile. Never had the boy called him that before. He went to sleep willing the stars to be diamonds in Haim's pocket. He went to sleep with the blankets over his head to muffle the sound of his only family's departure.

Haim waited for Abe's breathing to become regular. He was either asleep or pretending to be. What difference did it make, anyway?

He had no idea what to take with him on his journey and so decided to take nothing. Whatever he needed he would get in Palestine or do without, like a proper pioneer. Already his head was full of wonderful visions of himself astride a horse—or perhaps even a camel—with a pistol on his hip and one of those—what, turbans? No, a kaffiyeh on his head.

Haim stared at Abe's still form. Why wouldn't he come? There were times when try as he might, he could just not understand what made Abe tick. Haim was ruled by his instincts and impulses. Emotion was everything to him.

Abe, on the other hand, always had to think things through several times before acting. He would ruminate on a plan of action the way a cow chews its cud. Actually, Haim thought fondly, more like a billygoat, which Abe somewhat resembled.

Then it occurred to him that there was one thing in the ruined cottage he had to have. He moved silently across the floor to a wooden cabinet stuffed with papers of various kinds. The mob had tossed the documents about, hoping to find currency, family heirlooms, gold and silver jewelry.

Haim sifted through the untidy pile until he found what he had been looking for. It was still in the leather tube he had stitched up one afternoon both to protect it and to hide it from the tax collector.

On all things—matches, tobacco, schnapps, grain—whether bought, manufactured, grown or bartered for, there was a tax to be paid. When the tax collector came around on his fine horse, his bronze medallion of office hanging from his neck, he appraised all the peasant owned and announced the amount of the tariff. If the peasant could not pay, he had a choice of entering into a contract of slave labor binding on future as well as present generations or to surrender some of his wealth.

Haim and Abe hid the leather tube because they had no wish to lose the portrait inside.

By the light of the fire Haim carefully pried out the stopper and removed the rolled-up scroll of parchment. Last year a neighbor—an artist by proclivity, a farmer by necessity—had come to them with a proposition: three pairs of shoes for his children in exchange for a fine portrait of Abe and Haim. The cobblers agreed to the bargain and the artist produced a charcoal drawing that was astounding in its delicacy and accuracy. In Hebrew the man lettered their names, the name and location of their village and the date.

How the artist ever paid the taxes on three new pairs of shoes Haim could not say. In any case the tax collector, intent on tools, hides and thread, never discovered the drawing.

Haim gazed at the portrait and then glanced at Abe. He wished there were two drawings so each man could possess a memento, but there wasn't. There was only one, and Haim meant to take it with him.

Better it should be in the Holy Land than in America,

he told his conscience. Carefully he rolled up the parchment and slid it back into the leather tube. He pocketed the tube inside his coat, and holding it close to his heart, hurried off into the night.

Abe woke abruptly. At first he was confused. Where was Haim? Then he remembered and the immensity of loss threatened to overwhelm him.

The sun was just coming up from behind the distant hills, its radiance setting the forest on fire. By that glowing light Abe's eyes fell upon the wooden cabinet. He knew without looking that Haim had taken the portrait.

At first Abe was furious; then suddenly his anger lifted.

Guard the portrait and the memory of our life together, Abe wished to Haim. I've done my best for you.

A rooster, a mass of muddy mahogany feathers on scrawny legs the color of cheese rind, strutted past the gaping doorframe. It cocked its head sideways in order to eye Abe.

What do you see? Abe wondered. An animal concerned itself with external characteristics. To the rooster Abe was merely a two-legged thing like all the others in the village, no better and no worse. To the rooster he was the same as the tax collector or the czar.

I have lost everything in the last day—my shop and the only person I care for.

The absence of responsibility nagged at Abe; Haim had needed him, and that need was Abe's lifeline to humanity. For Abe responsibility was the only pleasure. He laughed only when it was important to cheer Haim. He had not entertained until it was clear that Haim needed friends.

The rooster flapped its stubby wings and threw back its tiny head to yodel in the new morning. Abe threw a

cracked shoe last at it and the rooster darted off, squawking in outrage.

Better you should view your life with the rooster's
eyes, Abe decided. Think only of externals. Put your
actions together the way you would cut and assemble a
boot. Do not look inside yourself, not until your heart has
had time to heal.

He took the leather pouch from the thong around his
neck and counted his remaining savings. He had lied to
Haim about the money and sent him away with over three
quarters of their cash. Abe had saved enough to pay for
two passages, but his budget was based on two men
traveling to the same destination. The cost of food, shelter
and bribes was not much more for two than for one.
Separate travel changed everything.

It was a question of each man going ill-prepared for
the journey or one going with proper funds and the other
postponing his departure. Abe knew that Haim could never
wait patiently until he could build up his savings. As soon
as Abe set off Haim would have thrown caution to the
winds and tried to go without money.

Abe made some quick calculations. With his shop and
tools ruined he could not hope to earn as quickly as before,
but earn he would, sooner or later. He had the patience
and temperament to wait until he was relatively certain that
he would get there. Unlike Haim, Abe had no taste for
adventure. He liked knowing in advance how things were
going to turn out.

Chapter 3

Things quieted in the area for the next few months. Still, the village was crippled. It was harder than Abe had imagined to make a living. He found himself relying on the hospitality of others more and more, and his savings began to trickle away.

Far from the pale, the rapid industrialization of Russia in the first years of the twentieth century, bringing with it the usual problems of harsh working conditions and low pay, made many converts to Marxism among students and intellectuals. Within these socialist revolutionary parties was a small group of radicals who believed that change could come only through terrorism and political assassination.

Once again Abe witnessed the formation of secret groups, but this time the topic of debate was not how to acquire a Jewish homeland but how to overthrow the czar and bring about changes in education, taxation and working conditions. Now not only the tax collector and army recruiter came, but also an official backed by soldiers. Young men were rounded up and hauled off to work in Nicholas' mines and textile plants, conscripted for life. Desertion was punishable by death.

High-ranking government officials were assassinated

in the name of socialism. The authorities, horrified by this show of defiance, once again plotted to distract the Russian people by blaming the nation's misery on the Jews.

In the latter part of 1904 a wave of pogroms cut through the pale's population of Jews like a scythe through wheat. Abe and his neighbors were reduced to hiding like rabbits as the mobs swept through, destroying what they could not steal.

Other events far beyond Abe's control were coming together in ways that were to have profound effects on his life. In 1900 Russia, along with the British and Americans, sent military forces to quell the Boxer Rebellion in Peking. Once the rebellion was broken Russia stayed in China, and by the summer a massive military expedition occupied all of Manchuria, which shares a border with southeastern Russia.

The czar's action infuriated the Japanese, who formed an alliance with the British in order to force back the "imperialistic Russians." The czar agreed to remove his army from Manchuria within eighteen months but did not.

In February 1904 the Japanese broke off diplomatic relations with Russia. Three days later they executed a devastating surprise attack on the czar's naval installations at Port Arthur, in South Liaoning Province, Manchuria.

The conflict was five thousand miles away from Abe. However, it was brought much closer to home with the arrival ahead of schedule of the army recruiter, a different man, not interested in bribes. This time he was backed by armed soldiers who saw to it that all of the remaining able-bodied males over five feet tall were assembled in the village square, which was still strewn with the wreckage of the last pogrom. The soldiers were tall, raw-boned, blue-eyed men; they stood like Satan's angels among the groaning, cowering Jews, who flapped about in their black coats like crows. The soldiers enjoyed the opportunity to conduct a pogrom, and under official sanction of the czar at that.

Terrified, Abe stood with the other men as they eyed the stern-faced soldiers in dark green uniforms and high leather boots. The soldiers formed a circle around the village men and kept herd on them like dogs rounding up sheep. One look at the Mosin-Nagant rifles in the soldiers' hands was enough to banish all thought of escape.

The recruiter never bothered to dismount. He was dressed like his men with the exception of two loops of gold lace in his collar and a gold tassel on his cap to signify his rank. He seemed to be looking somewhere beyond the assembled villagers as he began to address them. "Those of you over the age of thirty-five are exempted. The rest of you shall have the honor of serving in the czar's army—"

"This can't be," cried one of the astounded men. "Lord, sir, you don't mean every man under thirty-five? What will become of the village if all the men are taken?"

The recruiter rolled his eyes heavenward as the women, old men and children fell into each other's arms and began to keen.

A sergeant began to shout orders. "If I don't have quiet I shall give the command to begin floggings!" the recruiter roared over the noise.

"He can't do this," whispered a bookish young scholar standing next to Abe. "The law says only ten recruits per hundred men." He tapped his palm with an ink-stained index finger, looking for all the world as if he were safe in the yeshiva arguing a Talmudic point. "The law is quite explicit on this question."

"Don't risk a lashing," Abe warned him. "Obviously he doesn't care about the law. He has a quota to fulfill."

"But always before he has accepted our bribes." The scholar blinked rapidly, seeming to see the soldiers' guns for the first time. "Why won't they take our gelt as they always have, and leave us in peace? What good are men like *us* in the military? What can we do in a war?"

Abe looked dour. "We can stop the enemy's bullets, and clear a path for these other fellows." He gestured at the soldiers guarding them. "They'll do the fighting from behind the corpses of the Jews."

"No, no." The scholar stubbornly shook his head. "There is the law to be considered. There is the question of a bribe." His narrow features suddenly brightened. "Ah! It is simply a matter of offering this recruiter more money."

Abe stared at the scholar. For the first time he realized how sparse the other's long beard was, how young and helpless the scholar was in a world that had no relation to his scrolls. Normally a lowly cobbler would defer to such a learned fellow, but now Abe scolded the scholar like a child. "Don't you understand anything? This officer already has his bribe in his pocket. He's gone to the Christian villages first, and they've paid him well."

The scholar ignored him. "Obviously a mistake has been made, but the law will protect us."

Abe turned from him in disgust. "The law is for the goyim; don't you know that? You are not a wise man, you're an incompetent."

"Nothing is wrong. Nothing has changed. There is no trouble. We will simply offer more money." He began to approach the recruiter. "My lord? I have a bargain to offer."

"Stay back," Abe hissed. "Are you mad?"

A soldier moved to intercept the scholar, who tried to step around him. The soldier slammed the butt of his rifle into the scholar's stomach. Doubling over, the wind knocked out of him, the scholar sank to his knees before the grinning soldier. He coughed, groaning, as blood bubbled out of his mouth to bead like rubies on his whiskers. The soldier and his comrades began to laugh.

"It is the obligation of the village to pay for the outfitting of the recruits," the officer on horseback continued as if nothing had happened. "Now then, I ask you reasonably." He smiled, spreading wide his hands. "Will you surrender the money?"

There was an uncomfortable silence until finally one of the older men in the group spoke up. "My lord," he pleaded, "the village has been repeatedly ransacked. There is nothing."

"Well then, you must find something," the recruiter snarled. "You can't face the Japanese unarmed, with no uniforms, can you? Must I send these soldiers to search through your belongings?"

"You will do as you will. There is no money to buy even one gun here, lord."

The recruiter fumed for a moment but then smiled. "We'll shoot that young priest there," he mused, pointing at the scholar, who was still on his knees, his arms wrapped around his belly, his eyes squeezed shut in pain. "Surely even Jews respect their priests, do they not?" He looked away in distaste as the unfortunate scholar coughed up another mouthful of blood. "He'd be no good to us, so we'll leave him here—or we can shoot him. It is up to you people."

"There is no money, lord," the spokesman cried out in despair.

"Private?" the recruiter called to the soldier who had struck the scholar.

All of them silent, they could clearly hear the metallic click as the soldier worked the bolt of his rifle. He pressed the barrel against the scholar's bowed head. To his credit the young Jew did not plead for mercy. He began to rock back and forth in his kneeling position, murmuring a prayer. The soldier, winking at his comrades, used the tip of his rifle to flick off the scholar's skullcap. This time the young man did cry out.

Abe found himself reaching for the pouch around his neck. They'll take it from me anyway, he thought. At least

this way the money will buy a life as well as guns and
uniforms, and perhaps it will spare the village a further
search if I can convince the recruiter that I am telling him
the truth.

"My lord," he called out, holding aloft his leather
pouch. "This is all the money left in the village. The rest
was taken by—by—" Abe paused, afraid to lay blame
upon Christians.

"The rest of your resources have been confiscated by
good Russians doing the czar's work, seeing to it that
Jewish revolutionaries are deprived of funds," the recruiter agreeably finished for Abe. "But tell me, how is it
that you come to hold the wealth of the entire village?"

"My lord, I am the only one here with a really good
hiding place," he said simply. "No one else knew I had
this until now."

"So you are the only one left who has money, eh?"
The recruiter chuckled. "Well, bring the purse here, Jew,
and I'll keep my bargain."

He held out his riding crop. Abe came forward, looped
the thong of the pouch around the tip of the crop and then
scurried back to his place among the others.

The recruiter quickly thumbed through Abe's cash
and darkly announced, "There's not much here, but it'll
have to do. You may bring with you a few personal
possessions, but understand that anything valuable may be
confiscated. At this point you may consider yourselves
soldiers. If you disobey an order, you will be flogged. If
you attempt to desert, you will be flogged and sentenced to
life at hard labor."

The villagers joined a great mass of peasants trudging
along the main road to the railway depot under the watchful eyes of the soldiers. There were a lot of Jews, but
many Christians had also been unable to pay. Abe found
himself stared at by some of the rougher peasants, men

with matted hair and beards and greasy animal-skin tunics who reeked of manure and cabbages.

There was no trouble between the Jews and the Christians. Everyone was immersed in his own misfortunes. No matter what their religion, they all faced twelve years of active service and then another three in the militia.

In the army they would all endure poor living conditions and meager rations, but while these miseries would be shared, the Jews had to bear the brunt of some additional injustices. A Christian recruit could at least rise in the ranks according to his ability. A Jew could not be decorated or promoted. He could not be rewarded in any way for any act of valor. It was understood that Jews, being inferior to Christians, would be bunched in the front of any charge and would be the last to receive food and shelter. If beyond all probabilities a Jew survived his stint in combat, he could at any time be murdered by any Christian soldier. This was against the law, but the officers in charge invariably looked the other way.

The new recruits went by train to Kiev. Despite his predicament Abe was awed and excited by his first glimpse of a city. Kiev, with its shops, boulevards and massive crowds, seemed spectacular to Abe and the others, most of whom had never been outside their rural villages.

At the barracks Abe was issued a dark green uniform that fastened down the front with hooks instead of buttons, matching forage cap and rather shoddy boots. They were also issued knapsacks of tanned cowhide and bayonets, but no rifles.

While the Christian soldiers drilled the rumor swept the Jewish recruits that when battle came, they would have only wooden dummy rifles. For months the Jews—and some unfortunate Christians—dug sanitation ditches, cleaned streets and built rickety temporary housing for the hundreds of thousands of peasants shanghaied to the cities to

do factory work. The population of Petrograd had doubled
due to industrialization. That of Kiev had quadrupled.

The day finally came around when the soldiers were
loaded onto drafty straw-littered boxcars and transported to
Petrograd. From there they would journey almost five
thousand miles to the Manchurian front via the Trans-
Siberian Railroad.

The first part of the trip took a week. Elite squads
guarded the draftees as if they were convicts planning to
escape. Many did desert despite the harsh penalties if
captured, and the rumor mill had it that about half of them
managed to get away, at least for a little while.

Abe considered making a run for it, but he lacked the
spirit. He was no Cossack to go dodging bullets and
outsmarting trained manhunters. Anyway, escaping with
no money would be little gain. Most likely some recruiter
would stumble over him and conscript him again. Besides,
Abe had another plan.

They arrived in the capital to find the single-track
railway broken down. Their train would be delayed for at
least three days.

For the first couple of days Abe was assigned to a
ditch-digging detail. He began to despair of his chance
when his luck suddenly changed and he found himself
ordered to load supplies onto a train under the supervision
of a young captain, a quartermaster.

Like most of the officers Abe had come across, this
one had a shabby uniform. Abe noticed that the scuffed
leather uppers of the officer's boots had separated from
their soles. Like enlisted men, officers were required to
buy their own clothes and weapons, and although most of
them were nobles, they were too poor to replace or repair
what wore out. Any noble with money bought himself out
of the military in the first place.

The quartermaster, blond and fair-skinned, pretty
enough to be a girl, was not the first officer Abe had seen

with broken-down boots, but he was the first who was permanently stationed far from fighting. Abe waited until as few as possible enlisted men could hear him and then threw himself on his knees before the imperious captain, explaining that he was a cobbler and begging for the privilege of repairing the mighty warrior's boots.

"How long will it take you?"

Abe, still prostrate, his forehead almost touching the boots in question, thought fast. His regiment was due to depart for the front tomorrow afternoon.

"Tomorrow morning?" His eyes rose to the vicinity of the captain's knees.

The officer stroked his chin thoughtfully, then nodded and sat down on a crate to allow Abe to pull off the boots. The cobbler was careful to hide any exultation as he watched the proud nobleman gingerly take his leave in his stocking feet. As Abe suspected, the captain had only one pair. How many other officers were there like him?

Abe finished his duties, skipped the evening meal and worked through the night on the officer's boots. The camp was in confusion due to tomorrow's departure. Nobody noticed one man hunched over a stub of candle in the corner of an empty storage shack. Abe still had a couple of tools—a hammer, some heavy needles and thread, a small container of polish—he had been reasonably sure would not be confiscated.

His practiced eye scrutinized the boots. The leather had worn away in several spots, and the layers of the soles, while still thick, *thank God*, had started to separate.

Leather patches to bridge the gaps between the uppers and the soles and to refurbish the linings of the boots could be cut with his bayonet from his calfskin knapsack, Abe decided, but where could he find glue to repair the spreading soles? There was no way he could force his needle through so many thicknesses. The thread wouldn't hold anyway.

Abe hurried back to his barracks. The other men, exhausted, were sound asleep. Their snores blanketed any noise Abe made as he slowly maneuvered his lightweight but cumbersome wood and canvas cot back to the storage shed.

He flipped the cot over. Closely spaced brads held the taut canvas to the frame. Working very carefully so as not to weaken the brads by bending them too much, Abe extracted every fourth one with the claw of his hammer and used them to repair the splitting soles. It was dawn by the time he finished.

Russian officers did not usually rise at dawn, so Abe waited outside the captain's tent. As soon as he heard morning sounds coming from within, he approached.

The captain closely inspected the job. Abe, his eyes red and swollen with fatigue, was aching to point out that he'd also seen to the linings, but he didn't dare push the captain too hard. He had done all that he could. The next move was up to the officer.

"These will do, I suppose." He stared hard at Abe. "You don't imagine I will pay you, I hope."

Abe humbly dropped his gaze to the ground. "Of course not, sir. I am a cobbler by training and a patriot by nature. It is my wish merely to serve as best I can."

The quartermaster had the aristocrat's total lack of self-consciousness with people of lesser station. Abe might have been a barnyard animal the noble was thinking of buying. For one insane instant Abe thought the captain was going to force open his mouth in order to look at his teeth. All the while the cobbler could hear in his mind the constant tapping of his hammer as he struggled to repair those precious boots.

Think, Abe willed the officer. Consider how valuable I would be to a fellow vain about his appearance. Think of the money you could make charging your fellow officers for my services.

"Well," the captain said at last, "off with you then. Back to your regiment. You'll be leaving for the front in a few hours." Boots in hand, he turned and disappeared into his tent.

Abe, blinded with angry tears, stumbled back to his barracks. His scheme to remain far from the war had failed. He had no delusions about what would become of him in combat. It seemed as if he had two dismal futures from which to choose: desertion and most likely a life sentence at hard labor or the front and shooting by the Japanese.

Desertion was his best chance, slim as it was, Abe realized. He would make his try during the rail journey. It would have to be during the first days of travel. The longer he waited, the farther the train would carry him from the Austrian border.

He was on his way to the train when the quartermaster reappeared. Abe waited, agonizing, as words were exchanged between the young officer and Abe's sergeant. It was clear that the two were bickering over Abe. Helpless, he stood by, knowing that his life hung on the outcome of this argument. The captain held the superior rank, but the sergeant had personal responsibility for getting a certain number of men to the front.

The sergeant abruptly threw up his hands. He was scowling as he handed the increasingly giddy Abe over to the captain.

"Time's short," the sergeant muttered. "The train's leaving and one Jew more or less won't matter—as long as I know where to put the blame for his absence," he added meaningfully. He stalked off and Abe and the captain were alone.

"You are now my property," the captain said. "You will be a cobbler for me and for anyone I choose to send to you. You will not be paid. At any time I choose I can have you sent to the front. Is that clear?"

"Yes, my lord," Abe nodded, eyes on the ground. Meanwhile, he felt like cheering.

"Look at me, Jew."

"My lord?" Abe cautiously raised his eyes to the captain's face. The noble's pretty features were as smooth as glass.

"You have not deceived me, Jew. I know this is exactly what you hoped for. I don't mind that, not at all. I will continue to keep you alive only so long as it benefits me. Do you understand?"

Abe nodded so hard he almost snapped his neck. The captain smiled. "Yes, I thought you would."

Abe was surprised to find that he was not the first to use this particular ruse. The barracks to which he was assigned was devoted to the other household people combed out of the general military population by canny officers. In the barracks with Abe were tailors, cooks, winemakers, musicians and so on, men who plied their old trades for their patrons or for others, the fees for their work going to the officers. In exchange they were kept out of harm's way in the capital city.

The months stretched into years, but at least Abe was safe and sound. The war went badly for Russia, and strikes and pogroms ravaged the country. News of the Japanese annihilation of the navy in the Straits of Tsushima off the coast of Korea sparked a new wave of domestic disturbances as well as mutiny on the battleship *Potemkin*.

The war ended in defeat for the Russians. Czar Nicholas, anxious to placate the population, announced political reforms. Once again radicals and reactionaries— the former wanting more concessions, the latter far fewer— turned the streets into a battleground. Strikes and riots raged and thousands of manors were looted. Troops returning from Manchuria were directed to turn their rifles on their own people. Many soldiers refused. Battles over politics raged within regiments.

During this period Abe continually dreamed of running away. America was calling to him more irresistibly than ever. Fortunate Haim had been in Palestine for almost two years already, and Abe had yet to escape the confines of Russia.

Now that the war was ending there was no telling what might happen. The only certainty was that he still faced a decade of active service.

He would have deserted long ago except for the fact that he still had no money. Besides, the captain could issue a detailed descriptive warrant of arrest the moment he found his cobbler missing. Abe had no idea just how much the impoverished noble had made by renting out Abe's skills to his fellow officers, but the cobbler was quite certain that the young captain would be both angry and vindictive if he found his source of income absent.

In the latter part of 1907 a new wave of unrest swept through Petrograd, disrupting telephone and telegraph service and shutting down banks and hospitals. The riots got worse as the days progressed until finally Abe's captain appeared in the doorway of the barracks, saber in hand.

"All of you," the young officer shouted, "you are needed to patrol the streets."

This can't be happening, Abe thought as he found himself marching into the fracas behind the captain, flanked by bakers and musicians holding rifles no one had ever taught them how to load, much less shoot.

The streets were a madhouse. Shouts and the brittle music of breaking glass reverberated off the stone walls of the buildings. The pavement was littered with smoldering rubbish, and drifting black curtains of acrid smoke hid the rioters, who darted and skulked around the soldiers like wolves menacing a forest camp.

Abe ducked and crouched to avoid the rocks and bottles that came hurtling out of nowhere. Far away he heard a volley of gunshots and demonic shouts and cries of pain, but as far as he could tell, the captain and his make-believe soldiers were the only military presence in the vicinity.

The captain was shouting orders that no one could hear above the commotion. And then, faster than Abe could have believed was possible, the captain stopped shouting and waving his saber and instead staggered, caught in a shower of stones. The rioters, sensing a kill, pelted him with another volley. A large rock struck the young officer's head. The saber clattered to the cobblestones as the captain went down.

At once the soldiers broke ranks, scattering to go their separate ways. Abe threw down his rifle and began to run.

Then he paused. He looked back at the beautiful young officer, sprawled in the gutter's filth, blood pulsing from his broken head.

Abe stared at the still form. Was he actually even contemplating dragging the officer to a place of safety? Are you mad? he railed at himself. For two years this man has called you nothing but "Jew," and while for you it's the truth, for him it was a dirty word. He has made a fortune from your labor and has not seen fit to offer you a smile, let alone a ruble.

Scowling, Abe once more turned to run, but his feet refused to budge. Stones were clattering to the pavement all around him, but none were actually being aimed his way. An unarmed spindly timid little soldier of base rank was not about to stir the wrath of the mob. Many soldiers had even joined in the smashing and looting.

The captain, however, was a prime target. He was lying unconscious, unable to defend himself. How long before some passing rioter smashed another stone down on his head?

Abe started as a wild-eyed man dressed in work clothes noticed the wounded officer. The rioting striker raced toward the captain, screaming obscenities.

The captain deserves to die, Abe decided even as he began to run to rescue him. But two years ago he saved you from the front. Today you will save him and then you will pray to God that he doesn't have you arrested for desertion.

Abe reached the fallen captain an instant before the rioter. "Get away! Get away!" he shouted. The rioter was twice his size and mean drunk on vodka; Abe could tell from the way he was lurching about and the red glint in his little pig eyes. Did Abe think he could shoo the man off as if he were a housefly?

A nasty smile suddenly crossed the rioting laborer's flushed face. "Jew," he snarled. His big callused hands came up like grappling hooks.

Abe had a momentary flash of panic as he imagined his head crushed between those two hands like a walnut. Out of desperation he snatched up the captain's saber and began to swing it like a carpet beater. The heavy weapon's momentum almost spun him off his feet with each wild slash.

To Abe's relief his swordplay failed to come anywhere close to his adversary, who veered away from the attack and wandered off in search of easier targets.

The saber still in his grasp in case it was needed, Abe managed to lift the officer's shoulders and bloody, lolling head. The boots Abe worked on so hard dragged limply across the cobblestones as he hauled the captain into a nearby alleyway.

Abe set down the sword and started to run, but once again he hesitated. The captain was very still.

I should find out whether he's alive or not, Abe thought, returning to crouch beside the body and check for a pulse. There was none. The only man who might want to track him down was dead.

He turned his attention to the sword. It was a beautiful thing, the long steel blade polished to a mirror finish and engraved in Russian all along its face. Abe realized that the saber was an heirloom.

And what had Abe from his father? A shoemaker's hammer. Still, Abe had to admit that his cobbler's tools had done more to keep him alive than the fancy sword had done for the captain.

Just the same, Abe vowed, never again will I practice the cobbler's trade. Mending shoes belongs to the past. Soon I will be in America. I will find new work as a free man.

The hilt of the saber in his palm felt heavy. He glanced at it and his eyes widened and his pulse began to pound with excitement. He stared at the yellow metal handle. He squeezed it, stroked it; he even brought it to his trembling lips in order to taste it.

It was gold from guard to pommel, including the wide, delicately curved half-sphere of the basket.

It did not surprise or perturb Abe in the least how a man like the captain, with a mended uniform and worn-out boots, might come to own such a valuable object. The captain was poor, it was true, but surely his aristocratic family had once been very wealthy. The saber was the captain's birthright. Understandably, he would do without essentials to preserve his ancestral treasure, perhaps the lone reminder of happier times.

Now it belongs to Abe Herodetzky, he gleefully thought, leaping to his feet, clicking his heels and doing a jig in place, the saber clasped to his breast in a lover's embrace.

The thought that he was stealing from the dead gave him a moment's pause until Abe decided that God must want him to have the sword. Besides, the captain owed him something for his years of servitude and for his efforts to save the officer's life. Things hadn't worked out so well for the captain, it was true, but the noble could take that up with God.

The morality of the situation dispensed with, Abe settled down to mull over more pragmatic concerns. The saber was of absolutely no interest to him as a weapon or antique. The gold hilt represented his ticket to America. He had no use for the blade, which also made his precious find hard to conceal.

Finding a chink in the alleyway's wall, he wedged the blade into it. He sweated and groaned and pushed and pulled. At last the steel and gold came apart with a peal.

Abe shoved the hilt into his trousers and hurried away. He stripped off his dark green soldier's tunic as he ran, feeling utter joy as the uniform fluttered away behind him. Around the corner he came across a broken bundle of rags littering the riot-torn street. A threadbare coat was lying in a puddle of water. Never had a garment seemed so exquisite to him as he snatched up the civilian coat.

A fortnight later Abe had managed to put four hundred miles between himself and Petrograd. A wily shop-keeper in Minsk, knowing quite well what Abe was up to, paid him a mere fraction of what the gold hilt was worth.

To Abe, who'd received just enough to finance his border crossing and transport himself across the Atlantic to Ellis Island via a rusty Bremen steamship, the deal couldn't have been better.

Chapter 4

New York

All around Abe the machines hissed and puffed to life like dragons stirring from sleep. The lunch period was drawing to a close. Abe realized he'd been staring unseeing at his newspaper for twenty minutes.

Well, he could read about Palestine some other time. It was best that he get back to his pressing machine if he wanted to make any progress in his own new beginnings.

He stood up, stretched and tucked the folded copy of the *Forward* into his pocket. He took a sip of water from his can and lifted his sticky undershirt away from his moist skin. It was as hot as a jungle in the loft; mildew spread with abandon, and cockroaches the size and hue of cigar stubs ran all year round with an agility elsewhere demonstrated only in late July and August.

Abe was just returning to his machine when he felt a hand on his shoulder. He turned to face Stefano de Fazio.

"We gotta talk," the stocky Italian said. "I need your help with something."

"So? What's wrong?" Abe joked. "You ate too much for lunch, maybe? You should have shared with me, like usual." His mood had brightened since the awful confrontation with Sadie and Joseph early that morning. Perhaps it had to do with thinking about Haim; perhaps it was because he had done a lot of work before lunch.

Abe also felt better when he skipped the midday meal. Hunger sharpened his senses, made the world around him shimmer with vivid intensity. Fasting was self-denial, and there was in Abe's personality a curious streak that could turn deprivation into a form of spiritual and even physical pleasure.

"Well?" he demanded. "You going to talk or are you waiting for the foreman to come over and give us both a kick in the ass for wasting time?"

Again Abe was joking, but Stefano spun around almost fearfully. Now his normally happy-go-lucky expression was dark and brooding. "It'd be better for us to talk outside, in the hall," he muttered, eyeing the foreman, who was on the other side of the loft. "It's a private matter, a union matter. We go, okay?"

Union, shmunion, Abe thought. "Yeah." He nodded. "We'll go outside." He followed Stefano to the doors. The foreman glared at them but didn't say anything.

It was a grey, blustery sort of late spring day, bitter cold in the drafty hallway outside the loft. Abe felt the sweat stiffen on him. Goosebumps rose on his pale, thin arms as he began to shiver in his sleeveless undershirt.

The hallway had a single bare bulb hanging from the ceiling. The walls were tan where the paint hadn't peeled away. Stefano began to hoist himself up on the wrought-iron railing that overlooked the staircase, but then he hesitated. He prodded the rickety thing and thought better of trusting his bulk to it.

"I was at a union meeting last night," Stefano abruptly began, still experimentally shaking the railing, keeping his eyes glued to where it was fastened to the concrete floor.

"It was over on Eldridge, not so far from where you live."

"Stefano, I'm freezing out here," Abe complained.

"Okay, okay," Stefano said. "They read us a message from the joint board signed by the union president, Rosenberg. There's going to be a strike, Abe." Stefano finally turned his attention away from the bannister to stare into Abe's eyes. "This is a secret I'm telling you, okay?" He nodded vigorously, causing the harsh light to glint off of his black curly hair, wet with grooming oil.

"For such big news you dragged me out here to catch pneumonia? Stefano, there's been strikes before—"

"Bullshit strikes. Walkouts, wildcats, a spit in the bucket—"

"Drop, a *drop* in the bucket." Abe prided himself on his ability to talk like a real American.

Stefano shrugged impatiently. "This is going to be a big strike—all the locals, everyone! You understand? We're going to shut the industry down, okay? The locals, they get to vote on it, but believe me, it's gonna happen. This summer a big strike."

"It'll never happen." At least Abe hoped it wouldn't. "Every day new people are getting off the boats from my country, from yours, from who-knows-where. If the union strikes, the bosses will hire greenhorns." He brushed his hands against one another as if clapping dust from his fingers. "That's all for your union."

"The bosses will not hire greenhorns because we will immediately sign them into the union. And we will meet twice a day to make sure nobody scabs."

"Wonderful," Abe said dourly. "And what will this big strike accomplish, I'd like to know."

"Abe," Stefano scolded good-naturedly. "You gotta be cheerful, like me. What are we gonna get? First, we demand a forty-nine hour week and a day of rest, the choice of Saturday or Sunday, with no fear of being fired.'' He began to tick off points on his fingers. "We gonna demand a closed shop. The joint board say this is very crucial,'' he told Abe seriously. "We gonna get twenty-two dollars a week—''

"What?'' Abe gasped. "My best week, working a double shift, I only made fifteen.''

"Sure, twenty-two for pressers like us.'' Stefano's smile was beatific. "Others not so good make less, but everybody makes what's fair for them.''

"My best wishes for us, my good friend,'' Abe sighed, "but if you ask me what I think our chances are—'' He frowned and shook his head. "The police will not be on our side, Stefano. And what will we all do when we're hungry, when our rents are due?''

"The strike fund—'' Stefano began.

"Faugh!'' Abe cut him off with a disgusted wave. "The two dollars you took from everybody won't go so far, believe me.''

Stefano looked uneasy. "Well, that's what I wanted to talk to you about,'' he murmured, "why I asked you to come out so we could talk in private.''

"Yes?''

"Abe, my friend, you told me you have saved some money to start a business of your own someday—''

"No,'' Abe snorted. "You want my savings? I should give you my money?''

"Not give, lend,'' Stefano put in. "A loan, my friend, to the union strike fund. To be paid back''—he smiled fiercely—"with interest.''

"So much you know about Jews,'' Abe morosely grumbled. "You say 'interest' and I'm supposed to lick my lips?''

"Don't say such things,'' Stefano implored. "We are union brothers, honorable men.''

Abe, coloring, looked away. "I'm not even going to be in the union much longer.''

"You're in it now," Stefano pointed out.

"It took me two years to save that money."

"And it'll be another two years before you have enough," the Italian said. "You told me so yourself. Abe, believe me please, if you were ready to leave the sweatshop I would not ask this favor of you, but you are not ready. For two more years you must be a presser, which means you will remain in the union."

"I have only two hundred dollars." Abe heard the whine in his voice but ignored it. "How far can it go?"

"It could mean the difference between winning and losing for the men in our local. It could mean that their children—my children—don't go hungry." Stefano gripped his shoulder. "What's the danger? You can't do anything with the money until you double it anyway, right? It's a loan, Abe. You'll be paid back."

"The danger is that if the union fails, if this strike doesn't work, nobody will pay me back. What would I do then, Stefano?"

The Italian shrugged. "It's a chance," he admitted. "For me the decision would be easy, but we are different men from different worlds." He sighed. "Come, we go back to work. You think about it and decide. Let me know. I will not ask again. At the end of the day let me know."

Abe spent the rest of the afternoon in agonizing deliberation. He worked his pressing machine at his usual pace. He filled his racks, stacked his piles and tabulated his totals as the boys came to carry the garments away, but all he really saw was Stefano's anxious face; all he heard were the Italian's words, "We are union brothers, my friend."

I won't do it, Abe vowed. Why should I? The memories flooded over him like emotions—the way he gave the lion's share of his savings to Haim, denying himself. The way he gave what was left to the military recruiter to save that foolish young scholar's life.

I've already done my part for others, and too many times. He glanced over at Stefano, who was working hard at his own machine. There was a serpent hiss as the irons came together and then the puff of steam rose between them like a wall.

Look at him, Abe thought bitterly, him with his greasy hair and his suspenders and his dark skin. He is like something out of the funny pages of the newspapers. He calls himself my friend, that wop! He doesn't even know I'm about to lose my room. I have nowhere to live, but I should give him money? I wouldn't even tell him, for what if he invited me to his tenement? How could I live among Italians?

Abe started. His momentary hatred of Stefano was so intense that for a moment he wasn't quite sure if he'd merely thought those things or actually said them.

The intensity of his feelings had a sobering effect on him. I'm only angry with Stefano because he asked me for the money, Abe realized, but the decision is mine. Tonight before I leave work, I'll tell him that my answer is no and that will be that.

For a moment his decision brought relief, but then shame and remorse began. Did I come to America to act like a mean-spirited Russian peasant? Abe demanded of himself. Haim would give the money and be proud that he was asked.

Great sadness, majestic in its intensity, came over Abe, mixed with aching pride such as the weary shepherd feels when he has guided his flock home safely. It was not such a terrible fate, Abe supposed, to find it one's duty to carry the world on one's shoulders. He began to stand a little straighter before his pressing machine.

Haim had the physical strength to go to Palestine and conquer Turks and Arabs. Abe knew he could never be a fighter. The thought of an angry Arab, or even an angry New York City policeman, made him quake with fear.

But there was a way for Abe to be a hero. Someday he would be wealthy, but for the rich man to give away money was an obligation. No, the act of giving money could be considered heroic only when performed by a poor man.

Twice already Abe had saved a life—and that poor injured scholar. Abe had rescued these men not with physical prowess but with his hard-earned savings. Just like the rich German Jews, Abe had been singled out by God to help his fellow men through charity. Maybe, Abe thought with growing excitement, maybe God is preparing me for the day when I am fabulously wealthy. Maybe he is testing me now to see if I'm worthy of having money.

As important as God's opinion of him was, there was also Haim's judgment to consider. One day, Abe hoped, they would have a reunion. Haim would be able to brag about making his mark in Palestine, and Abe wanted to be able to point to some aspect of America—perhaps the labor movement—and say, "You see, little friend, look at what Abe Herodetzky has accomplished. These fellows in the factory owe their well-being to me."

He thought back to what Stefano had said to him. It was true that he needed to save at least another two hundred dollars to begin a storefront business. It had taken him two years to save what he had. How long before he would have the four hundred?

Meanwhile, the union could use the money. If the strike succeeded, Abe could save that much quicker. And if the union was willing to pay him back with interest, what was the big deal?

That they won't pay me back, Abe reminded himself. I am only halfway to my goal. That I can endure, but if I am forced to begin all over again—

It was a gamble, admittedly, but a gamble had to be

made if a man wished to be able to boast about winning.
Of course, first he had to win.

I hesitate because I am a coward, Abe thought
despondently. Unlike Haim, I cannot think of others, but
only of myself. Haim is a good-spirited man; I am weak
and petty. It is right that God constantly test me.

Finally Abe had to laugh. Being good was like being
a musician or knowing how to speak English. How much
more pleasure there would be in goodness if a man didn't
have to go through the misery of practicing the art.

The next morning, Sabbath morning, Abe appeared at
the loft for the day's work. Stefano de Fazio was waiting
for him outside. Abe handed him the two hundred dollars,
and Stefano, embracing him, handed over a slip of paper
upon which he had noted the amount, the date and the
union's obligation to repay the debt together with a nomi-
nal amount of interest. The paper was otherwise blank.
The only signature on it was that of Stefano de Fazio. Abe
briefly wondered if somebody more official from the union
should have signed, but he was reluctant to insult Stefano
by asking such a thing. Abe reverently folded the slip and
stowed it in his pocket. Later it would go into the now-
empty envelope as a reminder of future promise.

Last night, when Abe informed Stefano of his decision,
the exuberant Italian had lifted the squawking Abe off his
feet in a show of jubilation. He kissed Abe on both cheeks
like a proud papa on the day his son becomes a man.
Stefano's absolute certainty that Abe was doing the right
thing carried the worried lender through the rest of the
night and right through the morning—up until the moment
when he actually handed over the cash. Then Abe's despair rose like a fever.

Three times now, Abe cajoled God, three times I
have put others before myself. It has fallen upon me to

help others. So be it. But after this maybe I could get what
I want for a change?

That afternoon during lunch, Abe once more tried to
read the *Forward*. Stefano had disappeared.

Haim? Are you well? Do you prosper? Abe wondered
as he perused the articles on Palestine. His hand absently
rose to pat the pocket where his money had been. As for
me, little friend, I am exactly the same.

Chapter 5

The meeting house was a flat-roofed slab of a building with pink stucco walls that made it look like a cream cake. Indeed, viewed from the surrounding sand dunes, the settlement's lemon, lime and white cottages looked less like a town than a baker's display of pastries beneath the strong Mediterranean sun.

Far too many people were crammed into the sweltering confines of the meetinghouse. Sixty families from half that number of places in Europe and Russia were taking up the rows of wooden chairs, and a pack of cranky children careered around the perimeters. This meeting had been going on—in points of order, adjournments, tabled motions and secret ballots—for the better part of the last year. Today, however, there was going to be a resolution.

"The time has come," the Old Man decreed, his voice raspy, his pop eyes rolling. "Today we must vote."

Not quite yet. "Point of order," somebody—oh, no, Professor Chernak—called out. He rose, unfurled a scroll only slightly shorter than the Torah and began to drone his arguments.

69

It was too much. Haim Kolesnikoff began to squirm on his straight-backed wooden chair. His legs bounced in an excess of nervous energy. His ceaseless exertions were making the floorboards squeak as if even the mice had an opinion.

The squeak caused Professor Chernak to pause. People began to cast dirty looks in Haim's direction.

The woman next to Haim was also blonde. She was pretty the way unbleached Egyptian linen is pretty. She had a slightly crooked sunburnt nose and wide-set slanted eyes the lustrous hue of sable. When she was happy, her throaty laugh like birdsong could fill the air. When she was angry, her black-brown eyes were as sultry as the evening breezes from the sea. Haim could not decide which way he liked her better. Just now she was angry.

"What? You can't sit still?" she scolded, her tanned hand clamping down on his knee. "Stop, or else go run around with the children."

It wasn't such a bad idea. "I'm going for a walk." Haim stood up and began to excuse himself as he sidled past the others.

The Old Man, up behind the podium, called out to him. "I trust you will return to vote, Mr. Kolesnikoff?"

Haim nodded, reached the aisle and hurried out of doors. The evening sky was peacock blue. It was late spring and the temperature was mild enough to be comfortable in one's shirt sleeves.

However, Haim was wearing a suit and tie. He scowled, wandering the wide, hard-packed streets of the settlement, which Dizengoff and his followers had yet to name. Tonight's meeting would finally resolve that issue, or so everyone hoped. Haim would return in time to cast his vote on what to call the town, but he had no patience for further discussion.

He stripped off his tie and jammed it into his coat pocket. The prim and proper Dizengoff—the Old Man, as he was called out of earshot—had strict rules for dress at meetings. It all had to do with being middle class and respectable, except that Haim had not come to Eretz Yisroel to be respectable.

He made his way through the grove of wind-twisted sycamores that bordered the edge of the new settlement. Here the ragged paths gave way to sand. Haim kicked off his shoes, rolled up his trousers and headed for the beach.

Before him the surf rolled and crashed, shining like molten silver in the moonlight. Between waves Haim could hear Chernak's raucous voice from the open windows of the meetinghouse.

So walk a little more, Haim advised himself, strolling along the beach, his bare toes luxuriating in the cool, damp sand. Now it was the lights and music of neighboring Jaffa that beckoned. Haim gazed at the ancient Arab city. It was a familiar, even friendly place. How different it had seemed five years ago, the first time he saw it.

After his farewell to Abe, Haim traveled on foot to the rail station near his village. From there he went to Odessa, the port city, which he found crowded with Jews eager to escape the czar's pogroms. Cowed, Haim wandered amid the confusion, homesick and desperately missing Abe. He even considered giving up his dream of Palestine, but encouragement from Odessa's Friends of Zion bolstered his sagging spirits. He was told that he would have no problem leaving Russia. The Turks in Palestine had banned Jewish immigration, but Zionist Agency people at the end of his journey would smooth his entry.

Haim bought his steamship ticket and food to see him through the nine-day journey to Jaffa. He still had plenty of money left, so he gave half of it to the agency for less fortunate pilgrims. He ended up giving away most of the food as well, for he was far too seasick to eat much.

To take his mind off of the surging waves, the stink of the hold and the endless rocking of the crowded steamship, Haim spent endless hours gazing at the precious portrait. Abe's likeness comforted him. Dear, good Abe, off to America on his own adventure.

Today Abe crosses the Austrian border, Haim imagined as his own ship set forth upon the Black Sea. Soon he'll begin to cross the Atlantic.

Meanwhile, his own steamer chugged through the Bosporus to the Mediterranean. Haim imagined that Abe had only another week's travel the day his own ship dropped anchor in Jaffa harbor.

Lithe nut-brown Arab boys rowed out in little boats to ferry the newly arrived to shore. The Arabs wore long white shirts, flowing garments that fluttered like curtains in the warm wind coming off the bay. A halutz was riding in the lead boat of the Arab youths. He was fit-looking and deeply tanned, with a totally bald head and a shaggy salt-and-pepper mustache. Haim was consumed with jealousy and admiration as soon as he glimpsed the pioneer. The man was wearing light cotton trousers and an open-necked shirt, the sight of which made Haim want to tear off his own high-collared tunic and pitch it into the sea.

The halutz shouted that the Arabs would transport them to land. Once they were on the beach they were to say nothing to the waiting Turkish officials. They were to let the comrades on shore do all the talking.

Haim impatiently waited for his turn to board a rowboat. He was ready to dive from the ship and swim to land, so eager was he to taste everything including the warm waters of the Mediterranean. What stopped him was the leather tube containing the portrait. He had not taken it from Abe and carried it all this way to have it ruined by a salt-water soaking.

When he finally got to climb down the rope ladder to

a rowboat, he was surprised and delighted to find himself riding with the halutz. From a distance the man appeared young; this was an illusion created by his vigor. Up close Haim could tell that his mentor was in his sixties at the very least. The man had deep creases around his eyes and the corners of his mouth and brown age spots speckled his strong, capable-looking hands. His clothing was splattered with paint and smelled of turpentine.

The pioneer addressed the immigrants in Yiddish, but Haim knew that since the turn of the century Hebrew was becoming the language of the Jewish homeland. Thanks to Abe and the rabbi, Haim had regularly attended his village's heder and so had a basic knowledge of Hebrew, though there were still great gaps in the language as it was spoken in Palestine. Hebrew, like Palestine itself, was in a state of transition. Many everyday terms had yet to be invented.

"Please, sir." Haim addressed the guide in a faltering mix of Hebrew and Yiddish. "Where, please, may I buy a gun?"

The man's thick eyebrows lifted in bewilderment. "Boy, why would you want a gun?"

Haim decided the halutz was testing him. He thought back to what he had learned at the Zionist meetings in Russia and proudly spouted off. "Why, to kill the Arabs and Turks and reclaim our homeland, of course."

The halutz patted him on the shoulder, shaking his head. Indicating the Arab youths bending over the oars, he asked, "Then who would row?"

Haim was dumbfounded. "We could row ourselves."

The pioneer politely explained that he'd meant his question as a joke. "You won't need a gun here in Jaffa. The fellahin, as you can see, are quite friendly."

"And the Turks?" Haim asked, worried. He could see several uniformed Turkish officials watching from the beach.

"Ah," the halutz sighed, "the Turks are the Turks. It won't do to fight them. Baksheesh is what they're after."

Haim had never heard the term before. The halutz explained that even though the Turkish government had forbidden further immigration, Jews could get past the officials by paying them a bribe.

"Baksheesh stops them far more effectively than bullets could." The pioneer smiled. "By the way, my name's Erich Glaser." He extended his hand.

Haim introduced himself and asked Glaser if those were all agency people loudly dickering with the Turkish immigration officials.

Glaser puffed up his chest. "You could say they represent the agency due to me. You see, those are my sons and daughters."

Haim stared at the beach, and then looked back at Glaser. "All of them?" There were eleven men and women confronting the trio of Turkish officials.

"Six boys and five girls." Glaser nodded happily. "My three oldest boys were born in England—that's where my wife and I are from—but all the rest were born right here in Jaffa. True children of Zion."

There was a rough scraping sound as the rowboat beached. The Arab youths hopped out into ankle-deep water to steady the boat while Glaser led Haim and the others to the Turks.

"Remember now," he told them all in Yiddish, "stay quiet and let us do the talking. These fellows will act fierce, but it's just their way of upping the baksheesh."

Haim was happy to hang back and let Glaser handle things. The trio of Turks had split up, each officer, resplendent in uniform, scarlet sash, fez and pistol belt, heading off to confront a group of the newly arrived.

The officer facing Glaser kept shaking his head to the halutz's offers, but Haim, who had witnessed more than his share of bribe negotiations back in Russia, could tell from the Turk's tone of voice that they were not far from a compromise. He looked around, drinking in the sights as he squinted against the strong sun. Five of Glaser's boys were helping some of the immigrants with their bundles of possessions. Haim would have volunteered to help, but he dared not leave his group until Glaser had finished bargaining with the Turk. The halutz's remaining son was just concluding a transaction. Haim watched him pay the Turks, who turned on his heel and began to stride up the beach.

"Welcome to Palestine," Glaser said. Haim turned to see the halutz winking at him, and behind Glaser, the Turk already catching up with his friend. Both officials looked anxious to get out of the broiling sun now that their money was in their pockets.

"That didn't go so badly." Glaser nodded contentedly. He nodded at the backs of the departing Turks. "They don't even trust each other. They insist upon each negotiating his own bribe when they would most certainly do better by sticking together, asking one price and then dividing it evenly."

"That lady is having trouble," Haim observed.

"Lady?" Glaser spun around. "Where?"

Haim pointed down the beach at a blonde young woman wearing a dazzlingly white cotton sundress that left her slender golden arms bare. Things were not going so well for her. As he watched, she abruptly thrust out her chin to say something in a very sharp tone.

The Turk stiffened with shock. In an instant he was grappling with her.

"Oh, my God," Glaser murmured. "My daughter—"

Haim was already running toward them. He felt anger building to white-hot as he saw the Turk suddenly slap his opponent across the face with the back of his hand.

Not here, Haim vowed. His mind cast back to memories of women and children savaged by the czar's Cossacks in his Russian village.

He was dimly aware of Glaser begging him to stop. He ignored the halutz, intent upon reaching the pair before the Turk further abused the woman. The slap had sent her sprawling onto the beach.

The officer now unhitched his holster flap and drew his pistol. As Haim approached, the Turk aimed the gun at him, growling out curses in his own language. Haim froze, staring into the bore of the pistol, thinking that his end had come.

Glaser, puffing with exertion, was just reaching them. He stepped between the officer and Haim and began to talk in Turkish, putting his arm around the officer and drawing him away. Whatever Glaser was saying seemed to calm him.

Haim was still staring mesmerized at the Turk's pistol. Now, he thought, while Glazer has him distracted. He tensed himself for a leap.

"Stand very still," the blond warned him. She was cradling her cheek, which had turned an angry scarlet. "He'll shoot you if you provoke him."

Swallowing hard, Haim nodded. "Are you all right?"

"Better than you're going to be," she said, getting to her feet. "Why did you do that?"

Haim glanced at the Turk, who still had his gun drawn but was now pointing it down at the sand while he listened to Glaser.

"It's all right," she assured him. "The Turk understands no language but his own. Now tell me, why did you risk your life?"

"He was attacking you."

She laughed. "For a nothing slap on the face you're ready to take a bullet? You'd better go back to Russia. Here in Palestine you won't last, believe me."

"Don't worry about me," Haim said, stung by her ridicule. "You need manners, miss. I was coming to help you."

"Some help! My father just saved your life, mister. We need smart Jews here, not dumb ones."

"I owe the Turk an apology," Haim roared. "He showed restraint by merely slapping you—"

"I don't suggest you try it," she spat back. "From a yokel like you he would never accept it."

"Here now, calm down, both of you," Glaser cut in. The glowering Turk was right behind him. "Rosie, my darling, foul-mouthed daughter, I know you like a book. You're shouting at Haim because you're angry with yourself."

Rosie, smiling to herself upon hearing Haim's name, suddenly got very busy brushing the sand from her skirt.

"Why did the officer slap her?" Haim asked.

"It was her own fault," Glaser replied. "Here women are considered inferior to men—"

"Only by the Turks." Rosie's bare foot pawed the sand. "So get no ideas, Mr. Yokel."

"You see, the Turk considered it an insult to negotiate with a woman," Glaser continued. "Rosie, I told you it wouldn't work. Always you disobey me."

The Turkish officer, still sullen, began a surly exchange with Glaser, all the while keeping his pistol at the ready. The halutz reluctantly handed over a thick wad of bills. The Turk holstered his gun, said something else, glaring directly at Haim, and stalked off.

"We were in luck." Glaser sagged with relief. "The other two officers saw none of the incident. Otherwise he would have been forced to arrest you in order to protect his honor." He turned on his daughter. "Just the same, it was too close a call and too expensive. Rosie, next time you will not attempt what must be left to a man."

"Oh, Papa, it's too much," she wailed, then appealed to Haim. "Am I such an idiot that I'm incapable of taking my place in the world?"

Haim was wearing an idiot's grin. Rosie was unlike

any woman he had ever met. It was her bold, arrogant style as much as her appearance that captivated him. "Rosie Glaser," he said with heartfelt sincerity, "you are capable of doing anything you'd like."

"Oy," Erich Glaser sighed.

Rosie rewarded Haim with a smile and an apology. "My father was right. I was rude to you only because I was angry with myself for failing with the Turk. Please forgive me, Haim. I've caused you much trouble."

"Well, it's over now."

"No, I'm afraid it isn't," she told him. "The last thing the Turk said was that you had better get away from Jaffa while you still can."

"Yes, she's right," Glaser broke in. "You must go away until things cool down and the Turk forgets you."

"Maybe I'd better stay and let him arrest me," Haim offered. "If I run, won't he take things out on all of you?"

"Hardly," Glaser chuckled. "He'd have to testify to his own humiliation. No, he has his money, so we're quite safe. He's not a bad sort, just a Turk. He makes far too much in baksheesh to want to upset relations between himself and the Zionist Agency."

Haim nodded. "Then I'd better go." He found it difficult to tear his eyes away from Rosie. The wind had shifted to mold the thin white fabric of Rosie's dress to her thighs and hips.

"I'll have one of my boys take you to the coach to Jerusalem," Glaser offered. "There's stonecutting work there for strong men."

"Very well." Haim hesitated. "Rosie, until I come back—" The words stuck in his throat, but finally he managed to get them out, feeling quite bold even as he spoke. "Rosie, see to it that you don't fight with any more Turks, at least not until I can return to protect you."

"Hah! Listen to him, Papa," she laughed, blushing

furiously. "I dare you to come back, Mr. Yokel. I'll give you a slap like the Turk gave me."

"Enough, you two." Glaser pointed at the other new immigrants, who'd been patiently standing by. "We've got to get these people to town."

"Come," one of Glaser's sons said to Haim. "This way to the coach. There is one leaving in half an hour. The sooner you're away from Jaffa, the better off we'll all be."

Haim let himself be led away. "I'll come back in a month, Rosie," he called.

"And why should I care when you come back?" she demanded, brushing back her wind-tossed golden tresses. "Ben, take him away before I box his ears and make them ring."

Haim grinned at her. Then he felt the portrait of himself and Abe banging against his ribs. He pulled it out of his tunic and tossed it toward Rosie. It landed at her feet.

"I'm afraid I'll lose it in Jerusalem," he shouted above the crashing surf and cries of the gulls. "Hold it for me, please?"

Rosie brushed the sand off the case and held it aloft. "For one month only. I can't be bothered watching it forever. One month! Come back for it by then or else I'll throw it away." A smile played at the corners of her wide, sensual mouth.

I'll come back for it, Haim thought as he walked with Ben, and for you, as well.

The stagecoach ride from Jaffa to Jerusalem took all night. Haim felt like cursing the desert heat until the road began to wind uphill into the mountains and the coach passed groves of Aleppo pine and glossy green eucalyptus trees.

There were other passengers who tried to engage Haim in conversation. He was polite but replied tersely, turning away or pretending to doze in order to be left alone with his thoughts. As dusk fell, turning the bright blue sky to lavender and softening the arid, stony landscape, Haim contemplated his first day in Palestine.

The recollection of his attack upon the Turkish officer still had the power to quicken his breathing. Haim would never have dreamed of lifting his eyes before a representative of the czar or even a Christian peasant from the neighboring village.

It has to do with leaving home, Haim thought as the coach rattled through the night past lonely Arab villages hunched between the desolate hills. Now that I am among strangers, I feel free to behave like a different person.

But there was more to the day's actions than the sense of liberty felt by a stranger in a strange land. I behaved the way I did not because I am far from home, but because I have come home, he realized.

Haim still could not explain the intensity of the rage he'd felt upon seeing Rosie struck. Anger at injustice he had felt before, but never so deeply that he was compelled to unthinking action.

Why had he done it, then? The question had great importance to Haim, for he had grown up in docile acceptance of horrific violence. Attacks against his people were a part of life.

He had never been able to remember the events that led up to his being orphaned. It was as if his life began the day he appeared upon Abe's doorstep. Everything before that, including memories of his family, seemed a hazy hallucination. Haim was never sure how much of it had actually happened and how much he was making up.

Late at night during that strange interim between consciousness and sleep Haim saw images of a tall, balding man who wore tools on his belt. There came to him the sharp smell of sawdust and the smooth feel of planed wood. During half-sleep, while his head lolled on the pillow, Haim remembered being small enough to fit into a tin washtub with two other faceless children. A dark-haired woman with a mole on her chin was scrubbing his ears. Soap burned his eyes. The woman held him aloft and the tepid water dripped from his bare toes.

That was all—no memories at all of what had happened to those nameless people. And how could one *try* to remember something? His lack of a past had long ago ceased to be anything more than a vague bother to Haim. God had taken away, but God had also given. If Haim had lost his family, he had had Abe.

Now what concerned Haim far more than his past was the way he was reacting to the present. He had always imagined the day when he would use his physical strength to stand up for his rights. Now, within hours of arriving in Eretz Yisroel, the moment had come.

But I stood up for another, not myself. I risked my life for Rosie . . . and Rosie belongs to me. How Abe would laugh at me, Haim thought. I am not one day in Palestine and already I have chosen a wife.

Did she know? Haim decided she must. Such things were not hard to understand for people like himself and Rosie.

He remembered the way she looked at him, the way she blushed and the words she said. Yes, she had been waiting for him for just as long as he had been on his way to her.

Still, like anything prized, she would have to be earned. That was all right. Haim was not afraid of a fight. As surely as Palestine would belong to the Jewish people, Rosie Glaser would be his. Now that the decision was made, Haim could relax. His eyelids grew heavy as the movements of the coach lulled him to sleep.

Chapter 6

Shouts and whipcracks brought him awake a little after sunrise. Haim looked out the window, craning his neck to see where they were headed.

The sun was just perched above the golden domes and slender spires of the hilltop city of Jerusalem, still quiet at this early hour. The horses' hooves echoed off the yellowing stone walls as the coach passed through Jaffa Gate. Haim caught a glimpse of a sleepy Turkish sentry waving them through. The soldier could not know him, of course, but Haim found himself instinctively sinking back into the shadowy interior of the coach.

There was a tall rectangular clock tower, very new and very Turkish with its ring moldings and cupola, perched anachronistically upon the crumbling guardhouse. Haim scowled at it, shaking his head. The clock tower might just as well have been a line of washing hung out to dry, such was its devastating effect on the previous majesty of the ancient western gateway to Jerusalem.

"Terrible, isn't it?" clucked the slightly built passenger seated across from Haim. He was the only other person in the coach who was awake. "It looks like a tarboosh."

"Excuse, please?" Haim understood most of the other

82

fellow's rattling Hebrew, but that last word escaped him.

"A tarboosh? Means a fez. You know, those hats the Turks wear."

Haim shrugged. "All right, but I don't understand the reference." The diminutive man had a short black beard and a head full of closely-cropped black woolly curls. He had long thin arms and hands so incongruously large that they looked like shovel blades attached to the fellow's pencil wrists. The man was no older than Haim, but like a monkey he could in repose appear old, gnarled and wise.

"The clock was built to celebrate the thirtieth birthday of some sultan," the fellow was saying. "Anyway, it went up just last year. I always thought there was more to it than the Turks giving a birthday present to a sovereign. They wanted to show that Jerusalem belongs to them, that it's Turkish, see? So they put a big fez on it." He sat back, a proud smile stretching across his bearded face.

Haim shrugged. "When the city is ours we'll tear down the fez."

"I see you're just off the boat. Never mind, you'll get the hang of things soon enough." He stuck out his over-sized hand. "My name is Yol Popovich. I am from Poland, but for the last two years I have been a halutz," he added proudly.

"Me, I've been here only for a few hours, but already I have battled a Turk," he grinned, something about the brash good nature of the monkey-man drawing him out.

"This I've got to hear about," Yol Popovich laughed. The coach began to slow and the change in rhythm set the other passengers to stirring and yawning and stretching. "All out," the driver called as the coach came to a stop.

"Come, I'll buy you your first Zionist breakfast," Yol offered as he waited for the driver to hand down his suitcase, "and after you throw up you can tell me all about your adventure."

Haim's new friend took him to an Arab stall beneath the shadows of the ruins known as the Citadel of David. At Yol's suggestion they carried their meal to a nearby cypress looming over a bent fig tree. The halutz pointed at two mounds between the tree trunks.

"Graves," he said, his brown, beady eyes full of mirth. "Hope you don't mind." He peeled off his cotton shirt to spread it out on the grass for a blanket. "I don't know who is buried there, but the Arabs say it is two lovers from feuding families. Makes sense, yes? Oh, I forgot, you wouldn't know. You see, the trees? Well, the Arabs take the fig tree as a symbol of the female principle and the strong, tall cypress to represent the male."

"But they are merely trees." Haim shrugged. The least he could do for this funny fellow was be polite. "You are fond of the Arabs?" he asked, munching his breakfast.

Yol nodded. "They are clever and full of quirks— entertaining, the way I knew people to be in Lublin. A nice change from all the serious, dull Zionists."

Haim was too shocked to reply. He lowered his eyes and concentrated on his food.

"How do you like it?" Yol asked, gleefully watching Haim eat. "You're doing well. I couldn't stomach that stuff for weeks."

Haim shrugged again. "I've had worse. What is all this, anyway?"

"That flat bread is called *pita*, and the mush you're dipping it into is a crushed pea called *humus*. The salty stuff is *za'atar*; I don't know how they make that." He paused. "You're sure you're not going to throw up?" He looked disappointed.

"Positive," Haim chuckled. "And these?" He held up several small green oval objects.

"Come now, even in Russia they must have olives."

"What they had and what we had are two different things," Haim said. "Olives I've never seen."

"You'll have your fill of them here, my friend," Yol sighed.

"You really don't like this food?"

"What's to like?" Yol made a face. "In Lublin my father was a baker and loved food." His eyes went dreamy. "Ah, Haim, then we had what to eat—roast capons so tender they'd melt in your mouth. Flank steaks with tiny new potatoes cooked right in the pan with the meat. Fresh fish, and many kinds of cheese." Yol's bare, bony chest rose and fell in a massive sigh of resignation. "I've tried to get the halutzim to acknowledge the lack of anything decent to eat here, but they all consider fine food to be a sign of weakness." He shook his head. "What's the big deal over something good to eat?"

Haim frowned. "Why did you come to Palestine?"

Yol immediately was serious. "Now Haim, I make a joke or two, but when all is said and done, I am still a Jew, yes? Back in Lublin I got mixed up with the Friends of Zion, and through that group I joined the Zionist Workers. I helped forge passports for those who wished to emigrate. The Turks, as you've no doubt learned, don't look too closely at the papers as long as they get their baksheesh." When Haim nodded, Yol continued. "At first my clandestine work for the party was enough. I felt bold over it. It was the spice in my life"—he pointed at the remains of Haim's breakfast—"like the *za'atar*. A little goes a long way, yes?"

Haim agreed. "Then what happened? I mean, you're here."

Yol shrugged. "One morning I woke up and knew it was time for me to come."

"Your mother and father stayed behind?"

"Yes. They had many reasons. The goyim who came to buy challah were our friends, my parents claimed. Things were going to get better, they swore. The Turks would never let the Jews stay in Palestine." Yol frowned.

"Words, that's all. The reality was that my parents were too old to live anywhere but in Poland and I was too young to live anywhere but here." He brightened. "So. You must tell me what has brought you to Jerusalem."

"To cut stone," Haim said. "I heard there was such work available."

"Absolutely. Men are needed. I've come to do the same work, and you've reminded me that we are already late. The day starts at sunrise at the quarry."

"Shouldn't I find myself a room before beginning work? I don't have much money, so the search may take a while."

"All the more reason to stay with me. I have a room with board lined up, and it's big enough for two. I've stayed there before. It's a nice enough place, clean, at least."

Haim was hesitant. Solitude was still an enjoyable novelty to him. "Maybe I'll find something on my own. I don't intend to be in Jerusalem for very long."

"You needn't worry about having to pay my way," Yol promised. "The Zionist Workers' Party is paying me a subsidy, and in a fortnight we'll receive our first stonecutter's wages."

"Well—"

"Suit yourself, my friend, but two sharing expenses can live a lot cheaper in Jerusalem."

Haim found himself laughing. "You remind me of someone when you talk like that."

"Really?" Yol asked, charmed. "Who? Tell me."

"Come on," Haim smiled. He shouldered the smaller man's heavy suitcase. "Take me to the quarries. We can't be tardy on our first day there."

They walked north past the green gates of the Mosque of Omar and the Church of the Holy Sepulcher, where Jesus was said to have been crucified back when this site was called Golgotha. They walked through a labyrinth of twisting stone alleys where Haim found himself dizzied by the quick interplay of gloomy perpetual shadow and dazzling sunlight. In just moments he was hopelessly lost, but Yol, chattering all the while, seemed to know just where he was.

"Mark Twain has written that Jerusalem is so small that you can walk all around its walls in less than an hour. That is true, but inside the walls you can walk up and down and underneath and around. It takes awhile to get used to this ant's nest."

Haim was only half listening. They were passing through a marketplace and his attention was captured by the exotic Arabs selling strange purple and red fruits. Feminine black eyes above black veils seemed to follow him as he walked. The smoke from countless charcoal braziers collected under the worn stone spandrels of connecting archways, making it hard for Haim to breathe.

"Have you read Mark Twain?" Yol asked.

"I heard he met with the czar years ago. Who is he?"

"An American writer, very popular, a great man."

"You know English?" Haim was impressed.

"Absolutely." Yol looked to be a very proud little monkey. "I know everything."

He led Haim out of the Old City through the Damascus Gate and on towards Mea She'arim, the site of the most recently begun Jewish quarter.

Another Jerusalem was being built around the cramped confines of the old. The Jews, whose numbers had increased until overcrowding was intolerable and the landlords completely out of hand, were venturing from the security of the walls to establish new settlements just north and west of the Old City. At the same time the churches began putting up hotels and monasteries to accommodate growing numbers of Christian pilgrims.

Haim and Yol introduced themselves to the Yemenite foreman in charge of the stonework at Mea She'arim.

When he asked them what experience they had, Haim turned shy, but Yol cheerfully announced, "None at all."

The foreman sighed, indicated the expert Arab masons and instructed his newcomers to "Do as they do." Laboring alongside the Arabs were the children of Jews who had come to the Holy City during the last decades. These families lived like beggars, dependent on handouts from the Zionist committee in charge of distributing money donated from abroad.

Just how this money should be divided was a thorny question. For instance the Jews who had come from the pale insisted that all Russian donations should go to them. The dispute splintered the Jewish community into ghettos within the greater ghetto, each comprising those from a certain town or country and laying claim to the money that came from their place of origin.

The children of these feuding Jews were thoroughly demoralized. It was the hope of the various philanthropic agencies that hard work done on the behalf of all Jews would renew the spirit of these young people.

Haim, excited at the prospect of earning his first money in Palestine, stripped off his tunic and set to work. The Arabs all around him nudged each other and laughed.

An hour later the novelty of chipping stone had quite worn off. Haim's fingers were bleeding and his shoulders and face were stiff and sore with sunburn. By the end of the day his hands were too raw with blisters even to hold the hammer and chisel. All thought of finding a room of his own had vanished. When Yol renewed his invitation to share his quarters, Haim fought back the urge to kiss him.

The inn was in the Jewish quarter near the Western Wall. Yol led Haim beneath archways that were blessedly cool after the searing heat of the quarry and then down dark slippery steps until at last they came to a rotting wood facade that jutted out of a mossy limestone cavern.

Haim said he was too tired for supper, but both Yol and Mrs. Gertz, the gaunt, grey-haired landlady, insisted that he eat. He waited, almost falling asleep at the table, until a plate of fried eggs and bread was put before him. One taste of food and Haim realized he was ravenous. He ate half a dozen eggs, and finally pushed away from the table to follow Yol up the sagging, creaking staircase to their room.

The top-floor chamber had a vaulted ceiling with peeling plaster and one small window facing the wall across the narrow courtyard. Haim collapsed onto one of the thin straw-stuffed mattresses lying on the warped floorboards and tears of exhaustion seeped from his eyes.

"Here now, you'll get used to it," Yol said soothingly. As tired as Haim, he was sprawled half off the mattress and did not have the strength to right himself. The white limestone dust powdering his curly beard and hair made him seem to have aged fifty years.

"Haim? You wouldn't have maybe a bottle of schnapps in your pocket?"

"No." He smiled. "Again you remind me of Abe. He always liked to take a drink before going to sleep."

"Who?"

Between yawns Haim told Yol about himself. He left out yesterday's incidents in Jaffa. If and when the time came to describe Rosie, Haim wanted to have enough energy to do the job justice.

"So, Mr. Shoemaker," Yol teased as he stripped off his clothing and tossed it into a pile in the far corner of the room, "how do you like stonecutting?"

"I think I ruined more stone than I cut," Haim muttered.

"Don't worry, there's plenty more." Yol sighed. "You know the worst? Not the hard work but the way those Arabs kept laughing at us."

"How did you get stuck doing this?" Haim asked.

"For the last year I have lived in Zikhron, north of Jaffa on the southern spur of Mount Carmel. They grow grapes and olives there, also a little barley and wheat. The Workers Party asked for volunteers to work the land. The old Jews who own it all depend on Arab labor to do the work. You will find that the different generations of Jews here in Palestine have very different ideas as to how things should be done. Anyway, the party pulled a few strings and off we workers went, led by our manager, a nice enough fellow by the name of Ben-Gurion. In Zikhron I followed a plow," Yol continued. "It was a job I am even less suited for than stonecutting, I must admit."

"Then why did you go in the first place?" Haim asked.

Yol chuckled. "To impress the party a little bit, but mostly to get on Ben-Gurion's right side." Despite his weariness, Yol's voice took on an excited edge. "You see, my friend, Ben-Gurion had just returned from Galilee, where he helped form a watchman's organization called the Hashomer to guard pioneers from Arab attacks."

"Really? With guns and horses?"

"Absolutely."

Haim turned on his side to face Yol. "I don't understand why you would have to learn how to plow a field in order to join the Hashomer."

"We must be self-sufficient in all things if we are to make this country our home. We must know how to farm and build as well as fight." Yol shrugged. "Anyway, that is the party's belief. The plantation owners of Zikhron Yaakov see it another way. Jewish labor would cut their profits. Arabs will work very cheaply, you see.

"Places like Zikhron and Rishon le Zion are Rothschild colonies, and the great baron has done much for land settlement in Palestine, but the Jews who got here first have grown wealthy thanks to the baron's tzedakah and forgotten what it feels like to be poor. The party asks them what shall the thousands of newcomers do to make a living if only Arabs are allowed to work in the established colonies?'' Yol shook his head in disgust. "The farmers are locked in greed and suspicion of us young Zionists. On one hand they like to think that we are not capable of hard work in a warm climate—"

"They may be right," Haim groaned, feeling his aching body.

"No they're not," Yol insisted, "but there is more here than mere prejudice or even greed. The old generation scorns us for not praying every morning, for daring to go with our heads uncovered. They say we are not good Jews and so must not be trusted. When we tried to reason with them they looked down on us like we were fellahin. They called us intellectuals, and when we sang a song or danced the hora in order to relax after a hard day's work, the old Jews locked away their daughters from us."

"So what happened?" Haim asked. "Why did you leave Zikhron?"

"I was banished. They came for me with pitchforks."

"Why?"

"Remember those daughters?" Haim wordlessly nodded and Yol's grimy bearded face split into a lascivious, lip-smacking smile. "They didn't lock them up so good after all."

Haim sank back upon his mattress, chuckling softly as he shook his head. "Some watchman you're going to be!"

"What can I tell you? The girls of Zikhron thought I was something special. It was all very innocent, Haim. I merely danced with the lovely daughters of the bourgeoisie. With them I was not a plowman."

Haim rolled over onto his stomach and shut his eyes. "Good night, Yol."

"At first, when the angry fathers began a boycott of us halutzim, it seemed quite funny," Yol rambled on. "It was like a holiday, but soon we had nothing to eat. Something had to be done, so Ben-Gurion went to make peace with the old boys. It turned out that peace required me to take my leave of Zikhron. It was arranged for me to have a subsidy to learn stonecutting here in Jerusalem. I got rides down the coast to Jaffa, and from there I took the coach, which brings you up to date on me, my friend.'' Yol glanced over at Haim, who seemed to be sound asleep. ''At least I got to make an impression on Ben-Gurion. He won't forget my face so fast.''

''That's a certainty,'' Haim grunted. ''Yol, you are a clown.''

''So?'' Yol settled back and closed his eyes. ''If we're to be self-sufficient in all things, we'll need our own comedians, yes?''

''Go to sleep,'' Haim said smiling in the dark.

The days passed quickly. For Haim the work in the quarry never got easy, but with the aid of leather gloves his hands grew callused and hard and his skin baked bronze beneath the bright sun. None of the Jews ever came close to matching the expertise of the Arab masons, but each man, be he a halutz or a second-generation Jerusalemite, began to take pride in the fact that he was doing his part to build the homeland.

Both men grew hard and lean from moving and cutting stone. After several weeks Haim went to buy new clothes and was shocked to see how his waist had shrunk and his chest and arms had put on meat. Even little Yol looked less like a monkey and more like an ape. The other Jews had taken to calling them David and Goliath.

It wasn't long before they found themselves with the energy to wander the city in the evenings. Haim, playing the role of a true turn-of-the-century Marxist Zionist, belittled the importance of visiting the Western Wall. Yol forced him to go. The little man stood back grinning as

Haim became oblivious to the Arabs who'd built their huts against the remains of Solomon's Temple. Haim began to weep as he ran his fingers across the rough stonework.

"Do you believe, Yol?" Haim asked as they left the temple's remains. "Do you believe what the rabbis say, that God has never left the Wall?"

Yol scratched at his woolly curls. "I know that our hearts have never left, and now we are back again." He patted Haim's shoulder. "And God is with us, yes?"

When it became clear to Haim that he would not be returning to Jaffa so quickly he began to write to Rosie twice a week. Yol was curious but did not pry, wise enough to know that Haim would confide in him when he was ready. The bearded halutz had never heard how Haim came to fight with a Turk his first day in Palestine.

One clear starlit night Haim and Yol walked along Mount Scopus. They spent the evening on blankets spread beneath the wind-rustled silver leaves of an olive grove. For a while they were quiet, content to feel their kinship with the Hebrews who had walked this ground millennia ago.

Then abruptly Haim began to talk. He told Yol about his first day in Jaffa, what had gone on between him and Rosie and how he meant to marry her. Much to his chagrin, his heartfelt confession was met with a hyena-pitched peal of laughter.

"I think I'll hang you by your feet in a tree," Haim growled.

Yol wiped tears of laughter from his eyes. "If you do, you'll never hear about Rosie and her family."

"Just how do you know so much?"

"My friend," Yol protested, "it's a small country, and Erich Glaser and his children are well known. As for Rosie, she's the one we know best of all."

"What!" Haim exploded.

"Uh—Poor choice of words, my friend," Yol quickly said. "I meant 'know of her great beauty.' "

"Be careful," Haim warned, somewhat mollified. "You're talking about my future wife."

"Oy. Listen to me, Haim. You are not the first man to be taken with Rosie's charms. There exists a long line of potential grooms before you. Why, I myself proposed marriage to Rosie Glaser—"

"You?"

"And got my face slapped for my brashness, I hasten to add." Haim muttered. Yol looked sympathetic. "My friend, a goodly number of trees must be planted in Palestine before there are enough branches for you to hang by their feet all of Rosie's suitors."

"I don't know what to say." Haim was crestfallen. "Have I made a fool of myself?"

"Absolutely. However that isn't such a terrible thing. Girls of Rosie's sort like that in a man."

"Tell me everything."

"I'm glad you asked." Yol leaned back to gaze with great contentment at the moonlight filtering through the leafy olive boughs. "What a great country Palestine is. Even in Lublin I didn't have gossip on virtually every important Jew. Well, you know, of course, that Erich Glaser is a renowned artist."

Haim remembered the paint splatters and smell of turpentine. "I didn't know."

"A great painter," Yol repeated. "He has been successful since an early age, when he came under the patronage of Sir Moses Montefiore—"

"Of him I've heard." Haim nodded, impressed. "There is a settlement northwest of the city named Yemin Moshe."

Yol smiled. "That settlement bears Montefiore's name because he donated so much money to get it built. Anyway, Montefiore was interested in art, and since Erich Glaser was Jewish as well as talented, it was an excellent match.

In the forties Montefiore negotiated with Lord Palmerston for Jewish agricultural colonies in Palestine. By the time he met Erich Glaser, around 1870, I guess, the *Alliance Israelite Universelle* had been established near Jaffa.''

''What was that?'' Haim demanded.

''Just a fancy name for an agricultural school.''

''Get to Rosie.''

''Patience. Glaser had some money, a wife, a pair of sons and a reputation as an important painter, thanks in part to Montefiore, who'd also instilled in his protege Zionism. Glaser's the sort who never does anything half-way. He moved his family to Jerusalem in the 1880s. He is one of the first wave of repatriation.''

''And Rosie was born here, yes? She is a child of Zion?''

''She was born here.''

Haim thought back to his landing on the Jaffa beach, trying to remember Glaser's other daughters, but at the time he'd had eyes only for Rosie. ''Yol, she's not the youngest daughter, is she?'' If there were older girls in Glaser's family, they would have to be married off before Rosie could take a husband.

''Don't worry, she's the oldest, in her early twenties,'' Yol replied, reading Haim's mind. ''And Glaser isn't the sort to hold to tradition anyway. Keep in mind that the man is an artist, and artists flaunt tradition.''

''You think so?''

''Absolutely. Why, when Glaser first arrived he went to work teaching at Professor Schatz's Bezalel Art School. Of the Bezalel you must have heard?''

''No.''

''Ah, you're a dunce. Fortunately, you are also tall and handsome. It is the little ugly fellows like me who must be intelligent in order to get anywhere with the girls.''

"I see where your intelligence with girls has gotten you—chased from Zikhron to Jerusalem's rock quarries."

"I called you a dunce. Must you make of me a liar? Maybe I'd best continue my story. At the Bezalel, of which everyone but Haim Kolesnikoff has heard, Erich Glaser began painting scenes of Palestine. His works were placed in galleries overseas, where they sold to wealthy Jews who wanted a bit of the Holy Land to hang on the walls. The earnings allowed Glaser to purchase an inn in Jaffa, which has always been the gate through which immigrants passed. Since he was an artist, I suppose Erich had the right sort of temperament to get along with the Turks and Arabs. His inn became a place where immigrants were welcome to rest and get their bearings during their first few days in Palestine. He uses his own money in addition to funds given him by the agency to pay the baksheesh for newcomers."

"So?"

"So what?"

"What about Rosie? Tell me about Rosie."

"You know everything you need to know about her already," Yol laughed. "She's pretty—"

"I think she's beautiful."

"That's what I meant. Forgive me, my friend. She's beautiful, with good spirit, and her papa has a little money as well as a fine reputation. That's why when boys come to Eretz Yisroel, don't know what to do with themselves and decide to take a wife, Rosie's usually their choice." He wrapped himself up in his blanket. "We should go to sleep."

"Is that why you proposed to her, because you didn't know what to do with yourself?"

"Maybe."

Both men grew quiet. From somewhere in the grove came an owl's plaintive call. Haim idly plucked at the tufts of grass. "Did you love her?"

"I thought I did," Yol replied after a moment. "I loved her madly at the time, but thinking back, I suspect it was her father I really loved. You must understand how lonely I was my first few months here. I'm not like you, dear Haim, I don't draw people and make friends so easily. I make jokes but not friends." He sighed. "So here I was, far from my family and friends in Poland, surrounded by steely-eyed halutzim who had no time for jokes. Erich Glaser and I could talk about art and music; why, he even shared with me a bottle of French wine. Rosie is a darling, and it was easy for me to fall in love with her, for it allowed me to become another of Glaser's children." He sat up to face Haim. "Can you understand?"

"Yes. What did Rosie say to you when you asked for her hand in marriage?"

"The same thing she tells all her would-be husbands. She said, 'Not in a million years.' "

"Will she say that to me?"

"Absolutely. In your case, however, 'not in a million years' may well translate into 'after several months of courtship.' "

"You really believe that's true?"

"I have a feeling you're the man she'll marry, and my instincts about such matters are usually correct. In my case I would have had to wait the full million years." Yol laughed. "By then I'd be too old to join the Hashomer."

"You really do mean to join? The more I know you, the less I see you killing your beloved Arabs—"

"Then you don't know me," Yol declared. "They call us David and Goliath, but I mean to be a real David, a warrior. It has been my ambition for my entire life. For a Jew to become such a thing in Europe is unheard of, but here in a new land I can be a new person, and I intend to."

"You needn't get so touchy."

"Then don't make fun of me."

"To be a member of Hashomer is my goal as well," Haim reminded him.

"Hmmm. That you had best discuss with Rosie, yes?" Yol drew his blanket up over his head.

It was over a year before the stonecutting job was done. During that time Haim and Yol got acquainted with other young people who had come to rebuild and repopulate Palestine. Every night there were discussion groups to exchange news, practice Hebrew vocabulary and grammar and endlessly discuss the dialectics of Zionism. In Europe such meetings were for the most part political. In Palestine they struck a social note. Romances sparked, and marriages were made. A network of comrades was gradually formed.

Jerusalem itself seemed to welcome the influx of Jews. Haim had expected trouble with the Turks and the Arabs, but the Turks, if they paid any attention at all to the Jews, merely seemed amused, while the Arabs welcomed the construction work. Haim found himself picking up a smattering of Turkish and Arabic.

Haim kept up his correspondence with Rosie and found the time to make the journey to Jaffa to visit her every few months. Erich Glaser's inn was a rambling one-story whitewashed structure with flat roofs of red tile. Gardens, patios and terraces added charm to the wings that had been constructed over the decades. The place invariably teemed with new immigrants. Sometimes they were packed four and five to a room, but no one complained, since they were being sheltered and fed for free.

The Glasers had a wing all to themselves. The artist's wife was constantly flitting about the place, overseeing the Arab servants who did the cooking and housekeeping. Miriam Glaser had snow-white hair and leathery skin after years beneath the strong Mediterranean sun. Haim thought she was a few years older than her husband. She favored loose robes of Arab design.

Erich Glaser spent the mornings with his children doing agency work. Each afternoon he painted. He would disappear into his studio, a small outbuilding in a quiet corner of the main garden, and not emerge until dinner.

On his first visit to the inn Haim was surprised to find the portrait of himself and Abe framed and hung in the family living room. Erich Glaser asked if Haim had done the drawing and was disappointed at the answer. However, Haim was positive he detected a look of relief in Rosie's dark brown eyes.

His overnight visits with the family were always cordial, but that was to be expected. The Glasers welcomed many halutzim into their home. Haim knew he would not be able to tell how the family felt about him until he returned to Jaffa for good.

Rosie always saw him in private, if only in acknowledgment of the grueling trip. They would walk along the beach or stroll through the Arab bazaar. Rosie always raced ahead, forcing Haim to run to keep up with her. Taking her arm or trying to steal a kiss was out of the question.

Haim considered it an achievement if Rosie consented to talk to him without peppering the conversation with criticisms and insults. Haim did not take her taunts seriously; he was perceptive enough to realize that the members of Glaser's family felt overshadowed by the patriarch's strong will.

Rosie's spirit was too strong to be cowed by her father's—that's why she disobeyed him and tried to negotiate with the Turk—so she was relieved when Haim said he was not a painter. She was interested in him, but clearly she would never marry a man who marched in her father's footsteps. Rosie was waiting for the day when she could escape her father's shadow and be more than Erich Glaser's daughter.

Haim vowed to use Rosie's ambition in his strategy to win her, but first he had to capture her attention, and fleeting visits would never serve. Rosie was hardly able to grow used to him before it was time to return to Jerusalem.

Still, he had reason to hope, especially after an exchange that took place near the end of his last visit, while Rosie was walking him back to the coach depot.

"Why don't you stay here in Jaffa?" she suddenly demanded, her dark eyes serious. "If you care so much for me, why are you always running back to Jerusalem?"

Haim was tempted to forget Jerusalem and swear to remain by Rosie's side forever if she'd have him, but to neglect his duty was not a possibility. "Rosie, in Jerusalem we cut stone for a school. I wish to be with you, but I must see the job finished. All Jews, not just those who will inhabit Mea She'arim, have a stake in the settlement." He paused. His tongue grew thick and his heart began to pound at the audacity of what he was about to say. "Someday, Rosie, you and I will take our children to Mea She'arim, and we will point out that school and tell how I helped build it."

"How dare you," Rosie scolded, making as if to strike him, but her sable eyes were sparkling and her fingers on his cheek abruptly were something closer to a caress than a slap.

They walked the rest of the way to the depot in silence. Haim was unwilling to break the spell, quite content to savor sweet victory.

After that Haim tripled his correspondence to Rosie, who tended to answer about every third letter with a chatty but impersonal summation of happenings in Jaffa. Writing was torture for Haim. He never knew what to put down or how to express himself. It often took him an entire evening to compose a paragraph, and then he must agonize over its stilted phrases, positive that his clumsy style would only drive his beloved further from him.

"Don't worry about the coolness of her replies,"

Yol advised him. "Rosie will remain aloof precisely because she cares for you. When she turns friendly and treats you like a brother, give up, for a brother is all you'll ever be to her."

Rosie began to write that her father was involved in a building project with a man named Meir Dizengoff. Her letters spoke in such glowing terms about him that Haim started to worry about having a serious rival. Yol assured him that this was not the case; Dizengoff was not only married but old, and he looked like a toad.

Haim still brooded. Perhaps Dizengoff was not a rival, but who knew when someone else might catch Rosie's eye?

He was stuck here in Jerusalem and she was in Jaffa. What if some single fellow like Dizengoff came along? Against any penniless young halutz Haim was confident he could compete, but against a prosperous older man? In Russia the wealthy could take their pick of young women. Rosie could very easily talk herself into such a match. Of course she would end up miserable, not to mention himself. This new worry only made the time pass more slowly.

A week before the stonecutting was to end, Yol came to Haim with exciting news. The Jewish National Fund had been buying up land in Galilee. It came cheap, sold to the fund by Arabs who thought the Jews insane for planning to farm in a desert in the summer, a muddy mosquito-infested swamp during the winter.

"A bunch of us are going to Kinnereth," Yol began. "We'll be working under a fund supervisor, which isn't perfect, but it is better than laboring for some bourgeois plantation owner of a Jew who thinks Palestine is only fit for growing cabbages by Arabs."

Haim nodded, happy for his friend and more than a little envious. "When do you leave?"

Yol shrugged and looked down at his shoes. "Day

after tomorrow, old friend. I guess the stone will get along without me, yes?''

"We'll manage," Haim smiled. "You take care of yourself, now. There are Arab marauders—''

"I know. A couple of Hashomer will be assigned to our settlement, but all of us will have to take turns patrolling. Isn't that wonderful? At last I shall be trained with a gun and a horse.''

"Just stay away from the girls," Haim laughed, "or else they'll send you back to the quarries.''

"About that you needn't worry. Only one woman is coming along to manage the house, and I hear she is quite fat. Not my type at all, you know . . .'' Yol suddenly grabbed hold of Haim's shoulders. "Do you want to come?''

Haim shook his head. "You know why.''

That night they got drunk on wine made at Rishon le Zion, ignoring the disapproving looks of the Jews they passed as they staggered down the streets. The next morning they awoke with a sick feeling that had nothing to do with drinking. Yol did not go to work at the quarry that day. He had too much to do to prepare for his journey. Haim chiseled stone without his friend beside him and had a foretaste of how much he was going to miss the little monkey.

When he returned home that evening, he found Yol sitting on his packed suitcase in their room. "It turns out I'll be leaving tonight.''

"Good riddance." Haim pretended to scowl. In a way it was a blessing in disguise; he had not been looking forward to this last awkward night.

"I told Mrs. Gertz not to throw you out," Yol joked.

"That's good of you, considering that it's me who always remembers the rent's due.''

"I never held that against you. Anyway, money will be unnecessary in the settlements of the future. No one will possess anything, so no one will be lacking.''

"That's quite an Eden you're planning to build. Just don't die of swamp fever before it's finished."

"Do you doubt?"

"I envy you, Yol," Haim said. "Go and build. I would join you if I were not in love."

"Hmmm, love." Yol looked unhappy. "Aren't we friends?"

"The best."

"Then it is out of friendship that I presume to tell you so much about yourself. I wonder whether friendship isn't a pleasure with you but a necessity, a drug to maintain your sense of well-being, like the hashish maintains the Arabs in the bazaar."

"I don't understand."

"People like you need to be surrounded by admirers, Haim. Can you stand to be alone?"

"I came to Palestine by myself, didn't I?"

"And within the first couple of days found for yourself a lady love and a replacement for Abe."

"Are you saying you believe that I am not really your friend?"

Yol shook his head. "No. I don't question the sincerity of your feelings. I do wonder how much having been an orphan has to do with them. I wonder how your inability to remember your family affects you."

Haim took a deep breath and slowly exhaled, trying to control his fury. "Yol, I know you mean well," he said thickly, "and I will always be your friend, but I think you had better go."

Yol nodded. He picked up his suitcase and started for the door. "I will write to you in care of Erich Glaser," he called over his shoulder. He stopped to turn and gaze at Haim from the doorway. "Think things over carefully. Your dream has just begun. Once you marry Rosie, you will have to share that dream."

Haim listened to Yol's footsteps as he descended the

creaking staircase. At first they were loud, but too soon
they faded.

He looked around the room at the peeling plaster and
warped floorboards. The four walls were screaming at him
in deafening silence. He tried to sleep, but Yol's words—
his accusations—came back to him every time he closed
his eyes. Finally he gave up and went up to the flat roof of
the inn.

On the hottest nights he and Yol dragged their straw
mattresses up here to sleep beneath the moon and stars.
The night sky never failed to please him during those
times. The cool breezes wafted the flowery scent of in-
cense through the darkness, lulling him into drowsiness.

Tonight the Jerusalem evening was devoid of sweet
smells, and the pearly moon and cold, glittering stars
brought no solace. Haim restlessly prowled the roof. The
spires and domes of Jerusalem lay spread before him, stark
shapes and purple shadows. In the distance lay Mount
Scopus. Haim remembered Yol and himself walking those
hills and sleeping beneath the olive trees, and he felt
his heart begin to ache with the pain of separation and
loneliness.

If he had to share his dream with Rosie, so be it. And
what did he care why he loved her as long as that love was
real? Yol was knowledgeable, perhaps too much so for his
own good. Haim had to get through this one awful night of
loss, and then tomorrow he would think not about losing
Yol, but of winning Rosie.

Chapter 7

Haim arrived just after daybreak and wandered about, unwilling to call on the Glasers at such an hour.

The first indication that the ambience in Jaffa had changed was out on the bay. It was a windless day and the water was a flat blue mirror flecked with gold. Three steamships packed with immigrants were anchored together like herd animals. The small rowboats usually manned by Arab boys were beached upon the yellow sand; the youths themselves were nowhere to be seen. An older halutz—one Haim had never seen—was arguing with a Turkish officer. The Jew was wildly gesticulating, pointing to the steamers with a wad of money clutched in his hand. The officer stood with his arms crossed, shaking his head in refusal.

The second sign came after Haim bought breakfast in an Arab inn. The place was clean and it had tables and chairs instead of mats on the floor. Many windows afforded a view of the water. Finding the food to his liking, and the Turkish coffee thick and strong, Haim decided it would be a good place to stay. After all, he could not expect to move in with the Glasers while he was courting a daughter of the house.

He asked for the proprietor and was directed to an Arab seated at a small table in the corner. The man had a massive head with a thick shock of fleecy black hair. His right eye was badly swollen and wept constantly.

Haim asked for a room and was startled at how impolite the innkeeper's refusal was. The Arab made no apology nor even deigned to look at Haim.

"There are no rooms available here or anywhere in Jaffa for more Hebrews." As the innkeeper spoke he dabbed at his wet eye with a handkerchief. "Why don't you go to the Dar al-Yahud?"

"The Hebrew Inn is not suitable," Haim replied. He was careful to show no emotion and to keep his voice even. "That you do not welcome me is clear. Surely you know of a place that would welcome a paying guest?"

The Arab was not interested in that particular conversation. "Is it right that the workers answer to Jews in their own country?" he demanded, pressing his sodden handkerchief against his teary eye. "If I gave you a room you might complain. Jaffa is plagued with guests who insult our hospitality by complaining and turning us poor fellahin from the old ways handed down to us."

Haim had no more patience. "God be with you," he said before he returned to his table to finish his meal.

The innkeeper watched him in silence. "God go with you," he cried, sounding ashamed, when Haim rose to leave.

The glowering Turk on the beach who refused baksheesh and the innkeeper who was not interested in a paying guest puzzled Haim, but he began to understand their displeasure as he explored the town. During his infrequent overnight visits he'd had eyes only for Rosie. Now he was really looking.

When he first arrived in Palestine, Jaffa was a sleepy little place. Now the narrow, dusty lanes were clogged with shrill Jewish peddlers, hawking ribbons and pins right in front of the Arab stalls. Haim stared at these newcomers with their long beards, black coats and fur hats, at their sullen wives and screeching children. When he landed it was with a sense of wonder and an earnest desire to become part of this new land. How strange seemed these Jews from his own part of the world. It amazed him to realize that he felt more comfortable with the Turks and Arabs than amongst these upstarts.

He walked the Jewish neighborhoods. A year ago both the older communities and the newer had rooms and houses going begging. Now the twisting alleys were alive with homeless immigrants. The close, still air felt like wet wool on the skin and the flies and the reek of the garbage-strewn gutters assaulted the senses. Signs in Yiddish, Russian, Polish—every language but Hebrew—advertised beds for rent at impossible prices.

Haim hurried on to the Glasers' home. By this hour the inn and its grounds were teeming with activity. Haim made his way to the more sedate family quarters. A slender, elderly manservant named Kamel answered the door: he had been with the Glasers for years, so Haim was known to him. After a polite welcome he told Haim that neither Mr. Glaser nor Rosie was available but Mrs. Glaser was in the rear flower gardens.

Cultivating flowers was the only domestic routine Miriam Glaser had not delegated to her staff. She lavished as much care on her roses, violets and gladioli as she had on her many children. Just now, it was the gladioli to which she was turning her attention. Great lush spikes of salmon pink, scarlet, light green and violet-blue flowers lay in her wicker basket.

"Haim, how nice to see you," she cried, embracing him. "Are you here just overnight?"

"Actually, no. The work in Jerusalem is finished, Mrs. Glaser. I have come back to look for a place to live—"

"Please!" Mrs. Glaser stabbed the air with her pruning shears. "The Jewish quarter is intolerable and the Arabs will not have you these days." She frowned. "Things are awkward in the Arab district just now. You will stay with us."

"But you have so little room as it is," Haim protested. As much as he would like to remain under the same roof as Rosie, he didn't want to wear out his welcome. "Your sons may not want to share with me."

"My two eldest are not even here. Josh and Solomon are visiting family friends in Petah Tikvah. They've gotten it into their heads to be citrus growers, so they've gone to learn the art. You can have their room to yourself."

"I don't wish to be a burden."

Mrs. Glaser laughed. "You'd be doing us a favor. We miss the boys. Erich will look forward to talking with you." She winked. "Between us, the painting is not going so well just now. He's been an ogre. Your arrival is sure to distract him from his work."

"And Rosie? Do you think she'll be glad to see me?"

"That is something you must discover for yourself," Mrs. Glaser smiled, her brown eyes sparkling. As she turned back to her glads Haim began to get an idea of where Rosie had come by her tricks.

"Where is she now?" he asked.

"You know the Sha'arei Torah, the school in Neveh Shalom? In the back there are offices. That's where you'll find Rosie."

"What is she doing there?"

"That I'll let her tell you," Mrs. Glaser murmured. Haim knew it would be a wasted effort to try and get more out of such a sly woman. He thanked her for her invitation and said he would be back later in the day.

"Kamel," Mrs. Glaser called. When the servant appeared she said, "Kamel, see to Haim's bag. He'll be staying in Josh and Sol's room.

"Dinner will be at seven o'clock," Mrs. Glaser reminded Haim, "same time as always, but tonight there's an important guest coming—besides you, of course." she giggled. "Kamel, after you show Haim out, I'll want you to cut some tea roses for the centerpiece."

Haim waited until he and the servant were out of earshot before he stopped Kamel. "Tell me, please. What is happening in town?"

The old Arab looked uneasy. "You will say nothing to the master and mistress?"

"I swear."

Kamel nodded. His dusky skin crinkled like parchment as he offered Haim a wry smile. "Young fellow, I will tell a story in which neither of us figures, and in that way avoid all impoliteness. Say an unfortunate Hebrew pilgrim was drowning in the sea after being cast off of his ship by a cruel Christian master. 'Help! Help' the Jew calls out, on the verge of sliding beneath the waves. A kind Arab sailing by, a good Moslem, pulls him from the ocean. Before the Hebrew is dry he claims to be captain of the Arab's ship. Not only does he insist on the right to give orders to his savior, he even insists that he knows the correct course in which to steer this ship that he has commandeered."

"What if there are two Arabs on this ship, a sailor and the owner of the vessel? What if the owner sells the ship? Must not the sailor take orders from the new owner?"

Kamel had Bedouin blood. Now his face turned as fierce and unforgiving as those barren, rugged hills his ancestors had wandered. "You do not understand, young master. You know my language, but you do not see the pictures that I see inside my head when you use my words. Own? Sell? What does it all mean? The rich landlords sell the fellahin's land out from under them. Perhaps they throw a few coppers our way, but soon the money will be spent. The land will still be there, and clearly it must be taken back, for God has given it to the Arabs." The servant looked away and became his usual polite self. "I will take your bag to the bedroom, and then I must hurry to the garden, young master, for the mistress awaits me."

Haim let him escape as he considered Kamel's parable. A tiny ship bobbing in a vast ocean while the two on board fight to decide who shall be captain when what they both ought to worry about is getting to land.

Jaffa's second Jewish quarter, Neveh Shalom, was founded in 1891. It extended over about ten thousand square yards purchased from the effendis. With typical stubbornness the Jews of Jaffa, who had delightedly embraced the first quarter, Neveh Zedek, shunned Nevah Shalom for being "untraditional." The new houses remained empty until the rabbi of Jaffa bought one. Finally the district filled and the school, Sha'arei Torah, opened in 1896, funded by a predominantly wealthy class of newly arrived doctors, teachers and businessmen.

The school and its neighbors were closely packed in what the quarter's designers had dubbed the Parisian style. The school had an ornate facade but was nonetheless an Arab-style building, a cave of stone with thick walls and small windows. Inside it was dim and cool. Haim could hear children reciting lessons as he made his way to the offices.

In Sha'arei Torah secular as well as spiritual lessons were taught. Here large meetings were held in the evening and temporary space was given over to work for the community. If you wanted to know what was going on among the Jews of Jaffa, you came to Sha'arei Torah.

Haim considered this a good thing. Being a Zionist and not particularly religious, he was glad to see authority moving away from the rabbis toward the more innovative educators and wealthy merchant class. It took brains, muscle, and cash, not piety, to get things done.

Haim could hear Rosie's voice echoing down the musty corridor. The weak electric bulbs shone off the dark green floor tiles, adding to the musty feeling. He was far too anxious to see her for it to occur to him to knock. He swung the door open and sauntered inside the cluttered, brightly lit office. Rosie and an older man were standing side by side, scrutinizing a blueprint. She'd been asking questions and jotting down responses on a notepad. She stopped what she was doing and gaped at Haim.

"Yes? What is it, young man?" snapped the man in fluent Hebrew. He was stout, short and balding on top, with a horseshoe of clipped grey hair. He was dressed in a black wool suit with vest and velvet lapels, a boiled shirt with starched wing collar and a red silk tie. On the hat rack in the corner hung his black derby. The heavy clothes should have had the man gasping for breath, but his complexion looked as powdery dry as chalk dust.

"I'm waiting." He glowered. "Answer, please, or be kind enough to take your leave. Important business is being conducted here."

Haim ignored the man totally, his eyes on Rosie. Her skin was the color of coffee with cream, magnificently set off by the peach-colored cotton sleeveless dress she wore. Her pale hair was pinned up to reveal her long, graceful neck and the delicate gold chain around her throat. As usual, her dark brown cat's eyes were lustrous and her wide, slightly crooked sunburnt nose was a delicate coral pink.

Haim stood transfixed by the sight of her, feeling his heart swell with love.

"What the hell is wrong with you?" The little frog-eyed man was working himself into a frenzy. "What's going on here?"

"Rosie, I've come for you," Haim said, taking a step toward her.

"Please," she said quellingly, "I'm working!"

"What work? Come, we've got a lot to discuss." He took hold of her arm.

"Don't you dare," Rosie shouted furiously as she pulled free of him. "You can't just—" She stopped. "Haim, please. I'm glad to see you, very glad. Come by the house tonight—late tonight—and we'll—"

"I'm staying at your father's house," Haim interrupted. "Your mother has invited me to dinner this evening."

"What? Oh no," Rosie moaned.

"Rosie, why are you acting like this?" Haim demanded. He could feel his confidence ebbing. How could he have been so certain that she loved him? How could he have been so wrong?

The little man cleared his throat. "Perhaps the two of you ought to go somewhere more appropriate for this kind of thing."

Rosie whirled in a panic. "Please, Meir, I want to stay."

"What's going on here?" Haim heard himself shout.

"Oh, my," the little man gasped, misunderstanding Haim's concern. "My dear fellow, you don't imagine that Rosie and I are—? I mean . . . Why, I'm a married man, and what we're doing here is purely—"

"Haim, this is Meir Dizengoff," Rosie said, completely mortified.

"I knew that."

"Then please," Rosie implored, "go away."

He began to take offense. A declaration of love he did not expect, but a little encouragement—"It's not like you see me every day, Rosie. I could carry you out of here, you know."

"If you do I will never speak to you again. I mean it—never again."

"All right. I surrender. Good day to both of you. Rosie, I shall see you at dinner." Haim turned and left the office.

Dizengoff stared after Haim. "So he loves you, eh?" He seemed pleased with the notion.

"What was that?" Rosie asked, returning to the blueprint.

"Nothing. Let's get back to work, shall we?"

The Glasers' living and dining rooms had a slate grey stone floor scattered with colorful Persian rugs. It was sparsely furnished with large worn leather armchairs from England and low mosaic-inlaid tables from the bazaar. Ringing a massive oval table was an array of Sheraton chairs in dark wood with seat cushions upholstered in crimson chintz.

"Nothing in this house matches, but that's what I like about this country," Erich Glaser announced over cocktails. The *non sequitur* sprang a bit too loudly from the painter's lips, but that was understandable; he was working on his second tumbler-sized whiskey and soda. "The marvelous dichotomy of dark, pale Jews in this grand sun-charred *goldeneh medina*—"

"Goldeneh medina," Meir Dizengoff chuckled. "That's what most Jews call America." He sipped at his thimbleful of sherry.

"In America the gold does lie in the streets, they say," Haim observed, not touching his sweet sticky sherry. "Here in Palestine there is also gold; we just have to dig a little deeper to find it."

The room filled with appreciative laughter. Haim glanced at Rosie and then triumphantly eyed Dizengoff. They were only five for dinner: Rosie and her parents, Dizengoff and Haim. The younger ones had eaten earlier.

The tension between Haim and Dizengoff reinstated itself as soon as Dizengoff arrived. The formally dressed little man did not hid his amusement at Haim's shirtsleeves and open collar. Erich Glaser was also dressed in a suit and tie, but he had told Haim not to concern himself about it.

Haim had worried about it until he saw that smirk on Dizengoff's face. At that moment his unease was replaced with defiant anger. No bourgeois wearing a necktie could intimidate an honest Zionist worker here in Eretz Yisroel, he resolutely decided; he need never be ashamed as long as his clothes were clean.

As the laughter over Haim's remark died down, Glaser exclaimed, "You see, what did I tell you, Meir? This boy is unlike your run-of-the-mill young pilgrim who comes to Palestine as sour as an unripe orange." He gulped at his drink.

"He certainly doesn't look like most halutzim," Rosie began. "He's—"

"That's right, he doesn't." Erich Glaser's deep baritone filled the room. "With his muscles, golden hair and blue eyes he looks goyish, right, Meir? I shall put you in my paintings, Haim. I'm sick of dark hair and brown eyes except for my darling Rosie's." He smiled benevolently and drained his glass. "Kamel, more drinks."

"I believe we'll be sitting down for dinner at any moment now, dear," Mrs. Glaser said nervously.

Glaser ignored her and turned to Haim and Dizengoff. "Know what I like about women in paintings? They're beautiful and silent."

Miriam Glaser wore a long-suffering look and Rosie was plainly angry. Both women kept quiet, however. When Erich Glaser got a few drinks in him, he was unable to tolerate any voice but his own.

Kamel appeared with the sherry and another large whiskey and soda.

"What? No one else drinking with me?" Erich Glaser

glowered as Kamel's offer of sherry was refused. "Suit yourselves, but I've had a long day in my studio."

Haim occupied himself by gazing at the various paint-ings that crowded the whitewashed walls. They were mostly landscapes in oils, great slabs of burnt sienna and tur-quoise representing the earth and sky, dotted with green and peopled with figures wearing kerchiefs and jackets of bright red and yellow. In Glaser's paintings glinting hoes were invariably raised toward a bright sun; the clouds were always like fat, white sheep; women endlessly gathered oranges like tiny suns.

There were no Arabs, Haim cynically thought, be-cause the Jews in Europe and America had little interest in them. Not that he begrudged Glaser his success; for one thing, he did not know enough about art to judge the man's work, and for another, Glaser daily thanked God for his own good fortune by donating both time and money to poor immigrants.

Looking out of place surrounded by Glaser's garish landscapes, the finely detailed charcoal portrait of Haim and Abe hung in a place of honor. Dizengoff seemed to be inordinately interested in it, asking Haim a great many questions about his boyhood.

At last they went to the table. Haim was seated on Mrs. Glaser's right, across from Dizengoff and Rosie. Kamel and two other servants presented cold eggplant with pine nuts, roast chicken with rice and a green salad with tomatoes grown in the Glasers' own garden. There was a grapy burgundy from Rishon le Zion served with the chicken. Haim took a sip of his wine every now and then out of politeness. Dizengoff seemed to be doing the same. Most of the meal was taken up with compliments to the hostess and the dismal clink of silverware against china.

Halfway through the main course Rosie suddenly brightened. "Haim, why don't you tell Meir about helping build that school on the outskirts of Jerusalem? Meir too is involved in building new settlements around the old towns.''

Haim set down his knife and fork on the edge of his plate and rested his bare sinewy forearms on the table. He smiled at the spiffy little man. "Ever do any stonecutting?''

Dizengoff turned his froglike gaze on Haim. "Just what do you know about me, young man?''

Haim shrugged. "You have an office at the talmud torah, so obviously you are involved in community work. Beyond that nothing.''

Dizengoff nodded like a schoolmaster. "Let me tell you a little about myself and about Jaffa as well. In 1905 I came to Jaffa—''

"The same year I came," Haim interjected.

Dizengoff responded with a thin smile. "Yes, of course. But I first came to Palestine in 1885, young man, and from the looks of you, in those days, you were still your guardian's apprentice in Russia.''

"Meir once worked with Baron Rothschild," Rosie said, a bit too dreamily for Haim's taste. "He met the baron while studying engineering in Paris.''

Dizengoff took up the tale. "I was interested in glass production. You see, I had this idea of using the sand of Palestine to produce bottles for the baron's distilleries in Rishon le Zion.''

"There is such a factory?" Haim asked.

"There was, at Tantura, just above Zichron on the coast, but in '94 we closed it down. The sand there was not suitable, and the nearby Kabara marshes were filled with malaria mosquitoes. It was—a bad time. We were not prepared—'' For a moment the little man looked almost tearful.

"So what happened?" Haim asked, interested now. Erich Glaser caught his attention and was shaking his head. Haim took the hint and fell silent.

"Well, then," Glaser said heartily, "so you returned to Jaffa in 1905, right, Meir?"

Dizengoff nodded. He seemed to have regained control of himself. "My dear young man," he continued, "have you any idea how the population of Jaffa has grown in the two years since—we—arrived?"

"I only noticed it for the first time today," Haim nodded. "The Arab quarter is overrun, as is the old Jewish quarter."

"In a decade the number of Jews in Jaffa went from a thousand to over five thousand. Now the number is about seven thousand—not including transients, but only people who have decided to make their homes in Jaffa."

"And you think this is to be encouraged?"

"Who are we to encourage or discourage anybody?" Dizengoff spread his hands. "Our goal should be to prepare this land for the immigration to come."

"I disagree," Haim said angrily. "Have you seen them in the town? They come here expecting their lives to continue just as in Russia and Poland, except that here they intend to be the persecutors and make the Arabs their victims."

"But Haim," Mrs. Glaser said gently, speaking for the first time, "surely you don't champion the Arabs over your own faith?"

"Of course not." Haim thought hard, trying to translate what was in his heart into the proper words to convey his feelings. "We are the new captains of this ship," he began, smiling to himself as he recalled Kamel's parable.

"The Turks may have something to say about that," Dizengoff wryly interjected, "but actually I agree with you, young man." He began to ramble on. "Like you, I worry about friction between the Arabs and the newcomers."

Haim leaned back in his chair and sighed. Dizengoff's raspy voice lapsed into the rhythmic cadences of the professional orator. Haim stared up at the ceiling, examined his

fingernails and was studying the back of his dessert spoon
when a hard look from Rosie made him sit up and pretend
to pay attention.

"We must built a new adjunct to this city," Dizengoff
droned. "We must build a suburb that will free the Jews of
economic enslavement to Arab landlords, a place where
children can play free of Jaffa's filth and fellahin, a place
their fathers can come home to after a day in the factory."

"In the sordid slums of Jaffa?" Haim rolled his eyes.
"Yes, I think I'm beginning to understand."

"What I propose is a quarter quite unlike anything
either in Jaffa or Jerusalem," Dizengoff continued placidly.
"It will be built large and have more room for expansion.
We have already learned that it is far too expensive to
build tiny settlements that never catch up to a constantly
expanding population."

"It's also a good deal less expensive to build a large
quarter all at once, rather than several small settlements
piecemeal," Rosie contributed.

Dizengoff beamed with pleasure at his disciple as
Haim struggled to choke down bitter jealousy. "And the
Turks?" he asked. "You brought them up yourself. Are
they to stand by while you build a Jewish—" Haim was
momentarily at a loss for words. "Will the Turks let us
build a Jewish city?"

Dizengoff, to Haim's increasing fury, seemed far too
delighted to speak.

"You know the Turks." Erich Glaser dismissed Haim's
argument with a lazy wave of his hand. "We will give
them baksheesh. They will grouse all the while they have
their hands out."

You think a bribe will always suffice, Haim thought
but did not say. He could not let Dizengoff make him so
angry as to insult his host. Still, he began to suspect that
Erich Glaser's money made him a bit arrogant.

"The Turks will accept their bribes and leave us

alone," Dizengoff agreed. "The effendi are far too short-sighted to object."

Haim winced and glanced at the open portal to the kitchen, hoping Kamel, who understood Hebrew, was not within earshot. As he turned back, he and Rosie locked eyes. Her affectionate smile told him that she understood and shared his concern for the old servant's feelings.

"And of course the fellahin would be happy to have the construction work," Dizengoff went on.

Haim stared at him. For all of his bravado he felt inferior to the two wealthy, older men. Although he was young, Haim was no fool; young halutzim such as he and Yol were merely soldiers in a vast and ever-growing army commanded by generals like Glaser and Dizengoff. A general could be wrong, as Dizengoff was. Haim's indignation combined with Rosie's smile to give him courage. He found himself on his feet, staring down.

"Do you mean to say that you do not intend to use Jewish labor to build your Jewish city?"

Dizengoff was contemptuous. "Talk sense, young man. Are Jews meant to dig ditches, cut stone, plow fields? Of course not." Dizengoff looked at Glaser as if to say, listen to the nonsense being spouted by this hotheaded youngster! He shook his head. "Not all Jews are blessed with your strength. No, we are meant to supervise, to manage."

"You certainly have changed your tune since the day we first met," Glaser gently teased Haim. "Do you remember the first thing out of your mouth?"

Haim frowned. "I—oh, of course." He laughed, embarrassed. "I believe I asked you where I might buy a gun."

"Exactly." Glaser smacked the table with his palm, making the wineglasses jump. "Do you remember why you wanted a weapon?"

Haim blushed. "Two years is a long time. I've learned since then."

"*Half* the lesson you've learned," Glaser corrected. "You said that you wanted a gun 'to shoot Arabs.' " The artist smiled. "Now you know the folly in that, but you've forgotten the second part of the lesson. I pointed at the Arab oarsmen and asked you, 'If you shoot them, who will row?' "

"Erich, if we had rowed ourselves, we'd have sweat a little, but at least we'd know that we can transport ourselves across the water."

"God also gave you two feet, but on occasion you consent to ride a horse or a coach," Dizengoff put in. "Do not bleed for your precious Arabs. They will survive, but this time around it is the Jews who will envision the grand cities and the pharoahs' people who will move the blocks of stone."

Haim's eyes filled with tears of scorn and despair. Is this what Eretz Yisroel is destined to become? he wondered. Have the Jews suffered all this time only to become tyrants? Am I expected to crack the whip myself?

No, never, Haim swore silently as he glared at Dizengoff and Glaser. He would never lend himself to such a scheme, not even for Rosie. It would have been far better to go to America with Abe; at least there all men, no matter what their nationality, were promised freedom.

"Tell me this," Haim heard himself demand. "When you capitalist tyrants are seated upon your pharoahs' thrones, what shall prevent God from sending again the plagues? When the Arab Moses rises up and says, 'Let my people go,' and you reply, 'We cannot, for Jews have never learned to make bricks, grow fruit, cut stone,' will the Lord in righteousness strike down your firstborn?"

Dizengoff leapt to his feet, his eyes two embers glowing with shock and anger. Before Haim could react, the little man slapped him across the face.

Haim stared down at Dizengoff. He was twice the older man's size and could easily snap him in two. Of course he did no such thing, but merely touched his tingling cheek while gazing with wonder at Dizengoff.

He glanced at the others around the table. Mr. and Mrs. Glaser were clearly disapproving, but to his relief Rosie seemed just as bewildered as he was at Dizengoff's astounding behavior. Granted his words had been harsh; never could Haim have imagined that they possessed the power to shatter Dizengoff's composure.

Dizengoff slumped back into his chair and leaned on the table, his face buried in his hands.

"Rosie," Glaser whispered, "take Haim outside for a walk, please."

Haim felt Rosie's hand around his wrist, leading him away. Outside Haim breathed a relieved sigh as the cool darkness wrapped around him and the breeze soothed the hot flush of shame and perplexity.

"What happened back there, Rosie?"

They were heading for the beach. "You said a number of awful things." She tried to sound accusing, but her heart wasn't in it. "I know what you mean, Haim. I've never seen Meir like that. Certainly I recognize his anger and impatience, but never has anybody broken him this way."

"Some accomplishment. I've hurt an important man and probably soured your father on the idea of our marriage."

"Damnit, Haim." Rosie spun on him like a tigress. "It should have occurred to you that I'm the one to decide whom I shall marry—if I marry anyone. Despite my father's fondest wish I am not one of the beautiful, silent women in his paintings."

She ran off to vanish over the crest of a sand dune. Haim pursued her, calling out her name, not knowing whether she could hear his cries or if the crashing surf drowned them out.

The harbor was mist-shrouded. The stars were hidden, while the veiled moon hung like a pearl against the yellow-streaked blue-black evening sky. The air was damp with the briny smell of the sea and the sand beneath Haim's shoes squeaked and crunched as he sprinted after Rosie. By the time he caught up with her she was at the water's edge.

Chapter 8

"Look at me," Haim commanded. As Rosie obeyed he reached for her and squeezed her like a drowning man his lifeline; then he eased off and held her gently. The foamy swash swirled around their ankles, but they paid no attention. He kissed her for the first time and heard himself softly moan as her fragrant mouth yielded to his. Her lips were cool on that sultry night, while her cheeks were warm, damp, salty. He was tasting her tears.

She pulled away to turn her back on him, as was her way. Haim, who had felt her heart pound at his kiss, now saw before him a quivering, barely tame creature about to bolt.

He stood frustrated, helpless; his own thick passion made it impossible to think clearly. Then the realization came, and when it did it was like a lightning flash during a night storm.

She is all things to me, he thought, my lifeline, my treasure, but I cannot own her.

Yol's parting words came back to Haim. "Once you marry Rosie, you will have to share your dream."

"Listen to me," he called to Rosie. "I'm ready to

123

understand. I want to." He swallowed hard. "But first I've got to know. What are your feelings for me?"

"I do love you," Rosie said. "I did a little bit that first time we saw each other on this beach."

"A little bit?"

"To be swept off of my feet like a fairy-tale princess is not how I am. You said you were ready to understand. Please don't act like my father." Her voice began to rise. "He's far happier with my portrait than with his flesh and blood."

"All right, all right." Haim hesitated, glancing at her sideways. "Do you want to get married?"

Rosie stared back at him for a moment and then started to laugh. "Yes, love, eventually." She wagged her finger at him. "But not for a while, and not ever if you can't accept the fact that I intend to continue my work with Meir."

"What's going on with that?"

"You might have found out if you hadn't picked a fight with him. Come, we'll sit on the dry sand and I'll tell you."

They walked back the way they'd come and chose a spot where they could lean against the base of a sand dune. Haim stretched out his arm and felt his heart quicken as Rosie nestled against him.

She began to tell him about the meeting at the Yeshurun Club a little over a year ago. She wasn't there, but her father was, in common with more than a hundred of the most influential Jews in Jaffa. The idea of establishing a garden suburb outside of noisy, crowded Jaffa had been in the air for some time. Many ideas had been put forth, but it took the Yeshurun meeting to found Ahuzzat Bayit, a house builders' society.

Meanwhile, the Jewish establishment in Jaffa had strengthened with the openings of the Lewinsky Seminary for women teachers and local offices of both the Anglo-

Palestine Bank and the Zionist Organization. The latter controlled the purse strings of the crucial Jewish National Fund. Meir Dizengoff, a founder of the now-defunct Geulah Company, a land-buying group, headed up the steering committee. Rosie volunteered to be Dizengoff's personal secretary.

Haim kept nodding, doing his best to pay attention, but her words were a feeble distraction as compared to the scent of her and the feel of her warm thigh pressed against his.

"Haim, the bayit has bought the land," she said. "It is north of the town, and there will be empty space between Jaffa and the settlement. It will be a true suburb, the first of its kind in Palestine, and I will play a crucial role in its building."

"Rosie, we could go away from Jaffa—"

"Never!"

"We could play a crucial role elsewhere in the country, and as Zionists, not capitalists."

"You could, Haim. You, but not I. I would be the mother of your children, I would keep your house, but how would that be a significant contribution to this country?"

Her voice softened. "Oh, Haim, I said I loved you a little bit when we first met. That love deepened every day as I gazed at your likeness. Remember how you once told me you had to finish your work in Jerusalem so that one day our children could be shown the school their father had helped to build?"

Haim made a face. "And that's how you feel about your work with Dizengoff? You want to leave your mark, is that it?"

She smiled. "You do understand me."

"It will take years."

"But we can be married and—" She seemed to decide something. "Haim, what I said before about never leaving Jaffa? That isn't true. When this is done, we can go wherever you'd like.''

Haim frowned. In a few years it could well be too late to live the adventure that he and Yol had spent so many late nights talking about. In a few years Palestine might be so tame there would be no need for the Hashomer. He would only be able to envy Yol and his comrades when they recounted their exploits.

"Please accept, Haim, for both our sakes. You have your whole life to do important things. For a woman such a chance comes only once if at all.''

"Out from under your father's shadow, is that it, Rosie?''

"Is it so terrible? I love him, you know, but is it so terrible to want to accomplish something that will make him respect me? I can no longer be his little girl and I have no intention of becoming yours.''

Haim sighed. "I wonder what sort of work there is in Jaffa.''

"Oh, I imagine we can find you something,'' Rosie whispered. She pressed his fingers against her lips. Her sable eyes were shiny. "Maybe we should go back?''

"Yes,'' Haim agreed. "It's late.''

They strolled back to the inn with their arms around each other. Halfway there Rosie stopped to kiss him once again. "I'll never forget the sacrifice you're making for me.''

"I'll be around to remind you, don't worry,'' Haim said huskily.

They continued along the slate path to the inn's front door. As they waited there for Kamel to admit them, a figure stepped out of the shadows. It was Dizengoff, without his jacket and tie and with his shirtsleeves rolled up to his elbows. Briefly Haim thought the man had come to challenge him to a fight.

"I thought you'd have gone home by now, Meir," Rosie said nervously.

"I waited," Dizengoff said. "Haim, could we talk?" When Haim glanced at Rosie, the older man continued, "Come on, just me and you in the side garden. I want to tell you some things. I'm ashamed of the way I acted at the table tonight."

Haim felt Rosie squeeze his hand reassuringly. "Yes, Meir," he said evenly. "Let's talk."

They waited until Rosie was safely inside the house and then walked around the building to the side garden. Dizengoff led Haim to a stone bench beneath a fragrant orange tree.

"Here, sit," the older man rasped, wearily lowering himself onto the bench.

Haim took the other end. He glimpsed Dizengoff's suit jacket, neatly folded. Freed of its restraints, Dizengoff's starched shirt collar flapped in the breeze. "How long has it been since you took that herring from around your neck?" Haim gestured at the tie folded over the back of the bench.

Dizengoff eyed Haim and shook his head. "Youth," he grumbled. "The young always think they're the first to come upon the earth, like Adam—"

"Pardon me. I obviously upset you during our argument at dinner, but if you brought me here for a lecture, I'd just as soon—"

"You're much better at lecturing than I, my boy, and as for upsetting me?" Dizengoff shrugged. "Yes, you did."

"For that I apologize."

Dizengoff looked at him and nodded. "I appreciate that, but I have to apologize as well. Lucky for me you're a nice boy, else I'd be in the infirmary right now."

Haim chuckled. "I would never raise my hand to you."

"I know that. Now listen. Remember I told you about the bottle plant I tried to set up at Tantura? Well, my wife Zina came with me. During the mosquito season she was one of the first—but hardly the last—to come down with malaria. She was pregnant. The fever caused a stillbirth."

"Oh . . ." The sound issued from Haim's lips like a groan. "I'm so sorry—"

"You see, the child was our first and as it's turned out our last, so you were quite accurate if a bit after the fact in your prophecy."

Haim once again was full of remorse.

"There!" Dizengoff reached across and patted Haim's knee. "I have told you this not to shame you but to excuse my own behavior. You touched a raw nerve. You see, I've always blamed myself for losing my son."

"Still, I had no right to speak so disrespectfully."

"Nonsense." Dizengoff smiled. "You were extremely eloquent tonight, far more so than I ever was with the baron. It was no wonder he fired me for insubordination."

"You were fired for being disrespectful to Baron Rothschild?"

"Personally fired. Let's give credit where credit is due." Dizengoff laughed. "It was foolish of me, but it was just after the—the misfortune. In those terrible days I was in a mood to fight with anybody. I sent an extremely surly letter to my employer, accusing him of being self-seeking, of expecting his money to raise him above other men, of being haughty and prideful." He looked sheepishly at Haim. "The baron thanked me for my candor and added that my services were no longer required."

"Then what happened?"

"I came to Jaffa. Surely Rosie has told you about our project."

Haim nodded and on impulse added, "We're going to be married."

"Mazel tov! Wonderful."

"Her parents don't yet know."

Dizengoff froze. "I presume Rosie knows, yes?" When Haim said she did, the older man chuckled. "You're the sort of determined young fellow who might let it slip your mind to inform the bride of your intentions." He studied Haim. "I don't know how to put this. She must have told you that she is quite devoted to our project."

"We're staying here for the duration, if that's what you're trying to find out."

"I take it you're not very happy about the prospect."

"Let's not quarrel again. I simply don't see this project as a proper expression of Zionism—"

"Whatever that means," Dizengoff dourly interrupted. "Well, if it'll make you feel any better, you are not alone in your opinion."

"What do you mean?"

"Just that all the usual sources of funding have turned away from us, claiming just as you have that to be reckoned as Zionist pioneers we must plow fields—"

"We must make our own bread if we are to be self-sufficient."

"Please, spare me the doctrine, for I know it all by heart as well as you—"

"Really?"

"Yes, really. What do you think, that I was born a fat little middle-aged man? Back in Russia maybe fifteen years ago my political activities earned me some very unpleasant time in prison."

"They did?" Haim asked rather weakly.

"Yes indeed, and in my day if a comrade spent time in prison, his fellows gave him some respect."

"Of course. Absolutely."

"Well then," Dizengoff said smugly, "I'm going to ask you what I asked those insufferable Zionist fools with all the money. Tell me, Haim, when was the last time you tilled the soil?"

Haim swallowed. "Actually, never."

"Hmmm, that recently," Dizengoff mocked. "Don't fret, for few of you halutzim know anything about farming. Your parents reared you to devote your lives to study or learn a trade. Since you arrived here, you've learned a second trade, stonecutting. You've pursued it for rather a long time, yes? Why is that, Haim? I would think that all of your friends have long since scattered to the agricultural settlements."

"That's true. I remained in Jerusalem so I could save my wages. I wanted to come back for Rosie."

"In other words, you have not behaved as a pure, selfless Zionist."

"I'm ashamed of myself in that respect," Haim admitted. "But I was not holding myself up as the best example of how we should act—"

"Well, you shouldn't apologize for not being one of those drones," Dizengoff said. "Eventually they will discover that they are not suited to the farmer's life, and then they will want to return to the towns and villages."

Haim looked worried. "That's not the way that it's supposed to happen."

Dizengoff shrugged. "You must realize that up until now our cause has been a dream. An idea must be flexible if it is to survive. I was present when Theodor Herzl proposed that we all go to Uganda. Now, if the prophet of Zionism can preach that East Africa is the Promised Land, don't you think you might be a little flexible?"

"I don't know what to think," Haim complained. "All I know is that we must be self-sufficient if we are to survive. A house must have a firm foundation."

"That's good if you're a carpenter," Dizengoff said impatiently. "It's not so good if it's a country you're trying to build. I say it doesn't matter how we accomplish things as long as they happen. Let's build as quickly as possible and protect ourselves by becoming an indispensable part of the economy. The Arab who works for us will not attack us. The Turks will never banish us if their government depends on our baksheesh."

"But eventually we must hire Jewish labor."

"I agree with you if you mean slowly bring in Jews to do certain jobs. Our progress would come to a halt if all the settlements had to fire their Arab labor and bring in untrained halutzim. Where would we find enough skilled Jews to keep the agricultural settlements going, never mind construct the Jewish quarters in Jerusalem and Jaffa?"

Haim had no answer. After a moment he asked, "If the Zionist agencies turned you down, where did you get the money to fund your project?"

"A portion of it was raised among the members of the bayit," Dizengoff replied, "but most of it was loans through the central office of the National Fund in France. I still have a few contacts there, and so I was able to go over the heads of the local officials."

"I bet the locals were not pleased with you for doing that." Haim smiled. He was becoming fond of this fellow.

Dizengoff grinned back. "Few people have had occasion to be pleased with me down through the years."

Haim found himself extending his hand. Dizengoff shook it and asked, "Can I count you a member of the Ahuzzat Bayit?"

For a moment Haim was too astounded to speak. Finally he managed, "I have no money to contribute. How can I be brought in?"

"You have something more important to contribute— fresh ideas, fresh blood. We are all a little old, Haim, a little set in our ways."

"But what would I do to earn my membership?"

"You are an accomplished stonecutter, yes? And you speak Arabic. We shall need a construction foreman to oversee the Arabs." Dizengoff winked. "And don't forget, you are marrying Rosie. There's your greatest contribution.

She works for the bayit for nothing, and believe me, she is worth her weight in gold.''

''On that we can agree,'' Haim said.

They did not marry immediately. Rosie was willing and her parents gave their blessings, but Haim did not want to take a wife before he had the means to provide for her. Rosie was admirable, but she had never been asked to make do with little money. They might never be rich, but Haim had no intention of taking her out of her home before they could start their lives together in comfort.

How to accomplish this was the question. Haim had taken a room in the cheaper Arab quarter, where the effendis warmed to him now that he was hiring fellahin. Thanks to the building on Karm Jabali's land, the fellahin were earning at last.

Late every night after visiting Rosie, Haim would walk back to his digs, lost in thought. How could he earn money? Neither was being paid. The understanding was that they'd be allowed membership in the bayit in exchange for their labor. When the time came, they would be portioned out a housing plot in the new suburb, just like the other members. Haim had to figure out a way to earn enough money to be able to build a house.

A letter from Yol, still toiling at Kinnereth in Galilee, gave him the idea. Most of his friend's correspondence was taken up with amusing anecdotes and outrageous bragging about his exploits with a gun, but one letter happened to mention in passing some of the things the settlement was lacking. Food they had more or less, but dry goods like clothing and shoes were wearing out and decent replacements hard to come by. Now, the one trade that Haim knew better than masonry was cobbling, but one man could never hope to supply all the work boots for the agricultural settlements.

He went to Dizengoff with his idea. The Old Man, as most had taken to calling him, furnished Haim with an introduction to an assistant of Arthur Ruppin, who had recently arrived in Jaffa to head the Zionist Organization's office for Palestine. What Haim proposed was that the organization supply its settlements with shoes manufactured in Jaffa at a far lower cost than imports.

The idea was enthusiastically received, but there was a considerable delay due to bureaucratic wrangling before he was officially awarded a limited contract on a trial basis. It was even longer before the promised advance was paid. Haim used his savings from his stonecutter's job in Jerusalem to rent a hall and equip it with benches, tools and leather.

He went out to hire Jewish cobblers, but to his stupefaction and Dizengoff's glee he was unable to find halutzim willing to work at the wages he could offer. The fellahin at the building site told Haim of Arab shoemakers, skilled men who would be happy to get the work. Haim hired the Arabs and at last was in business.

At first he tried to be in two places at once. Mornings he spent at his shoe factory and afternoons at the building site. The Old Man soon spoke to him about neglecting the bayit. Addressing him as Mr. Kolesnikoff, as was the exceedingly proper Dizengoff's habit when discussing Ahuzzat Bayit business, the Old Man suggested that Haim choose his best cobbler and make him manager of the factory.

Within a year Haim had forty Arabs working for him and was supplying virtually all the leather goods needed by the settlements: shoes, belts, gloves, aprons, livestock harnesses. He reinvested some of his profits in imported machinery to increase his factory's production and hired two halutzim to oversee the sale of surplus goods in the bazaars of Jaffa and Jerusalem.

He soon found that he no longer had the time to be foreman of the bayit project. A vote was taken by the membership and Haim was allowed to resign his position after hiring an Arab to take his job. He then bought in as a full member of the bayit.

At Dizengoff's urging he began to dress "appropriately" for a "man of his position in the Jewish community." Haim found himself going around in a white linen suit, a tie and a straw boater. When he and his fiancee were invited to dinner parties, he wore a black suit. Whenever he ran into Dizengoff he remembered their first meeting and imagined that the Old Man was smirking at him.

On April 11, 1909, the housing plots were portioned out by lottery. Haim immediately contracted for a house to be built on rutted, muddy Herzl Street.

On a warm, bright Sunday in June he and Rosie were married in the Glasers' side garden. The chupah was set up beneath the fragrant, blossomy orange tree. Each of the four poles of the canopy was held by one of Rosie's brothers; Dizengoff stood by Haim.

The groom wrote to Yol inviting him to the wedding and paying him the honor of requesting his services as best man but mail could take months to travel even short distances in Palestine. Haim suspected he'd be a married man by the time Yol knew what was happening.

The night before the ceremony Haim walked by himself through the shifting sands that lay between the old town and the new suburb. He thought a little about Yol, who had a gun, the use of a horse and the adventurous life he himself had always dreamed about. If Yol could only see him now, with his suit and tie and his ridiculous straw boater instead of a kayffiyeh, how the little monkey man would laugh!

And then Haim thought about Abe, somewhere in America, undoubtedly fabulously wealthy after all these years. Abe would probably scold him. "For this you came to Palestine? If you'd wanted to wear a necktie you could have come with me to America."

Thinking about Abe only made Haim miss his friend

all the more. Since coming to Palestine he'd learned that it was possible to send letters to America in care of the Zionist Organization offices located there. But the addressee had to be expecting mail in order to pick it up. Haim had tried writing a couple of times, but his letters were returned to him unopened. It worried Haim. He prayed that Abe was all right, just as he prayed that someday the two of them would be reunited.

The next day during the wedding Haim imagined that Abe was standing in Meir Dizengoff's place. As far as he was concerned it was Abe's hand that placed Rosie's wedding ring in his and Abe Herodetzky's witnessing signature on the fancy marriage certificate.

Haim and Rosie Kolesnikoff moved into the Glaser household for a month until their house was finished. Then Haim took leave of his father-in-law's residence and carried his bride across the threshold of their new home.

The surf was soaking the bottoms of his rolled-up trouser cuffs. Rosie would scold him for letting the salt stain the white linen. Haim, still staring at the lights of Jaffa, stayed where he was. He could afford all the linen suits he needed.

Five years, he thought, five years since I came to Palestine. It was hard for him to believe. He found himself continually ticking the years off on his fingers and shaking his head in wonder.

It was May 21, 1910, the night of the big meeting to name the suburb. He and Rosie had been married nearly a year.

And that year had passed the quickest of all. Haim's days consisted of little more than meetings with other Jewish businessmen and hours at his desk in the leather factory. At twenty-eight he felt prematurely old. Deskbound, he watched his stonecutter's physique shrink and fade while his belly grew. Yol, fit and tanned, visited since the marriage. Their friendship remained as strong as ever, but something had changed. Yol was truly a halutz; Haim no longer felt like a pioneer.

If his days at the factory were a dreary disappointment, his nights made up for it. Rosie was worth sacrificed dreams. Rosie was worth everything. Their marriage was blissfully happy. She was proud of him and proud of herself. Her work with Dizengoff had given her new self-confidence. This and her changed circumstances allowed her to shed her animosity toward her father. Daughter and father were getting along fine. Rosie had even begun to paint, and her father's critiques bothered her not at all.

"Haim!"

He turned to see Rosie coming toward him along the beach. He went to meet her, gathering up his shoes and suit jacket on the way.

"I know, I know. The meeting . . . I'm coming."

Rosie went to him and put her arms around his waist. "Forget it," she chuckled, giving him a kiss. "It's over."

"What? The voting is finished? They chose a name?"

"Ummm . . ." She slid beneath his arm and together they began to walk home. "Do you mind not getting to vote?"

"Not in the least."

"I didn't think so. That's why I didn't come fetch you."

"So?" Haim demanded.

"So what?" Rosie teased him, pulling away.

"Rosie," he growled, pretending to chase her. "Slow down," he commanded. "You know the doctor told you to take it easy!"

"Haim, we just found out that I'm pregnant. There's time yet before I turn into crystal."

"So start now, and when it is time you'll have trained yourself not to run around like a wild animal. Now then, tell me what was decided at the meeting."

"Mrs. Sheinken's choice won by a landslide."

Haim shook his head. "You think I remember every—"

"She suggested the title of Herzl's novel, *Altneuland*, except, of course, that we'll use the Hebrew."

"So it's to be Tel Aviv? The 'Hill of Spring.' " He smiled. "You like the name of your city, my love?"

Rosie nodded and leaned against him as they trudged through the winding path that led through the dunes to their home.

Chapter 9

New York

The tenth convention of the ILGWU was held in the first part of June 1910. A week into the convention a delegate introduced a resolution for a general strike against the garment industry in New York City. The resolution passed overwhelmingly. There remained only the formality of polling the increasingly militant rank and file and the choosing of the day the strike would begin.

The joint board, made up of nine locals, began its preparations. It was up to this body to hire the halls and organize the relief, information and picketing committees. One of these was Cloak Pressers' Local 35, Abe Herodetzky's shop.

Abe had heard little from Stefano about the coming strike since he handed over his two hundred dollars. He knew about the convention, which was held in Boston, but only because he read about it in the *Forward*.

The usually easy-going de Fazio was looking haggard these days and had no time to talk. He was putting in full days at the Allen Street sweatshop and long, late nights at secret union meetings. Stefano de Fazio was no longer very productive at his pressing machine, and once or twice the loft's foreman threatened to fire the Italian, although everyone knew he wouldn't. The situation at Allen Street and the other sweatshops scattered throughout the city was like dynamite. The shop foreman was not about to light the fuse by firing a union representative. The looming strike was on everyone's mind although no one spoke of it. Of course, unlike those horrors, the strike was going to end up being good for everyone. At least that was what everyone hoped.

Abe had long since moved out of the Kraviches' Montgomery Street apartment. He did not miss the bearded slaughterhouse worker's pompous advice or Sadie's rantings, but he did often think longingly of his blessed private room. He'd moved to nearby Jefferson Street, where he had to share his room with two other boarders.

Abe's thoughts also dwelled on Leah Kravich. On the day he left, sweet Leah burst into tears as she shook his hand in farewell. Abe did think of her, but truth to tell, he far more missed the private room.

On June 25 Stefano came around to each worker to whisper that there was going to be a mass rally at Madison Square Garden in three days. Abe nodded, promising to be there, and was rewarded with a pat on the shoulder. Abe was ashamed of himself for hoping the rally would be a failure. As the day approached, he managed to convince himself that this talk of a big strike was absurd. How could thousands of Jews, Italians and Poles who'd never laid eyes on one another hope to stand together against the combined money and might of the owners, the government and the police?

It was not that Abe was against unions, and he certainly desired the benefits Stefano spoke of. The problem was that Abe was sorely missing his savings. Stefano never mentioned it and Abe was reluctant to pester him about it, but in his bed at night, while the other two boarders slept, Abe would stare at the receipt. He would read and reread it, taking slim comfort from it. That Stefano was scrupulously honest Abe had no doubt. That the union would repay him— Well, Stefano said it would, but what if the strike failed and the union was shattered?

And so Abe brooded. His decision gnawed at him. The fact that it was over and done with did not matter. It ached like a scar in the rain. When he did finally fall asleep, uncertainty would jab him awake. Then he would brood about that. He'd done a good deed, but he was ruining it in God's eyes by his niggardly doubts. That train of thought would set him off in bitter recriminations about why he wasn't a good man and all chance of sleep would be lost for the night.

June 28 was a ghastly, humid day with a grey sky and stale air like wet wool against the skin. Stefano had asked that the men meet at the corner of Orchard and Grand.

Abe was one of the last to arrive. The others greeted him quietly as they stood about with their hands in their pockets, skittish as colts at missing work and self-conscious because of the stares from the Orchard Street merchants. The day seemed preternaturally still as they walked to the streetcars for Madison Square Garden. All Abe could hear was the clacking of their shoes against the pavement and the sudden liquid fluttering of the pigeons overhead.

They boarded a trolley and watched nervously to see if other workers were going to the rally. The street began to thicken with fellow unionists long before the arena came into view. The streetcar gave up trying to inch its way through the throngs. Abe and the others had to walk the last part of the way, and when they finally got to the Garden, they were informed that there was no more room inside.

Thousands were milling about waving picket signs. They swarmed like locusts across the green lawns of Madison Square Park and packed the streets all the way to the oddly triangular Flatiron Building three blocks away.

Inside the arena Samuel Gompers, the president and a founder of the American Federation of Labor, was exhorting his vast audience to press for higher wages and shorter hours, not social revolution. Outside far lesser union officials were repeating the same message. It was a circus. Stefano jumped up and down, tossing his hat into the air, delirious with excitement and joy. "I told you all! I told you to believe," he cried between lapses into Italian.

Stefano laid eyes on Abe and set upon him to grab his sleeves and whirl him around the jam-packed sidewalk in a dance of triumph. "Now aren't you glad you gave the money?" Stefano shouted into Abe's ear.

Abe nodded, for right then he was glad. It was a grand thing to be a part of all this activity. He felt giddy locked in Stefano's robust embrace, the center of everyone's attention.

Then Stefano released him. The Italian veered away to join a trio of men Abe didn't know and blended into the crowd. Abe's other Allen Street compatriots were also gone. He was alone and he began to feel claustrophobic from the press of bodies and the weather.

He fought his way to the edge of the crowd and began to head down Fifth Avenue. Past the Flatiron Building the throngs thinned out and Abe was able to breathe a little easier, but with the distance came loneliness and depression.

It's unfair, he told himself, I belonged back there. But he did not. He didn't care about the union, not really. His dream was far different from the common one shared by the celebrating unionists.

Stefano de Fazio and the other men he worked with wanted nothing more than higher pay and more time to spend with their families and their God. Let others have the responsibilities of ownership as well as its rewards.

Responsibilities were what Abe needed, to fill the

difficult days and the far worse nights. A busy man would not have time to dwell on his personal shortcomings. A wealthy man, no matter how lacking in personal appeal, grace and warmth, could send out his money to win respect and even affection in the community.

The kind of woman he wanted to marry would expect him to have money, proof that despite his unprepossessing appearance he had what really mattered in the world, intelligence and shrewdness.

He expected the same qualities in a woman, along with durability. Abe wanted good value in a wife as in all things.

Abe kept walking downtown. He cut east on Twenty-first Street, past the locked gates of lush Gramercy Park, down Irving Place past the brownstones and an Irish policeman who gave him a hard stare.

This was a wealthy area, but Abe had not come this way to view the architecture. Parked on the tidy streets were many automobiles, the magnificent playthings of the very rich. Abe saw two Pierce Arrows and a shiny Welch Tourer. He managed to peek inside the vehicle before being shooed away by its chauffeur, most likely a former coachman.

Abe walked the next mile in a daze, dreaming about what it might be like to sit in such a contraption. One would be cushioned on soft, fragrant red leather upholstery—there was enough fine leather in that Tourer to make fifty pairs of shoes. One would issue curt orders to the chauffeur, "Right, left; fast, slow"—but no. It would never do to direct the vehicle. The chauffeur must know the way on his own.

The daydream collapsed of its own implausibility and its dreamer's ignorance. Abe did not know enough about automobiles even to imagine the realities of owning one. He did not know enough about anything except what it was like to be poor.

I might just as well have stayed in Russia, he thought. The lament had occurred to him many times before, but now he was beginning to believe it.

Abe walked clear home. To ride the dingy, crowded streetcar after seeing those automobiles was an impossibility. Besides, saving the trolley fare made him feel correct, even virtuous in his behavior. It was a small pleasure, but these days, with so little in his pocket, not spending was the only pleasure he could afford.

The weeks following the rally at Madison Square Garden were filled with progress reports from Stefan. To Abe's astonishment more talking than working was going on at the Allen Street factory loft and the foreman seemed resigned.

Voting day finally came around. Stefano approached each man individually to record his vote on a small pad. No names would be attached to their votes, he promised. Only he would know, and he would promptly forget. There would be no recriminations.

When it was Abe's turn to voice his opinion, he hesitated, wondering if a vote against the strike would have any meaning.

"Well, my friend, yes or no?" Stefano asked. The Italian looked drawn and nervous but also excited, like a man who was about to savor hard-won success.

Abe hesitated, a trifle hurt becuase Stefano's eyes were already on the next fellow.

"Yes or no?" Stefano demanded.

Abe flinched at his friend's harsh tone. "Yes," he whispered. "I vote to strike—with the others," he couldn't help adding.

Stefano grinned and moved on to the next man.

Abe glumly returned to his pressing machine, aware that his moment had come and gone; his vote had been cast. Once again, as in his years in the army, his money and fate were caught up in a struggle too vast to comprehend. He thought briefly of the aristocratic quartermaster who rescued him from the Manchurian front and who lost his life in a brave but stupid attempt to quell a street riot. Abe wondered if he was being just as foolhardy.

His dismal reveries did not keep him from doing his work. He needed to earn as much as possible before the strike began.

Throughout the city votes were taken and tallied. Men and women voted over their machines in the various sweatshops. At night many gathered in cellars, apartments and cafes to talk it out over cups of espresso, over glasses of Chianti or tea. Afterward they toasted their decision in schnapps or good Polish vodka.

They voted to strike and then went home where they tried their best to hide their uncertainty and worry from their anxious families. It was hard for these new immigrants to stand up against the American establishment.

The final vote was nearly nineteen thousand in favor of striking and just over six hundred opposed. The date chosen was Thursday, July seventh at two in the afternoon.

The strike leaders had no idea what to expect. Would the workers lose their courage at the last minute and stay on the job? They needn't have worried.

By half past two on that Thursday, the lower part of Manhattan had to close the streets to traffic as thousands of people streamed from their workplaces. Singing and laughing like children at the start of a school holiday, the workers congregated at their local halls, where the dole from the union coffers was announced.

Those who needed it would get two dollars a week if single, four dollars if married. The initial euphoria faded quickly at that announcement. Abe was one of the many who scratched their heads in disbelief and felt sick with worry. Just his rent—and he was sharing his boarder's room with two others—was three dollars a week. How was he to live?

There was constant negotiation as soon as the strike began. Rumors abounded. Things were going well; things were terrible. We've won; we've lost—it was better not to listen. No news at all was easier to bear than the unending, inaccurate whispered reports.

Roll calls were held during the day to discourage scabbing. Roving bands of picketers made the rounds to bolster morale. Impromptu concerts were staged on street corners throughout the Lower East Side to take people's minds off their troubles.

It was not only the sweatshop workers who were suffering. When the unionists' pockets were empty, so were the cash registers of the merchants who served them. So it was that idle shopkeepers were able to stand in their doorways and listen to music along with the workers.

The strike lasted through the summer. The leadership negotiated with the manufacturers, who meanwhile took out newspaper advertisements to carry their side of the argument to the public.

Abe read those advertisements in the antistrike *New York Times* as well as the prostrike editorials and news in the *Forward*. Like the great majority of the rank and file, he got his progress reports from the dailies. Since he no longer went to Allen Street every day, he no longer saw Stefano and he didn't know who else to ask about union business. The others who loitered about his local's hall on East Broadway seemed to be as much in the dark as he was. The strike committee was headquartered at the Victoria Hotel at Twenty-third and Fifth Avenue. Abe ventured up there only once. He felt out of place in the hotel's carpeted corridors. Besides, all the important union officers were far too busy to pay attention to him.

By the beginning of August more than three hundred of the smaller manufacturers had settled with the union, recognizing most of its demands, including a forty-eight hour week and employment of a shop steward. It still remained to settle with the giants of the industry and to decide the overriding question of the closed shop.

The strike dragged on. Abe read the papers and walked the streets. The family he was boarding with was allowing him to pay a dollar a week toward his rent. Since Abe was drawing a two-dollar dole, he had some pocket money, but he was slipping into debt.

Others told him not to worry. How much could he owe—eight dollars, twelve dollars? When the new salaries began, he could repay that sum in just one week and still have almost as much in his pocket as he used to have—and that was after one week.

Abe nodded, smiled and did his best to be a loyal unionist. It was hard, though. He didn't know what to do with himself all day long. He wanted to spend as little time as possible in his room. It was August, the tenement was sweltering, his two fellow boarders were invariably there, stinking up the place with putrid herring and chattering so Abe couldn't concentrate to read. He began to while away the hours at the public library. At least there he was somewhat sheltered from the weather and could read books on retailing as well as the newspapers.

The big department stores soon entered the act as they found themselves without stock to sell. Filene's of Boston brought in the jurist Louis Brandeis, who along with lawyers for both sides tried to define "closed shop," while the manufacturers asked for and got an injunction against the strike from New York's Supreme Court.

There was violence. Goons attacked the pickets. Some of the strikers fought back, but the majority depended on their fellow members to prevail by sheer numbers.

The police were not sympathetic to the union. The strikers, many of whom could not speak English, were from countries where a uniform was the symbol of absolute power. They gripped their signs, closed their eyes, said their prayers and stood their ground. Abe was one of those who was asked to interpret for these greenhorn picketers. He did not carry a sign and thus avoided being arrested. It was Abe's job to explain to the arrested picketers that they were not headed for execution or deportation but would be released in a few hours.

Abe was pleased for the chance to help, relieved to have something to do and profoundly thankful that his job prevented him from picketing. He did not want to risk jail.

The strike lasted nine weeks. On September second, amid much fanfare, the settlement was announced. Bandwagons rolled through lower Manhattan informing the workers, and once again the streets filled with joyous people celebrating what amounted to a qualified victory.

There would be no closed shops, but union members would be "preferred" for all jobs. There would be legal holidays and holy days off with full pay, but the work week would be fifty hours. The raises amounted to an average of three dollars per week.

Abe could have told them that in a negotiation you get maybe two thirds of what you ask for in the first place, and that's if you're very lucky and your opposite is a dummy. Along with everyone else Abe cheered, and when someone offered, he lifted up a drink of schnapps, but he thought, the sweatshops are no paradise, but they are a little better. The strike is over, thank God. Now let's all get back to work, and let the union pay me what it owes.

September second was a Friday. On the following Monday Abe returned to Allen Street to report for work. The day started out jolly enough, but by midmorning all the workers were stripped down to their undershirts, sipping away at their tin cans of drinking water and sweating over their machines as if the strike had never happened.

At lunchtime Abe approached Stefano and asked for a

word in private. The organizer led him to the dingy hallway with its peeling walls.

"They could have painted this place while we were
out," Stefano joked, winking at Abe. "What can I do for
you, my friend?"

Abe found himself respectfully lowering his eyes. He
hated himself for it, but such deference seemed called for.
The first order of business on Allen Street that morning
was to elect Stefano shop steward. For one instant during
the voting Abe had imagined that the workers would turn
to him to do the job, saying, You are our hero, Abe. You
lent us the money to hold out against the manufacturers.
But of course they unanimously elected Stefano.

Now he presented his tattered receipt. "Can I be paid
back, since everything's over?"

De Fazio reluctantly took back the paper. "The money
. . . Abe, it's not like I got the money on me, you know."

"Of course not."

"I gave it to the treasurer at the local hall."

"I go there for it?"

"Nah. They turned it in to the committee at the
Victoria Hotel."

"What committee?" Abe asked. A queasy feeling
was beginning to form in the pit of his stomach.

"The welfare committee." Stefano gave back the
receipt. "That's where you got to go with this."

Abe tried to control his anger. "I didn't go to Twenty-
third Street to hand the money in. Why I got to go all the
way up there to get it back?"

"That's where all that kind of money went, my friend."

"What do you mean?" Abe demanded, confused,
alarmed and suspicious. "I gave you American money."

Stefano heaved a great, patient sigh. He'd learned
many things during these last nine weeks. He liked union
business and he had a talent for it. He saw a place for
himself in the organization, an important place. The big

shots now in control were good men who meant well, but they were more like professors than fellow-workers. For now such men were needed, but shrewd working-class champions would eventually rise from the ranks to guide their brothers to prosperity. If he wanted to be one of those champions, he would have to maintain his reputation as a regular guy.

"I meant that the money was used for different sorts of things," he explained. "There was dole money, like you gave—"

"I lent it."

"I mean lent. Anyway, there was dole money, lawyer money, advertising money—like that."

"Okay. But they'll honor this?" Abe demanded, waving the receipt. "They won't give me trouble?"

Stefano shook his head. "You'll get your money. If you don't, come back to me." He decided to reveal his secret to Abe. After all, it was the Jew's two hundred dollars that had impressed the big shots with his ability to organize his men. "Because we're friends, I tell you this. I am making a career in the union."

"For a job, you mean?"

"Sure."

"They got a job for you?" Abe shrugged. "I mean, there's something to do for pay now that the strike's over?"

"The job is just beginning." Stefano realized that for all Abe's intelligence his mind was inflexible, closed to many things. He began to fear for his friend's future. America was not for the meek of heart or the staid.

"So they'll give me my money if I go to the hotel to claim it?" Abe repeated.

Stefano frowned. "I promise you, they'll give back the money. Go tomorrow before work, about eight o'clock, and see someone at the relief committee. All right?" When Abe nodded, he said. "Now I gotta eat lunch. I'm starving."

Abe followed him back into the loft. It occurred to him that it had been a long while since his friend invited him to share his roast chicken.

The next morning Abe took the trolley up to Twenty-third Street. His palms were wet as he walked into the hotel. As he crossed the bustling lobby toward the elevators, he kept patting the receipt in his breast pocket. The crackle of the paper was reassuring.

The smirking elevator attendant made him repeat the floor three times. Eventually Abe shuffled down the corridor toward the pebbled-glass door and went inside. His heart was pounding. How he hated confronting authority. He thought fleetingly of Haim; a bit of his brashness would come in handy now.

A man in a suit and tie stood guarding the entrance to the inner offices. Abe asked him if he might see somebody on the relief committee.

The guard sized Abe up, asking if he might know the nature of his business. Abe nodded, tried to speak and found that his throat was too dry. The guard was big. Abe caught a glimpse of a pistol on the man's belt beneath his jacket. Trying his best not to look at it, he began to explain about the loan.

The guard interrupted to suggest that Abe talk to his shop steward; the union was in no position to make a loan. Indignation gave Abe courage. He pointed out that he'd come to be paid, not to borrow.

At that point the guard gave up trying to make sense of this funny-looking little man. He gestured over his shoulder with his thumb, telling Abe, "See Miss Grissome, down the hall on your right."

Miss Grissome, Abe mourned as he wandered into the warren of offices. So much for seeing a Jew. This person was clearly a Christian as well as a woman.

That a woman should work was nothing new to Abe. In Russia wives slaved alongside their husbands, and in

New York plenty of women were in the garment workers' union. There were even sweatshops where men and women labored together, although Abe had never been in such a place. What astounded him was that some women had authoritative positions. All over New York women were getting jobs as secretaries and sales clerks. They were even telephone operators. Obviously a socialistic progressive place like union headquarters would employ women, but for a man like Abe, who found it nearly impossible to talk to women in any situation, to have to come before one in a business matter was hell on earth.

Which was where Abe found himself as he approached Miss Grissome's desk. She had dark brown hair pinned up, a weak chin and wire-framed spectacles with thick lenses. She was wearing a brown skirt and a high-necked white blouse with ink smears on its frilly cuffs.

"Hello," Abe began. "I—" She was ignoring him, seemingly engrossed in the papers before her. He colored, chiding himself for his ignorance. A bureaucrat was a bureaucrat in any country—except that in Russia one was spared the additional indignity of standing in supplication before a woman.

"Yes, what is it?" Miss Grissome asked. She tucked her papers into a drawer and folded her hands on the desktop.

Abe awkwardly shifted his weight from one foot to the other as he explained. He took the receipt from his breast pocket, carefully unfolded it and placed it upon Miss Grissome's desk. She stared at it with unmistakable gloom.

"Mr. Herodetzky, we all made sacrifices during the strike. I myself am earning far less money here than I could as a bookkeeper in an accounting firm."

Abe had absolutely no idea what she was talking about. He decided to make another start of it. "I lent this money, you understand." He tapped the receipt with his finger.

"You must understand that we have a duty to each other to pull together." She glanced at the smudged, tattered receipt, partially torn at the folds. When she looked back at Abe, her small, weak pale blue eyes swam like fish in an aquarium behind the thick glass of her spectacles. "You come in here presenting this paper that I can hardly read, signed by somebody I've never heard of, demanding two hundred dollars? I hardly know what to say."

"It's my money. I lent it," Abe heard himself rasping.

"You say you did, but frankly, Mr. Herodetzky" —her smile was as thin as a straight razor and just as lethal—"where a man of your station in life could come upon two hundred dollars escapes me."

"I earned it." His tone was so plaintive that she momentarily believed him, but as she contemplated the scrawny laborer in his too-large shabby suit, her initial concern turned into contempt.

"I saved every penny of it out of my wages," Abe was saying. "Two years it took me."

"I hardly think so," Miss Grissome sniffed. "But for the sake of argument let's say that you did donate some money to the union—"

"It wasn't donated, it was lent."

Miss Grissome smacked her desk top with the flat of her hand. "I am just about out of patience with you, sir! If you gave that money, it was donated, just the way restaurants donated free meals, and college students went from door to door soliciting donations. Why, do you know that the workers who settled early with their employers donated fifteen percent of their earnings to the strike fund? Over a quarter of a million dollars was collected in that manner. If you somehow managed to raise some money for the cause, you ought to be ashamed of yourself for asking for it back. Hasn't your union done enough for you?"

"The paper," Abe pleaded, "read the receipt. It's there before you."

"I have read it, Mr. Herodetzky." She shook her head. "Whoever gave you this, he had no right to do so, do you understand? No right whatsoever. He would be in great legal trouble with us—we'd have him arrested for fraud—if I believed your story in the first place, which I don't." She crumpled the receipt and tossed it into her wastebasket.

"Give that back to me!" Abe started around the desk to retrieve his receipt.

"Trouble here, ma'am?"

Abe spun to confront the guard he'd passed at the entrance.

"I do hope not," Miss Grissome said, her voice quivering with anger. "This man was just leaving. Would you please show him out?"

Abe tried to think, but the touch of the guard's thick fingers on his sleeve panicked him. He felt himself being led away from Miss Grissome's desk, and the only English he could seem to remember was, "My money, my money!"

"Come on, mister," the guard urged. Abe moved along the corridor in a dreamy haze, only barely aware of the office personnel watching him from their doorways. Then he was in the foyer, and then he was on the other side of the pebbled-glass door. The empty hotel corridor seemed to tick with silence.

Abe suddenly realized that Miss Grissome had to have a ledger where all contributions were noted. Somewhere there had to be a record of his two hundred with de Fazio's name.

I should have thought of this before, Abe stormed at himself. As he re-entered the suite he wondered to himself in Russian why he'd let that supercilious woman frazzle him so.

He was hardly through the door before the guard

moved to block him. The big man stood with his arms crossed. "On your way. I don't want to hurt you."

"I just want to see that woman once more," Abe said, trying to sidestep the man. "I thought of something—"

"Get out."

Abe was petrified, but he stood his ground. He held his hands up before him in a placating gesture—all the while trying to sidle past the big man.

The violence came with obscene abruptness. Abe distractedly wondered how some were able to marshal their reflexes to defend against such attacks.

The guard carried him by the scruff of his neck, as he would a kitten, and propelled him out of the office. Abe saw the man shove open the glass door with his free arm. He caught a glimpse of the guard's hamlike fist drawing back and sickening pain thudded into his lower back.

Abe found himself on the carpeted floor on his hands and knees. He settled down on his belly, inhaling the musty odor of the worn carpet's nap, and waited for the agony to fade.

From somewhere above him came the guard's gruff voice. "It's my job to see that there's no trouble here. I can't risk my job. You stay out, mister, else I'll really bust you up."

God's angel, sent to drive Adam and Eve from Eden, Abe thought almost wryly, for the assault had drained his nervousness, leaving him feeling oddly hollow inside. The pain was fading. Behind him the glass door clicked shut. The dust in the carpet made him sneeze.

He sat up. His palms were red and stinging, raw from the friction of the carpet. The baggy knees of his trousers were torn. "Not enough I got to lose the money," he complained to the empty corridor.

Slowly, wearily, he got to his feet. It was going to be dreadful, but he had no choice. Steadfastly he went to the closed door. He had to see Miss Grissome and ask about that ledger.

The door was locked. Abe rested his sweaty forehead against the cool pebbled glass. "Hah," he murmured to the guard on the other side, "so you're afraid of me."

He began to laugh. The sound of it in his throat was soft, diffident, but it was definitely a laugh. I might as well laugh, as cry, Abe thought. The money is lost.

He would not tell anyone what had happened. He would lie to the steward. He would tell him everything went just fine.

Abe wandered the seventh floor until he found the stairwell. He could not bear the thought of that smirking elevator attendant.

The deserted stairwell was very warm. It was still summer in New York, one of the hottest Septembers ever. It had to be as hot within these unventilated confines as it was in the sweatshop.

The sweatshop—back there again, and for how long?

Between the sixth and fifth floors Abe found himself growing dizzy. His vision darkened and he had to clutch at the banister to keep from falling. He doubled over and vomited, and through it all he was petrified that someone might hear. They would think he was a derelict, seeing his torn pants. They would think he was a drunk and call the police. He would be arrested and thrown in jail.

His spasms subsided. Gasping, he scuttled like a crab down to the ground floor. His side was aching terribly and his mouth tasted terrible.

At the ground floor another staircase descended into the basement and the gentlemen's washroom. The attendant, a black, eyed him stonily but said nothing. Abe stepped into a cubicle and locked the door behind him. He stripped off his suit jacket, lowered his trousers and twisted around to examine his aching lower back. There was a large purple bruise over his kidney. Abe wondered if he'd been injured internally. He hitched up his trousers, put down the lid on the toilet and sat with his head in his hands, wondering what he was going to do.

One thing was certain, he would hold to his decision not to tell Stefano. Miss Grissome's words kept echoing in his mind—"Whoever signed that receipt committed fraud." Stefano could end up in prison if Abe made trouble. Abe could not be responsible for ruining his life.

Could he expect Stefano to pay him back? "Come see me if the union gives you trouble," he had said. The idea initially attracted him, but he discarded it as unworkable. It would take years to pay back such a sum. Sure, Stefano would commit himself to it, for he was a man of his word, but how many months would it be before that commitment turned to resentment? The other workers would find out about it, and before very long Abe would be treated like a Shylock even by his fellow Jews.

No, Abe thought, there are some things in life more important than money.

He left the cubicle, rolled up the sleeves of his sweat-slick shirt and went to a basin to wash his face. He cupped water in his hands and rinsed the foul taste out of his mouth, not caring if the attendant was watching and disapproving.

The attendant wore no expression at all as he handed Abe a towel. Abe thanked him and dried off. He saw the man's dark eyes flick down to his torn trouser knees.

"I fell."

"Yes, sir. Sorry, sir," the man said. He cocked his head. "You with the union, sir? The union's a good thing." He held Abe's jacket for him.

Abe knew that he was supposed to tip, but he had just enough money in his pocket for carfare downtown. He hurried out of the washroom, calling out a thank you over his shoulder without looking back.

He made a beeline through the lobby, eyes straight

ahead, and after an eternity found himself out on the sidewalk. On the street at least if someone noticed his torn pants they wouldn't speak to him about it.

A clock in a store window told him that it was after ten. He hurried to catch his streetcar downtown. It had been quite a morning, and the thought of a full day on Allen Street nauseated him all over again, but he couldn't skip work. Not now, not when he was penniless.

He managed to avoid Stefano for the rest of the morning, but during the lunch break the Italian came over. "It all go okay?" he asked.

Abe swallowed hard and nodded. "Fine. Everything is fine."

"They paid you? No trouble?"

Abe nodded.

"They give you the interest?"

"They gave me everything," Abe said, too quickly, too harshly. "I'm sorry to sound nasty," he added. "I'm tired today."

Defazio stared at him curiously, then shrugged. "Okay, then. I'll see you later, my friend."

Abe watched him go off. Twenty minutes later he and the other workers were back at their machines. The clatter and hiss of Abe's pressing irons seemed to taunt him with the same chant over and over again: You'll be here forever. The money is gone.

Chapter 10

Tel Aviv, 1910

It was a sultry sixty-five-degree evening in November. Haim Kolesnikoff, his heart fluttering with excitement, skipped down the stairs and out the front door of the Jewish National Fund office. He stood on the creaky wooden planking that served as the sidewalk and dug his gold watch out of his satin waistcoat.

It was just after seven. Haim sighed with relief. He would not have to go back to work. His factory manager would have shut the place down for the day. Anyway, Haim was far too excited by the results of the meeting he'd just had with the fund's director, Dr. Arthur Ruppin, to return to his desk.

Haim slid his hands into his pockets and started home. He found himself whistling happily as he strolled along.

Calm down, he warned himself. You may have convinced the Jewish National Fund, and last week you worked things out with the bank, but the hardest part is still ahead of you. You've yet to confront and convince Rosie.

Tel Aviv's streets were bustling; crowds of workers were returning home from their jobs in Jaffa and stopping

158

to shop. The little city was thriving. More small suburbs were sprouting around the nucleus, where mud and sand were slowly giving way to blacktopped roads and new waist-high toothpick-slender eucalyptus, which somewhat helped to halt the constant shifting of the sand dunes.

As Haim walked past the shops of Zangwill Street, he wondered what Meir Dizengoff would say when he heard of his plans—assuming he could convince Rosie, of course. Meir probably wouldn't much care. He was too busy. These days Dizengoff seemed to be everywhere at once, tending to every aspect of his beloved Tel Aviv. He interviewed the teachers at the Herzlia High School; he hired municipal workers; he scrutinized every blueprint for a proposed building.

That the Old Man had any legal right to control these matters was questionable, but one might as well ask a parent if he had any legal right to meddle in the affairs of his grown offspring. Like the proud papa he so longed to be, he continually extolled Tel Aviv's virtues while ignoring its shortcomings. For example, the straight, shallow shore of the city could not compete for shipping with Jaffa's existing natural bay, and the shifting sands and crumbly stone made building difficult, but these things did not matter to Dizengoff. As far as he was concerned, Tel Aviv was the best place on earth.

Dizengoff had never been cheerful or gregarious, and these days he'd almost totally cut himself off from the original members of the Ahuzzat Bayit. The few who did see him said that he'd soured even more except when it came time for him to address new Jewish immigrants. Then he became the inveterate optimist, expending his considerable charm until his voice was hoarse, encouraging wealthy newcomers to begin building in Tel Aviv and instructing the not-so-wealthy on how to borrow the money to do the same.

Haim had been dropped from Dizengoff's social list,

and at first he was hurt and upset. After all, Meir had been the guest of honor at his wedding and had witnessed the certificate. Eventually, however, Haim came to understand that Dizengoff was wrapped up in a dream. Haim could understand, for he was working hard to bring about a dream of his own.

He passed a shoe store and saw the products of his own factory displayed in the window. His business was successful, as were all the other Jewish businesses in Tel Aviv and Jaffa, including Dizengoff's new shipping company. Tel Aviv welcomed commerce and clamored for more. It was next to impossible to go bankrupt in Tel Aviv, for the city's interdependent business sector considered itself to be one big family.

Haim was gradually phasing in young Jewish trainees at his factory. He was also attending weekly planning sessions at the Jewish National Fund office. Unlike the private get-together he'd just had with Dr. Ruppin—Haim was no longer obliged to deal with an assistant to the director—these weekly sessions were attended by all the community's business leaders.

Haim, feeling stuffy in suit and tie, would sit with these men, all of them far older than he. Dizengoff would preside and Dr. Ruppin would sit in, now and then quietly offering his comments. Important business would be discussed. Baksheesh for the suspicious Turkish authorities was arranged in the attempt to ensure that the tenuous relationship between the Ottoman Empire and the first Jewish city since Biblical times did not further deteriorate. They also worked out agreements with the Anglo-Palestine Bank to see to it that the newly arrived working-class halutzim could borrow to establish themselves.

When he wasn't participating in city planning, Haim was at his factory. At the end of the long day his back ached, not from honest physical labor but from bending over ledgers and endless sheaves of orders and bills. With wealth came responsibility, and Haim cared for neither. In Russia it was Abe who wanted wealth and who took pleasure in seeing to the accounts.

Haim frequently found his mind wandering during the workday. He would look at his hands, holding them up to the light to see if they still showed any of the calluses he'd built up when he cut stone. He would daydream about those days in Jerusalem when he and Yol worked together, strong and tanned beneath the hot sun. True, the work was grueling, but Haim had been the equal to it. In those days he could rightly call himself a halutz. No, it was not money that he needed but hard work and comradeship.

Haim paused as several workers stepped from a doorway into his path. There were no cafes in Tel Aviv, for the rabbis had forbidden them, but there were innumerable workers' clubs where a man could get coffee or a glass of wine on credit. The men blocking Haim's way were just leaving such a club, rowdy with happiness over the end of the day. They were laughing over a shared joke, but their raucousness quickly faded as they noticed Haim behind them. They began to fall over themselves to get out of his way. "Excuse us, Mr. Kolesnikoff."

"Nothing to excuse," Haim said heartily. "A little fun is natural after a hard day's work."

"We were careless not to see you," the speaker insisted, not listening to Haim. The worker was big, about Haim's height, though not as broad in the shoulders. He wore an open-necked cotton shirt with rings of sweat in the armpits and a leather-visored cloth cap, which he doffed. "If you'll excuse us now, sir, we'll be on our way."

Haim watched them hurry off. How he longed to invite them back to the club so he could buy them all more coffee and bask in their conversation.

Such madness, he reproached himself. He gazed inside the club. The place was dense with blue cigarette smoke and redolent with the aroma of fresh coffee. The bare wooden tables were all ringed with halutzim enjoying each other's comradeship.

If he entered, all conversation would end. The proprietor would clear a table for him and he would sit all by himself staring into his coffee as the halutzim filed out in groups of two and three, muttering to themselves and shaking their heads.

It was no use trying to pretend he was still one of them. He could shed his jacket and tie, but much more than his attire separated him from the workers. The halutzim who came to Palestine were socialists, just as he had been—and still was in his heart—although he blamed none of the working class for scoffing at that. After all, he owned a factory. That made him an exploiter, benign or not. At twenty-eight he was far more like Meir Dizengoff than like any of the young men in that workers' club.

Haim felt miserable now, estranged and lonely. He was willing to trade everything he had except Rosie once again to count himself among the pioneers. The point of coming to Palestine in the first place was not to grow rich but to help establish a homeland.

Yol Popovich had recently come to Tel Aviv for a fortnight's visit with Haim and his wife. Rosie warmly welcomed him. Yol, gloatingly eyeing her obviously pregnant state, slapped Haim on the back.

The friendship between the two men was as strong as ever. A steady stream of letters flowed between them, so there was none of the awkwardness that often attends such reunions.

Yol looked gaunt and beneath his tan his skin had a yellowish cast to it, since he had contracted malaria very soon after he got to Kinnereth.

"Of course at Kinnereth malaria is merely a nuisance, hardly a debilitating disease," Yol boasted, swaggering about Haim and Rosie's front parlor in his red Arab shoes and baggy cotton work clothes. On his head was a kaffiyeh, held in place by a leather thong and draping loosely over his neck and shoulders. "So despite my fever I planted trees and dug ditches, and in between I ate perfectly loathsome food and drank no schnapps, not even a little wine. Well, what do you two say? Am I a mensch or what?"

Yol told them the initial experimental project at Kinnereth had gone so well that Dr. Ruppin at the National Fund decided to hand over a tract of land for them to develop with no fund supervisor present. They were given three thousand dunams—seven hundred fifty acres—on the east side of the Jordan River. The settlement was called Um Jumi, from the name of a nearby Arab village. The workers who took it on, Yol included, were among the most experienced in the country. Their goal was not to settle permanently at Um Jumi, but to make a start of it and then hand it over to another settlement group in a few months. The original pioneers would then go on to tame another tract.

Late one night after Rosie was in bed, Haim and Yol sat up talking. Yol fetched his valise; packed inside were his cartridge belt and revolver. Haim was enthralled with the weapon and with Yol's anecdotes of his self-defense training among the Hashomer, the closest thing to a Hebrew warrior class since the time of Masada.

"And what do I have to show you in return," Haim moped out loud, "my ledgers from the shoe factory?"

Yol, usually flippant, grew serious. He studied his friend and then softly asked why he wasn't happy. "Remember, you knew marriage would mean you'd have to share your dream."

Haim protested that he'd never once regretted marrying Rosie and that he looked forward to their first child. He then told Yol about Rosie's promise that if he allowed her to complete her work as Dizengoff's secretary, she would give him his chance to do what he wanted to do.

"I would join you in an instant," Haim said, longingly hefting Yol's revolver, then shrugged in resignation. "But I fear it is too late."

"Maybe not," Yol murmured. "Haim, fetch us a drink."

Haim brought to the table a bottle of wine. By the time the flagon was dry, they had hatched their plan.

Haim turned the corner onto Herzl Street. He opened the whitewashed picket gate in front of the blue two-story cottage that was his home. The front lot was still nothing but sand, but from the back yard came the musty odor of composted soil. Haim arranged for the stuff to be carted in so that Rosie could begin a flower garden under her mother's tutelage. Miriam Glaser supplied her daughter with seeds, bulbs and incidentals, including a servant to do the heavy work. Rosie diligently puttered around the seed beds, but it would be at least another season before the garden's promise was realized.

Haim walked the side path around the cottage into the back yard. Rosie, seven months pregnant, was seated in a wicker chaise lounge with a sketch paid on her lap. She wore a heavy scarlet muslin caftan and had a grey wool shawl wrapped around her shoulders against the slight breeze. During her pregnancy she chilled easily during the evening.

Haim stood quietly for a moment. Rosie, engrossed in her drawing, had not yet noticed him. He loved to watch her like this; it allowed him to study her every feature. If he tried to gaze at her while she was aware of it Rosie would start to fidget, blush and finally scold him.

Now he had the chance to notice how the last rays of the setting sun brought out the glinting coppery highlights in her golden hair. He smiled at the way her perpetually sunburnt nose wrinkled and her lips pursed as she pondered her work.

She took her painting and drawing very seriously. Some of her work had gone to her father's agent in London, but none had yet been sold. Nevertheless, Rosie kept at it. She meant to surpass her father's artistic success. Haim wondered out loud why that would matter to her if she enjoyed the work, and Rosie just smiled and kissed him.

Moving silently, Haim was able to approach unnoticed. His wife, intent on her sketching, was deaf and blind to the outside world. Finally he was close enough to tickle her bare brown toes.

Rosie's sable eyes widened with surprise, and then she grinned. "You're home late. Everything all right, love?"

Haim nodded, coming around to perch on her armrest and give her a hug. Rosie rested her head against him for a moment, shutting her sketch pad.

Haim noticed her action, but he had long ago learned not to take offense. Rosie could not bring herself to show her work before it was finished. Often she sent it off to London via her father without showing it to him at all. Maybe she would gain some confidence when something of hers finally sold.

"Would you like me to go inside until you're done drawing?" Haim asked, nuzzling the top of her head.

"No, I want to be with you. The light's gone, anyway," she added, squinting at the twilight sky. "What I'd like for you to do is to continue to kiss me for a while," she murmured, "and when you've grown tired of that—"

"That's not likely—"

"You can help me out of this chair. Your child has seen to it that I can sit down easily enough, but getting up is quite another matter."

By the time they were ready to go in, it was dark

enough for the first stars to be seen. In the quiet between day and night they could hear the Mediterranean crashing upon the beach and then the cough, clatter and momentary roar as the city's lone generator surged into life. Haim considered it an interesting novelty, but like his neighbors, he had no desire for one in his home; they made too much mess and stink. Tel Aviv's residences still depended on lanterns and candles for evening light.

Rosie started dinner as Haim went upstairs to change his clothes. When he returned to the ground floor Rosie called out, "What was so important to talk about that we couldn't go to my parents this evening?"

Haim entered the kitchen and Rosie turned from the stove. "Well?" She looked at him quizzically. "Haim, are you well? You look pale."

"Leave what you are doing and come sit with me a minute."

"Dinner will burn."

He moved the pot from the fire and led his wife to the kitchen table, already set for dinner. "Sit. We must talk about the future."

Suddenly suspicious, Rosie shrugged. "What's to talk? This is our future." She patted her big belly. "Our children, the factory—"

"Rosie, tomorrow I am putting the factory up for sale." He picked up a teaspoon and tapped it in his palm.

She stared at him a moment. "Maybe I'd better sit down," she muttered, taking a chair. "Husband, please explain to me."

Haim stared at the tablecloth. "It's been years already since your work with Meir—"

"Barely two."

"About a few months I don't want to argue."

"Then what?"

"Rosie, that night on the beach when I proposed to

you, you made me a promise.'' He slid the blade of his knife between the tines of a fork and wiggled it.

She shrugged. "I have not forgotten. So what about it?"

"You said that when your work with Meir was done—"

"Please don't quote me back to myself."

Haim stubbornly plodded on. "That when the work was done, you would leave Tel Aviv and go with me where I wanted to go."

"Please tell me what is on your mind."

Haim nodded, his blue eyes anxiously searching her face, the cutlery forgotten. "You heard from Yol all about Um Jumi. Remember, he said the original pioneers would turn the settlement over to permanent workers. Well, that transfer will soon take place. I've talked about it to Yol and with Dr. Ruppin, who controls the project. I've requested that we be allowed a place at Um Jumi and today Dr. Ruppin agreed."

Rosie stared at him aghast and then broke out laughing. "Don't frighten me so with your jokes." She trailed off as she realized he was serious. She smiled at him almost condescendingly. "Haim." She shook her head. "You are my husband, whom I love and respect—"

"So you will come with me?"

"Darling, listen a minute, please. You have been in Palestine for five years, but I was born here, yes? Perhaps, if you'll excuse my saying so, I know a little more about the land than you. It is barren wilderness in Galilee. In winter, when the Jordan is in flood, it is difficult even to get to Um Jumi. It is swamp there in the spring and fall and in summer nothing but scorched earth. There are vermin and fever."

"It is part of the homeland and it must be colonized."

Rosie wearily rested her chin on her hand. "What could you do in such a place?"

Haim shrugged. "Whatever is needed. I'll dig ditches, plant trees, farm; it is not up to me to decide what to do. I'll be told."

"You'll break your back."

Haim's blue eyes began to glint with anger. "I was a stonecutter in Jerusalem and again right here in Tel Aviv, you'll remember, young woman. My back did not break then, nor will it in Um Jumi."

"Enough, Haim. You are talking nonsense. You have responsibilities right here. What will happen to the business?"

"The business is for sale," Haim stolidly repeated.

"And what about me? You sit like a stone and make your pronouncements, but what about me? Am I to be sold as well?"

"Don't be so foolish." Haim scowled.

"Me foolish?" Rosie screeched. "It's you!" Her face contorted with bitterness. "What about our child?"

"Stop, Rosie—"

"Shall I come with you to that horrid swamp so that our child is born dead like Meir Dizengoff's?"

"*Stop!*" Haim's fist came crashing down on the table. A water tumbler tottered, rolled, and shattered on the floor.

Rosie's own vehemence shocked her. Her hand went to her lips and she shook her head. Now she stared down at the broken glass. "From our wedding set, the first one broken." She began to cry. "Oh, God forbid what I said, Haim. I didn't mean to say such a horrible thing."

"I know."

"I know you don't wish the baby any harm."

"Sha! It's over, calm yourself . . ." Haim saw that she was pale and trembling; she was on the verge of hysterics. "You'll understand everything in a minute."

"I want to hear it all."

"All right, but first you've got to relax, for the baby,

yes? Take deep breaths." He reached across the table to take her hand. "It gives me no pleasure to upset you, Rosie, but there is no time." He shrugged helplessly. "These matters must be discussed. One question you must answer for me right now, and after that the problems will be solved one after the other. You'll see.

"First I have to know. Will you—" He stopped, shaking his head. "Wrong words. Not will, but can you keep your promise to me?"

"You mean follow you to—that settlement?" Rosie began to cry all over again. "I don't know . . . yes, of course I will. *I love you.*"

Haim squeezed her hand. "And I love you." He winked. "Now that we've got the most important matter settled, the rest will be easy."

"Hah!" She sniffled and then laughed, swiping at her red eyes with her sleeve.

"You want I should finish cooking the dinner?" Haim asked.

"I want you to explain how easy it's going to be."

"Well, like I said, the biggest problem is time. I've got to be there a little more than a month from now."

"Why?" she implored. "Haim, what will happen to me? I must have our baby all alone?"

"Oh, Rosie, I'm sorry, but Dr. Ruppin was quite firm on that point. The women can come later, but the men must be there when the transfer of control takes place. I can't expect Yol and the others to do my share—"

"Yol is staying? I thought he was going to move on with the other pioneers."

Haim smiled. "It's something Yol and I cooked up during his visit with us to help sweeten the deal with Ruppin. He was begging for volunteers from the original group to stay behind and advise the newcomers. They all refused, but now Yol has agreed to stay on condition that I be included as a new member."

He became short of breath in his eagerness to tell her about it. "I found out that my desires, my ambitions are not so farfetched after all. Around Dizengoff and the other capitalists of Tel Aviv, faced with their scorn, I had begun to think I was just an idealist. Thank God Yol came to visit. It proved to me that there are others who share my beliefs. Palestine is Eretz Yisroel, Rosie, our ancient homeland from which we were sent into exile. This land and the Jewish people are like a husband and wife too long separated. Now that the Jews have returned, we must embrace the land, make love to it; only then shall our spirit be restored and healed."

He shook his head. "It cannot be done in cities like Tel Aviv, where the fortunate Jews posture like aristocrats, where our people are divided up into the oppressors and the oppressed. We Jews cannot afford to be our own worst enemies. We must all be brothers and sisters to each other and let our reclaimed land regenerate us."

"Haim, we are relatively well-to-do," Rosie began.

"I don't care about wealth."

"Maybe not, but think of our child."

"I am thinking of our children. I want them to grow up at one with their homeland and their comrades."

"But right now you've begun a great business. Is it fair to throw it away? Isn't it something to hand down to your children? Haim, you've worked hard to build up the factory. I am proud of you, but don't imagine that you didn't have a tremendous advantage over others. When you went to Arthur Ruppin's assistant so long ago, they gave you a chance, yes? That initial contract was the key to everything that followed. Why were you so favored over a thousand other young men, Haim?"

"It was my idea, Rosie," he said, slightly defensive. "A thousand others didn't think to go to the assistant."

"That's true. You are clever, and as I said, I'm proud of you." She hesitated, thinking twice about what she was about to say. "But clever ideas are not always enough, especially when one has no reputation. Darling, your proposal would have been turned down flat if it had not been for my father and Meir Dizengoff, who spoke up for you. I don't tell you this to belittle you, but only to point out that what you have accomplished here in Tel Aviv has had as much to do with our connections in this city as with your ability . . . If you throw away what you've built so far, you may find—should the time come when we want it again—that it is impossible to replace."

"I don't care about—"

"Wealth," Rosie finished for him, laughing. "I know, I know." Her voice softened. "I don't care about it either, not as long as I have you. It's our children I worry about. Do we have the right to make them paupers? Will they hate us for not allowing them the choice?"

Haim smiled. "I've thought about it and worked out a way to provide for them, should it turn out that the cooperative settlement program is a failure or should they decide to pursue a different life. It'll all be clear to you when the time comes."

She gazed into Haim's eyes and then heaved a great, resigned sigh. "Our house must be sold too, I suppose."

"The house too."

Rosie nodded, but the tears welled up again. She cursed herself for crying, roughly blotting the tears trickling down her cheeks. "Sometimes I act like a child. Don't mind me."

"There's nothing about you I mind," Haim said tenderly. "To me you are perfect. I am very fortunate to have you as my wife."

"That's a certainty," Rosie murmured, and then giggled. "You know what most breaks my heart? I'll never see that silly garden in bloom."

"Eretz Yisroel shall be our garden," Haim swore.

* * *

The next day Haim began the paperwork to transfer ownership of his business to his prospective buyer. He'd lied to Rosie to spare her feelings, leading her to believe that he'd not yet begun the selling process pending her approval. Actually Haim had already completed most of the work through confidential meetings with his buyer, a wealthy young immigrant from Germany, and the Anglo-Palestine Bank. Selling their cottage took only a week. There were always prosperous would-be citizens arriving in Tel Aviv, and many of them preferred to buy a solid cottage in the center of the city rather than build in the outskirts.

Rosie's parents were at first disturbed by Haim's decision, but eventually Erich Glaser came around. He was, after all, possessed of an artistic temperament and had been a pioneer quite as daring as Haim. Miriam Glaser remained furious and was only slightly mollified when it became clear to her that Rosie would be moving back into the family's house for the duration of her pregnancy. Their daughter had been spending several nights a week there anyway as her time grew near.

Meir Dizengoff sent Haim a curt note expressing his disapproval but beyond that showed no interest. Haim was relieved. Meir could have caused real trouble, for example by using his influence to impede the sale of the business and the house.

When negotiations were completed, Haim sat Rosie down in her parents' garden and explained to her what had been worked out. The Anglo-Palestine Bank had fed the sum into Erich Glaser's account. From there it would be transferred into Rosie's London account, established when she began to ship her pictures there. In London their capital would be invested in British and American concerns by Erich Glaser's business advisors, under Erich's supervision.

Rosie objected, wanting to know why the money was

not being put in both their names. Haim explained that it was a condition placed on them by the Turkish official in charge of currency transfers. The man was quite willing to look the other way during the transfer in exchange for a substantial bribe, but he insisted for his own protection that the money go out under the surname of Glaser.

"He said that his department is used to such activity under your father's name," Haim told her. "Anyway, you sign your work Rose Glaser and the account in that name already existed. There was no sense in further complicating matters. The important thing is that the money will be safe for our children."

It was late December. They sat wrapped in sweaters on a bench beneath a gnarled, ancient sycamore. Mrs. Glaser's gladioli lay dormant until spring. Rosie, watching the wind ruffle her husband's blond, curly hair as he revealed what was in his heart, desperately fought back her tears. He was going to be leaving for Galilee in just a few days. It would mark the beginning of their first separation since the wedding.

"When I join Yol and the others I want to be the same as them," Haim was saying, his voice dreamy. "Let the money be in your name. I want only to share what belongs to my brother haultzim."

The weeks following Haim's departure were dismal for Rosie. She hated herself for doing nothing, but she could not even bring herself to pick up her pencils or paints. Now that her house was gone, she tormented herself over the garden she would never see in bloom and the nursery her baby would never inhabit.

She would get furious at Haim for disrupting their lives; her pregnancy was enough to endure. Then she would find herself feeling guilty for being angry with him. Surely it was only because she missed him so.

She felt almost disgraced without him. She dreaded

shopping in Tel Aviv, dreaded even leaving the grounds of
the inn. Everyone in the community knew where Haim had
gone. The wives smirked at her when she passed.

It was worse when she was with her mother. Miriam
Glaser could not for the life of her understand what possessed Haim. She endured the taunts and gossip from the
community for a time but then finally suggested to her
daughter that for the sake of the family it might be better if
Rosie stayed close to home.

Rosie, tight-lipped, was glad to agree. She did not
want to humiliate her mother or herself.

Her friends cut her off, seething over Haim's rejection of their way of life. Her brothers and sisters were
well-meaning but awkward with her. Their sister Rosie
was different—weak, unhappy, even weepy.

Then there was her mother. Before Rosie married, the
two women were allies against Erich Glaser's remoteness.
Mrs. Glaser felt betrayed when Rosie moved out of the
house. Her sons could not distract her and her other daughters were too young for her to turn to.

Now Rosie had returned. At first Miriam was pleased,
but as she became aware of her daughter's misery, fierce
satisfaction seemed to set in.

"Aren't you ashamed of the way everyone is laughing at you?" Miriam would demand. "Why do you let
him run roughshod over you?"

When it got to be too much, Rosie would hurry out to
the garden, where she could be alone. It would not do to
cry in front of her father, as he would only be embarrassed,
and she would not give her mother the satisfaction.

On the stone bench under the twisted old tree she
would quietly weep, her fingers laced across her distended
belly. It comforted her to feel the life kicking within her.
Keeping company with the baby in her womb eased the
dreadful loneliness.

Chapter 12

Galilee, 1911

It took Haim Kolesnikoff three days in a horse-drawn cart to reach the Arab village of Um Jumi, just east of the Jordan River and close to the Sea of Galilee. His transport ran supplies between the towns and settlements; consequently it followed a meandering route. Haim wondered if he was ever going to arrive at Um Jumi and whether the handful who were already there would think badly of him for being tardy.

He was looking forward to good, honest, physical work, and though he was saddened not to be present for the birth, he was firmly convinced that he was doing the right thing.

Haim felt reborn. Let the capitalists back in Tel Aviv think what they might; his money and power had been chains on his soul. Now that his wealth was out of his hands, he felt unfettered. Stripping himself of his material assets had returned his youth and strength to him. He still had his wife and soon would have a child, but his days of sitting behind a desk were over. He was going to be a pioneer again.

Haim grinned to himself as the squeaky cart rolled northward. Yol, old friend, he reflected, it looks as if you were wrong. It appears that I've managed to win beautiful Rosie without having to compromise my dream.

Slowly the terrain began to change. The evergreen oaks gave way to leathery, gnarled carob trees and then to low scrub and thorny bushes. It became colder as they approached Galilee and it rained a lot more.

Five miles from Um Jumi they found that the Jordan had overflowed its banks. There was only swamp and blood-crimson mudbeds as far as the eye could see. The mud sucked at the cart's wheels like something hungry. Haim had to push from behind as the brace of horses, heads lowered and hooves kicking and slipping, strained to pull the cart. Haim gave it all he had. Several times the horses abruptly found firmer footing. The cart would lurch forward several yards, leaving Haim stretched full length on his face in six inches of mud. Soon he was crusted over with it.

It took the cart nine hours to cover the last five miles. When they finally rolled into Um Jumi beneath a pelting, icy rain that soaked Haim to his skin, the new pioneer wanted nothing more than a long sleep in a warm, dry bed.

The cart made its way through muddy garbage-strewn streets lined with low clay huts and tattered tents. Dark Arab eyes stared out at Haim as he rode past. Now and then a mangy dog would dart between the plodding horses' legs or a scrawny chicken would flap its wings, clucking in outrage. From some hovel came the sound of a child crying. From all the huts and tents greasy smoke curled up into the rainy sky.

This is worse than how the lowliest serfs lived back in Russia, Haim thought. These poor fellahin—we must do something for them as soon as we can.

When the cart reached what the driver mumbled was the Jewish portion of the village, things seemed little better. There was no garbage, but the streets were just as muddy and the clay huts just as wretched. A rickety wooden building stood on the very outskirts of the Jewish encampment. Haim glimpsed Yol leaning against the rain-shiny planking, totally unprotected from the weather. Water was dripping from the end of his nose to join the rivulets streaming down his beard.

Silly little monkey, Haim thought fondly. He may be in charge, but he doesn't know enough to build a roofed porch. I'll get on it first thing.

Yol detached himself from the building and walked over to meet the cart. He was dressed in his simple work clothes, red Arab slippers and his kaffiyeh. His revolver was nowhere in sight.

Because of the rain, Haim told himself. Why ruin the gun by getting it rusty? Besides, those poor souls I passed seemed peaceful enough.

The cart came to a stop. As Haim rummaged around to collect his belongings, he wondered why the rest of his comrades had not turned out to greet him. During the last leg of his journey it had been in his mind that the others would gather around him like a family welcoming a long lost member; this was to be the ultimate homecoming. At last he would be with people of his spirit if not his blood. At last he would be with kin.

"Shalom," Yol said, not smiling at all. "Grab your stuff and follow me. There is work waiting for you."

They went directly from the cart to a large, mildewed, leaky canvas tent. There for the rest of the day he oiled and sharpened rusty scythe blades. He was so tired he couldn't see straight, and several times he cut his grimy fingers. Cold, wet and miserable, Haim wondered where all the others were and cursed himself for thinking of coming to this hellhole.

He thought that first day at Um Jumi would never end, but at last Yol came to fetch him for dinner. The large wooden building turned out to be the communal dining hall. Haim timidly took his place upon a long bench and sat quiet and withdrawn. Water dripped down his neck and onto his plate from the leaky roof. The others talked around him. There was lamb stew, flat bread and dried fruits soaked in hot water. The dried fruits had come in on Haim's cart and were garnering far more attention than he.

When the meal was over Yol called a meeting to order. Haim saw that his normally easy-going friend was not enjoying his position of leadership. Yol looked supremely uncomfortable guiding the discussions, recognizing speakers and calling some of them out of order.

Haim was asked to stand up and was introduced to the group. A scattering of scowling faces glanced at him and turned away.

All right, Haim told himself, don't worry. You know how meetings are. Remember Dizengoff's endless assemblies to discuss a name for Tel Aviv.

He sat quietly, biding his time to speak out and make a good impression. Yol suggested that Haim make his bed in the dining hall until the rains were over and a hut could be built for him. Haim offered to have Rosie bring along a tent to save everybody the work. He expected gratitude, but the others only shook their heads knowingly. Yol merely shrugged and said it was time to discuss new business.

Haim impatiently listened as the others discussed pesticides, kitchen duties and work details out in the fields. During a lull in the conversation he raised his hand.

Yol hesitated but finally recognized him. "What, Haim?"

"I had an idea coming in this afternoon," he said loudly. "The dining hall has no porch. I know a little about building. Why don't I put one on? It'll keep us dry in the rainy season and give us shade in the summer."

"And where should the lumber for your personal project come from?"

Haim turned. The speaker had long black hair and a beard with no mustache. His name was Isaac; Haim had used all his concentration to memorize names as he heard them.

"There are no trees here," Isaac said with amused contempt. "If there were, we would cherish them, not cut them down to make a porch."

"This spring we will begin planting seedlings to reclaim the swamps," Yol added kindly. "Haim, perhaps you should get the hang of the way things are around here before offering comments."

Half an hour later the meeting ended and the halutzim filed out to their beds. Only Haim and Yol were left.

"They hate me," Haim blurted.

"What did you expect?"

"But why?" Haim shook his head in bewilderment. "What have I done to them? Why should they treat me so coldly?"

"My friend, listen to me. All of us have slaved for years to earn this opportunity. To us this misery is a privilege. Do you understand? This is an experiment, my friend, one that the National Fund is watching very closely. The fate of other proposed settlements rests on our shoulders."

"This is the great experiment," Haim scowled, nodding. "I know that. Arthur told me about it."

"Arthur!" Yol exclaimed. "You call him Arthur. To us he is Dr. Ruppin. These people you ask to accept you as an equal have never laid eyes on Ruppin, and yet you call the great man by his first name."

"Is it my fault I worked for him back in Jaffa?"

"It is not a question of fault, Haim, but merely that you are the newcomer and you must fit in." Yol smiled sadly. "We offer to build you a hut and you say, 'Don't bother, I'll buy one.'."

"One little mistake," Haim muttered.

"I'll build you a porch," Yol mimicked, chuckling. "My friend, I was waiting for you to suggest that the lumber be delivered from Tel Aviv."

Haim blushed. "What, then, little monkey? Help me. This is so important to me—their approval too."

Yol came over to Haim and put his hand on his old friend's shoulder. "If you want to be accepted, try to see their side of things. Right now the men are suspicious of your success in Tel Aviv and jealous of your blue eyes and curly blond hair. 'Here is a handsome bigshot among us,' they grumble. 'Will our wives think less of us compared to Haim Kolesnikoff?' "

"Absurd," Haim scoffed. "The women glared at me worse than the men."

"Absolutely," Yol nodded. "The women are thinking, 'Here's the one who married Rosie Glaser, the rich girl.' Don't forget, the Glaser family is famous in Palestine. 'Where is this rich girl?' the women are asking each other. 'Is she too good for us or is she waiting to come when the weather is more to her liking?' "

"You know why she isn't here," Haim said reproachfully.

"Yes, I do," Yol agreed. "The other married couples have vowed not to have children until a permanent settlement is built. Also a couple just last week announced that they were expecting a child but that woman will work until delivery is imminent, and only then go to the clinic at Tiberias."

"So!" Haim snapped. "It was necessary for me to risk the lives of my wife and unborn child to prove I have the right spirit—is that what you are saying?"

"No, my friend. What I am saying is that everything takes time. Eventually you as well as Rosie and the baby will be accepted. For now I can only give you this advice: I know that your heart is in the right place, but you have been wealthy for a long time. Maybe you've given up that wealth, but you still think and act like a rich man.''

Haim looked rueful. "How'd you get to be so wise, monkey man?''

"Leadership, responsibility, maturity—terrible things like that.'' Yol made a face. "Hurry up and become a leader here the way you have everywhere else. Then I can go back to doing what I do best: getting drunk, shirking and making jokes.''

Haim seemed not to hear him. "I thought it was going to be like one big family,'' he moped.

"It is exactly like that!'' Yol laughed sardonically. "Your problem is that you know nothing of family life. You imagine it to be love and kisses all the time, but it is rivalry, jealousy, intense hatred until a crisis threatens, and then everyone pulls together.''

"If that's what it takes, then I pray that a crisis comes soon,'' Haim said forcefully.

"Don't worry,'' Yol chuckled. "That's like praying for the sun to rise. Which it's going to, and not so many hours from now. I'm going to bed, and so should you. Tomorrow is going to be a long day.''

Left alone, Haim found that he was far too agitated to sleep. He decided to write to Rosie. The letter would go out on the returning supply cart and would likely take a month to reach Tel Aviv, but sporadic communication was better than none at all.

"My most precious love,'' Haim began his missive, everything is wonderful here.''

It was mid-January before Rosie received Haim's first letter from Um Jumi. Late one morning one of the servants brought it up to her bedroom. Rosie was still in bed. Her time was drawing near and it was doctor's orders that she stay off her feet as much as possible.

The doctor was coming every day now. Arrangements had been made to transport her from her parents' house in Jaffa to the new infirmary in Tel Aviv. The port city had seen the arrival of its first gasoline motor trucks, and Meir Dizengoff had seen to it that one was standing by for her, its canvas-enclosed cargo area rigged out as a makeshift ambulance.

Rosie read Haim's letter, carefully folded it and placed it on the nightstand. Later, when she was dressed, she would put it in her pocket, where she could touch it from time to time through the day.

She missed Haim desperately and found herself heartened by the good news in his letter. According to Haim he and the other halutzim were transforming the agricultural settlement into a place of primitive but unspoiled beauty.

"Like the Garden of Eden," as Haim described it in his letter. Rosie, reclining against her feather pillows, smiled at her reflection in her vanity mirror.

"The Garden of Eden," she murmured, patting her huge belly. "A nice enough place for you to grow up in, yes, my son?"

She rang the bell, for it was time to dress and go downstairs. Her mother had invited several women for luncheon. Normally Rosie found herself bored by her mother's circle, but she had been housebound for a week and was hungry for diversion of any sort.

Her mother's guests began arriving at noon. Kamel showed them into the dining area one by one.

As the meal wore on, Rosie began to suspect that her mother had laid down specific ground rules for conversation. Miriam Glaser kept the focus firmly on baby clothes and Tel Aviv society gossip in general; not once did the subject of Um Jumi or Haim come up. This was patently absurd, for the whole notion of a self-sufficient commonly owned agricultural settlement was so antithetical to the middle-class European sensibilities of Tel Aviv that the matter was literally the talk of the town. For days the newspapers had been full of Dr. Ruppin's comments on the program. It was widely known that he was a staunch advocate of settlement.

That the subject did not seem to exist at her mother's table was highly amusing to Rosie. She perversely decided to raise the issue at her first opportunity. Haim's encouraging letter had made her feel bold. She was also eager for news.

Mrs. Wasserman, seated on her right, was the wife of one of Tel Aviv's foremost newspaper publishers. Rosie leaned towards her, whispering, "You must be very proud of your husband's exclusive interview with Dr. Ruppin."

"Rosie . . ." her mother admonished.

"Let the girl talk, Miriam," Mrs. Wasserman interjected. She was an overweight plain-featured woman with crooked teeth. She had always felt inferior among her friends and tended to bolster her standing by recounting her husband's successes. "Teddy hasn't printed half what Arthur told him," she boasted.

"What do you mean?" Rosie asked, not liking her tone.

"Just that Arthur is very disappointed in how things at Um Jumi are going."

"Dr. Ruppin sounded so optimistic in the interview."

"Darling, he has to be optimistic," Mrs. Wasserman explained. "He can't let on how poorly things are going, can he? Not if he wants to hold onto his position as head of the National Fund. He's invested quite a bit of money in the farm machinery and all that land."

"Please! You're upsetting Rosie," Miriam Glaser cut in. "My dear, don't you pay attention," she told her daughter. "I'm sure Mrs. Wasserman is exaggerating," she added, but then abruptly realized that in her haste to keep her daughter calm, she was saying exactly the wrong thing to quiet the insecure Mrs. Wasserman.

"Rosie, I know your mother thinks I'm a braggart," the newspaper publisher's wife said huffily. "Why I'd ever make things up I'll let her say. But one thing I can tell you is that Dr. Ruppin is very worried about the climate at Um Jumi. Never mind the malaria—everyone outside Tel Aviv is fair prey to malaria—Arthur confided to my husband that Um Jumi also has yellow fever."

Rosie's heart began to pound with awful fear. She clutched the letter in her skirt pocket. It had been written weeks and weeks ago. Was Haim even now laid up with fever? Was he calling out for her as he lay dying?

Rosie gasped, positive that her beloved was a jaundiced corpse.

"You see what you've done, you big cow?" Miriam screeched at Mrs. Wasserman from what sounded like a great distance.

"Now, Rosie, don't cry like that," somebody whispered directly into her ear. She felt hands grasping her as she began to sway off the chair, and then quite suddenly she felt herself struck by a lightning bolt of pain.

She cried out, doubling over with such force that her forehead slammed against the edge of the table. Had she left blood on her mother's lace tablecloth? She couldn't tell, for she was far too overwhelmed with labor pain.

"Oh, my God," Miriam murmured. "Kamel," she shouted, "send for the doctor. Rosie's having her baby!"

Somehow they got her upstairs to her bed. Then her mother was there, whispering reassurances. There were cool wet clothes pressed against her forehead. They stung at first. *I guess I did cut my forehead on the table*, Rosie thought distractedly. *I hope there isn't a scar.*

The doctor arrived. He asked about the interval between contractions, and then, disbelieving, timed them himself.

"Forget the ambulance," he said brusquely. "Tel Aviv is out of the question; she can't travel. She'll have it at home."

Rosie spent all that day and half the night in labor. During the first hours she called for the charcoal sketch of Haim and his friend Abe, which had been taken down from the wall and rolled up to be packed in Rosie's trunk. She'd packed some weeks ago, to occupy herself and to feel that she was making some real progress toward joining her husband.

Now the rolled parchment in its leather tube went beside her on the sweat-soaked sheets. During the bad periods, when her world was nothing but grunts and contractions, she gripped that tube as she would her husband's hand had he been present.

She began to have delusions. She imagined that she had yellow fever, that Haim had it. She imagined she was back on that sandy stretch of Jaffa beach, being assaulted by the Turkish immigration officer. Haim came racing to her rescue all over again, but then the scene shifted and it was a Bedouin marauder confronting Haim. They were all at Um Jumi and the nomad wanted the baby.

A few minutes after dawn on January seventeenth, 1911, a boy was born to the Kolesnikoffs.

At Um Jumi winter gradually mellowed into spring. The cold rains turned the roads between Tel Aviv and Galilee to impassable mud. No supply carts could arrive until the sun had the opportunity to bake the sticky earth dry, and no carts meant no mail.

Haim could only wonder about Rosie. Had she carried to term? Had she come through all right? Was it a boy, a girl? Was there a child at all?

The others watched him, fascinated by his stoicism as he stubbornly maintained a cheerful manner. He was the first to volunteer for a work detail, to risk his own health nursing fever patients. For every bucket of water the others carried from the turbulent Jordan back to the huts and dining hall, Haim carried two.

The others watched and when he was away nodded reluctant approval. Maybe the capitalist from Tel Aviv wasn't so bad after all.

Of all the halutzim at Um Jumi only Yol understood Haim. He knew his old friend was throwing himself into his work to avoid thinking about Rosie and the baby. Yol knew it had been Haim's way not to brood but to lose his sadness and worry in hard labor.

The Arabs of Um Jumi were employed by an absentee landlord who had sold a portion of his land to the National Fund. At first, the fellahin assumed the Jewish newcomers would themselves be landlords, hiring others to do the work. When they saw the Jews—men and women—providing for themselves, they respected them for it.

However, there was still a great deal of mistrust between the ethnic factions of Um Jumi. Most of the blame for the tension lay with the Jews. The halutzim were strict Zionists; they were well educated and could not help looking down on the Arab peasants. During their meetings in the dining hall they assured each other of how happy the Arabs would one day be under Zionist protection.

One night Haim approached Yol after the meeting disbanded. Popovich looked drawn. He had been up most of the night on guard duty.

Lately there had been an increase of nomad robbers from the Transjordan menacing the village. The two members of Hashomer, the professional watchmen, had left Um Jumi long before Haim arrived, after training the halutzim in the use of firearms. Now the men, in addition to their regular duties during the day, took turns on guard. It meant standing in the dark, tightly gripping one of the three twenty-year-old Lee-Enfield rifles provided by the National Fund office in England.

Haim had also received firearms instruction and took his turn. At first he found it fun. At last he was a soldier in the Jewish cause.

Then late one moonless night he heard a sound like a hornet buzzing past his head. A split second later a sharp cracking sound reached Haim's ears. He'd been shot at, he suddenly realized. Oh please, no, he wanted to cry out, not until I know what happened with my Rosie. Not until I see my son.

But he kept silent, taking shelter in a ditch. The next bullet never came, and he was never shot at again on watch. From then on, however, being a warrior ceased to be fun, and the heft and scent of the well-oiled rifle failed to bring him pleasure. He also understood why Yol no longer proudly brandished his pistol.

"What is it, my friend?" Yol asked as the last of the halutzim left the dining hall.

"It's no good, our dealings with the fellahin," Haim exploded. What he wanted to say had been pent up in him for a long time. "I accept the fact that I am a newcomer to Um Jumi—"

"So far I have nothing to add to this conversation," Yol observed.

"But about living with Arabs and profiting from the relationship I do know a little something," Haim continued. "I know it from my time as a factory owner in Tel Aviv."

"Stop a minute." Yol held up his hands. "I know what you're intending to say and I agree with you. We've made a mess of things with the people living here."

"So?"

Yol shrugged. "Our coworkers don't know Arabs the way we do. To them the Arabs are merely a nuisance to be coped with, like the mud in winter and the snakes in summer. They can't even speak with the Arabs."

"You have the language," Haim pointed out.

"I know, I know, but with all my other responsibili-

ties as the damned patriarch of this project, I simply have
not had the energy to convince our comrades that we ought
to negotiate with the villagers and then actually do it.''

"Poor old Yol," Haim said. "You hardly laugh
anymore. You've had to grow up very quickly, haven't
you?'' He gazed at his friend, lost in thought. "Tell you
what. I've got the language to talk with the fellahin. I'll go
see their mayor tomorrow."

"No. First we must discuss it with the others."

"We don't yet know what to discuss. Please, leave it
to me. I'll bring back something we can vote on."

"It's risky," Yol warned. "The workers here are just
starting to accept you."

Haim pondered it. When Rosie finally came, she too
would be afforded a trial period, and then the others would
vote to accept or blackball them.

"Remember what you told me, Yol, that all this
bickering and jealousy was the way of it in a real family?
Well, I think I've been here long enough to speak up for
myself. At tomorrow night's meeting, assuming I have a
profitable talk with the mayor, I'll present what I've
accomplished. If the haluztim refuse me—if they see night
and I see day on the issue—then I'll know I'm so different
from them that this isn't my family after all."

Yol smiled thinly. "Go on then. Have your visit. I
have just two bits of advice. Don't wear clean clothes, for
there are lice in those huts, and do make a big thing of
refusing all gestures of hospitality once or twice. The rural
fellahin are far more traditional than those who live in the
cities."

The next day after his morning chores were done,
Haim walked over to the Arab sector. He did not manage
to get very far before he was surrounded by a flock of
gawking children who wore only flimsy rags despite the
coolness of the day. They were all pitifully thin and most
had open sores on their nut-brown skin.

The mayor's house was a small stone cottage in an out-of-the-way part of the village. Adult male Arabs passed Haim, giving him hard looks, but none stood in his way as he opened the gate, threaded his way past several scrawny goats grazing in the yard and knocked on the door.

An old woman with two blue dots tattooed on her forehead listened intently as he explained why he'd come and then left him on the doorstep while she relayed his message to her husband. As Haim stood waiting, he felt countless eyes drilling holes into his back.

Presently the old woman returned and ushered him inside. Haim found the mayor reclining on grimy cushions in the dark, stuffy low-ceilinged living room of the cottage. The village mayor looked to be in his seventies. He was bald and wore a white goatee. His belly was big enough to be obvious. He did not stand to greet his guest.

"You are welcome," Kareem al-Hassad said in Arabic, smiling. "Jews were welcome when they came unasked to Um Jumi, land of our ancestors, and you are welcome now that you have come uninvited to my home."

"I am in debt to your kind hospitality," Haim said meekly. The old man, he noticed, was wearing a thread-bare caftan and was missing three fingers of his left hand. There was a bubbling hookah at his side.

"Sit," al-Hassad said as the old woman reappeared with two tiny cups of coffee on an ornate lacquered tray.

Haim sat cross-legged on a cushion, repeatedly re-fused and finally accepted the thimbleful of thick black brew, sipping it and pronouncing it delicious. At the same time he took a packet of cigarettes out of his pocket and lit one. He did not smoke, but he had to go through the motion. The mayor would be offended if he thought the cigarettes had been brought purely for his benefit, as an act of charity. When he was finally persuaded to accept a smoke, Haim was careful to place the packet halfway between them.

Haim had snitched the cigarettes from the cupboard in the dining hall. Tobacco, like everything else, was stored in a communal supply. There were only two packs left. Haim hoped his taking the cigarettes wouldn't poison the others' objectivity when he presented his case at tonight's meeting.

"Yes, then?" the mayor asked, waiting.

Haim thought back to his beginnings with the shoe factory. During those days he needed fellahin workers as much as they needed jobs. Like most people, their pride grows with the depths of their poverty, he thought. He mused upon the Arabs' ragged clothing, their primitive farming implements, the sickness among their children.

"Sir," Haim began, "I've come to ask you to help my people."

That night at the meeting, when Yol asked if there was any new business, Haim raised his hand.

"You are recognized, comrade," Yol said.

Haim nodded respectfully and got up to move toward the front of the hall as he announced. "I was in the Arab quarter today. I had coffee with the mayor."

Normally the halutzim spoke from their places at the long benches, but Haim's work in city planning during his Tel Aviv days had made him savvy. He wanted the front of the hall, which would lend authority to what he was about to say.

"I went there to see if we could come to some agreement of cooperation with the Arabs."

"We didn't vote to authorize this last night," Deborah Felicks called out. Her stony-faced husband Jack sat beside her, nodding agreement.

"Haim has the floor," Yol interjected.

"Here is what I've worked out, subject to everyone's vote, of course," Haim said brightly. "As you all know, we've been carrying our own water. The Arabs will rent us some mules, which can carry water cans, saving time as well as our backs."

"The National Fund office is sending us mules this spring," one of the workers pointed out.

"That's true," Haim said, "but now we can tell the fund we've figured out a way to save the money. The Arab mules are already here. It is within the spirit of socialism to use what is available. Also, these mules thrive in Galilee. Better to stick with them than bring in new animals that may not thrive in this difficult climate."

There were no objections, and Haim quickly continued. "The Arabs have a boat on the Jordan. They've agreed to let us hire it on occasion. This means that once we have freight to ship, we can send it by river. Our potential market for surplus products will double, and in the winter, when the roads are closed, we'll be able to maintain trade links."

There was a table behind him. Haim perched on its edge. "There's one final benefit we will get from cooperation with the fellahin," Haim announced, letting his eyes make contact with his audience. "We will begin to understand them as our neighbors in this land. If we are here to become one with Eretz Yisroel we must also accept the Arabs."

"So far you've told us what we'll get from this new partnership," Isaac Nemoy called loudly, looking like a stern sea captain with his black beard and no mustache. "Please inform us what we must do for them."

"I will," Haim nodded. "One thing is teach them agriculture. These poor devils are still farming the way it was done in Biblical times. If we lend them our plows and our harvesters when we aren't using them, what's the harm? Another thing we can do is heal their sick children. All of us keep ourselves clean and eat correctly. True, we suffer from fevers, but we have none of the diseases the Arab children have. Our medicines sit on the cupboard shelf. They grow stale, useless. Let's heal the children.

The more Arab youngsters who grow up trusting Jews, the less our children will have to fear Arabs.''

"What you've so far asked of us is not very much," Isaac admitted after a pause. "Is there anything else?"

"Only that we stand guard duty over the villagers as well as ourselves," Haim answered. "You see, the fellahin are even more fearful of the Bedouin robbers from Transjordan than we."

"I still maintain that you were wrong to approach the Arabs without taking a vote," Deborah Felicks insisted.

"For that I apologize," Haim told them all, "but no harm has been done. My agreements are tentative, depending on your ratification. Nothing has been lost except for my time and a few cigarettes."

"You took cigarettes?" came a howl of outrage from the rear of the hall. Skinny, hatchet-faced Moses Pool jumped to his feet, wagging a trembling finger in Haim's direction. "Stealing from the cupboard is a serious breach of rules."

"Wait, now. There's an interesting point of contention here," Jack Felicks, a lawyer, spoke up. "Haim does have a right to a share of the tobacco—"

"He doesn't smoke," Pool snarled.

"So?" Felicks shrugged. "Just because he doesn't smoke—"

"If Haim isn't ill, can he still claim medicine?" Pool scoffed.

Others began to shout their opinions on the matter until Yol called for order. "It's late," he said. "I suggest we all think about what Haim has presented and vote on it tomorrow night. This meeting is adjourned."

Haim, all alone in the dining hall, found himself unable to sleep. His bedding was rolled in one corner of the building, but he had no desire to lie down.

Maybe it was being all by himself in the cavernous, utilitarian hall. When the rest of the halutzim were about, the place took on a warm, friendly, familiar glow. Now the rough, bare planking, the long hard benches, wobbly tables and dark corners seemed to intensify Haim's feelings of estrangement. How he missed Rosie, and some sort of home of his own. And when would he know about his child?

How can I have come so far in my life and still be an orphan? Haim wondered during the early hours of the dawn, when his only company was the ticking of the building settling and the piercing wail of the wind blowing down from out of the hills. When will my comrades accept me? When can I sleep the night through with Rosie back in my arms, where she belongs?

The next night during the meeting the agreements Haim had made were approved unanimously. There was little debate, but Moses Pool did insist that it be duly recorded that Haim Kolesnikoff had been reprimanded for improperly requisitioning one pack of cigarettes.

It was a warm sunny day in May when the first supply cart made it through to Um Jumi. There were plenty of long-awaited goods to be unpacked, but this time the dried fruit took second place in interest. All the halutzim formed a circle around Haim. He tore open the long-awaited letter from Rosie and scanned it quickly. Then he threw back his head and roared his happiness.

"It's a boy!" Haim shouted. "Born the seventeenth of January, a healthy ten-pound boy with blue eyes and light coloring." He paused, astounded by the realization. "My God, my son is four months old already."

"His name?" Yol demanded, eyes aglow.

Names had been decided before Haim left Tel Aviv. Rosie got to choose the first name; she wanted to honor the memory of her departed Aunt Harriet, who'd been very kind to her when she was a child. Haim got to pick the middle name.

"His name is Herschel Abraham."

"Herschel Abraham Kolesnikoff," a fellow grinned as he stood beside his pregnant wife. "It's good our little one will have someone to play with."

That day was declared a holiday. Yol miraculously produced several bottles of wine, and in the spirit of sharing fostered by Haim, sweets newly arrived on the supply cart were distributed to the Arab children. The Arabs watched and laughed delightedly as the Jews danced the hora; a few even joined the circle.

And for the first time since Haim arrived, all the halutzim made it a point to embrace him. They shook their comrade's hand in congratulations, in welcome.

Chapter 11

New York, 1910–1911

That winter was a grand time for the garment workers on Allen Street. In December there was the Feast of Lights, Hanukkah, which commemorates the Maccabees' victory over the Syrians in 168 B.C. Not a few Jews in the sweatshops around the city equated the fledgling union's victory over the manufacturers with the ancient rout of the Syrians.

This year the economic gains won by the summer-long strike allowed the Christians to treat their families to a most generous and festive Christmas.

For both the Christians and the Jews the approach of the New Year was a happy, hopeful time. They had good reason to celebrate on New Year's Eve; 1911 looked to be bright with opportunity.

Abe Herodetzky spent New Year's Eve alone. Stefano had invited him to his home for a family dinner, but Abe was too melancholy to desire to intrude upon a happy family's celebration. Besides, what if Stefano asked him when he was planning on opening his store? Abe had no stomach to lie again; as far as Stefano was concerned, the union had paid Abe back his two hundred dollars with interest.

Having refused Stefano's invitation, Abe found himself walking the streets. He was even more withdrawn since the end of the strike and the destruction of his dream. He had no friends besides Stefano—if one could call the Italian a friend.

Abe had been asked to leave his digs on Jefferson Street. The other two boarders didn't like him, his landlord said. Abe did not blame them for their antipathy. He'd always been quick to complain when they talked or laughed and had always refused their invitations to shul or to the settlement houses to flirt with the girls.

To shul Abe still could not bring himself to go, not even on Rosh Hashanah and Yom Kippur. He was accepting God's treatment of him, and God could take or leave him as he was.

As to girls, the pretty ones would laugh if he dared to approach. He was an ugly little man who'd been robbed by the union.

Well, there was Leah—sweet, quiet, pretty Leah. She was far too shy to flirt at the settlements despite her family's prodding. No, there was no way he could call on Leah, not without his own business. Leah wouldn't care one way or the other, but Abe could not endure the wicked glimmer of satisfaction in Sadie's eyes when he confessed that he was still a presser on Allen Street. He would stay away from Leah. He was too proud to face her family.

East Broadway was a mass of happy people hurrying to New Year's Eve festivities. Abe let himself be swept along through the chilly darkness to Chatham Square. He angled eastward and left the crowds behind as he headed toward the river. He stopped into a saloon on South Street near the Fulton Fish Market to get warm and have a drink.

The saloon had no name. It was dimly lit, it lacked tables, and it sported pale green peeling walls, sawdust on the floor and a long, splintery bar where dockhands and fishermen lifted glasses of whiskey and beer. The saloon stank of smoke and spoiled catches, but a whiskey here, even on New Year's Eve, was only a dime. Elsewhere, Abe knew, you could pay two bits for a drink on a holiday.

Tonight the saloon was packed with Irish, Portuguese and Italians elbowing for a place at the bar. Abe was the only Jew. If the other men had recognized him as such there could have been trouble, but Abe was clean-shaven and hatless. He knew from past experience that Italians and Portuguese often mistook him for a fellow countryman. Nobody would bother him nor even speak to him.

Abe had started coming here every night around October. It was a waste of money, he knew, but he indulged himself anyway. Whiskey helped him relax after working all day on Allen Street. He didn't like the goyish saloons very much, but there were no better cheap places around and certainly no bars in the Jewish neighborhoods.

Abe wouldn't have gone to them even if there were. He wanted no company when he drank. He preferred to drift back in time to those days when he and Haim shared a bottle of schnapps before falling asleep in the back of their shop.

Taking the bottle to bed with him was still the way that Abe most liked to drink, but he was once again crammed into an extra bedroom with another boarder. As was usually the case, he and his roommate were jockeying for favor with the family. Abe could just hear the outraged howls and demands that he pack up and leave if it was known that he drank.

He couldn't face having to move again. While it was one thing to be rich and hated, it was quite another to be excluded from the rest of the world when one was poor. Once he'd had his savings to keep him company. Now that he had nothing, he could feel himself growing old. Once

he'd been envious of the happy family life of his landlords;
now he was just bitter and often preoccupied with sour
musings on why he was a failure.

Besides, it was expensive to move. Each family asked
more rent than the one before, especially now that garment
workers were making more money. A boarder was at the
mercy of the landlord family. Abe had increased his weekly
savings out of his heftier salary. In the four months since
the strike ended he had cached away forty-eight dollars,
but moving again would cut into these savings.

Forty-eight dollars, another beginning. So many
beginnings. If only he were a better man, or at least
tougher, but his misery tormented him.

If he was a good man, why was he so unhappy? Was
it because he'd been a fool? Perhaps lending the money
hadn't been a good deed, but only a stupid one. In that
case he truly had lost everything, including his self-respect.
He had no peace, no peace at all.

Abe leaned heavily against the bar. He'd not eaten
since the morning, and his three whiskeys went straight to
his head. The blessed numbness began in his lips and
tongue and finally crept through his brain, dulling his
jagged pain. He paid the bartender and went outside. The
sidewalk seemed to sag beneath his feet as he walked
toward the river. From some far tower a clock chimed ten.

The night seemed crisper and the stars brighter than
before, but Abe was no longer cold. The weather, like the
anguish, was on the far side of the whiskey.

He walked south on Front Street, past dark buildings
and deserted docks. From the shadows came the rustling of
rats. He also heard the water slapping against the pilings,
and occasionally himself, laughing out loud for no particular reason. He heard nothing else. This part of the city was
deserted on New Year's Eve.

He walked all the way to Battery Park and loitered
there, leaning on a railing, letting the wind sing to him as

he gazed out at the inky chop of the bay. The lights of Ellis Island glimmered in the distance. The whiskey was holding sway within him; for a moment it made him dizzy. He imagined that the suddenly unsteady ground was the heaving deck of a steamship. He thought about the day he'd first set foot on American soil.

For one brief but horrifyingly intense moment he thought about hurling himself over the balustrade. The black shifting water below seemed to yawn like a mouth, promising blessed oblivion after brief moments of icy agony. Abe went so far as to tighten his grip on the wooden railing. His leg muscles tensed for the leap—

He turned away and began to walk rapidly home. He would not kill himself. What if Haim someday found out?

On Wall Street he passed a group of celebrants. They wished him a happy New Year and allowed him several pulls from their flasks. The whiskey fueled him for the rest of his long walk home. It was well after midnight. Abe's first decision of the New Year was to buy himself a flask.

Winter softened into spring. Abe was putting in his days at Allen Street and more and more nights at the waterfront saloon. He was saving less money now and spending more on whiskey. He didn't care. It was the thought of a drink that got him through the day.

In April Abe discovered that God had not forsaken him after all. The miracle occurred on a Wednesday afternoon. Abe would remember not only the heat and unpleasantness of the sweatshop but also the way the April wind drove the cleansing spring rain against the black window panes. The sound of the rattling glass was a reminder that in a hairsbreadth God can change everything; that His alone is the power to renew the world by renewing a dream.

It was a little before five o'clock and the shop was

steamy as the pressers feverishly worked their irons. A shipment of coats had to be gotten out before the end of the day.

The manufacturer's foreman was not there. He was less and less in evidence these days. Mostly he just checked in with de Fazio at the end of the day. Stefano was able to get more out of the men through their loyalty to him and the union than the foreman could.

Stefano himself no longer worked a pressing machine. As union representative he spent his days overseeing shop productivity and watching out for his members' interests. Stefano counted every garment finished by every worker and kept a careful tally of each man's total in a ledger.

Abe, sweat-sodden and exhausted, was waiting for the long day to end two hours from now. The humidity, combined with his hangover from the previous night's bout of drinking, had left him extra thirsty. He'd already drained his tin can of drinking water and thought about going to fill it, but the sink was on the far side of the loft. In the few minutes it would take to complete the errand he could press three more coats.

I'll do ten more coats and then get the water, he decided. When those ten were done, he told himself just ten more. He was very thirsty now, and he used his discomfort as a goad to force himself to keep up the pace.

Ten more and I'll have a nice, cool drink; ten more; ten more. It was tricks like that that got a man through the day.

His corner of the loft, where all the pressing machines were grouped together, was as cloudy as a Turkish bath. Abe could not see past his own machine. He could hear the hiss and sigh of his neighbor's pressing irons, but the man himself, who'd been hired to take Stefano's place, was lost in the fog.

As Abe worked he found himself absentmindedly reaching for the drinking can, only to remind himself that it was empty. At that point he'd fall back on his "ten more coats" ploy to keep himself going. A few minutes would pass, his thoughts would move onto other things and he once again found himself reaching for the can out of habit.

It was during one of these intervals that Abe, reaching out, found his hand colliding with that of another worker. The man tilted the tin can as if to assure himself that it was empty and then dropped something into it.

"Some of us heard what happened," the man said in Yiddish. "It was a mitzvah, what you did."

Abe tried to see who it was, but the sweat in his eyes combined with the clouds of vapor rising off of his machine to obscure the man's features.

"You should take this from a few of us with thanks," the man added, and then he was gone.

Abe pawed at the tin can. Inside it he found wadded together five crumpled, soggy dollar bills.

He stared at the money and then squinted after the man who'd given it to him, all the while shaking his head in disbelief. How did that fellow, whoever he was, find out what had happened?

Somebody tapped him on the shoulder. Abe half turned. It was the new man who worked Stefano's presser. "I heard what you did," the man said in English thickly tinged with Polish. "I'm grateful to join a union, and I know it's thanks to you." He shook Abe's hand, pressing a dollar into his palm. "I saved this out of my first few weeks' pay."

Before Abe could think of a reply, he was distracted by two other men who stepped out of the steamy fog to drop money into his tin can and then silently disappear.

"Abe, this is for you with thanks," yet another man said, dropping money into the tin. The two right behind him only nodded shyly, smiling as they added their contribution to the can.

"For you, Abe."

"Thanks, Abe."

"To make it up for what they pulled on you, Abe."

He watched, his shoulders slumped and his baggy undershirt hanging from his scrawny frame. He stared in stupefaction as a procession of men glided like ghosts out of the steam fog to pay their respects. Some spoke to him; others gripped his hand or shoulder in affection; many merely nodded gruffly, but all dropped currency into the tin can.

He stood dumbstruck, a mute, enchanted spectator. Not me, he thought in wonder. It's not me they mean. He realized he was sobbing; then he began trembling like a lover in the throes of passion, a suitor finally the recipient of sweet ardor too long unrequited. He did not think about the money. He was content to bask in gratitude, as warm and dazzling as golden sunshine. They were all clapping him on the back. He was the center of attention.

I'm a hero, Abe gradually realized. In the dazzled far reaches of his thoughts Haim reared up, smiling affectionately.

"Hero!" Haim was saying, "I'm proud of you, hero."

Stefano de Fazio suddenly appeared at Abe's side. The stocky Italian put his arm around Abe's shoulders and guided him away from the pressing machines toward a relatively cool area of the loft given over to long work tables piled high with finished garments. This was where the union representative maintained his "office."

"Why didn't you tell me?" Stefano gently slapped Abe's cheek. "You feed me all kinds bullshit, eh, my friend? Why I got to go uptown to headquarters to find out you never got your money back?"

Abe didn't know what to say. The Italian had taken to wearing a suit with a vest and tie to work, a different one every other day. Abe had begun to think of Stefano as a superior, which only added to his tongue-tied awkwardness.

"I didn't want to cause no trouble," Abe finally stammered. "Didn't think it would help any, and—"

De Fazio shook his head disapprovingly. "We ain't greenhorns, right? The squeaky wheel gets the grease, Abe. You got to talk up if you want your due."

"I didn't want no trouble," Abe repeated. "Making trouble never helped nothing."

"You never had trouble before, Abe? I mean, what's the big deal if you complain?"

"For you, I meant. I didn't want trouble for you with the union."

Stefano stared at him for an instant. "You're not kidding, are you? Sweet Mary, you're not." His rotund features brightened with genuine pleasure. "That's nice, Abe, really. I got to tell the other guys about that kinda loyalty."

"Here, you mean?" Abe asked, puzzled. "These workers?"

"Nah," Stefano laughed. "These guys I got. I mean at the other locals. There's an election coming up, right?"

Abe stared blankly.

"Anyway, I figured something wasn't right about you saying you got your money on account of the way you were down in the dumps. I asked myself, 'Why ain't he happy 'stead of sad?' So I went uptown and found out all about it."

"They threw me out and the guard beat me."

"They told me." Stefano made a face. "I gave them a piece of my mind about that." He straightened the knot in his necktie.

"So they gave you back the money, Stefano?"

"Nah, I didn't ask for it back. It woulda taken too long to work it all out, going through channels."

Abe had no idea whatsoever what de Fazio was saying. "That Miss Grissome," he began obliquely, "she didn't make no trouble for you, I hope?"

"All you worry 'bout is causing other people trouble." Stefano ran his hands through his glistening black curls. "You were afraid of Miss Grissome—She is just a bookkeeper, my friend. You let the guard that works for your union rough you up, and you take it quiet 'cause you're afraid a bookkeeper is gonna make trouble." He scowled. "Ain't you ever stood up to anybody in your life?"

Abe considered the question, stung that what he considered heroic stoicism might be viewed by others as cowardice. In Russia he'd been respected for his circumspection, but also for his ability to speak up for himself. There was the time he defied the village rabbi, and once he argued with the tax collector, and hadn't he valiantly stood over the body of his fallen captain, defending the officer against the rioters of St. Petersburg?

"I guess I never stood up to any Americans," Abe said. "To fight with Americans would be like making a fuss in somebody else's house, you know, Stefano?"

"This ain't somebody else's country, it's ours," de Fazio told him. "What are you behaving like a guest for?"

Abe was noncommittal. "Maybe you're right."

"You'll never get anywhere being polite," Stefano warned him, then shrugged.

"Let me tell you what happened." He beamed at Abe. "First I told all the guys right here what you did for the union. I bet you got about fifty dollars in that tin can."

Abe smiled. "I'm grateful for what they done for me."

"You ain't heard it all yet," Stefano laughed. "I went around to all the other locals, telling your story to the rest of the membership. Now, come the next elections, everybody will know who Stefano de Fazio is, and everybody will know that he takes care of his friends." He reached into his pants pocket and came out with a fat bankroll. "Union membership all over the city gave to replace what you lost, my friend."

Abe stared at the money. He'd never seen so much. Stefano thrust it at him. Abe tentatively reached out for it and then withdrew his trembling fingers, shaking his head, once again wondering if it wasn't some kind of mistake.

"Go on, take it," Stefano chuckled.

"That is my two hundred?" Abe whispered.

"Hell, no," Stefano grinned. "I got here exactly three hundred and eight dollars for you, my friend." He thrust the roll of currency into Abe's hands.

"They gave you this for me?" Abe squeezed the money as if to prove to himself it was real.

Stefano nodded. "Even the big shots uptown. Even Miss Grissome threw in fifty cents of her own money when she heard the whole story."

Abe heard himself giggle, felt himself begin to weep. He was dimly aware of the other workers forming a semicircle.

"I got some bad news for you, though," Stefano said loudly. "I'm advising the manufacturer's foreman that you should be fired, and I ain't calling no strike on your behalf."

Abe heard the surrounding workers' laughter. It came in two waves as those who understood English translated the joke to fellow-countrymen who had yet to learn English.

"You're through at Allen Street as of today, Abe," Stefano continued. "My advice to you is to forget about all this and open up a business of your own."

Men all around Abe congratulated him and patted him on the back.

"I'll walk you home myself," Stefano announced. "We got to see to it that your fortune stays safe."

Abe said his farewells to all the friends he'd never known he had. Then Stefano, true to his word, saw him safely home like a shepherd tending his flock.

Chapter 13

New York, 1911–1912

Leaving the Allen Street sweatshop marked a new beginning for Abe Herodetzky. Abe was not of a philosophical bent. He believed that self-examination was a time-waster bordering on the obscene unless it took the form of castigation and led to self-improvement. Accordingly, it did not occur to him that those few weeks during which he scoured the neighborhood for a property suitable for his as yet undecided-on business constituted his honeymoon with the future.

All he knew was that he was hugely enjoying himself, that he was no longer drinking and that the transformation of his dream into reality was imminent.

On Cherry Street Abe found what he needed, a vacant storefront with a big plate-glass window and an available apartment just above it. A back staircase led up to the three-room railroad flat, which although small had its own water closet in the kitchen, tucked between the pitted enamel sink and the cast-iron bathtub.

The landlord was glad to sell the storefront's existing fixtures—shelving, a scarred wooden front counter and a dented cash register—for twenty-five dollars. He also offered Abe a lengthy renewable lease at a reasonable rent for both the store and the apartment.

Abe signed the papers that same day. How proud he felt as he scrawled his signature on the dotted line.

His new address housed a jumble of different nationalities on its six floors. The various families reached their apartments via a rickety, ill-lit staircase that led up from a separate side entrance. Abe considered the mix of nationalities to be a good omen. It had been Russian Jews and Polish and Italian Christians who contributed the money to give him his start, and so it suited him to have varied clientele.

Of course before there could be customers, there had to be something in the store for Abe to sell. The tenant before him had run a hardware store. There were still two stacked rows of empty open bins along one of the walls. Once they'd held nails, screws, bolts and so on. Abe hadn't the slightest notion what to put in them. He couldn't run a hardware store; he knew their most valuable commodity was advice, and he didn't know enough to offer it. Besides, the previous owner had been unable to make a go of that business and it made no sense to repeat a failure.

He had already vowed never to return to cobbling, and his years as a presser had instilled in him similar aversion to lapels and suit linings.

For a few days he mulled over the problem as he busied himself furnishing his apartment. He bought the bare essentials from a rummage store on Ludlow Street. Up until that point he'd been taking his meals at cafes and sleeping on his shabby overcoat spread out on the hard wooden floor. Now that he had a bed to sleep in and a kitchen table, he went out to shop for food.

It amazed Abe to find that with the exception of Breakstone's Dairy up the street, there was no place to buy provisions on Cherry Street. True, the pushcart vendors

sold spoiled produce, stale bread and fly-blown mounds of
fish, but decent food was available nowhere in the vicinity.
The nearest grocery was several blocks away. Abe saw
that it had no push cart competition, for carts could not
match a store's variety, nor could heavy tinned goods be
wheeled around.

With growing excitement he hurried back to his own
store and scrutinized the place. The shelves that had once
stocked hardware could just as easily display canned goods,
and the wooden bins would do nicely for potatoes and
onions, sugar and flour. Someday the rear of the store
could house a meat cabinet, Abe mused. To kosher Jews
he could never sell, but on Cherry Street only a small
number of his customers would be kosher Jews . . .

He skipped up the back stairs to his apartment and
hurried out to the front fire escape. Staring like an owl
from his iron perch, Abe watched Breakstone's Dairy. The
customers left with loose-cut butter and cheese and milk
ladled into their own containers from huge drums. If
Breakstone could make his fortune selling comestibles on
Cherry Street, so could he.

From then on he spent his nights making long lists of
inventory and sketching floor plans on scraps of paper.
Days he spent scrubbing. He was quick to welcome all his
curious neighbors. Despite his heart-stopping shyness, Abe
boldly implored them to patronize his business when it
finally opened.

His days found him at the provision wholesalers and
the Washington Street produce markets. It did not take him
long to learn where the best deals were.

That he knew nothing about the business on which he
was about to embark did not faze him. He trusted his own
natural shrewdness and his almost mystical devotion to the
idea of commerce.

At first the clerks in the wholesale food markets
considered the scrawny fussbudget of a Jew to be a joke,

but gradually they began to respect him. When Abe examined what they sold he used all of his senses. He sniffed, prodded and tasted their samples—including the smoked and salted hams and pork sausages—as if he intended to eat them himself.

It gave him pause to taste pork. Even during Abe's stint in the czar's army he'd managed to avoid eating unclean meat. Often he went hungry, but he did it.

Now he was willingly tasting sausages and hams. He just hoped God understood that he was doing it for the store.

He opened for business at six-thirty on a Tuesday morning in June. His hardwood floors and polished wooden shelves glowed richly beneath milk-glass light fixtures. These were a treasure he'd found buried beneath the rubbish in the back storage room. Three of the four glass bowls were broken and all were coated with dust and grease. Abe cleaned them all—every shard of glass—and painstakingly glued the shards together.

It took two days and a night to repair the fixtures, but it was worth it. The milk glass floated like white puffy clouds over Abe's inventory.

He set up his waxed and buffed, but still worn, scarred wooden counter near the entrance. Here Abe put his cash register and a high three-legged stool. Near it were displayed the more popular patent medicines, needles and thread, cigarette papers, loose tobacco and matches, hanging from cardboard sheets on the wall. On the far end of the counter he kept three glass jars filled with peppermints, licorice and horehound to tempt the children when their mothers came to shop.

Along the rear wall of the store was bread and squat wooden barrels containing smoked and salted meat and fish. The center of the store was taken up with free-standing shelves. Upon them were displayed a colorful

array of tinned meats and vegetables. The hardware bins
on the wall opposite Abe's counter overflowed with golden
onions, russet potatoes and shiny red apples. A white
enamel scale with a government seal stood ready to weigh
purchases.

On that first day he did a wonderful amount of business.
He sold over sixty-five pounds of bread, which he cut to
order from twenty-pound rounds, three barrels' worth of
smoked meat and two barrels of salt herring, which he
wrapped in old newspapers, saved for weeks, for his
customers' convenience. He spoke Yiddish to his Jewish
customers, English to those who had no Yiddish and sign
language to the few who knew neither. His canned goods
flew from the shelves and his bins of produce steadily
emptied. His customers asked for milk, eggs, cheese and
butter, but Abe shook his head, directing them up the
street to Sam Breakstone's. Abe knew enough not to antagonize a far better-established neighborhood merchant.

The only loss Abe took was on the candy, which he
gave away. As he'd suspected, the children clamored for
the sweets, and he decided the goodwill generated by a
small gift was worth more than the penny or two he might
have charged.

Abe locked his doors at seven that evening. He was
exhausted but elated, spilling over with ideas for improvements.

He stowed the day's receipts beneath a loose floorboard
in a cavity lined with paper. He kept back just enough to
replenish his inventory in the morning. If this volume
continued in a few weeks he could expect the dealers to
extend him credit and start making deliveries to his store.

On the second day his business remained constant.
Abe rewarded himself by spending some precious cash on
the finishing touch to his new store. The next morning a
sign painter arrived to letter in bright red the plate glass
window:

CHERRY STREET MARKET
A. Herodetzky
Proprietor

He looked forward to the day he could have "&
Sons" added, but there could be no sons until there was a
wife. There was no getting around it; it was time for him
to marry.

Then came thoughts of Leah Kravich, the shy, diminutive spinster sister of his first landlord on Montgomery
Street. Thoughts of Leah would steal over Abe at the
oddest times, until he didn't know what to make of his
preoccupation with the quiet twenty-year-old.

This he believed for certain, that it was not love. He
was not the sort to be consumed by passion. But then why
did Leah haunt him so? Occasionally they had a chance
encounter on the street, not often, but frequently enough
so that Abe found himself disappointed when he did not
run into her. Always they paused to exchange pleasantries.
On these occasions Abe could scarcely control his heart-
thumping nervousness, nor could he recollect just what
nonsense it was he'd stammered to her.

Their sporadic random meetings seemed to last for an
eternity and then end far too soon. Afterwards Abe's day
seemed filled with reveries of Leah. At night while half-
asleep he heard snatches of her laughter and could even
picture the way she blushed at the sound of her own mirth,
so shy and prim and proper was she.

In the morning he would find himself stirring at the
thought of her touch. He would tremble, ashamed that he
should covet her, astounded and frightened that this magic
could be worked upon him. It was too much, too dangerous.

Dangerous? Nonsense! Leah would make a docile,
hard-working wife. She seemed to like him, and Abe, for
his part, could see beyond her unprepossessing exterior to
the quiet, subtle beauty beneath.

To Abe it was astounding that no one else seemed

able to appreciate the depth of her gaze or the dark sheen of her long, wavy tresses. How could others be so oblivious to the promise of her lips, to the swell and curve of her bosom beneath her frumpy garments? Her timidity made it possible for him to approach and talk to her. Leah's hunched vulnerability made Abe want to stand tall and protect her. Even Sadie and Joseph wanted him to court her, so why not follow his feelings?

No, he was afraid to give himself so completely. Love was not for him.

Abe chided himself for even thinking of giving in to such temptation. Love was the province of only two sorts, handsome young blades and self-deluding fools. If he allowed himself to love he would be hurt. Experience had taught him that. He loved his parents and then was orphaned. To ease that pain he took in Haim and loved him, and now Haim was gone as well.

No, from now on he would protect himself. He would choose his wife as he had the location for his business. He would choose prudently, coolly, with good value foremost in his mind.

He would do the sensible thing and take himself to a matchmaker. He would buy a wife, for buying was the only certain way to possess.

One miracle in his life—the return of his savings—was enough. He would not expect another, that he might find love.

Abe's fear of intimacy made it easy for him to rationalize waiting "a prudent amount of time" before marriage. How much wiser it seemed to him to get the business established and to build up a bank account before taking on more responsibility.

The fall and winter passed and Abe waited on his customers. The days flew by, but each solitary night seemed to last for an eternity. He spent his evenings reading, finding his taste changing from business primers and newspapers to romantic novels. He would put himself in the hero's place, murmur the words of love out loud to his own imaginary lady.

Then he would look up from the page, see his scrawny image in the mirror on the wall and blush with mortification. How pitiful he felt, a yearning hermit in a cave.

Finally loneliness overshadowed fear. Thus it was on a Wednesday morning in July 1912, a year and a month after his store's opening, that Abe found himself fidgeting in the outer foyer of the matchmaker's office.

Abe was wearing a brand new brown suit. Blue might have been more appropriate, but he already had a blue one, so why not get another color?

He was also wearing shiny new shoes and for the first time in his life an American-style necktie.

He wanted to look his best for this important interview. At long last he had the money in his pocket to do so.

So much has changed in my life, Abe found himself musing. I wake up in my own apartment, don new clothes and on my way out check the locks on my own business.

Change was difficult for him. In Russia change rarely came for the serf or peasant. In Abe's village a humble thatched hut stood for a hundred years, passed down from a father who also passed down his livelihood. In Russia for serfs and peasants only the seasons changed.

But America was founded on the theory of change. For instance, the marriage broker's office was on Orchard Street, and Abe remembered reading that Orchard Street had been named for the groves of fruit trees that thrived there in 1806, when the tract belonged to an Irishman named Delancey.

1806—just one hundred and five years ago. To a Russian Jew such a period amounted to the briefest blink of the eye. In a land where villagers routinely labored to pay the avalanching interest on loans incurred by their grandfathers, one hundred and five years was nothing at all.

And yet in just that period the rich black farm soil of Orchard Street had been entombed beneath unyielding pavement. If Abe had not read it, he would never have believed that trees had stood where now loomed nothing but drab tenements and street lamps.

If the street had seen better times, so had the matrimonial agent, Abe surmised. The office was four flights up in the rear of a tenement that rumbled and shook with the sound of knitting machinery. The foyer had peeling brown paint and grimy pink linoleum. The hard wooden bench on which he sat was littered with orange peels and crusted with spilled food.

For this I bought new clothing? Abe asked himself sourly. He'd always considered matchmaking to be one of the best-paying businesses possible, but evidently this too had changed.

When the Jews first came to New York, forcing the Germans from the Lower East Side, they brought with them all of their old country traditions, including the matchmaker. A proper Jewish man concerned himself with religious studies, the community and making a living, in that order. No one expected a studious, hard-working, moral man to seek out a member of the opposite sex and propose matrimony face to face.

For a fee, usually ten percent of the bride's dowry, the broker would call on the parents, present the groom's case and bring back an answer. The broker, if successful, was paid his fee upon the announcement of the engagement. If the answer was no, the groom was spared the embarrassment of a personal rejection, an important consideration in a tiny village.

If the suitor had no particular bride in mind, the broker would take down his specifications, advise his client as to how much dowry he could reasonably expect, and then explore the community looking for a suitable match. This role became even more crucial in America at the turn of the century, when Jews from many different villages were thrown together, strangers to one another.

The door to the inner office opened and Yuri Charnov ushered out an old woman. During his wait Abe had been forced to hear them through the thin partition that separated the foyer from the inner office. The old woman was illiterate and had been dictating a letter to her daughter in Canton, Ohio.

Signs downstairs on the street and up here in the office advertised Charnov's services as a scribe and as a business interpreter on a walk-in basis. Abe was somewhat surprised. Once it had been essential to make an appointment far in advance to have an interview with a marriage broker, but the era when this one, at least, enjoyed that kind of prosperity had evidently long since passed.

Charnov turned to Abe as the old woman left, tucking her freshly inked envelope into her black string bag. He was in his sixties, Abe guessed, tall, and heavy-set, his physical bulk emphasized by the garish combination of a blue striped seersucker suit, red waistcoat and bright yellow tie. He had weak green eyes behind thick steel-rimmed spectacles and a bald head as round and sickly pale as an unripe honeydew melon.

The broker warmly welcomed Abe in Yiddish, shaking his hand and holding on in order to tug him into his office. This inner sanctum wasn't much cleaner than the waiting area, but at least it had a window thrown open to admit sunlight and fresh air. The office shelves were lined with books on various subjects and his desk was piled with the black ledgers.

Everyone knew that a marriage broker's ledgers were the repository for his primary stock in trade, the names and addresses of potential mates. Staring at the ledgers, Abe felt a twinge of sadness. In one of those black books was written the name of his future wife, but her name would not be Leah.

Abe seated himself on one of the hardbacked chairs in front of the broker's desk and for a few minutes they exchanged pleasantries. Charnov had a glittering gold incisor that added a disturbing touch of lewdness to what was obviously meant to be a friendly smile.

Finally the broker said in English, "Now then, tell me about yourself." He listened intently, jotting notes as Abe recounted his background and his status.

"Good, very good," he smirked. "Now describe for me the sort of young lady you have in mind."

Abe confessed in faltering, embarrassed phrases what he was looking for in a wife, including a physical description.

"Dark she should be; a copper-haired freckled girl is not for me."

"Fat? Thin?" The gold tooth was hardly visible now; this was business.

"Thin," Abe mused, "and not too tall. Especially not taller than me. She should have dark eyes and long black hair."

"Yes, you've told me that." Charnov tapped his notes.

Abe paused. "She should be intelligent, for she must help me in the store," he began, "but she should also be a quiet girl, one who knows to respect and honor her husband." Here he grew shy all over again. "She should know to appreciate him even if he is not forceful or virile. . . . Understand what I'm saying?"

"Perfectly."

"Good."

Charnov eyed him. "Really, you shouldn't be so upset."

"What?" Abe started. "Oh, no, you misunderstand,"

he said, his tone melancholy. "I'm thinking about something else."

"Come now." Charnov was obviously unconvinced. "You'll excuse me for saying so, but a man your age who has never been married—well, it is natural for such a man to be concerned with the as yet unknown demands that a wife will place on him."

Abe was hardly listening, for what was disturbing him was the realization that the "perfect" woman he'd been describing was none other than Leah.

He stood up, reaching into his pocket for some money, which he placed upon the desk. "This has been a mistake," Abe said. "Or maybe it hasn't; maybe it was just what I needed." He smiled. "Anyway, please take the money for your time."

Charnov looked glum. "Where you going so fast? You're making a mistake. Sit. Let's talk it over at least."

Shaking his head, Abe was already on his way toward the foyer.

"Then take back your money," the matchmaker scowled disgustedly. "For nothing I don't need this pittance."

"You keep it," Abe insisted, standing in the doorway. "You earned it. Without you I might never have made a good marriage."

Abe floated past the shops and stalls of Orchard Street, but as he turned onto Hester and cut across the cropped lawns of Seward Park toward East Broadway, his initial enthusiasm turned to unease.

"I'm doing the right thing. I know it," he muttered through clenched teeth, "but why do I feel sick to my stomach?"

His interview with the marriage broker had inspired him. He was on his way to propose marriage to Leah, but once again he was losing his nerve . . .

He loitered for a bit in the tranquil greenery of Seward Park, hoping to stiffen his resolve by watching the children playing and listening to them.

These were healthy children wearing decent clothing, school children on summer sabbatical. They knew nothing of the sweatshops.

He wandered eastward, out of the park, his thoughts dark and brooding. To be face to face with a woman and ask her to marry him—it seemed impossible. He was simply not that sort of fellow. His tongue would cleave to the roof of his mouth if he tried to sweet-talk a woman. Only tall, handsome men like Haim could be so brazen with the opposite sex. For men like him were the services of the world's Charnovs.

Abe stopped walking. He had brought himself to Montgomery and was across the street from where Leah lived. Paralyzed with fear, he stared at his reflection in the first-floor windows. What a ridiculous little man he looked.

He would not go inside. It would be hard enough to get the words out without having to suffer Sadie's formidable presence. He would wait right here and intercept Leah when she came out or came home. Abe decided, if Sadie ventured forth, he would hide behind the garbage cans.

He sat on a stoop that afforded him a view of Leah's building. While he waited he desperately tried to think of a way out of his predicament. If only he could fall asleep and wake up already married, with fine sons ready to help him in business, then he would not have to go through this humiliating proposing or the other things a husband had to do to become a father.

He briefly considered returning to the matchmaker's office and having him act as the intermediary between himself and Leah. But the broker would want to talk to Leah's parents to assure himself that the engagement was secure, and for them to give a blessing, or even to understand what was being asked, was an impossibility. Charnov would have to turn to Sadie, and she, as usual, would be wickedly obstinate in demanding conditions and would take perverse pleasure in gossiping about Abe.

"Abe Herodetzky?" she would moan, feigning despair, as if she'd been asked to eat bacon. "I should let my precious treasure of a sister marry that little creep? Why, he lives like a convert. You should have seen how it was when he boarded with us. He shaved and he worked on the Sabbath—he still does. I hear that in his store he sells *trayf* food."

In the end she would give her blessings, and gladly, but not before she had shredded his character. Not only that, but Leah's family was poor. Joseph could afford no dowry, which meant that Abe would have to pay the broker's fee out of his own pocket.

Then Abe had no more time to brood. Leah turned the corner onto Montgomery and hurried along the far side of the street, a big basket of sewing in her arms.

"Oh, God," Abe murmured softly. He pushed himself up onto his feet and angled across the street to cut her off. Leah was wearing a dark cotton skirt that swirled around the tops of her black high-buttoned shoes. Her plain white blouse was buttoned to the neck, and she had a dark blue apron knotted around her slender waist. Her gleaming black hair was braided into two pigtails that hung down to the small of her back. Her dark eyes sparkled and her pouty pink lips widened into a surprised, shy smile as she spotted Abe.

Her smile faded and by the time Abe had reached her she was frowning uneasily. It did not occur to Abe that Leah might be even more timid than he, only that she was unhappy to see him.

She will never love me; she will refuse me; I am going to fail, but at least it will be over and done with.

"Hello," he began, dismayed as Leah flinched at the sound of his voice. Years living with Sadie had turned her into a fearful creature, poised to retreat at the slightest provocation.

Abe understood none of this. It seemed to him that Leah's behavior expressed dislike of him.

He was not blind to her pleasing looks, however. As he gazed at her flawless ivory complexion, her finely chiseled features, he was honestly amazed that he could even dream that she might accept him.

Something must have communicated his aching love, for Leah, watching him, tentatively offered up her ephemeral smile, and that smile gave Abe the courage to follow through, although the moment before he had decided to offer his greetings and slink away.

She was still holding her sewing basket. Abe chivalrously took it from her, realized that he could hardly propose with his hands full and set the basket down on the sidewalk.

"You are doing piecework?" he asked, stalling for time.

"Yeah, sure," Leah said. Sadie allowed no language but Yiddish in her house, so Leah practiced her English as much as was possible when she went out. "I walk over to Rivington and they give it to me."

Abe nodded. "Over there they pay okay." He was grinning like an idiot. Compliment her on something, he coaxed himself. Say her blouse is becoming or her hair looks shiny and pretty.

A heavy steel basement door clanged open and a stream of laughing, rowdy boys ran up the steps to street level, swung around the iron railing and skipped across the sidewalk, tumbling Leah's sewing basket in the process. Half a gross of men's white shirts spilled across the grimy pavement.

"Oh, no," she moaned, "they'll get dirty. I should go in." She bent to gather her work. "It'll take me twice as long now, for I'll have to wash them too."

"Stay another minute," Abe implored as he righted the basket and scooped up the shirts.

Leah dejectedly examined one of the shirts for grime. "If you get them dirty, they don't pay you for the sewing," she said.

Abe gently took the shirt from her and tossed it into the basket. "Listen to me. I want to tell you—to ask you something."

He could feel the sweat trickling down the side of his face. His hands were so tightly clenched that his nails were drawing blood from his palms.

Leah stared at him. "What is it, Abe?" she asked, sounding frightened. "What's wrong?"

"Nothing Leah, I want to marry you," he blurted, staring down at the basket of shirts. He heard her gasp but kept his eyes locked on the ground. "You're not so surprised, are you? We liked each other when I was a boarder in your sister's household, didn't we?" Finally he glanced at her and felt his terror rise as he regarded her blank expression. I am in a nightmare, he thought.

"We've seen each other so often on the street," Abe continued. "You looked at me during such meetings; I looked at you—" He shrugged. Leah was still staring, still silent, and he had nothing left to tell her. He had feelings aplenty but no words, or at least he didn't know how to say them. He'd made a fool of himself by attempting this, though another kind of man, more confident and daring, might have reached her.

Leah seemed lost in rumination. She absently reached behind her for one of her long braids, twisted the flagged end around her fingers and brought the coil up to her lips to chew on it.

"Stop that," Abe said mildly. "Your hair is too pretty . . ." His tongue suddenly thickened; no more words would come out of his mouth.

Leah let go of her braid, smiling at the compliment.

She tentatively reached out to take his hand. She noticed that his fingers were trembling in hers.

That was when she began to understand Abe. For the first time in what was to be the pattern of her life with him, she offered Abe what he wanted and needed. "I love you," she said.

Sadie and Joseph seemed little surprised by the announcement. "It's about time," Sadie grumbled. Joseph merely smiled, offering a celebratory schnapps. Arrangements were made with the rabbi to marry the couple in the Kraviches' front parlor in one month.

It would be a modest private ceremony; Abe briefly considered inviting Stefano de Fazio to be his best man, but Sadie forbade it, vowing that no Italian would ever step foot in her home. Abe acquiesced; he didn't want to start a commotion, and he wasn't sure Stefano would accept.

Abe hadn't seen much of Stefano since he left the sweatshop. A few times Stefano had stopped by the market, once to ask a favor of Abe. Elections were being held to select a board of officers to administer the locals and represent them to the national office. De Fazio was running for secretary-treasurer.

"It's gonna be a full-time job," said de Fazio, looking prosperous in his expensive suit and tie, polished leather briefcase under his arm.

"No more Allen Street?" Abe asked.

"Nah. An uptown office comes with the job. It'll be up to me to record the dues paid by every member in New York." De Fazio tried to look modest. "I'll be the guy who disburses funds, as well."

Abe was impressed. "I'll bet that'll be thousands of dollars, Stefano."

The Italian nodded. "But first I got to get elected." He smiled then, stroking his mustache, which had sprouted prematurely grey, matching the grey that salted his thick, black glossy curls. "I've a favor to ask of you, my old friend."

Abe felt honored. "Whatever I can do for you, Stefano, just ask."

"Good!" De Fazio beamed, patting Abe's shoulder. "In this election I got my own people and the Polish in my pocket. It's the Jews I'm worried about. Some will vote for me, but there's another guy, a Jew, who's running against me. What I want is for you to come to the meeting next week and tell 'em how I handled that whole money thing with you—"

"You mean, talk in front of all of those people?"

"Nothing to it, my friend. Just tell 'em what happened." Stefano gripped his hand. "I'll be grateful, Abe."

"Then of course I'll be there."

The night of the meeting came around, and with Stefano watching Abe stood on the stage, gripped the podium and did not dare to look at the audience as he stuttered out the story of how Stefano organized Allen Street, borrowed his savings to help finance the strike fund and then personally saw to it that he was paid back. Afterward Abe took a drink with some of his former union acquaintances and went home to Cherry Street, and that was that. A little while afterward he read in the paper that Stefano had won his election by a considerable margin.

That meeting was the last time he'd seen Stefano, but with such an important job it made sense, Abe reasoned, that de Fazio had no time to come around to Cherry Street or attend a modest wedding in a tenement apartment.

Chapter 14

On her wedding day Leah sat in the kitchen of the neighbors across the hall, waiting for it to be time for the ceremony. She didn't have to watch the clock, for Joseph would come for her at the proper moment. She didn't have to talk with anybody, for the neighbors had been invited to the ceremony in exchange for allowing the use of their apartment as the bridal chamber. Sadie, thank God, was too busy to sit with her.

Sadie had warned her that the day of her wedding would pass dreamlike, but Leah had never felt wider awake in her life. As she sat all alone in this strange apartment, stiffly upright upon a chair to avoid wrinkling her wedding dress, she could feel her pulse pounding and her nerves singing. The tan walls and chipped porcelain and enamel of the kitchen seemed to throb with vibrant color.

I'm going to be a wife, have a husband, a home of my own and a family.

She'd given up on marriage a long time ago, accepting spinsterhood as God's will. If God had disappointed her by refusing to provide her with a husband, she could understand His side of the issue; she was, after all, rather plain. True, she had made the most of her attributes by keeping her hair clean and being pleasant at all times, but at twenty-two she had seen enough polite disinterest in the eyes of the eligible bachelors at the settlement house socials to understand that God's hands were tied in this matter.

As late as last night, when Sadie and Joseph thought she'd fallen asleep in the parlor, she heard them whispering together in the kitchen.

"Thank God for Abe," Joseph told his wife. "It's lucky for us; I'd given up hope for her. She creeps around like a little mouse and she's got hips like a boy."

"Stop it," Sadie scolded him. "She's got plenty to recommend her. . . ." She trailed off.

"That's what I thought," Joseph knowingly chuckled after a few moments of silence. "Believe me, Sadie, that little mensch is a godsend. We'll save a lot of money by not having to support her."

"Well, Abe is getting a fine girl," Sadie argued, miffed. "He's in his middle thirties, don't forget, and not a handsome man."

That was true, Leah mused as she waited, nervously drumming her fingers on her neighbor's kitchen table. Abe could never be called good-looking.

She remembered the first time she'd set eyes on him, years ago, when he came to board in Sadie and Joseph's spare room. Just thirty years old, he was endearingly full of himself, a feisty bantam rooster homely as sin, crowing at the world.

His years in the sweatshop blunted his edge. His narrow shoulders rounded and his long face began to sag into a perpetual frown. There was a growing bald spot at the back of his dark brown head. Leah very much doubted that Abe had ever seemed especially young; already he was verging on old.

"Do you think she loves him?" Sadie whispered to her husband last night. Leah was able to hear the hand-wringing in her voice. "He won't mistreat her, will he? Poor Leah. You're right Joseph. She is like a little mouse."

"Who knows from love? This much I can say: She's made a good match. She has no dowry, she's in her twenties already, and she's caught for herself a fellow with his own business. You got to give Abe that much—he swore he'd have his own store and he's done it." Joseph's voice softened. "But don't worry. One thing about Abe I know. He'll do the best he can by her, that's for sure."

"I hear that apartment above his store has a private toilet." Sadie sighed wistfully.

Leah had smiled at that final exchange last night, and she was smiling now. How Sadie used to lord it over her, having a husband and children! She'd been dominated by her older sister for as long as she could remember. How wonderful to get a husband in a higher station than Joseph— not that she had any grudge against Sadie's husband, who had always been kind to her and who often stood up for her against Sadie's bullying.

Sadie took pleasure in bullying her, Leah knew, and had since they were little girls living with their parents in a drab Lithuanian village on the Baltic. Sadie used to take her down to the beach in winter to pin her down and sit on her belly. Sadie would sprinkle sand into her mouth as the cold wind whipped away her childish screams of outrage and chapped her cheeks beneath her streaming salty tears.

Years later Leah brought those childhood incidents up, but Sadie denied that they had ever happened. Leah was incredulous. How could Sadie have forgotten?

"You made it up," Sadie insisted, and finally, to keep peace in the home, Leah allowed that perhaps she had.

Adulthood had not put an end to the intimidation, but merely turned it to more subtle forms. For instance, not a day went by that Sadie did not find a way to point out

Leah's second-class status in the Montgomery Street household.

"It's not enough I've got our infirm mama and papa to care for," Sadie would rant. "I also must care for you like a child. Poor Joseph works like a dog in that trayf slaughterhouse to keep a roof over all our heads. Don't you feel ashamed, Leah? Don't you feel grateful to me? Why don't you do more around here, Leah? Why can't you find a man?"

There was nothing Leah could say. She would stand silent, biting her lower lip to keep from crying, absorbing Sadie's abuse. Through it all her parents would be coughing and groaning, lost in senility. Sadie's youngest children would be squalling so loudly that Leah could not think, and her own hands would be raw and her head spinning from the stench of Joseph's bloody slaughterhouse work clothes as she scrubbed them clean in the sink.

At those times Sadie's shrewish attacks were worse than anything she'd inflicted upon her younger sister during their childhood. Leah would feel so ashamed that it would seem to be her fault her parents were senile, her fault Joseph had a disgraceful job.

Then Sadie, abruptly softening, would calm and kiss Leah affectionately, saying, "It's nothing, dear, just me. Sometimes my feet swell up and my legs ache so much I don't know what I'm saying. It must be because I'm so fat. God willing, a skinny thing like you will never know such agony."

Sadie's explanations only made it worse, for Leah could no longer assuage her misery by hating her bully of a sister.

Now all that was changed. Abe had rescued her. It was just like a prince rescuing a damsel in the storybooks she'd pored over in the settlement house reading classes. Never mind what he looked like; to her Abe was a prince.

There came a light knock on the door, and Joseph, resplendent in his finest pin-striped suit, came in.

"Ready?" he asked, looking exceedingly nervous. For the hundredth time that day he reached up to assure himself that his yarmulke was in place upon his curly mane. "Come, Leah, they're waiting for us."

She nodded, straightening her white gown, and arranged her veil. Joseph looked pale. It fell to him to take her ailing father's place in escorting her halfway across the parlor. Abe would take over at that point, leading her the rest of the way to the canopy beneath which they would make their marriage vows. Then after it was over Abe would take her to their home.

"Leah . . ." Joseph was looking down at her, his eyes full of concern above his glossy black beard. "If you ever need anything—if things don't go right with you and Abe . . . Well, we want you to know, Sadie and I, that you are still our family. Do you understand?"

She stood on tiptoe, lifting her veil to kiss his cheek. "Thank you, sweet Joseph, for everything."

"Sha," he commanded gruffly. "No crying. A bride is not supposed to cry." Then he took her arm and led her out of the kitchen and across the hallway into his own apartment.

Sadie's kitchen was deserted. The oven was on, keeping the food warm for after the ceremony, but everyone was in the parlor. Leah caught a glimpse of their expectant faces through the partly drawn curtain that divided the apartment.

"Ready now," Joseph breathed. "Here we go."

At once Leah was racked with a spasm of nerves. Sadie's kitchen with its pink floral wallpaper and worn floorboards covered by area rugs had never seemed so inviting.

It's just that it's all so familiar, Leah thought. It's safe, even if it is unpleasant, but God sent Abe to me; a prayer has been answered. So what if I'm nervous; I shouldn't be nervous on my wedding day?

Joseph gently pulled her through the curtain, and with shining eyes and God's hand on the small of her back, she was presented to her husband.

The days after the wedding seemed like a dream to the new Mrs. Abe Herodetzky. There was the Cherry Street apartment to get used to, furnishings to purchase, and of course the store. During the first week of married life, in which Leah learned how to work the cash register, make change and keep the accounts book straight, it seemed that her new home was not upstairs but amidst the potatoes, onions and barrels of smoked meat.

She was not disturbed by the hard work. It was all going to lead to something grand, Abe promised, and his dreams stirred her. She was impressed by the uncharacteristic passion he showed when confiding them to her. Besides, she was of a generation that looked upon hard work as due, even a blessing, as long as a free soul could reap the benefits of his own labor.

The customers were warm to her, and she found herself enjoying her dealings with them. Like Abe, she was very shy but also fond of people in general and eager to please. Serving the customers, making them smile and seeing them return was extremely satisfying after the drudgery of piecework sewing. The fragrance of each morning's delivery of freshly baked bread, the pungent aromas of the smoked fish and meats, the head-spinning variety of canned goods and abundance of produce combined to make the market an exciting place.

It wasn't long before Leah decided that owning a grocery store was the finest business in the world. As a housewife takes pride in her well-stocked larder, Leah took pride in seeing to it that the shelves were well stocked and clean. She and Abe were closest when they were working together.

"At least," Abe once told her, "come good times or bad, with a grocery store we'll never starve." It became their private joke and could lighten any day-to-day frustration, any upset, conflict or problem.

No, work was not at all the problem for Leah. She welcomed the start of each day, for it meant the end of the previous night's agonizing.

They had been married a month, and Abe had yet to make love to her. At first she accepted his coolness as normal. Truth to tell, she'd even been relieved. She was a virgin, of course, and beyond the basic facts entirely ignorant. Sadie had told her certain stories guaranteed to make her petrified of being "split open" by a man.

So on their wedding night, when Abe mumbled something about being tired from all the excitement and the drinking, Leah thought it was just as well. Her own head was spinning with nervous exhaustion and too much schnapps. She undressed and put on her nightgown in private—Abe suddenly found something to do in another room—and fell asleep at once. When she awoke the next morning, Abe was downstairs and the store was open for business.

The next night he explained that he had to stay up late working on the accounts. Around three in the morning Leah tiptoed downstairs to find him sound asleep, sprawled across some hastily assembled sacks of potatoes and onions.

Angry and afraid, she confronted him. Her own insecurity made her cry. Abe swore that he'd only decided to nap for a moment, that he was going back to work. Finally he came upstairs, but only after she pretended to have fallen asleep.

It went on like that. Only by feigning sleep could she coax him to lie beside her. In their month of marriage he had yet to touch her. In that month neither had seen the other naked.

Leah didn't know what to do, and she couldn't discuss it with Abe. She sensed that speaking of the problem would only worsen it, just as she sensed that Abe was equally miserable. She could tell he loved her. That love was far more important to Leah than the physical passion Abe was afraid to express; no, afraid to release.

All the same, a marriage without its physical aspect was like a painting with no color. What she could do about it was the question. She had to find a way to build her husband's confidence, to bridge the yawning chasm.

It was not a bad marriage. They were certainly companionable during the day. It was only at night that they became estranged.

Big deal. So my man and I are good business partners, she fumed. What good is that? I've got to shake things up. The ice has to be broken. Something very good or very bad has to happen to make him see me differently. Maybe if someone attacked me and Abe had to rush to my defense—

God forbid! She shuddered. How could she even briefly imagine such a catastrophe? Poor Abe could never stand against that sort of scoundrel.

As the days wore on Leah helped in the store, cooked and cleaned upstairs and thought hard about how to solve the problem. For the first time in her life she had no one to turn to for help. It was all up to her, simple as that. Her future happiness, not to mention Abe's, depended on her ingenuity.

Whatever was to be done, it had to happen soon. Like slow-acting poison, their nightly estrangements were gradually coloring their relationship in the store. If Leah didn't act, there would be no marriage left to save. She settled down to think of a solution.

*   *   *

Leah was at the back of the store cutting bread for a customer when the bell above the door jingled and Joseph walked in. It was a late summer's evening, just a few minutes before the store was to close for the day.

Listening as Abe welcomed his brother-in-law, Leah totaled up a housewife's bill, wrapped her purchases and showed her out.

"All finished for today?" Leah asked Abe.

"Yes, time to lock up." He winked at Joseph. "Especially since we have a guest."

Leah turned the key in the door and put the "CLOSED" sign in the window. Behind her she heard Abe inviting Joseph upstairs for a drink and some supper.

"No, let's stay here," Joseph said. He had come directly from his job at the slaughterhouse, so he was still dressed in his summer workclothes. His cotton shirt with the sleeves rolled up showed off his powerful physique. He had always been a large man, but years shouldering heavy carcasses added inches to his already broad chest and wrapped thick layers of ropy muscle around his arms. Joseph's thighs looked as thick as Abe's waist, Leah noted. Standing before them in his blood-spattered clothing, sporting his long tangled beard and his wild mane of curls, he reminded Leah more of an old-time frontier pioneer in Texas than a Jewish immigrant on the Lower East Side of New York.

"Yes, we'll stay downstairs." Joseph was grinning, looking around. "This way I can get used to things."

Abe glanced quizzically at Leah, who shrugged. "Get used to what?" he asked Joseph pleasantly.

Joseph's rough, sinewy hands spread wide. "Your store, of course." His teeth gleamed against his black beard. "I'm going to be your partner."

"Joseph," Leah gasped, "what are you talking about?"

"Leah," Abe said firmly, "please, I will handle

this.'' He turned back toward Joseph. "Now then, please tell me what you have in mind.''

Joseph shrugged. "Well, now that you've married Leah, we're all one big family, yes?''

"We are related by marriage,'' Abe acknowledged.

"All right, then.'' Joseph helped himself to an apple and began to chomp. "Sadie has been after me to get out of my job,'' he remarked between mouthfuls. "This business would be perfect. I have decided to come in as your partner.''

"Now just a minute, Joseph,'' Leah fiercely cut in.

"Leah, please go upstairs,'' Abe said calmly.

"But—''

"Please do as I ask.''

Sulking, she trudged past the two men to the rear of the store. Halfway up the staircase, out of the line of sight, she settled down on a step to listen.

Abe stood with his hands on his hips regarding Joseph. He was a little afraid of the huge fellow. His virile, confident brother-in-law seemed to be Abe's better in every way. He's got no problems siring sons, Abe taunted himself, for his lack of intimacy with his wife gnawed at him constantly.

"Of course there will be some changes,'' Joseph announced before he ate the core in two quick bites.

"Really? What will they be?'' As Abe spoke he undid his apron and tossed it onto the counter. Normally he liked his shopkeeper's attire, but right now it was making him feel self-conscious.

"First of all, Sadie will not allow the sale of trayf foods,'' Joseph explained, "and she will want to keep the books—''

"Get out of here,'' Abe said. His voice was steady, but he could feel himself trembling with fury. "Get out of my store.''

Joseph's eyes narrowed. "You don't talk to me like that," he growled. "Soon I'll be the one giving the orders, little man. You may as well accept your new partner and let that be the end of it."

"Never," Abe shouted. "I won't have it." He was so angry he slid into English. "Go on, get out from here before I call the cops on you."

Muttering an oath, Joseph took a menacing step toward Abe, who darted away, swinging around his counter. There was a hickory club stashed away on the shelf beneath the cash register. Abe had put it there when he first opened, vaguely figuring that it might be a line of defense against a robbery.

Now he took up his club and stood his ground with the counter between him and his opponent. "Stay away, Joseph."

Joseph eyed the little shopkeeper warily. "You going to hit me with that, Abe?" he asked softly. He took another step closer to rest the tips of his blunt fingers on the scarred countertop.

Abe wanted to retreat a step, but he stood his ground. He tightly gripped the club and rested it on his shoulder the way the boys held their broom handles when playing stickball on the street.

"God forgive me," Abe muttered hoarsely, "but I'll crack your skull to keep what's mine."

Joseph nodded and backed off, heading for the door. "All right, you win. I'm not prepared to have my head broken over this matter, Abe." He turned the key to let himself out, and as he pulled open the door, he looked back and smiled. "No hard feelings, right? Maybe I misjudged you." He was gone.

Abe was still clutching his club and still shaking as Leah ran down the steps to embrace him.

"How wonderful you were!" she told him, her tone

and eyes overflowing with relief and tears. "How brave to stand up to that bully!"

Abe nodded a trifle uncertainly. He was panting for breath and his blood burned due to the excitement. What had he been prepared to do? He realized he was still holding the club and dropped it to put his arms around his wife. The warmth and softness of her beneath his exploring fingers, her scent as he pressed his face into her dark thick hair, made him dizzy.

Why should her touch be so unfamiliar? he wondered sadly. Why am I so afraid to hold her—to reveal my feelings, be they love or anger? I stood up to Joseph, didn't I? There is nothing to be afraid of.

"Leah," he said thickly, "if it hadn't been for you— I would also fight for you. . . ." He held her at arm's length, staring earnestly into her eyes. "You understand that, don't you?"

He hesitated then. The anger had vanished—no, it was still surging within him, but it had been transformed into desire for Leah. He wanted to cry out with the intensity of it. He felt changed, renewed by his earlier fury. He felt as giddy as he had in the whiskey-drinking days.

Leah was gazing up at him, a look of yearning in her dark eyes. "Husband," she murmured, leaning against him, "all the excitement—I feel dizzy. Help me upstairs."

Abe, his arm around her waist, led her toward the back staircase. His own limbs had turned rubbery. The adrenaline was draining out of him now, but he still felt clearheaded and invigorated.

Just like being drunk, he thought, like being drunk and walking outside in the frosty winter air.

"Leah, I love you," he whispered to her at the foot of the stairs. "I do love you, you know."

"Come upstairs."

In their bedroom only a single candle flickered. Abe watched mesmerized as his wife disrobed. He had never seen a naked woman before. He gazed awestruck at her breasts, at the soft swell of her belly, her hips, her thighs, the thatch at her center.

I am so afraid . . . he thought as he began to undress, and then he remembered how he'd just stood up to Joseph.

Naked, they stood face to face, tentatively discovering each other's body, at first smiling and then giggling as they elicited in each other sensations neither one had ever before experienced. Finally Abe led his wife to their bed. Leah drew the coverlet up over them and leaned over Abe, unpinning her braids, shaking them free, so that her long tresses cascaded over him like a soft, gleaming waterfall.

When Abe slid into her at long last, they both cried out, rejoicing in each other. Their celibate time together was impossible to fathom, even to imagine.

They loved each other until daybreak. There was no such thing as exhaustion. Each satisfaction only led to desire that was stronger than before. When they finally fell asleep, their slumber was deeper than either had ever known.

The next day in the store they could not look at each other without breaking into blushing giggles, and the customers all thought the marriage was off to a good start. At last they were behaving like newlyweds.

There was usually a lull in business during the midafternoon. Leah told Abe she wanted to shop for material to make curtains. She'd be back before things got busy again around five o'clock.

She headed west to the Hudson, where the slaughterhouses and meat-packing plants lined Washington Street. It was a long walk and the day was very warm, with the sun shining in a clear, deep blue sky, but Leah was far too full of happy energy to sit still on a trolley. As she walked her eyes drank in the colorful pageant that was Manhattan on a September day, while her mind languidly replayed the exquisite pleasure of last night. As she walked she felt a slight twinge between her legs. How delicious to know that womanly ache at long last!

Leah got to her destination just in time. It was four o'clock and the slaughterhouse was releasing its workers for the day.

When Joseph appeared she waved, catching his eye. He waved back and angled across the street to where she was waiting.

"Well?" he demanded. "Tell me."

How tired he looks, Leah thought. Joseph's clothing and even his beard were glistening with fresh blood. He stank like the carcasses he spent his days hefting on his back.

"Everything I won't say," Leah smiled demurely.

"That well it worked, eh?" Joseph threw back his head and roared. "You have turned into a witch, little Leah. I must say, when you came to me saying, 'Joseph, you must pick a fight with Abe,' I thought you'd gone mad. Then when you told me why, I was ready to give up on both you *and* your meshugga husband." He laughed again. 'Come to the store,' you begged. 'In the evening come, just before we are to close. Tell Abe you expect a partnership and that you intend to be the boss. Make him mad, make him lose his temper.' "

Leah grinned like a cat full of milk. "It worked," she said smugly.

Joseph, laughing so hard the tears rolled down to wet his beard, put his arm around Leah to hug her. She endured his embrace despite his awful stench, for she was very fond of this fierce-looking fellow who was really so compassionate and kind. Not once had he mocked Abe when she told him about the trouble. Not only had he helped her, he also kept it a secret from Sadie.

"You'll come home with me for supper?" Joseph suggested. "I know Sadie would like to see you."

"I can't. The store gets busy at five. I'll be late if I don't hurry back. Another time Abe and I will both come."

"Another time," Joseph nodded agreeably. Then he eyed Leah. "You think Abe will ever talk to me again?"

"Of course. He's already told me he hopes you'll make up with him. He likes you better now that he's stood up to you."

"This is too mixed up for me," Joseph complained. "One thing I do know: That husband of yours has got plenty of guts. He didn't know I was fooling when I chased him around the store."

"I'm glad you've forgiven him for threatening you with that club," Leah sighed, relieved.

"Big deal, a club," Joseph snorted. "What else should he have done against a man three times bigger than him? Right here at the slaughterhouse there are strong men who do not stand up to me. Yes, your husband is all right, I'm glad to say." His smile gradually faded. "Except that he thinks too much."

Leah shrugged noncommittally. "I've got to go. Thank you, again, sweet Joseph."

He waved her off, calling, "Don't ask me again; Abe will murder me." The last Leah heard of him was his laughter, booming deep as thunder.

As she hurried home she considered what Joseph had said. Abe thinks too much, does he? Well, maybe so. He can do our thinking and I'll do our feeling, and between the two of us we should prosper, God willing.

The sun was lower in the sky; it burnished the tall buildings and splashed orange and crimson fire against the high windows. As Leah walked, she thought about all the nights of love to come. Just when, she wondered excitedly, will I feel our first child within me?

Chapter 15

Um Jumi, 1912

Rosie Kolesnikoff waited until fall to take her son to the kibbutz by the Jordan. She longed to rejoin her husband and present him with his son, but her own desires were overshadowed by her maternal instincts. She would not risk Herschel's health. There was less chance of contracting fever in the cooler weather of the fall.

The Galilee settlement of Um Jumi was quite a different place than when Haim arrived nearly a year ago. For one thing there were many more people. Some of the newcomers applied for membership, but most were itinerant volunteers, ready to lend a hand and then move on to the other frontier outposts springing up in Palestine.

Over the summer a new, permanent site six miles from Tiberias had been chosen. Thanks to Haim's agreement with the fellahin of Um Jumi, building materials could be brought in by boat. The membership was eager to impress the sponsoring National Fund, so the long, dry summer days were taken up with construction as well as agriculture. With the extra help the settlement quickly raised a barn, a new, larger dining hall—with a roofed porch—a kitchen, and a cistern to hold water. Private cottages were erected for the married couples and a barracks for the unmarried and transients.

Everybody was very busy and a new face was no longer a novelty, so Herschel and Rosie's arrival caused very little excitement. Herschel was not the first child at the settlement. That honor belonged to another baby boy. With two around the rule against having children was ignored. The wives began to announce their pregnancies to great applause during the nightly meetings.

It was the meetings that most astounded Rosie. How so many people could meddle in one another's private affairs and how so many different personalities could ever decide on a specific course of action always amazed her. If they weren't voting on an issue, they were discussing it—and they discussed everything from what color to paint the walls to where the settlement stood concerning global affairs.

One night she had to gnaw her lip to keep from laughing as the membership bitterly debated over whether they should draft a formal letter of support to the *London Times*, endorsing the Triple Entente, which had last year chased a troublesome German gunboat out of the Moroccan port of Agadir.

Sitting beside Haim with Herschel on her lap, she would listen quietly as the arguments droned on. To her the entire idea of committee rule was ludicrous, but she kept her opinions to herself for Haim's sake.

She had only to see the gleam in his eyes as he sat basking in the nightly tumult to know how happy he was. In Haim there was a hollow place where the memories of his lost family should have been. The closeness and commotion of the kibbutz, the angry shouts and raucous laughter nourished Haim's hunger for brothers and sisters, a mother and a father.

For Haim's sake Rosie struggled to gain acceptance.

Gradually she made friends by working hard and never complaining. When the other women flaunted their seniority to avoid the lowly jobs, Rosie cheerfully cleaned the chicken coops and shoveled out the livestock stalls. She honed her cooking and sewing skills and learned how to milk a cow and coax a stubborn mule into its harness. Her hands grew calluses and her back ached from hauling her year-old son in a swatch of canvas tied around her hips. She dug irrigation ditches, cultivated vegetable gardens and even attempted a bit of carpentry.

She rarely knew what she was doing, but at Degania—the membership had chosen a new name, which meant "cornflower," for the settlement—inexperience was the norm. All of the work being done by both the men and women was accomplished through trial and error. Roofs leaked, food was scorched, crops failed, saplings withered, animals died. If things didn't work out, have a good laugh or maybe a cry. At Degania spirit was what mattered.

Gradually things did improve. Crops were harvested, trees took root, egg and milk production was increased. A flower garden was planted. Rosie crawled on her hands and knees with the others, carefully burying the bulbs. One night despite the fence wild boars managed to penetrate the flower beds. The next morning upon discovery of the ravaged garden Rosie found herself weeping as if for lost children. One step forward, two steps back—Degania managed to exist, and that was progress.

One day while working in the laundry Rosie realized she'd been at the settlement for almost a year. It was not a very long time, but already her previous soft life in Tel Aviv was a faded, distant memory.

She found herself growing angry. In a few months the kibbutz would vote on her membership. I hope they black-ball me, she thought.

Life here was so drab, so primitive. She belonged in Tel Aviv, where she could paint and give parties and have servants. If she was blackballed Haim would have to take them back to civilization. She hated this life. She hated Degania and voting on everything and eating in the communal dining hall, and most of all she hated the danger.

The permanent settlement had attracted more attention from the Bedouin robbers who struck from across the river. The men in the fields had been shot at, but none, thank God, had taken a hit.

Someone will be killed eventually, Rosie warned herself. All of us know it, especially the women.

In Galilee violence could descend like sudden rain. On the nights when it was Haim's turn to stand guard over the settlement, Rosie lay awake mewling with terror. Six hours until he's here beside me in bed, she'd think. Five hours, four, three . . .

Once when he was out patrolling the fence, she felt a chill and for an instant was certain that a robber had crept up behind Haim to plunge a dagger into his back. On that terrible night she fought back the impulse to run and find him. When he came home, tired but safe, she merely kissed him, never letting on what she'd been through.

It was always that way after Haim's tour of duty—a kiss, a hug, and then dark, dreamless sleep for the hour left before the dawn. They never made love on those nights. Haim was always far too weak with nervous exhaustion, and the smell of the gun on his hands made Rosie choke.

Thank God shots never seemed to be fired during Haim's watch. On other nights, when shots were heard, Rosie could never fall back asleep. She would look at her husband and son, sound asleep, and wonder how they could lie undisturbed by the gunfire. Then she would silently pray that it was Jews doing the shooting and that if the watchman had a wife, God was somehow comforting her.

One day Rosie stood before the big washtub with

tears streaming down her face. This time she was not crying for ruined flowers, but for herself. A passing woman peeked into the steamy laundry room but kept on walking.

Nothing unusual, correct, comrade? Rosie thought bitterly. Why shouldn't I weep when faced with a lifetime at Degania?

At least Rosie cried herself into a state of numbness. If only there were a way out of Degania, but there wasn't—not if she wanted Haim's love. She resumed the washing.

She glanced at Herschel, who was playing with a wooden rattle Yol had carved for him. He was sitting on a blanket in the far corner of the room, tan and fat with curly hair like spun gold and startlingly blue eyes that seemed far too wise and perceptive to belong to a toddler. They spent virtually all of their days together. Herschel's eyes habitually followed her after she put him down.

Now Herschel sensed his mother's loving gaze. He set down his toy and turned toward her, smiling.

"Yes, I know," Rosie murmured. "You like it here as much as your father does." She sighed and wiped her eyes, getting soap suds in them. She muttered a curse as she rubbed at her eyes with a towel because the soap stung and because she knew that Degania was where she and her family were going to stay.

September 1913 marked her first anniversary at the settlement. She was accepted as a member without incident. Haim asked her how she felt about it one evening after they returned home from supper at the dining hall.

"I feel guilty," Rosie confessed. "It has more emotional relevance than our wedding anniversary." She looked wistful. "I hope you're not angry."

"I told you you'd love it here." Haim laughed delightedly. He'd been sitting on the floor, playing with Herschel, now twenty months. Haim would hold out his hands and Herschel would totter forward, his chubby arms windmilling the air.

Haim scooped up his son with one arm and with the other embraced his wife. "Wait until I tell them what you've said," he babbled, clearly beside himself with happiness. "Only a true member could say such a thing. Oh, Rosie, I love you."

"I love you too, Haim," she whispered, thinking she would gladly spend the rest of her life telling lies if they could make her husband this happy.

The first rains of winter began early that year, bringing an onslaught of illness. Haim and his family were spared the fever, but others were not so lucky. Their stored medicines were useless against the illness, and the only doctor in the area lived across one of the Jordan's twisting, rain-swollen tributaries.

Haim volunteered to go fetch the doctor, but he was turned down on account of his having a family. It was considered a dangerous journey, for there were said to be Bedouins in the area. Finally a young, single man named Moshe offered to go. He set out on muleback early in the morning. If all went well he would be back with the doctor or at least the proper medicines by nightfall.

The entire settlement started to worry about Moshe as soon as he'd ridden out of sight. He was a friendly twenty-year-old from a poor family in Russia, always ready to lend a hand and very well liked. When night fell, Degania had been anxious for hours.

It was midnight when Yol came to the door of Haim's cottage. Rosie answered his knock, frightened when she saw that Yol was dressed in his work clothes and a leather jacket, with his pistol belt strapped around his waist. She was about to tell a lie—that Haim had come down with the fever—when she heard her husband stir. Suddenly he was standing behind her, looking over her shoulder into Yol's dark, brooding eyes.

"Come outside, Haim?" Yol asked softly. "We must talk, and I don't wish to disturb Herschel."

"Wear something warm," Rosie commanded, wrapping a coat around her husband's shoulders. Haim was wearing only a thin nightshirt, and it was drizzling.

Out of Rosie's earshot they hunched against the chill and damp as Yol explained.

"Moshe's mule returned without him. A search party is to go out, but only three. Too many are already sick. We cannot risk the health of the rest by making them ride around in the cold and rain and probably bullets. There's too much work to do tomorrow."

"Only three." Haim frowned, shaking his head. "And it's night."

"It's volunteers, of course," Yol murmured, looking away.

Haim patted his friend's shoulder. "So who else is coming with us?"

Yol grinned, then continued. "Trumpeldor raised his good arm even faster than me."

"Of course." Haim chuckled. "I'm surprised he doesn't want to go by himself."

Joseph Trumpeldor had come to Degania the year before. He was a dour Russian in his early thirties with streaks of grey in his close-cropped coal-black hair. At first the membership did not know what to do with him. His left arm was missing and he refused to speak anything but Hebrew, a language he did not know. He might just as well have been deaf and dumb, and with his one arm, what sort of work could he do?

Trumpeldor was an amazing man. He had lost his arm in the service of the czar during the Russo-Japanese War. Despite his terrible injury he asked to be sent back to the front. His request was granted. After Port Arthur surrendered Trumpeldor found himself in a Japanese prisoner-of-war camp. In 1906 he was returned to Russia, where he was made an officer, an incredible achievement for a Jew.

In 1912 Trumpeldor came to Palestine as a militant Zionist. He wandered the country for a bit before finding his way to Degania, where he proved himself able to work harder and fire a rifle more accurately than any of his able-bodied peers.

"That an old soldier like Trumpeldor would volunteer doesn't surprise me," Haim said, "but why are you going, Yol? There are so many others, and you've done your part over the years."

"The truth is that I feel compelled to volunteer for the dangerous jobs. When we were younger, I used to brag about what sort of warrior I intended to be. Well, I had my fill of fighting the first time I was sniped at while on guard duty. Now when trouble comes I can hear God's laughter in my mind. 'Yol,' He tells me, here, I give you a chance. Go be a warrior.' " Yol smiled. "Haim, you know I have always been the jokester. I can't allow anyone, not even God, to have a joke on me."

"Little monkey, you are quite insane," Haim whispered, shaking his head.

"Absolutely."

"Either that," Haim continued thoughtfully, "or you are joking with me. Which is it, little monkey?"

Yol winked at him. "A big, strong, handsome fellow, you don't need to be intelligent. Now then, go get dressed. I will collect your rifle and saddle our mules."

Haim pulled on warm clothes and kissed his ashen-faced wife good-bye. Rosie said nothing, merely embraced him. At times like this Haim was thankful he'd married a woman who understood these things.

He shrugged on his coat and turned to his son, fast asleep in his cradle. Haim bent low to kiss Herschel's forehead and then hurried out of the cottage. The other two would be waiting for him at Degania's main gate.

Trumpeldor and Yol were already mounted up. The former gave Haim a curt nod in greeting as he swung himself astride his mule. Yol handed him his rifle and the three rode out in the direction Moshe had taken many hours before.

As soon as they'd turned the bend in the trail Haim felt a hundred miles from the settlement. Once Degania's lanterns were out of sight there was no light at all, for the clouds obscured the stars and the moon. It began to rain more steadily. Yol and Haim had leather-visored caps, but Trumpeldor did not wear one. He rode in the lead with coattails flying, sitting ramrod straight upon his jouncing mule, letting the rain drip from his stern, craggy features as if he'd been carved from stone. His empty left coat sleeve flapped like a raven's wing. He carried his rifle, barrel downward against the rain, across his right shoulder and had his Russian officer's saber thrust through his belt.

Haim kept his own rifle at the ready, balanced across the horn of his saddle. He briefly wondered how Trumpeldor, with his one arm, could work the bolt on his Lee-Enfield. He didn't have the courage to ask, and devoutly hoped there would be no occasion to find out. He glanced behind him. Yol brought up the rear. He was armed with just his revolver, for he had a first-aid kit across his shoulders in case Moshe was injured.

It took the trio two hours to reach the ford. The village with the doctor was another hour's ride beyond. They had to coax their mounts across several steep gullies and thread their way through thorny scrub before they were actually at the water's edge.

"We needn't ride any farther," Trumpeldor announced as he surveyed the crossing. "Just listen to those currents raging! Moshe's mule returned on its own to Degania. A riderless mule would never have crossed that torrent."

Haim nodded. "You're clever, Joseph. So if Moshe is here, he fell somewhere along this bank of the river."

"We can narrow it down a little more," Trumpeldor remarked. "This ford is only a hundred yards or so in length and it's the only place Moshe could have crossed."

"How do we find him?" Haim wondered. "It's so dark we can't see very far—"

"And everything I can see looks alive," Yol complained. He drew his revolver. "If Moshe's calling to us we'll never hear him over the river's roar."

"Quiet, both of you," Trumpeldor ordered. "First of all, nobody is to call to Moshe. If he was ambushed, the enemy may still be nearby, waiting for the rescue party."

"Wonderful." Yol swallowed hard.

"Here's what we'll do. Haim, you and I will search. Yol, stay here with the mules." Trumpeldor swung out of the saddle. He left his rifle across his shoulder and drew his saber. "Two men can search a small area like this and keep an eye on each other. If all three of us start wandering around, we'll likely shoot each other for Bedouins."

Haim dismounted. For some strange reason planting his shoes upon the wet ground made him feel more vulnerable. For the tenth time that night he checked to see that a round was chambered in his rifle.

"Keep your eyes open, Yol," Trumpeldor warned. "We'll call to you before we return so you'll know who it is."

"Don't forget or I'll shoot you," Yol said.

Haim could hear the strain of fear in his friend's voice. "Poor Yol," he commiserated, "you've got the toughest job, just waiting here by yourself."

"That's true," Trumpeldor agreed. "It takes nerve to do this. Are you game?"

Yol shrugged, then grinned. "Absolutely."

"Good man!" Trumpeldor smiled briefly.

"If only there were a moon," Yol complained, "I could see something."

Trumpeldor's smile was gruesome. "If you could see something, then something could see you."

"Go already," Yol urged them. "Even I know when to joke and when not."

"We'll walk ten meters apart," Trumpeldor quietly instructed Haim as they moved forward. "Parallel to each other and the river. I'll ask you to walk along the water's edge. It's slippery there, rather difficult for a one-armed man holding a weapon." Haim nodded and Trumpeldor continued. "If we don't find him on this sweep, we'll cover the next ten-meter strip working back toward Yol. Understand?"

Haim nodded. "And if there's trouble?"

"If I can, I'll get to you. If I can't, work your way back to Yol. Don't forget to let him know it's you. Then make Yol do what you think best."

Their eyes met. Haim nodded. "He's not weak, you know."

Trumpeldor did not answer. He glided away and after a few steps was lost in the shadows.

The rain pelted the branches of the scrub, making it move as if camouflaging an army of Bedouins. Haim gripped his rifle tightly, squinting against the darkness, trying to watch all around him while keeping an eye on the treacherous footing along the riverbank.

I'm really doing this, Haim thought as he moved along in a semi-crouch, his rifle across his chest. He remembered what Yol had earlier confessed to him, that the little monkey man had had his fill of fighting after one incident of sniper fire.

Yol was afraid and is afraid now, Haim mused. I'm wary but not exactly afraid. This isn't like being sniped at; this is real fighting.

He felt a tiny fire within him, a spark akin to the fire he'd felt when he first laid eyes on Rosie, and when he knew at long last that his Tel Aviv factory was a success.

This flame within him warmed and sustained; it whispered to Haim of his prowess. You cannot lose, it told him.

He stumbled on the body before he saw it. He jumped backward, fumbling his rifle. Then he dropped to his knees, feeling the wet earth bite into his trouser legs as he twisted around, trying to see if he'd blundered into an ambush. He strained to hear movement above the rain.

All was quiet. Haim got to his feet and crabbed sideways, putting his back to the river for protection. Where is Trumpeldor? he wondered anxiously. Now that he knew where to look, Moshe's body stood out clearly. He was lying sprawled on his belly a meter or so from the water's edge. Haim cautiously approached. There was something beside Moshe's head.

"Joseph," Haim hissed. He set down his gun and groped at Moshe's neck, trying to find a pulse. His fingers came back wet with something that was not rain.

He's dead. He's got to be dead, he's lying so still.

An image flickered in Haim's mind. It was long ago. There was a child and the night was moonless, just like now. Many bodies lay still. "Oh please, get up please, Father, Mother." I am that child—won't remember. Don't want to.

"Joseph."

"I'm here," Trumpeldor murmured, hunkering down beside Haim. "Get hold of yourself. It's Moshe, all right. You look like you've seen a ghost."

Trumpeldor rolled Moshe over. There was a stick beneath the body. "The boy's dead. Look here—they stoned him, and after he fell they slit his throat." Trumpeldor glanced at Haim. "Come on, now, snap out of it."

Haim shook himself and nodded. "I'm all right," he said weakly. "It was . . . It reminded me of . . . I don't know what." He frowned. "I'm all right though." He pointed at Moshe's head. "What's that beside him?"

Trumpeldor smiled in grim satisfaction. "Shoes. It's the Arabs' way of honoring him. Evidently little Moshe managed to kill or wound one of his attackers, with this stick, I'd wager."

"They took his rifle, I guess."

Trumpeldor shook his head, scowling. "He didn't have a rifle. I was at the meeting when he volunteered to go. It was decided by the committee"—he spat—"that he must go unarmed so as not to provoke the Arabs. Jews! When will they stop depending upon the good intentions of others and learn that a strong offense is the best defense?"

"You talk like you were not Jewish yourself, Joseph," Haim scolded.

"Of course I'm a Jew, but the rare one who knows that sometimes you ought to shoot first and ask questions later."

"It's not so simple, damnit. We can't just clear out the Arabs like rocks from a field—"

A report from Yol's pistol cut Haim off.

Haim crouched frozen, but Trumpeldor, saber in hand, was off and running. Snatching up his rifle, Haim quickly followed.

Yol was standing with his back to them beside the kicking, bucking mules, his gun trained on a cluster of boulders.

"What is it?" Trumpeldor demanded.

"Over there—a man!" Yol chattered, shivering with fear or the cold, for his leather jacket was slick with rain. "I heard a noise and I turned to see him climbing over those rocks. He had a rifle. I fired. I heard him cry out. I'm sure I got him."

"Stay with him," Trumpeldor instructed Haim before he went off to investigate.

"I was so frightened that it was you who got shot," Haim said, embracing his friend.

"You were frightened." Yol laughed a trifle hysteri-

cally. "I got him, though, I'm sure of it. I saw him fall."
He hesitated. "I heard you calling, Haim. Did you find
Moshe?"

Haim grimly nodded. "Yes, he's dead. But be of good
cheer, little monkey. Perhaps you have killed his murderer."

"Yes, of course." Yol brightened. "It must be so. It
was exactly as Trumpeldor said. That damned nomad was
waiting around for us. I'm a warrior after all."

At that moment Trumpeldor rejoined them. "There's
nothing there. You must have imagined it, Yol."

"No!"

"Then you missed and the beggar's run off," Trumpeldor said impatiently. "Come on, now, let's fetch Moshe's
body and get home."

Yol refused to be denied his victory. Trumpeldor tried
to block him, but the nimble little man scooted around him
to disappear behind the boulders.

"God have mercy," Trumpeldor softly grumbled. "I
tried."

Yol's wail was a drawn-out sorrowful cry. It echoed
plaintively against the rocks in that desolate place.

"He's being murdered!" Haim rushed to Yol's rescue.

Trumpeldor watched for a moment and then wearily
trudged after them. "More likely he's murdering himself,"
he muttered.

Haim scrambled over the rocks. He saw Yol kneeling
beside a still body. The corpse was not garbed in flowing
Bedouin robes but in the simple rags of the fellahin.

"It's just an old man from Um Jumi," Yol mourned,
"just a shepherd. See, there's his staff. There was no rifle,
just his staff."

"What was he doing here?" Haim wondered as he
climbed down to stand beside his friend.

"Who knows?" Trumpeldor replied, joining them.
"His sheep are somewhere about, I'd wager. At this time
of year the grazing fields close to Um Jumi have been

exhausted. He probably came here to find some decent grass for his flock. Then either he got caught in the rain and took shelter or he witnessed the battle between Moshe and his attackers and decided to lie low until things quieted. He probably smelled our mules and came poking around, hoping to claim them. Moshe's mule ran away, don't forget. This old fellow probably thought he'd found that one and could bring it back to Degania for a reward.''

"I'm no hero, am I, Haim?" Yol hugged himself, gently rocking back and forth, lost in grief. "God has played on me a good joke after all. I'm a murderer.''

"Come now," Trumpeldor chided. "You couldn't have known. A staff looks like a rifle in the dark. I know about these things.''

"It wasn't your fault, Yol," Haim added gamely. Still, he couldn't help feeling pity and horror for his friend. Thank God it wasn't I who did this thing, he thought.

"Perhaps the fellow wasn't even from Um Jumi but some other village," Trumpeldor suggested. "Who can say?''

"I can," Yol replied dully. "I knew him.''

"Yes, well—" Trumpeldor cleared his throat. "You were rather friendly with these beggars, teaching them things and all.''

"I'm a murderer and I shall turn myself over to the Turkish authorities," Yol told them both, getting to his feet.

"You'll do no such thing," Trumpeldor snapped. "Listen to me. You've always wanted to be brave, Yol, and now you must be braver than anyone. You must tell no one about this. The people of Um Jumi will assume that the same robbers who killed Moshe murdered the old man, and that is how it must remain. If you confess this killing, you'll begin a blood feud between the fellahin of Um Jumi and the people of Degania. The alliance you and Haim have struggled to build between the two peoples will crumple.''

"He's right, Yol," Haim said. "You know as well as we do that a blood feud, once begun, can never end. Many lives depend upon your silence."

"I understand," Yol said thickly. "Come, I want to go home."

"Good man!" Trumpeldor slapped his shoulder. "Haim, take Yol and get poor Moshe's body across one of the mules. We'll take turns walking back."

Haim waited until Yol had stumbled away. Then he turned to Trumpeldor. "Don't we take back the Arab's body?"

"No. The villagers will come looking for his sheep. We'll let them find the corpse." He hefted his saber. "I've got to dig Yol's bullet out of the man's chest and make his body look like the murder was done by Bedouins. It's a nasty job. Now, off with you."

Haim turned to go. Trumpeldor called to him.

"Keep an eye on Yol for a few days," the one-armed man said, "until he gets over this."

"What makes you think he'll get over it?"

Trumpeldor smiled. "I know about these things."

"Yes," Haim sneered, "we see what you know. We see, for instance, what comes of shooting first and asking questions later."

Before Trumpeldor could reply, Haim stalked off and rounded the boulders in time to see the splash as Yol hurled his revolver into the Jordan.

Chapter 16

New York, 1913

Abe and Leah Herodetzky celebrated their first wedding anniversary in August. As far as Abe was concerned, it was the happiest event in his life, overshadowing even that day long ago when ten-year-old Haim wandered into his cobbler's shop.

In celebration Abe closed the store for the afternoon. He wanted to shop for a present for Leah.

"What should I buy for you?" Leah asked him, watching as he set the locks on the door and hung the "CLOSED" sign in the window.

"You give me enough," Abe said. It came out almost gruffly. "Now come, I will carry you upstairs."

Sighing, Leah let him lift her and stagger beneath her weight as he headed toward the staircase. He huffed and puffed his way up to the second floor, while Leah steadfastly pretended to ignore how he was straining.

It was so silly, Leah mused, but better to humor than to argue with a husband. Besides, his solicitude was very sweet, even if she was only three months pregnant and hadn't begun to show.

Abe stubbornly refused to set her down on the landing, insisting upon shlepping her through their apartment so he could lay her upon their bed. Leah kept her arms around his neck, refusing to release him until after many kisses.

"When you come back I'll have supper ready," Leah smiled. "I'll see you in a couple of hours."

After he left, she took her hairbrush from the dresser and stroked her long black hair until it shone. She wanted her hair to look its best tonight, for Abe loved it when they were lying in bed and she leaned over him, letting her tresses envelop them both like a curtain. A few months after they were married, Leah asked him if he wanted her to cut it and don the wig worn by the most devout women to show their piety. Abe forbade her to do any such thing.

He had never been a religious man, he explained. He had no use for rabbis, preferring to deal with God directly. It mattered little to him whether she went to the ritual pool to purify herself after her time of the month; that was up to her. If she didn't go, well, they had a bathtub of their own right in the kitchen.

She let the matter rest, trying hard not to show Abe that she was disturbed. Her years in her sister's household had made an impression. Sadie had always been fiercely orthodox; going to shul was a regular part of life.

It really did not matter if a woman went anyway. A woman's religious duty was to make a good home for her husband and children . . . it did no good to lie to herself. Not going to shul was a definite lack in her life. Abe must have noticed, for he offered to take her on Rosh Hashanah and Yom Kippur, the most sacred holy days.

Abe's compromise put her troubled heart and conscience at ease. God's blessing was clearly on the bargain, she decided, and so the matter of religion was settled.

After assuring herself that she looked her best, Leah went into the kitchen to start supper. For their anniversary meal she had an expensive cut of beef from the kosher butcher. That was another understanding between herself and her husband. He might sell trayf, but in their home they would keep kosher.

As she peeled the potatoes she thought how lucky they were that everything had worked out so well between them. How easily tonight could have been a sad affair.

Last September Leah had expected to get pregnant right away, but as the months passed she began to worry.

Abe did his best to be kind and considerate during those first interminable months of fretting and waiting. He tried to conceal his disappointment, but Leah knew he yearned for sons.

For the second time since the wedding Leah needed someone to turn to for advice. This time Joseph was out of the question. She dreaded confessing her difficulties to Sadie, but there was no one else.

To Leah's great surprise Sadie was genuinely sympathetic. "You should wait at least a year before worrying so much. Your type has difficulty, and your husband, God bless him, is not so young, if you'll pardon my saying so."

Leah colored. "I know what you're thinking, that we—are together—not so often. That's not the case."

Sadie cackled, shaking her head in admiration. "All the more reason for you not to worry," she repeated. "Wait a year, that's what I say." She smacked her palm on the table like a judge bringing down his gavel. As far as Sadie was concerned, the matter was resolved, but for Leah the difficulty still existed. Abe was approaching forty. How could she expect him to wait another year?

She made an appointment to see the doctor without consulting Abe. When she told him about it one evening after supper, he nodded and resumed reading his newspaper. It was impossible for him to acknowledge the matter.

Later that same evening Abe suddenly embraced her,

whispering in her ear how much he loved her. He always whispered his endearments.

Nevertheless, Leah took what expressions of love Abe could make, knowing full well that the little he could bring himself to murmur was worth far more than what other, more facile lovers might effortlessly pour forth.

Abe's weaknesses brought out her strengths. What she could not find the courage to accomplish for herself, she could bring herself to do for him.

So she went alone to her appointment. She had briefly considered going to the clinic at Gouverneur Hospital, but the facilities there were too modern, too bustling for Leah to face. How could she reveal her concerns to a physician who was Gentile and perhaps her own age or even younger? The man one got at the clinic was strictly luck of the draw. No, she would go to the neighborhood physician. Dr. Glueck was elderly. She could confide in him with far less embarrassment. Besides, he was an Orthodox Jew. He understood the importance of children in a household. He would understand how crucial it was to her marriage that she not be barren.

His office was just around the corner from the store. Dr. Glueck answered her knock himself—he did not employ a nurse or receptionist—and asked her to take a seat on the bench in the outer office. Already waiting were a mother holding a sniffling daughter on her knees and a stout man cradling a toothache.

Dr. Glueck attended to a broad range of ailments in his community, for like Leah most in the neighborhood preferred his personal approach to Gouverneur Hospital. The doctor had received his training in Germany and as a young man had traveled to America in first class. Now, in addition to his black bag as a symbol of prosperity, he had a black automobile. Dr. Glueck's car on house calls was a familiar sight around the Lower East Side.

Eventually Leah found herself in an ominously

medicinal-smelling windowless room. There was a wooden examination table fitted with evil-looking straps and cranks. Along the walls were glass-door cabinets inside which a great many sharp-looking objects glinted.

Dr. Glueck had sparse grey hair brushed straight back and a bushy grey beard. He wore odd spectacles that perched on the bridge of his nose without the benefit of earpieces. As he shrugged off his suit coat he muttered in Yiddish that the last time he'd seen Leah was on a house call long ago, when she was just a little girl. She'd had croup, as he recalled.

Leah was not listening. Her stomach was lurching at the thought of those wicked little blades in the cabinets. She managed to blurt out that she was not sick—at least she didn't think she was. She had come to ask his advice.

The doctor nodded. He slowly donned his coat and led her into his office. The room was carpeted in crimson and lit by fine brass lamps crowned with green glass shades. Two leather armchairs faced an imposing mahogany desk. There was a curtained window behind the desk's swivel chair. Along one wall was a worktable on which rested a scale, weights and measures, trays and supplies. The innumerable vials of brightly colored pills, powders and liquids looked very much like the loose candy on display at the Cherry Street market.

There were tightly packed floor-to-ceiling bookcases, and against a side wall, lined up on a series of shelves, was a collection of large glass jars in which various rubbery monstrosities floated in preservative. There was an eye ringed with filaments of nerve tissue beside some kind of snake or worm. There were other things that Leah thanked God she did not recognize, and one prize trophy, pink as a valentine and all curled around on itself like the head of a fiddle; it had glossy black eyes.

Of course, Leah reassured herself, it's not human. It's just a baby chick or something.

She turned away and forced herself to stare at the doctor's green desk blotter as she told him why she'd come. She tried to block out the image of the pink thing, but it kept intruding.

She began to feel better as she stammered out her confession. Dr. Glueck was in his eighties. With his long grey beard, funny spectacles and dark study walled with leather-bound tomes, it was like talking with the rabbi.

The similarity was underscored when Dr. Glueck, his gnarled white blue-veined hands resting placidly on his green blotter, asked if she and her husband observed the rule of abstinence and enjoyment. Did they abstain prior to and after her menses? the doctor asked.

He is old, she reminded herself, unable to meet the doctor's level gaze as she told of every aspect of her lovemaking with her husband. He is a physician. For Abe's sake as well as your own, you must get through this. But the doctor might as well have extracted the information with a scalpel, so painful was it.

She kept her head bowed as he began to murmur to her. His instructions were specific and quite clinical. She thought of how she might impart them to Abe, of the look of bewilderment and humiliation in his eyes, and she began to weep. Their intimacy had been a magical thing. What if the doctor's instructions spoiled it?

Dr. Glueck, a compassionate man, paused and escorted her to the washroom. He told her to take her time and compose herself. He would be waiting.

When at last she could, she found that he'd written out the instructions for her. Leah folded up the sheet of paper and stuffed it into her purse. She paid the doctor and took her leave.

All the way home she kept her purse clutched beneath her arm, thinking of what was inside and feeling as if she had in her possession some of those filthy picture cards the degenerates sold up on Fourteenth Street. She said nothing to Abe about her interview with the doctor for all the rest of that day, and she knew he wouldn't ask. That evening after they locked up for the night, Leah unfolded the sheet of instructions and silently pushed it across the kitchen tablecloth to her husband.

Abe read in his slow, thorough way, as if it was the editorial page in one of his newspapers. He pursed his lips and nodded at her.

"The doctor says this is how it must be; then this is how it will be," he said at last. "When is supper, Leah?"

The words came out halfway through the meal. Abe uttered them so softly that he could easily have denied speaking if Leah had pressed him. "Leah, I love you very much."

In May she suspected that she was pregnant. She did not say anything to Abe because she had always been irregular in her cycles and she did not want to disappoint him. In June she went to see Dr. Glueck, who confirmed her hopes. She rushed home to tell Abe and their celebration was joyous.

Now, on the eve of their anniversary, Leah put their supper in the oven to roast and went into the parlor to await her husband. She sat down in an old overstuffed sofa they'd bought secondhand, glad for the opportunity to put her feet up on its matching ottoman.

These days she was spending less time in the store and more time resting. She'd been alarmed by how tired she was feeling so early in her pregnancy, but Dr. Glueck told her not to be concerned.

"This will be difficult for you, my dear," the doctor warned her. "You are of narrow girth and delicate disposition. Other women may continue to work or keep house well into their term, but you must conserve your strength for what may turn out to be an ordeal."

Dr. Glueck insisted upon seeing her often. He warned that she would have to deliver at the hospital. Leah followed all his commands and accepted his decrees. It was due to his magic that she had conceived. Nothing else mattered and no sacrifice was too great.

She heard the downstairs door open and then the click as it was relocked. Abe's footsteps sounded on the squeaking stairs. He came into the parlor with his arms full of parcels wrapped in brown paper.

"All those for me?" Leah laughed.

"First this," Abe handed her a small tissue-wrapped packet.

Leah tore away the wrappings. It was a string of pearls. "They're beautiful," she cried.

Abe, beaming proudly, came around the back of the sofa to clasp the necklace around her throat. As he bent to his task he paused to press his lips against her neck.

"It's a lovely gift," Leah murmured tenderly. "Thank you, my love."

Abe sat down beside her on the sofa so he could watch his wife's face as he handed her a sheaf of papers. Leah unfolded the documents and tried to read them, but the close-spaced English-language legalisms meant nothing to her.

Grinning, Abe put his arm around her and with his free hand tapped the papers in her lap. "What it says there is that Stefano de Fazio and I are now partners in ownership of this building," he announced. "Some weeks ago I went to see him. He had some money he wanted to invest, and I—"

"Wait," Leah interrupted. "Stefano is a union officer. He had union money he wanted to invest?"

"No. I saw him in his private office on Sixth Avenue. This had nothing to do with the union."

Leah frowned. She had met Stefano only once and had instantly mistrusted him. Now, watching her husband duck her gaze, she became suspicious. "Abe, what is it you are not telling me?"

"It is nothing to be concerned about. Stefano confided in me about where the money came from. He wanted to be straight with me, you understand? Always Stefano has been straight with me. So. He has control of so much money coming in and out of the union's coffers. It is possible for him to put into the ledgers that a certain amount was to go to a fellow holding a job in a local. Perhaps that person did not come to work except to collect the money, and then gave all but a little of it back to Stefano. It often happens that as treasurer Stefano has to pay out a disability benefit to a worker, but then the fellow only gets half of the allotment. The rest of the money ends up in Stefano's pocket. Then he has many relatives who have come over from Italy," Abe continued. "And all of them might go to work for the union, and Stefano would control their salary allotments . . ."

"What you are trying to tell me is that Stefano has stolen the money from the union, is that it?" Leah demanded.

"What is stealing?" Abe scowled. "Who is to say? It is how it works in America, that's all. Stefano had money that he wished to invest, but not in his name. He had his lawyer approach this building's owner and they agreed on a sale price. Then Stefano, wishing to pay me a favor, says to me, 'Abe, my friend, I will put the building in your name. You will collect the rents and give them to me and look out for the place, and in exchange you yourself will pay no rent at all.' " Abe paused. "Stefano's lawyer will take care of my obligations with the law. Many years from now it will be arranged that I sell the building back to him, and I will receive some money for that, as well. So what is the harm, Leah? I have helped my friend invest his money, and he has seen to it that we have more money to put away for our children."

"But Stefano has stolen his money, Abe," Leah sorrowfully repeated. "And now you have been made a party to the stealing."

"I don't care," Abe declared. "Every day the policemen come here to take home groceries without paying for them. Is that not stealing, Leah? The police, do they not steal from us?"

"A few groceries is not the same as money—"

"Please!" Abe turned away from her in disgust. "So from somebody else they take the money. Believe me, Stefano explained everything to me. This is how it works in America. This is how you become successful in business, Stefano has assured me, and I trust him. He has always been good to me."

"I'm afraid," Leah whimpered. "What if you have to go to jail?"

Abe chuckled, albeit nervously. "For what would they put a nobody like me in jail?" Then he hugged Leah, admitting, "Maybe I'm also a little frightened." He shrugged. "Who knows, maybe when you start to be successful you're supposed to be frightened. This much I can tell you, for you are my wife and you probably have already realized it about me. I was bragging to you just now when I said I was Stefano's partner. I could never be the partner of a strong fellow like that, for I'm a little man—"

Leah pressed her fingers to his lips. "Stop. You've done very well for yourself."

Abe shook his head. "Over two years I've been in this store. We have enough, but now we have children coming and our expenses will increase. I make our customers happy, but as hard as I think, I can't figure a way to make more of myself than being a retail merchant. If something happened to me—"

"God forbid."

"If I got sick and couldn't open the store, we'd be

out in the street.'' Abe smiled. ''Now that can't happen. It would not be in Stefano's interests to let it happen.''

''I understand.'' Right or wrong, the papers had been signed. Perhaps she was wrong in mistrusting Stefano.

''There's another thing too. Stefano mentioned that he intends to own other businesses someday. He said that maybe if I learn the food business thoroughly I could someday do the same thing for him that I'm doing now, but with a larger business, for more money. If I'm ever to leave something behind for my sons, it will come about through serving a man like Stefano de Fazio.''

''You are my husband,'' Leah said. ''I leave our welfare in your hands.'' She turned her attention to the other parcels, closing the discussion. One by one she unwrapped a succession of little boy's attire: shoes, shorts and shirts. ''Abe,'' she scolded, this time in amusement. ''These clothes are for a three-year-old.''

''They were on sale.'' Abe shrugged. ''He'll wear them when he grows.''

''And what if it's a girl?''

''What do I know from dresses? You'll buy for the girl and we'll put these things away for the boy when he comes.''

Leah bit her lower lip to keep from telling him what Dr. Glueck said. She'd kept the matter from Abe so as not to worry him and because she was still denying it to herself.

''Your physical constitution is not a match for your force of will, young woman. No more children after this one. Not if you want to live to see your firstborn thrive.''

''Supper is almost ready,'' Leah said brightly. She swung her legs down from the ottoman and got to her feet. She took a few steps then staggered.

Abe was at her side. ''Are you all right?'' he begged. ''Should I get the doctor?''

''I got up too fast,'' Leah mumbled. ''I'm fine.'' She

leaned against Abe for a moment and then let him escort her into the kitchen.

"I was just teasing you, my love," she whispered to Abe. "This first child is a son for you. It must be."

September brought in a spell of cool, blustery weather. Leah stayed upstairs in the apartment as much as she could, but there were times when she had to mind the store.

She dressed warmly, but it was drafty there by the cash register as the customers came in and out. Leah felt a sore throat develop. Soon she was coughing and sniffling and cursing her bad luck to have caught a cold.

Her cold seemed to drag on. Between its effects and her pregnancy she had no strength left at all.

One night during the third week of September she awoke with stomach cramps, moaning softly.

Abe came awake at once. He had always been a light sleeper, but since Leah got pregnant his eyes opened if he felt the least stirring beside him in the bed.

"Go back to sleep," she urged. "It's nothing. My cold went down to my stomach, that's all."

"Go see the doctor tomorrow," Abe muttered.

"I'm to see him at the end of the week anyway. What can he do for a cold?"

Abe grunted and turned over as Leah got out of bed. It was not so dark in the bedroom that she couldn't see that his eyes were open, watching her.

"Go to sleep."

"When you come back to bed I'll fall asleep."

"I'll be back in a minute."

She skipped barefoot across the icy cold linoleum floor on her way to the toilet. She did not bother to turn on the kitchen light. She could easily find her way in the dark to the little water closet.

Another series of cramps hit her. She pressed her

belly, bent her knees and waited for the pain to subside. Maybe I will go see the doctor tomorrow, Leah decided. A head cold was one thing, but in her mind, an illness moving down toward her belly was like an invading army.

As she pulled open the water closet door she had a wave of dizziness. She felt warm liquid cascading down the insides of her thighs, sopping her flannel nightgown.

I'm peeing on the floor, she thought distractedly. A high, keening noise had begun to build in her ears. I'll have to clean this mess up.

It was suddenly very much darker in the shadowy kitchen. Her hand rose to swat the air in search of the pull-chain that dangled from the overhead light fixture. She felt herself losing her balance and fell. She cried out, deciding that she was having a bad dream and wanting very much to be awake. She did not feel herself hit the floor.

Abe jackknifed out of bed at her call. He ran into the kitchen and lost his footing as his bare feet skidded out from beneath him. He landed spread-eagled, taking a nasty crack to the back of his head. What the hell was on the floor? The entire back of his nightshirt was soaking wet.

"Leah, where are you?" He got to his feet and pulled the light chain.

Blood—an impossible amount of blood as bright as fire had spread across the floor. More of it was seeping from between Leah's legs as she lay semi-conscious, curled up on her side.

They must have given her a sedative. All she possessed were hazy recollections, memories just beyond grasp. Leah had vague remembrances of a weeping Abe in his bloody nightshirt being comforted by their downstairs neighbors. She remembered Dr. Glueck looking very sad as he explained something to her, but his words were lost.

Then she was swathed in blankets and carried downstairs and through the store. There was a short ride through the deserted streets in the back seat of the doctor's black automobile.

And then there was Gouverneur Hospital. The ward was brilliantly lit, a vast, glaring cavern echoing with moans. They wheeled four walls of canvas screen around her bed and cut away the clotted, crusty flannel nightgown. She smelled acrid antiseptic and felt its sting as they scrubbed between her legs. Then came the stink of the ether across her nose and mouth. Her widely rolling eyes glimpsed a white tray arrayed with knives. Just before the ether swept her into oblivion she remembered Dr. Glueck's words to her as she writhed upon the kitchen linoleum.

"An incomplete miscarriage, I'm sorry to say. You must go to the hospital. I'm so sorry, my dear."

She came out of the ether late in the day. Her eyes sprang open. She knew where she was and what had happened to her.

She also knew what had happened to her baby. An image came to her of a room deep in the bowels of the hospital. Inside that room there was a shelf, and on it rested a new glass jar containing something pink as a valentine and all curled around like a fiddlehead.

She began to weep, but softly, so she wouldn't disturb the other patients. She wanted the nurses to leave her alone with her grief.

They kept her in the ward for one more night. Abe arrived early the next morning looking haggard, with a paper sack stuffed with her clothing under his arm. He waited impatiently for the attendants to wheel the canvas privacy screens into place. When they were sheltered from view, Leah began to get dressed.

"You talked with the doctors?" she asked.

Abe nodded.

"It was a son, yes?"

"Yes," he replied, shaken. "How did you know? You also spoke with them?"

Leah squeezed her eyes shut, willing away the image of that pitiful little thing in the jar. "No, I talked to no doctors, but I knew."

Abe scrutinized her, worried by the unfamiliar edge in her voice. He noticed how pallid she was, like a ghost of her former self.

"We must forget this terrible thing, Leah," he began, his manner almost formal.

She winced, waving at him to be quiet, and finished dressing in the awkward silence that followed. He pities me, she thought, and probably himself, for marrying a woman with hips like a boy, who can't even give him healthy sons. I should have died along with my son. A woman like me is better off dead.

Abe walked around the bed to her. He was going to embrace her. "Don't," Leah warned, shrugging off his touch. She'd endured enough pity in her life. Any response from Abe—even hatred—was better than pity.

Abe jerked back as if he'd been slapped. The anger and recrimination he'd fought to repress welled up in him. *You stupid woman, how could you have lost my son?* he wanted to scream at her.

But he didn't. He said nothing to her; he didn't know what to say at such a time. As well as they knew each other, in tragedy they were still strangers.

Always Leah had been the one to reach out. Why wouldn't she now? Where was her compassion? He needed her to help him understand what had happened and what it meant.

Say you love me, Abe willed. Help me understand.

"Let's go," he said thickly. His initial humiliation had faded. Now there was nothing within him but a dark void.

Chapter 17

Degania, 1914–1915

One evening in January Haim Kolesnikoff received a mysterious summons to attend a closed session of Degania's governing board. The summons made it clear that Haim was to appear at Yol Popovich's request, but it did not explain the purpose of the meeting.

On his way to the dining hall Haim concluded that the meeting had something to do with that terrible night they'd searched for Moshe. As Trumpeldor predicted, there had been no trouble over the shepherd. The mourning fellahin of Um Jumi blamed their loss on the nomads.

Yol's sense of guilt had not eased. Haim well understood what his old comrade was going through. Yol had dreamed of being a righteous warrior and wound up killing a harmless old man.

It gnawed at him. The cocky, joking monkey man was a shadow of his former self. There was no joy in his life.

On his arrival at the late night meeting Haim was shocked to learn that his friend was requesting a leave of absence from Degania. The reasons for his mysterious summons to the closed meeting became clear to Haim. For Yol to make such a request was a serious matter.

In the past Degania's officers had granted limited leaves so members could receive technical training or for such personal reasons as visiting one's parents in the old country. No one had ever asked to go without giving a reason or saying when he would be back.

Yol's request was summarily refused. The board lectured him on what it viewed as his profligate behavior. Yol countered by threatening to resign his membership.

At that point Haim spoke up. He reminded the officers that Degania's morale was to be considered. The settlement already had its first grave, poor Moshe's. Was this the right time for one of the founding members to leave under a cloud? Haim suggested that the board call Yol's leave Degania's first sabbatical. The Old Testament specified that there should be a year-long period every seven years during which the plow is put away and the fields left fallow. Yol Popovich had been in Galilee for seven years. "Yol," Haim loudly announced, "has been here longer than anybody."

The board relented and Yol's leave was granted.

"I've only been here six years," Yol told Haim after they left the dining hall, his breath making vaporous puffs in the cold night.

"The board members have all been here less than four," Haim laughed. "They'll never find out."

"Well, I thank you." Yol smiled thinly. "That sabbatical business was very clever."

They walked on side by side with their coat collars turned up against the cold. Despite winter's being the rainy season the weather had been dry the past fortnight. Degania's usually muddy pathways had hardened, and keeping one's footing was not much trouble.

It was late enough for them to make their way in solitude, casting inkspills of shadow as they crossed an occasional square of yellow light cast from a cottage window. Overhead were myriad diamondlike stars and a milky crescent of moon against a canopy of black velvet.

Once they heard the dry cough of a jackal prowling the other side of the perimeter fence. Several of the settlement's dogs picked up the scent and began to bark.

"Would you really have resigned?" Haim asked, "Or was it just a bluff?"

Yol sounded weary. "I would have done it, even though it would have broken my heart. I must get away from here, where everything reminds me that I am a murderer."

"What happened was very sad, but it was not murder—"

"I've told no one about it. I've accepted Trumpeldor's reasoning that my confession would bring about a blood feud between Um Jumi and Degania. But I cannot stay where the old man's ghost haunts me."

"When will you leave?" Haim asked.

"At dawn. My things are packed. I have a place on the boat to Tiberias."

"I knew that I never should have arranged our using the fellahin's boats," Haim said ruefully.

Yol chuckled. "I told you only trouble would come of it. Anyway, from Tiberias the roads are better. I can be on my way."

"Where to?"

Yol shrugged. His curly hair and beard looked gunmetal blue in the moonlight.

They were reluctant to part. Both were aware that it would be a long while, if ever, before they would be reunited. They stood, eyeing each other almost crossly, hunching their shoulders and stamping their feet against the cold.

"Little monkey," Haim finally grumbled, embracing Yol, "we are fine comrades, yes?"

"Absolutely." Yol patted Haim's shoulder. "Now go home to your wife and son."

"What will I tell them? Rosie will rail at me for letting you go, and Herschel, he'll cry for his uncle—"

"Thanks for reminding me," Yol exclaimed. "Wait one second." He dashed into his room and reappeared a moment later with something wrapped in an old cloth. "I carved this for Herschel's birthday next week." He thrust the parcel at Haim. "When you give it to him, be sure to say I made it, yes?"

"Of course I will," Haim promised. He carefully unwrapped the birthday gift. It was a small prancing horse hitched to a wagon that could be rolled along on its delicate spoked wheels.

"This is magnificent work," Haim murmured. "I'll show it to Herschel and then put it away for when he is older and can appreciate it. This is far too delicate for a three-year-old."

"Do what you think best." Yol's mouth twisted into a sad smile. "Now go home."

Haim took one last long look at his friend and turned away. He could hear Yol calling softly to him as he walked back to his cottage, his boots crunching the brittle mud. "Tell them Yol got bored with this dreary place and went off to look for some fun."

In the spring it was voted that the original founding kibbutz disband itself and reform to embrace all of the newer, permanent settlers. Degania, it was thought, could more smoothly and equitably function if there was no distinction between the most recently accepted and the charter members.

Another problem to be resolved was how to care for the children. Each mother kept her own with her throughout the work day. This was acceptable as long as women stayed in traditional roles, but some of the more radical ones had begun to insist that they do the same kinds of work as the men.

"We didn't come to this country to cook, clean and do laundry," these women maintained.

At first the men argued. "You have your gardens to till and cows to milk," they pointed out. "We could never again hold our heads up if it became known that the men of Degania allowed their women to push plows."

Gradually it became clear to everyone that work details had to be mixed if a cooperative program was to succeed, and something had to be done with the children. A mother could keep track of her children in the laundry room or the garden, but not in the fields.

None of the women would hear of giving up their hard-won right to do communal work in order to look after their children. Finally it was agreed that each child was the responsibility of the kibbutz. A building was set aside as a nursery, and two women—one of them Rosie—volunteered to look after the children. At the end of the day the mothers came to collect their offspring and take them back to their cottages for the night.

The day-care arrangement worked well for everyone, especially Rosie. She had never really enjoyed doing domestic chores or the arduous agricultural work, but she loved children and they loved her. The governing board complimented her on the job, and Rosie, regaining her self-confidence, once again felt the desire to sketch and paint. She referred to the children as her "puppies" and confessed to Haim that if she'd known she was so well suited for this kind of work, she would have used her time in Tel Aviv to train as a teacher. As it was, it would be several years before any of the children were old enough to require formal schooling.

The spring and early summer of 1914 proved to be a good time for Degania. Slowly the cobblers, merchants and lawyers who'd come to settle the land began to understand how they could profitably cultivate the Jordan valley. Strategies were devised, a special system of crop rotation was implemented, and all at once there began to occur a real improvement in the quality of life.

For one thing, the years of work had begun to eradicate the surrounding swampland. This cut down on the number of flies and mosquitoes, reducing in turn the incidence of fever. Pepper tree saplings were planted and took root. This encouraged the kibbutz to plant an avenue of cypress trees leading from the gate to the water tower. The flourishing cypresses became a sort of symbol. Every day the workers could walk past them, remarking to each other how much taller they looked since yesterday.

A flower garden was once again attempted, and this time the wild boars stayed away. One day, quite suddenly it seemed, bright flowers appeared, contrasting nicely with the pale green of the saplings. On that day the workers of Degania realized that they had begun to transform their desolate stretch of Galilee into a place of beauty.

Degania's success had led to the establishment of similar agricultural settlements. Arthur Ruppin, head of the National Fund, made the trip from Tel Aviv to inspect what he had helped bring about at great risk to the fund's meager resources, and even his own reputation.

Degania, he told them, was the first land to be truly owned by Jews, and now Jews could be proud of that ownership.

On June twenty-eighth Archduke Ferdinand was assassinated in Sarajevo. The murder and subsequent outbreak of war in Europe were closely followed by the Jewish community of Palestine. Many of the most influential people, property owners in Tel Aviv, for example, argued that the Turks would stay out of the war and that if the Ottoman Empire did fight, it would be on the side of the Allies. Many Jews in Palestine had taken Turkish citizenship and now loudly proclaimed their loyalty to Turkey no matter which side that country took.

It was Joseph Trumpeldor, anxiously perusing the stacks of tattered weeks-old newspapers brought in on the supply carts, who understood the significance of the widening war. For fifty years the storm had been brewing. Now it was just beyond the horizon. Trumpeldor's warrior bones told him that the rain was about to fall.

Haim was in the tack room caring for the saddles and the leather harnesses for the mules when Trumpeldor came to talk with him. It was the end of September but still blazingly hot. The sky was bleached white. Here in the Jordan valley the earth had baked hot enough to raise a blister on the bottom of a bare foot—except for the feet of the Arabs, and the children of Degania.

Haim liked working in the tack room. It was relatively cool and pleasantly lit. The harsh sunlight filtered golden through the burlap curtains, bringing a rich sheen to the burnished leather.

He took each harness from its peg and carried it to the worktable. He scrubbed the tack down with a rag soaked in saddle soap and then waxed the leather. He polished each bit of leather and brass until it gleamed, the simple, soothing work carrying him back across the years to his apprenticeship in Abe's cobbling shop and their little village in the pale.

Next year would mark a decade in Palestine. Ten years! So much time passed, miles traveled, money earned and given away. He had cut stone, run a factory, helped build the first Jewish city and the first kibbutz.

But for all that no work satisfied him as much as when he cut and molded the leather, affixed the brass and polished the piece until it glowed.

"You made of me a fine shoemaker," Haim remarked to Abe, whose presence seemed to hover amidst the cut hide and pungent tins of soap and preservative. It was in the tack room that Haim could best remember Abe. Since Yol's departure seven months ago he had begun anew to long for Abe's company.

In the tack room, through a kind of meditation brought about by the simple but soul-satisfying work, Haim found that he could talk to Abe. He could describe what had happened to him so far in his eventful life, and he could talk of Rosie and of his pride and joy, his son Herschel. As Haim worked he found himself better able to remember conversations with Abe.

His work in the tack room had taken on such a private significance that Haim considered it an intrusion when Joseph Trumpeldor barged in, a creased newspaper in his right hand. Haim had done his best to avoid Trumpeldor since that terrible night last fall. He—admittedly irrationally—blamed the Russian for Yol's misfortune.

"Read this." Trumpeldor thrust the newspaper in front of him.

Haim glanced at the front page as he continued with his work. "It is in English, yes, Joseph? I do not know English."

Trumpeldor nodded. "It's a British-funded paper out of Tel Aviv. It just arrived on the cart. I'll read it to you."

Haim listened as Trumpeldor rambled on about a battle at a river called the Marne, near Paris. The French and some English—the British Expeditionary Force—had won a decisive victory over the Germans.

"The Kaiser's forces will fall back now," Trumpeldor continued. "The Germans' strategy of crushing the West so that they can turn all of their might against Russia is finished."

Haim was unclear if Trumpeldor was still reading or was offering his own opinion. He carefully ran his saddle-soaped rag the length of a harness rein, making sure to clean the edges of the leather as well as both sides.

"There's no question now that a long and costly war on two fronts is unavoidable for Germany," Trumpeldor went on.

There was a horsefly buzzing figure-eights around the tack room, occasionally thudding against the slanted white-washed ceiling. Haim wished that both the fly and Trumpeldor would go away and allow him to work in peace.

"Joseph, what is the point you are trying to make?" As Haim spoke he scrutinized the harness. "I don't quite see the significance of this Marne," he absently murmured.

"Perhaps if you gave me your attention, I could help you to understand it," Trumpeldor curtly replied.

Haim set down his polishing rag. His work in the tack room was special. He would not spoil it by continuing while another person—especially Trumpeldor—was nattering at him.

"Here is what I can deduce from the newspaper," Trumpeldor began, folding it in half and shoving it into a pocket. "With two fronts going the Germans will want to give the Allies a little more to think about. The Kaiser will redouble his efforts to get Turkey to ally itself with the Central Powers."

Haim shrugged. "If you say so, Joseph, for you know far more about military matters than I do, but I've heard people say that Turkey is leaning toward the Allies because of French investments in that country. I've heard that many Turkish ministers are pro-Entente, or at the very least neutral."

Trumpeldor's stern, hawkish features relaxed into a thin smile. "You're wrong, my boy, but at least you've begun to think."

"I'm not your boy," Haim glowered.

Trumpeldor's smile turned into a smirk. "Sorry."

"You may disagree with me, but don't say I'm flat-out wrong, Joseph."

"Actually, I will say that, and here's why." Trumpeldor's fingers hammered the tabletop as he made his points. "Number one, the Turkish army has recently been restructured by a German general. Number two, there are leaders of the Young Turks Revisionist Party, War Minister Enver Pasha among them, who have taken on the Prussian style. I suspect they'll be taking fencing lessons and sporting monocles before very long. Third, there is long-standing animosity between Turkey and Russia over the former's claims to ancient territory now held by the Russians. The Germans will bewitch the Turks with glorious tales of what could be. The Turks would rather listen to such promises than face reality. Already we've seen which way the Turks are leaning. Consider the events of just a few weeks ago, when those German battleships evaded their British pursuers by entering the Dardanelles—''

"Everyone knows that story." The German cruisers had been immediately "purchased" by the Turks and the German sailors issued fezes. "And everyone has an explanation for the Turkish action. It could have been that the Turks wanted to teach the British a lesson for having seized those two battleships being built for Turkey in British shipyards—''

"Or that Turkey wanted to put pressure on Russia to cede those territories," Trumpeldor scowled. "The immediate motivations are far less important than the result, which will be Turkey's entry into the war on the side of the Central Powers."

Haim feigned a yawn. "Whatever you say, Joseph. There's nothing we can do about it. Now please, may I get back to my work—''

"Damn you, listen to me!" Trumpeldor barked. "I know you blame me for your friend's troubles on that night, but put aside your grudge for the moment and listen. Believe me, that war is coming here. Believe that I have lived through enough war to know how it can—'' He hesitated, his arm impotently sawing the air as his mind groped for the right words to express himself. "I've seen how war can accelerate the course of history—"

"You're a soldier, Joseph. To you war is the solution to every problem." Haim grimly shook his head. "That's why I can't trust your interpretation of events." And that's an outright lie, Haim thought. Why am I frightened to confront him with my feelings concerning Yol? He's already brought it up.

"I am a warrior, it is true. But above everything I am a Zionist. When Turkey enters the war the Allies will have to divert forces to defend Egypt. They will need help. There are eighty thousand Jews living in Palestine at this moment. How the Zionist movement aligns itself in the immediate future will affect the likelihood of establishing a Jewish homeland for generations to come."

"You were right, you know," Haim heard himself admitting. "What you'd said before, concerning Yol, you were right. I do blame you."

He expected Trumpeldor to make a face, to shout, to belittle the accusation. He even expected the hard old soldier to ridicule Yol for carrying on like an old woman over the incident. If he does that I'll smack him one, Haim vowed. Never mind his one arm and the fact that he's a hero.

What Haim did not expect was for Trumpeldor to nod, looking suddenly very grey and tired, nor to see compassion in his brooding hunter's eyes.

"I don't question you for blaming me, because I've already blamed myself," Trumpeldor said. "You don't know how often I've wished it were you I'd left to watch over the mules."

Haim nodded sullenly. "Thanks very much. Then the shooting would have been on my conscience."

"Perhaps, but then again perhaps not. Perhaps you

wouldn't have shot so quickly, Haim. You're not like Yol.''

"Yol is a good man, Joseph," Haim began in tones of warning. "Don't you—"

"Oh, stop it," Trumpeldor implored. "Yol is totally unsuited to be a fighter. It's not a question of whether he is a good man or a bad one. He simply isn't cut out for the job. For one thing, he has far too much imagination. A head full of ideas is an asset for a jokester, a detriment to a man who has to face an armed enemy in the dark. Believe an old soldier, Haim. You may think that when it comes to war I am like a drunk clutching his bottle, but the truth is that I do not enjoy killing or watching my comrades being killed or maimed. It is simply that I have a talent for the military." He paused, his dark eyes intent upon Haim. "And so do you, you must realize, so do you."

"Joseph, I'm confused." Haim stared at Trumpeldor. "I was terrified that night."

"I was watching you. You did well. I saw what you were made of. If it had been you who shot the Arab, you would have gotten over it. Unlike Yol, you would have come to realize that such accidents are unavoidable during wartime."

"We're not at war."

"But we are," Trumpeldor insisted. "Now we fight the Bedouins. Soon we will fight the Turks, and someday we will be against all the Arabs. Believe an old soldier, Haim. There is only so much land. If we are to have some of it, we will have to fight for it."

"We have Tel Aviv right now," Haim argued. "Degania is ours; we have the papers to prove it on file at the National Fund office."

"We have only illegal status in this country, which allows us to build and turn wasteland into farmland because we pay the Turks. We are no better off than the serfs in Russia. They pay the landlords for the right to improve

and work the land. A bribe is a bribe, Haim, and paying it
is not the way to earn a homeland.''

"There aren't enough Jews in Palestine to defeat the
Turks,'' Haim said. "We must cooperate, get them to trust
us—''

"They never will,'' Trumpeldor said flatly. "They
will use us if they can, but they'll never accept us. We've
paid baksheesh far too long, and most of us are from
Russia, their enemy in this war. Our only hope lies in an
Allied victory, especially if we can help to bring it about.
Our leaders must bargain with the British and the French:
Jews to fight against the Central Powers in exchange for a
homeland after the war. I intend to organize and lead those
volunteers, and I want you with me, Haim.''

"But Joseph—'' Haim was flabbergasted. "Why me?
I'm a poor farmer and a better leatherworker, but hardly
worth my salt as a soldier. Why not recruit the Hashomer?''

"They are good at fighting Bedouins,'' Trumpeldor
replied, "but I wouldn't want to be the one to tame those
wild men into a disciplined military unit. The Hashomer
will have their place in the struggle, but what I have in
mind is to form a model corps of regular troops. Don't
forget, I got my experience fighting against the Japanese.
I've trained many men in my day, and I'll take ordinary
fellows with raw talent any time over undisciplined toughs
who can't follow orders.''

"What good could so few men be to the Allies?''
Haim asked.

"Every man counts. On the other hand, you're right,
so few men are certainly not going to win the war.
That doesn't matter, you see. The volunteers will be a
symbol of the Jewish presence on the Middle Eastern-
Palestine front. 'Here are some men to help you fight,' the
World Zionist Organization can tell the Allies, but what
they'll really be saying is, 'Here is the support of Jews all
over the world.' ''

"Any Palestinian Jew who comes out against the Turks could be hanged for treason," Haim warned.

"Eventually, but not until that Jew has sworn his loyalty to the Ottoman Empire." Trumpeldor grinned ferally. "Anyway, they have to catch you before they hang you."

"That's the other part of it." Haim seized the point. "We'd have to leave Palestine. It's easy for you, Joseph, but I have my family to consider. If I went with you, there could be reprisals—"

"You know better than that. The administration in this country has kept no records on us. They don't know who you are or if you're married. When you entered this country, you paid your bribe and that was that."

Haim sighed; it was the truth. "When do you need to know?"

"Hard to say," Trumpeldor replied. "There's some time, but not very much."

"Well, I can't give you my decision right now."

Trumpeldor nodded. "You have a difficult time ahead of you, my boy. Come with me, and it may be years before you see your wife and son again."

"Assuming I'm not killed."

"Always assuming that," Trumpeldor wryly acknowledged. "But consider this, Haim. If you stay in Palestine, you will have to knuckle under to Turkish authority."

Haim nodded. "I have to discuss it with Rosie."

"As I said, there's not much time."

Haim felt no peace in the tack room after Trumpeldor left. He'd lied to the man. He had no intention of discussing Trumpeldor's offer with Rosie because he had no intention of accepting it.

He picked up his rag and resumed his work. He rubbed at the leather as if it were a magic lamp and by stroking it Haim could make a genie appear to solve the dilemma he faced.

Trumpeldor had seen through him. Haim despised

what the Turkish government represented in Palestine. If he were single, Haim would immediately have volunteered against the Central Powers just on principle, never mind what his efforts might accomplish for Zionism.

But I'm not single, Haim thought. I've already missed most of the first year of Herschel's life. He hardly knows me yet. How can I leave him for what might amount to years? I'd be a stranger to him. He wouldn't recognize me, and he wouldn't love me, and that would be exactly what I'd deserve.

And there was his darling Rosie. The year he spent apart from her had dragged for an eternity. How could he leave her again, especially having taken her from her family in Tel Aviv?

And what if I'm killed? he wondered. I know what it is to be an orphan. I was lucky enough to be taken in by Abe, but who would be a father to Herschel?

He rubbed harder and harder at the leather until his arm ached and it gleamed like new. Then he put it aside and started on another. As Haim worked he imagined Abe dourly smiling at him.

You alone understand the truth, don't you? he thought. You know I've gotten older, gotten to be very much like you. I've been lucky, and now I've come to think in terms of what's to be lost rather than what's to be gained.

He wanted to stay with his family. Haim finally had to accept the fact. He wanted to put in a day's work right here in Degania and come home in the evening to play with his son and make love to his wife.

In October the Turkish fleet, led by German commanders, staged a surprise attack upon Russian ports along the Black Sea. A week later Russia, England and France all declared war against the Ottoman Empire.

Rumors swept Degania. The Turks were going to imprison the Jews; the Turks would draft all able-bodied men. Their army offered horrors which, Trumpeldor was quick to warn, would make the the Russian army look like a picnic.

"We'll be safe here in Galilee," the anxious settlers of Degania assured each other. "The war will not touch us here."

All across the settlement work increased. Gardens were dug, buildings begun and repairs made. Rosie applied for and got permission to paint a mural detailing Degania's history across one wall of the dining hall. She asked for help and was flooded with offers. Everyone, it seemed, was intent upon keeping himself busy and his mind off what no one could control.

In November Trumpeldor came to Haim. "It's time," the soldier said. "Come with me to Jerusalem. Ben-Gurion and the others are there. They've submitted a prosposal to Djemal Pasha, the Turkish commander." Trumpeldor's eyes were bitter. "They too wish to raise a Jewish army, but attached to the Ottoman Empire."

"That is foolish." Haim frowned. "The British have Egypt under a protectorate. It's almost a certainty that they will sweep through Palestine in a matter of weeks."

"I totally agree. The Turks have no navy or artillery to stop them, and as yet no decent soldiers. And the population would certainly welcome the chance to overthrow the corrupt Turkish government."

"Our fate should not be tied to that of the Turks," Haim went on. "My father-in-law is English, and he believes there are strong sympathies for us in the British government."

"Come with me, then, Haim. Together we'd have a chance of convincing Ben-Gurion and the others."

Haim shook his head. "I'm sorry, but I believe my place is here with my family."

"A pity, my boy." A smile played across Trumpeldor's hawkish features. "I could have turned you into quite a soldier."

"Joseph, know that I no longer blame you for what happened with Yol. I can also say that Yol himself never blamed you." He shook hands with Trumpeldor. "Shalom."

"Shalom means 'peace,' and that I don't think we shall have, Haim, not for a long time."

Walking home from that last meeting with Trumpeldor, Haim felt strangely hollow inside, also strangely settled. For the first time in his life he had put his responsibilities ahead of his desires.

Haim thought, how Abe would have approved.

On impulse he turned down a side path that led to the nursery. The children were playing in front of the building; Rosie, sitting on a bench with her sketch pad on her lap, watched over them.

Haim waved to his wife and called out to his son, suddenly seized with overwhelming certainty that he'd done the right thing.

Herschel ran toward him. The boy would soon be four years old. Haim watched Herschel's legs pump like pistons under his large, baggy shorts. The boy's pudgy arms windmilled for balance as he ran; he looked like a baby bird intent on getting airborne for the first time.

Haim hunkered down to catch Herschel up in his arms. The boy spoke to him in English. Rosie was teaching their son her mother tongue in addition to the Hebrew and Arabic.

"Say it to me in Hebrew," Haim gently reminded Herschel.

"Papa, take me with you to work?" the boy obediently piped.

It was not allowed; the principles of the collective overrode all things, even parental authority. "You will stay here with the other children."

Herschel nodded and Haim ruffled his hair, as golden as the grain for which the settlement was becoming renowned. He looked into his son's yearning upturned face, into his eyes, bluer than his own.

"We will play after the day is done," Herschel offered.

"Yes, papa?"

"I will be here."

As the new year approached, Degania heard that the authority to muster a separate Jewish legion to fight alongside the Turks had at first been granted and then abruptly rescinded by Djemal Pasha. Jews were declared to be foreign traitors, and hundreds of Zionist activists—among them Ben-Gurion, Trumpeldor and Arthur Ruppin—were rounded up and deported to Egypt.

The people of Degania passed an anxious winter wondering when the British would come to rescue their country. The Turks continued to expel Zionist activists and slowly but surely looted Palestine to support the troops. The Jews were ordered to surrender any weapons they might have, and most did so, desperate to convince the Turks of their loyalty and survive the nightmare.

In Tel Aviv Dizengoff implored his eligible male citizens to enlist in the Turkish army to prove Jewish loyalty. Many brave young men did enlist, aware that they were sacrificing themselves as cannon fodder to appease the savage Turkish temper. Meanwhile they silently vowed to surrender their rifles to the British—if only they would come.

In the spring of 1915 the sinking of the *Lusitania* shocked and horrified the world. The Jews of Palestine were further rocked to learn that the Allies were making their assault at Gallipoli, a peninsula in European Turkey. Churchill, then First Lord of the British Admiralty, intended to seize the strategically crucial Dardanelles in order to enable the combined might of the Greek and English navies to sink the German-Turkish fleet.

That same year the first refugees were driven into Palestine's interior by the pillaging Turks. The war was coming to Degania after all.

Chapter 18

New York, 1914

In January Abe tried to contact Haim. It was a little over three months since the miscarriage and a storm cloud of sorrow had descended over Cherry Street. Leah was withdrawn and subdued. She was in mourning, leaving Abe to sort out his own grief as best he could.

He was not up to the task. He didn't know how to confront his own anger about what had happened. Leah had always been the one to reach out to him. Now that she wouldn't or couldn't, Abe was unable to cope.

He briefly considered swallowing his pride and going to see the rabbi. It would have been nothing but a gesture, though, to have to sit through the story of Job, to be told that God's will works in mysterious ways, that it is not for man to question. He was not religious enough to take solace in the assertion that God likes a good loser. Abe had lost too much as it was; he was sick to death of the taste of loss.

First the child and now Leah. Yes, she was lost to him, or at least her radiance was, and that was the aspect of his wife that Abe had loved the most.

She was still dutiful, accommodating her husband in their bed, but without passion; she still did her share of the work in the store, but the market no longer rang with her rich laughter.

Abe had depended on nothing since his childhood except the exuberance that Leah had brought to his life. Now the loss of that joy had left an awful void. Abe tried to fill it by locating Haim to persuade him to come to America and become a partner in the market. Of course if pressed Abe would admit that Haim was in his thirties by now and probably settled, but in Abe's heart his ward was still the headstrong youth who needed guidance. Perhaps things had not gone well for the boy. Perhaps Haim was pining for him even now.

He went to the *Jewish Daily Forward*'s offices with his idea. Perhaps there was a newspaper similar to the *Forward* in Palestine that would run an advertisement directed at Haim Kolesnikoff, asking that he write to Abe Herodetzky at the Cherry Street address.

The *Forward*'s people did as much as they could, but they were busy putting out their paper and handling appeals from Jews looking for their families all across America and the world. It was two months before the advertisement in Hebrew was sent overseas along with the money to pay for its run.

Abe waited for an answer, but his hopes faded. The answer never came. Who knew if the advertisement had ever been published in the first place? The people at the *Forward* offered no guarantee. Anyway, Palestine was not the Lower East Side, where you could buy a dozen different dailies on any street corner. The editors cautioned that newspaper circulation was spotty outside the coastal areas.

In August, for their second anniversary, Abe presented Leah with a pair of gold earrings. She smiled faintly, kissed him on the cheek and refused to put them on. He also gave her another sheaf of papers, again drawn up by Stefano de Fazio's attorney. These were applications for citizenship, Abe explained to Leah. For their anniversary he intended that they officially become part of America.

Abe's omnivorous readings had long ago acquainted him with the legislative process and civics in general, sufficient to pass the examination. Leah, on the other hand, was totally ignorant about such things. It soon became evident that long evenings of study would be required before she could answer the questions.

She didn't even want to try. Since the miscarriage she'd been nervous and unable to concentrate on anything for very long. Abe found that he had to make a game of the lessons to get her to pay attention to the dry facts. He made jokes and they found themselves laughing. It was the first time they'd laughed together since the loss of the child. Abe made more jokes; he did foolish things; he found himself courting his wife all over again, not to win her heart, but to rescue it from the darkness.

For two weeks they spent each evening drilling themselves for the test. No matter how hard Leah tried, she made little progress. The night before the hearing, more confused than ever, Leah burst into tears. It was no use. If she remembered that the number of United States representatives depended on the population and that there was a blessedly uniform pair of senators per state, she forgot that representatives served for only two years as opposed to the senatorial six. If she remembered who served how long, she forgot that the House and the Senate made up something called Congress. And what *was* the President's name?

"I give up," she cried, exhausted. It was three in the morning. They'd been sitting at their kitchen table with their books and papers in front of them since nine. "Take the test without me, please. And I'll thank you very much—"

"Nope." Abe crossed his arms and shook his head.

"They'll fail you too, if I go with you," she warned. "I'm stupid and hopeless and there's no more time."

"If you don't go, I don't go."

"You want to vote, don't you?" Leah sniffled. "I don't care about it—"

"Women can't vote," Abe said, distracted. "Anyway, we're doing this together."

Leah swallowed her arguments and nodded. Since they began to study for the citizenship test she'd found herself forgetting about the miscarriage for hours at a time. Abe had been trying so hard to see to it that she passed the test. The work every night had been for her; he could pass the hearing without trying. During the days and weeks immediately following her stay in the hospital Leah had grown remote from her husband because she couldn't endure his pity. Now it occurred to her that she'd been mistaken, that what she thought was pity was really his attempts to let her know that he still cherished her even though he was sad.

"Who is the President?" Abe asked. "Not the Governor of New York," he warned before she could speak. "The President of the United States, I'm asking you."

"What difference does my being a citizen make to you?"

"It just does. Now, who is President?" Abe insisted.

"Because why? Is it such a big deal to go to the test alone?"

"I don't want to go alone. There's already enough things alone in our lives." He hesitated. It seemed the time to say he loved her, but he'd always had trouble saying it, and the few times he had recently, Leah had pretended not to hear. It wasn't a husband's love that he wanted to communicate, or not just now at any rate. What he wanted Leah to understand about their relationship involved more than love. It involved the loss of their son, and what happened with the store, and their future in America, and all the happiness and disappointments that life would throw at them, singly and together.

"Leah, listen, please. We're doing this together because we are partners, as Haim and I were partners at one time. The way I would like to be partners with him again. That's how you and I are partners, in addition to being husband and wife—"

"Woodrow Wilson," Leah interrupted. If he could give the right answer, so could she.

They studied until it was time to open the store. Abe washed and shaved, using plenty of cold water to shock himself awake. While Leah made him coffee he dressed in his best suit, and then she napped and he tended to the morning's business.

He closed up at eleven-thirty. They had to be at the district courthouse at half past noon, and Abe wanted to get there in plenty of time to have a final go-round drilling Leah on Congress.

He heard her coming down the back stairs, turned and thrilled at the sight of her.

Leah's waist-length black hair was braided and tucked up beneath a high-crowned floppy-brimmed hat of maroon felt. Her turquoise dress was pretty enough with its flat white collar and its flounced skirt that ended above her ankles, which were covered by her high-heeled, high-buttoned shoes. Still, it was the hat that gladdened Abe.

She'd bought it well over a year ago in celebration of becoming pregnant, after an afternoon shopping on Division Street, nicknamed Millinery Lane. When she brought it home Abe thought it made her look both seductive and like a little girl. He said it made her look like Mary Pickford, who was one of Leah's favorites at the moving pictures.

It was a silly, totally useless hat, ready to cause a

nuisance by blowing off and cartwheeling down the street at the slightest puff of wind. It was the sort of hat a woman would wear purely for the joy of it, to make a man notice her.

And thank God she's wearing it again, Abe thought. "You look very pretty today," he said.

Leah shrugged, making a face. "I should be a frump on the day I become an American?" She stalked past him, stiff-legged and self-conscious.

Abe said nothing else as he locked up, afraid to break the spell. His heart was thumping like a newlywed's; as Leah brushed past him he noticed that she was wearing the gold earrings he'd given her for their anniversary.

That evening, in celebration of their new citizenship, they drank a bottle of wine with their dinner. Then, slightly drunk, emboldened by the wine and the events of the day, Abe led Leah to their bed. They undressed each other with trembling fingers; they felt extraordinarily naughty and nervous. It had not been so very long since sex, but an eternity since they'd made love.

They relearned each other, lingering over touch and taste. The cruel and raucous world retreated as they loved each other. Later, when they were resting, they felt renewed and reborn, dreamers ready to wipe the sleep from their eyes and face a bright morning after the passage of a long dark night.

"We must try again to have a child," Leah whispered, her sweet lips brushing his ear as they shared a pillow.

"The doctor said no more children," Abe objected.

"Doctor Glueck said no more children after this one we lost, but a loss shouldn't count," Leah was continuing, her logic exquisite. "We will have another."

"I love you so much, my Leah," Abe said, and from her delighted laugh he knew that this time she'd heard. He rose up, twisting upon her. As she moaned, her nipples rising to meet his hungry mouth, Abe felt himself grow strong again. The hope was relit inside his heart. There would be a son.

Any possibility that Haim might have written in response to Abe's appeal in the Palestine newspaper was swept away by Turkey's entry into the war. There had been only the slightest of chances in any event, assuming that the advertisement was ever run in the first place, and now that chance was shaved even slimmer. Abe doubted if correspondence could enter or leave Palestine until after the war.

The war fascinated Abe because he felt so remote from it. He bought armfuls of newspapers every day and spread them out on the counter to read during his free moments in the store. That America could ever get involved in the insanity overseas struck him as totally absurd. America was the New World. The war belonged to the old.

In April of 1915 Leah confided to Abe that she was once again pregnant. The visits to the doctor were resumed. Leah did not tell Abe that Dr. Glueck was very pessimistic.

Abe once again relegated his wife to the upstairs apartment. By day he minded the store, read his newspapers and argued current events with his customers. After the *Lusitania* was sunk, many of the people who came to his store argued with Abe that America would soon be at war.

"Never," Abe declared to them all, echoing what Stefano had told him the last time Abe delivered his building's rent receipts. "Next year comes up a Presidential election. No politician worth his salt considers a war during his campaign."

"Maybe yes, maybe no," Abe's customers would cluck.

"Take it from a United States citizen," Abe would brag. "You might as well worry about a pogrom on Cherry Street."

In June Leah had another miscarriage. This time it was not nearly as debilitating as the first, but Dr. Glueck insisted that she spend a couple of days in the hospital to be certain there were no complications.

Abe visited her both evenings. He sat by her bed and held her hand. They both said little, having known there was a strong chance this would happen. This time they could face their sorrow together.

On the second evening in the hospital, Leah squeezed Abe's hand. "We will try again."

"Of course we will."

"We will die trying." Leah mustered a look of weary determination.

"I certainly intend to." Abe leered until Leah had to beg him to stop, for it still hurt too much to laugh.

As the war progressed, the Yiddish newspapers devoted great coverage to events on the Palestine front and the exploits of Joseph Trumpeldor and Vladimir Jabotinsky. Abe read that both these men were Jews who had fought their way to respectability in Russia despite strong prejudice. Trumpeldor had done it through valor in battle, Jabotinsky through his prowess as a philosopher-writer. Neither man had allowed his own relatively comfortable circumstances blind him to the plight of his people. Both became staunch Zionists.

Their paths crossed when Jabotinsky, employed as a correspondent for a Moscow daily, went to Alexandria. His assignment was to report on the refugee camps the British set up to shelter Palestinian Zionists, but the Russian journalist had a far different personal motive. Jabotinsky's dream, according to the accounts in the Yiddish newspapers, was similar to the one the departed Trumpeldor had recently espoused but went far beyond.

Most Yiddish newspapers carried a certain photograph of Jabotinsky. The grainy black-and-white likeness revealed a slightly built clean-shaven man of indeterminate age with rather large ears and intense-looking eyes behind thick spectacles. From his picture he didn't look much like a fighter, but he must be one from what the various articles went on to say.

Jabotinsky believed that the war was the Jews' golden opportunity to forge an army of their own and earn the Allies' goodwill by helping to defeat the Central Powers. In return the Allies would endorse the postwar creation of a Jewish national home. This same army would then guarantee the security of the Jewish people. Jabotinsky dubbed his army a Jewish legion.

The newspaper articles recounted how Trumpeldor and a majority of the Palestine Refugees' Committee—the governing body—endorsed Jabotinsky's idea. Training of five hundred volunteers began immediately, with the understanding that they would fight beneath a special Zionist ensign as a British detachment in the liberation of Palestine.

Things stalled, Abe read, when General Maxwell, the British commander in Egypt, announced that an assault on Palestine was unlikely and that there was a question as to the legality of foreign nationals entering His Majesty's army.

"The best we can do," the newspapers quoted Maxwell, "is allow the Palestinians to serve in some support capacity on some other Turkish front."

Jabotinsky and others immediately rejected Maxwell's offer. Trumpeldor, however, agreed to help train the sort of unit Maxwell had in mind. Trumpeldor believed it to be better than nothing and not so different from his own far more modest concept of a symbolic Jewish presence in the war.

Under the auspices of the British Trumpeldor formed and led the six-hundred-fifty-strong Zion Mule Corps, which provided supply and artillery transport during the Gallipoli campaign.

That Trumpeldor and his volunteers worked behind the lines instead of grappling hand to hand with the Turks made little difference to Abe and his Jewish neighbors. The very idea of Jews like themselves wearing uniforms and standing side by side with soldiers from the foremost nations of Europe captured their imaginations.

The Yiddish dailies knew what sold newspapers. Until the ill-fated Gallipoli venture came to an end in the first quarter of 1916, there were articles on the subject in each issue.

Abe read them all. He convinced himself that Haim had joined the Mule Corps and was obsessed with the younger man's safety. When in February one of the dailies published a list of the corps' six casualties, Abe fully expected to see Haim's name on it and thanked God that it was not.

Throughout the rest of that year Abe kept abreast of developments in the war by reading both the Yiddish and English-language newspapers. The Yiddish papers focused a great deal of attention on Jabotinsky's lobbying efforts on behalf of a Jewish legion in the various European capitals of the Allies. Along with other Jews and Christian immigrants who realized in one form or another the horrors of a pogrom, Abe was appalled at reports of the Turkish slaughter of a million and a half Armenians, a helpless minority within the Ottoman Empire. As Germany's use of U-boats increased, more and more Americans, including Abe, began to suspect that America would be forced to step in despite President Wilson's campaign pledge to keep America out of the war.

Stefano told Abe that no President would declare a war while running. True, but what might happen after Wilson was safely returned to office was another thing entirely.

America, Abe read, had a huge economic investment in the Allies. The politicians and businessmen put forth that the nation would maintain its neutrality by selling to the Germans if they could break through the Allied naval blockade, but it was becoming clear from the slant and tone of the newspapers that this country was siding with the Allies. Suddenly Abe's Old World seemed not so far away.

In December, the election behind him, Wilson attempted a peace initiative, but the new year 1917 was an increase in German U-boat activity leading to the sinking of the British liner *Laconia* and the loss of three American lives. In February an irate United States learned of a month-old telegram from German Foreign Secretary Zimmerman to the German minister in Mexico City. This "Zimmerman Telegram," as the newspapers dubbed it, proposed a Mexican-Japanese-German alliance against the United States should she enter the war. By the end of March word of the "pro-democratic" revolution in Russia convinced many Americans that entry into the war was essential if the newborn Russian people's government was to survive. War appeared inevitable as the Germans sank three American ships.

Despite it all the newspapers were full of Wilson's efforts to keep the country neutral. Abe prayed that the President would succeed in his goals. It had been a decade since Abe entered the Russian army, but the talk of a military draft vividly brought back those dreary memories.

It does not matter what you want, Abe firmly told himself. You became a citizen, you voted, and now you must pay for that privilege if asked.

But what would become of the store, of Leah? In March she had come to him, tense, hopeful, with the news that she was two months pregnant.

Chapter 19

Degania, 1917

Early in the year the interior agricultural settlements were overwhelmed with refugees. Many were people Haim and Rosie knew from Tel Aviv. The Turks expelled nearly all the Jews from the coastal cities. Dizengoff himself, the Mayor of Tel Aviv, was deported to Damascus.

About Rosie's family there was at first no word. Then as the anxious weeks passed, rumors began to abound. Every new arrival at Degania had a different story to tell about the fate of the Glaser household, and every bearer of bad news swore that his version was the truth.

The Glasers had been deported to Egypt, to Damascus, to the interior. They had been arrested as British spies, had bought their freedom by turning in a Jewish resistance group to the Turks. They had been killed.

Rosie calmly listened to every story and did her best to believe only the more optimistic accounts. Meanwhile, there was plenty of work to keep her mind off her own troubles. The valley was filled with people who knew nothing about survival in Galilee. Degania's shelters were overcrowded and its sanitary facilities were overtaxed.

Fever began to spread. At night the settlement was filled with the moans of the sick.

Rosie worked hard in the nursery. There were many more children, and their health did not permit them to run barefoot or play outside with the thoughtless energy of Degania's own offspring.

The mural remained uncompleted, a symbol of life disrupted by war. As she endeavored to be both a teacher and a nurse to the frightened, miserable children, many of them orphans, she found herself struck several times throughout the day by the realization that her own family was lost to her. For the first time she comprehended a little of what her husband had suffered his entire life. Now both of them might be orphans.

They are not dead, and you know your mama and papa are not spies, so they could not be imprisoned, she sternly lectured herself. At the very worst they have been expelled to the camps in Alexandria or Damascus. Perhaps they are just a few miles from here at one of the other settlements.

By day her pragmatic self-assurances had weight, but at night, when the sick called out from their flimsy tents and the children, stirring in their nightmare-ridden sleep, wailed so loudly that the jackals in the hills picked up and returned their cries, Rosie could believe the worst. In a world turned upside down by war, a world where the children of once-prosperous Tel Aviv families now wandered pitifully thin and dressed in rags, her parents could well be languishing in a filthy Turkish prison. Her brothers might be forced into the Turkish army and her sisters scattered among the harems of the pashas.

Or somewhere in Jaffa there could be a public square where the bodies were hanging from their heels, half-eaten by buzzing flies, innocent victims of the Turks' anglophobia.

In May a new evacuee presented Rosie with a tattered

envelope that had passed through many hands on its way to Degania. It was a letter from her father. The Glasers were alive and well in Jaffa. Despite their British origins and their religion the Glasers' long-standing relationship with the Turkish authorities had earned them as much goodwill as was possible in the circumstances. That they had never moved from their inn in Jaffa to the Jewish city of Tel Aviv was also in their favor. The Turks promised the Glasers protection and allowed them and a few other remaining Jews to set up a committee and watchmen's group to protect the evacuees' property. For the next few days the children at the nursery wondered why Rosie would suddenly begin to weep.

Haim admired the strength his wife had shown. The land had molded Rosie's character, turned her from a spoiled rich girl into an indomitable heroine of the Zionist struggle.

There had been a cost. Strands of grey had appeared in Rosie's hair and lines were beginning to deepen at the corners of her sable eyes. The soft, dewy-skinned, laughing sprite had been worn down by the wind and sand, as everything was eroded in Galilee. Her laughter was rare, replaced by only the faintest of smiles at the corners of her mouth and by the slightest glint in her eyes. Her curves had shrunk to gauntness. Her slender, graceful fingers were knotted with scars, rough with calluses.

The changes saddened Haim, but he loved his Rosie none the less for the changes worked upon her. In fact he loved her more, if that was possible, and for a curious reason. She had become the practical one of their family. These days it was Rosie, not he, who made decisions by logic as opposed to emotions. Perhaps it had always been that way; perhaps she had always been the responsible one.

Haim found himself thinking about Abe a great deal, at work and in the evenings while playing with his son. He told Herschel about Abe and his own boyhood in Russia—as much about it as a six-year-old boy could be expected to understand. He often showed Herschel the portrait of himself and Abe.

"That man is your grandfather," Haim told his son. "I lived to be a man thanks to him, and you have descended from me. The two of us are the result of that man's kindness toward a ragged orphan many years ago in Russia."

"Orphans like the children here in Degania?" Herschel asked his father, his eyes wide as his young mind made the connections.

"The same, my son. Galilee has become very much like the Russia of my boyhood."

Haim told Herschel nothing more. He hoped the war would end before the boy was old enough to form strong memories. There was no need for his son to comprehend just how much progress had been rolled back for the halutzim of Degania.

First there was the amount of work to be done. Systems of crop rotation had been devised by the various agricultural settlements to bring about the replenishment of the soil. With the coming of war and the subsequent cutoff of Palestine's ability to import food from the Allied nations, a bread shortage developed. Every settlement set to work growing as much grain as possible, and only grain, so that in a short while the beneficial effects of crop rotation were reversed and the soil was again depleted.

Now, three years after the war came to Palestine, the bread supply was meager and its quality poor. It was supplemented by only a few eggs and not much milk, a diet not so different from what peasant Jews had been forced to live on in Russia.

This sort of farming called for every worker with the least knowledge of agriculture to go out to the fields. It was difficult to maintain the proper Zionist spirit when one labored hard all day only to return at night to a settlement made intolerable by overcrowding. Soon it would be another rainy season, and once again Degania's carefully laid paths would be churned to mud by too many feet. The evacuees would complain about discomfort and lack of food, not understanding how difficult it was to wrest anything from unyielding Galilee.

At such times it was hard for Haim and the others who belonged to Degania to remember that they were all Jews and ought to band together. As in Russia, the Jews could not afford to be their own worst enemy, and as in Russia, there was somebody to remind them of that fact.

Several times since the beginning of the war Degania had been overrun by detachments of Turkish troops. Sullen, arrogant soldiers in Prussian-inspired khaki tunics and tropical helmets would march through the gates, ominously silent except for the stomp of leather boots, the creak of equipment belts and the rattle of bayonets.

Degania had seen to it that its own few were in a safe place. The guns would be uncovered and turned on the Turks when the British came.

Despite the fact that Degania was behind Turkish lines, news from the outside world did occasionally get through. It was known that the British were advancing from the south toward Jerusalem and that the glorious, long-awaited people's revolution had taken place in Russia. The future once again held promise. For now, however, the Turks ruled.

Each time they invaded it was the same. First the storehouses, granaries and kitchens would be stripped and the people driven out of the buildings to make room for the soldiers. Then the interrogations and tortures would begin.

Haim went through it once. They took him to the dining hall and tied him on his back on one of the long tables so that his feet hung over the edge. Then they slowly removed his shoes and stockings, all the while questioning him about the whereabouts of Degania's hidden money, British spies, arms caches.

Then they beat him on the soles of his bare feet with the flat of a sword.

What went far beyond the physical pain was having the torture take place in such fondly remembered surroundings. As Haim was being beaten, he found himself gazing at Rosie's partially completed wall mural.

Money, the Turks demanded. British spies, guns. The soldiers would leave off for a bit and then the beating would resume.

Haim kept himself docile by thinking of his son. If I insult these bastards they'll kill me and my boy will be an orphan, he reminded himself.

When it was over Haim had no memory of screaming, but the others said he had, and Haim didn't doubt them. Others screamed as well, and helplessly listening to their anguish seemed as bad the torture itself.

The Turks always confined their interrogations to the male members of the kibbutz. There was an epidemic of fever going around the evacuees. The Turks, not wanting to expose themselves to it, left that group alone, and Degania's women, aware of the Turks' fastidiousness, always announced to the officers that they had been nursing the sick. The officers would invariably issue an order for their soldiers to leave the women alone.

There was no protection for the men. The soldiers would round them up and jail all of them in one building. They would huddle together, singing songs and nervously joking in a futile attempt to drown out the screams coming from the dining hall.

The Turks always left after a week. There were plenty of other settlements to raid. The physical injuries they inflicted eventually healed, but the shame endured.

*   *   *

One September day while working along the edge of a field bordered by rocks, Haim heard somebody calling him by name. There was an Arab boy close by, peering out at him from behind a limestone boulder.

"A friend has sent me," the boy said in Arabic. He looked to be eleven or twelve, wizened by malnutrition. He had close-cropped bristles of hair and sunken onyx-black eyes.

Haim glanced around. His nearest coworker was about fifty meters away and had not heard the boy. The closest thing to a weapon Haim had was his hoe. He kept a tight grip on it in case he was being set up for an ambush.

The boy seemed to read his mind. "Don't be afraid. I am to lead you to your friend, that's all." His hollow-cheeked grin looked disconcertingly skull-like. He was wearing a baggy striped caftan, ludicrously large for him. The fabric draped his skeletal frame like a collapsed tent around its pole.

That the boy knew his name meant nothing. Haim was well known to the fellahin of Um Jumi. He approached, but cautiously. The Arab was a skinny little nothing, but who wasn't these days? He didn't look like he belonged to the Bedouins, and it wasn't like the Bedouins to lure a man into an ambush for no reason. They wouldn't expect a field worker to be carrying anything of value. Anyway, the Bedouins had made themselves scarce since the Turks came.

Haim followed the boy as best he could, but he had to walk around the boulders while the boy capered up and over the silvery limestone like a lizard. Haim soon found himself out of the line of sight of the other field workers. The boy cut across a bone-dry wadi whose surrounding vegetation was as shriveled as dried sponges. In just a few months, when the rains came, all this dusty marl would turn to mud and the scrub would swell and turn green.

"There."

The boy pointed his pencil-thin finger at a Bedouin in striped caftan and black coat. The man was slouched against a large stone, a rifle across his knees. The man's kaffiyeh was drawn across the lower portion of his face, obscuring his features.

The hoe fell to the ground as Haim eyed the man's rifle. He spread his fingers wide and raised his hands above his head. "I have nothing of value," he called in Arabic. "Have the boy search me if you like."

"All I want is my comrade's embrace," the Bedouin said in Hebrew.

Haim stared. *That voice*—"Yol? That's you?"

The kaffiyeh fell away as Yol leaned his rifle against the stone and got to his feet. Time had put some grey in his beard and he looked very thin and weathered but also fit and healthy. In all he seemed to be in far better condition than on that January night four years ago when he departed Degania with his burden of guilt.

"I'm very glad to see you," Yol murmured as the two men embraced.

"Everyone will be glad to see you," Haim laughed. He held on to his friend as if he might vanish. "Especially, in that getup you're wearing. I swear, little monkey, you had me totally fooled."

Yol pulled back. "I can't return with you to the settlement."

"What?"

"I've come for you," Yol replied. "Haim, go back to your work. Tonight after supper tell Rosie you want to go for a walk and—" He stopped. "But you must tell me. How are she and Herschel? The boy is well?"

"Everyone is fine, and Herschel is almost bigger than you, little monkey. You're welcome at Degania, Yol. You're still a member; there's no need to worry."

"You don't understand, but you will after tonight if you'll meet Jibarn"—he gestured toward the Arab boy waiting patiently—"just beyond Degania's gate. He'll lead you to my campsite. Will you come?"

Haim made a face, then shrugged. "Of course I'll come, although I still say you're being foolish."

"Remember, no one must know I'm back," Yol warned. "Now go back to work before the others miss you and come searching. It'd be just my luck to be stoned for a Bedouin."

Haim reluctantly started back. "Tonight? You'll be here?"

"Absolutely. I'm not a ghost, you know."

"And I'm not dreaming." Haim grinned. "You're really back."

The rest of the day crawled by. He could not imagine the reason for Yol's mysterious behavior. He hardly heard the conversations during supper. He just stared at his plate, pushing the food around with his fork. Several times he glanced up to see Rosie watching him.

At last the meal was over and Haim and his family were strolling back to the cottage in the twilight. "I think I'll go for a walk," Haim began.

Herschel, walking beside his father, tugged at Haim's fingers. "Take me, Papa."

"We'll all go," Rosie agreed.

"Well, I'd like to go by myself."

"By yourself," Rosie repeated, her expression deadpan.

"Yes."

"Haim, you want to tell me what's going on with you? What is this new silliness?"

"Rosie, don't talk that way to me." Haim glared at his wife, the anger raging within him. Lately there had been an almost imperceptible but definite change in Rosie's attitude. He saw the change in the way she looked at him; it was evident when she listened to him speak, obvious when she replied.

It was a mixture of impatience, aloofness and maybe

even a little contempt. Their lovemaking banished it for a
time, but always it returned. It chilled Haim the way her
wide, sensual mouth hardened into a thin line, while her
warm gaze cooled to an icy, impenetrable sheen.

"I'll see you in a little while." Haim made his voice
calm so as not to upset Herschel, who was anxiously
peering up at his parents.

"Maybe later you can confide in your wife," Rosie
said through clenched teeth. She'd been on the verge of
apologizing, but she was losing her temper all over again
to what she perceived to be his insolent indifference. "Go,
do what you want. Your son and I will go home."

Why does this happen? she wondered. How have I
changed? He's a good man, but I constantly hurt him.

It was the war that was mostly to blame, she believed,
the war and the way it had ravaged Degania. She had
gotten used to the spartan, self-sufficient kibbutz way of
life and had learned to love the harsh, rugged splendor of
Galilee, but this valley was no place for the sick and the
weak. The evacuees were turning this rough-hewn paradise
into hell. How much longer could the membership provide
for so many helpless people? And if Degania collapsed,
what then?

There was the Turkish menace too. Those periods of
occupation sapped her spirit more than anything. You had
to contain your hatred of the soldiers if you wanted to
survive. When they came to torture the men, to spread
their filth throughout the cottages, to take the food out of
the mouths of hungry children, you had to make yourself
go numb inside. Denial of the bitterness was the only way
to keep it from eating away your heart.

"Mama?" Herschel whispered fearfully. "Don't cry."

Rosie bent low to hug her son. "Come on." She
forced brightness into her voice. "We'll go home and wait
for Papa."

The danger of shutting out your hatred is that you also shut out the other emotions, Rosie thought on the way home.

Haim began to calm down as soon as he'd passed through the gate. The setting sun gave the hills a purple glow, while the distance made their barren turns look as soft as pillows. He stood awhile, letting the cool night breezes wash away the last vestiges of his anger. Then he walked on until he'd turned the bend in the road that put Degania out of sight behind him.

No lanterns were lit in the compound at night. The Turks had confiscated all the kerosene. In a little while one of the night watchmen would light a torch to mark the gate, but for now the countryside was as dark as God had created it. Haim listened to the crickets massed along the reedy banks of the Kinneret and the cawing of the black-birds settling down for the night in the fields.

Then from someplace very near came the summons from Yol's little Arab runner. Haim moved toward the sound until the boy's form detached itself from a black and twisted shape that turned out to be the stump of a gnarled carob tree.

"Not so fast this time," Haim cautioned the boy. "I'll lose you in the dark."

"All right." The boy obediently stayed at Haim's side. "It is not so far."

"Your name is Jibarn, yes?"

The boy nodded.

"And your surname? The name of your father?"

"I have no father. Yol will answer all your questions, I do think."

Jibarn led him through a limestone gorge. Haim smelled burning wood and a moment later caught sight of a small, flickering fire surrounded by stones. Here was Yol's camp. Several blankets were spread out upon the dust beside the

barest trickle of a stream overgrown with cattails. Haim
thought he heard a mule's soft, nervous whinny.

The site was deserted. Haim was about to ask Jibarn
where Yol was when his old comrade, still in Bedouin
garb, stepped from the shadows.

"I heard you coming," Yol said. "Of course I expected you, but—"

"We came very quietly," Haim said. He smiled
approvingly. "You've learned a great deal since you left.
Tell me everything."

"Of course, but first please sit." Yol indicated the
blankets. "I will brew us some tea."

As Haim took a place near the fire he saw Jibarn
wander off into the darkness and he glanced inquiringly at
Yol, who smiled and shrugged.

"Jibarn does not care to be still for very long. He will
patrol the area and if intruders approach, either warn us or
take appropriate action to stop them."

"That little beanpole?" Haim chuckled.

"Jibarn has slit half a dozen Turkish throats in the
last two years," Yol said, scooping some water from the
stream into a small pot. He added a handful of tea and set
the utensil on the fire.

"Something tells me my old friend has changed since
his Degania days."

"Somewhat." Yol smiled modestly.

"How did Jibarn come to join you?"

"I'll start at the beginning. When I left you on that
winter's night in 1913, it was my plan to journey to Um
Jumi and from there take the boat to Tiberias. Well, the
boat was delayed for several nights. I found myself stuck
in the last place on earth I'd wanted to be, the village of
the dead shepherd. At first I despaired, but gradually
perverse curiosity got the better of me. I was well known
in Um Jumi, so it was not hard for me to have a talk with

the mayor. I asked him if the shepherd had left any family."

"Oh, no, Yol."

"The headman told me the shepherd—his name was Mohammed Ahmed, by the way—had only a grandson, a boy named Jibarn no more than eight years old.

" 'Then he is an oprhan, this Jibarn?' I asked. The headman nodded and told me that all that could be done for the boy would be done, but— Well, Haim, you've seen the miserable existence the most well-to-do fellahin lead."

Haim nodded. The boy would have been doomed to an early death, there was no question of that.

The tea was ready. Yol poured it into two small brass cups and set one before Haim.

"I went to see Jibarn," Yol continued. "I stayed several nights with him in his grandfather's hut. In my mind I was appeasing the old man's ghost. The boatmen came to tell me they were leaving for Tiberias, but now I was not ready. I ended up staying in Um Jumi for a month. Little by little I got Jibarn to trust me. Then one night I told him what had happened to his grandfather."

"Yol," Haim gasped, "You didn't! You risked a blood feud?"

"There was no chance of that," Yol declared. "I was right there in the village. The fellahin could have executed me and closed the matter if Jibarn had chosen to speak out."

"You put your trust in an eight-year-old Arab?"

"I prefer to think that I put my trust in God," Yol said earnestly. "Jibarn was only the instrument God might have used to punish me had that been His decision."

Haim nodded. "But obviously it wasn't."

Yol smiled. "Jibarn listened, as silent and intent as an owl, as I stumbled through my halting explanation. It was quite strange, Haim, quite cathartic." His tone was distant as he remembered. "Jibarn has always been precocious. He's an odd boy—"

"That I've noticed."

"Well, he was even more that way when he was younger. Sometime during that confession I broke into tears. Suddenly it was as if he was the man and I the little boy. He put his arms around me as best he could and told me that from now on we belonged to each other."

"I shouldn't doubt that he saw it that way."

"I thought you'd understand," Yol snapped, suddenly angry. "I thought you of all people would understand about an orphan who needed somebody to take care of him and a man who needed somebody to care for in order to absolve his own grief."

Haim was ashamed. Many years ago, when he and Yol first met and were sharing living quarters as stonecutters in Jerusalem, he had told the story of himself and Abe. Yol was indeed right. He of all people should have understood.

"I'm sorry," he said. "It's the war perhaps. I've seen so many orphans. I guess I've forgotten—or want to deny my own origins."

Yol patted his hand and for a moment Haim caught a glimpse of the warm-hearted jokester his friend had once been.

"So I take it that Jibarn left Um Jumi with you?"

Yol nodded. "The mayor did not hesitate to put him into my care. The boy and I wandered together, working on farms and in the towns. We stayed a good long time in Jerusalem. Jibarn had always wanted to visit the Holy City. It was my great pleasure to show it to him. I taught him Hebrew and all about Zionism. Together we both learned a bit of English. I also enrolled him in a mosque school so he could learn his own religion. It was not my intention to turn him into some sort of mockery of a Jew. I owed it to his grandfather to raise him to be true to his own God.''

Haim was quiet for a few moments. He realized his tea had gone untouched and was now cold. He had been too engrossed in Yol's story to drink it.

''Do you love this boy as your son? I must know, Yol, so that I don't further insult you . . . I mean, he is an Arab, and I must learn to think of him differently if I am not to offend you.''

''He is not my son, Haim. Our relationship is based on debt. I killed his grandfather and now I take care of him. Do I love him? I suppose I do, but indirectly I am loving myself—or rather, I can consider myself worthy of living because of what I do for Jibarn. If he loves me I can't say. He is an Arab, after all, and sees and feels differently than we do.''

''You mentioned that Jibarn has killed Turks?''

''Absolutely, and so have I. So shall you if you choose to join us. Eighteen months ago Jibarn and I linked up with a number of Hashomer. The Watchmen are skilled horsemen; they speak Arabic and know how to live in the wild. I daresay they've battled Bedouins for so long they've come to think and act like nomads.'' Yol winked. ''That's why I'm dressed up like a Bedouin. If you were to cross the Jordan and journey about six kilometers, you would find an encampment of forty mounted men similarly dressed, but every man of them is a Jew and all members of the Hashomer, as I now am, I might add.''

''You're a raiding party?''

''Like the Britisher Lawrence with his Arabs to the south of us,'' Yol agreed. ''We do what we can to harass the Turks. We cross the Jordan, hit them and retreat before they can organize a defense. The Turks are convinced that we are nomads, so there is no danger of retribution against the settlements.''

''Until one of your band is captured or killed,'' Haim

pointed out. "Then the Turks will see quite well that you
are no Bedouin tribe."

"But so far they've not caught or killed any of us." Yol
shrugged. "It's a chance we're willing to take. The British
have Jerusalem; Jaffa may soon fall. The Allies are
slowly advancing, but the rains are coming. The mud may
do what the Turks cannot—stop the British in their tracks.
When the roads dry the British will again advance, and it
is our hope to have sufficiently weakened key Turkish
positions to make that advance all the easier."

Haim made a face. "And you've come to ask me to
join you?"

"I've come to offer you the opportunity to join us,
old friend. The Hashomer will accept you at my behest.
Jibarn, you see, fights with us but is loyal to me. An Arab
boy is a great help to a band of Jews desiring to appear to
be Bedouins. He is talented at stealth, and on the rare
occasions when he is discovered, his appearance and charm
usually persuade the soldier to lower his guard. That's
when Jibarn's knife does its work."

Haim shuddered. "This is a thirteen-year-old boy
you've turned into a killer."

Yol shook his head. "I've not done anything of the
kind, but perhaps the world has, just as it's made a killer
of me. Jibarn is an Arab, and they hate the Turks as much
as we do. Anyway, he won't be thirteen until next year."

"All the worse, Yol. My Herschel is going to be
seven. Would you like to recruit him?"

Yol took a deep breath to control his temper. "What I
would like to do," he began quietly, "is offer Herschel's
father an opportunity to fight for his homeland."

"The British are doing well without our help—"

"*I* wouldn't do it just for the British," Yol said.
"*I'm* doing it for myself. I think any Jewish man who
does not fight for Palestine in its time of need is going to
be heartsick for the rest of his life."

Haim nodded, acknowledging the truth. "You know, sometimes we get news at Degania. Maybe a Jewish soldier in the Turkish army will tell us something, or somebody passing through has seen a newspaper. One way or another a little news reaches us. Last month we heard that Jabotinsky has finally persuaded Weizmann to go along with his idea for a Jewish legion and that Weizmann has changed the British mind about it."

Yol shrugged. "You hear more than we do. We can't make contact with any of the settlements for obvious reasons. But if Weizmann is behind the idea, then the entire Zionist Federation has come around to it."

"This fellow who brought us the news also said the Allies were about to announce something big. He didn't know what, but he thinks it has something to do with the British Foreign Secretary, Balfour, and his country's turn-around on the legion."

"I don't know about any of that," Yol said, "but I did hear about Trumpeldor's Gallipoli venture."

"He asked me to go with him," Haim said, "after you left. I should have gone."

"And if you had, you'd have been covered with mule shit and your back scarred by a British whip. They flogged the Jews, you know, whipped them as if they were no better than the mules."

"At least the Jews in the Mule Corps earned some respect. You said it yourself, Yol. Nobody knows about you and your Hashomer friends. The Bedouins you pretend to be will most likely get the credit for your victories."

"I'll let Ruppin and Weizmann worry about such matters," Yol replied. "I'm for the Allies, my friend, but I have no confidence in the British letting us fight alongside them. They'll have this Jewish legion—if it ever comes about—learning how to parade for the rest of the war. I don't know about you, but I'd rather kill Turks than learn to salute."

"*Would* you?" Haim did not want to look his friend in the eye. "Monkey man, I'm afraid."

"Nothing wrong with that. Everyone's afraid."

"Not like me. I hate the Turks. They beat me last time they were here, Yol. I want to kill them, but I'm afraid I'll be killed. I want to fight, but I'm afraid to fight. I'm afraid for Herschel's sake—"

"Stop," Yol commanded. "Don't carry on so. You don't owe me any explanations." He paused. "Remember that last night together in Jerusalem? I was for Kinnereth and you were going to Jaffa to court Rosie Glaser. I told you marriage would change your dreams."

"Rosie has changed me," Haim admitted, smiling ruefully. "She's taught me to think twice. I enjoyed life more when I didn't think so much, and I think Rosie liked me better that way as well. She seems disappointed these days."

Yol looked away, embarrassed and helpless to advise his friend. "In a week I will send Jibarn to this spot. I don't want to risk him any closer to the kibbutz. Can you find your way back here alone?"

"I could."

Yol smiled. "Well, you've got a week to decide if you want to. Jibarn will be here with a mule and suitable clothing. You speak Arabic, can pass as an Arab and will be with the boy, so nobody will bother you. Jibarn will wait until dawn and then return to the Hashomer camp. If you are with him, all well and good. If not, then I say farewell to you, my friend, until this war is over and we can drink wine and joke together like we did in the old days."

Haim got to his feet. "Maybe I'll come at that."

At one time Yol's dark eyes would have glinted with sarcasm, but now he made no jokes at Haim's expense. He just nodded, the picture of equanimity, and began to gather up the teacups and tiny pot.

*   *   *

As Haim walked back to the settlement, he sensed an accompanying presence somewhere in the dark. "Jibarn?" he called.

There was no answer. Haim scanned the rocks but saw nothing. That was hardly surprising. An army, let alone one boy, could hide itself in those crags and shadows.

He walked on, concentrating now, and picked up the faint scratching sounds of the boy's fingers and toes scrabbling for purchase against the limestone. Now and again there was a rattle, dry as old bones, when a pebble came loose.

Why is he playing this game with me? Haim wondered. There was nothing good-natured about it. This was a stalk.

The moon rose and cast a ghastly pallor over the twisted, primitive landscape. Haim, searching for a glimpse of the boy, neglected to watch where he was putting his feet. He tripped on a stone and staggered forward for several steps before regaining his balance.

The boy's high-pitched trill of laughter wafted through the night, nasty music. Haim hurried on.

He's slit half a dozen Turkish throats—a twelve-year-old boy. And he's frightened me half to death tonight, Haim mused. If Jibarn were not within Yol's protection I would—

Would what? He's a twelve-year-old boy, an orphan like yourself. Are you so afraid of fighting the Turks you'd kill a boy?

As he rounded the bend that put the torch-lit gate within sight, he heard Jibarn's call. "Next week then, Allah willing."

Haim neither replied nor turned around. He lowered his head and hurried toward the light and safety of Degania. Next week was next week. Tonight he wanted his own bed.

*   *   *

Seven days—they lasted forever and passed quickly, like predawn hours spent in fitful sleep. Three days to make up his mind, then two, then one—Haim still did not know what to do. He had until tomorrow dawn to decide. By the next sunrise Jibarn would be on his way back to the Hashomer camp and Haim's opportunity to join them would be gone.

That day he found himself volunteering to work in the tack room. The cool dark was redolent with the rich smell of well-worn leather. Haim was seized with a sense of tranquility. Working with his hands had a way of shrinking problems down to size. Haim took down a harness from its peg, laid it out on the rough worktable and began to clean it. His mind filled with memories of all the many things he disliked doing but had accomplished for a good purpose.

He left his beloved Abe to come to Palestine. He made friends with Dizengoff—and profited by it—to appease Rosie and for the same reason built up a fine business, the profits from which would someday go to his son and any other children of his. On that terrible night when Moshe was missing he answered Yol's call for a volunteer to go with him and Trumpeldor and conduct the search.

"And now I am asked to go to war," he told Abe, whose presence he had conjured up via the feel of the leather and scent of the polish. "No, you needn't scold me. I know you would never willingly fight, but I also know you would do so if you had to." After receiving a startled look through the door from a passing stranger, Haim continued silently.

While you might be angry with me for volunteering, I think you would also secretly approve a little. It was that way when I left you to come to Palestine. You wanted me to go with you to America, but still you gave me money. You did it out of love, I know, but also I think you were proud—sorry to see me go but proud that I dared.

Abe, I wish you could meet Rosie. She is so much like you.

Haim spent the rest of the day working in the tack room. He was at last in peace. His decision was made.

He waited until late that night after he and Rosie had made love to tell her that he was leaving. In this he was being selfish, he knew. He wanted his wife to give herself freely so he could memorize every nuance of their passion to sustain his soul through the long nights to come. He had another, more earnest reason for waiting: their lovemaking momentarily healed the rift between them. It was impera-tive that he and Rosie be as close to one another now as they were in the old days if she was to understand.

She listened quietly. The sheen of sweat they'd worked up through their hushed, sweet tussle dried fast in the cool night air. Ordinarily she'd have cuddled against him, but now she remained uncomfortably cold and stiff upon the damp, twisted sheets as she listened. Haim's day's growth of beard rubbed against her cheek and his breath tickled her ear in an insane parody of romantic intimacy as he whispered of their imminent separation.

As she listened she harbored fury as white-hot as Galilee's pale disk of a sun in July. She found herself hating Haim as well. All this nonsense about Palestine and Zionism—he was doing it for himself, running off to join a bunch of irresponsible dreamers. He would get himself killed in the process.

She stared into the darkness, listening to the rhythmic breathing of her sleeping son as well as to her husband. He had to go tonight, he was saying—within an hour or two. Was he planning to disappear without explaining to Herschel? Was he going to gather his things and sneak out of his son's life?

"You're just angry because the Turks beat you," Rosie hissed at last. "This whole crazy notion is just revenge for that. I suggest you get over your sulk and put this nonsense out of your mind.''

The ferocity of her response surprised her. *Acting like a shrew is not going to keep him by your side,* she admonished herself. *Somehow I must understand what is going on inside him.*

''Rosie,'' Haim whispered, ''as the British advance, the Turks will retreat north, toward Galilee. They will occupy Degania. If I'm here when they arrive, one of two things will happen. Either they'll kill me for defying them or our love will die because I've submitted.''

''That is the craziest thing—''

''It may be crazy, but it is true. You fell in love with a man who thought nothing of defying the Turkish immigration officer who slapped you—don't you remember that day on Jaffa beach, my love? I was with your father when it happened. I ran to you—''

''And I told you then that what Palestine needed were live Jews, not dead ones.'' Her tone softened. ''You were so brave.''

Haim smiled to himself in the darkness. ''And you loved me for it; I know you did, Rosie. Deny it if I'm wrong. I know you can't lie to me.''

''I can't.'' She felt his arms slide around her and then she was sobbing against his chest, for she began to comprehend what had been causing such trouble between them and realized why he had to go.

''It's so foolish,'' she mourned as Haim stroked her hair.

Haim felt her warm tears running down his bare chest. He hugged her tight, marveling that he could think of leaving her and that his very decision had healed the breach.

''It isn't smart or foolish or good or bad,'' he whispered. ''You need a man you can respect and I need to conquer my fear. There was a time I was not afraid to try anything. That's the man you fell in love with and married and that's the man I must try to be again."

"What about Herschel?"

"I'll wake him before I go."

Rosie smiled. "He'll say, 'Papa take me with you; I'll help you fight.'"

Haim thought of Jibarn, creeping through the darkness with a knife between his teeth, and shuddered. "I'll talk to him. Somehow I'll make him understand."

"But there is time before that?" Rosie asked.

"There is," Haim said, and drew the coverlet over them.

Chapter 20

September marked Leah's eighth month of pregnancy. She and Abe had progressed from guarded optimism to delirious joy as she moved closer to term. Even Glueck's usually dour mood brightened as she entered her third trimester. "I guess practice does make perfect," he found it within himself to quip.

The physician was coming to see her once a fortnight now. Leah, her belly swollen and hard, was a queen bee, rarely moving from her bed in the upstairs apartment. Abe fussed over her, and his careful, awed attention pleased her no end.

She felt voluptuous and womanly as she dreamed the days away, her hands caressing her swelling breasts. At last, Leah thought, after so much trying, I'm proving myself as good a wife as Sadie, as any woman.

Every night Abe would kneel beside her on the mattress, his ear pressed against her abdomen and his fingers gently, wondrously exploring.

"Listen, feel!" he'd laugh, astounded. "The boy is dancing around already. For his wedding he's practicing."

322

Leah would smile approvingly, quite satisfied. Very late, after Abe had fallen asleep and she was dozing, she would journey inside herself to join hands with her baby and wheel around in a dance of life that made her feel like the Mother of the world.

The baby made her as physically miserable as proud. She suffered morning sickness the equal of her seasickness during the Atlantic crossing. She had cramps, not in her belly, thank God, but in her legs. The little walking she managed to do made her ankles swell and her back ache. She was quite content to take Glueck's advice when he decreed that she stay in bed. "Being pregnant is about as much as a skinny little girl like you ought to handle," he insisted.

Glueck took Abe aside on one of his visits to the apartment and suggested that arrangements be made for Leah to deliver at the hospital with an obstetrician in attendance. "There could be complications," he explained. "Your wife has very narrow hips. The baby may not be able to move through the birth canal."

It was all Abe could do to listen without fainting. On the edge of Glueck's explanation was the possibility that the doctors would have to cut his Leah, cut her!

Leah begged and pleaded to have her baby at home, but Abe was adamant. Glueck himself was reluctant to deliver, and they must not force him. She would go to Gouverneur. Abe had money enough to pay her way there, if not at the expensive Jewish hospitals. She would not be in a ward and she would have a good doctor, but she would be in Gouverneur despite the unhappy memories the place held for her.

The obstetrician who saw Leah on her preliminary visit was a young Irish Catholic named Henderson. He had the lightest coloring of any human being Abe and Leah had ever seen. The first time she laid eyes on Dr. Henderson's ash blond hair and fish-belly complexion she burst into tears. Haim excused his wife's behavior to the startled physician and led Leah outside into the hospital corridor to ask what was wrong.

"Abe," she sobbed, "how can I let that goy touch me? He's got white eyelashes."

In time both Abe and Leah came to think the world of Dr. Henderson. Despite his religion and strange appearance he was conscientious and compassionate. He did all he could to put them at ease. He even invited them to ask questions.

Abe and Leah politely thanked Henderson and assured him that they had no questions. It did no good for Abe to remind himself that he'd been in America for a decade and was a citizen; when speaking to a big man like Henderson, his accent seemed to thicken, his clothing became absurd, and for all practical purposes he felt like a greenhorn just off the boat. As for Leah, whenever Henderson examined her she just squeezed her eyes shut and thought about what to make for dinner that night.

With Henderson taking care of Leah and the bed in the hospital bought and paid for, Abe had nothing to do but wait for the birth while he ran the store, and that was fairly routine. Most of the goods Abe had once fetched from the wholesalers now were delivered. Business was good, although the talk around the wholesale markets and from the delivery men was that the United States' entry into the war would soon affect the supplies of groceries available.

Last June Abe and millions of his fellow citizens reported to local polling places to register for the draft. The dark, stuffy basement of Public School 31 was crammed with newly naturalized men who were bewildered with the bureaucratic process. The officials running the board seemed just as confused and clearly were frustrated with their slim pickings, for on the Lower East Side it tended to be mostly older men who had been in the country long enough to be naturalized. In the confusion Abe, who could speak English and who though over forty seemed a youngster compared to the long white beards all around him, found himself scheduled for a preinduction medical examination.

He was unable to sleep the night before the ordeal. What would happen to him? Abe had never been examined by a doctor in his life, except for the cursory look they'd taken before letting him into the country.

He came home from the examination clutching an exemption certificate. The doctor told him he had a heart murmur. The word "heart" he knew. He also understood that a "murmur" was like a whisper, but what the two words meant together he had no idea. He decided to ignore the whole thing, and told everyone that he was exempt due to his age.

The 4-F certificate was proudly displayed in the store's front window, where it never failed to provoke gales of laughter from Stefano de Fazio, who had begun to stop by Cherry Street on a regular basis. Stefano had left his union post and opened an office on the Hudson River docks, where he had part ownership in a warehouse.

Abe had no idea why a man as prosperous and important as Stefano de Fazio enjoyed hanging around a modest grocery store. When he visited, a sleek black Pierce-Arrow waited for him at curbside. Behind the wheel slouched a fellow with a tough look about him despite his suit and tie. The car was really something to see.

Stefano, fatter than ever, his mustache and thick head of curls completely grey, would come in and go directly upstairs to see Leah. He never failed to bring her candy or flowers. He'd come back down, slap Abe on the back and help himself to some fruit. Then he'd toss his expensive pin-striped suit coat behind the counter, loosen his tie, roll up the sleeves of his silk shirt and help put the tins on the shelves.

The whole notion of Stefano acting the stockboy at

first confounded Abe. Here was a man who hobnobbed with important people—Stefano's name was always in the newspaper financial columns, and once the papers published a photograph of him shaking George M. Cohan's hand at a Liberty Bond rally in front of the great entertainer's own theater in Times Square.

So why is he hanging around making small talk and dusting my stock? Abe found himself wondering.

Stefano did own the place. At first Abe feared Stefano was coming around to break the news that he was going to sell the building. When Abe finally worked up enough nerve to ask about that possibility, Stefano laughed and promised that he would not sell for a long time, if ever.

"I like this store," Stefano said. "I like owning a piece of this old neighborhood, and I like having you around, Abe. You know what you are? You're my good luck charm. When I was nothing I came to you and asked that you trust me with your savings—and you did. You trusted a little shit like me."

"I knew you had good intentions," Abe shyly said.

"That's true, I did," Stefano nodded thoughtfully. "You know, the union changed as it got bigger. Sometimes I had to do things, or have things done, that weren't very nice." He grinned. "But when I come here I get to see some of the old guys from Allen Street. I get to relax and enjoy myself. That's why I come here and that's why I wouldn't sell this old tenement. Now where do you want the canned peaches?"

Once Abe knew the visits were nothing more than they seemed, he began to relax. With Leah upstairs the two men had ample time alone to talk, or rather for Stefano to talk and Abe to listen.

"I had to get out of the union," Stefano began one day. "I love this country very much, Abe. I love what it stands for. When we started the union it was to get the workers their fair share, but now with that damned revolution in

Russia there's guys—mostly Jewish guys, you'll pardon
me for saying—who think America oughta be socialist.
That's not for a guy like me. I mean, there's got to be
workers and there's got to be bosses—and you know I
stood up to the manufacturers in 1910?''

Abe did indeed know that. ''Everybody in America
has the opportunity to improve his situation.''

''Yeah, exactly right,'' Stefano said excitedly. ''Look
at me. I was a presser, and then I held union office, and
now I got property and part ownership in a warehouse on
the Hudson. And this week I'm closing on two more
facilities, one in Brooklyn and one on the Jersey side of the
river. A guy like me would still be a presser in the old
country.''

''Maybe not.''

Stefano beamed. ''You stick with me. Whenever you're
ready I'll find something better than this market for you to
run.''

''I thought you liked this store.''

''I do, but you gotta grow with the times, Abe. You
gotta be always thinking, always looking for a way to
make a buck. Just last week I put a guy I knew from my
union days—a manufacturer of hosiery—in touch with one
of Uncle Sam's buyers on the War Service Board. That
guy's now making socks for our doughboys. The finished
goods go to my warehouse in my trucks. I got the right
connections with the Teamsters to make sure everything
goes smooth at that end. I also lent the guy some money to
get extra knitting machines so he can fill his new orders. So
now I got a piece of a sock company along with everything
else.''

''I don't know, Stefano,'' Abe sighed. ''When you
explain it, it sounds easy. I just don't know how to do it
for myself. Maybe after my son is older and I teach him
the grocery business, the two of us can move on to something bigger.''

"It's always a son with you," Stefano chuckled. "God makes daughters too, you know. There's nothing wrong with a nice little girl."

"You can say that. You already have sons."

"You can have both sons and daughters."

Abe nodded noncommittally. Some things were just too personal for him to discuss with Stefano, such as the doctors' opinion that Leah should not risk another pregnancy.

On October 18, a brisk sunny Thursday afternoon, Leah called down to Abe that it was time. Both Stefano and Glueck had offered to drive Leah to the hospital, and Glueck was closest. Abe completely forgot about the pay telephone by the front door and sprinted up the block and around the corner to Glueck's office. In ten minutes the doctor's Ford was idling in front of the market.

"It's such a wonderful, beautiful day," Leah gushed as they brought her outside. "Please, can we put the top down on the car?"

It was a short ride to the hospital. Leah basked in the golden sunshine as she cuddled next to Abe in the back seat of the open touring car. How she'd missed being out of doors these last few months.

"I'll take the baby for a stroll in its carriage every day," she confided to her husband.

Abe hardly heard her. He was too busy praying that it would be a son.

"Is it?" he blurted out to Leah as they were pulling up to the hospital's entrance. "You never actually said it all these months. Is it a boy?"

"God made that decision nine months ago," Leah said demurely. "I really don't know."

"Why not? You knew well enough that first time," Abe wanted to shriek, but he didn't. It wouldn't do to remind his wife of that awful first miscarriage now of all times.

As soon as Glueck escorted them inside, the nurses came to take Leah away. The two men awkwardly stood about for a few moments, and then Glueck offered to drive Abe home.

"You're not staying?" Abe asked, incredulous. "You're the doctor—"

"Not here," Glueck said somewhat wistfully. "Henderson is her doctor."

"All right, but I'm staying. Keep me company."

Glueck shook his head. "I've got to go back to my office."

They had been speaking Yiddish, and now Glueck looked uneasy when an orderly, passing by, smirked in amusement.

In our neighborhood he's The Doctor, a pillar in the community. Here he's just a funny-looking old Jew, Abe thought, no better than me as far as the goyim are concerned.

"Go," Abe said. "I'll stay."

"It could be a whole night and day before the baby comes."

"I'll stay."

After Glueck left Abe waited patiently for an hour until Dr. Henderson could see him. "She's comfortable," the young physician said, hardly pausing as he swept through the waiting area. "I suspect it'll be a long labor."

What else should I have expected? Abe thought dourly. He called out his thanks to the departing doctor, swore that he would be here come evening and went out for a walk.

He was oblivious to the cold and the surrounding scenery as he walked along the East River and beneath the Brooklyn Bridge all the way to Fulton Market. He sat at the counter of a waterfront cafe and ate roast chicken and mashed potatoes without tasting the food. The crowded, smoky cafe was filled with weary longshoremen and clipboard-toting supervisors wearing the uniform of the United States Army. From here it was not very far to the

West Side and Stefano's waterfront office, but Abe was apprehensive about going there. It was one thing for Stefano to come see him, but who was he to drop in on a big shot?

You are his good-luck charm, don't forget, Abe reminded himself as he drank his coffee. He was not too dimwitted to comprehend that Stefano considered him more of a pet than an equal. Still, why shouldn't it be that way? Stefano had made something of himself, and Abe owed everything to Stefano.

If he wants to throw me a few crumbs as the years go by, I'll take them and be grateful. That way I'll provide for my wife and have the time to enjoy my son. Then when he's older, the boy can go to work for Stefano and learn to be a big shot. That's not such a bad life. Plenty would be glad to trade places with me.

"Only one child," the doctors warned.

I haven't asked for much, God . . . Let this one be a son.

He paid for his dinner and elbowed his way out of the cafe.

The sun set. As he wandered with his nerves on fire through the evening he passed a spirits shop whose bright windows lined with green and brown bottles beckoned him.

A drink—a real drink—was just what he needed. He had not had anything stronger than wine for many years. But I'm alone tonight and I need something to calm myself, he thought as he entered the shop. *One bottle won't hurt me after all these years. I'll have a few drinks, sit by the river and dream about my son. When I go back, who knows? Maybe he'll have been born. A father can have a drink on the day his son is born; of course he can.*

"A quart of vodka," he said to the man behind the counter.

Outside the heft of the bottle felt lovely in his hand. He was at once seized with an overpowering craving to let a long draught of it sear his throat on its way to lighting that friendly fire in his belly.

He pulled the cork and tilted the bottle to his lips. He swallowed and swallowed. The vodka went down like water. He sighed, wiped his mouth with the sleeve of his overcoat and slipped the bottle into his pocket.

As he walked toward the river the pavement softened beneath his feet as the stars overhead got brighter. Everything was going to be all right, Abe thought, and wasn't buying the bottle such a good idea!

He awoke to the harsh steam whistle of a barge on the river, horrified to discover that he'd passed out. He'd spent the night curled on a wharf, his face in the dirt, a derelict, a bum.

His eyes fell on the vodka bottle. It was lying on its side, about three fingers of drink still in it. Snarling, Abe kicked it away. It skidded several yards and then began to roll with the natural incline of the pier, slipped beneath the railing and splashed into the river.

Leah, Abe thought, my son! He moaned aloud, sick with remorse. What time was it? Oh, God, what time?

Abe got to his feet. At once the pounding within his skull began. He staggered away, savoring the pain, considering it his due.

He made his way toward Chatham Square to catch a trolley. He paused to examine his reflection in a shop window. As bad as he felt, he looked reasonably presentable. He needed a shave and his hair was disheveled, but his dark overcoat did not show the dirt.

My eyes must be red, but that can't be so unusual for a worried husband, Abe reassured himself. I can tell them I fell asleep on a park bench. I can tell Leah I worked myself into nervous exhaustion and fainted.

I can lie my way out of this, Abe thought, and then, God, I'm so ashamed.

He turned away from the shop window. Somewhere a clock tower began to chime. Abe stood frozen, counting the bells. It was twelve o'clock, noontime! Leah would surely be calling for him.

He rinsed the sour taste from his mouth at a public fountain and flagged a taxi. The driver eyed him suspiciously but relaxed when Abe showed him his money, babbling that his wife was having a baby at Gouverneur Hospital.

He was out of the cab and tearing up the steps of the hospital before the vehicle came to a full stop. He dashed through the front lobby, toward the maternity area.

Maybe she hasn't had the baby yet, he told himself. If she's still in labor, no one will have missed me. I must still be drunk. How can I hope for such a thing? Please, let her be finished with it, he prayed. Let her and my son be all finished.

The woman behind the desk looked at him like he was a maniac. "My wife, Mrs. Herodetsky? My son?" Abe pounded the desktop in frustration. Why wouldn't she answer? Then he realized that he was speaking Yiddish.

"Mr. Herodetsky?"

Abe spun around. It was Henderson. The physician looked tired and drawn and even paler than usual. "There you are." Henderson stifled a yawn. "We've been looking for you."

A dozen excuses flitted through Abe's mind before he realized that he no longer cared what the doctor thought of him.

"My wife?" he demanded hoarsely. "It's finished?"

Henderson permitted himself a slight smile. "Yes, indeed, Mr. Herodetsky. It was touch and go there for a while last night. Surgery was called for, but your wife and daughter are resting comfortably.''

''Daughter,'' Abe echoed. ''Daughter.''

Repugnance filled Henderson's watery sky-blue eyes. ''You needn't look so disappointed, Mr. Herodetsky. Your wife will be all right and the baby is perfectly healthy—''

''My wife can have more children?'' Abe demanded.

Henderson frowned. ''We've discussed that and my recommendation was—''

''I didn't ask what you recommended,'' Abe snapped, then paused, realizing his tone would not do. He took a deep breath. ''My wife can have more children?'' he asked, his voice calm, his teeth clenched.

Henderson nodded once curtly. ''I did not perform a hysterectomy. So yes, technically your wife can have more children.''

''Where is she?''

''I'll take you to her in a moment, but first you'll listen to me,'' Henderson declared. ''The only reason I didn't do it—against my better judgment—was that your wife specifically asked me not to unless it was a healthy boy. 'Do what you think best,' she said to me, 'but only if it's a son.' '' Henderson shook his head. ''Mr. Herodetsky, I'd like to understand. Is it some sort of religious matter?''

''I'd like to see my wife now, if you don't mind.''

Henderson scowled. ''This way.''

They walked down a corridor painted pale green. ''Here we are,'' the physician said, but he held the door closed as Abe reached for the knob. ''One final word of caution and then I'm going home to sleep. Last night your wife came very close to dying, Mr. Herodetsky. That's why we were looking for you. For a time we were sure we were going to lose her. Now you know. Whether Jew or Christian, Mr. Herodetsky, we would do well to count the blessings that the Lord bestows upon us. Good day, sir.''

Abe waited until the doctor had turned the corner. Then he went inside.

He found Sadie and Joseph sitting on the wooden bench by the desk in the maternity area. The receptionist looked just as unhappy as when Abe confronted her.

"They told us nobody can see her but the husband," Sadie squawked in Yiddish. She was wearing a floral print dress and a black wool coat with a scruffy fur collar. "What's wrong? A sister can't visit a new mother? What is this nonsense? Joseph took off from work to come."

"She had a difficult delivery," Abe explained, nodding a greeting to the silent, anxious Joseph, looking uncomfortable in his suit. "She'll be here a week. Tomorrow you can sit with her, Sadie."

"And the little girl?" Sadie was quivering with happiness. "Everything's all right?"

"She's a beautiful baby," Abe told them. "We're going to name her Rebecca after your grandmother." Abe smiled. "All right by you?" He assumed it was, as Sadie began to weep with joy.

Joseph clapped him on the back. "A daughter then." He nodded, about to say more, but Abe turned away.

What can you tell me that I don't know? Abe thought. That a daughter cannot aid a father in his business nor provide for her parents in old age? That a daughter has to be sheltered, until the time comes for her to desert her family for a young man—and that there had better be a dowry to attract the husband in the first place?

When Abe went into Leah's room—crowded with two other recovering mothers, squalling babies and attendant husbands and relatives—Leah was gazing serenely out the window. Abe was stunned by how old she looked. He could have sworn the grey strands in her long black hair had not been there yesterday. Her lower lip was swollen and torn where she'd bitten it during labor.

She turned toward him, smiling. "A fine girl, Abe," she said, her eyes intent upon his. "This time a girl. Next time will be—"

"Sha." Abe tenderly cupped her cheek, and then his eyes fell upon his daughter, a tiny, wrinkled, squirming thing, sighing in contentment as it nursed with eyes shut at its mother's breast.

"Abe—"

He leaned forward to kiss his wife's damp forehead. "If she's as good as her mother, she'll be worth a dozen sons."

He was afraid she was about to apologize to him, and that would be unbearable. Who was he to be apologized to? Last night while his wife almost died delivering their child, he was drunk.

"Abe—"

He snapped out of his brooding as Joseph steered him to an out-of-the-way area of the lobby. "I got here a little flask of something," Joseph confided, patting his coat pocket. "What do you say? A little drink on such an occasion never hurt anyone." He drew the battered metal flask and handed it over.

Abe twisted off the stopper and took a long pull. It was whiskey, not vodka, but it would do. He handed it back to Joseph, who took a sip, smacked his lips and asked, "You want more?"

"Yes," Abe nodded. "I do."

Chapter 21

Degania, 1918

On March twenty-fourth Rosie Kolesnikoff and her son
Herschel attended a raucous Sunday evening dining hall
meeting. There they heard a visitor report that the British
were preparing to move against Turkish positions in the
Transjordan. The next few months would be hard, but the
end was in sight. Last year Jerusalem and Tel Aviv had
fallen to the British. The Turks seemed to be losing interest in Palestine as they concentrated on Russia, which was
in a shambles due to the Bolsheviks. With the Turks so
eager to seize coveted Russian territory it was conceivable
that northern Palestine could be liberated within the year.

The twilight sky still flashed fiery hints of the blood-
orange setting sun as Rosie and Herschel left the exuberant
singing and dancing in the dining hall to walk back to their
cottage. Herschel was preoccupied and quiet. Usually that
meant he was missing his father, but Rosie could sense
that he was intent on digesting the news that they had just
heard.

At seven Herschel was a skinny miniature of Haim.
His blond hair was straighter and lighter than Haim's but

still his father's gift, as were his handsome features and blue eyes.

Rosie watched Herschel as he walked with his hands thrust into the pockets of his baggy shorts, eyes narrowed in thought. He was all gangling arms and scabby knees, but there was something very grown-up about him.

She knew what Herschel was thinking. She'd seen the way he perked up when the speaker mentioned Transjordan.

He knows that's where his father probably is, Rosie thought.

It had been six months since Haim left them, half a year since that night when husband and wife loved each other so exquisitely, and teary-eyed father and son exchanged their private farewells outside the cottage, beyond Rosie's hearing. During those months the Turks had come and gone twice. As always, their presence was odious, but with the Balfour Declaration and the Central Powers' promise that they too would provide for a Jewish homeland in exchange for Zionist cooperation, the beatings and other mistreatments had lessened.

There was still disease. The years of overcrowding and malnutrition had taken their toll on both young and old, and medical care was hard to come by. The Turks and Germans restricted movement about the region. People had to depend upon the compassion of individual soldiers; some, both Turk and German, would allow a mission of mercy such as transport of the sick to a hospital. Other soldiers would order the carts back and threaten to shoot if their decree was not obeyed.

Herschel ran ahead of Rosie to pull open the door of the cottage. No key was needed, for there were no locks in Degania. That the members might steal from each other was unthinkable, and locks were useless against enemy soldiers.

As Rosie crossed the threshold into the dark cottage she knew Haim was back. Later on she analyzed her

Israel

intuition as a composite of the smell of cordite and gun oil in the one-room cottage, the creak of the floorboards behind her, the glimpse from the corner of her eye of Herschel frozen in place, staring past her at someone stepping lightly from behind the door.

"My love," she whispered even as she was turning to meet Haim's embrace.

"Papa?" Herschel was not at all sure of the identity of the fierce Bedouin hugging and kissing his crying mother.

"Papa?" The boy's voice still shook with uncertainty, though the joy began to expand inside him. The Bedouin was wearing leather slippers and baggy canvas trousers cinched at the ankles. There were the filmy cotton brussa shirt, the striped caftan and the black cotton coat. On the man's head was the kaffiyeh, cinched in place with an ornate braided headband, called an akal.

The Bedouin looked down at Herschel and the boy began to shiver—in fear, in love, in awe. It *was* his father! He had been fooled by the nomad garb and by the full honey-colored beard, but Herschel knew his father's eyes.

"Papa!" His father was moving toward him, brushing back his coattails as he hunkered down to scoop up his son. Herschel's eyes widened as he took in the scuffed gunbelt glittering with brass cartridges, the leather holster and the worn wooden butt of the revolver.

A gun, Herschel thought. His father's rough beard was tickling his face and he sobbed his greetings between kisses. My father is a Jew, but he has a gun like the Turks. I thought Jews could only farm and let others hurt them, but my father has a gun. He fights!

He knew his father was gone to fight the Turks, but only in an abstract, unreal way, as he knew that he'd been born seven years ago and that in a forever from now, they said, he would die. His formative time on earth had been spent since the advent of the war. No one had ever thought to tell him of the Hashomers' early role in the defense of the settlements. He didn't know the kibbutz had a cache of rifles or that the bowed, meek farmers had the knowledge to use them.

Now as he hugged his father, Herschel made the connection between his father's absence, his father's gun, and the defeat of the Turks that everyone said would soon come. Herschel, his young mind reeling with reports of war and his heart set ablaze by the touch of his father's huge strong loving hands upon him, realized that the ability to endure hardship was only the half of it. A man also needed the wherewithal to fight back.

Seven-year-old Herschel did not have the words to express what had happened to him, but he had just made the transition from a resigned, long-suffering Jew to a Zionist.

"Are you back for good?" Rosie asked hopefully, wiping away her own tears.

Haim shook his head. "No, my love. Yol is waiting for me in the rocks a little way from the compound. The rest of the band is camped along the Jordan. We've come north because the Turks are falling back. I wanted this chance to see my family."

"You've not come home, Papa?" Herschel asked.

"I can't stay, but it'll only be a few months more, my son, and then I will be home for good. Meanwhile I want you to take care of your mother. Is that understood?"

Herschel, gazing up at the sun-burnished giant, nodded wordlessly. He drank in every detail of his father's appearance, struggled to memorize his voice and the way he walked. These memories would be all he would have to sustain him during the next interminable absence.

"Has the boy been all right?" Haim asked. "He studies? He's healthy? There's food for him?"

"He learns his lessons because I've told him that his father wishes it. He has Hebrew, Arabic and English; he's shown an aptitude for mathematics and the sciences. We

teach him and the others what we can from the textbooks.''
She shrugged. ''As for the other questions, he eats what
everyone eats, which is not enough. Thank God the fever
leaves him alone. He's as healthy as any boy who so
desperately misses his father—''

''Oh, Rosie,'' Haim turned away from her.

She threw her arms around his neck. ''Forgive me. I
said that only because of my disappointment that you can't
stay. It is only because I love you.''

Haim kissed her lightly. ''Your idea of love talk
always has been a little rough.''

Rosie rested her head against his chest. ''I've been so
worried.''

''The Turks have yet to get a shot at us.''

''But you shoot them, yes, Papa?'' Herschel insisted.

''Yes, we shoot them, but you mustn't say anything
to the Turks when they come.''

''I won't, Papa, I promise.'' Herschel's hand reached
up and his small fingers tentatively brushed the holster—he
could not bring himself to touch his father's revolver—and
then jerked away.

''Everyone here is proud of you and Yol,'' Rosie
said.

''So the man at the gate told me. I understand why
you had to explain my disappearance. I'm just afraid the
secret will leak out. It's for you and Herschel and the
others that I worry.''

''No one has ever told the Turks anything they wanted
to know, and no one ever shall,'' Rosie assured him. She
took a step back in order to look him over. ''You've not
been wounded, God forbid?''

Haim laughed. ''Just once did I even come close. We
were waiting for a Turkish patrol. We didn't know it, but
this particular patrol had a real Bedouin of its own acting
as a scout. We'd never heard of such a thing, you
understand; the Arabs hate the Turks as much as we do.

"Anyway, this nomad came around behind our position, and as luck would have it, I was the one he discovered. Evidently he was going to plant a knife in my back when Jibarn—he's an Arab boy who travels with us—saved me by—"

Haim stopped abruptly as the memories flooded back: Jibarn riding the Bedouin piggyback; his glee as he slit the nomad's throat. "Let me just say that Jibarn killed the man before he could harm me."

"If an Arab boy fights with you, why can't I?" Herschel implored.

"This boy is older. He's thirteen—a man already. If you were thirteen it'd be different." Haim winked at Rosie, who was glowering at him. "Anyway, that was the only close call. You know what he said to me, Rosie? 'Haim, I will not allow anyone to harm you.' " He shrugged, smiling. "He seems very much attached to me, even more than to Yol, who— Well, it doesn't matter."

"Haim, what if you just didn't go back?" Rosie pleaded, hugging him. "What if you just stayed? Yol would understand."

"Listen to me," Haim said gently, holding her at arm's length. "Many Jews have volunteered to fight. Since the liberation of Jerusalem and Tel Aviv, Palestinians have flocked to Jabotinsky's call. The Jewish Legion has been formed and is being trained in Egypt, but it has seen no action. I've come to believe what many have said, that it never will. The Balfour Declaration promised us a home in return for our aid in this battle. My group is fulfilling the Zionist part of the bargain. The more fighting we do now, the sooner this will be over. Besides, when the Turks and Germans withdraw to Degania—and they are coming this way, I'm sorry to say—could you expect me to hang my head and polish their boots?"

"No." Rosie colored. "You are too brave and strong . . ." Her voice grew thick. "Too fine for that—Oh,

Haim, I feel shy with you. Like a bride. I wish we could
. . .'' She trailed off, her eyes on Herschel, who was
staring up at them.

"I love you," Haim murmured, "and I long for you.
Soon we will be together again and there will be time,
proper time. For now it is more important that we three be
together as a family."

"I could come to your camp later, when Herschel
sleeps," Rosie suggested. "It is not so far—"

Haim was tempted. Yol and their makeshift camp
were only half an hour's ride from here. He frowned. "It's
too dangerous. Why take such a risk? Come, now, let's all
sit together and talk, for I have only a little longer. Yol,
Jibarn and I must be across the river with the others by
dawn."

It was after midnight when Haim returned to the small
camp by the same narrow stream Jibarn had led him to that
first time. As on that night, there was a small fire burning
and a pot of tea warming in the glowing coals. Both Yol
and Jibarn were still awake, sitting crosslegged on their
blankets as they watched the flames.

"Everything okay?" Yol asked as Haim entered the
clearing.

"Everything is fine, and you were asked for," Haim
told his friend. "You should have come."

Yol shrugged. "I have no family waiting for me."

"My family is waiting for you."

Yol smiled. "You know what I mean. To go calling
on all our old friends while you were with Rosie and
Herschel and then to have to leave again would have
caused me more pain than pleasure. When this war is over
I shall return to Degania for good."

"Well." Haim reached beneath his tunic and set a
bottle of wine before Yol. "All the halutzim said, 'Here,

take this bottle to Yol to show him that we still remember what he is like—' "

"Haim, it is a bottle from Rishon le Zion—why, it must be one of the last!"

"Degania has a few cases hidden. They're saving it to celebrate liberation, but they insisted that we have one."

"Now here we have a moral question, Jibarn," Yol began. "Our comrades wait for us by the Jordan. Should we save this bottle—this tiny bottle—to share with them?"

"I think not, Yol," Jibarn replied thoughtfully. "Such a tiny bottle would allow only one sip each for forty men. A mere taste of home would be just like your visit to Degania, it would cause more pain than pleasure."

Yol had already pulled the cork. He took a long swallow and said, "I toast you, Jibarn. I can teach you no more."

"You've already done enough to corrupt him," Haim joked as he was handed the bottle. He and Yol laughed, but Haim noticed that Jibarn did not. The Arab merely watched them, his smile inscrutable.

"A drink, Jibarn?" Haim asked.

The boy shook his head. "The Koran forbids it."

"Absolutely it does," Yol exclaimed, snatching the bottle from Haim's grasp. "I'll drink his share."

"Yes, go ahead and drink," Jibarn agreed, his skull-like face disquieting in the firelight. "It will help you to sleep. Don't worry, I will wake you when the time comes."

The wine did help Yol to sleep, but Haim, still caught up with thoughts of his family, was far too restless to close his eyes. He kept the fire going and thought about his visit home until Jibarn silently rose and came around the flames to sit down beside him.

"I am glad you got the chance to see your wife and son," the Arab said in his own lilting tongue.

Haim glanced sideways at Jibarn and returned his gaze to the fire. "Family is important," he replied in Arabic. "You will have a wife and son one day."

"Oh, perhaps." Jibarn shrugged. His shaved skull dipped down between his narrow shoulders. "It is hard to imagine such a thing, though. I have no home, Haim."

"You know I was an orphan, too—"

"Yes, but to lose one's family goes far beyond personal tragedy for an Arab. We put great stock in tracing our lineage, you know. Like the horse, like the falcon, we are only the sum total of our fathers and grandfathers."

Haim was silent for a moment. "I was there that night, you know."

Now it was Jibarn's turn to glance sideways and nod shyly. "I know."

"It was an accident, as Yol has told you. It could not have been avoided. It was dark and we were afraid of the Bedouins. Yol was all alone, guarding our mules. He heard a noise, he turned, he fired—"

"Stop," Jibarn softly ordered. "The circumstances do not matter. Either something happened or it didn't. It is not masculine to cloud the matter with circumstances." He paused. "This I do say: I know that it was a blunder. Yol is prone to blunders."

"I think he made a blunder when he told you."

Jibarn smiled ferally. "I also think that." He shrugged. "But it is in the past, yes, Haim? Come, hand me your revolver and I will clean it for you."

Haim nodded, reaching behind him for the holster lying on the blanket. He drew the pistol, an ancient Webley, and handed it to the boy, who nimbly extracted its cartridges, spilling them onto the blanket. Jibarn cleaned the firearms of most of the men in the group. Tonight there was no danger in being without a sidearm. Haim's rifle was nearby and there were no Turks in the area as yet.

"I turned thirteen last month," Jibarn said as he

wiped the weapon's action with the hem of his caftan. "In my religion, as in yours, that is the age when a boy becomes a man. Until that age a boy can be neglectful if he wishes. After then, however, he is responsible for the honor of his family as well as himself." He unscrewed the cylinder from the revolver's frame. The Webley was in two pieces. Jibarn set both down on the blanket as he turned to confront Haim.

"It is important to me that you understand everything," the boy said, his tone oddly formal. "I respect you."

"I'm fond of you as well," Haim said, not altogether truthfully. There was a quality about Jibarn that he did not care for, but tonight the mellow warmth of the wine he'd drunk, combined with his sympathy for the boy's orphaned state, opened Haim's heart. "I've not forgotten the way you saved my life. When the war is over, I'll make it up to you." He stretched to put his arm around Jibarn's shoulder.

Jibarn ducked beneath Haim's outstretched arm and rose behind him with lethal grace and speed. Haim had no time to react before Jibarn's sinewy forearm hammerlocked his throat and the boy's glittering seven-inch blade materialized from the flowing cuff of his caftan to press against Haim's ribs.

"Blood feud," Jibarn whispered like a lover into Haim's ear. "As my enemy makes me cry, so will he weep. What he takes from me, I shall take from him. A man shall have his revenge."

Haim tried to speak, but only hoarse, fitful croaking came out of his throat. He tried again and managed, "You don't want to do this."

"I do not, but that fact changes nothing. At first I thought to kill Yol. I thought this years ago, when he stayed with me in my grandfather's hut in Um Jumi. 'When I am thirteen,' I vowed to myself, 'when I am thirteen this womanly, weeping Jew will die for my grandfather's murder.' When you joined us I realized that the most exquisite revenge would be not to kill Yol, but to make him mourn for his great friend as I have mourned for my grandfather. In truth I did not count on becoming fond of you, Haim.''

"Jibarn—'' Haim rolled his eyes, trying to catch a glimpse of Yol. He could hear his friend snoring loudly. He's drunk, Haim thought. You know how soundly he sleeps when he is drunk. You must keep the boy talking to gain time.

"Why did you save my life that time?'' Haim asked as loudly as he could.

"I saved you in order to kill you myself. You must die by my hand if my grandfather is to be avenged.'' He tightened his hold on Haim's throat. "Don't try to awaken Yol. If you do, I will kill him too. You know it is likely that I could, long before he could figure out what was happening.''

This is a dream, Haim thought, just a joke. Herschel! Rosie! I won't—can't—die!

"I will not let you beg. There is no dignity in that. We are too good friends. That is why I delayed this reckoning until you had a chance to see your wife and son—''

"Jibarn—'' Fight him, Haim thought, panicking. Fight for the knife!

Jibarn kissed Haim's cheek as he thrust home the dagger, leaving it buried in Haim's ribs. Then he was on his feet and looking down at his work.

Haim slumped over onto his side, driving the knife in to its hilt. His fingers blindly groped for the Webley and closed around it, but then he remembered that Jibarn had dismantled the revolver. The rifle was somewhere behind him, but he didn't have the strength to lift it, even if Jibarn allowed him to.

He gazed up at the boy. He felt no pain, hadn't felt any when the blade went in; just an icy sensation. The worst of it was hearing the grating noise as the steel ground against a rib.

"Grandfather, you are avenged," Jibarn said softly. "Haim, I wish you a good death." Then he turned to vanish into the darkness beyond the fire.

The world was spinning. Haim felt as pliant as rubber. He was warm and wet where his body rested in his own pooled blood.

Got to stop the bleeding—He futilely plucked at the blood-slick handle of the knife and then gathered up a handful of the blanket and pressed it against his wound. Jibarn had twisted the knife as he plunged it in, making a wide, gaping hole. Haim's blood quickly soaked through the coarse woolen blanket no matter how much of the cloth he bunched around the protruding knife handle.

"Y-Yol . . . *Yol!*"

"What—?" Yol stirred. "Time to leave already?" He sat up, stretching and rubbing his eyes, then stared at Haim, who was on his knees with Jibarn's knife still in his side. The blood gleamed black in the firelight.

Yol screamed.

Take care of my boy, Haim said or thought; he was too far gone to know which. He settled himself, curling into a fetal ball, and closed his eyes.

When he awoke, the sky had taken on a leaden glow that presaged the dawn. He thought it was a nightmare until he tried to move and realized he couldn't. He felt very sleepy and his arms and legs were numb. I'm so tired, he thought, as a sharp, incessant throbbing began where the knife had gone in. He felt for it and found that where the dagger had been there was now a bandage strapped tightly around his middle.

"Haim?"

It was Rosie. The sound of her voice cleared his mind. He blinked, trying to focus his eyes. There were other people around him. Rosie was kneeling by his side and Yol was close by. Behind them stood two others from Degania.

"We're here to take you back," Yol said. "I went to get Rosie and some men with a cart to take you home."

"I'm dying, Rosie." Haim gazed perplexed at his wife.

"No," Yol said too heartily, "you'll be fine."

"No lies," Rosie said. She brought Haim's fingers to her lips. "You are dying, my love."

"Damn Jibarn! Damn him to hell!" Yol cried out.

"Yol told me why he did this," Rosie said to Haim. "Now listen to me. I won't let them take you back to Degania—" She paused as Haim's eyes closed.

"He should die in his own bed," Yol said reproach-fully.

"No!" she snarled. Bending close to Haim's ear, between kisses and clutching his hand, she said, "Can you hear me, my love? Can you understand? It's for Herschel I'm not taking you home. Last night he saw his father as a hero. I want you to live for him that way for a long time." She felt the tears running but did not wipe them away, afraid to let go of Haim's hand, to stop talking to him. She tried hard to smile; even if he couldn't see her expression, he might be able to hear it in her voice. "Every day I'll tell him of your adventures. I'll make Herschel so proud of you—"

Haim's eyes fluttered open. "He'll be an orphan . . ."

"No, he won't be. I promise."

"Orphan like me . . ."

"Like you, he'll be, but never an orphan." She kissed him on the lips. "I'll take care of our son," she whispered, "but what shall I do without you?"

Haim stared up at her.

He's dead. The realization sent a shock wave of panic through her. She sniffed and rubbed at her eyes until they were raw and stinging, but the tears were gone. I have too much to do to cry, she thought. I have my son to raise.

"We've got to take his body back, Rosie," one of the men said.

"No."

"He must be buried in Degania's cemetery—"

"I said no!" Panther-like, she sprang up to confront them, and so fierce did she seem that without thinking the men stepped back from her. "Bury him here! Throw his corpse on the rocks! I don't care." She realized she was crying again. It was no use trying to forbid her tears. "I won't break my promise to Haim. Herschel will not know, and none of you shall tell him that his father has died. Let everyone think Haim and Yol have gone back to the fighting. I swear, if either of you two—or you, Yol— reveals what has happened, I'll kill you, even if it takes years, just like that Arab waited so long to kill my beloved—"

"Stop it, Rosie," one of the men pleaded, embarrassed by her grief. "We won't say anything if that's how you want it."

"But sometime Herschel will have to know," the other added.

"That'll be months from now," Rosie said. "Given just three months I can make his father live in Herschel's memory forever. There will be plenty of time to say Kaddish and burn candles. For a while longer my boy and I will celebrate his life."

The two men looked at each other and shrugged.

"Now then," she went on, "there are shovels and a pick in the cart from today's farm work. I hate to ask you, but I cannot bury my husband alone."

"Again you insult us," the men chided. "We are halutzim. We will bury our brother here and now if that's what you want."

"It is. Thank you. I'll walk back alone. The sun is coming up. It'll be safe enough."

Yol glanced up at her from where he sat beside Haim's body. "I won't see you again until the war is finished. I'll tell the Hashomer what Jibarn has done. We'll get the bastard for this—"

"As Jibarn has gotten Haim for what happened to his grandfather? My husband is dead. What happens to his killer will not bring him back and so is a matter of indifference to me."

They waited until she had left to begin digging the grave. As they worked one of the men said, "She is cold like that because she has British blood."

Yol disagreed. "She is like that because she is born and bred a Palestinian."

Chapter 22

"Don't cry, don't cry," Abe Herodetsky mumbled in his sleep. "I'll fix it. Don't cry—"

"Abe, wake up!" Leah prodded, startled awake by her husband's moans. "Wake up, wake up."

He came out of his nightmare soaked with sweat, gnawing at the back of his hand to keep from screaming. He bolted upright, eyes wide and wild as they peered into the bedroom's shadowy corners. "Haim—"

"You were muttering in Russian," Leah told him, "dreaming of the old days in Russia, that's all."

Abe, still dazed, nodded vaguely. "Yes, a dream." He shuddered. "What a dream, Leah. It goes back to when I was a youth—"

"Not so loud. You'll wake the baby."

"Becky's sleeping in the parlor with the door closed. She can't hear me." Still, he turned on his side and put his head close to Leah's on the pillows so he could whisper.

"I was in my village in Russia. I was maybe seventeen and Haim about eleven. I had begun to teach him to be a cobbler." He laughed a trifle hysterically. "All this is

351

the true part, you understand. . . . One day he was cutting leather and the blade slipped, giving him a nasty gash between his thumb and index finger. It bled something awful. Haim began to cry and I went to tend to him.''

"Nu?" Leah sleepily demanded. "That's all of it?" She turned over, wiggling her backside until it was pressed against his belly. "Sleep . . ." she yawned.

"No, wait. Here's the nightmare part," Abe whispered. "In between Haim's cutting his finger and my going to him, he ended up in Gallipoli with the Zion Mule Corps. Remember when that was in the newspapers and I was so worried about whether Haim was there? Well, in my dream he was, but as a little boy, you see? Remember that photograph they published? That battlefront scene with all the dead men and the blown-up wagons—well, that was where I was looking for poor little Haim. He was crying for me, and there was all that blood, but to reach him I had to step over the corpses of those dead soldiers . . . Leah?"

He couldn't see her face, but he could tell from her shallow, rhythmic breathing that she'd fallen back asleep.

And why shouldn't she sleep? Abe asked himself. The baby runs her ragged the whole day.

He reached over to the nightstand, brought the alarm clock close to his face and squinted. It was eleven o'clock.

"It's still Sunday night," Abe muttered to himself, "still March twenty-fourth. That is what's real. My dream is not."

He leaned back against the pillows and closed his eyes. They popped open. He was haunted by the image of that hazy corpse-strewn battlefield with little Haim in the middle of the carnage, covered with his own blood as he cradled his cut hand and called for Abe to come soothe him.

Haim, something is very wrong. I know it is, Abe brooded. Something has happened to you.

Across the bedroom the clothing heaped upon a chair

began to slither like snakes. That's my eyes playing a trick in the dark, Abe thought. It's an illusion, as was my dream. Leah is right. There's nothing to be concerned about. Haim is no doubt quite fine. My dream is not about Haim but about my own unhappiness.

He got out of bed quietly so as not to disturb Leah. There was no point in trying to sleep. He stepped into his slippers, wrapped a flannel robe about his nightshirt and went out into the parlor.

Their daughter Rebecca, five months old, was sound asleep in her crib. She was a good baby that way, rarely waking before they got up.

Abe gazed down at his tiny daughter. I love you, he thought. I am very happy to have you, my Becky. Then he silently rapped his knuckles on the wooden railing of the crib.

Knock wood, Abe said to himself. Count your blessings, just like Dr. Henderson advised you. Let God know that you are thankful in case He should misunderstand.

His nightmare concerning Haim had sprung from his own disappointment over not having a son. His disappointment made him feel guilty, which ruined his sleep, causing nightmares. It was quite simple.

He went into the kitchen, closed the door and switched on the overhead fixture. Squinting in the harsh glare, he stooped down to open the cupboard beneath the sink. He reached back, stretching and straining to get his hand into the narrow space between the wall and the pipes. His fingers touched the neck of the bottle. He carefully threaded the quart of vodka through Leah's maze of cleansers and brought it over to the kitchen table.

He sat down heavily and stared at the bottle in front of him. My secret friend, he thought, despising himself. He had opened the bottle Friday evening and it was already half empty. I hate you, he told the bottle. He'd smuggled it into the apartment while Leah was in the bedroom getting dressed for Sabbath dinner at Sadie and Joseph's.

He took a swig. The stuff went down like the tonic he sold to the children in the store, or at least the stuff he used to sell before President Wilson's food administrator, Herbert Hoover, instituted his voluntary food rationing. The "wheatless Mondays, meatless Tuesdays," and so on made an empty-shelved grocery store a dreary place to be. The war had even led to suspension of the manufacture of liquor.

Abe helped himself to another drink. "Here's to you, Stefano," he toasted his friend. Stefano seemed to know where to get everything, including hard drink. There was no shortage of coal in Stefano de Fazio's buildings during this chilly spring, and he always had plenty of gasoline for his trucks and his automobile. Everything Stefano touched turned to gold.

A little while ago there had been something in the newspapers concerning his most recent acquisition. The owner of a meat-packing plant on Washington Street claimed that certain business mishaps and union troubles that plagued him had been instigated by Stefano. The newborn news tabloids enjoyed a field day with their "meat war" headlines, but the whole matter blew over when the *Daily News* published an exclusive, the meat packer's public apology and retraction of all of his accusations.

He sold his business to Stefano at a reduced price and moved away. Stefano won, but the affair cost him. No longer did his name make the respectable papers. There were no more pictures of him shaking hands with celebrities. Stefano seemed hardened by the experience as well. He confided in Abe that friends of the packer had made threats against his life. He'd hired men to protect him—bodyguards, not thugs, despite what the rags printed.

Abe didn't doubt what Stefano told him, and even if

he had, the time had long since passed—if it had ever been—when he would dare to contradict Stefano de Fazio.

Abe had another drink. If only I had Stefano's luck. Just a couple of weeks ago Stefano's wife had presented him with his fifth child. Granted, it was a girl—christened Dolores—but there was nothing wrong with daughters when a man already had two sons.

And there is nothing wrong with only having the daughter, Abe chided himself. Becky is healthy, thank God.

How he hated himself when he was ungrateful like this. His ingratitude was a stain upon him. No matter how he tried to train himself to be happy, to be thankful, his disappointment cropped up.

No son. Never a son—The realization soured him. He was mean to Leah. He would nag her until she cried. She never defended herself, and that compounded his remorse.

Have another drink, Abe told himself as he sat alone with his bottle in the kitchen of the silent apartment. Drink and count your blessings.

But he couldn't, and that made him wonder when and how God would punish him, not only for his ingratitude, but also for being a drunkard. Drinking brought him some relief by rescuing him from his own mind, but always the alcohol wore off, leaving him even more miserable than before. Never again will I take a drop, he'd swear, but soon his unhappiness drove him back to the bottle and the beginning of another cycle of despair.

He pointed the bottom of the bottle toward the ceiling, draining it of its last drops. The vodka had done its work. He would sleep now.

Abe put the empty bottle on the back staircase. He'd take it downstairs when he opened the store a few hours from now. Tomorrow when Leah wasn't there to see him he'd hide another someplace in the apartment.

Stefano had given him a case. Next month another

one would be delivered, just like the one Abe had furtively, desperately drunk the month before.

A case a month; twelve cases a year. He could survive.

Meanwhile he would run the Cherry Street Market and care for his family. He would do his best to keep his bitterness inside, where it could do Leah and Becky no harm.

Eight bottles to the case; two quarts a week. When the war finally ended business would pick up. He would fall back into the old routine, fueling himself with Stefano's liquor.

Haim, what has become of you? Abe wondered. "And what has happened to me?" he asked the empty kitchen. He sat down again.

Twelve cases a year, year in, year out. Abe began to cry. He sat alone in the kitchen, his head cradled in his arms, his face pressed against Leah's embroidered tablecloth. He wept and wept, locking his sobs with his sorrow deep inside, so as not to disturb his family.

Chapter 23

"Abe's my good luck charm," Stefano de Fazio liked to tell everyone, including Abe himself. When Stefano considered how far he'd come since his start as a lowly presser fifteen years ago, he knew that what he'd always said about Abe was true. The Jew had brought him luck.

Back in 1910 it was a two-hundred-dollar stake; in 1912 it was Abe's testimonials during the election. Once he was in, it had been relatively easy to "borrow" funds from the union's coffers, and once he had some money to work with, the connections had come easy.

Things got a little shaky for Stefano after the war. The government was no longer shipping materiel, the scandal about the takeover of that packing plant caused a lot of his side business to dry up. His warehouses sat empty, and Stefano tried to sell them, but luckily, he'd been unable to find a buyer with the funds to pay cash during the postwar recession.

Then came Prohibition as of January 16, 1920. There were suddenly millions of gallons of legally made booze to be stored away for safekeeping. A lot of it went into federal warehouses, but there was still an overflow, and the word went out that Uncle Sam was accepting bids for storage contracts. Thanks to his War Department connections, Stefano was able to get a sizable piece of that action. His warehouses on both sides of the Hudson were soon filled with barrels and cases of premium liquor. The government was paying him top dollar for his space besides coughing up a surcharge to cover a security force to guard the valuable property.

The small army of security personnel were all handpicked by Antonio Bucci, Stefano's most trusted business partner. It was Tony who supervised the operation, seeing to it that the security men were equipped to steal the liquor out of the warehouses and transport it to a network of speakeasies and under-the-counter sales outlets. A case a month went to Abe's grocery store free of charge. It was Stefano's way of making up for the fact that he was far too busy to continue his visits to Cherry Street. De Fazio's organization under Tony Bucci's stewardship charged everyone else a bundle.

Tony was ten years younger than Stefano. He had been a fabric cutter back in the old days and had served as Stefano's campaign manager during the run for treasurer. Tony was a homely, prematurely bald man who wore extremely thick eyeglasses from which he acquired the nickname Tony Gemstones among his cronies. These included Dutch Schultz and young Al Capone, who had once belonged to Brooklyn's Five Points gang but had gone on to better things in Chicago as Johnny Torrio's second.

The thick glasses, taken with his glistening scalp, sallow complexion and vacant expression, made people underestimate Tony, which was a bad mistake. He was an avid reader, an expert at accounting, totally ruthless and as loyal as a dog to Stefano de Fazio.

It was Tony who understood the ramifications of the

Russian Revolution in '17 and convinced Stefano that he should quit the union before the activities of the socialistic Jews brought unwanted public attention.

In 1918, when Stefano wanted to buy out the meat packer, it was Tony who orchestrated—as he had several times before—the harassment and violence meant to cut the selling price and coerce silence. When the scandal broke, leading to embarrassing publicity and hushed, urgent telephone calls warning of an imminent federal investigation, it was Tony who kidnapped the meat packer from his home late one night and took him to one of Stefano's warehouses.

It had been not Tony but Stefano who pressed a revolver to the man's temple and warned him that if he did not cooperate, his brains would splatter across the cement floor and his corpse would be found bobbing in the inky waters of the Hudson.

The meat packer agreed to retract his accusations and sell out at a rock-bottom price, believing correctly that Stefano was quite capable of carrying out the threat. He had already done so five times.

Abe Herodetsky did not know this any more than Mrs. de Fazio did. Maria, a chubby, kind-hearted woman, considered her husband a god for having moved the family out of Little Italy to a home of their own near Sheepshead Bay in Brooklyn. The move took place in September of 1923, approximately a month and a half after President Harding died in the White House in the aftermath of the Teapot Dome scandal. Calvin Coolidge took over so successfully that he was easily elected in November 1924.

On election night Stefano threw a party, though Abe and Leah Herodetsky were not invited. Stefano had contributed heavily to various campaigns, and most of his candidates were considered shoo-ins. That night he capered triumphantly, like a tout at the track on his lucky day. Stefano had always been an advocate of the fix, and now he'd bought himself more protection than any man he knew.

Tony Gemstones was also in a good mood that night. He asked if Stefano would see him later on, after the guests had taken their leave.

Maria de Fazio had been given a free hand to decorate her home, and she'd leaned toward red velvet, white marble and a great deal of gilt. There were ponderous crystal chandeliers and Louis XV armchairs; there was no wallpaper that was not flocked. Mrs. de Fazio used the manner of a little girl let free in a toy store, letting gaudiness and expense serve as her criteria of quality. She and Stefano loved the result, as did their friends and Stefano's business associates. The de Fazio home was a merry place.

Maria completely reversed herself in Stefano's study. Here the floors were covered with a staid blue wall-to-wall carpet and the walls were lined with banker's dark brown paneling. The heavy armchairs and sofas were set out in a circle in the manner of a men's club lounge.

The desk was massive and as barren of clutter as a desert mesa. Decorating the walls were framed mementos— union campaign posters, complimentary clippings from newspapers Stefano controlled, pictures of him with various important people, civic awards and so on. The study looked the way Maria and he imagined it ought to, but in truth Stefano was not comfortable in it. It was too dark and somber for him. He was a lighthearted, sentimental man and much preferred the movie hall atmosphere of the rest of the house to his gloomy den. The only good thing the study had to offer was a magnificent view of the bay.

Still, it was to the study Stefano brought Tony on that November night. Tony opened his briefcase and removed a bottle of vintage Scotch—no alcohol had been served at the party in deference to the police officials who attended— and an accounts ledger, the sanctity of which Tony would have protected with his life.

Tony poured them each a shot, using the crystal glasses from the mahogany sideboard. He put his hand on the ledger as if it were a Bible and toasted his boss.

"Stefano, it gives me great pleasure to inform you that you are officially a millionaire."

Election night 1924 was nine months ago. It was now a steamy summer day at the beginning of August 1925 and Stefano was sitting behind his chipped, dented steel desk in his warehouse office on the Manhattan side of the Hudson. He was staring at Tony Gemstones, who had thrust his homely four-eyed features through the doorway that led from the outer office to announce, "Abe's wife is here with a kid, and just who the fuck is Abe?"

"Abe's my good luck charm," Stefano blurted without a moment's thought. Then he laughed. "Why would Leah be here?" he wondered out loud. "With Becky, you say? Well, show 'em in."

"Who the fuck is Abe?" Tony repeated.

"A guy I know." Stefano scowled. "From the union. He's got nothing to do with anything, you know? So be a gentleman and show Mrs. Herodetsky in."

Leah clutched a paper shopping bag with one hand and tried to hold onto Becky with the other as they waited in the lobby. Initially Leah had thought of leaving her daughter with Sadie, but she wanted no questions. Besides, she decided that having her daughter with her might help gain Stefano's sympathy. She was about to ask a great favor of him, assuming, of course, that he had time to see her.

"Mommy, what's that? What do they sell here? Why can't we go in?"

At seven—"Seven years and eight months," Becky would announce if anyone asked her—Leah's daughter was at the stage where everything in the world fascinated her. She was a pretty child with dark brown hair and eyes to match and a creamy, flawless complexion. Short for her age, she was roly-poly round and moved much as a turtle might if it could walk on its hind legs. She was overweight due to unrestricted noshing on the penny candy and fruit in the store. Baby fat everybody called it, including Leah.

Next year Becky would start school, which would restrict her time in the store and cut down on her snacking. Until then darling Becky could have what she wanted, her parents had decided. She was their only child, and they spoiled her no end.

"Mommy, what's that buzzing noise? Why can't we go in?"

"The buzzing is an electric lock on the door. That lady who is sitting behind the glass window works it, and—"

Leah paused as the bald man with incredibly thick glasses returned. When Leah told the receptionist that she wanted to see Mr. de Fazio and that her business was personal, this man had been summoned.

"Stefano can see you now," the man said, holding open the door.

"Mommy, why is he wearing cheaters?" Becky asked loudly.

Leah blushed. "I'm sorry," she told the man. "She gets that slang from the radio. Children will ask such embarrassing questions—"

"Hey, kids—" Tony Gemstones said, not exactly smiling. "Forget it, ma'am." Stefano had said to be a gentleman, but Tony was remembering the last guy who had merely referred to his eyeglasses, never mind having the audacity to call them cheaters. Nobody saw that guy around anymore. "Watch yourself, Mrs. Herodetsky," he warned as he led her through the crate-lined corridors towards Stefano's office. "Them boxes could do you some damage—"

They reached a large room cluttered with steel desks. Several men in suits and ties were smoking cigarettes and playing cards here. They did not look to Leah like they were clerks. *Just as I thought.* She nodded to herself.

"Right through here," the man with the thick eyeglasses said, steering her quickly through this outer office and through a short vestibule to a wooden door marked, "Knock First."

The man knocked. "It's me," he said, opening the door.

Stefano came around his desk to embrace Leah. "What a pleasure," he grinned. "You look wonderful—and look who else is here." He put his hand on Becky's head. "Remember me, cutie?"

"No," Becky mumbled, taking a step closer to her mother. It was her habit to be brash until she'd attracted a stranger's attention and then go exceedingly shy.

"Well, you were just a baby when I saw you last," Stefano chuckled. "You want something, Leah? Coffee maybe?"

"No, thank you." Leah looked around. The office was windowless, its walls light green and lined with cardboard file cabinets on top of which were stacked lopsided piles of yellow invoices.

"What do they sell here, Mommy?"

"Sha," Leah hissed, anxious to silence her child, because she had a very good idea indeed what it was Stefano sold here. *Coming here is a great risk,* she reminded herself, as she had countless times in the past when contemplating this action. *The risk was worth it, though; her marriage and her husband's well-being were at stake.*

"She thinks every place is a store." Leah smiled at Stefano.

"She's her father's daughter," he chuckled. "Now, what can I do for you?"

"I'd like to talk to you," Leah began, and then glanced over her shoulder at the man with the eyeglasses, who was leaning against the doorjamb. "In private."

"Of course. Tony, would you excuse us?"

Leah smiled apologetically as the man left the office, shutting the door behind him. At Stefano's invitation she took the straightbacked chair in front of his desk, waiting until he had settled himself in his own swivel chair before starting.

Here we go, she thought. She reached into her shopping bag and put the empty vodka bottle on the desk. "I found this in my bathroom," she said. "It was stuck behind the toilet. It had liquor in it when I found it, but I dumped it out."

Stefano nodded. "I guess Abe likes to take a little nip now and then. A lot of men do."

"Stefano, I'm very frightened to say this, but there is a lot at stake for me and for Becky."

Becky looked up at the mention of her name. She had removed Stefano's stapler from his desk and taken it into a corner to play with it. Now that the adults were talking about other things, she lost interest in the conversation and returned to the fascinations of the stapler.

"Stefano, Abe sees what he wants to see. He knows what suits him. I'm different. I read the papers and I know all about the Prohibition. I think you know about it, as well." She eyed him inquiringly, waiting for him to say something. He didn't, but merely sat stony-faced, watching her. She pressed on lest he get the wrong impression. "This is your private affair, I understand."

She took a deep breath to control her thumping heart and then bit down on her lower lip, which had begun to tremble. "But this I beg you, Stefano, please do not sell any more of it to Abe. This liquor will be the death of him."

Stefano smiled. "Wait a minute, Leah. You're getting carried away. Maybe the Jewish religion doesn't approve of drinking, but a little nip now and again won't hurt." He shrugged. "Anyway, Abe's grown up. I can't stop him."

"You could refuse to sell it to him—"

"I don't sell it to him, Leah, I give it to him. I'd never charge Abe. I've been sending him a case a month since the war—"

"That's years ago." Leah blanched.

"Right. And I bet he's bought you a lot of nice things with the money he's made selling it under the counter—"

"But he doesn't sell it!"

Stefano stared at her. "What do you mean? I've been sending him a case a month since Becky was born—"

"He doesn't sell it, Stefano, he drinks it." Leah pointed to the empty quart bottle on the desk. "This is not the first one I've found. I've known about his secret vice for months. There have been others hidden in my closets and my cupboards. Once I even saw him take a bottle from beneath the cash register in the store and put it to his lips and gulp it down. He didn't know I was watching him. It could have been his daughter who was watching."

Stefano was dumfounded. There were eight quarts to a case, being delivered once a month to Cherry Street. If Abe was drinking two quarts a week . . .

"He's become a different man," Leah told him. "He's very different. You don't know. You've not visited him for any length of time for years, and when you have stopped by, he's been on his best behavior with you." Leah smiled. "That's why I've come to you, Stefano. I don't dare talk to him. He's always finding fault with me. Of course he has good reason, I guess."

"That's not true," Stefano said gruffly.

Leah shrugged. "We both know how Abe pines for a son. He loves his daughter, but a girl is not a boy.

Anyway, I want him to live to see his daughter grow up. He's not a well man, you know. He has his heart thing . . ."

"The heart murmur, yeah." Stefano nodded thoughtfully. "The sauce is no good for a guy with a weak ticker." He tapped his fingertips on the metal desktop. "You did right to come to me, Leah. I'm going to talk to Abe."

Leah sagged in her chair with relief and gratitude. "Thank you," she whispered. "You're not angry with me, I hope?"

Stefano winked at her. "Nah. Like I said, you did right. Now, you don't say nothing to him about this, and of course you don't tell nobody about where this"—he touched the empty vodka bottle—"comes from."

"I would never do that, Stefano, no matter what."

He nodded again. "I know that, Leah. Me and you and Abe go back a long time. I owe him a lot, and I'm going to get him out of this. Don't you worry. I got some ideas on how to do it, and I think you'll be real pleased. I'm not saying I'm gonna do it tomorrow, it'll take some setting up, you understand, but I'll straighten this thing out for you." He stood up.

"Thank you so much. Come, Becky. Mr. de Fazio is busy."

Stefano smiled down at Becky. "My little Dolores is just a few months younger than your daughter—"

"I'm seven years and eight months," Becky said.

Stefano went to the door, opened it and summoned Tony. "Show 'em out and then come see me," he instructed. He kissed Leah on the cheek. "Remember, you can count on me."

After she and the little girl had left, Stefano walked back to his chair. He stared at the empty vodka bottle, then took it from his desktop and tossed it into his wastepaper basket. Who would have thought a guy like Abe would become a juicer? He had such a nice wife—a little skinny for my taste, Stefano mused, but nice, all the same. And Rebecca—what a little doll.

"Poor Abe," he muttered to himself. "What a stupid bastard."

"What's up?" Tony Bucci asked, coming into the office.

"Sit," Stefano ordered. "I got some stuff for you to do, some details to iron out."

That night Leah sat at her vanity in the bedroom, staring into the mirror. She was thirty-two and there was a good deal of grey in her long black hair. When she smiled, the laugh lines framing her small mouth and the crow's-feet at the corners of her eyes were deeply etched.

Nu? So life is hard and the girl soon becomes the woman. I feel healthy, and that's what's important, she thought.

She could hear Abe's voice coming from the parlor, where he was reading the comics to Becky. Listening, Leah was overcome with love for him. Abe was such a good man! This drinking habit was serious, but no real harm would be done as long as it was stopped. Going to Stefano was the right thing to do. She had been frightened, not knowing how Stefano would react. She had long ago sensed what Stefano was capable of. She knew that he could kill and probably had. She shuddered, then remembered that with Abe and her Stefano was gentle and kind. Ganef or not, he was going to fix things.

As Leah stared at her reflection she found herself deciding that it was time to fix things from her end. "You could die," the doctors had warned her, and for a long while their dire predictions frightened her. But in seven years—seven years and eight months, as Becky would say—the fear had faded. Doctors didn't know everything, after all. After her miscarriages they had warned against trying again, but she had, and there was darling Becky to show for it. No, the doctors did not know everything.

Abe came into the bedroom. "What are you looking so excited about?" he asked.

"I've decided something."

"What?" Abe demanded suspiciously. "How to spend money, I bet," he laughed, kissing the top of her head.

Leah gazed at both their reflections in the vanity mirror. "I've decided that we should have another baby. It's time I gave you your son."

Chapter 24

Abe was touched by Leah's determination to give him a son, but he did not really expect her to get pregnant. After her previous troubles bearing a child it seemed nearly impossible. She was in her thirties, after all, and he was forty-nine. Who knew if he still had what it took?

No, Abe did not believe it could happen, and as the months passed it seemed to him that he was being proved right. He said nothing of his pessimism to Leah, she was so excited, so full of hope. Her exuberance had instilled within him new hope of his own.

He curtailed his drinking during that first month and soon swore it off completely, so that he still had two quarts of vodka hidden in the store behind some fruit crates, even though the monthly deliveries had mysteriously ended. He had thought to pour the vodka down the drain to ward off future temptation, for he was far too full of renewed dreams to want to dull his mind with drink. He ended up keeping the two quarts to remind himself how low he had sunk and how Leah had raised him up.

In October she announced the grand news to one and all at a supper at Sadie and Joseph's apartment. Joseph took one look at Abe's flabbergasted expression and burst into uproarious laughter. "You didn't know?" he managed to gasp.

Abe wordlessly shook his head while Becky sang "Mama's having a baby," again and again, ever more loudly as the rest persisted in ignoring her.

"But Leah, it's only been a few months since we started trying—" Abe whispered to his wife, seated next to him at the table.

"So by now we ought to know what we're doing, yes?"

"—Having a *baybee!*"

"Becky, please," Sadie complained, "why can't you sit quiet like my children?" She gestured at her silent brood.

"Are you sure, Leah? I mean—" Abe scratched his head.

"Of course I'm sure." She threw her arms around him. "Darling, you are exactly the opposite of Job. When bad things happen you accept them without question. When God sees fit to bless us, you shake your fist to the sky shouting, 'Why? Why?' "

"I hope I get a little sister to play with—Ow!" Becky cried out. "Mama, Aunt Sadie pinched me!"

"This calls for a drink," Joseph announced. "Abe, a schnapps?"

"Not for me, Joseph, thank you."

"Mama?" Becky asked plaintively, "why are you crying?"

Later Abe sent his family upstairs to the apartment by themselves, saying that he'd be up after restocking a shelf. He waited until he heard the apartment door click shut and then moved those empty fruit crates. The two quarts of vodka sparkled invitingly. He touched one of them. It felt so cool—

If any man has a right to celebrate it is me, Abe thought. Even pious Joseph said I should have a drink.

But he left the bottles where they were, carefully recovering them with the fruit crates. As he did so he noticed that the wooden boxes' end labels depicted a pink ripe peach the size and hue of the setting sun. Framed within it was a tow-headed, freckled farm boy, mopping his sweaty brow with a red bandanna. Beneath the illustration was the legend: "Thirsty Boy Peaches."

Abe, his pulse racing and his mouth bone dry with his despicable craving, tittered, a high-pitched, almost feminine sound in the empty, silent store.

I won't dump those bottles, he thought. I'll keep them, as a reminder to be strong. Then he switched off the overhead light fixture and climbed the stairs to his family. He hurried as if there was something in the dark store that might reach out to pull him back.

Leah's pregnancy progressed normally. She helped out in the busy store throughout the winter, only allowing herself to be banished upstairs in the spring, when she began her third trimester.

In May Stefano telephoned the store to suggest that he and Abe get together to discuss a business matter.

"What do you think he wants?" Leah asked after Abe told her of the call. To herself she wondered if this was the start of Stefano's attempt to straighten Abe out. If it was, she was sorry she'd involved Stefano. His help was no longer needed. She could tell Abe had stopped drinking. Then again, she reminded herself, since I went to see Stefano the liquor has stopped coming.

"I hope he doesn't intend to sell the building," Abe fretted. "Well, we'll know soon enough. I'm to see him tomorrow."

The next day Abe made the trip across town to Stefano's warehouse. It was his first time there. He arrived punctually and was greeted by Stefano's partner, who introduced himself as Tony Bucci.

"I've heard a lot about you from Stefano," Tony said as he escorted Abe through the warehouse complex.

It was almost three months since Abe had touched liquor, and he hadn't missed it until now. Catching glimpses of the men who worked for Stefano made him long for a shot of vodka to steady his nerves. These men were gangsters, he knew, ganefs, like he read about in the tabloids.

Stefano is a one too, he mused, a racketeer, but he is your friend and you knew him when, so don't be afraid. If he wants to sell the building it will be sold, for it does belong to him, but be a mensch and negotiate a little money for yourself. There is Becky to think of, and the new one as well.

"I'll get right to the point, Abe," Stefano began after he'd welcomed his visitor into his office. "Business has been terrific—so good that I've had to divert those monthly cases I've been sending you all these years to a bigger customer. I hope you're not mad at me?"

Abe shook his head. "To tell you the truth I don't do very well with selling it. I guess it's the neighborhood."

He thought he heard Tony Bucci snicker, but when Abe turned in his straightbacked chair to glance at the man, there was no smile on his face.

"It's not only the hooch that's going good, but the market is climbing and real estate is booming," Stefano said, pushing back his swivel chair and putting his feet up on his battered steel desk. "With both those things the secret is to buy cheap and sell dear. For instance, I paid chickenshit for the Cherry Street property—"

Abe heard rough laughter coming from the outer office, where the thugs were lounging. Behind him he heard a match scrape and catch and then smelled the pungent scent of burning tobacco as Tony Bucci puffed on a cigarette.

What am I doing here? Abe thought. I feel like I've wandered into the lions' den.

"And now I've got a big chance to make a nice profit on the property," Stefano was saying, "so I'm gonna sell it."

"Oh . . ." Negotiate, Abe commanded himself, but his mind had gone totally blank. "I guess I'll lose the store, huh, Stefano? It's a shame. We're doing a lot of business—"

"Forget the store, Abe," Stefano said. "It's yesterday's newspaper. You can't compete against the chains—A&P, Safeway, Piggly-Wiggly, they're all taking over. I ought to know, I got a piece of a chain of drug stores, and I just became the sole supplier of meat to the Went's Grocerterias outfit. That brings me to what I wanted to talk to you about. Abe, I got a problem. Just like always, I'm in need of your help."

Lost in dark musing, Abe hadn't been listening all that closely. What will I tell Leah? he wondered. He perked up, however, when Stefano said he needed help.

"Me?" Abe peered at Stefano. "I can help you?"

"He sounds so amazed," Stefano joked to Tony. "Hell, my friend, I wouldn't be here if it hadn't been for your trust. And now again I'm in a jam and need my pal's help to get clear."

"Whatever I can do for you, I'll do," Abe said.

For Stefano, who had encountered so much duplicity in his rise, Abe's sincerity was a novel, pleasant response, one to savor. He looked past Abe, eyeing his partner, smiling faintly as if to say, "See, what did I tell you?"

Tony nodded, thinking, son of a bitch, Stefano was right about this Jew. Tony Gemstones considered himself a good soldier. He recognized the quality of true loyalty in another when he witnessed it.

"Here's the thing, Abe," Stefano began. "I got the meat plant on Washington, and now that I've got this contract to supply Went's, things at the plant have got to run smooth. The guy who runs it now can't handle the job. I need somebody who can replace him. Someone I can count on.''

"Me?" Abe gasped. "You want me to supervise the plant?"

"Nah, I already got a good enough supervisor, a guy by the name of Louie Carduello. What I need is somebody to take over as manager—somebody to keep the books, watch over the whole place, keep it running smooth, you know? Maybe I'm imposing on you by asking you to take on the job, and it's probably more than a friend should ask, but I'd sure make it worth your while financially—''

"Stefano, it's a great opportunity. Of course I'll do it.''

"That's fine." Stefano grinned. "Tony here will handle all the details. We'll start you training gradually. I want you to continue taking such good care of Cherry Street until we find a buyer—''

"I thought you had a buyer," Abe said, puzzled.

"Oh sure I do," Stefano replied, "but these things ain't certain until you get the guy's signature on the dotted line. You know how it is, Abe. So I'll want you to keep the store going—keep it looking profitable and busy—until after the building has changed hands.''

"I'll get a neighborhood kid to help out at the market," Abe said.

"Yeah, sure." Stefano shrugged, glancing at his gold pocket watch. "Tony and you can discuss the details in his office." He escorted Abe to the door. "It looks like things are gonna work out real nice." He shook Abe's hand. "You've probably figured on moving into a bigger apartment anyway. When's the baby due?"

"Month after next.''

"Well, give Leah my best," Stefano said, "and tell her not to work too hard.''

* * *

The fact that Leah would have to work at all weighed heavily on Abe's mind. Tony Bucci suggested that Abe begin his on-the-job training at the packing plant on the first of June. "We'll need a couple of weeks to smooth things out for you," he explained. Abe didn't argue. He could use these last couple of weeks in May to interview and hire a clerk to help out at the market.

"But we can't trust hired help behind the cash register," Abe explained to Leah. "I don't know what to do. You can't work in your condition, and I've got to spend at least a part of each day over at the plant—"

"I will work if you need me," Leah declared. "No harm can come to me. I don't feel nearly as exhausted as I did before Becky was born. The doctor says everything is fine with me. All I'll do is sit behind the counter and watch things. The boy you hire will do all the physical work. Anyway, we have no choice. You can't be in two places at once, right?"

"Maybe Stefano will let me delay the training—"

"You can't ask him that. What if he decides to hire someone else? No, Abe. He said that he needs you now. You must begin."

"Then I'll close the store."

"Stefano said you mustn't. That would make it harder for him to sell the building."

"All right," Abe sighed. "There's nothing for it, I guess. You can work, but only sit at the register, yes? Absolutely no lifting or fetching."

"I promise."

Abe ended up hiring Mario, the sixteen-year-old son of the Italian widow who lived on the third floor. His nationality seemed like a good omen to Abe, and he hoped the fact that the boy was his tenant—on paper the building belonged to Abe—would help keep him honest. Unfortunately, it didn't turn out that way. Several times Abe caught the boy stealing cigarettes or orange tonic and candy, but said nothing. An accusation would force him to fire Mario, and if Mario left, who would Abe find who would be any better?

No, I'll just live with the problem until the store is sold, Abe thought. The boy at least makes our customers' deliveries on time, and if he loiters with his friends on the way back I can put up with it. He has a strong back to lift the crates, and that's all that matters.

In truth Abe no longer wanted to be bothered with the store. The future beckoned to him. He looked forward to his afternoons on Washington Street, learning his way around the plant with the assistance of Tony Bucci and Louie Carduello. There was so much for him to learn— who wanted to think about the store?

All the unpleasant symptoms of pregnancy that Leah had so far managed to escape converged upon her with a vengeance in her eighth month. She let Abe know about none of it. He had enough on his mind. Anyway, if she let on how poorly she was feeling he would at once quit his training to take her place behind the counter at the store. She could not let him miss this big chance. Stefano was bending over backward to afford Abe this opportunity. She could not let Abe pass it by. He was going to be fifty years old soon. Even a man as powerful as Stefano de Fazio would be hard pressed to come up with another position so suitable for Abe.

Mrs. O'Malley is such a stubborn old crone, Leah thought. It was July second, a Friday afternoon, and the elderly grandmother had just placed a large order for groceries to be delivered tomorrow morning. There were a few things she wanted to take with her, however, like the ingredients to bake her pies for the Fourth of July holiday supper she prepared for her large brood. The flour and shortening were within easy reach on a lower shelf.

"I need the baking soda, too, dearie," Mrs. O'Malley insisted, pointing up at the small cans lining the top shelf behind the counter.

The shelf was nine feet off the floor. Leah tried to grasp a can with the reach extender, but she was just too short. She would need the stepladder.

"Mrs. O'Malley," Leah pleaded, "Mario should be back from his deliveries soon. He's been gone over an hour. I'll have him bring it right over to you."

"No. I want it now, young woman. And if I can't have it now, you can just cancel the entire order, including the ham. I'll go elsewhere to spend my money, where they have proper clerks to serve their customers."

"All right, Mrs. O'Malley! Just wait one moment for me to fetch the stepladder."

Where was Mario? Leah wondered as she dragged the folded stepladder from its place beside the produce bin and brought it around the front counter. If only he would come back. She knew she had no business climbing the stepladder in her condition, but Mrs. O'Malley's food order was over sixteen dollars. It would be shame to let such business go elsewhere. There was no use trying to stall. Mario was most likely at the corner candy store smoking cigarettes with his friends, and Abe wouldn't be back from Washington Street until around five.

She had maneuvered her swollen body halfway up the rungs before she realized that she'd forgotten the reach extender.

"Mrs. O'Malley, would you—?" Leah pointed to the thingamajig.

"I'm an old woman," Mrs. O'Malley scowled, "and I don't work here."

If you and your daughters-in-law didn't do so much shopping here—Leah thought as she worked her way down.

It was hard going; her big belly forced her to lean backward to balance herself. Even this small amount of physical exertion after so many weeks of inactivity was exhausting. She leaned against the stepladder for a moment to catch her breath. She was feeling dizzy. She fought off her fatigue. I can do this, she stubbornly insisted to herself. I will get this old hag her baking soda, and I will be able to tell Abe how much money we made today.

She grabbed the reach extender and climbed back up. The tool was designed to be used with one hand, but Leah's fingers were not strong enough to compress the spring grips that caused the pincer mechanism to expand. She had to use both hands, working the grips like a bellows.

To do so she had to release her steadying hold on the stepladder. She concentrated on working the unwieldy reach extender. She didn't want to climb more than two thirds of the way up the ladder. That meant rising up on her toes.

She felt herself on the brink of a dizzy spell. As her vision darkened she let go of the reach extender and tried not to panic. You're only a few feet off the ground, she thought desperately, but as she tried to climb down her foot missed the next rung.

Leah cried out as she felt herself toppling backward. She pinwheeled her arms, trying to regain her balance, and then she was falling. The back of her head struck the edge of the counter. There was a moment's numbing, sickening pain and then nothing at all except for Mrs. O'Malley's faraway frightened yammering and her impact with the floor, which seemed as soft as a feather bed.

Mrs. O'Malley stared down. There was blood seeping from her nose and ears and more of it dripping from beneath her skirt.

"Little girl?" the old woman called up the back stairs to Becky. "Little girl, come down here! Your mother needs help."

At that moment the bell above the front door tingled musically as Abe strode in. "Leah! They let the new manager in training go home early because of the holiday weekend—"

The horror was enhanced by Abe's giddy nightmare sense of it's all having happened before. Just like that first miscarriage, Abe found himself thinking as he sat in the hospital waiting lounge. That whole thing is happening again.

There were some differences, of course. Old Dr. Glueck had passed away in '22. The unconscious Leah was carried out of the store on a stretcher by two grim-faced attendants. She went to the hospital by ambulance. There was no Dr. Henderson at the hospital. Henderson had no doubt long since gone on to better things than a staff position at Gouverneur. The young obstetrician Leah had been seeing this time had been far more sanguine about her pregnancy. No semiprivate room had been reserved weeks in advance.

As it turned out, none was needed. Leah went directly from the ambulance to the operating room. In addition to the obstetrician a surgeon had been summoned. There was something wrong—an injury to the head—a nurse told Abe. She has a concussion, they said darkly. There was bleeding inside her brain.

Please, God, Abe thought over and over as he sat alone, reliving the nightmare, don't let her die, I've got nothing if she dies.

Becky was with Sadie. Joseph had gone to services to pray for Leah.

And I'm having my own service right here on the wooden bench outside from where the doctors are cutting my wife to keep her alive. God, I've tried to be better. I really have. If you want me to make it, don't let her die.

He waited ninety minutes before the obstetrician came

out to say that the baby was breech and a Caesarian section called for.

"Meanwhile, the surgeon was operating on your wife's head. You must understand, Mr. Herodetsky. I considered it my responsibility to deliver the baby as quickly as possible because—"

"My wife is dying, is that it, doctor?" Abe asked softly.

"The surgeon will talk to you about that. But you have a healthy son, Mr. Herodetsky."

Do not do this to me, God, Abe warned. Do not give with one hand and take with the other. I will not accept it; I won't. None of your tricks. Give her back to me.

Twenty minutes later the surgeon came out to say that he was very sorry but that Leah Herodetsky had died on the operating table.

Abe did not carry on; he showed no emotion. He thanked the surgeon and quickly left the hospital. He did not go to Sadie and Joseph's, but to Cherry Street.

"Mr. H, I'm real sorry," Mario, pale and frightened, stammered when Abe came into the store. "I cleaned up, you see?" the boy said, pointing to the spot where Leah had fallen. "I didn't take nothing, Mr. H. Honest I didn't."

Abe nodded and managed a thin smile. "You're a good boy. Now go home."

"Mr. H? How is she?" Abe did not reply and the boy began to blubber. "Oh no, it's all my fault! I shoulda come back sooner."

"Go home, Mario. It's not your fault." *We know whose fault it is, don't we, God?*

Abe pushed the sobbing boy out of the store, then locked the door and pulled the shades. He went to the back of the market and moved aside several boxes in order to uncover the two empty Thirsty Boy Peaches crates. He took the two quarts of vodka and thrust one into each side pocket of his jacket. Then he left the store.

He couldn't stay at Cherry Street. Too many people could disturb his drinking if he remained there. He would head for the waterfront. Just the river and his vodka could keep him company.

"Abe," a customer called to him as he locked the door and pocketed his keys, "I need a few things. Open the store."

"I'm closed up," Abe snarled, hurrying down the street. There was no Leah, no expanse of life for him to contemplate without her—there was only that first swallow of vodka to think about.

Abe's eyes fluttered open. He stared into total darkness. Where am I? What has happened?

Leah—The realization that she was gone thudded home to him. "Oh, no," he moaned. Leah was gone, the vodka was gone, and he was all alone. He remembered how he'd wandered to the waterfront area and searched out a secluded spot from which to watch the river as he drank. Then he must have passed out.

Where am I now? he wondered. He was lying spreadeagled on his back on a rough cement floor. I'm inside. There's a roof over my head. I must have crawled into some sort of warehouse.

"Leah?" Abe began to sob. "Leah, how can you be dead?" His despair tore loose within him. He wept until every tear was expended. He wept himself sober. He did not think of his daughter or his infant son. He wept only for himself.

At some point Abe heard the squeal and clang of a steel door moving on rusty hinges. The noise should have been as abruptly shocking in that still, cavernous darkness as the cry of a great beast in some nocturnal jungle, but, Abe ignored it. He felt invincible, wrapped in the hard shell of his grief.

Directly above him flared a bare electric light bulb.

Abe shouted out, covering his light-sensitive eyes with his hands. The glaring bulb seemed to sear through his brain.

He heard footsteps scuffing toward him and turned to the sound. He squinted up at a man dressed in long-shoreman's garb.

"Get up if you can," the man said. "He's waiting for you."

"Who is?" Abe demanded. "Where am I?"

"He'll answer all your questions, I guess," the man said. "My job is to take you to him, and then I can go home. Can you walk or should I carry you?"

Abe rose unsteadily. The longshoreman eyed him. "You all right?" Abe nodded and the man said, "Follow me."

Abe stumbled along, but then he began to black out. The longshoreman caught him and half-carried, half-dragged him through a maze of crate-stacked pallets to the outdoors and onto a dockside loading bay. It was evening. Abe saw the stars, bleached of their brilliance by the competing illumination cast by the city at night. Across the river glimmered the lights of the New Jersey waterfront.

He had a moment's peace to listen to the water lapping against the pilings, and then a match flared and touched the wick of a kerosene lantern. Several figures, demonic-looking in the wavering light, stepped out from behind the stacked boxes to close around Abe.

"What? What's happening?" Abe blurted, frightened and disoriented. *How long have I been drunk?*

"It's Stefano de Fazio, Abe."

"Stefano?" Abe shielded his eyes against the lantern light.

"You're at my warehouse," Stefano said. "It's July third, Saturday."

"L-Leah died yesterday night, yes?"

"You've been drunk since then, wandering the waterfront," Stefano said. "As soon as I heard about what happened, I had my men look for you. They found you three hours ago, curled up like a damned worm behind some trash bins. They brought you to my warehouse and we've been waiting for you to sober up.''

"I'm sober now, Stefano," Abe said mournfully. He smiled tentatively. "You got plenty of hooch here, yes, Stefano? I could have a drink, couldn't I?''

"That's what you want, is it?" Stefano muttered coldly. "Not to know how your daughter is, or your son, for God's sake? What you want is a drink.''

"Oh, don't, Stefano.'' Abe shook his head. "You don't know— Just leave me be.''

"Sit down, Abe.'' Stefano indicated a couple of boxes stacked in the middle of the loading bay.

"I don't want to. I want a drink!''

Stefano uttered a command in Italian. Abe felt strong hands propel him to the stacked boxes. "Sit down," somebody snarled into his ear. Abe sat.

"What the hell are you doing?" Abe demanded of Stefano. "What is this?''

Stefano reached out to press his fingers against Abe's lips. "Shh. Listen to me," he said quietly, "because you could die tonight if you piss me off any more.''

When Stefano removed his fingers, Abe asked, "What's going on? Why are you doing this?''

Stefano scowled at him. He began pacing back and forth in front of Abe. "I'm doing it because I owe you. Besides, I cared about Leah, God rest her soul. I'm doing it because you got a daughter the same age as my Dolores, and now you got a helpless baby boy. I have to straighten you out, Abe. Now that Leah's dead there ain't nobody else to do it. It ain't right you going on a bender at a time like this—''

"Who are you to tell me what's right?" Abe demanded.

"Never mind that," Stefano snapped, running his fingers through his grey hair in exasperation. "Look at it this way. You belong to me, my friend. From the day you agreed to be the dummy owner of my Cherry Street building in exchange for free rent, you became one of my people. Your personal business is my business. I don't let my people lose discipline. I'll kill you myself before I let drink do the job.''

"But we're friends. I thought—"

"Oh, brother," one of the men behind Abe—Tony Bucci, he thought—muttered in embarrassment.

"Yeah, sure you're my friend," Stefano shrugged.

No, I'm not, Abe thought. I understand now. I've been a fool, but now I understand. You called me your good luck charm, and that's all I am, an underling, a pet.

"You never needed me for that manager job, right Stefano?"

"Need you?" Stefano laughed. "I was killing myself figuring out ways to fit you in without pissing off the people who really ran that place for me. It cost me a bundle to keep everything jake with Louie Carduello. 'Louie,' I told him, 'you're gonna be the real boss, but make this new guy think he's important.' Need you? That's a fucking laugh.''

"I hate you for this, Stefano." Abe stood up. "I'll never forgive you for this.''

Stefano's eyes glittered dangerously. "Sit down.''

"Go to hell, Stefano," Abe uttered hoarsely. "What will you do, kill your good luck charm? I think you are too superstitious to do that. Yes, I think I will leave here now.''

Stefano glared another moment, then shook his head and started to laugh. "I swear, Abe, I don't know what it is with you, guts or stupidity or maybe a little of both." He slapped Abe on the back. "You're right, I won't kill you.''

"Then leave me alone," Abe demanded.

Stefano grew serious. "Oh no, never that, Abe. I'll

never leave you alone. I can't. I'm too superstitious, as you put it. You're nothing to me now, but I owe Leah a promise I made. I'm gonna see to it that her kids are taken care of, my friend. That means no more drinking, Abe. That means if I find out you've been hitting the booze I'll have my guys come around and hurt you—not kill you—but beat you up enough to make you think twice about disobeying me again.''

Abe stared at Stefano in shock. ''You've got no right. You can't do this to me.''

''Sure I can,'' Stefano grinned good-naturedly. ''What can you do to stop me? You know better than to go to the police, I hope. There's no one who can protect you against me, my friend. I am your master. I'm gonna watch over you, Abe. From now on it is not our Old Testament god you must fear, but Stefano de Fazio. Forget about the job at the meat-packing plant. We'll keep you in your little grocery store for now. You'll have enough on your hands dealing with your kids for the time being. We'll forget about selling the building. Maybe I'll send somebody over with some papers for you to sign. It won't make any difference to you. You'll have the store.''

Abe tried to think of some way to counter Stefano's power. It was no use. Going to the police was unthinkable. For now Stefano was indeed his lord and master. Once again Abe was a serf.

You must prove you are strong, Abe told himself. You must earn back your pride. Think of Becky; think of your son.

''Stefano; I must go. There is the funeral for Leah—things I must take care of.''

Stefano nodded to Tony Bucci, who stepped forward to take Abe's arm. ''Tony will see to it that you're driven to your sister-in-law's place. If you need any money to take care of the arrangements, call Tony.''

''This way,'' Tony said, pulling him along.

Abe started walking, then broke free of Tony's grasp to turn back to Stefano. "I'm a good father," he fervently declared. "I am, Stefano. I'd let nothing hurt my children."

"That's what I wanted to hear," Stefano said.

Abe nodded uncertainly. Then he walked toward Tony, who was waiting for him.

Think of Becky. Think of your son. "Please don't put your hands on me."

"Whatever you say," Tony Gemstones replied, amused. "Follow me. The car's waiting for you."

Oh, Leah, how can I live without you? "I don't need help," Abe muttered. "I can walk by myself perfectly fine."

PART II

DREAMS DEFERRED

Chapter 25

Jerusalem, 1939

The crowded marketplace in the Arab quarter of the Holy City was vibrant with sound, redolent with odors. It was a place of catacombs and tattered pastel awnings. Breezes blowing through the dripping stone warrens of the ancient bazaar filled the dim claustrophobic spaces with heavenly fragrances and raw stench by turns. When the wind blew from the east there were the heady aromas of cinnamon and cloves wafting from the spice stalls. When it blew from the west, the high stone archways and narrow thoroughfares reverberated with the steady droning of the flies as they swarmed to the rotting meat whose odor emanated from the open-air butcher stalls.

The proprietor of a stall that displayed prayer rugs had long endured the winds of the marketplace. His clothing was grimy and rank. He was unshaven and his sandals were held together with twine. He had been in his stall across from Sultan's Coffeehouse since boyhood. The stall opposite the modest coffeehouse so grandly named had belonged to his grandfather and his father. He would have handed it down to his own son, but the youth was killed trying to drive those sons of death, the Jews, out of Jerusalem in the uprising of '29.

The rug vendor brightened as a prosperous-looking young Englishman came in. The Anglo looked to be in his twenties, but from the way the fair-haired gentleman was dressed, in finely tailored tropical-weight worsted wool and silk haberdashery, one could tell he was a high-ranking official in the British administration.

The proprietor, pleased that the gentleman understood Arabic, launched into a torrent of flowery oratory, eventually rounding the near bend of his soliloquy by detailing the quality and workmanship of his rugs as compared to the lackluster competition elsewhere in the bazaar.

The Englishman nodded. He wore a wide-brimmed hat and smoked-glass spectacles. The shopkeeper was all the more convinced that the gentleman was an aristocrat as he explained in excellent British-tinged Arabic that he needed a great many prayer rugs to send back to his family and friends.

"I'll be making notes on the quality of your goods," the gentleman said. "I wish not to be disturbed. If I like what I see, I may well buy out your stock."

The proprietor respectfully lowered his head, taking the opportunity to appraise the Englishman's hand-stitched crocodile shoes. "Take all the time you wish, effendi."

"Go about your business then." The Englishman shooed the merchant away. He glanced at his pocket watch, the gold chain of which draped across the points of his vest. "It is eleven-thirty. I'll poke around here until noon or so."

The proprietor backed off, his head full of dreams. He watched the Englishman saunter down the cramped aisles of his stall, already savoring the feel of English folding money between his fingertips.

The Englishman turned, feeling eyes on his back. The Arab murmured an apology and disappeared into a tiny private area in the rear of the shop, drawing a curtain across the doorway.

The Englishman sighed in relief. At last he could remove his dark glasses. They'd been a hindrance in the dimly lit, shadowy alleys of the bazaar, but Herschel Kol—he had shorted his surname when he joined the Irgun—needed them as a disguise.

Haim's son blinked his blue eyes, waiting for them to adjust to the light. He fingered the two hand grenades in his pockets. They were British-made, stolen from a police station by Irgun operatives he had never met. Today at noon he would hurl them into the coffeehouse across the way during its crowded noon rush. Then the "British gentleman" would vanish.

For an operative of the Irgun Z'vai Leumi to engage in such an elaborate charade was unusual. Today at noon, for instance, Irgun men and woman would be hurling bombs into crowded Arab quarters all across Palestine in retaliation for attacks on Jews. None of these other operatives had donned a disguise as Herschel had done; the others would simply detonate their explosives the first chance they got and then run away.

Arab women and children were going to die today, Herschel knew, and the spilling of innocent blood troubled him, but he struggled to put his doubts out of his mind. Enough Jewish women and children had died at Arab hands to justify it. This was a war, which meant that one could attack as well as defend, contrary to the policy of self-restraint preached by Haganah.

Anyway, indiscriminate killing in a terrorist action was not Herschel Kol's mission. The ramshackle coffeehouse across the alley looked harmless enough with its open windows, low tables and stools and its peeling sign of a fat turbaned sultan siting cross-legged and smoking a narghile, but it was a very special target. The Irgun's informants had named the place as a rendezvous for an

Arab activist cell led by a lieutenant of Arab terrorist Fawzi Kaukaji.

The British had been hunting Kaukaji for years. He commanded a widely dispersed force and was funded by the wealthy land-owning clans, who got along so famously with the British.

For years Kaukaji had satisfied himself and his sponsors by attacking isolated Jewish settlements, but now he had expanded his operations into the coastal cities. Hand-picked men from his inner circle went to the Arab quarters of Jerusalem, Jaffa and the other towns, inciting the fellahin to riot by spreading anti-Semitic lies and then organizing and arming them against the Jews.

The man who controlled the Arab quarter of Jerusalem in Kaukaji's name was known only as Eagle Owl, supposedly because of his ferocity as a slayer of Jews and for his elaborate caution and cunning. It was not known what Eagle Owl looked like. All the Irgun knew was that he met his agents daily at noon in this coffeehouse and that he was one of Kaukaji's most trusted and experienced aides.

"This Eagle Owl fellow is good, you realize," Herschel's superior in the Irgun argued during the special private briefing a month ago. The superior was an elderly man who ran a religious goods shop in Mea She'arim. "We are staging a country-wide blanket reprisal against Arab aggression. In all of our other targeted areas the appearance of Jews will be noted, but nothing will be made of it until it is too late. But there is no chance that Eagle Owl will keep his rendezvous if he notices one of our own nearby."

"Is this to be considered an assassination?" Herschel asked.

"Certainly not," his superior snapped. "We do not assassinate; we execute."

"It is a word game you play."

"No, Herschel. First we circulate a death warrant, and only then we execute the condemned man. We can hardly issue such a warrant for a man we cannot recognize and whose name we don't know."

"So I am asked to kill many in the hopes that the man we want will also perish?"

"This is just one operation among many. If you should succeed in killing Eagle Owl in your operation—"

"You mean when I blow up the coffeehouse," Herschel scowled.

"Yes." The officer nodded. "That's what I mean. If at that time we happen to kill Eagle Owl, our enemies will take it as an unfortunate coincidence. They will not suspect our informer." The superior peered at Herschel. "It still disturbs you? So why are you here?"

"You know why."

"To avenge your father's death. I allow you the means to accomplish it. I even afford you a clean target. There will be few innocents in that terrorist-infested coffeehouse. I understand your feelings, you see. I thought you'd be more appreciative of this particular mission."

"Stop it." Herschel winced. "I intend to do my job, so stop talking to me like a fool. You couldn't care less about my sensibilities. You said yourself that Eagle Owl would be on the lookout for Jews. You have no other operatives who can accomplish this execution, or reprisal, or whatever you want to call a mass killing."

The Irgun officer hesitated, becoming embarrassed. "Eagle Owl would never suspect you. He might even feel safer, assuming that we would never dare attack if it meant jeopardizing a British subject in the vicinity."

Herschel understood. He could pass as English. He had his father's blond hair and blue eyes, but his finely chiseled features were a product of British ancestry on his mother's side. As a youth he vacationed with his maternal grandparents at their inn in Jaffa. The visits allowed him to practice his English and pick up a reasonable facsimile of the clipped inflections the seasoned Anglo civil servant brought to his Arabic.

At the end of his briefing Herschel followed as the old man in mended sweater, yarmulke nestled on the sparse white tufts of his liver-spotted scalp, shuffled in backless slippers toward his storeroom. Herschel watched as his superior officer moved boxes of prayer shawls and phylacteries from a shelf to reveal six hand grenades lined up like toy soldiers. He took two and handed them to Herschel, who stowed them beneath his shirt.

"Now then, some tea and a honey cake, maybe?" the old man smiled. The briefing was over.

"No thank you," Herschel said, turning to go. Before he left, he turned back. "It's clear that we're in for another war. No matter that the Chamberlain government gives in to Hitler the way it gives in to the Arabs."

"Nu?"

Herschel eyed his superior. "Well, I was just curious about our plans. I remember that the Jews helped the British during the last war."

"We're helping them now as well," the old man asserted, "by not killing them."

As Herschel hurried from Mea She'arim he trailed his fingers along the cool limestone walls, thinking: My father toiled to cut the stone that shelters our people. He is everywhere in this country. Mama has taught me well. I am a Palestinian and can never be fatherless in this place.

"You have made your selections, effendi?"

Herschel started. It was the rug merchant, tugging at his sleeve. "What? What did you say?" Herschel asked in Arabic.

"Pardon me, but I saw that you were no longer examining my wares. I thought perhaps you had made your selections and were waiting for me."

"No, I'm not ready," Herschel stammered. "More time. I need more time."

The merchant eyed him curiously. "As you wish, effendi." He backed away to his inner sanctum.

Damn, Herschel fumed, he's seen my face without the dark glasses. I mustn't let this assignment rattle me so.

Violence was not new to Herschel, but he still hated it. This would not be the first time he'd spilled blood. He had used his rifle to defend Degania during the Arab riots of '29.

He and the other youths of Degania slept in their clothes with their rifles beside them during the Arab rioting. News of massacres in Hebron and Safed came to the kibbutz; they heard tales of how the rampaging mobs murdered or mutilated defenseless Jews. The British reacted to these atrocities by locking up the surviving victims "for their own safety." There were few arrests of Arabs, who chanted and carried banners that read, "The British are with us."

Herschel and his comrades drilled with their rifles. When Degania was challenged they killed those who would have killed them. Like most adolescents, they dreamed of the future; like most, they thought they would live forever. After the attacks, Herschel and his friends found themselves obsessed with thoughts of dying.

But the young men gritted their teeth and rode with their elders, pursuing the Bedouin marauders to the banks of the Jordan River. They soon learned that it was possible to beat the nomads at their own game. Indeed, they learned that it was necessary to do so if they were to survive. The British had replaced the Turks, but little else in Palestine had changed.

Papa, it is all just as it was when you died, Herschel brooded as he absently picked over the prayer rugs, waiting for it to be noon. We are older. Mama has grey hair

and old Yol is bald on top, with a beard salted white. I
have had to learn to be a desert fighter just like you. There
is still no peace, Papa, never any peace.

When Herschel Kolesnikoff was twelve years old his
mother told him the truth about his father's death, that
Haim Kolesnikoff valiantly served Zionism during the war
but did not die in battle.

"You are old enough now to understand how it is for
us in the world," Rosie sorrowfully explained to her son.
"I am confident that you can understand, for I have tried
to make you strong with memories of your father."

Yol, who had returned to Degania after the war, was
present when Rosie told her son the circumstances of his
father's murder. He explained Jibarn Ahmed's motive and
confessed his part in the blood feud that cost Haim his life.

"That boy?" Herschel gasped. "That boy Papa said
saved his life—it's the same one?" His elders nodded and
Herschel asked, "Where is Papa's grave?"

They took him to the spot. Herschel knelt by the
unmarked mound of earth. Rosie and Yol exchanged glances
as the boy pressed his lips against the ground and then
stood up, grim-faced but dry-eyed.

"Herschel," Rosie asked, "do you wish to put a
stone here?"

He shrugged. "If the Arabs see that a Jew is buried
here they will desecrate the site."

"We could have him brought back to Degania to be
buried in our cemetery."

Herschel shook his head. "Papa's happy here." He
spread his arms wide. "This land is his home. He is part
of Palestine, just as we are."

Rosie stroked her son's blond hair. "I'm proud of
you, Herschel. Long ago I made a promise to your father
at this very spot, may he rest in peace. Your father is with
you always."

Herschel stared down at the earth. Papa, I would kill that boy if I could, he vowed. Someday when I'm grown I will kill him, I promise.

When Herschel turned thirteen, Yol asked him what gift he desired to mark the occasion. "History," Herschel replied. "Teach me, Uncle Yol—tell me what my father fought for and died for. Tell me what he won. Tell me what I won't learn from my teachers. From them I get the facts. You can tell me the truth. I remember a little about the war, mostly how miserable everyone was and how bad to us the Turks and Germans were. But why do the British treat us so poorly now? Why don't they keep their promises?"

Herschel and Yol were seated across from one another at the table in the cottage. Rosie's paintings and drawings lined the walls, and a small bedroom for Herschel had been added. Rosie sat in her son's bedroom with the door open. She was pretending to read, but she was really listening to Yol.

"It is absolutely true that the time immediately after the Turks were defeated was a honeymoon between the English and the Jews," Yol explained. "Unfortunately, it was a very bad marriage in the first place. We Jews are a robust, forthright people. The British?" He dismissed the empire with a contemptuous flick of the wrist. "They make a very frigid bride."

"My dear friend," Rosie called from the other room, "I will come in there and pull your beard out by its roots if you do not stop filling my son's head full of your filthy analogies concerning honeymoons and frigid brides."

"Excuse me," Yol grumbled. "He is thirteen years old, isn't he?" He turned back to Herschel. "Your mother, a lovely woman, forgets that she is no longer the school-teacher for our kibbutz. She forgets that we are now Degania Aleph and Beth and that our two villages share a proper teacher for our children."

"I agree with everything you have said," Rosie called back to him, "but I will still pull your beard if you don't stop that dirty talk."

"All right." Yol winked at Herschel, who delighted when these two grownups bantered for what he took to be his amusement. "In the beginning the British meant well, you should understand, Herschel. They fully intended to live up to the Balfour Declaration, but they are a funny people. In many ways they are far more like Arabs than like Jews. For instance, both the Arabs and the British believe in class distinction. Both put great stock in elaborate courtesy and hospitality. Most important, both hate change. To tell either people that the change might do them good only makes them hate it more.

"The British were pleased with the Arabs for helping them against the Central Powers during the War," Yol continued. "Finally you must realize that we Jews seemed quite able to take care of ourselves. The Arabs are a rather primitive lot, and the imperialistic British like nothing better than to shoulder their so-called white man's burden and colonize a backward people for their own good."

"But they promised us a national home," Herschel interrupted.

"Who, boy? Who promised?" Yol shook his head. "The British government? Men in the government said certain things, that I'll grant you, but the local British administrators can either carry out or impede London's policy, and what they choose to do influences and changes that policy. The Arab riots of '20 and '21, which you probably do not remember so well—"

"I remember. I remember the watchman's calls waking us up, and the shots and Mama crying."

"Those uprisings went pretty much unpunished by the British. Somehow it was made out to be our fault. We'd asked for trouble, the British told us. We were too pushy; we wanted too much. As you might imagine, the

Arabs were greatly encouraged. If a few riots could accomplish so much, why not keep it up? More and bloodier attacks on Jews took place, and when we—the Z'va Haganah, the Army of Defense, which was formed from the Hashomer—attempted to protect our lives and property, it was we who were arrested, not our attackers.

"The Arabs were elated. New men flocked to join Fawzi Kaukaji's marauding bands, while the wealthy effendis, who had always hated us for threatening their privileged position as feudal lords, financed the attacks.

" 'Hunt down Kaukaji,' we implored the British.

" 'Very well, we shall try, but then we must also arrest your Haganah members. That is only fair,' the British said." Yol sighed. "Of course, we were not running away, so the British had a little easier time confiscating our guns." He smiled. "When they could find them, of course."

"Teacher's pet," Herschel murmured.

"Eh?"

"In school there is one boy—his name is Jossel— who is always misbehaving, but the instructor is fond of him and figures out a way to explain all the bad things he does so he won't have to be punished. It's like that with the British and the Arabs, yes, uncle?"

"Teacher's pets," Yol chuckled. He patted Herschel's hand. "Absolutely."

Late that night after Yol returned to his own cottage, Rosie told her son, "I have a birthday present for you as well." She went to the closet and reached up for something hidden away on the top shelf.

Herschel watched as she brought the worn leather tube to the table. "Is it a spyglass?"

"No." Rosie laughed kindly. "Well, maybe in a way it is like a spyglass. With this you can see far into the past."

She carefully extracted the rolled parchment from its protective casing and gently spread it flat on the table.

Herschel's eyes widened. "It's Papa's likeness. I remember when he showed this to me. I was so little. Papa looks very young in that picture. He looks like me."

"You do resemble your father," Rosie amicably agreed.

"Mama, I can't remember—did you draw this?"

"No, it was done by an artist in your father's village in Russia. Here, see?" She pointed to the Hebraic characters. "This tells you when it was done and where."

Herschel wrinkled his nose. "He drew very well, but his Hebrew wasn't much."

"In Russia Hebrew is not for every day, but only for prayers."

Herschel chuckled at that. "Who's that man?" He squinted at the smudged writing. "I can't make out his name."

"Your father's papa died when he was very young. That man, Abraham Herodetsky, took care of your father. Don't you remember hearing about him?"

"No. Was it like how Uncle Yol takes care of us?"

"Yes."

"Mama?" Herschel squirmed. "Are you going to marry Yol?"

"What?"

I've made her angry, Herschel thought, frightened.

"I am very fond of Yol, but there will be no other husband for me, not ever. Can you understand?"

"Yes, Mama." Herschel smiled, relieved. "I am also fond of Uncle Yol, but I also won't have another father—just like you."

Rosie kissed her son, and then asked, her voice suddenly grown gentle, "Do you like your present?"

"Yes, very much. Is it really mine to keep?"

"I'll take care of it for you until you're older, but it is

yours. For a while I considered sending it to your grandfather in Jaffa, but it seems to me that you should have it.''

Herschel grinned and gazed at the drawing. He said nothing out loud for fear he would upset his mother again, but he thought, Abraham Herodetsky, I would like to meet you someday.

It must be coming close to noon, Herschel Kol thought as he loitered in the stall. He checked his watch: two minutes to go. He peered at the coffeehouse through the crowds thronging the narrow, hard-packed street. The place was filling up with patrons. They sat bent over their board games, furiously rattling dice in leather cups and sipping at tiny cups of Turkish coffee.

Only I know how all those games will end, Herschel brooded. The two grenades had grown warm to the touch in his pockets.

How much easier it is to belong to the Haganah as opposed to the Irgun, Herschel thought. How much easier to act in self-defense than to plot an attack.

Once again he gazed at his soon-to-be victims, feeling his pulse quicken and the sweat trickle down his spine beneath his fine silk shirt.

One minute to go, he thought, and began to count backward to himself from sixty.

Take the grenades out, pull the pins—no, too soon. You'll be spotted. Thirty-five, thirty-four, thirty-three . . .

His own heartbeat filled his ears, drowning out the commotion of the bazaar. Now! he thought. I don't care what time it is; I can't bear to wait any longer.

Herschel thrust his hands into his pants pockets. His fingers wrapped around the cast-iron serrated bodies of the grenades. He began to stride toward the coffeehouse and then froze.

A short, slightly built Arab wearing a suit and tie and a Turkish-style fez had been on his way into the coffeehouse.

He noticed Herschel standing across the alley, did a double take and froze.

Herschel stared back at the man, his hands half out of his pockets. Who was he? Why was he looking at Herschel like that?

The Arab took a tentative, horrifying step toward Herschel, but then blessedly changed his mind. He turned and went into the coffeehouse. Herschel caught a glimpse of him in the large window, taking his place at a round table occupied by several men.

Now. Herschel steeled himself. The grenades were out of his pockets. He pulled the pins with his teeth and hurried forward, keeping hold of the safety levers. He dimly heard the rug merchant crying out for him to stop and then shouting for the police. He saw in the coffeehouse window that same Arab wearing the fez. The man saw the grenades in Herschel's hand and then feinted sideways, disappearing from view.

Herschel zigzagged into the middle of the street. All around him Arab shoppers hurried to get away. He had a clear throw to the coffeehouse's gaping windows. He released the safety levers and bowled both in a smooth, underhand motion. He caught a glimpse of one of the grenades bouncing on a table, scattering the crockery. The other skittered out of view amidst the furnishings of the place. Herschel spun and ran.

The twin blasts were concentrated and intensified within the confining stone walls of the bazaar. Herschel had prepared himself, or so he'd thought, but the shock wave knocked him off his feet. He was up and running again in an instant. He did not look back.

He had three different escape routes planned out, just in case. In minutes he was out of the market into the sweet open air, leaving the smoke and the anguished cries far behind.

Chapter 26

Herschel loitered in a quiet alley just long enough to strip. He kicked off the crocodile shoes and hurled them deep into the dark recesses of the alley. Off came the suit pants, jacket and tie. He wore his usual khaki shorts underneath, and a pair of sandals tucked into his belt. He threw away the wide-brimmed hat. As he discarded each garment he felt a little safer. He rolled up his shirt sleeves and unfastened his collar. Finally he smudged dirt on the gleaming silk. When Herschel emerged he looked like what he was, a student at Hebrew University.

He headed for the university now. He was pumped far too full of adrenaline to return to the apartment he shared with his mother. She would be waiting for him, and he didn't trust himself to face her while he was so on edge. She knew he'd joined the Irgun, and quite soon word of the organization's country-wide reprisals would reach her.

No, he could not yet return home, not until he had sorted out his thoughts and tumultuous emotions as the ramifications of his actions took hold. At one time he could have discussed such things with his mother, but they'd grown apart.

So, you helped kill women and children? Herschel could imagine the accusation in his mother's eyes. The question hovered in his own mind. His had been a so-called 'clean' target, but what of his complicity in the organization's actions as a whole? What of his moral responsibility?

Herschel boarded a motor bus and settled into a seat in the back as it began the slow journey north, up the winding road to the campus on Mount Scopus. As Herschel gazed through the bus's grimy window, covered with wire mesh to deflect hurled stones, or worse, grenades, his thoughts drifted back.

Early in his education Herschel showed a strong talent for mathematics. His teachers took him as far along as they could, and after that they compiled book lists for him. The volumes were ordered from Tel Aviv.

His mother was pleased that Herschel wished to pursue his education. She explained to him that there were two decisions he would have to make.

Was he willing to leave Palestine in order to go to school? Was he willing to resign from Degania if the membership, which had the authority to veto the kibbutz children's career plans, failed to agree?

Herschel thought hard. He knew that their money had been wisely managed over the years; paying for an education abroad was not a concern. But if he left Palestine there was no promise that the British would allow him to return. Besides, how could he resign from Degania? He told his mother that he would remain in Palestine and abide by the kibbutz's decision.

Permission was granted. Herschel would attend Hebrew University in Jerusalem.

The kibbutz decreed that Herschel should stay on until there were youths old enough to take his place in the defense of the settlement. The delay chafed at him, but it also worked to his advantage, for Hebrew University at that time focused on graduate-level research. The older Herschel was, the better he would do there.

In 1934 Rosie accompanied her son to Jerusalem. Degania granted them both leave, insisting that she go along to look after Herschel, so she said. Herschel suspected that his mother encouraged him to choose Jerusalem over Haifa as much for her own benefit as his. She seemed as excited as he. She would paint, she told her son, take classes, talk with other artists and stretch her mind and talent. New surroundings would inspire her. Degania was her home, but she needed a change.

Herschel welcomed his mother's company. The harsh demands of settlement life matured him beyond his years, but in another sense he led quite a sheltered existence within the rural family atmosphere of Degania. He knew how to track his way across Galilee and how to kill, but the thought of an urban maze of cobblestoned streets dismayed him. How could he haggle with a shopkeeper? No money changed hands at Degania. Farm life had afforded him an eyewitness understanding of the facts of life, but the girls on the kibbutz possessed the passion-numbing familiarity of sisters, and Herschel had never had a girl friend, never been in love.

But it was not merely a matter of finding Jerusalem intimidating; he wanted his mother with him for her sake as well as his. Since the death of his grandparents and the sale of the family home in Jaffa, his mother was feeling very much alone. Some of her brothers and sisters had left Palestine and some had stayed, but all were occupied with their own lives and families, and all had grown apart from Rosie since she moved to Degania.

Herschel was, quite simply, the only family his mother had left. He relished the role and the responsibility that went along with it. In that expectant, happy time, Herschel assumed that he and his mother would forever be happy in one another's company, watched over by his father's ghost.

The bus to Mount Scopus groaned to a halt before the ponderous castlelike buildings that made up the university. News of the terrorist attack in the Arab quarter preceded Herschel. Several students collared him as he stepped off the bus, demanding to hear the latest.

Herschel told them he knew nothing, even as he itched to correct the rumor that the Irgun had blown up a coffeehouse filled with "innocents." Nearby a student anxiously wondered when the police would make an appearance on campus. The university had only recently returned to normal since the last sweep. In that one the police, many of whom were fascist veterans of the repressive Black-and-Tans sent to quell the Irish Rebellion in the twenties, arrested Abraham Stern and David Raziel, former students and Irgun founders. An overzealous police inspector named Cairns ordered both men tortured when they refused to be interrogated. The Irgun issued Cairns a warning and then put forth his death warrant. Soon after that Cairns and another police official were killed by an Irgun bomb.

"The British will be coming up here again," the student said worriedly. "They'll arrest someone—anyone— just to have a culprit."

Herschel wandered away, heading for the shaded limestone courtyard behind the science building. *"They'll arrest someone—anyone . . ."* The ramifications of his actions were beginning to dawn on him. The adrenaline had worn off, leaving him tired, anxious, remorseful and angry at himself for suffering the weakness of uncertainty.

He entered the courtyard and sat down on a bench before pulling a book from his pocket. Pretending to read so as to avoid being disturbed, he tried to sort out the jumble of conflicting thoughts and emotions washing over him.

Raziel and Stern were rotting in jail under torture, he reminded himself. Any action was permissible to protest such injustice, the atrocities committed against Jews and the British government's white paper, which capitulated to Arab demands that Jewish immigration be curtailed and that the Jews be forever condemned to minority status in Palestine. He ought to be proud of himself, not mired in this confounded funk.

Then he remembered the look of fear in the eyes of that Arab in suit, and fez, and his resolve to be a "good soldier" once again began to waver. To kill in a fair fight was one thing, but his spirit could not endure the thought of any more bombing attacks. It was true that Herschel wished to avenge his father's death, but bowling bombs into the midst of unarmed, unsuspecting victims hardly honored his father's memory.

If only Frieda were here, Herschel thought wistfully. I could do with some of her strength, her certainty.

They met during the spring of 1936, during Herschel's second year of school. He was lazing on the grass, his back against a tree and his nose in his calculus text, when he heard his name called. He looked up from his numbers and equations to see a pretty girl grinning down at him. She had a scattering of freckles across her apple cheeks and a bushy mane of coppery, wiry curls beneath a bright blue kerchief.

"You are Kolesnikoff, the English Jew?"

"I am descended from the English on my mother's side," Herschel coolly allowed. He tried hard not to be mesmerized by the points of her nipples showing through the gauzy cotton of her blouse, but her grey-green eyes followed his fidgety stare, and she smiled, obviously reading his thoughts.

"B-but I was born here in Palestine," Herschel continued, flustered and sounding it. "As was my mother."

"A sabra!"

"What?"

"You never heard the term?" she asked, incredulous. Then she plopped down beside him, sitting crosslegged, carelessly hiking her calico skirt high above her knees.

Freckled also, Herschel thought, his pulse pounding, her thighs are freckled too.

"I'm Frieda Litvinoff." They ended up talking for an hour discussing politics, school and their pasts. Frieda had come to Palestine in 1933, the year of Hitler's rise to power, when the Nazis were just beginning to blame European Jewry for the world depression. Frieda emigrated without her parents as part of the Youth Aliyah program financed by Hadassah. Now she was studying to be a nurse at the university hospital, also funded by Hadassah.

Herschel told her of growing up at Degania. They talked of his renowned grandfather and his paintings on exhibit at the university. It was during a lull in the conversation that Herschel remembered. "Frieda? Before, you were calling me by name. You were looking for me." He smiled. "I'm glad you found me, but why—?"

"Many students here know English, but not so well as you, I've been told." She tugged a packet of papers from between the pages of her nursing tomes and passed them over to Herschel. "Read them later, at home, in private," she commanded.

"What are they?"

"Later, at home. Be sure no one sees them, understand, Kolesnikoff?" she repeated, her green eyes suddenly hard. "Those writings need to be translated into Hebrew, but not just any Hebrew—The language must be passionate, as fervent in expression as the English is now. It will take someone fluent in both languages, and perhaps somebody with some understanding of how those English words of exhortation came to be written.''

Dumfounded, Herschel nodded.

''You can meet me here tomorrow at this same time to let me know if you'll do it.'' Frieda patted his hand and stood up.

''Wait,'' he called as she strode away. ''Where do you live? How can I get in contact with you?''

''You'll see me tomorrow when you let me know,'' she called over her shoulder. ''Then we'll see, yes, Kolesnikoff?''

That night in the privacy of his bedroom while his mother cooked supper, Herschel read the documents. They were propaganda fliers from the Irish Republican Army demanding that the British leave Ireland and that it be declared a free state. The most recent was dated 1920, but Herschel was astounded at how up-to-date and relevant the words sounded when ''Palestine'' was substituted for ''Ireland.''

By the time Rosie knocked on his door to tell him the food was on the table, Herschel was halfway through a Hebrew version of the first leaflet. After the meal he finished the work and then slid it between the scribbled pages of his lecture notebook. He hid the originals deep in his closet—safe, he hoped, from his mother's eyes. Then he went to bed, but he found himself wide awake. The passionate words he'd translated swirled endlessly in his brain, gradually melding with another sort of passion. When he finally dozed, it was to dream of Frieda. The night passed in a giddy half-sleep in which he and Frieda danced and laughed, in which they tumbled endlessly as his trembling fingers traveled her length, learning all the secrets of her body.

A virgin, he had yet to be romantically kissed. He hungered for that of which he had only a hazy knowledge.

By the next morning Frieda was his universe. Rosie

complained that he was acting thick-headed and demanded to know why, but Herschel did not tell his mother that he was in love.

That day he gave Frieda the translation and was thrilled at the pleasure she took in it. He began to spend part of every school day with her, and once or twice a week he saw her during the evening.

He quarreled with his mother about Frieda. Rosie at first attempted to reason with her son, warning him that a girl friend would distract him from his studies. When that failed to deter him, Rosie flatly forbade him to see Frieda. Herschel just as flatly refused to obey. Mother and son did not talk to one another for three days. It was the first time they'd ever seriously quarreled.

For all the turmoil Herschel's relationship with Frieda caused his mother, it was for a long while a chaste love. Herschel felt very unsure of Frieda. He was careful how he acted, even what he said. It was months before he even let on that he knew she was an operative for the Irgun.

"I couldn't tell you," she confessed to him. "Your grandfather was a key figure in Zionism. You yourself were raised a socialist on a kibbutz. How could I expect you to be sympathetic to a revisionist platform that goes against everything—"

"Quiet a minute," Herschel began, then paused. He'd been on the verge of saying that the differences between Zionist philosophies meant little to him, but he thought better of it. He knew Frieda well enough to realize that disagreement would make her far less angry than apathy.

"You're a nice boy, Kolesnikoff," Frieda murmured, patting his cheek.

"Boy!" Herschel was stung. "I'm older than you."

"Chronologically, yes, but that's all. You grew up a sabra. I grew up in Poland. I've been the butt of anti-Semitism, and not isolated hatred for Jews, but organized, government-condoned violent hatred. Believe me, what

Ben-Gurion preaches is wrong. There is no time to negotiate a political solution, not while millions of Jews in
Europe wait to escape Hitler's net. Ben-Gurion and his
supporters are prepared to accept whatever whittled-down
scrap of territory the British see fit to hand us, but there
are Jews who believe that the British must abide by their
word. They promised us all of Palestine, including the
Transjordan, and that is what we need to absorb the
millions who must flee Europe. We need it and we shall
have it, and now, not later, by force if necessary.''

Herschel was staggered by the intensity of her
convictions. He knew of the rift between the mainstream
Zionist movement and the fervently nationalistic revisionists
led by the renowned Vladimir Jabotinsky. The autonomous
Irgun Z'vai Leumi had loosely aligned itself with the
rebels, but he'd never known their motivations. Yol and the
other elders at Degania only ridiculed the revisionists as
fascists. When he explained this to Frieda she laughed.

''Is is fascist to be more concerned with rescuing and
protecting Jews than managing rural collectives or maintaining solidarity with the Russian Communists? I say that
they are the fascists, not we. I left my parents behind in
Poland; you know why? Because the Jewish Agency refused them papers on account of their revisionist beliefs.
Only Jews with the appropriate ideological viewpoints were
encouraged to emigrate.''

She began to tremble. Herschel, lost in her grey-green
gaze, wondered if this was how she might look in his
arms. ''I love you,'' he choked, and felt rising from his
loins the glassy, thrilling sensation of his declaration soar-
ing away.

Frieda patted his cheek. ''Kolesnikoff, we have something very special. With you I am comfortable as with no
one else. You must not spoil it.''

Herschel closed his eyes to hide his pain and then said

the same thing all over again, but in different words. "I want to join the Irgun."

Frieda cocked her head in appraisal. "Why?" She must have realized, for she tried to be kind. "It doesn't matter. We can use you."

Herschel's reveries shattered when a chattering group of students invaded the cobblestoned courtyard. They were loudly debating the grenade attack on the coffeehouse. Herschel had no stomach to listen to their views and dreaded being snared into the argument. He shut his book and left.

After a moment's indecision he decided to head for the gallery where his grandfather's paintings were on view. The brilliant optimistic landscapes of the Holy Land never failed to cheer him. Besides, Herschel spent a good deal of time in the gallery with Frieda, who greatly admired Glaser's work.

It was several weeks after his initiation into the Irgun that Frieda at last took him to her bed. They had been at a hushed candlelit cell meeting in the musty basement of a university building. There was a debate about something. Herschel could not remember what, all he remembered was the way he'd fathomed Frieda's point of view and championed it. She tried to argue for herself, but she'd never been good at that sort of thing. With one other person she could be persuasive, but addressing an assemblage her heady sexuality betrayed her. The women disagreed with her to punish her and the men ignored what she had to say to bask in her aura.

So Herschel rose to the challenge, taking the floor and speaking for his beloved. He debated, cajoled and harangued for over ninety minutes, alternating jokes and shouts to put her point across to them. All that while he knew Frieda's eyes were on him. He noticed another Irgun member leaning toward Frieda and heard the man murmur in admiration, "He's very good."

Frieda smiled and Herschel saw her nod.

Afterward he shyly stood before her, his head lowered, waiting for her benediction. He felt small and vulnerable, but also excited and expectant; he was still elated from his triumph in bending the meeting to his will. His throat tightened as he asked her to have coffee with him. He was ready for her to say no, she was busy, she was going with one of the other boys—Herschel had known from the start that she went with other boys—but she said yes, taking his hand.

They hurried, tense and silent, to Frieda's small rented room in the Jewish quarter. They made love on her thin mattress on the floor beneath her room's single gauze-curtained window. The moonlight washed over them as they twisted together. Frieda's experienced, lushly sensual body enveloped him. He clutched at her, almost frightened as he discovered what delicious physical sensations his own body was capable of. She cried out when he'd moved within her. It was his first time hearing a woman's passion, and that high, feline sound brought him more pleasure than his own climax.

He'd heard frightening tales about a man's first time: that he would be unable to love or else it would be over too quickly. Nothing like that had happened, however. When at last they lay quietly, Herschel's head resting on her soft hip, he nervously asked her if he'd been all right. Frieda's throaty, purring laugh filled the gloaming.

She marked him as her own right then; he felt her etching ownership onto his heart's pristine surface and rejoiced. "Sweet, sweet boy," she murmured, her fingers in his hair, "sweet boy . . ." He drew himself up to lie on her; he suckled at her full bosom; he pressed his ear against her ribs to listen to her heart. He was half drowned, embracing the shore after struggling out of the turbulence of a roiling sea.

"Sweet boy—"

His low, guttural moan rose from his core as Frieda's fingers recaptured him, inexorably drawing him back into her warmth.

Much later that night, as dark velvet gradually lightened to leaden grey and the first expectant bird song greeted the morning, Herschel told her how much he loved her. Frieda said nothing in return, and during that awful silence, as the hopelessness of Herschel's devotion became evident to him, he left her side and ran to the rusty sink in the corner to wash his face.

He left his face dripping wet so that she could not see that he was weeping.

And so at first Frieda refused further advances. She didn't want to encourage him, she insisted. It was not fair to him. He should find another girl. She was married to the Irgun. She would never take a man until the homeland was established.

Herschel persisted. He was head over heels in love, but that did not make him foolish. He set about wooing his reluctant lady. Love had not blinded him to Frieda's weaknesses. She was a slave to her own sensuality, and Herschel had made love to her in an exquisite inspired fashion. No other man could so love her. It was inevitable that Frieda would grow at first to desire and then to need his loving.

Before another month passed Herschel was able to lay claim to her bed. For a week at a time he'd disappear from the apartment he shared with his mother.

"Have you ever heard of the Betar?" Frieda asked him one night in bed as they shared a cigarette in the dark. "It's a youth organization founded in Latvia by Jabotinsky back in the '20s. Betar's ideology combines Jabotinsky's

and Joseph Trumpeldor's ideas on forming a Jewish defense legion—''

"I knew Trumpeldor," Herschel remarked. "I was
only nine years old when he was killed in the Arab riots.
Anyway, he lived for a time at Degania. It's said that he
and my father were friends." He glanced at her profile,
inches away on the pillow they shared. "Is that where you
became politicized, in Betar?"

"Yes." The tip of her cigarette glowed red as she
inhaled.

"A handsome young fellow probably seduced you
into joining," Herschel grumbled. "Another man—I can't
bear it." He leapt upon her, tickling her ribs and rolling
his tongue about her nipples. Frieda began to screech,
letting the cigarette fall to the mattress. She brushed the
burning embers to the floor, where they burned bright
cherry for a second and then slowly cooled to ashes.

"The fellow who 'seduced' me, as you put it, was
not handsome, but he won me all the same." Frieda
planted an affectionate kiss on his brow. "It was my mind,
he won, not my body. Truthfully, we never met. I was
thirteen when I attended a Betar membership meeting in
my village in Poland. A Betar commander, a university
student, spoke. What an orator, Herschel—better even
than you, and I know how good you are," she giggled.
"The commander's name was Menachem Begin. The entire
audience rose to applaud when he was through. Imagine, a
young man barely out of his teens. It was a difficult time
for Betar in Europe. The Socialist-Zionists and Betar used
to have terrible street fights. Names were called and heads
broken."

"Jew fighting Jew?" Herschel shook his head in
disbelief.

"Begin exhorted us to be strong, to be proud, to train
and to wait patiently for vindication," Frieda continued.
"We revisionists have been patient, and behold, we have

been vindicated. Since the Germans and Soviets signed their nonaggression pact, the Socialist-Zionists think twice before condemning us.''

Herschel's voice sounded small. ''Frieda, you have inspired me the way that fellow Begin inspired you. We are soldiers together for Zionism. We are lovers . . . I want to marry you, Frieda.''

There was silence for a moment. Frieda struck a match to light another cigarette. In the flare Herschel saw her furrowed brow—her frown.

''They say Begin will be Jabotinsky's successor as leader of the movement,'' she began, trying to change the subject.

''Frieda, I've asked you to marry me!''

''Oh, Herschel, how can we? You've told me you intend to return to Degania. Those kibbutz socialists would rather you bring home an Arab than my sort. They'd ask me my beliefs and I'd tell them. They'd blackball me.''

''Then to hell with Degania,'' Herschel declared. ''I'd renounce it for you.''

''You would, Herschel? Your home?'' Frieda murmured. ''You're a sweet boy, but what of your mother? She despises me. You can't give up your mother.''

''Frieda, I am all my mother has left,'' Herschel began. ''The day she admits that I am grown and ready to leave her nest is the day she must once and for all say good-bye to my father and the past. Surely you can understand what pain that will cause her.''

''Yes, of course, but—''

''Nevertheless, I shall take leave of her nest. I already have,'' he said firmly. ''My mother has nothing against you but the notion you've stolen me away. When she realizes that my loving you does not amount to rejecting her, she'll come to adore you.'' He grinned. ''How could she not?''

''That much I accept,'' Frieda chuckled.

"So? It's settled then?" He kept his tone light to control and conceal his anxiety. She could not abide uncertainty. "You accept, I presume? We will be married?" He held his breath.

"Herschel, in the Betar we took an oath. It went, 'I devote my life to the rebirth of the Jewish state with a Jewish majority on both sides of the Jordan.' "

"So?"

"When I devote myself to something I do it totally, excluding everything else. When I marry my husband shall take precedence."

"What does that mean?"

She embraced him. "It means that you have conquered me, Kolesnikoff." Although he'd pared his surname down to Kol at his Irgun initiation, Frieda delighted in teasing him. "I thought I could twist you around my little finger, but I see that you have turned the tables on me. When our struggle is over, I will be your wife."

The picture gallery connected to the university's library was empty at this time of day. Students were either in class or studying. To be enrolled here was a great privilege. Few students would jeopardize their standing by wasting time looking at pictures at this hour.

Herschel walked the deserted marble corridors, gazing at his grandfather's landscapes and desperately missing Frieda. It seemed that he could hear her ghostly laughter echoing in the still hallways, could remember exactly her comments about each painting.

If only you were here, he thought, you could tell me I did the right thing in the Arab quarter. You could tell me that destroying a terrorist headquarters struck a blow for our cause and brought us closer to marriage. If you were here I could feel like a hero.

But Frieda was not here. Three months ago the Irgun had ordered her to report to a cell somewhere along the

Mediterranean coast; she was not allowed to tell Herschel exactly where.

Since the Nazi invasion of Poland, leaky, overloaded ships flying the Greek or Turkish flag had begun to transport desperate Jewish refugees to Palestine. The ships brought their cargo as close to shore as they dared; then Irgun boats ran the British blockades.

The Arabs were howling in disapproval and the British were increasingly determined to stop the influx. Frieda's cell was doing all it could to keep the people from being drowned or sent back.

Herschel was at the mercy of his guilty conscience. Perhaps all the people in the coffeehouse were Arab terrorists, but what if they weren't? What if that one fellow, the one in the suit and tie and the fez, was an innocent?

That poor man stared at me like he knew me, Herschel recollected. He saw his death in me, and in him I saw stark fear.

It was no good. He couldn't live with the thought of more attacks like this one.

A particular painting by his grandfather caught Herschel's eye. It was a view of Galilee. Herschel did not know if Erich Glaser had ever visited Degania, but he had captured the burnt umber of the pillowy hills and the cerulean blue of the sky. Herschel had heard the usual criticisms leveled at his grandfather's work: that it was highly idealized, often saccharine. In some Herschel could see how such comments were justified, but with this his grandfather had succeeded. The almost fantastic pleasantness of the scene corresponded to the pride, affection and solicitude a son of Degania felt when gazing at the land he and his fellow members had tamed.

As Herschel took solace a childhood memory came to him. He could have been no more than ten. He and another boy were together in the schoolyard, which afforded a view similar to the one in the painting. This other boy was seven and was named Moshe in memory of the brave young halutz who in 1913 rode out alone to fetch medicine.

The more Herschel concentrated the more vivid his recollection became. He and the younger boy were arguing, Moshe bragging that he'd been named after a hero. Stung by Moshe's boasting and still raw with sorrow over the loss of his father, Herschel reacted with a child's ferocious intensity.

"That man Moshe was dumb to be ambushed. My father is the true hero. He fought in the war, facing the enemy man to man. He had a pistol—yes, he did! I remember he showed it to me."

The younger boy was no match for Herschel's fury. He apologized, agreeing with him. "A man who fought in the army is certainly a hero." They shook hands and parted as friends.

"Shalom, Herschel Kolesnikoff."

"Shalom, Moshe Dayan."

A short while after that the Dayans, one of the original families of Degania, moved to another settlement with their three children, of whom Moshe was the youngest.

Herschel stared at his grandfather's painting, musing on the memory it had evoked. Seven-year-old Moshe misunderstood and assumed that Herschel's father was in the British army. *"A man who fights in the army is certainly a hero . . ."*

Herschel hurried out of the gallery and cut across campus to the bus for Jerusalem. He knew what he had to do to assuage his conscience.

It was three o'clock in the afternoon when Herschel Kol returned to the apartment he shared with his mother near the Western Wall. He steeled himself for confrontation as he climbed the dim stairs to the third floor. He hoped his mother had painted well that morning. When her time at her easel was profitable she was in a good mood.

Their rooms faced the rear courtyard and did not receive much sunlight after midmorning. The ceiling light was off in the living room as Herschel entered the apartment. He heard a chair creaking and saw his mother, bathed in shadows, sitting in a rocker in the far corner of the room.

Rosie reached out and clicked on a table lamp beside her chair. Herschel saw that her eyes were red-rimmed from crying, her lined face drawn and pallid. How old she looked. She was just fifty, but her years in Degania's harsh climate had turned her skin leathery and her hair prematurely grey. What had become of his beautiful mother? Who was this haggard crone in a shapeless, paint-splattered frock? When had mother and son become such strangers to each other?

"It was you, wasn't it Herschel?" Rosie's trembling voice, husky from disuse, shattered the dark stillness. "You blew up that coffeehouse. Oh, I know it was you."

"I don't want to fight about it with you, Mama," Herschel began.

"It's that girl—she's turned you into a murderer. I warned you about her, didn't I?" She stood up. "She has made you a wild man. You grew up in Galilee, learning to use weapons just as you did farm tools. I remember how you cried, your head buried in my lap, that first time you had to kill to defend our settlement." She shook her head bitterly. "You don't cry now, though, do you, boy? Why are you here? Why don't you rut with your whore to celebrate—"

"Shut up!" Herschel shouted. "What I did was for our people! I didn't enjoy it!" His anger vanished. "How can you, Mama? How can you speak to me this way?"

Rosie's shoulders sagged. She turned away from her son. "Are you safe at least? No one is chasing you, I hope?"

"No one. Mama, let's not argue anymore. I love you."

Rosie nodded. "I'm sorry, Herschel, but I can't forgive her for transforming my beautiful, clever son into a terrorist. You had a future, but now it's only a matter of time before the British arrest you. If not for this crime, for some other one that girl—"

"Frieda. You know her name, just as you know that she is away from Jerusalem. Don't be this way."

"All right," Rosie said scornfully, "Frieda." She shook her head. "I heard ten people were killed in that blast and six more injured. Your father would not have approved."

"That's not fair—"

"Your father would never have joined an organization like the Irgun."

"But he would have joined the Allied Army," Herschel snapped. "Wouldn't he have joined to fight the Turks if he could?"

Rosie stared at her son. Something in his eyes frightened her. "I don't understand," she murmured. "Herschel?" Her fingers rose to her lips. "Herschel, what are you getting at?"

"On my way home I stopped at the Jewish Agency office. They are taking names for volunteers to join the British Army. Most Jews are having trouble getting inducted, but with my light features and my British ancestry, I should have no trouble, I was told. The agency people are anxious to get as many Jews into British uniforms as they can." He smiled. "They think it will persuade the British to side with us against the Arabs later on. That's what Papa thought. I guess history does repeat itself. Personally, I don't care what the agency people think. I'm only joining so I can fight our enemies honorably. You see, Mama, I do care what you think and what Papa might have thought. I'm quitting the Irgun tō follow in my father's footsteps."

Rosie said nothing. What could she tell him? He wouldn't listen anyway. As her son retreated to his bedroom and shut the door behind him, Rosie thought that history did indeed repeat itself. The first war had taken her husband and this second would lay claim to her son.

Chapter 27

The grenades' destructive power was contained by the thick walls, but the resultant panic made a shambles of the marketplace. Fleeing bystanders toppled the charcoal cooking brazier in front of a food vendor's stall; the accident went unnoticed in the confusion. The scattered coals began to smolder in their nests of straw and sawdust and soon tendrils of blinding, acrid smoke were winding through the catacombs.

A pair of bodies lay where the twin explosions had flung them. A wounded man wandered in shock; others managed to stagger outside and lay sprawled in the narrow thoroughfare, moaning and crying. The explosions caved in part of the roof. Frenetic would-be rescuers shouted contradictory orders as they tried to dig out the crumbled masonry and toppled timbers.

The rug merchant across the way was one of those who hurried to lend a hand. He was unharmed except for the ringing in his ears.

The British police soon arrived, but there was little they could do except step gingerly about the rubble. The vaults of the marketplace could not accommodate motor vehicles. The ambulances idled an eighth of a mile away.

Those too badly injured to walk would have to be loaded onto stretchers and carried up twisting passages out into the open.

"Who saw what happened?" one of the policemen bawled in Arabic. "Who has information about this mess?" He rocked on his heels, his thumbs hooked into his pistol belt. "Come on," he shouted, "how do you expect us to catch the bloody Jews if you won't help us?"

The rug merchant timidly approached the officer. He tugged at the policeman's khaki sleeve. "He was not a Jew," the rug merchant murmured after he'd garnered the officer's attention. "He was an Englishman."

"What's that? English, you say?" The policeman chewed on the ends of his mustache as he thought it over. Just the other day his sergeant had lectured them on the possibility that certain British, sympathetic to the Zionists, might throw in with them. That sort of thing was certainly not unheard of. Why, Captain Orde Wingate of British Intelligence had thrown in with that Haganah lot, teaching the Yids things they had no business knowing. It was a short leap from advising the Yids to an active role in their operations.

"Perhaps you'd better tell me about it." The officer pulled out a leather-bound notebook and a stub of pencil. "Start with a description." He licked the point and began to write as the merchant spoke.

"Blond hair and blue eyes, handsome, very tall and well built."

An Arab in suit, tie and fez listened as the merchant stammered his description of the attacker. He was seated on the cobblestones some yards away with his back against an overturned table. Directly in his line of vision was a severed arm in the blood-slick gutter. The hand lay palm up, the fingers curled. The Arab wished someone would take it away or at the very least cover it.

He had no need to eavesdrop on the rug merchant's

description. He quite well remembered what the attacker looked like; he'd taken a good long look at him just before entering the coffeehouse. The fellow's haunting looks had lured him to the coffeehouse window for a second glimpse, and that saved the Arab's life. His black eyes and the attacker's blue ones locked for a moment; he saw the grenades clutched in the man's hands.

The Arab did not utter one word of warning to the others in the coffeehouse; to create a panic might have blocked his escape route. He made a beeline for the side entrance, just reaching the threshold as the grenades exploded. The blasts hurled him against the opposite stone wall of the narrow alley, giving him a sound jolt. He'd fell to his knees, tearing holes in his trousers as he grazed his skull against stone. He blacked out for a moment, and when he came to, he felt dizzy. He crawled out to the street and sat down on the curb to rest against the salvaged table. He was unharmed except for a slight bump on his head. In a few minutes his dizziness would recede and he could be on his way.

Another Arab dressed in a long striped caftan and billowy trousers quietly seated himself next to the one in European garb. This newcomer's name was Assiya; he had within the folds of his garment a pistol and a knife. He was ready to use either to protect the man beside him, who was his master.

"Forgive me," Assiya murmured. "I was in position, watching as I was instructed." As he spoke he looked straight ahead and hardly moved his lips. If any of the British policemen glanced their way the officers would have seen two mute, shocked victims of the attack.

"I saw him," Assiya continued, "but I never suspected him; he was English."

"He wasn't."

"Not English?" Assiya wondered if his master was injured worse than he seemed. "I tried to get a shot at him as he attacked, but there were too many people blocking my aim. Afterward I considered pursuing him, but I thought my place was here with you."

The other man nodded. "The others are all dead?"

"All dead."

"I would have died as well if I'd not recognized the attacker."

"You know him?" For the first time Assiya glanced in his master's direction.

The suited man smiled. I know his blond hair and blue eyes, he thought, I know his face. Oh, it's finer-featured, the nose less aquiline, the lips thinner, but of course the mother is Anglo, and that would cut the father's Slavic blood. "I killed his father," he said. "Don't be fooled by his looks. He's a Jew, all right."

"Jibarn Ahmed, you are incredible." Assiya breathed, so overcome with awe that he forgot himself so far as to call one of Fawzi Kaukaji's operatives by his real name.

"Yes, he is a Jew. I want you to go over to that policeman and corroborate the rug vendor's description—it is quite accurate. Only say that the attacker was not Anglo but a Jew. Say his name is Kolesnikoff, first name—" Jibarn Ahmed searched his memory—"Herschel. Tell the British policeman he wants a Jew named Herschel Koles-nikoff."

"The authorities will want to know how I came by this information."

"No. They will be so relieved that it was not one of their own that they will ask no questions. Assiya, you realize that after you testify at the Jew's hearing you will be known to the British and accordingly of no further use to us."

"I understand."

"You know what must become of a man who leaves our services?"

"Do not worry," Assiya assured him. "I long to

receive my hero's welcome in Paradise and take my place at Allah's side. The day I send this Jew to his death will be the day I willingly embrace my own.''

''Assiya, will it be necessary for me to send someone to escort you to Paradise?''

''No. I will take myself there.''

Jibarn Ahmed nodded, satisfied. ''Allah be with you, Assiya. Now do as I've told you.''

He sat awhile longer, listening as Assiya told the British officer his piece. Oh, how exquisite it was going to be! The British would surely hang the Jew responsible for such carnage. Herschel Kolesnikoff, Jibarn thought, the only sour notes are that your attack was so successful—my best operatives are dead—and that I cannot remain in Jerusalem to see you hang.

Haj Amin el-Husseini, the Mufti of Jerusalem, had succeeded in joining clans into the Arab High Committee. An important meeting was taking place in Beruit in just seventy-two hours' time. Nazi representatives would be there; the Mufti had promised Hitler Arâb support in exchange for German arms. Jibarn Ahmed had been accorded the high honor of signing the secret alliance on behalf of Fawzi Kaukaji.

''Well, now we've got the bastard dead to rights, don't we?'' the British officer chuckled as Assiya finished his story. As the policeman continued jotting down the rug merchant's and Assiya's particulars, the Arab bodyguard turned for a farewell glimpse of his master, but Eagle Owl had already vanished.

Chapter 28

The worst argument Abe Herodetsky ever had with his son Daniel occurred several months after Daniel's thirteenth birthday, by the front counter of the Cherry Street Market. It took place during the midafternoon, so there were no customers to interrupt or slow the steadily escalating rounds of spite.

Danny was failing in school. According to his teachers he was also disrespectful and in danger of being expelled.

"Who cares?" Danny demanded. "I don't care about that crap."

"Don't talk like you're from the gutter," Abe scolded.

Danny shrugged. Abe, staring at his son, thought: You look like a punk, like the hooligans I chase out of here. Danny was thin and short for his age, scrawny in his dingy turtleneck sweater and shiny wool knickers.

Danny must have seen the disapproval. His lips curled into a sneer. Abe tried desperately to think of some way to persuade his son to apply himself. It wasn't that Danny was stupid, he was very clever when he put his mind to something. He knew how to fix machines, for instance.

428

When the cash register broke Danny had disassembled it and got it working.

The same stalemate between father and son had occurred over the boy's bar mitzvah. The teachers had warned that unless Danny applied himself he would not be ready, and he hadn't been, despite Abe's pleading not to dishonor his mother's memory. There was no bar mitzvah and what a bitter fight they'd had over it. He and his son did not speak for a week.

If only Abe knew how to reason with the boy. If only he could get across to him how his dear mother felt about education and religion.

Abe began attending synagogue soon after his wife's death, both because of his belief that it would have made Leah happy and as a response to the reprimand dealt him by Stefano de Fazio. Abe came away from that late night waterfront confrontation determined to show the Italian he could be a worthy father. To that end he struggled to control his drinking and to make annual contributions to the synagogue to honor Leah's memory. The latter was his way of making peace with God. It was especially difficult for Abe to give money during the first years of the Depression, but he managed, unable to brook the loss of the small brass plaque commemorating his wife. It brought him such pride and pleasure.

If he were willing to make the sacrifices required to be good in honor of Leah, so should his children. After all, they owed their existence to their mother. As in all things, his daughter Rebecca dutifully deferred to his wishes. That his son constantly defied him enraged Abe. Nevertheless, today he would try.

"To be a good student is what your mother wanted for you."

"You always say something like that, Pa," Danny countered. "It isn't fair. I gotta sit in a stuffy classroom for somebody who's dead and doesn't know the difference—"

"Somebody?" Abe was aghast. "Is that how you talk about your mother, who died to give you life?"

"I'm sick and tired of hearing about it," Danny stormed.

That was when Abe said the worst thing a father could say to his son. "I curse the day you were born! To think that she died to bring forth an animal like you."

The look on Danny's face stopped Abe. The color had drained from the boy. His brown eyes burned with hatred. He's going to cry, Abe thought, softening, willing the tears from Danny's eyes. Cry, and then I can embrace you and say I'm sorry.

"I hate you." Danny's tone was feral, deep and low beyond his years. "Why don't you die, old man? Then you'll be with her. You'd rather that than here with us."

"That's not true, Danny—I—" Abe, at a loss for words, merely shook his head.

Danny turned on his heel, looking for something—anything—to lash out against to relieve his fury.

"Danny, listen to me—"

The boy swept a row of canned vegetables from the shelf.

"That's money, damn you," Abe shouted, his anger refueled and flaring more intensely than before.

Danny viciously booted the tins out of his path and stomped out of the store. The bell above the transom gaily jingled as he straight-armed the door open. It quietly closed itself in his wake.

Abe sagged against the counter, his breath coming in ragged sobs. Sixty-three years old and he felt like a hundred. His heart was pounding and in his mouth was the metallic taste of adrenaline mixed with bile. He had to be careful. The doctor had told him not to get excited, not to put a strain on his heart.

His medical rejection certificate was still in the front window. The paper was torn and yellowed and the inked medical terms had faded to illegibility, but now Abe knew what the draft board doctor meant. For several years his heart had been whispering of death.

"He never knew her," Rebecca said, "not like we knew her." She was standing at the foot of the stairs that led up to the apartment above the store.

"You heard? He won't got to school. You watch. It's going to be the same thing as with the bar mitzvah. Did you hear him wish me dead?"

"He didn't mean it."

"Oh, sure."

"Just like you didn't mean it when you cursed him."

Abe nodded. "Yeah, you're right. I'm too old to have such a son. What can I do to understand a thirteen-year-old boy? When I was his age I wouldn't have understood him—"

"Oh, Father." Abe watched his daughter as she walked toward him. He remembered his vague but real disappointment when it was evident that Becky was not going to look like her mother. Oh, there was some of Leah around Becky's nose and eyes and in her thick, dark hair—how absurdly angry Abe had been the day that Becky cut her hair to shoulder-length. But Leah was a slight, thin woman with narrow hips. Becky was big-boned with wide hips and a buxom figure. She wasn't plump; her baby fat had been just that, now she was a strong, healthy girl with a flat belly and firm arms from helping with the boxes in the store. Even though she was demure of manner and dress, Abe had seen the way she caught the young men's attention and was glad of it. He wanted his daughter to have the conjugal bliss that had been his while his wife was alive. He loved his daughter and he wanted her to be happy.

"We knew Mama," Rebecca was saying as she hugged Abe. "She's a real person to us. To Danny she's just that strange woman beside you in the photograph. When you tell him to do things or not do them on account of Mother, it's like—'' Becky furrowed her brow. "It's like what the goyim go through when their priests warn them not to betray Jesus.''

Abe pulled away, putting his hands over his ears. "Please! You want to put me in the wrong?'' He pointed at the tin cans, some dented, scattered on the floor. "When that animal did this, did he betray me? Tell me what I've done that's so bad for him. I feed him and clothe him and give him a roof over his head. He goes to school and every year I put something away for his college education. But he acts like a dunce, insulting his teachers, and he wishes me dead.''

"You wished him dead first.''

"Shut up,'' Abe growled, angry because he knew she was right. "Don't be a wiseacre. Are you going against me as well?''

Becky bent to pick up the cans.

"Are you?'' Abe demanded.

"No.''

Abe nodded, satisfied, and then sighed. "I'm exhausted. I'm going upstairs for a while. You'll manage here?'' Without waiting for an answer Abe left the store to trudge upstairs to the apartment. He kicked off his shoes and stretched out on the cot in the kitchen. Since Becky's adolescence she'd had the privacy of the bedroom. Danny slept on a foldout couch in the living room and Abe slept here, his old bones kept warm by the gas stove. They could have moved to larger quarters—Stefano had insisted that Abe continue on as the figurehead owner of the building, but he didn't mind if Abe and his children chose to move. Stefano also offered to have one of the larger apartments in the building vacated, but how could Abe give up these rooms where Leah lived? I would freeze to death in any other apartment, Abe mused drowsily. Here Leah keeps me warm. I should let strangers live here?

As he drifted off, Becky's recriminations rose in his

mind to haunt his dreams. God, forgive me for what I said to my son. Make me better. I'll do what's right for Danny if I can, but it's not my fault if I don't—can't—love him.

Abe fell asleep the way he always did, in his fantasy world. Leah was alive; they cuddled together every night, and by day they laughed and played with their children, magnificent Rebecca and their laughing, loving, respectful blond and blue-eyed son Haim.

Becky finished reshelving the fallen tin cans just as the late afternoon rush began. With the exception of the glass-fronted refrigerated meat counter, which her father had installed several years ago in the rear of the store to replace the barrels of smoked meat and fish, the market was set up to be self-service. Adult shoppers did serve themselves; still, later afternoon invariably brought a flurry of children bearing shopping lists from their mothers. Sometimes a dollar bill or so was wadded up in the folds of the note, but more often the lists closed with a directive to put it on the bill.

Making up orders while the children waited was a nuisance. Becky also had to run the meat counter and check out the customers at the cash register. Still, the children's shopping lists had to be filled, just as credit had to be given. It was these extras that gave a small independent grocery a chance against the larger, much better stocked supermarkets with their cut-rate prices and newspaper advertising.

The afternoon wore on. There were jam-ups at both the meat counter and the cash register, but the majority waited patiently for Becky to get to them.

Becky resisted the temptation to call her father to lend a hand. He needed what little rest he could get. She knew he wasn't sleeping very well at night, and the fight with Danny had clearly taken a lot out of him. Besides, she worked better when her father wasn't around to peer over her shoulder and criticize everything she did.

Danny came back a little after seven. He used his key, for Becky had locked up for the night. She was kneeling behind the meat counter, scrubbing the big squat wooden chopping block. He stood watching her, his hands in his pockets. "Want me to finish that for you?"

"I'm almost done." A tendril of hair had fallen across her eyes. She tried to blow it off of her face but couldn't. Her hand rose to brush her hair behind her ear, but then she hesitated. Her fingers had been in the scrub water. Becky hated the smell of it on her hands and certainly didn't want it in her hair. Danny came around the side of the counter and brushed back her hair.

"Thanks." Becky smiled. Danny stood beside her, affectionate yearning in his eyes and posture. Becky dropped the scrub brush into the bucket and straightened up, wiping her hands on a towel. Danny stood just chest high to her. He seemed small and defenseless against their father's aloof, gruff manner. "I'll say to you what I told him. Neither of you really meant what you said."

"Doesn't matter," Danny said too brightly, "but I think he did mean it, Becky. Pa's not proud of it, but it's still the way he feels." He gazed at his sister, his eyes hard, daring her to contradict him. "I can't stand it when we get into fights like that. My guts get all tight, you know?"

"Maybe you should try to please him a little more."

"I can't. He hates me! He can't stand to have me around. You know that."

"I don't." Becky clasped his shoulder.

"He won't let me help in the store."

"That's because he wants you to use the time to study. He wants you to have an education."

"That's what he says. The real reason is that he

doesn't want me here with him. At night at the supper table he never looks me in the eye or talks to me.''

"He'll change," Becky said, "and so will you. You'll see.''

"He'll never change.''

"I did. About you, I mean. When Father took me out of high school to work in the store I hated you.''

"You did?'' Danny looked up at her, his eyes wide with apprehension.

"Father said, 'You're the oldest and can help me best, and you're a girl, so what do you need with an education? To get married, to have babies? For that a girl doesn't need school lessons.' ''

She twisted her face into their father's scowl and her raspy voice perfectly captured Abe's tone and inflections. Danny giggled in appreciation.

"Anyway, I used to cry in bed every night, missing my schoolmates, thinking I was never going to be anybody all because you were the boy and I was the girl—''

"I'm sorry.''

"Hush. I didn't tell you to make you feel bad. For one thing, working in the store has turned out to be good training for me. I wanted to study retailing in school. Here I do most of the ordering and keep the books, just as Mother once did. I've learned plenty that will be useful someday, when I can get a real job in a big store.

"No, Danny, I told you about my feelings only to prove to you that people do change. Someday when you're a little older, you and Father will act differently to one another.''

"That's forever from now.''

Becky chuckled. "Not so long, and in the meantime I'll speak to him.''

"You will?'' He gazed up hopefully.

"Uh huh. I'll see if he'll let you help in the store.'' She took on a mock stern expression. "But you've got to prove that you're a man. You study hard and make Father proud, and we'll see about you helping out around here.''

"That's a deal. You know, if Pa let me help, you could look for that real job you wanted."

"Yes."

"It'd be sorta like I was making it up to you for having to leave school."

"Oh, Danny—" Becky hugged her brother. "I love you, Danny."

"I love you, too," Danny murmured. After a moment he asked, "Are you going to the library later?"

Becky glanced at the Coca Cola wall clock. "If I can," she said. "It closes at nine-fifteen."

"Then I'm going back out too."

"Danny, it's after dark."

"I don't want to be here alone with him."

"Well, at least get your coat. You'll freeze in a sweater."

Danny looked reluctant. "I'd rather not go upstairs for it. He might wake up."

"I'll get it for you." Becky tiptoed up the stairs and passed quietly through the kitchen into the living room. She pulled Danny's coat out of the closet, checked to see that his muffler was stuffed into its sleeve and returned downstairs, pretending she hadn't heard Abe calling for her. If Danny heard her talking to her father he might run out without his coat.

"Thanks." Danny tugged on the garment and patiently suffered Becky to wrap his scarf around his throat.

"Not too late coming home," she called to him as he ran out.

Becky was going over the credit accounts when Abe came downstairs. She'd turned off the opalescent ceiling fixtures to save on electricity and worked in the small pool of light cast by the goose-neck lamp clipped onto the cash register. She'd emptied the cigar box of credit vouchers onto the wooden counter. She was in the process of sorting the slips by name, adding up the amounts, and stapling the vouchers together when she noticed her father. His wrinkled face was still puffy with sleep, his right cheek scored by the pillow. His hair had gone iron grey after his wife's death, and in the last couple of years it had pretty much thinned out so that there was a horseshoe fringe around his ears, and a few feathery wisps on top. He hadn't shaved in the last day or so.

"We were busy tonight," she reported. "We ran out of chopped meat."

Abe grunted acknowledgement. His baggy rumpled trousers hung around his hips and his cardigan was misbuttoned across his paunch. "The Schwartzes pay?" he asked, fingering the neat stacks of credit slips.

"You kidding?" Becky chuckled absently, her mind on her addition.

"Sons of bitches," Abe said mildly. He stuck a pencil above his ear, licked his finger and began to rifle through the slips of paper. "You give to Ronzi?"

"I gave," Becky replied, "because you told me to, but look at their bill. Six dollars they owe us. Today they bought two pounds of sirloin, two pounds at thirty-nine cents a pound. Rib roast at a quarter a pound wasn't good enough."

Abe chuckled: "You sound just like your mother."

Becky looked away. "Please, Father, you know I don't like it when you say things like that."

Abe shrugged. "Anyway, she always wondered why I gave credit. She forgot how all the boys in the union chipped in to give me the stake to open this place. And then in '33, you remember the day the banks closed, how people were running wild in the streets? All those drunken Irish gangs came to Cherry Street and for a few bad minutes we thought they would break our windows and loot the store.''

Becky nodded. ''I was crying, I was so frightened. Everybody from the neighborhood lined up in front of the store. 'Get out,' they told the Irish ruffians. 'This is our neighborhood and our store and you're not going to wreck it.' ''

''And they weren't just our Jewish customers,'' Abe added. ''There were goyim as well. They made that Irish bunch hesitate long enough for me to telephone Stefano, and he sent some of his men to chase them away. But it was our customers—including Mr. Ronzi—who saved us.''

''Because even then we gave credit?'' Becky smiled, egging him on. Talking business was one of the few things that could bring the light to his eyes. ''They owed us, Father?''

''Because when the seller treats the buyer right it's like magic. Buying and selling is what made the first civilization. Love, hate—all emotions—as well as the act of taking by force—animals can do all that. But to work out a system where goods and services are exchanged in a fair manner—this only mankind can do. It's what separates us from the animals.''

Abe winked. ''Every night you go off to the library. I see the books you bring home, every one of them on retailing, but there are still a few things I can teach you that maybe the big shots who write the books don't know.''

''Like letting the customers run up six-dollar tabs they haven't a hope of paying?''

'' 'Cut 'em off when they don't pay,' is that what those fancy books tell you? Well, if I did tell Mr. Ronzi that he couldn't charge anymore, you know what would happen? He'd be ashamed to face us, which means that he'd do his shopping somewhere else. Now, somewhere else probably wouldn't give him credit. He'd have to use his cash to feed his family, which means that he wouldn't be able to pay us anything at all on the bill. We'd lose a customer and the six dollars. The way we're handling it now, he pays us a little and he charges a little. Eventually he'll make good on the whole thing, believe me.''

Becky was charmed. She'd studied revolving credit, but here was her father explaining it to her as if he'd invented it.

Abe was collecting the credit slips and putting them away. ''Believe me, I can't get nervous about being owed a few dollars now that people have money in their pockets again. God bless Roosevelt. Not when it was so bad a few years ago. You remember those days, yes?'' Abe shook his head.

''We gave nothing but credit in those days, and the wholesalers gave credit to me. Everybody was so happy just to keep each other from going under. If a customer could pay me a little something or else trade me a pair of pants from his business or a nice dress for my little girl, that was all right too.''

''I remember how all of a sudden the men started pushing the baby carriages and shopping for their wives, who were taking in sewing.''

''All the sweatshops had laid off their workers,'' Abe interjected.

''They used to hang around to talk with you about politics. Remember the to-do when the Arabs revolted in Palestine? It must have been ten years ago, the summertime. I remember because it was so hot. The Jews held a big demonstration in the city against the British. You wanted to march and carry a sign, but you couldn't go because you didn't want to close the store and I was still too young to stay here alone. I remember one of the men who used to hang around shot off his mouth that he was a Communist and that the Arabs were right to fight for the liberation of their land from the capitalist Jews. I never saw you get so mad. That was the first and only instance of you throwing out a customer."

"A putz like that, his business I didn't need. Besides, he was the second one. You should have heard what I said to Mrs. O'Malley, who made your mother fall off that ladder."

"Father," Becky began, "you have taught me a lot about business."

"That's for sure," Abe agreed, turning to the cash register.

"Maybe you could teach Danny some things."

"Hah!" He rang up "No Sale" to open the cash drawer and removed the rumpled dollar bills.

"Really, Father. He wants to work here."

"Come upstairs. It's time for supper." Abe put the sheaf of bills under the loose floorboard that had served as his safe for so many years.

"I was already working weekends at his age."

"He can't do anything except mouth off to me," Abe snapped. "I can't trust him. He's not reliable."

"Father—"

"We'll see." Abe waved away the conversation. "Maybe when he's older."

Becky sighed. It was hopeless. Her father hadn't even asked where he was so late at night.

"Come on, turn out the light and we'll have supper."

Becky glanced at the clock: eight-twenty. "I was hoping to get to the library."

"I can't cook the supper like you do. You make it just like your mother used to—what? Why are you looking at me so funny? Come, I'm hungry." He shuffled away toward the stairs.

Sighing, Becky followed. There was always tomorrow night for the library.

* * *

It was a cold night, but that suited Danny. He walked with his hands jammed into his pockets, his coat collar turned up, an unlit Lucky Strike dangling from his lips. In cold weather coats and scarves bulked up a scrawny fellow's build, making him look tougher. An upturned collar helped as well, as did the cigarette. As soon as the cigarette got damp and began to shred, Danny would throw it away and replace it with a fresh one. He never lit up, it made him cough and that was not tough. He had half a dozen assorted packs in his pockets, filched from the store while Becky was upstairs fetching his coat.

Danny strode along Division Street. It was nine o'clock, and for the hour and a half since leaving Cherry Street Danny had been loitering outside the branch of the New York Public Library located on Jefferson near East Broadway. That was the branch Becky used, and Danny had been watching for her to show up. He did that most nights, never letting his sister know that he was watching for her, but taking comfort all the same in knowing her whereabouts on his nocturnal wanderings.

Tonight she hadn't shown. Danny guessed his father had thought up some excuse to keep her home. The old man often did stuff like that, and Becky always took it.

Danny made a right on Eldridge. Two doors up was Jerome's Luncheonette, a dingy hole-in-the-wall with a long black counter and high-topped stools bolted to the black and white checkered tile floor. Other than Jerome, the old geezer of an owner, Danny had never seen an adult in the place. It was where Rudy Lipsky and his chums hung out, drinking Cokes and smoking cigarettes, when they weren't out cracking Irishmen's skulls.

"Here he is," Rudy told his friends as Danny entered the luncheonette. Rudy Lipsky was fifteen years old and stood six feet tall. He was pimply and fat but also strong. He didn't mind being hit in a fight as long as he could give back what he got. The other boys in the gang—Alan, Leo and two named David—were all in their early teens. All were smaller than Rudy but much larger than Danny, whom they called the little pisher.

"You got 'em?" Rudy demanded.

Danny, a doglike grin creasing his features, nodded. "Two Pall Malls, three Chesterfields—" He was making a conscious effort to slur like Rudy. He put the cigarettes on the counter. "It's thirty-five cents."

Jerome eyed the exchange, but a hard look from Rudy sent the elderly counterman back to polishing his soda glasses. Cigarettes were selling for nineteen cents a pack, so Rudy and his boys were getting a good deal.

"You know, kiddo, I'd buy more if you'd bring 'em," Rudy offered.

Danny nodded. "I can't take any more than this at a time, Rudy. My old man'll get wise."

"Yeah, well—" Rudy shrugged and lit a match on his thumbnail to puff a Chesterfield.

"What you doin' with the money, anyways?" one of the other boys asked as he slit open a pack of Pall Malls. "Bet you get all the candy and tonic and Pall Malls you wants from your old man's place," he continued enviously.

"He don't sell—" Danny shut up. What he needed the money for was a secret he was not about to share, not even with Rudy's gang.

"You beat it, now, pisher," Rudy muttered, blowing blue cigarette smoke into Danny's upturned face. "Come back when you're growed."

The other boys laughed, just as they always did. "Unless you got more smokes to peddle," one of them added. Danny shook his head, turned and trudged out of the luncheonette. Outside he turned up his coat collar against the wind and hurried up Eldridge.

Always it was the same hope and always the exact same disappointment. How he longed to join Rudy's gang, to belong, to walk full of pride with the other boys,

patrolling the neighborhood, keeping it safe from roving
gangs.

He was too small. He just didn't measure up, not to
the other boys and not to his father.

He turned left on Delancey and continued to where it
intersected with the Bowery. He walked uptown past the
darkened shops until he reached the East Village.

He got careful here. No cigarettes hanging from his
lip, no tough sauntering. When he crossed East Houston
he'd entered into an ill-defined strip of no-man's land, a
buffer zone between the Jews of the Lower East Side and
the Italians who owned the West Village. A Jew, even a
tough guy like Rudy, could get hurt if the wrong sort got
hold of him. Danny furtively darted along, staying out of
the streetlamps' glow. At times like this being puny was
an advantage. He breathed a sigh of relief as he entered the
candy store on East Fifth between Second Avenue and the
Bowery. In a few minutes he would have what he'd come
for and be on his way home.

The confectionery was owned by an old woman, a
Christian—his father would have said goy, Danny con-
temptuously thought. She was Polish and always seemed
to be knitting. Danny had rarely seen anyone else in the
store, but then he was invariably here at night. A glass
counter display of penny candy occupied the front of the
little store. The wall opposite was full of shallow wooden
shelving above which peeked the colorful mastheads of a
vast assortment of slick picture magazines and pulps.

The middle rows of the display comprised *Life*,
Collier's and *Time*. Danny ignored them all, as he ignored
the crime and western pulps, the automotive periodicals
and the ones that featured sports personalities. Behind him
the old woman's steel knitting needles clacked implacably.
She had the biggest assortment of current titles.

He zeroed in on the lower left-hand corner of the
display. That was his special territory, the aviator pulps.

He was in luck. The new issues of *Bill Barnes, Air Adventurer* and *G-8 and his Battle Aces* were on sale. He snatched a copy of each off the rack, feasting his eyes on the cover paintings. As usual, G-8 and his crew were fighting their eternal World War One, skidding their British-built Sopwiths, Vickers guns blazing, through smoky mauve shooting-gallery skies filled with the Huns' blood-red Fokkers. The *Bill Barnes* cover depicted futuristic aircrafts, sleek mono-winged torpedo-shaped flying machines, that existed only in the pages of the pulps and a boy's imagination.

When it happened Danny couldn't say—when the notion of being an aviator took hold in his soul. All he knew was that on the rare occasion that an airplane passed overhead, Danny stopped whatever he was doing to crane his head and shield his eyes against the sun in the hope of catching a glimpse of it.

When you were high in the clouds, higher even than the Empire State Building, it didn't matter if you were puny. When you were behind the control stick you called no man your better and you left your earthbound cares behind.

He'd read everything on aviation in the children's section of the library and devoured what was to be had in the adult section, thanks to Becky's cooperation. He was an avid follower of *Scorchy Smith*, *Barney Baxter* and *Smilin' Jack* in the daily and Sunday funnies. Last year for Hanukkah Becky had given him the Big Little edition of *Tailspin Tommy and the Sky Bandits*. How he loved that book and loved his sister for getting it for him.

He paid the old woman a dime apiece for the two pulps, stuck them in his jacket and zipped it up. He was halfway out the door when he paused, thought a moment and then returned for *Mechanix Illustrated*.

His father didn't make such a stink about the flying books if he also had something "educational" to read. He always told his father he found the magazines and the old man either believed him, or didn't care.

Anyway, if all it took was *Mechanix Illustrated* to shut his father up, Danny was willing to pay the cover price. Making his father happy kind of soothed his conscience over swiping the smokes in the first place.

Anyway, that stuff in *Mechanix Illustrated* was kind of interesting.

Chapter 29

Jerusalem

It would be some weeks before his induction into the army could be arranged, the people at the Jewish Agency told Herschel Kol. With active participation in the war looming before him, it made little sense to Herschel to attend classes. He stayed up for most of every night reading—tracts by Jabotinsky, newspapers that covered the crisis events in Europe, David Raziel's manuals on small arms and the Old Testament, the prophecies of which the Irgun considered manifestos of the future.

He would drag himself from his bed toward noon and stay at the apartment until he could no longer bear his mother's icy despair. Then he would wander the streets of the Old City.

Herschel believed that his decision to enlist was right, but he fretted over Frieda's reaction to it. Frieda hated the British, and with good reason. To Jews too young to remember World War One and any recently arrived in Palestine, the British were not merely political adversaries but murderers. Even before the publication of the white

446

paper, the British had turned refugee ships packed with Jews back to the concentration camps.

Herschel stayed out of contact with the Irgun after his attack on the coffeehouse, and what they might think of his decision to enlist did not concern him. Not that he imagined they'd think much about it one way or the other. The Irgun had exploited his talents while they were available and would do so again if the opportunity presented itself. The discipline of the Haganah did not exist for the followers of Raziel and Stern. Members came and went—the fact that the organization was so loosely knit had allowed it to survive the arrest of its leaders.

Herschel was solely concerned with Frieda's reactions, and somehow he would make her understand that if the Nazis defeated the Allies, the question of a Jewish state would be academic.

There was plenty of time for Frieda to come to terms with Herschel's decision once she learned of it. She said that she wouldn't marry him until Palestine was liberated, and what point was there in taking a wife when he had a war to survive?

One morning just after dawn the police came for him. It was a nightmare. Herschel opened his eyes to see half a dozen police officers crowded into his tiny bedroom. They were grouped around his bed, revolvers drawn on him as he cowered naked beneath the sheet.

Through his doorway he could see two more struggling to hold back his mother. One of them had his hand clamped across her mouth. Herschel could see that his mother's eyes were wide with panic. The other officer did something to her wrist, and her eyes squeezed shut against the pain.

"Let go of her, you bastard!" Herschel roared, his fear forgotten in his anger over the mistreatment of his mother. He jackknifed from the bed, but they must have hit him.

He dimly heard his mother's cry, muffled by the policeman's fingers across her lips, and a gruff order, "Search the place!"

To Herschel it all seemed very remote as he settled softly onto the planks of the bare wooden floor and into blackness.

He came to propped upright in a hardbacked swivel chair. He tried to raise his arms, but found his wrists cuffed behind his back and chained to the chairback. At least they'd clothed him. He was wearing rough hemp pants and a pullover smock, prison garb, he realized.

The room was windowless; its walls were cinderblock. Got to think, he warned himself. How did they find out?

He flinched, startled, as a hand snaked past his ear and came down upon his shoulder.

"Back with us, eh, Mr. Kolesnikoff?" came a man's British accent from behind him. Herschel was spun around in his swivel chair—unnerving with his hands pinned behind him—to confront three men. All wore the khaki of the British police. The one who had spoken stood uncomfortably close. The other two sat behind a plain wooden table laden with books and papers—his books and papers, Herschel realized.

"Is my mother all right?" Herschel demanded.

"Not relevant," the officer beside him proclaimed.

"Who are you? What's your name?" Herschel stared up at the man, who was in his fifties and had icy blue eyes and the florid complexion of his kind. He had a white bottlebrush mustache precisely clipped along the line of his upper lip. Herschel glanced at the stripes on the man's sleeve. A sergeant.

"Sergeant," Herschel began, "there's been a terrible mistake. I'm just a student—"

"You're a terrorist, lad, a murderer, and that's the whole of it." The sergeant scowled. "We've all but measured your neck for the hangman's noose, of that you can be assured. Now then, the corporal over there is a stenographer. What I want you to do, lad, is tell us nice and quick the names of your friends in the Irgun."

"I don't know what you're talking about."

"Lad"—the sergeant's tone held menace—"don't make me beat it out of you."

Herschel took a deep breath, trying to control the trembling in his voice. "If you beat me, you'll get nothing but screams, sergeant. I can't tell you what I don't know."

One of the others at the table laughed. "Well said." Herschel peered at him and saw captain's bars on his collar. "Yes indeed, Mr. Kolesnikoff, well said, even if it is a lie. Now, first we'll tell you what we know, and then it will be your turn."

The captain looked to be no more than thirty, Herschel thought. He found himself idly wondering if the sergeant was jealous of his young superior. Anything was better than attending to the captain's revelations.

"We had you tracked—right down to your address—within forty-eight hours of the attack on the coffeehouse," the captain was boasting. "We could have picked you up at any time, but we waited in the hopes that you and your Irgun mates would have a get-together."

"Why? Why me?" Herschel blurted. Frieda, he thought, thank God she's been away. "P-please, captain, if that's true, you must know that I'm innocent of these charges. I've gone to no Irgun meetings." He smiled tentatively. "I've even volunteered for the army."

"We know that, lad." the sergeant nodded. "That you Yids hate Hitler makes sense to us, all right. But there's no point in your going on about not belonging to the Irgun."

The Captain held up the IRA leaflets and the crudely

carbon-copied small-arms manual by Raziel. "We found these items in your closet, Mr. Kolesnikoff."

"All right," Herschel sighed. "I flirted with the idea of joining the Irgun. But I never did join, honestly."

The sergeant and the captain exchanged weary smiles. "We have two witnesses, Mr. Kolesnikoff," the young officer said. "The rug merchant has already come by— you were unconscious—to identify you as the man who threw the grenades."

Herschel stared, dumfounded, sick at heart. Up until now he had entertained a hope of talking himself out of this mess. Now that hope was gone. That the rug merchant might identify him Herschel could understand, but how did the police manage to nab him in the first place. "You said there were two witnesses?"

"Aye, lad," the sergeant replied. "An Arab at the scene identified you by name."

"But how?" Herschel cried out. "That's not possible."

"Lad, the two witnesses support one another, don't you see? We've got you."

"Now then, let's have that list of names," the captain said.

"I'm not going to tell you anything."

The sergeant and the captain exchanged glances. "What the hell, lad." The sergeant gave him a comradely pat on the shoulder. "There's no real hurry. We can postpone your hearing for as long as we like. We'll let you stew over your predicament for a while. Let you talk with your mother—oh, yes, your mother's fine. Perhaps she can talk some sense into you. Cooperation with us might rescue you from the gallows."

No longer any point in pretending, Herschel thought. "As an Irgun soldier I demand to be treated as a prisoner of war."

"That's not likely," the sergeant said almost kindly. "If it were up to me—" He shrugged. "It's true you Irgun blokes have yet to hurt a British subject, and I appreciate the fact that you personally volunteered. It's a pity you didn't think of it before you threw those bloody grenades.''

Herschel felt worse faced with sympathy than with bluster. He began the Irgun anthem. *''In blood and fire did Judaea fall/In blood and fire Judaea shall rise again.''*

''Perhaps,'' the captain acknowledged brightly, ''but unless you supply us the information we're after, you shan't live to see it, Mr. Kolesnikoff.''

''Kol,'' Herschel said fiercely. ''My name is Herschel Kol.''

The captain smiled thinly. ''Quite. When the time comes, we shall see to it that the hangman gets it correct, won't we, sergeant?''

Chapter 30

New York

It had long been Abe Herodetzky's habit to sit in his rocking chair behind the meat counter and study the newspapers for mention of Palestine. With Becky handling things up front he often had an uninterrupted hour early in the morning to skim the English-language papers and then peruse the Yiddish press. The American papers ran little about what was happening over there, but the *Forward* and especially the *Freiheit* offered regular dispatches from the Holy Land.

The *Freiheit* was the Jewish Communist paper, and while Abe despised the Communists for what they were doing to the unions, he bought the paper for its coverage of Palestine. Ever since the Palestinian Zionists staged the bombing reprisals against the Arabs, the anti-Zionist *Frieheit*—despite Stalin's devil pact with Hitler the Communists insisted that post-revolutionary Russia was the Jews' Promised Land—afforded expanded coverage of the British administration's efforts to "track down the terrorist fanatics."

"Father," Becky called for the third time. Giving up,

she left her place behind the counter and walked back to the meat counter. "What's wrong?" she demanded. "Didn't you hear me calling you?" She stopped abruptly. Her father was ghost-white. He was staring at his newspaper like a man reading his own obituary. "Father, are you ill? What is it?"

Abe looked up at her and chuckled. "Nothing. I'm fine." He breathed deeply and laughed again. "I gave myself a good scare, that's all." He gestured to his daughter to come around the counter and read over his shoulder. "See here? Look what it says: Herschel Kol, just like in Kolesnikoff, yes Becky? I was reading about this poor fellow who got arrested for blowing up the Arabs, and then I got to his name and for a moment—"

"In your head you thought his name was Kolesnikoff." Becky murmured. "Oh, I'm sorry . . ."

Her father had long ago confided in her that he studied the papers not out of Zionist fervor but because he still held onto the hope of finding mention of Haim. "One day his name—with a picture—will be in there," her father predicted, wagging his finger. "With my luck the day I don't buy will be the day it gets published."

Becky scanned the article. It seemed that the man had yet to be sentenced. There was some flap about his being the grandson of a deceased famous painter, once a big shot in England, for that matter. Considering his crime, the young man's heritage made for a good story. The British were afraid that if they hanged their prisoner, the publicity would exacerbate a sensitive political situation.

"Look, Becky," Abe grumbled. "These Commies are saying the young man did it because he came from a wealthy background. They say that a boy from an honest worker background would never do such a thing." Disgusted, he quit reading to crumple the paper into a ball. "Now, why were you calling me?"

"Just to remind you that I've got something to attend to this afternoon."

"What, today? You're leaving me alone in the store today?" Abe frowned, shaking his head. He remembered the crumpled newsprint still in his hand and set to work polishing the slanted glass windows of the meat counter. "You can't go today. You know the freezer is coming."

"Oh, Father, you can handle it." The General Foods wholesaler was supplying the store with a small freezer to display frozen packages of fruits and vegetables labeled "Birdseye." Abe had made room for the freezer by tearing out some of the old wooden produce bins.

"All right, go," Abe said with a long-suffering sigh. "I'll manage."

At one o'clock Becky untied her apron and went upstairs to change her clothes. She'd been giving careful thought to her clothes for the last few days, so there was no indecision as she shucked off her skirt and sweater and put on her best navy blue dress with its white collar. Her best shoes were brown and low-heeled, but they would have to do. Becky sighed. At least they matched her coat, if not her dress.

She turned on the radio and absently hummed along as she looked at herself in the vanity mirror. She had no makeup of her own, but the drawers of the vanity were filled with her mother's cosmetics. She selected a lipstick and carefully put it on, then peered doubtfully at her reflection.

She could not remember when she had last thought to wear makeup. She no longer attended school, had no beaus; there was no call for it in the store. There had been nobody to teach her how to put it on; all she had to go by were the photographs in the magazines.

Becky turned away from the mirror, feeling depressed. She was certainly no glamor girl. Her nose was too big, for one thing, and she was far too fat. Compared to the angels in strapless evening gowns who filled the society pages, she was a cow. But at least her lipstick was on straight and her hair was clean and shiny. She was so happy she'd found the gumption to defy her father and have it cut into a fashionable shoulder-length page-boy.

She grabbed her coat and purse and was halfway down the stairs before she remembered the radio. She hurried back to the apartment to cut off the warbling and then thought to wonder about the time. The alarm clock in her bedroom read a quarter past two. She'd frittered away over an hour at the vanity, as if all the lipstick in the world could help her if she was late.

She flew down the stairs and rushed through the store, stopping at the cash register for a dollar. She hated taking money, whether it was to buy something for herself or just to have a little in her purse. Her father never commented on it, but he never failed to notice and winced at the amount, however small, as if his heart had begun to act up.

Today she had no choice. She had to have carfare if she was to be on time.

"I'll try to get back before it gets busy," she called to her father, who nodded morosely. She hurried out the door.

She took the subway to Fourteenth Street. As she rode she went over her strategy, trying to bolster her flagging courage. If this worked out, she would find the resolve to stand up to her father. He'd have no choice but to allow Danny to help out after school and on Saturdays.

She got out at her station and skipped up the stairs to street level. She ran the few blocks to Malden's, the sprawling five-and-ten, crossed her fingers and searched the store's plate glass windows. The small sign was still there. "Applications to be accepted for part-time sales

clerks,'' it read, and then the succinct instructions to apply
on today's date at three o'clock.

Inside Becky negotiated the maze of aisles through
Notions, past Dress Goods, Costume Jewelry, Clocks,
Hosiery, Stationery. She began to panic. It was just a few
minutes before three. Where was Personnel?

"Help you, sweetie?" It was a matronly woman with
silver hair and a badge that read "Floor Supervisor."

"Oh, please," Becky gasped, breathless with anxiety,
"the personnel department?"

The light died in the older woman's eyes. "Straight
back, sweetie, just after Domestics. When you get there
you can follow the thundering herd."

"You mean, somebody's here before me?"

"You poor kids." The woman clucked sympathetically.
"Go on, you've no chance at all standing here."

"Thanks," Becky called, hurrying off. In Domestics
a woman dusting throw pillows directed her to a set of
double doors marked "employees only." Becky pushed
through into pandemonium.

At least a hundred and fifty women from adolescents
to grandmothers were crowded in like cattle in a box car,
chattering to each other as they filled out applications with
pencils tethered to clipboards. There were only three short
rows of folding chairs and the women who'd claimed them
showed no signs of budging. A woman tapped Becky on
the shoulder and thrust a clipboard into her hands.

"Fill it out and wait till you're called," she said, her
eyes darting past Becky toward the two women who had
just come through the double doors behind her. "Move to
the front," she ordered. "Make way for the rest."

At the opposite end of the room a bald, fat, weary-
looking man in a three-piece suit sat behind a desk smoking a cigar. "It's three o'clock," the man called out, his
tone harried. "I'll be interviewing those with experience
first."

This is hopeless, Becky thought. I don't have a chance. She began to burn with humiliation, pondering how naive she must have seemed to that floor supervisor—". . . Somebody here before me?"

Furious, she bore down hard with her pencil as she began to fill in the application. Before she had finished printing her name the lead point broke. She looked around for the woman in charge of the clipboards and noticed a young man carrying a sign under his arm come from an interior office. The sign was of similar size and shape to the one Becky had seen in the store's front window. She craned her neck, trying to read what it said. "Shipping," "wanted" and "apply" were the only words she could decipher before he was past her.

She made her decision in an instant and dropped her clipboard to the floor to stride out of bedlam. There was no point in waiting around here; they'd fill the job before they ever got to her.

She made her way to the basement, past House Furnishings and through the dented steel doors to shipping.

It was a man's job she was going after, of course. A woman had no more business working in inventory or on the loading docks than a man had on the sales floor, but down here at least she could talk to the man who ran the department. If she talked fast, perhaps she could demonstrate her knowledge of ledgers, of packing and unpacking goods—if he'd just give her the chance she'd lift something for him and her best dress be damned. She lifted heavy boxes in the store all the time, especially since her father's heart condition was worse. She doubted that Malden's sold anything much heavier than a cardboard carton containing three dozen ten-and-a-half-ounce cans of condensed soup.

The shipping and loading areas, which were closed to the public, differed greatly from the rest of the store. Here illumination was provided by bare bulbs encased in wire, and the institutional green paint on the cinder block walls was chipped and peeling. Wooden pallets of goods were stacked to the ceiling. The loading bays, where the trucks pulled in, were up ahead. Becky heard the lusty shouts of men calling and joking with one another. These were men who relied on the strength of their backs to earn a living. They swore, they spat; they probably forgot women existed for the eight-hour workday.

Of course Becky knew she had one chance in a million of getting a shipping clerk's job. Even if by some miracle she managed to persuade the supervisor to hire her, management still had to agree to it. No, she was over-optimistic; her chances were closer to one in a billion.

But at least she would have the satisfaction of knowing that she'd tried everything. For the past couple of days she'd been able to entertain a wonderful dream of breaking free of the Cherry Street Market and starting an exciting new life of her own. That had ended now, but even if she did have to admit to failure, she was going to try everything.

"Hey, lady, you ain't supposed to be back here."

Becky ignored the shout and hurried toward the wide open bays of the loading dock. She saw two men talking as workers hurried to unload the cargo from several trucks backed up to the docks. One of them was older-looking and had close-cropped reddish-brown hair and silver-rimmed glasses. He was dressed in sturdy work clothes and a necktie. Holding a clipboard he unconcernedly puffed away on a briar pipe. Becky had spent enough time at the grocery wholesalers to recognize the boss when she saw him.

It was the man he was talking to Becky couldn't place. He was in his early thirties, of middling height and wearing a splendid tweed suit with pleated trousers and a jacket with a belt in the back. He was clean-shaven, but even from a distance Becky could discern the blue-black shadow of his heavy beard along the strong line of his jaw.

His hair was charmingly tousled, thick and black. There was a glossy sheen to it beneath the overhead lights.

He's got to be a salesman, Becky decided. Nobody employed at Malden's five-and-dime could possibly earn enough to afford a suit like that.

At that moment the well-dressed man noticed her. His hazel eyes stared into hers for a moment. He smiled and tapped the pipe smoker on the shoulder, pointing in her direction.

The manager glanced her way, did a double take and stared. "You shouldn't be around here, miss. Did you lose your way?"

Becky took a step forward. "Hold it right there," the manager squawked. "Don't come past that there yellow line painted on the floor. There's heavy loads here. This is no place for a woman."

Oh, God, Becky thought. All around was the noise of bantering men, thudding boxes, idling truck motors. A driver, grown impatient, began to lean on his horn.

"Hey, I think you've scared her," the man in the suit chided the manager.

"No, I'm not scared," Becky shouted, trying to make her voice carry over the commotion. "I've come to apply for the job."

Suddenly there was silence all around as the men stopped what they were doing. She could feel them staring at her. Only the impatient truck driver, who'd not heard, continued to lean on his horn. "Cut that," the man in the suit commanded. The honking ceased.

"Honestly, mister," Becky said to the manager, "I can handle this kind of work." She realized that she was still shouting, and lowered her tone. "I mean, if you needed someone to sort out the manifests or—"

Behind her, someone had started to laugh. "Yeah, Charlie, why don't you hire her? We wouldn't mind a skirt around the place."

Others joined in the laughter. Becky felt herself blushing, and cursed everything—emotions, gender, parents—that a person could not control.

"Hey." The man in the suit swept his hazel eyes around the room and the laughter died down. He regarded Becky. "Come here."

Becky cautiously eyed the supervisor, but his downcast expression combined with his sudden preoccupation with his pipe told her that in this particular instance he was not in charge.

As Becky approached, the other man cocked his index finger in her direction. "Ain't you Abie Herodetzky's little girl?"

"She ain't little no more," one of the workmen cracked.

"Hey, wiseacre," the man snapped, "get back to work."

"Yeah, everyone, back at it!" the supervisor echoed. He nodded at Becky. "You'll see to the young lady and show her out?"

"Yeah, Max. Don't worry about it, all right?" He turned to Becky as Max walked off. "You shouldn't put Max on the spot like that. He's okay, but he can't hire you. You gotta understand that—" he closed his eyes, snapping his fingers, "—Rebecca, right?" When she nodded, he continued, "Yeah. Becky, they call you. I never forget a name, not when it belongs to somebody in the neighborhood."

"Why don't I recognize you?"

"Well, I've only been in a few times, buying smokes or chewing gum, you know? Anyway, usually I come by when your father's around. We discuss business."

"With my father?" Becky asked, puzzled. "What sort of business are you in?"

"Trucking," he said smugly, rocking on the heels of

his two-tone suede bucks, his hands thrust into his pants pockets.

Becky giggled. "You mean, 'trucking' like in dancing?"

He laughed. "Right, trucking." He launched into a finger-waving, hip-rolling dance step, his two-tones moving quick as lightning across the rough concrete flooring of the loading dock. Becky offered a mile-wide smile in appreciation.

"Oh, yeah," he grinned. "You an alligator?"

"What?"

"You cut the rug? Jitterbug?"

Becky's mind went blank. "I listen to the swing on the radio."

He stopped dancing. "Just listening to it on the radio ain't no good, Becky. You have to experience swing. You like to dance?"

"I never went," she admitted. In front of this handsome man it seemed a shameful confession.

"You want to go with me?"

This is flirting, Becky numbly realized. He's asking me—me!—out on a date. She stared into his eyes, locking his gaze, because his tawny eyes were lovely and because she didn't want him glancing down to notice that she was wearing brown shoes with a blue dress.

"I'm a stand-up guy, Becky," he said quickly, evidently mistaking her confused hesitation for reluctance. "You see them trucks?" He gestured over his shoulder with his thumb. "They're mine. And I got plenty more like 'em."

"Is that how you know my father?" Becky cut in. "Because your trucks have made deliveries to the market?"

"Yeah, sorta like that."

"I don't know why I've never seen you then," Becky mused. "I mean, you look familiar, but I'm sure I've never seen you in the store."

"Like I said, you've never been there when I stopped

by. Anyway, what brought you to Malden's in the first place? Why'd you ever think you'd get hired as a shipping clerk?''

The date! Becky silently pleaded to him. Ask me out again on the date! Oh, why had she hesitated in the first place?

''I originally came to get a part-time sales job, but there were too many applying, and they wanted experienced help.'' She shrugged.

''So you thought you could jive your way into the shipping department.'' He shook his head in admiration. ''Listen, the guy who was doing the interviewing, was he bald and fat?''

''Yes, and smoking a cigar.''

''Yeah, yeah,'' he nodded. ''That's Wilkie.'' He winked at Becky. ''Mr. Wilkerson to you. He's just a flunky. We'll go through him the way a hot knife cuts through butter. I'll telephone Pinckameyer—''

''Who's that?'' Becky asked. The date—the date, she willed him. She'd already picked her dress for the big night.

''Pinkie's a big shot at Malden's,'' he explained. ''He'll see to it that you're hired.''

''What?'' Becky wondered if she'd heard right. ''Me? Hired?''

''Sure.'' He shrugged. ''You come back here tomorrow to see Wilkie—Wilkerson, right? The guy with the cigar. You just tell me what schedule you want to work. It'll go smooth as glass, I promise.''

''But they want experienced help.''

''Hey, you work in your pop's store, right? That's experience. That's how I learned everything, working for my pop.''

''They'll listen to you? I don't mean to doubt you, mister—'' She realized that she didn't know his name.

''Benny Talkin. Call me Benny. Don't you worry.

Jews help Jews. They'll listen to me. I do a lot of transport business for these people. They don't make me happy, my trucks don't roll, and that means empty shelves for Malden's. Get it?''

"Got it." Becky grinned.

"Come on." Benny began walking her toward the steel doors that led out to the basement sales floor. "You gotta get going. I've still got some things to discuss with Max."

"It'll be all right? The job, I mean—"

"Piece of cake."

"You'll call—whoever it was you said you'd call—?"

"You come see Wilkerson tomorrow afternoon. Tell him when you want to start; it's as simple as that." He held open the door for her.

"I don't know how to thank you."

"Anything for Abie Herodetzky's daughter."

Becky chuckled ruefully. "Now I just have to get my father to let me work here."

"You mean he doesn't know?"

"Uh-uh."

"You'll have to finagle that on your lonesome. Now beat it."

Becky felt a pat on her haunch and then she was through the doorway alone, managing only a quick final glimpse of tweed stretched across Benny's broad shoulders before the dented steel doors swung shut.

She floated home on a cloud, feeling as if a handsome archangel had swooped down on indomitable wings to lay miracles at her feet.

The job! Tomorrow she would have the job!

Tomorrow night she would have to break the news to her father, but for now she was entitled to savor her exultation. And so she would. There'd be no clouds in her sky at all if only Benny Talkin had thought to ask her out that crucial second time.

*   *   *

The next afternoon she put on the same dress and shoes and returned to Malden's personnel department. As soon as she'd identified herself to Mr. Wilkerson he handed her some papers to fill in and asked her when she wanted to start. Any time and any schedule was fine with him.

Becky chose Monday, Wednesday and Thursday afternoons from three till closing and all day Saturday. When she thanked Wilkerson he scowled suspiciously; Benny Talkin's intercession had offended the personnel manager. Once again she thanked him, doing her best to show her gratitude for the chance he was giving her. When Wilkerson saw that she meant it he took the cigar from his mouth long enough to smile and say she was welcome.

On her way home Becky decided she'd stumbled upon a cardinal rule for a woman who meant to make her way up the ladder of success. To lose graciously was admirable, but to win graciously was crucial.

Now, if only she could apply the rule to tonight's confrontation with her father.

She broke the news to him after supper. She was careful to present her tale the way she had rehearsed it, as a *fait accompli*. Not once did she ask his permission or opinion of her decision, nor did she imply that her mind could be changed. Her father said nothing as she calmly explained the hours she'd be working at Malden's. Danny listened silently, his wide eyes restlessly shifting between his stony-faced, sullen father and his wondrous sister.

When Becky was done Abe asked, ''You'll work in the store until you go to the nickel-and-dime?''

''I said I would.'' She caught the strident note in her voice. Calm down, she told herself. I think you won.

She watched her father gaze at Danny. How cold and aloof his eyes were. Danny began to fidget, and Becky felt for him, remembering all the times she'd suffered their father's dispassionate evaluation.

"Right from Hebrew school you'll have to come to help me," Abe warned. "No more running with the other boys."

"I know."

"When you'll have time to study I don't know," Abe sighed. "Ask your sister. Maybe she knows. She's got all the answers."

"Pa, I don't study anyway—"

"You hear?" Abe grumbled to Becky. "And who'll make the supper?"

"When I come home I'll make the supper," Becky said patiently.

Abe shook his head, rapping his knuckles on the table. "You don't ask my permission so I don't give it. Do what you want."

After her initial enthusiasm wore off, Becky found working at Malden's disappointingly dull. Wilkerson seized upon her experience to make her a cashier. Becky hardly talked to the customers and never got a chance to try and sell them anything. All she did was punch in the numbers on her register. She found her days at the Cherry Street Market to be more fun. There she knew who she was selling to and got to move around at least.

It was Thursday night three weeks after she began her job. Becky was leaving with the other girls via the employees' entrance. She heard a car horn beep, and saw Benny Talkin grinning at her from the driver's seat of a maroon convertible that glistened like a garnet beneath the streetlamps.

"Who's that?" one of the girls cooed enviously. "He's waiting for you?"

"I guess," Becky said, feeling nervous as she crossed the street.

"I thought I'd come by to see how you were doing," Benny greeted her.

"I'm okay." Becky said shyly. Since the first and last time she met him she'd compiled imaginary lists of clever things to say in case she got this chance. Now her mind was blank. She should have written those lists down. Looking at scraps of notes was only half as foolish as standing like a tongue-tied idiot.

"I know who you look like," she blurted. "It's been bothering me—I mean, you looked familiar, but I knew we'd never met. You look just like John Garfield in *Four Daughters*."

"An actor!" Benny laughed, not displeased.

"Did you see it?" Becky demanded. "I saw it twice—"

"Get in." Benny didn't get out of the car, but leaned across the gleaming leather front seat to open the passenger door. When he sat upright he saw that Becky had not moved. "Come on, it's cold out there. I ain't going to bite you."

"Okay." She came around and got into the car, shut the door and leaned against it. The interior of the car smelled of leather and Benny's cologne. His suit was grey flannel. His arm and shoulder muscles strained the fabric as he ran his hands over the steering wheel. His hands were large, strong and capable-looking. The gold pinky ring with its large, glittering stone looked out of place on such fingers.

"You like it?" Benny asked.

"What?" Becky asked, startled. "The car? Sure, it's great."

"It's a '39 Cadillac. I get a new one every year. Do you know how much it cost me?" When Becky shook her head, he laughed. "I didn't think so."

The conversation lagged for a moment. "You want a

smoke?" he asked, taking a packet of Chesterfields from the top of the dash.

Becky accepted a cigarette and Benny lit it. She was very conscious of her fingers touching his as she steadied the flame. He watched her exhale.

"You don't look old enough to smoke."

"I'm old enough to vote," Becky sighed. "But I know what you mean."

"I like how you look," Benny murmured. "A pretty girl don't need much to set her off, and you're real pretty, Becky." He was sliding closer to her across the leather.

During the silence that ensued, Becky set her cigarette into the ashtray and leaned back. *This-is-it-I'm-going-to-be-kissed*—

Benny Talkin froze with his arm halfway around her shoulder as a long, gurgling growl reverberated from the depths of Becky's stomach. He began to hoot with laughter as Becky blinked back mortified tears.

"When did you eat last?" he managed to demand.

"This morning. I don't have time to eat lunch."

Benny waved her quiet. "You're gonna waste away to nothing." He made a point of giving her buxom figure a lascivious once-over to make her laugh. "A girl like you oughtn't to be skin and bones." He winked.

"Not much chance of that," Becky demurred.

"I guess the first stop is this little steakhouse I know." He pulled away from the curb.

Becky felt a brief twinge of guilt. Her father and her brother were waiting for her at home, waiting for their supper. They're not crippled, she told herself. Let them make their own supper for once. She would telephone from the restaurant and tell them that she and some of the other girls had gone out for a bite.

And if her father complained, he would just have to get used to the change. She'd been his dutiful daughter long enough.

"You'll like it better in the spring," Benny said, cutting through her thoughts.

"Pardon?"

"The convertible," he said cheerfully as he put the powerful Cadillac through its paces. "When the weather turns warm and we put the top down, that's when you'll really enjoy it."

At a stop light Benny finally did kiss her. He patted the seat next to him, and Becky sidled close as if she'd been doing it forever.

Chapter 31

The British police held Herschel for two months and sub-jected him to daily interrogations. Sometimes he was beaten. Often the promise of imprisonment instead of execution was held out to him. Throughout the ordeal Herschel thought of Frieda and told his captors nothing.

He was tried before a military tribunal. A British major served as prosecutor and three other officers were his judges. No spectators were allowed, not even Rosie.

The trial lasted less than twenty minutes. The rug vendor identified Herschel as "the man who pretended to be English, the man who threw the bombs." Another Arab seemed to know Herschel by name and also placed him at the scene of the explosion. Herschel's attorney waived the right to cross-examination. The best they could hope for was to keep him from the gallows, so the attorney had no desire to antagonize the court.

After the witnesses were heard the judges whispered among themselves for a few minutes. Herschel was or-dered to stand. He would not hang; it was not the administration's goal to create martyrs. Herschel was sen-

469

tenced to twenty-five years in prison. The gavel came
down, he was led away, and that was that.

At Jerusalem's Central Prison they shaved his head
and issued him brown sandals, baggy trousers, a collarless
pullover shirt and a cloth cap. He was assigned to a
communal cell in which there were already four Jews and
two Arabs. The first week Herschel was cautious, keeping
quiet until he knew what was what. Then one of the Arabs
took sick and the Jews joined with the other Arab in
donating a portion of their meager food to the invalid until
he was well. The clash between the two peoples could
wait. The inmates' common enemy was the British prison.

The days took on a numbing sameness as Herschel's
world shrank down to dark, narrow vaulted halls, iron
grates and grey stone. There were no books allowed, no
writing materials. At sunrise there was morning exercise, a
brief walk in the yard under guard. Next came a work
period until the first meal, at midmorning. There was
another brief walk, more work until late afternoon, a final
meal and sleep until roll call at sunrise the next day.

Anyone on good behavior was allowed a visitor once
a month. Herschel's visitor was invariably his mother. She
was only in her fifties, but a long hard life had prematurely
aged her and his sentencing had sapped the last reserves of
her youth and strength. During one of her visits she broke
down.

"I remember when we first moved to Jerusalem,"
she wept. Herschel stared at the multitude of fine lines
etching her translucent skin. "I remember how we would sit
on the bare wooden floor of my studio with a plate of fruit
and cheese between us. You would tell me about the
university. How you made me laugh. How silly we got,
like drunkards. You remember, don't you? It's not just an
old woman remaking her memories, is it? We were friends,
yes?"

"It happened, Mama," Herschel quietly agreed. "We're still friends."

"No!" Her fingers were like claws rattling the mesh. "Mother and son, perhaps, and we still may love one another, but we are no longer friends." She smiled, wiping her tears, and suddenly despite her wrinkles and grey hair the ghost of her youth seemed to appear in her red-rimmed sable eyes.

"I'm a painter, yes? Not a great one, perhaps, but nevertheless an artist. You, my son, were my greatest work. When your father was killed you became my creation, one that I would never finish. I thought I could never lose you. Then along came that girl—"

"Mama—"

"She stole you away, she did. And now this prison has you for twenty-five years. Never again will we embrace. Herschel, there is no point to my existence if yours is to be spent in a cage."

Months passed. His mother's visits continued. Herschel became increasingly concerned over Frieda's well-being. Rumors had circulated the prison that new ordinances allowed the British to fire on ships carrying illegal Jewish immigrants to Palestine. Many discounted the rumors. Even the most virulently anti-British Zionists had a hard time believing that defenseless refugees would be shot. Still, Herschel worried. As best he knew, his beloved was still smuggling in Jews. His mother knew nothing about Frieda, of course, and Herschel understood that even if Frieda had returned to Jerusalem, she could not visit him without drawing suspicion to herself.

In the fall the prison's grapevine buzzed with the news that a refugee ship, the *Tiger Hill*, had been attacked by the Palestine Coast Guard. Two people were killed. A scrap of newspaper was smuggled in and passed along through most of the inmate population before it was confiscated by a guard. The scrap quoted the British colonial secretary, Malcolm MacDonald, as saying that the responsibility for these and future deaths rested with those who were organizing illegal immigration.

One month Herschel was surprised to find that his visitor was none other than Yol Popovich. The old man had come all the way from Degania.

"How fine you look," Herschel laughed as Yol smiled at him from the other side of the wire mesh. "Like a patriarch, like Moses himself, with your walking stick and that grand grey bushy beard."

"Patriarch, eh?" Yol grimaced. "It's baldness. Makes the skull look bigger."

"How is Degania?"

"It thrives, boy. You see how old I look, and now I'll confess how old I feel—I cannot wait to get back to that quiet little corner of the world." His dark eyes narrowed as he peered through the mesh. "Herschel, you are so gaunt."

"The food is poor, and there's not enough of it."

"But you're holding up? You can survive?"

"We're strong, so strong that on Yom Kippur we fasted."

Yol was truly appalled. "Good socialists like you fasted?"

Herschel laughed. "You should have seen the looks on the faces of the guards when we all refused our meals—us! With our ribs sticking out, yes? Of whom not one had ever fasted when we were free. The guards were curious, so we explained to them that it was the Day of Atonement. The guards nodded. They thought we were atoning for our crimes, but it was really for getting caught."

"It's good your spirit is strong," Yol grinned, then began to fidget in his chair. "I'm afraid I've got some bad news for you," he muttered uneasily.

Herschel felt the chill of Yol's words dancing along his spine. "What?" he demanded.

"Your mother received a message. I'm sorry to say that your friend Frieda Litvinoff is dead."

"Oh, no."

"The letter was brief and there was no signature. It seems that Frieda and her comrades were in Jaffa, rowing out to ferry refugees from their steamer to shore. It was night, of course. There was no moon and the sea was rough. The little rowboats, as always, were overcrowded. The one Frieda was in capsized. In the dark, in the confusion, in the tossing waves—well, she was lost. The next morning her body was found on the beach."

"You came to tell me because my mother could not. Is that it, Yol?" Herschel asked. It was a struggle to control his grief, but he was not surprised. That was the worst of it, that he was not at all surprised. "You came all the way from Galilee. I'm very appreciative."

"I would have come no matter what," Yol replied, "before this unpleasantness, but that would have meant depriving Rosie of one of her visits to you."

"She's very lonely."

"Yes, boy, she is lonely. That's something I want to talk to you about." Yol took a deep breath. "I intend to ask her to return with me to Degania. She's wasting away here, and to tell the truth, I myself find life very drab when deprived of her companionship."

Herschel nodded. "Have you always loved her?"

"Long before your father met her. When he confessed his love to me I realized that they were perfectly suited for each other, so I lied. I said I no longer cared for her."

"She'll never marry you, you realize."

"Marriage! Please, boy." Yol shuddered. "Why do I need to get married at my age? No, I just want to protect your mother, Herschel, to keep her company, to keep her

as happy as possible. I can do that at Degania." He looked
into Herschel's eyes. "I loved your father, I love Rosie
and I love you. You're all my family. Do you understand?"

"Have you talked to her about it?"

"I've broached the subject," Yol said. "I think she
would like to come, but it would mean the end of her visits
to you. She feels awful about that."

"Take her to Degania. You have my blessing. When
she comes to see me next month I shall tell her as much."

"Thank you."

"Please, make her happy. She deserves it."

Yol winked. "Absolutely."

One month later Herschel's mother paid a final visit
to her son, who did his utmost to assure her that she was
doing the right thing. During this last visit they did not
speak of Frieda nor of any unpleasantness between them.
Their love was a vast, dark ocean, and mother and son
stood on opposite shores. Each took solace in the pulse
and thunder of that sea, but the time when either could
make the voyage across had long since passed.

With his mother's visits a thing of the past there was
nothing in Herschel's routine to break up the passage of
time. The days belonged to the British jailers, but the
prisoners owned the night. They did secret exercises by
moonlight, and in the shadows they talked and taught one
another. Sporadically, as the months passed, news of events
beyond their prison walls reached them.

During the summer of 1940 they learned that Abraham Stern, newly released from prison, had split off from
the Irgun to form a new, far more aggressively violent
group, Lohmey Heruth Israel. The Sternists would not
honor the Irgun's unofficial truce with the British for the
war's duration. Soon British policemen would find themselves shot down on street corners.

The Irgun, meanwhile, continued its frantic efforts to aid the illegal refugees fleeing Hitler. The ships converged on Palestine. The displaced persons camps administered by the British were soon filled to overflowing.

In November of 1940 two leaky refugee-packed steamers, the *Pacific* and the *Milos*, were intercepted by the British in the bay at Haifa. The refugees were loaded onto the slightly more seaworthy British steamer *Patria* to be transported to the DP camp on the tropical island of Mauritius until they could be returned to Germany. On November 25 in full view of the population of Haifa the refugees aboard the *Patria* blew up the ship. Hundreds of blast-mutilated corpses bobbed in the blue waters as still more refugee-laden ships steamed over the horizon toward Palestine.

When the news of violence was against the British it inspired the prisoners. When, as was much more often the case, the violence was against their own people, it fueled their determination to drive the British from Palestine. Hatred gave the inmates the strength to persevere; hatred seeded their reveries. What sprouted in the hardened souls of these young Jews, inured to violence, was beyond all control.

One sunrise Herschel awoke from a dream of himself and Frieda making love. Even now, wide awake, the taste of her mouth seemed to linger on his lips.

Outside during the exercise period the dream still haunted him. He was heartsick, his loneliness intensified by the knowledge that he had been visited by a ghost.

He must have been walking too slowly. A guard prodded him to hurry his pace, and the next thing Herschel knew his arms were manacled behind him. The guard was bloodied, lying curled on the ground.

Herschel was flogged and put into solitary confinement for one week. He spent his time in the dark, cramped cell meditating on the sort of being he had become.

He thought back to the Arab riots of '29. Still an adolescent, he killed for the first time in defense of Degania. How he cried over it. He brooded on the shame he felt after his grenade attack on the coffeehouse, and then he pondered how he would have killed that guard if the others hadn't dragged him away. His assault had been pure reflex, with no hesitation and no regret. He didn't even remember doing it.

Chapter 32

New York, 1940

After their first rendezvous Becky Herodetzky discovered Benny Talkin's maroon convertible idling across the street from Malden's every Monday, Wednesday and Thursday night. At first Becky was able to convince herself that Benny's interest in her would be fleeting and that her life had not taken an extraordinary turn. In the beginning she constantly steeled herself for the night when the convertible would not be waiting for her, but there it always was. Gradually she began to rely on those late suppers and evenings at the movies with Benny.

After a couple of months the trunk of his Cadillac began to spew forth marvelous dresses. "I ain't trying to be forward," Benny would murmur bashfully, "but when this guy on Seventh Avenue showed 'em to me, all I could think of was how nice you'd look." Becky would run back into Malden's to change her clothes, and off the two would go to dance to Count Basie or Charlie Barnet at the Famous Door or another club along Fifty-second Street.

Benny was always the perfect gentleman, and that added to his allure. His occasional kiss, his touch could thrill her, but it was the limits he set for himself that allowed Becky the confidence to surrender her heart. Benny's fabulous tours of nighttime New York always ended with Becky safe in her bed at Cherry Street. Was it any wonder that on the mornings after as she performed all the mundane chores of readying the market for the day's business, her evenings with Benny seemed impossible? If the dresses had not been hanging in her closet as proof of his affection, she might have considered herself mad for daring to hope for the day when she would be his wife.

As the relationship progressed Becky found herself totally captivated. When business at her father's market was slow she would replay the previous night's activities in her mind as she puffed away on the Chesterfields—his brand—she'd taken to smoking.

Benny nearly broke her heart by failing to ask her out for New Year's Eve. She spent that night in tears, her face pressed into her pillow, while on the other side of her locked bedroom door her father begged to know what was wrong.

New Year's Day 1940 was a Monday and Malden's was closed, so Becky had until Wednesday to mourn her loss and to ponder whether life could be worth living without Benny.

Wednesday night the maroon convertible was there, and in the spring Benny kept his word. The car's top came down and the couple spent several glorious Sundays cruising out to Flushing Meadow and the World's Fair.

So Becky's Cinderella romance continued, her happiness uncomplicated and unalloyed. One warm spring night Benny met her after work to take her to a picture everyone was talking about, *The Wizard of Oz*. They'd been meaning to see it for quite a while, but now that they were there Becky had a hard time concentrating. Her own life and her time with Benny seemed far more fascinating than the gaudy goings-on in Oz.

During the movie Benny took her hand. She wondered if tonight they would indulge in their recently begun bouts of petting that turned the Cadillac's windows steamy and left Becky's emotions and clothing in disarray. Becky had been secretly relieved at Benny's passion—they'd been seeing each other for almost half a year—but she was also frightened and uncertain about what she was supposed to do to further their romance. She stared blindly at the screen as she reviewed their relationship, trying to fathom a way to strengthen her claim to Benny's affections. She'd grown up a lot these last six months, begun to have more confidence in her looks and in herself. She'd begun to think she deserved a prize like Benny Talkin.

Those recent balmy Sundays at the World's Fair were the exceptions to the rule of their relationship. At Benny's insistence they met only on the nights she worked at Malden's, excluding Saturday. Benny had yet to make his appearance as her beau at Cherry Street.

"It's best that your dad doesn't know about us," Benny would assure her whenever she brought up the subject. "It'd cause trouble if he knew."

Benny told Becky about his own father during one winter evening. They were at the Downbeat on Fifty-second Street. They had a corner table, cigarettes and the obligatory cocktails, from which they rarely sipped. Becky had no taste for drinking after her father's struggles with alcoholism. Benny simply had the traditional disdain for drunkards.

"My dad was born in '84," he began. "My grandparents were broke, of course, like most in those days. My dad's name was Mendel. He was their only child. He started roaming the streets pretty early, lifting goods off delivery wagons, stuff like that. He was always big for his age, and he got to be known as a brawler. He began to collect protection money from the pushcart peddlers. It was all on the up and up; I mean, the peddlers figured it was a good deal, paying Mendy Talkin a little to keep the Irish hooligans from stealing a lot. By that time my father had guys working for him. Then along came the movement to unionize the garment industry.''

"Did your father work in a sweatshop, like mine?" Becky asked.

Benny grinned. "My dad believed in working for himself. Anyway, you know the word *shtarke*?''

"Nope.''

"Good. A sweet thing like you shouldn't know, but I'll tell you. Some might say that a shtarke is just a punk, a tough, but in those early union days he was more like a soldier. Those disputes were really wars.

"A lot of gangs worked both sides of the street. Sometimes they'd break up a strike and sometimes they'd enforce it. Not my father, though. Right from the start he threw in with the unions. He and his boys carried cards, and the United Hebrew Trades and the ILGWU paid him a regular salary. If a local was causing trouble, my dad and his boys talked some sense into them. If some scabs tried to cross a picket line, my dad taught them a lesson. And no striker had to worry about goons when my dad was around. What I'm trying to say is that Mendy Talkin had principles. He never forgot his origins. He was always for the working man.''

Becky fought back the most horrendous impulse to laugh. Imagine a hoodlum showing support for the working man by clubbing down any attempt to defy the union. It was at times like this that Becky appreciated her own father, who was poor but honest. She wished her brother Danny could hear what Benny was saying and realize how lucky they were to have a decent man as a father.

"You think my father was just a hood, right? And that means I must be as well, right? That's just how your father would feel, Becky. That's why you can't tell him about us. Abe probably thinks it was sign carriers like him who won the union's battles.''

"This is a ridiculous argument.'' Becky interrupted. "My father did more than carry a sign. He lent his life savings to his union—''

"Through Stefano de Fazio, right? He's chums with de Fazio.''

"Not anymore,'' Becky replied. "Not since Stefano became known as a—well, you know . . .''

"A gangster?'' Benny asked softly. "Your daddy would never have anything to do with a gangster, would he?''

Becky looked into his face and was frightened. His hazel eyes were cold, even cruel. Like father, like son— the phrase leapt into her mind to make her shudder. "Listen, I didn't mean to insult your father. I'm sure he's a good man.''

"He's been dead for years.''

"Oh, I'm sorry,'' she stammered, thinking how little she knew about her love.

"He died young, but what life he had was good. He made a lot of money from the unions, and they profited from his services. Things started to change after the war. That's when he lost his health and his eyes started to give him trouble. They diagnosed diabetes, but what took away his will to live was the changing times.

"By then the Communist influence had begun to tear at the ILGWU. Hatred made everyone crazy, willing to do the worst to each other. There weren't enough shtarkes to go around.

"Then came the Depression. You know who had the only cash? The bootleggers. The industry had already turned to them for muscle, so why not borrow too if some were willing to lend?''

"And your father was too sick by then to continue?''

"Partly that, but there was more to it. When the

industry moved uptown people like my dad were left
behind.'' He chuckled. ''He was pretty much blind by
then, just a relic of the old days when a word to the wise or a
punch or two was enough to keep order. You know,
Becky, he never owned a gun. He never had need of
one.'' Benny was leaning forward in his chair. He had
taken hold of Becky's hand and was squeezing it hard.

''It's all in the past now.''

''Yeah, sure.'' He leaned back and lit a cigarette in
order to compose himself. ''My dad had some friends,
though, friends who thought well of an old-timer who'd
always kept his mouth shut. So when he bought some
trucks, they threw business his way. My dad knew enough
to do them favors in return. You own the trucks, keep up
contacts in the drivers' unions, and you can shut down any
industry any time you want. That's power. As soon as I
was old enough I quit school and went into the business.
As my dad got sicker, I took over more and more and
made it grow.'' He smiled. ''Now you know everything.''

''Do I?'' He was too good to be true. ''Dance with
me,'' she begged almost desperately. He was her love and
she couldn't bear to doubt him.

Benny led her to the floor, wrapped her in his arms
and began to sway to the slinky chords. Now it was easy
for Becky to banish her doubts as she lost herself in his
intoxicating closeness.

''Was your father as handsome as you?'' she murmured against his chest.

Benny laughed. ''My dad took quite a few punches in
his day.''

''And you?''

''Let's just dance, okay?''

''Tell me, Benny,'' she prodded softly. ''I've got to
know. Are you like him?''

''I'm a businessman, Becky, but I would like to think
I am like my father.''

"Like him. That means no guns. You don't hurt anybody?" Anxious, she stared up into his eyes, thinking, I'll know if he's lying. If we're really in love I'll be able to tell.

"No guns. Last fist fight I had was when my father was still alive and I was driving one of his trucks. I won, incidentally. There—now you really know everything."

Becky nibbled kisses along the line of his jaw. Sighing, Benny held her tightly. She kept her eyes closed, trusting to Benny to keep her safe from uncertainties as they danced. His reply had reassured her, but there were still demons lurking in shadowy corners.

That revelatory evening at the Downbeat took place last December. Then came that dismal New Year's Eve, followed by the far brighter spring. Now they strolled arm in arm from the Broadway movie palace. A light rain began to fall, softening the lights of Times Square and sending the evening crowds scurrying.

"Damn," Benny muttered. "I think we left the top down on the car." It had been a prematurely warm spring day and Becky was wearing only a light cardigan over her blouse. Benny peeled off his jacket and draped it across Becky's shoulders. As they walked he cheerfully whistled the movie theme.

Becky decided that the time had come to put a stop to Benny's hesitancy about revealing their relationship to her father. She knew he loved her, but if he was too timid to confront her father, how could she hope he would find the courage to propose?

"My father knows about us," she announced.

Benny stopped whistling. "I thought we had an understanding."

"We did—I mean, I guess I let you think we did," she stammered, feeling a twinge of guilt. "You've got to believe me, I've hated deceiving you all this time, but my father has known for months, long before you told me about your father. Oh, Benny!'' She pulled away from him as he frowned at her. ''You needn't look so worried.''

''This is bad.'' He shook his head.

''At first I told him I was spending my evenings with the girl at work. As we continued to see each other I'm sure he got suspicious, but he didn't say anything. Then, well—when we didn't spend New Year's Eve together, I guess I got upset. I figured I would never see you again.''

''Oh, Becky,'' Benny groaned.

''Wehl, why didn't you ask me out?'' she demanded. ''Anyway, my father saw how angry I was and begged me to tell him what was wrong.''

''And you did?'' When Becky nodded, he winced. ''That was a terrible mistake.''

''No,'' she insisted, ''really, it wasn't. You've got the wrong idea about my father. That night he comforted me, and when we got back together he said nothing at all about it to me. He is not the type to hold you accountable for your father's—'' she hesitated.

''My father's what?'' he demanded sharply. He scowled up at the rainy night sky. ''Come on, it's getting cold.''

''Want your jacket back?''

''No. And stop pouting.''

''I didn't mean to insult you,'' she said reproachfully.

''I know.'' He shivered. ''Let's get to the car.''

''Then stop acting like there's been some kind of tragedy,'' she scolded, standing right where she was.

''We can talk about it in the car, in private. Not out here on the sidewalk, for crissakes.''

Something's very wrong, her intuition told her. Suddenly she was very sorry indeed that she had brought up the whole topic, but now she had to follow it through to the end. ''Benny? It's not like you don't already know my father. I'm really confused, Benny. It's not like you to act so . . . well, frightened!''

"It's a mess, honey," he said listlessly.

"Why can't you look at me?"

He turned and squarely confronted her, placing his hands on her shoulders. "All right. You're gonna find out real soon anyway. I don't know why you haven't already. Oh, God, Becky, I do love you. It's a goddamn shame—"

"Benny, what?" Becky stared at him. "You're scaring the hell out of—"

"I'm engaged, Becky."

The rain tapered off to a light mist and the people who'd been bunched up under the awnings began brushing past as Becky stood paralyzed with shock. "A joke, right?" she smiled tentatively, ready to laugh. All around her Times Square was vibrant with life and color, the people and the hum and purr of the cars cruising along the drenched asphalt. A score of thousand-bulbed theater marquees cast glistening reflections on the wet sidewalks, while swirling nimbuses wreathed the traffic lights.

"I was engaged the day I laid eyes on you."

"You bastard."

"The wedding is June sixteenth, in five weeks."

"You bastard!" Becky cried, twisting free of his grasp. She ran as fast as she could, bumping into people and not caring, until she reached the end of the block. At the curb she hesitated and hated herself for doing it, even as she looked back at him over her shoulder.

Benny's rain-soaked shirt clung to his torso. His curly black hair was plastered to his scalp. He was standing just where she'd left him.

He's not going to chase me, she realized. Engaged all this time— She wanted to weep, to clutch at her belly and double over from heartache.

A yellow Checker taxi, turned the corner and slowed. The driver stretched across his front seat to roll down the window and peer out at her. "You okay, miss? Need a cab?"

Becky nodded and got in.

* * *

Abe Herodetzky and his son Daniel were in the parlor, reading and listening to the radio when Becky got home. Seated in his armchair in a pool of lamplight, Abe looked up from his newspaper as he heard his daughter's tread on the stairs. He folded away the news of the Nazi blitzkriegs and of the exasperating bellicosity of the Japanese in the Pacific. Becky looked exceedingly bedraggled as she came in carrying her purse and a man's damp, wrinkled grey tweed herringbone jacket. Her eyes were red-rimmed and her face was more streaked with tears than rain.

"You were with Ben Talkin this evening?"

"Yes, Father."

Abe eyed her. "I gather that you quarreled?"

Becky hurried across the parlor toward her bedroom. "It's too terrible to talk about."

"I gather that he told you about his commitment."

Becky froze and stared incredulously at her father, then crumpled into a straightbacked chair. "You knew?" she gasped. "You knew and didn't tell me?"

"What's goin' on?" Danny demanded from his place on the sofa. "Hey, Becky, that's a sharp jacket." His voice was changing and every sentence ran the octaves from reed-thin tenor to a bulldog's husky growl. "Where'd you get it, sis? Can I have it?"

"Never fit you, shrimp."

"Hey! Anyhow, I could grow into it," he suggested hopefully. "I'm not gonna be a shrimp forever, I hope."

"Danny, I want to talk to your sister," Abe interrupted. "Go for a walk, all right?"

"Pop, it's late, and raining to boot."

"Then go downstairs and take inventory."

"Of what?"

"Danny—"

"I'm goin'." He got up, tucking *Tailspin Tommy* under his arm. "I'll read downstairs."

"He calls those funny books reading," Abe grumbled after Danny left. He took his son's place on the sofa. "He's almost fourteen and still he's with those funny books. He got his report card today. All failures he got, except for two A's, in you know what? Machine shop and woodworking."

"He's who he is," Becky said, "and he's a good boy."

"Yeah," Abe admitted, "but now I'm worried more about my good girl." He patted the sofa cushion beside him. "Come, talk to me."

"I'm too angry—with Benny and now with you." She sat beside him anyway. "How did you know about his being engaged and why didn't you tell me?"

Abe put his arm around her. "I didn't know until two days ago, when I went to see Stefano—"

"You went to de Fazio, Father? Why?"

"Stop asking so many questions and let me tell you. It's not easy for me. New Year's Eve, when you were so unhappy and confessed to me that you'd been seeing Ben Talkin but thought it was over, I was sympathetic, but secretly I thanked God he'd given you up. His father was a gangster, and the son is no better, you can believe me."

"That's not true. I don't care who Benny's father was. It's Benny I love—" She paused, embarrassed. "Anyway, how he's treated me is terrible, but that doesn't make him a gangster. He's in the trucking business—"

"Bah! He delivers from racketeers to other racketeers—"

"He delivers to you."

Abe shrugged. "Baked goods, meat and produce his trucks bring me." He smiled at Becky. "That's legitimate. Even a gangster has some business that's not crooked, I guess."

"What I can't understand is why Benny came to see you," Becky mused. "It's the wholesalers who contract with a trucking concern to make their deliveries to their customers, not the other way around.''

"I never met Ben Talkin," Abe hotly declared.

"Benny said that you did."

"I don't believe it."

"I'm certain, Father," Becky replied, bewildered by his vehemence. "He said you two did business together, and more than once as I recall."

Abe scowled. "Oh, yes, of course," he blurted, brightening. "Yes, that's true, we did—but just a few times."

"What about?"

"It's not important," Abe said. "When you got back together after New Year's, I was upset, but I didn't say anything. It took you so long to tell me about him, I figured that if I nagged you you'd never tell me anything again."

"I'd still tell you everything." Becky kissed his cheek. "I would have told you about Benny sooner, but he didn't want me to—"

"Yeah. So I kept my mouth shut and hoped that your feelings toward him would cool. Finally I couldn't stand it. I was afraid that—well, I had a father's fears about his daughter in the hands of a—a sharpie." Abe blushed. "Let's leave it at that. So a couple of days ago I went to see Stefano at his office."

"Why him? What does he have to do with anything?"

Abe waved that aside. "Stefano is powerful, and a powerful man can have to do with what he wants. Besides, once he was a trusted friend. I was going to appeal to him to protect my daughter."

"Oh, Father . . ." Becky, her head resting on Abe's shoulder, began to weep. "I love him so much, and now he's gone forever."

"You'll get over this."

"I don't want to," she sobbed. "I don't want my life

to go back to the way it was before I met him." She pushed away from Abe. "Father, look at me," she commanded, wiping her eyes. "I'm begging you. Sell the store."

"What?" Abe nervously laughed.

"I can't spend my life here, Father."

"Becky, please," he snapped, "we've been over this too many times, and tonight you're hysterical. Get some sleep."

"Just sell it, Father," she persisted. "Find somebody to take it over. With the money they'd pay you and the rents you collect we'd be fine—"

"I can't sell."

"Why not?" she cried in frustration. "It's yours, after all. Father, listen, I'm doing so well at Malden's, really I am. They want me full time"

"Out of the question. Danny's no good as it is."

"They want me to train as an assistant supervisor. We'd probably end up with more cash in our pockets—"

"I don't care about the money. Tell them you can't do it."

"I'm warning you, Father," Becky said evenly.

Abe glowered. "This is how you talk to your father? Thank God your mother can't hear you—"

Becky sagged. "I guess I am pretty tired. I'm going to bed now."

"That's a good girl." Abe knew a surrender when he heard it.

Becky trudged toward her bedroom, still clutching the jacket. She reminded Abe of the days following his wife's death, when Becky, still a chubby little girl, took to dragging around a tattered scrap of blanket for comfort and security.

At her door she held the jacket aloft for Abe to see. "I was going to throw it in the gutter, and then I was going to leave it in the cab. I checked the pockets. No wallet or keys. Just a solid gold cigarette lighter.'' She laughed wearily. ''But each time I got ready to throw it away, I found myself thinking, such a waste, a nice jacket like this. That's what you would think, yes, Father?''

''Becky, I love you very much.''

''I know you do,'' she sighed, ''but you don't know what's best for me. Only I know that. Good night.''

The door closed. Abe sat, his mind a blank, his brain and emotions exhausted by the strain of telling lies to his daughter. He could not bear to have sweet Becky know the extent of her father's involvement with Ben Talkin nor the fact that the store and the building that housed it belonged not to him but to Stefano de Fazio. Becky had grown up thinking her father owned property. Always it had been later, when she was older and could understand, that Abe was going to tell her the truth, and now it was too late. Abe could never tell her without looking like a liar as well as a failure.

And so I am Stefano de Fazio's dog, Abe brooded. I am his pet, and well provided for, but I must do as he tells me or else lose my business and my home.

Six months after Leah's death Stefano's attorney had come around with papers for Abe to sign. Ownership of the Cherry Street building was transferred to Stefano's business associate Antonio Bucci. Occasionally sums of money were ''invested in improvements'' to the Cherry Street property. The cash was delivered to Abe and it was his job to pay out specified sums to the various contractors who came by the store. In exchange for this service and for continuing as landlord, collecting rents and watching over the building, he continued to pay no rent for his store or apartment.

Becky, wrapped in her robe, returned to the parlor. ''One thing I forgot to ask. How did Stefano know Benny was engaged?''

Abe couldn't bring himself to look at her. ''He's promised to Stefano's youngest daughter.''

Chapter 33

Brooklyn

Benny Talkin punished the Cadillac on the way out to Sheepshead Bay in Brooklyn. By driving hard he hoped to work some of the anger out of his system. He chafed at the way he'd been summarily summoned to the home of the de Fazios.

He received the note from Stefano the morning after his disastrous blow-up with Becky. Abe had evidently gone to Stefano some time ago, and that visit had resulted in the note that "strongly suggested" that Benny come to Sheepshead Bay this Saturday afternoon to discuss his "serious breach of faith."

Benny savagely pounded the horn as he passed a battered Plymouth Road King, almost forcing it onto the shoulder. The driver swore at him, and Benny had a fleeting but intensely vivid image of pounding the offending driver's head against the dented, rusted fender of his crummy Plymouth.

Benny had waited twice for Becky at Malden's, hoping for a chance to apologize, to confess how the thought of never seeing her again made him yearn for her.

On both occasions Becky had either stayed late in the store or left by some other entrance. He could have seen her easily enough at home, but Benny had no stomach for that.

Unfortunately, this afternoon it was he who would be cornered. Benny frowned as he drove past the piers lining Gravesend Bay. How it galled to be lectured to about matters of honor and morality by someone like Stefano de Fazio.

And to make matters worse, I deserve it, Benny told himself. The fact that he loved Becky counted for nothing when his own self-interest had kept him from breaking off with Dolores de Fazio.

He'd met Dolores eighteen months before at one of her father's parties. She was in her early twenties, a lanky brunette wtih alluring blue eyes and a tomboyish way. She still lived at home. Benny asked her out a couple of times, but there were no sparks and the relationship languished.

Then there was another party, which led to a dinner date in Manhattan, which led to Dolores' long colt's legs wrapped around Benny's hips as they rutted on his double bed. He had not been the first, Dolores informed him as she reapplied lipstick to her wide, sensual mouth. She'd run with a succession of willing males from the time she was fifteen. Her father knew about none of them, of course.

Benny was a good lover, Dolores informed him. If he was willing, they could get together on a regular basis. Benny needn't fear getting involved too deeply with her, Dolores assured him. After all, he was Jewish.

Benny began calling for her at Sheepshead Bay on a regular basis. He took her to dinner the first few times, but when Dolores confessed that it made no difference to her, they soon dispensed with the restaurant and went directly from Brooklyn to Benny's apartment on the Upper West Side of Manhattan.

She was a sophisticated woman with a quick sense of humor, easy to like, and at some point, mixed in with the laughs, the champagne and the silken texture of her thighs as they tussled on the double bed, Benny decided he loved her. Dolores admitted that she'd begun to feel the same way about him.

Of course that was before he met Becky, before he learned what love could be. He felt more passion holding Becky's hand than he ever had in bed with Dolores.

But eight months ago, when Stefano de Fazio asked Benny to come into his study for a little talk while he waited for Dolores to finish primping upstairs, Rebecca Herodetzky was just some girl from around the old neighborhood.

"Look, I ain't gonna beat around the bush with you," Stefano began as he moved to pour Benny a Scotch. The Italian was wearing shabby work pants and a cardigan sweater with a hole in one elbow. The old clothes, combined with his thick grey hair, mustache and accent, made him seem totally out of place in the ostentatious luxury of his home. "This kind of thing ain't easy for a father, but on the other hand, I kinda like the fact that she came to me in the first place."

"What's this about, Stefano?"

"Hah! And me saying I wasn't gonna beat around the bush, right?" de Fazio laughed. "Well, Dolores has told me how fond of each other you two are. I think my daughter has her sights set on you, Benny. I think she wants to marry you."

"Dolores told you that?" Benny asked in disbelief.

"Hold on. She don't know about this conversation," Stefano warned. "She'd be furious with me if she ever found out about it. All I'm saying is that if you asked her, she'd say yes, okay? And if you're the man to make my daughter happy, well . . . I'm not one to let religion mess things up. Get me?"

After the initial shock of Stefano's suggestion had worn of, Benny did understand. Like any father, Stefano was anxious to see his daughter happy, but it was Benny's trucking business that had prompted Stefano's suggestion.

All Benny told Becky about his father was true, but he'd left some gaping holes.

For instance, the friends who set Mendy Talkin up with his profitable delivery routes were Benjamin Siegel and Meyer Lansky. In those days there was plenty of territory, and these same men, along with some others, felt sanguine enough about the future to form a crime confederation or syndicate, that alloted each boss his own territory. The Jews were given the job of enforcing the peace, and to do it they formed Murder, Inc.

That was during the thirties. To Lansky, Benny Talkin had always seemed like a good kid. While Benny's father was ailing, young Benny moved to curry favor with Lansky. When Mendy Talkin died, Benny was quick to assure Lansky that his trucks and union contacts would continue to be at Lansky's disposal.

Lansky could easily have prospered without small potatoes like Benny, but Lansky appreciated the fact that Benny was eager to ingratiate himself. Since Benny was useful as a buffer between Lansky and the unions and industries, since he was Mendy's kid and a fellow Jew, he found himself under Lansky's protection.

It was this protection that allowed Benny to hold on to his father's business. No other racketeer, no matter how hungry for trucks and power over the transport unions, would dare to try and muscle in on a protege of Meyer Lansky.

That included Stefano de Fazio, who hungered mightily for wheels. He had to move restaurant and building supplies, and of course there were his bakeries, meatpacking and warehouse holdings. Stefano had trucks of his own and some union connections from his old days as treasurer of the ILGWU, but nothing that approached Benny Talkin's fleet.

Right now it made no sense for Stefano to attempt to establish his own trucking business; Lansky would move to stop him. Like the other syndicate members, Stefano used Benny's trucks, and a healthy portion of Benny's profits were finding their way into Lansky's coffers.

But if Benny Talkin were Stefano de Fazio's son-in-law, the Italian would take over as Benny's feudal lord. Stefano would have the trucks and contacts he wanted as well as Lansky's share of Benny's profits. Benny knew this because he had wisely asked for Meyer's blessing on his impending marriage, and while Lansky advised against an interfaith marriage, he did not forbid it. Lansky then proceeded to act as Mendy would have in arranging things with de Fazio. In exchange for Benny's trucking business Stefano agreed to make his son-in-law a full partner in all of his holdings.

As Benny drove up the winding driveway bordered with evergreens, he noticed that Dolores' bright pink Hudson coupe was missing. Thank God she wasn't home. Benny sighed to himself as he parked and walked up the cobblestone path to Stefano's front door. He believed himself to be up to confronting an angry Stefano de Fazio, but he had no stomach just now for Dolores' wrath.

The door opened before Benny had a chance to ring the bell. "Come on in," Gemstones Bucci said. Tony was dressed in golf clothes: brown knickers and a bright yellow sweater with a crimson argyle pattern across the front and back.

Yellow was a bad choice for Tony, Benny couldn't help thinking, it brought out his baldness and the slick sallowness of his homely features. Benny himself was wearing a three-piece suit of dark green worsted. His shirt was mint green Egyptian cotton and his silk tie was the color of ivy flecked with gold. His shoes were custom made two-tones, the color of strong tea with dark green saddles. Benny considered this to be his lucky outfit. The girls said the greens did something magical to his hazel eyes. Benny figured that it must be so, for so many had said the same thing.

Tony Bucci led Benny through the movie-palace ambience of the big house. The flocked wallpaper, white rugs and red velvet draperies were all unchanged. As usual, Benny felt jarred as they passed from the eye-aching gaudiness of the main part of the house into Stefano's somber mahogany-paneled study.

Stefano was standing by the big window, gazing out at the bay. He turned, nodding to Benny. "Come see. Beautiful view today."

Benny dutifully moved to the window. The sunlight glittered on the mirror surface of the bay; gaudy boats bobbed in the water, tied to buoys like fat marshmallows.

Benny felt Stefano's hand on his shoulder. "How about a drink?"

"I wouldn't say no."

"Atta boy. Tony," Stefano called, "make us some of them—oh, hell, what were they called? You know, that new drink we had at the St. Regis."

"Red snappers they were called," Tony said. "I gotta go downstairs for the stuff."

"Look at you, all dressed to the nines like you was going to work at some bank or something. It's Saturday. You people don't work on Saturday, right? You're making me feel like a bum," he laughed, gesturing at the ink stains across the front of his old white shirt and at his corduroy trousers, rubbed smooth at the knees and across the droopy seat. Stefano stroked his chin. "I ain't even shaved today. Come on, at least take off that tie."

Benny demurred. "The tie is what makes it."

"Yeah, I guess. You got a lot of style, kid. Except of

course for this mess with the women. Except for that, huh, kid?''

Before Benny could reply Tony Bucci returned with a tray laden with a pitcher of tomato juice and spices. He went directly to Stefano's well-stocked sideboard and began to mix the ingredients with vodka.

"Wait'll you try this," Stefano boomed. "Maurice, the headwaiter at the St. Regis, told us it's the latest thing in Paris."

Benny suppressed his smile. "They start serving those during the wee hours at the all-night joints in Harlem. They call 'em bloody marys."

"Hear that, Tony?" Stefano pouted. "And we thought we could impress Benny. Bloody marys, eh?" He chuckled. "No wonder they call 'em red snappers at the St. Regis. Can't have no blood in a classy joint like that. Well, sit down. Make yourself comfortable."

Benny settled himself into a leather armchair and balanced his glass on the brass-studded armrest while he lit a cigarette, flicking the match into the standing ashtray beside him. My lighter, he thought, Becky still has my lighter. Oh, Becky, how I miss you.

He took a sip of his drink. "It's good." He nodded to Tony.

"Be a cold day in August I can't mix a drink better than some goddamned nigger in Harlem," Tony declared.

"I sent my wife shopping with Dolores," Stefano began. "Maria and my daughter don't know nothing about any of this, and as far as I'm concerned they never will. I don't want Dolores holding nothing against you before the marriage. Get it?"

"I've got to tell you something." Benny had already rehearsed what he wanted to say. He would get it across to Stefano that this marriage would be a terrible mistake. There'd been so many women in his life. Benny had felt more or less the same vague fondness for them all, includ-

ing Dolores. He'd truly believed that there was nothing
more to feel for a woman, but then he met Becky. This
marriage to Dolores had started out as a marriage of
convenience, a business deal; such a marriage was no
longer adequate now that he'd fallen in love with Becky.

Of course he couldn't tell Stefano he didn't love his
daughter. He had to be diplomatic.

"Stefano, after what's happened I wouldn't blame
you if you called off the wedding. I'm not good enough
for Dolores," Benny mourned.

"You hear that?" Stefano asked Tony. "I told you
he's a good boy. Benny, you made a bad mistake, but it's
an understandable one. I was young myself once. I ain't
gonna hold this against you."

"Really, Stefano. Call it off. I'm not worthy—"

Stefano smiled. "Let me explain something, kid. I
mean, your father, may he rest in peace, hasn't been
around to show you the ropes. This whole marriage thing,
it's for the women, you know? They give you sons—
daughters too, of course—but it's the sons that count.
Anyway, in exchange for bearing your children they expect a little security, so they invented marriage. Now,
what a woman don't know won't hurt her. Just like the
cops or the government. For instance, I got enough dough
to live in a joint that'd make this place look like a garage,
but I don't need to attract attention to myself, right? I got
Tony here to juggle my books so it looks like all my
profits get plowed back into my businesses. I pay very little
tax this way, Benny, and when the IRS comes snooping
around they see that I live good, but not too good for what
my books tell 'em. Get it? In other words, I'm discreet. In
everything. That's how you gotta be. Understand?"

This was not going the way Benny had hoped.
"Dolores should find herself a man worthy of her.

Stefano waved him quiet. "Bullshit. For one thing,
there ain't no man worthy of my daughter; for another

thing, the fact that you're so broken up about cheating on her makes you a saint compared to some guys I know. I'll tell you the truth, Benny. I ain't so mad at you for cheating on Dolores, 'cause what she don't know can't hurt her. I'm mad because of what you've done to poor Becky. I've known her since she was a little girl. She's an innocent, Benny, and I hear you messed her up but good.''

"I know that.''

"She'll get over it," Stefano continued. "She's got a lot of spunk.''

"Maybe I'll tell Dolores what's happened," Benny said, beginning to panic. "Let her make the decision—''

"Shut up and listen to me," Stefano said, his voice suddenly like steel. "This marriage is going to take place. Don't give me no crap about honor and worthiness and love. None of that has anything to do with it. You know it and I know it. Even Meyer Lansky knows it. The only ones who don't are my wife and my daughter. You made a business deal, Benny. You got to keep it. Meyer can't help you now. He wouldn't try, and even if he did, I'd go to the syndicate and they'd vote Meyer down. A deal's a deal. That's the only way we can operate. Nobody has the right to go back on his word. Do you understand?''

Benny stared at him. "You can't force me to—''

"You ever kill anybody?" Tony Bucci interrupted, his glasses flashing fire from the sunlight streaming in the window. "What I'm wondering is, you got any idea at all what you're talking about when you use the word 'force'?''

"Lansky can't protect you anymore," Stefano repeated. "When he blessed this marriage he was giving you to me.''

"What if I ran?''

Stefano shrugged. "Go ahead. I don't care. If that's what you gotta do, then do it. Just make sure it's far enough away so I don't see you around no more. I'll make up some kinda story to Dolores and to save face around

town, and the syndicate will give me your trucks and
routes to make it up to me. Lansky won't like it, but he'll
go along to keep the peace. Like I said, kid, a deal's a
deal.''

"You want to take some time to think about it,
maybe?'' Tony Bucci asked, licking his lips. "Personally,
I ain't got much use for you, but we could use them
trucks.''

"Yeah, think about it,'' Stefano agreed. "But frankly,
I don't see a guy like you slinging hash in Chicago or
somewhere.'' He shrugged. "Say good-bye to them fancy
suits and Cadillacs, right?''

Benny slumped in his chair, knowing he was trapped.
His choice was to marry Dolores or end up penniless
somewhere far away. Stefano wouldn't put out a contract
on him, but he'd be as good as dead nevertheless. He'd
have no money, no business, no home. Everything his
father had built up would be lost.

"Don't take it so hard,'' Stefano said soothingly.
"You like Abe's daughter? No problem. I'll confess something to you, father-in-law to son-in-law. I got me a little
apartment on the East Side with a chippie in it. Yeah, me,
Stefano de Fazio.'' He laughed. "She calls me Poppie.''
He traced an hourglass figure in the air and smacked his
lips. "She's a blonde. She knows how to make a man feel
good. You know what I'm saying?'' He pondered it. "I'm
talking about doing things a nice girl wouldn't dream of.
Personally, I don't see Becky being that kind, but who's to
say? After all, she's got a drunkard for a father.''

Tony Bucci glanced at his watch. "They'll be back
soon, Stefano.''

"Yeah. You take off now, Benny. Call me in a
couple of days and let me know how you want to play it.''

Tony stood up to escort Benny downstairs and out to
his car. "A word to the wise,'' he whispered to Benny as
the latter started up the Cadillac. "Meyer don't know

about any of this and I wouldn't tell him if I were you. You wanna stay on his good side, don't mention how you're thinking of letting him down.''

Tony Bucci watched Benny drive off and returned to the house, where he found Stefano downstairs in the kitchen, washing the glassware that had been used for their drinks.

''That wife of mine would want to know who'd been here with us if she saw three glasses,'' Stefano muttered good-naturedly. ''Dewey ain't got snoops as good as Maria.''

''Want me to do that?'' Tony asked.

''Nah, my hands are already wet.''

Tony nodded but stood by uneasily; it didn't seem right that his boss should be washing dishes. ''I hope that Yid does cut and run,'' he offered experimentally, not sure where Stefano really stood on the matter.

''I don't,'' Stefano replied as he sponged out the pitcher. ''The trucks are worth plenty, but not as much as Benny.''

''I don't get it,'' Tony scowled. ''You're talking like you want a Yid for a son-in-law.''

Stefano shrugged. ''All my other daughters married Italians, so I can take it if Dolores has her heart set on that guy.''

''It galls me that he's coming in as a full partner.''

Stefano continued to rinse the glasses. ''Hey, my sons are in as partners, too, but so are you. You got nothing to fear from Benny. He's a baby. You heard it yourself. Lansky has always taken care of him. He's been in a couple of fist fights and that's it. He's never made his bones and he never will. He can't kill nobody.''

''But a Jew—''

''Jews and Italians have worked together since Rothstein.''

"This ain't just work, this is marriage. What about your grandchildren?"

"They'll be raised in the church."

"Does Benny know that?"

Stefano shrugged. "He'll know when I tell him. Don't worry, Benny will be a help to us. He works hard. That business didn't thrive all by itself. Benny built up what Lansky and Siegel threw Mendy Talkin's way. And then there's politics to be considered."

Bucci scratched at his slick scalp, totally confounded.

"You ever read Shakespeare?" Stefano finished rinsing the last glass and wiped his hands on his worn corduroys. "I know you haven't. You only read accounting books, God love you."

"Get to the part where you explain why we need a Yid in the family," Tony implored.

"A lot of them Shakespeare plays have got to do with a bunch of royalty running around to see who's gonna be top dog while the king's away. That's like the situation now with Luciano in jail. Meyer Lansky is definitely a duke. What he says goes because Luciano backs him. I'm only one of the earls or whatever. My word doesn't cut it unless Meyer backs me. Now, the way I'm seeing it, Lansky and me are like two houses of royalty about to be joined together through marriage. What Lansky has to gain from this escapes me, but we do very good. Through Benny we get links to both Lansky and Bugsy Siegel out west. We also get closer to Luciano by being closer to Lansky."

"And the trucks," Gemstones chortled. "Don't forget them. There's a war coming, Stefano. Don't forget how good we did with our warehouses during the last war."

Stefano, nodding agreement, crossed the kitchen to open the refrigerator. "Maria's got some roast chicken in here from last night. How about a snack?"

Chapter 34

New York

That same Saturday Becky told her father that Malden's was closed half a day for inventory and the cashiers did not have to report to work until two-thirty that afternoon. She left Cherry Street at two o'clock with a shopping bag under her arm.

She'd told her father a white lie. She did not did not have to go to work at all that day. Instead she took the subway to the Upper West Side and emerged at Sherman Square.

In the shopping bag was Benny Talkin's jacket. She'd come uptown to return it to him. His apartment in the Dorilton was just steps away at Seventy-first and Broadway. Becky headed that way but then faltered. Returning the jacket with a note pinned to the lapel suggesting to Benny that they be friends had seemed like a good idea, but now that the moment had come, Becky lost her nerve.

She reversed her direction and wandered uptown along Broadway. As she walked she let the excitement of this part of the city wash over her, momentarily banishing her turmoil over Benny.

Becky had always enjoyed wandering the Upper West Side. Her favorite tour took her past the Astor, the Evelyn and finally the Apthorp, at which point she left Broadway to head east toward Central Park. Becky would pass Mount Neboh synagogue, its Byzantine dome and roughened exterior suggesting that it had been standing there far longer than twelve years.

Becky considered its newness something to crow about. A magnificent synagogue in a well-to-do section of the city the Jews claimed for themselves. How wonderful to leave Hester and Orchard and Cherry streets far behind and wander here, along the majestic wide avenues.

She continued all the way to Central Park West. Becky was wearing her smartest day dress and drawing nods and smiles from passersby as she turned their heads with her bright eyes and shiny dark shoulder-length tresses swinging in the soft breeze. On such a day her dreams swelled to fill the flawlessly blue sky.

She would become a buyer in a major department store like Macy's or Gimbels or Pickman's in Herald Square. Oh, what a marvelous job being a buyer was. There was travel, even to places like Paris, and an expense account and the opportunity to meet marvelous gentlemen who would invite her to intimate candlelit dinners in the dining cars of streamlined trains.

There would be a good salary, of course, enough for fine clothes, car and an apartment in one of those marvelous buildings identified by glamorous name, not nondescript street number. Perhaps her rooms would have a window high above Central Park. She would gaze out at the majestic landscape and the fire escapes and rank alleyways of the Lower East Side would be memory of days long past.

Often had Becky strolled this area, pretending her dream had come true, that before her at last was the delicious task of choosing the building in which she wished to live. It was during such a stroll that a lost soul came up to her and asked for directions—actually asked her, confident that she would know because she looked like just the sort of woman who belonged here.

Someday, Becky vowed, I will get here someday.

Suddenly she realized she was once again close to Benny's address. The jacket in the crumpled Malden's shopping bag was a weight dragging her down to dismal reality. She had not so much as a salesgirl's job at a real department store. She was just a cashier at a five-and-dime, and a part-time cashier at that.

Becky felt trapped. She desperately wanted the offered supervisor's job, but it seemed that there was no way to turn her dreams into reality without disobeying her father, and how could she do that? She loved her father; besides, she knew full well that in his old eyes she was a partner in the store.

Becky was her father's only real happiness in life. Their time together in the store was a sorry imitation of what Abe had at one time believed he would enjoy, but it was all he had, and he wholeheartedly tried to make the most of it. How could Becky make her father give up the store? He couldn't run it alone and wouldn't run it with Danny. The dilapidated building on Cherry Street was her father's entire world. Giving it up would break his heart, even if selling did give him enough money to live comfortably for the rest of his life.

Becky's dreams would turn bitter if she realized them by destroying her father—and that meant her dreams might never come true.

A clock in the window of a dry-cleaning establishment on the corner of Seventy-second and Central Park West told her it was close to five. She'd procrastinated enough. Drop off the jacket and be done with it, she scolded herself. The note pinned to it had been written days ago, and while the thought of making this gesture was humiliating, Becky loved him so much she had to give him this last chance before his wedding to ask her forgiveness and propose.

"If you want something, go after it," Benny used to tell her. Well, she wanted him, and while she was appalled at his duplicity, she simply refused to believe he didn't love her.

Love can win out, Becky told herself. She walked south one block along Broadway, took a deep breath and entered the Dorilton's marble lobby.

The desk man informed her that he didn't think Mr. Talken was at home but that he could ring up to check if she wished. That wasn't necessary, Becky replied, greatly relieved. She had no intention of seeing Benny. All she wanted was to drop off the jacket—with her note—affording Benny an opening to contact her.

She was willing to meet the man she loved halfway, but she'd never crawl to anyone.

She had the empty shopping bag folded up under her arm and was on her way out when she ran smack into Benny coming in. He looked so handsome in his dark green suit and so surprised and happy to see her that Becky's heart melted. She forgot her earlier resolve, and after stammering out her reason for being here, she heard herself agree to come upstairs for a drink.

Benny retrieved his jacket from the front desk and took Becky's arm to lead her to the elevator. He was quiet, reading and pondering her note as they rode up to his floor. Becky had ample time to imagine Benny apologizing and proposing marriage to her right now and to listen to her own pounding heart.

Benny waited for the elevator attendant to let them off and shut the car doors, and then he swept Becky into his arms and kissed her. Becky was aware that such behavior in the public hallways was scandalous, but she didn't care, not when Benny held and kissed her this way.

"I missed you so much," he whispered.

Becky, shivering at his touch, nuzzled his cheek. "I want you to miss me. I'm glad you did."

In the foyer of his apartment he took her coat. The foyer was done in dark blue and white and had a pair of tall mirrors lit from their pedestals.

The rest of the apartment was also blue. The living room was large and painted a lighter shade than the foyer. The wall-to-wall robin's egg carpet was thick and lush. Flanking the fireplace were two high-set bulls-eye windows. Beneath each was a burl-veneer walnut chest upon which rested a porcelain lamp with rectangular ivory shade.

Facing the fireplace were a sofa and armchair in walnut and blue leather separated by a low table set on a mirrored base. An open archway at one end of the room led to a small dining room and more walnut furniture. There was a small highly polished square table accompanied by smart modernist Italian Empire chairs with blue leather seats. One door, slightly ajar, led to the kitchen, while another closed one had to take one to the bedroom.

Benny opened that door. Becky glimpsed the reflection of an awesome circular bed captured in a huge mirror hung above a built-in dresser. She turned away, both thrilled and frightened, wondering what she was doing here when she knew he was about to marry another woman.

In the dining room Benny mixed drinks, then took them back to the living room. As usual, he barely sipped at his, but Becky, who had been careful to seat herself in the armchair, not on the sofa, found herself gulping the Scotch. It was far too strong, and it was going to go right to her head, but God knew she needed something to calm her nerves if she was to get through this ordeal.

"I'm sorry," Benny began.

"Don't tell me how you feel. Tell me what you're going to do." Was that she being so forward? How bold the Scotch was making her.

"I don't understand what you mean."

"Are you going to marry her?" When Benny averted his eyes, she nodded. "I see."

"I just came from seeing Stefano de Fazio," Benny said. He went to the mantel and took two cigarettes from a box. He lit them both and handed one to Becky before returning to the sofa. "I tried to get out of it. I really did; you've got to believe me."

"I believe you, but I don't understand. He can't force you to marry his daughter."

Benny smiled bitterly. "Do you have any idea what the word 'force' means?" he muttered.

"What?"

"Nothing, Becky." He sighed. "There's so much you don't know and I don't know how to tell you. You know about Stefano, of course?"

"That he's a gangster?" Becky nodded. "I always knew that. My father and Stefano were once friends, but that was long ago, before Stefano turned dishonest."

"My father was more involved with people like Stefano than I led you to believe."

"But that was your father. It's not you." Becky nervously fingered her empty glass. She couldn't remember ever finishing a drink before.

"It's not that simple, Becky."

"Yes it is," she snapped. "You lied to me." She stubbed out her cigarette and stood to go. "Are you just a racketeer, or do you murder people as well?"

The look on Benny's face, the speed with which he rose from the sofa frightened Becky. He caught her arm as she shrank back and pulled her close to embrace her.

"Don't be afraid of me," he implored. "Never be afraid. I'd never hurt you. I'll always be here to help you—I swear it."

He's going to marry her, Becky realized. It's true. I've lost him. She began to cry.

"There's a lot I didn't tell you, Becky, and a lot I can't tell you, but I didn't lie. My father's heyday was long ago. He was never a real big shot because he wouldn't kill anyone, just like I told you. I've always drawn the line at that kind of rough stuff as well. Yeah, I'm involved in the rackets. Maybe right now I'm sorry I am, but that doesn't change the fix I'm in. Stefano will ruin me if I back out of this marriage."

"Does that matter if we can be together?"

"Give up my business?" Benny shook his head. "First off, we'd have to run. Stefano told me so. We'd be running while Stefano took everything. I can't give up what my father earned. I can't and I won't."

Becky pulled away from him. "Then it's over. I'd better go." Her face was stiff with dried tears. She didn't want to go home looking like a wreck. "Please, can I freshen up?"

"Through the bedroom."

The effects of the Scotch had lessened, leaving Becky with a sour taste and the beginnings of a headache. She got her purse and walked a bit unsteadily through the bedroom and into the bathroom. The walls were blue tile. Like the rest of the apartment, the bath was immaculate and splendid, and Becky found that what she had moments ago considered exquisite she now hated. This luxury, not Dolores de Fazio, was her true rival. He could not give up the trappings of wealth.

She washed her face and reapplied her makeup. When she was done she was presentable enough not to arouse suspicion when she returned home. She would not be able to bear it if her father started questioning her.

She picked up her purse and left the bathroom. Benny was in the bedroom, blocking her way out. He'd removed his jacket, vest and tie. His shirt was unbuttoned and the sleeves rolled up, exposing his powerful forearms.

Once again Becky's heart began to pound. She found

it hard to breathe. The circular bed was beside her, just
beyond the periphery of her vision. "Let me out of here."

"Listen to me," Benny said. "It doesn't have to be
finished between us. I've been thinking."

Becky held her breath. He'd reconsidered! Elation
surged through her. He was going to marry her after all.

"After Dolores and I are married I'm going to be a
lot richer than I am now. I saw the way you lit up when
you saw my place. I could set you up in an apartment just
as nice as this—even nicer, maybe. And, well—then I
could come see you . . ." He peered at her face and fell
silent.

"I'm so sorry I came here," she said faintly. "I'm so
sorry you said that to me. Before at least I had our time
together to remember. Now all I'll be able to remember is
you asking me to be a whore."

"Who are you to be so high and mighty?" Benny
snapped. "You weren't that way when I met you. I guess I
taught you pretty good—Maybe I treated you too good! I
shoulda left you in that crummy grocery store with your
nobody old man—"

Becky took a step forward and slapped his face.

Benny's eyes widened. "Damn you, I'll show you."
He rushed at her.

Becky shrieked at him to stay away and tried to
defend herself, but his strong hands locked about her
wrists, pinning them to her sides.

"Treated you right, Becky . . . Always been good to
you . . ."

Becky twisted her head, trying to avoid his mouth as
it closed upon hers, his tongue thrusting. He brought up
his knee to pry apart her legs. In her struggle she upset
their balance. Locked together, they toppled sideways onto
the bed.

"You're mine, bought and paid for, Becky. Mine,
and I'm claiming you."

He released one of her wrists to tear at the buttons of her blouse, at the zipper of her skirt. Becky tried to rake his eyes with her nails. Swearing, Benny blocked her attack and then easily recaptured both wrists. Twisting them behind her back and holding them with one hand, with the other he wrenched apart the hooks of her bra. Now her breasts were bare and his lips upon them, his tongue teasing at her nipples.

Becky writhed in his grasp. The sound of her own exhausted breathing filled her ears. She tried to kick, but his legs had hers pinned. She arched her back, squirmed and twisted; she cried in pain as the sharp edge of his belt buckle dug into her naked belly.

Fighting him was useless. He was too big, too strong. His hands seemed to be everywhere on her at once. She was staked out, spread open and vulnerable beneath his bulk and strength.

"Benny, please! Oh, God," she wailed, "don't do this!"

He was possessed by demonic savagery, unable to comprehend her. He was intent on subduing her.

Briefly she was paralyzed with shock, less at the danger to herself than at his behavior. He felt her yield slightly and relaxed his grip a little, not enough to let her wrench free but enough to let a little blood flow into her hands.

At this she heartened and started to think. As an experiment she let her legs relax a little. It worked; he eased off more too. Becky calculated swiftly. If she shifted so, he would compensate thus; she would be in as good a position as she could hope for to make her move.

Becky raised her right shoulder so that her whole arm slid up a little in spite of Benny's grip. The strap of her purse stayed put and wound up just below her elbow instead of just above it. He had to lean off her a little or lose his grip.

She stopped struggling entirely and lulled him for a moment. He took the opportunity to let go and reach for his own zipper as Becky unobtrusively hooked her elbow into the strap and got a good grip on it.

I'll teach this creep to break my heart, she vowed, and she swung her purse hard at the side of his head.

The blow startled him more than anything. He reared up on his knees, his handsome face twisted into an ugly grimace of shock and frustration. He snatched at the strap and Becky surrendered it to grab the corner of the bag and thrust it into Benny's face. She felt the metal clasp catch the skin beneath his left eye, and she twisted and scraped it across his cheek with all her strength.

Benny shrieked and rolled off her, his hand over his eye. Blood welled up between his fingers.

He pulled away from her and left the bed. Across the room, fly undone and belt buckle dangling, he collapsed into a chair. The blood was trickling down his cheek onto his shirt. He took his handkerchief from his back pocket, wadded it up and pressed it against his cheek.

Becky, still on the bed, stared at him. The room was thick with silence. She heard a door slam and a faraway voice gaily wished someone good night.

Benny said, "I'm sorry . . . I'm . . . Really, I don't know what to say. I don't know what you want to do right now. I mean—"

"Go away so I can dress," Becky said coldly.

"Of course." Benny looked very pale. "I'll go out in the living room. You shower, whatever you want . . . You can lock the door after me."

"I certainly will—if you ever go."

"I'll—" Benny stared at her and shrugged helplessly. "I'll get you a drink," he said thickly, and left the room.

Becky turned the lock. She rushed into the bathroom, locked that too, and barely got the toilet seat up before she vomited. Fortunately, there was a new toothbrush in the medicine cabinet.

She washed her face again. Reaching for her purse, Becky recoiled as she noticed blood on the clasp. Shuddering, she wiped it clean with an embroidered linen towel—take that, you rapist—and breathed deep to steady her shaking hands enough to reapply her makeup.

"You're mine, bought and paid for."

She stared at her reflection in the mirror as her dark eyes once again filled with tears. Her knees were trembling; it was a delayed nervous reaction, she supposed. She sat down on the closed lid of the commode, stared at the blue tile and for one scant second clearly saw herself taking his safety razor, removing the blade and slitting her wrists.

"Serve the bastard right if I bled to death all over his fancy marble bathtub," she muttered, and then laughed and knew she was going to be all right.

She dug into her purse for her cigarettes. The pack was rumpled and flat, but there was, thank God, one left. No matches, though.

She went back into the bedroom and spied the jacket she had brought, lying over the back of a chair. She patted its pockets until she found his lighter, lit her cigarette and then pondered the gold bauble lying on her palm. She turned it this way and that, capturing the light on its burnished surface. Like all Benny's possessions, it exuded his style.

She slipped the lighter into her purse. She needed a memento of this day to keep her from softening toward him; it would take awhile to root out her love, even now.

Benny left the bedroom and headed directly for the drink he'd left on the coffee table.

He shuddered, unable to understand what he had been about to do. He'd never before lost control of himself like that.

You never felt like this before, he told himself.

He was on his way to the dining room to mix them both another drink when he heard his bedroom door close and then the click of the lock. He pondered the situation, set down the glasses, lit a cigarette to steady his nerves and went to the telephone.

His address book contained the telephone number for a separate line in Stefano's study. He dialed and let it ring, imagining Stefano's cumbersome progress up the long, wide curved staircase to the second floor of the house.

"Yeah—" Stefano's guttural voice on the line.

Benny glanced at his closed bedroom door. "It's me. I've decided to take your advice. But I want a wedding present."

"What?"

"I want the building on Cherry Street. You know what I'm talking about. The one that houses Abe Herodetzky's store. It belongs to you, right?"

"Sure it belongs to me. It's in Tony's name, but—"

"I want it."

"Talk to me, Benny. Tell me why."

Benny's fingers gingerly explored his cut cheek. The scab broke beneath his touch, and his face once again began to seep blood. "I got a score I want to even up."

"This something to do with Abe's daughter?"

"Yeah. Well, do I get my wedding present or not?"

"Sure, sure," Stefano sighed. "What the hell. It's yours. Do what you want with it. I'll have the papers sent over to your office. Okay? You happy?"

Benny pressed his bloodied handkerchief to his face. "Not yet," he said, "but I will be." He heard the bedroom door open behind him. "I gotta go."

Benny hung up. He turned to see Becky watching him. She was wearing one of his crewneck sweaters.

"Sorry about the sweater," she murmured. "I needed something to cover up my torn blouse."

"Jesus, I'm sorry. Let me pay you for the blouse—"

Becky's eyes closed. "Stop it." She crossed to the foyer and took her coat out of the closet. Once again Benny was treated to the sound of Becky shutting a door between them. This time it was his front door, and this time she was gone for good.

Chapter 35

As the weeks passed Becky threw herself into her work. At Malden's one evening a few minutes before closing Wilkerson called her into his office. The stout, balding personnel manager acted inordinately gentlemanly, actually inviting her to sit down. He fumbled with his cigar as he spoke.

"There's no easy way to break this kind of news, Miss Herodetsky. I'm sorry, but we're going to have to let you go. You've been doing a fine job here, but we just don't need so many part-time employees right now. I offered you the chance to train as a supervisor. I still don't understand why you didn't."

"I was proud you wanted me to train," Becky said. "Really, I was, Mr. Wilkerson. It's just that there's a problem at home. I've got to help out there, so for now part-time is all I can handle."

"I see." The personnel manager frowned. "I thought it was just that you were looking for something better than Malden's."

"Oh!" Becky was so startled that she laughed. "No, no, sir . . ."

"Now don't be embarrassed about it. Malden's is just

a five-and-ten, after all. As we both know, floor supervisor is as high as a woman can go around here, and that's not very high at all. I've watched you, Miss Herodetsky. In the beginning I confess I was looking for a pretext to fire you because of the way you got your job.

"But you've turned out to be one of my best workers. I've got to let you go, but if I need more help you're the first I'll call." He opened his desk drawer to remove a slip of paper. "This is the name and telephone number of the personnel manager at Pickman's in Herald Square. He's a friend of mine, and when he mentioned he was interviewing sales clerks, I told him about you. He was so impressed that he suggested you call him for—"

"Oh, Wilkie, how wonderful of you!" Becky gushed, so excited she broke the manager's cardinal rule and called him by the nickname he despised.

Fortunately, he seemed not to notice. His robust, shell-pink blush suffused his jowls, rising to encompass his balding dome. "It's nothing at all, my dear. I'm glad to do it. The only problem is that Pickman's is hiring full time only."

"I understand. I think I'm going to try for it anyway. There's no guarantee I'll get it, after all."

"None at all," Wilkerson smiled. "Then again, I wouldn't bet against you, Miss Herodetsky."

Beaming, Becky said, "Thank you, sir. I'll always be grateful."

"It was nothing. It's all up to you, really. You can finish out the week if you'd like."

The next day she called Pickman's while her father was upstairs. She made an appointment for a preliminary interview the following week.

After her job at Malden's ended, Becky still left the store until the early evening three nights a week and all day Saturday. She saw no point in taking a giant step backward, letting on that she'd been fired, especially if she wanted to work at Pickman's full time.

She decided to ignore her father's opposition, at least for the time being. What point was there in getting into a raging battle over a job she was still a long way from getting? Most likely she'd be crossed off the list of Pickman's prospective employees after her first interview, considering the way her luck had been running.

Pickman's dominated Herald Square. Once in a blue moon Becky's mother had run to Pickman's to take advantage of the big sales. Sometimes Becky would get to go along. She remembered how impressed she'd been by the tall, slender salesladies, to a little girl from the Lower East Side as glamorous as princesses.

And soon I may be one of them, Becky thought. Sales clerk was the first rung of the ladder to buyer.

She spent her former working hours in the library, poring over texts on fabrics, the garment industry, wholesaling and retailing. She had no idea what questions might be asked, so she prepared for everything she could think of. With Wilkerson's personal recommendation behind her Becky would never have a better chance at landing a job, but these days competition was stiff, as it was fashionable for the daughters of the wealthy to play at work behind the counters of the better stores. The department stores competed to see which could put the prettiest and most sought-after young ladies on its sales floor and show ramps and in its buyer-trainee programs.

During those exhausting evenings at the library Becky tried hard not to think about the debutantes who might get her job, only to quit after a month or so. With all those beauties they've got to hire at least a couple of girls with brains, she grimly told herself, and then she redoubled her efforts at her books.

*   *   *

On Wednesday afternoon Becky left the personnel department of Pickman's and wandered in a happy daze among the throngs in Herald Square. She was past the preliminaries. They'd asked her back for a second interview a week from today, on the nineteenth.

During the next seven days Becky made innummerable false starts on breaking the news to her father. Each time she began to tell him, she lost her nerve and changed the subject. No point to telling him now, she would decide. I don't have the job yet.

Becky gambled some of her savings on a Pickman's dress for her second interview. It cost a staggering twenty-five dollars, but it was well worth it. Pale grey with white collar and cuffs, it was at once businesslike and elegant. A shirtwaist, it would never go out of style, and its closely woven fine linen would wear for years. Besides, she had new white accessories, so the dress was her only expense.

All Sunday it rained and Becky pored over her notes from the library. She woke at dawn, around four-thirty, and got right to work. She seemed driven to concentrate solely on preparation for her interview Wednesday. She was quite fierce to Abe when he mildly suggested that she stop and get dinner. Finally Danny made sandwiches, but Becky would not stop to eat hers.

When she went to bed at midnight she was exhausted. She collapsed between the sheets and was asleep at once and for nearly ten hours thereafter.

On Monday morning she woke feeling vastly relieved, which puzzled her, for her interview still loomed ahead. Then suddenly it dawned on her—Benny was married now. She could not relent even if he asked her and she wanted to. Yesterday she had toiled her way through the ceremony, the reception and in all likelihood the consummation.

Becky congratulated herself on having forgotten the date and turned her head into the pillow, which she pounded

and bit as she wept for her lost lover with the feet of clay.
Finally she slept a little more and woke thinking of lip-
sticks and her new grey linen.

On Wednesday morning, just hours before her all-
important final interview, a letter addressed to Becky arrived at Cherry Street—not a catalog or a library notice,
but a letter—the first ever with Becky's name on it.

Becky skipped upstairs to read it in private. In the
sanctuary of her bedroom she tore open the thick envelope.
Wrapped around a sheaf of papers was a note:

> Dearest Becky,
>   I made some mistakes. I hope this helps a
> little to make things right.
>
>   Love,
>   Benny

Trembling, Becky examined the rest of the papers.
There was a handwritten explanatory history of this
building's ownership, which ended with Benny's admonition,
"Destroy after reading." And there was the deed. Becky
read everything twice, including the brief note from Benny's
attorney asking her to stop by his office to sign a few
documents and remit the sum of one dollar for the building
that housed the Cherry Street Market.

Becky was stunned. Benny's bombshell of an envelope might just as well have contained evidence that she
was adopted or a bastard or a princess or heir to a fortune.
She tried to come to terms with the bewildering implications.
She was not elated, but more hollow and numb.

There was no doubt that the deed was genuine, which
meant that the property really did belong to her. Benny
might well have betrayed her, but now he'd also supplied
her with the key to her prison.

If the deed was genuine, her father had been lying to
her all these years. He owned nothing and never had.

Becky fought back the impulse to rush downstairs and confront her father with the evidence. She had her interview at Pickman's in just a little while. It would be foolish to upset herself; she would face him after she got back.

She went to her closet. There hung her courage, and as she dressed she blessed herself for buying it. At last she dashed down the stairs and out of the store without so much as a word to her father. She didn't trust herself to speak to him. In her purse Becky carried the deed, hoping it would bolster her courage during the interview.

On the way home from Pickman's she stopped at the attorney's office to complete the transaction. It was still early when she was through; she decided to walk downtown. It was a nice warm day and walking would give her some time to think things over.

All through her interview she'd been afraid she seemed too remote and uninterested, but she'd been unable to help it. Her thoughts were taken up with her letter and the story that went with it.

And yet here she was, a bonafide property owner, and it now seemed conceivable that she might some day be a department store buyer, for the personnel manager at Pickman's congratulated her at the end of the interview, admiring her cool poise, and gave her the job.

As was Becky's habit, she waited until that night after supper and after Danny had gone out to discuss matters with her father. She ignored his glower as she explained that she'd be reporting to work bright and early Monday morning and that he would have to manage by himself each morning and with Danny during the afternoons until school let out and summer vacation began in just a few days.

"And what then?" Abe thundered.

"Then Danny can be here full time, just as I was."

"That's no good. Danny's going to enroll in a special summer school to help him pass—"

"Well, he can't do that now, Father." It would not do to get angry, not when she still had her second bombshell of the evening to drop.

"I see how it is. You're selfishly taking away your brother's chances for college even though you know that for years I've been saving for his education—"

"Stop it! Just stop. You know as well as I that all the money in the world couldn't buy Danny into any college, and even if it could, he'd flunk out. Face it. Danny is no scholar."

"So be it. I'll sell the store," Abe announced.

"You can't sell it," Becky snapped.

"Pardon me," Abe said sarcastically, "so why can't I sell?"

"Because you don't own it, and damn you for lying to me all my life." Becky slapped the deed down on the table between them.

Abe reached out to touch the paper, then jerked back his hand as if it could bite. "What is it?" he asked weakly.

"That paper and some others Benny Talkin sent me explain everything. What it didn't explain I could guess. Now I understand why Benny came to see you, although never when I was around. Stefano de Fazio has been your landlord, hasn't he, Father? All the years of my life, when you held this damned building over my head to make me do what you wanted, you were just a little man working for a ganef. Right? You looked down on Benny and his father, but all the time you'd been paying out blood money from Stefano to Benny. How many others come to you for their murder money?"

Ashen-faced, Abe sat with his shoulders hunched, his eyes downcast. "There are plenty who come," he said hoarsely. "Whether Stefano was paying them for murder,

I don't know. I was merely a messenger, a go-between. Nobody sees fit to tell me anything. Oh, *goddamn* Benny Talkin for sending that to you.''

''Did Mother know?''

''Everything, always. She was my strength. Oh, Becky, don't hate me,'' he pleaded. ''I had to lie to you. I wanted you to think I was special—''

''Why couldn't being a good father have been enough?''

''*Ahh*—'' His keening tore at her. He sagged toward the tabletop to lay his head in his hands. ''You know how many times I was a big hero? Never. So often in my dreams I was important, a somebody. So often I was applauded, admired. But only in my dreams. In real life, never.''

''That's not true, Father,'' Becky said. ''Remember when you gave the money to Stefano to save the union?''

''Look what it brought me.''

''I can't talk to you.''

''All it made me was Stefano's dog.''

''Not anymore. He no longer owns the building.''

''Who, then?'' Abe asked fearfully.

''I do.'' Becky tapped the deed. ''Somehow Benny got ownership, and he's given it to me.''

Abe shook his head. ''Gave it to you? Why?''

''Never mind why. From now on the rents you collect will really belong to us. With the rents, the profits from the store and my salary at Pickman's, there'll be more than enough to pay a helper come fall.''

''Please, Becky, don't leave me.''

''I'm not leaving. I'll still live here, after all.'' She smiled, attempting to reassure him.

''Now you'll live here, but for how long? Don't go, Becky.'' He tried his best to smile. ''You're the owner now, yes? We can make changes in the store—improvements.''

"Father, I'm sorry I yelled at you. I don't care about the past. I love you. But I don't want to work in a grocery for the rest of my life."

"Everything changes too fast," Abe complained. "Everything before I'm ready. Haim's leaving, your mother's death—everything."

"Father, I've got a chance to be something I've always wanted to be. Can't you be happy for me?"

"Everything changes too fast . . ." He wasn't listening. Becky took the deed and went into her bedroom. The last thing she did before going to bed was carefully unfold the note Benny had sent.

He had made a handsome gesture, and she was on the verge of forgiving him after all when she recalled that the deed to a house was a traditional way of paying off a discarded mistress. She clung to that thought as her last line of defense against him.

PART III

DREAMS RENEWED

Chapter 36

Jerusalem, 1941

Herschel Kol huddled in the corner of his dark cell, listening to footsteps echoing along the dank corridor of the solitary confinement block. The sounds registered on his brain, but he paid them no mind. Surviving a spell in solitary called for ignoring the unpleasant externals and focusing on one's center.

The footsteps grew louder and then stopped. Herschel briefly imagined that somebody was standing on the other side of the windowless steel door.

A hallucination, Herschel decided. It had to be.

A fellow locked up by himself in the dark was easy prey to hallucinations unless he disciplined his mind. Say he let his thoughts wander, got to thinking about the roaches, spiders and the like. He couldn't see them, of course, any more than he could see his own hand in front of his face, but he knew they were there, and if he concentrated, he could hear the tiny clicks of their legs as they scrabbled across the concrete—toward him.

So if a fellow knew what was good for him, he didn't think about the blasted bugs that might or might not be there. He calmly refused to acknowledge the itching along his spine, resisted the impulse to scratch, because giving in to that itch would spawn a dozen more, and before long he would be tearing at his skin in the dark, convinced that he was being eaten alive.

The footsteps, Herschel reminded himself. Had they stopped before his door? Not likely. It seemed too soon for release, although these days he did not have the best grasp of time. Was this his fifth or sixth spell in solitary? It was bad not to be able to remember.

What day was it? What month? Let's see, the usual stretch in solitary was seventy-two hours, but after a man's third offense the sentence was often extended to a week. When had he gone in? Before. When would he be released? After.

Goddamn it, Herschel thought—or had he actually said it out loud? He couldn't tell. Was he awake or asleep? He pinched himself. Pain—he was awake. He knew his name, and that this couldn't last forever. Consciousness, identity, the knowledge of time's passage—these three formed the tripod on which Herschel Kol's sanity rested.

The door slot slid open. Herschel winced and shielded his eyes. The slot slammed shut and the door to his cell was wrenched open. Somebody half-dragged, half-carried him from his cell, back into the world.

"What day? What month?" Herschel begged.

"April twenty-fifth, a Thursday. You've been in five days," someone with a British accent replied. "You'd be in for another two but for your luck. Come on, liven your pace. We've got to get you cleaned up, mate. Someone very important is here to see you."

Herschel was allowed to shower and shave. They gave him clean clothes, not the usual prison garb, but trousers, a shirt and sandals, reasonably well-fitting. They gave him a meal he could only pick at because he had been on starvation rations so long. Then a doctor came and gave him an injection that made him itch worse than the imaginary bugs but feel very alert and strong.

Finally he was escorted to the office of the chief magistrate of the prison. It was a spartan room with stone walls painted yellow, a metal desk and file cabinets and several straight-backed chairs with missing rungs.

The chief magistrate was absent. In his place, seated behind his desk, was a British colonel in his sixties with grey hair and a matching iron-hued slash of mustache. Standing respectfully to one side was a youngish captain with a number of file folders clasped under his arm. The captain was pale and gaunt, clean-shaven and bespectacled. Despite his uniform he looked far more like a bank clerk than a military man.

"Mr. Kol, how nice to see you." The colonel beamed, actually standing and extending his hand.

Herschel hesitated, mindful of the guards around him. Moving without permission usually earned an inmate a painful taste of a guard's baton.

The colonel evidently understood Herschel's hesitation. "You men wait outside," he ordered. The guards saluted, turned and marched out of the office.

"Now then, Mr. Kol, why don't we shake hands like gentlemen, eh?" the colonel remarked pleasantly. Herschel, nodding dazedly, did as he was told. When the colonel invited him to sit down, Herschel sat. "Would you care for a drink?" He indicated a bottle of whiskey and one glass on the desk.

"I don't drink."

"A cigarette, then?" The colonel took a silver case out of his pocket and offered it.

"I've given up smoking. Please, who are you and what do you want from me?"

"Yes, of course." He snapped the cigarette case closed and returned it to his pocket. "I am Colonel Ian Richards of General Sir Archibald Wavell's staff. Do you know who that is?"

"No."

Colonel Richards glanced at the captain. "How long has he been in?"

The captain scrutinized the contents of a cardboard folder. "Twenty-one months, sir."

Richards nodded, his smile reappearing as he turned back to Herschel. "General Wavell is Prime Minister Churchill's chief of staff in the Middle East, and the general himself has sent me from Cairo to see you, Mr. Kol. To ask for your help. Things have been happening while you were our guest here."

"Yes, and some of it I know about. For instance the way you have been condemning my people to death by refusing to grant them sanctuary from Nazi persecution—"

"Be quiet and listen, Mr. Kol," the colonel said patiently. "I have not come here to debate my country's immigration policies with you."

"Why are you here?"

"Get some respect," the captain warned.

"What if I don't?" Herschel laughed. "What can you do to me that hasn't already been done? Now then, Colonel Richards. You've said you want my help. How so?"

"Several weeks ago we suffered a bad setback in Iraq," Richards began. "Our treaty afforded Britain two air bases and the right to transport troops across Iraqi territory. In exchange Iraq was granted independence. At our request the League of Nations terminated our mandate to rule—"

"The Anglo-Iraqi Treaty was ratified over a decade ago," Herschel said.

"A treaty is a treaty," the captain exclaimed.

"I'm amused," Herschel smiled, "at how the British

have so little understanding of Arabs when they profess to have such an affinity for them.'' He glanced at the captain. ''Was that respectful enough for you?''

''Mr. Kol, we are well aware that you are finding this interview as distasteful as we are, so let's get on with it,'' Richards said. ''There has been an Iraqi coup d' etat. We thought we had a strong pro-British government in place, but a bloke named Rashid Ali, backed by some nationalist fanatic types, ousted our people.''

''Rashid says he'll hold to the 1930 treaty, but we know he's in Hitler's pocket,'' the captain added. ''When the time is right Nazi military assistance will flow into Iraq via the Vichy forces holding Syria. The mufti's holy war against Britain will—''

''Just what the Prussians promised the Turks in World War One,'' Herschel mused. '' 'Side with us,' they coaxed the Ottoman Empire, 'and we will give you back your former glory.' ''

''Yes, I suppose,'' Colonel Richards agreed absently. ''In any event, Rashid Ali would dearly like us to recognize his government. Accordingly, he's allowing us to land our troops, but the Germans are at him. Yesterday Rashid informed our ambassador that from now on there would be a quota—only so many British troops in for so many leaving Iraq—something strike you funny, Mr. Kol?''

''It is satisfying to see Britain chafing under a foreign nation's immigration policies,'' Herschel smiled. ''What was your government's reply?''

''That we will decide how many troops will land and Rashid had best keep his nose out of it. That is where things stand. We believe Hitler will soon officially endorse Rashid's government—that is something we cannot do, of course. Rashid will most likely put his facilities at the Nazis' disposal, the most important of which at the moment are the oil installations near Baghdad.''

''I still don't understand what you want me to do.''

Colonel Richards smiled coldly. "Only what you do best, Mr. Kol. That is, blow up those oil installations before the Germans can make use of them. You're rather keen on blowing up things Arab, aren't you?"

Herschel stared at the two officers and burst out laughing. "Surely there are British soldiers who far surpass me in grenade-hurling ability."

"It would be—embarrassing—if Englishmen were caught destroying Iraqi property," the captain said stiffly. "There's the treaty, of course."

"Of course," Herschel crowed. "None of your Arab allies would undertake such a thing, so who else can you send but Jews?"

"Not just any Jews," Colonel Richards said. "We've already recruited a few of your Irgun associates. We've released them from various prisons and detention camps and have grouped the team at our RAF base at Habbaniyah, approximately fifty miles west of Baghdad. The plan is for the team to pose as Arabs. Like you, the rest have received Irgun terrorist training—"

"You mean military training."

"Commando training then."

"Colonel, look at me," Herschel commanded. "I have blond hair and blue eyes. I had limited success pretending to be British, but I would have none at all playing an Arab."

"Now, now, Mr. Kol. Fair coloring never stopped your father," the captain put in, tapping one of his folders. "We know all about Haim Kolesnikoff's exploits on behalf of the Allies during the First World War. If your father could pass as a Bedouin, we see no reason why you—"

"Don't tell me about my father," Herschel snapped. "What happens to me if I agree to join your team?"

"Assuming the Iraqis don't kill you, you will be amnestied."

"I go free?"

The colonel hedged. "We'll see about getting your sentence reduced."

"Amnestied means go free."

Colonel Richards shrugged. "A lot would depend upon your willingness to perform other missions for the Allies."

"Consider the altenative," the captain said. "We say good-bye to you and you remain here for—" he stroked his chin thoughtfully. "For twenty-three years and three months, give or take a few days."

"Tell me one thing," Herschel asked. "You have gone to a great deal of trouble to persuade me. Why? Any number of imprisoned Irgun members could do it."

"Quite right, Mr. Kol." Richards nodded. "But the so-called commander in chief of your Irgun, David Raziel, specifically requested your participation. Raziel is leading the team, you see—"

"I'll do it."

At dawn the next day Herschel was flown under guard to the RAF base on Lake Habbaniyah, which itself was just a few miles from the Euphrates River. From the air the base looked more like an English resort than a military outpost. Herschel saw a polo ground, a swimming pool, cricket and football fields and rows of neat bungalows with red tile roofs and garden plots. There was also a large white villa. Herschel was informed by his guards that it was the residence of Vice Marshal Smart, air officer commanding in Iraq.

Habbaniyah looked like a resort, but one that had fallen on hard times. Due to the confrontation between the British and Rashid Ali's nationalist-backed government, British dependents had been evacuated from Baghdad, with hundreds taking refuge at the base. Iraqi forces had established positions on a high plateau a scant half-mile south of the base. There were Iraqi armored cars within sight of the air strips.

It was time for Habbaniyah flight school to become a combat-ready unit. Air Vice Marshal Smart had eighty planes, more than the Iraqi air force did, although the planes themselves—ancient Gladiators and worn-out Audax and Oxford trainers—were far from battleworthy.

Besides, there were no experienced pilots to fly them. Almost all the pilots were students, and the instructors were too rare and precious to send into combat.

As Herschel's transport plane taxied to a halt he spied a pair of rusted World War One field guns and several antiquated armored cars. This was the extent of Habbaniyah's heavy ground defense. Out on the golf course the greens were trampled and volunteers fumbled their way through hastily improvised rifle drills.

Herschel's guards escorted him to the white villa, which they called Air House. There, amid fine furniture and exquisite Persian rugs, Herschel was greeted by Major Thomas Lemon, the officer in charge of the raid. Lemon had thinning dark hair and watery blue eyes. He was in his forties and stocky in a soft sort of way. He had a potbelly and wore his revolver high on his right hip in deference to it.

"Glad to have you with us, Kol," Major Lemon began, then paused to sneeze. He took a balled-up handkerchief from his trousers pocket and dabbed at his weepy eyes. "Blasted oleanders," He muttered. "Come along then."

"Where is Raziel?"

"I'm taking you to him," Lemon managed before the next sneeze. Herschel was seized with anticipation as Lemon and the guards led him from the villa to a waiting car.

David Raziel, with the poet-warrior Abraham Stern, had guided the Irgun after its split from Haganah. Both men were imprisoned in 1939. Raziel had been released from Latrun Detention Camp in exchange for his willingness to cooperate with the British against the Axis powers.

Herschel had never met Raziel. As the car drove past a church and a cinema, dark since Habbaniyah's siege began, he remembered how Frieda used to talk about Raziel, how jealous Herschel once felt. That was all long ago, or so it seemed to Herschel, despite the way he missed his lost love.

The car pulled up in front of a barracks flanked by two more old armored cars and by a squad of British regulars on guard duty. Herschel noticed bars on the barracks windows and the heavy-duty hasp and padlock on the outside of the door.

"This will be your home for the time being," Major Lemon said, sniffling. He did not get out of the car.

Herschel's guards removed his handcuffs and then escorted him to the entrance, where the door guards lightly frisked him.

"Just routine," the sergeant-major in charge told the insulted guards who had gotten Herschel this far. "You're my responsibility now, Kol," the noncom went on. "My name's Foster. We'll get along fine. Don't you worry."

Foster opened the door for Herschel, who stepped inside and saw three men lounging on canvas cots. One stood up and approached Herschel, his hands outstretched in welcome. He was a swarthy man with thick black hair, wide-set eyes and a broad, fleshy nose.

"I have been looking forward to meeting you," the man said in Hebrew. "I am David Raziel." He paused as the door slammed shut and the padlock was fitted into place. Raziel grinned. "Welcome to the kennel, Herschel Kol."

The mission, it turned out, was delayed in the hopes that some peaceful way could be found out of the deadlock between the British and Iraqi governments. However, compromise became extremely unlikely when Air Officer Smart sent his squadron of trainer aircraft fitted with makeshift bomb racks to attack the Iraqi positions overlooking the base.

The Iraqis responded with antiaircraft and artillery fire. One British plane was shot down and the base itself was pounded. The Iraqi shells fell for a week. Herschel and the others spent their days digging trenches and hauling aircraft as far as possible from artillery range.

They received a daily briefing from Major Lemon on their mission, which was indefinitely postponed. They received no training and would receive none, the major told them. Weapons practice was out of the question. They would be supplied and armed just before departure. Guards with submachine guns watched them all day, and at night they were locked into the kennel.

It was just like prison to Herschel, except that in prison nobody had been trying to kill him. Habbaniyah had undergone periodic air attacks since Hitler recognized Rashid Ali's government, and now the tired Iraqi Gladiators were being replaced by sleek, lethal Messerschmitts. The planes carried Iraqi insignia, but from the way they were flown it was painfully obvious that experienced Luftwaffe pilots were at the controls. The twin-engine ME-110 fighter bombers came infrequently to Habbaniyah in an almost desultory fashion, but when they did come they chewed the base to pieces.

"This is the proof. To the British we are merely useful animals," Raziel fumed one night during an air attack.

He, Herschel and the others—a Pole and a pair of dusky-skinned Sephardim chosen by the British because they spoke Iraqi—were huddled inside the kennel. It was torture to be locked inside the flimsy building while all around them bombs exploded and incendiary machine-gun fire set similar structures ablaze.

"We are just like their guard dogs," Raziel was muttering, "like the Alsatians that patrol the fence. We are kept chained until it is time for us to be turned loose to bite somebody, and then back on come the chains—"

The rest was lost in a nearby explosion. Herschel snuffed out their one candle as the blackout curtains were jarred loose from the window moldings. They sat in the dark, listening to the whine of the planes swooping over the base in the night, and told each other that with any luck this would be their last such attack.

The silver lining was that Command had been jarred into putting their mission back on rails. They would be starting out any day now, according to Major Lemon's latest briefing.

Since Herschel had the best English of the team, he would accompany Raziel to the villa tomorrow morning for an intelligence report on the oilfield's defenses. They would also receive their maps.

Raziel guessed they woud depart tomorrow night.

It was a few hours before dawn. The air attack had ended and only Raziel and Herschel remained awake. At Raziel's request Herschel explained how he came to be an Irgun member. Without meaning to he found himself talking about his father and growing up at Degania, about those heavenly first years living in Jerusalem with his mother and then his brief, intense affair with Frieda Litvinoff.

He spoke intensely and sincerely of all of his passions and his grief over Frieda's death.

Raziel listened intently. He was deeply interested in Herschel; he was interested in all his men as commander in chief, but the cream of the crop of Palestinian manhood merited special attention.

Raziel said as much. Whatever path had led Herschel Kol to the Irgun was a path Raziel wanted to know about.

Finally Herschel was finished talking. His throat dry, he stared at Raziel.

"What?" the Irgun commander coaxed.

"I don't know how to ask. I don't want to appear disrespectful, but—" Herschel shrugged. "We could be dead a couple of days from now."

"See how things improve?" Raziel chuckled. "A little while ago we might have been dead last night. Come, Herschel, I have no secrets from a fellow fighter. Ask me."

Herschel nodded and nervously cleared his throat. "When the British came for me at the prison, I was ready to go back to solitary rather than help them. Then they said you were involved, and that settled it for me, and here I am."

"I am flattered," Raziel said dryly.

"No you're not. You don't respect my decision, and frankly, neither do I. What I want to know is why you're here. It's been years since you made your truce with the British, and still they keep you locked up, guarded all the time, like—"

"Like their patrol dogs."

"Yes. That they cannot trust Jews is obvious, but why do you help them? Merely because the Germans are worse enemies?"

"That they are against the Nazis is a good reason. Chasing the British out of Palestine will not bring about a Jewish homeland if it is the Nazis who do the chasing." Raziel paused. "But I have a more personal reason for helping the British despite the way they treat me. I simply don't want to hate."

"I don't understand."

"The Irgun Z'vai Leumi was not formed out of hatred but because of a difference of opinion with the Zionist Socialists."

"That I understand."

"Do you understand why Abraham Stern is not here with us?"

Herschel swallowed hard. "You've read my mind. In prison I thought to desert the Irgun and join the Stern group."

Raziel nodded. "Every man must follow his own conscience. I declared a truce, while Stern declared war. I will not judge my old comrade's actions." He pondered Herschel for a moment. "Do you remember when you were defending Degania in '29, how the Arabs attacked impulsively, lacking all strategy; mere mobs?"

Herschel grinned. "They were easy to defeat."

"They were—and are—like that because they believe the glory of battle is diminished by too much preparation. Concerning oneself with mundane details is an aspect of ordinary life, not of warfare. To the Arabs fighting is like lovemaking: too much prior thought makes both the will and the ability vanish."

"That is why we will ultimately win."

"Win the war, but at what cost?"

"Lives will be lost."

"Lives, yes, but souls as well?"

"I don't understand."

Raziel sighed. "I see that you don't. Be comforted. Stern does not understand either. This is the reason I asked the British to recruit you. There was much publicity surrounding your case. Imagine, the grandson of the renowned Erich Glaser, a terrorist. I was curious about you and wondered what conclusions you had come to concerning the struggle for a homeland."

"I'd like to know your conclusions." Herschel began to feel uneasy. He wanted—needed—Raziel's strength and certainty, just as he had once needed Frieda Litvinoff's.

"Mine, eh? Very well." Raziel shrugged. "I've come to believe that the very qualities that make the Arabs weak will ultimately allow them to prevail. They do not brood the way Jews do. They somehow remain lighthearted and pure while we grow bitter and spiritually stunted as we apply ourselves to the art of killing as we once might have pursued careers. I think about the combat manuals Stern and I wrote. I have seen former Yeshiva boys memorize every word the way they once might have studied the Talmud—''

''Well, they—*we*—have to,'' Herschel argued. ''Guns are what we need these days.''

''Of course you are right.''

''You don't sound so happy about it.''

''That's because I've seen Jews take delight in killing. We have always excelled as students. Now we shall advance to the head of the class in violence, and we shall see what God will have to say on the matter.''

At nine o'clock that morning Sergeant-major Foster called for them by car. He sat up front beside the driver. In the back seat Herschel and a guard flanked Raziel.

''I imagine you boys are looking forward to being off,'' Foster said over his shoulder as the car pulled away from the barracks. As they sped past the villa and through the main gates, Foster told them there had been a change of plans. ''The Iraqis have blown the dikes on the Euphrates. The bloody main road to Baghdad is flooded. The briefing is going to be held at the RAF Boat Club. Major Lemon thought that you two ought to get a look at the skiffs available during daylight so as to chose the one you'll be using come nightfall.''

''So we are leaving tonight?'' Raziel asked.

''Looks like it, old boy.'' The sergeant-major wagged his finger. ''But you didn't hear it from me, right? I expect you'll take one of those skiffs across the river, float across the flood area and end up in the town of Falluja, halfway to Baghdad. From there reportedly the roads are dry.''

''Boathouse just ahead,'' the driver warned.

"Right." Foster reached down to the floor of the car and came up with two pairs of handcuffs. "Sorry about this, chaps. Major's orders, seeing as how we're off base. He wanted me to fetter you for the whole trip, but I didn't—"

"I understand," Raziel said calmly. He held out his wrists.

The guard sitting beside him made a face. "You hear a plane?" he asked the sergeant-major, rolling down his window. He stuck out his head, trying to get a look at the sky.

"No more chains," Herschel said angrily. "You ask us to risk our lives and now you insult us—"

"None of that, Kol," Foster scolded as he snapped the cuffs on Raziel's wrists.

"They will have their way no matter what," Raziel whispered in Hebrew, leaning toward Herschel. "There is no point in giving them the satisfaction of manhandling you."

Foster tugged experimentally on Raziel's handcuffs. "Right. Your turn, Kol. Get your bloody head in the car and give me a hand," he ordered the guard. "Kol is being stubborn—"

The guard jerked his head inside. "Messerschmitt!"

Herschel was staring at Raziel as the rear window of the car imploded. There was a sound of myriad angry hornets and the driver's head suddenly splattered against the windshield. Foster was screaming and then he stopped and quietly slumped forward out of Herschel's sight. The driverless car was swerving, and Raziel, apparently off balance, fell against Herschel, who bent beneath the weight. Herschel's door sprang open. He tumbled out of the car in time to watch it slam into the back of Major Lemon's automobile, which was parked in front of the boathouse. The car's hood flew up and steam or smoke began rising from the engine. The horn began to blare.

Herschel was sprawled on his belly. His palms were raw and his trouser knees were torn, but he was otherwise unharmed. He lay still, pressing himself into the dirt. The landscape was flat and the boathouse itself afforded little protection. Herschel did not want to attract the attention of the circling Messerschmitt.

A stunned and appalled Major Lemon and his two men were outside the boathouse and saw the attack. His two soldiers threw down their rifles and scrambled up a ladder to the flat roof. Herschel saw the fear distorting their faces as they struggled to bring a machine gun to bear on the enemy.

The soldiers' efforts were hopeless. Their machine gun was a World War One vintage drum-fed Lewis. It managed to loose one short, stuttering burst before the German plane opened fire, shredding sandbags and men and sending the Lewis gun somersaulting into the lake.

Major Lemon was running along the edge of the lake, away from the boathouse and the Messerschmitt and toward Herschel. Clearly the major was panic-stricken; he would only draw fire on himself.

The ME-110 had streaked past the major before the pilot could react, but the plane also carried a tail-gunner. He zeroed in and water spouts began erupting all around the panicked major.

"Get down! Fall down," Herschel shouted. The major was still heading toward him, and so was the machine gun fire nipping at Lemon's heels.

Finally the gun caught up with Lemon.

Herschel lay paralyzed as bullets kicked dirt in his face, and then the enemy plane was past him. It made a final run over the boathouse to shoot apart the skiffs along the pier, and then it flew off.

Herschel unsteadily got to his feet and made his way to the car. Its engine had stopped smoking, but the horn was still blaring. He went around to the engine compartment and yanked out a handful of wires.

The noise stopped. Now there was nothing to break the stillness but the sound of the water lapping against the pilings.

Raziel's body was dangling half out of the car. Herschel knelt over him, though he knew he was beyond help. He'd been hit at least six times. Herschel glanced at the guard who'd first spotted the plane; he was dead as well.

He noticed Raziel's handcuffs and went around to the passenger side of the car and opened the door. Sergeant-major Foster spilled out, just as bullet-riddled as everyone else.

Except me, Herschel thought, thanks to Raziel falling on top of me and absorbing my share . . .

He patted down Foster's corpse until he found what he was looking for. He took the handcuff key and removed Raziel's manacles, which he hurled into the lake.

"You are free now," Herschel told the body, and then he wandered over to Lemon's automobile. The rear trunk area was fairly bashed in, but the car still looked sound enough. He got in behind the wheel and pushed the starter. The engine caught. Herschel put it in gear and drove it clear of the accident.

He left the engine running and returned to Sergeant-major Foster. He took the man's revolver, a .38-caliber Webley, and his money. Then he went around to all the other dead men and collected their money as well.

Herschel knew what he was going to do. The way Raziel had died—handcuffed—was what decided him. With money and a gun he could try to make his way back to Palestine. Lemon's car would get him part of the way there, and when it gave out, Herschel would trust his boyhood training at Degania to survive the rigors of the Transjordan. There were villages and towns too small to be on the map where money or a gun would get him clothing, food, transportation.

Perhaps he would stop and see his mother and Yol. Then he could make his way along the coast and look up an Irgun or Lehi cell.

Perhaps he would be accosted by a British patrol. In that case he would be shot before he allowed another sergeant-major to chain him like a dog.

Chapter 37

New York, 1942

Becky Herodetzky's second anniversary behind the handbag counter at Pickman's convinced her that she would have to do something more than her job if she wanted to succeed in retailing. Her abilities were not exactly going unrecognized or unappreciated, for her department's finicky merchandise manager had recently commended her for moving some atrocious wartime excuses for leather handbags. Every six months like clockwork she'd received her merit salary raise. For all that, she was still exactly where she'd started.

If Becky had learned anything working for her father on Cherry Street, it was patience. If it were not for two occurrences she would have patience now and never dream of rocking the boat.

First there was Grace Turner's rapid rise. Grace was a woman her own age, a tall, attractive, dizzy debutante with enormous green eyes and silky blond hair. She was the daughter of a stockbroker and enjoyed the advantages of finishing school and a college education. Grace had had a princess' upbringing in Westchester, which she left for a share in a roomy apartment on the East Side, where two other young ladies of similar breeding were her roommates.

Grace had started at Pickman's nine months ago. Becky was her trainer on the sales floor, and despite the dissimilarity of their backgrounds they had become friends, exchanging sandwich halves in the employee's cafeteria and giggling together about all sorts of things, not the least of which was their immediate superior, Winston Kelly, the prissy tyrant who was their department's merchandise manager.

Becky wasn't seeing so much of Grace lately. Now they were taking their lunch breaks on different schedules and Grace was spending only half-days on the sales floor. She'd been promoted into the buyer-trainee program.

Becky wasn't surprised. Grace Turner was who she was. Some people were just born blessed; opportunity came to them on bended knee, like a starry-eyed suitor. Others, like Becky herself, had to do the proposing if opportunity was to pay them any mind.

Besides, Grace deserved to be a buyer. The finer things in life were second nature to her. She was also generous and sweet. Upon her promotion she invited Becky out for a celebration. They went to a wonderful French restaurant where Grace gaily chatted with the obsequious headwaiter in his own language—and they ordered champagne. When Becky confessed that it was her first taste of it, Grace laughed with her, not at her. Becky didn't know how to eat escargots and Grace discreetly showed her. Later, when Becky discovered what escargots actually were, Grace comforted her and they laughed until they cried.

The fact that Becky was poor and Jewish didn't matter at all. Becky was happy for her friend's success. She just wanted to be happy for herself as well. Grace Turner's rapid rise spurred Becky, but not nearly as much as the specter of the war, which overshadowed everything.

The war transformed Pickman's, along with its

competitors, from post-Depression emporiums of plenty into shadows of their former selves. Pickman's major-appliance department was now a large empty space. The walls were bare where once shiny toasters and irons gleamed beneath the lights. The apparel departments were in tatters. Not selling in the least were men's so-called victory suits, pricey, shapeless garments cut with narrow lapels and no cuffs or vests. Ladies' fashion was paralyzed both by the fall of Paris and by government regulations strictly limiting the amount of fabric the manufacturers might use. Whiskey, glassware, stockings, hairbrushes, alarm clocks—everything once taken for granted was now in short supply. Why, even on Cherry Street the line for cigarettes extended out the door when they grew scarce, as happened from time to time. The one advantage to the grocery store—*her* store—was that she was assured of a steady supply of cigarettes. It was Grace Turner's promotion, but especially the dangers and deprivations of the war, that instilled Becky with her sense of urgency.

Reluctantly she began to give up her dream of being a buyer, a useless position while the war was on. In any event she'd begun to realize her disadvantage in trying to compete with women like Grace for the few available positions.

What Becky set her sights on was a niche on the sixth floor as Millie's assistant. Millie Kirby was secretary to both Carl Pickman, the president, and Philip Cooper, the vice president and general manager of the store. Millie was an overweight grey-haired spinster who had devoted her life to Pickman's.

Messrs. Pickman and Cooper were undoubtedly the brains of the operation, but Millie was its heart. There was nothing she didn't know about the day-to-day workings of the store. Most of the sixth floor was taken up with bookkeeping and accounting, but no information reached Pickman or Cooper without reaching Millie.

Just outside Millie's office were a desk and typewriter, vacant for the last few months, since Millie's old assistant joined the WACS. This was the job Becky wanted.

She considered it common sense to make friends with a person like Millie and had done so during her first year at Pickman's by letting her know whenever particularly nice purses were in stock. Millie for her part, was careful to let Becky know she knew she was being soft-soaped. Nevertheless, today Millie went out of her way to repay Becky's small favors.

Today the executive assistant made a rare sojourn from the sixth floor to track Becky to the employees' lunchroom. "I've finally convinced them that I need some help," she confided. "Interviews will begin next week." Becky understood that Millie's personally delivering the information was her way of encouraging Becky to try for the job.

"It will entail scads of typing and filing," Millie warned, "but whoever is chosen will be in a position to learn what makes Pickman's tick. Now, before you get too excited, Becky, I've got to warn you that choosing my assistant is not up to me. Mr. Cooper will be interviewing, and I'm sorry to say he's got a bug about picking a Phi Beta Kappa." With that Millie wheeled her large bulk around and sailed out of the lunchroom, leaving Becky to wrestle with the obstacles in her path.

Belonging to an elite scholastic fraternity was quite an obstacle indeed for someone who had never finished high school. Mr. Cooper's fascination with Phi Beta Kappa members likely stemmed from the success of advertising director Bernice Fitz-Gibbon over at archrival Gimbels, for it was well-known that she considered only such women.

Advertising, she thought, pushing aside her uneaten lunch. Pickman's advertising was stuck back in the twenties and consisted of dreary, unillustrated full-page newspaper spreads filled with simpering pledges to uphold "our long tradition of egalitarian service."

Egalitarian, really. Becky took the time to go to the library and look up the word, but she was willing to bet a week's salary that not one in ten of her fellow New Yorkers ever had or ever would.

And it was not just in advertising that Pickman's was losing ground. Even prior to the wartime shortages the store's inventory was—well—dowdy. It was not that Pickman's had changed, but that the world had. The sturdy, utilitarian goods that had enthralled Becky's immigrant mother were not the sort of merchandise that could set her own heart afire. Younger shoppers were less and less in evidence at Pickman's, and the corresponding shortage of profits had begun to affect upkeep. Becky had seen it all before on Cherry Street. When there were no customers there was no money to replace a cracked window, and a cracked window drove away customers.

Pickman's, due to its plain goods, its yellowing walls and often dusty, fingerprint-marred display counters, had turned into an old women's store. The problem was that in 1942 even the elderly had the sense of style to prefer Macy's and Gimbels.

The shame of it was that Pickman's had plenty to sell: it just didn't know how to go about it. Her friend Joey in Shipping and Receiving had told her about the enormous inventory of nylon stockings, Scotch and even major appliances and furniture languishing in the warehouses. Carl Pickman had amassed the stock before the war, tying up a fortune in the inventory, and now Becky surmised that he didn't know how to sell it without appearing to be a black-market profiteer.

Becky left the lunchroom obsessed with the problem of proving herself worthy of being Millie's assistant. Whatever she came up with, she had to do it fast. Her one

chance rested on winning the position before Mr. Cooper
had the opportunity to interview those college graduates.

So Becky went directly from work to the main branch
of the New York Public Library. She combed the old
newspaper files; she hadn't forgotten the magic Pickman's
had created for the public back when she was little. Perhaps in the past she could find the key to the store's
potential in the present. She especially studied the newspapers
during the First World War. Wars—and people—were
different, but they were also very much the same.

By closing time she had her idea.

She passed a restless night staring up at her bedroom
ceiling and rehearsing her lines. The next morning she
wore the crepe blouse with the drawstring waist that Grace
had made her buy and she tried to remember the makeup
and hairstyle tips Grace had given her.

At work she made sure that her glass-topped counter
was immaculate, then settled down to wait for Mr. Cooper
to make his daily rounds, as he did every morning before
the store opened. She could see him coming, pausing to
chat with the staff in millinery. She caught a glimpse of
him among the mirrors and faceless white forms on which
were displayed military-inspired berets and caps and those
newly fashionable coolie hats. He was laughing; he seemed
to be in a good mood. Becky crossed her fingers. *Please
make him be in a good mood.*

Philip Cooper might have been Grace Turner's brother.
He had the same silky blond hair and blue eyes: he was
baby-faced, youthful and blessed with a light beard. He
was in his forties, Becky guessed, and always behaved in a
courtly manner. He was never angry, but at the most
disappointed, and no matter what, he never raised his
voice.

"Good morning, Miss Herodetsky," Philip Cooper
said as he strolled past her counter without pausing. "I see

everything is in order, as usual. You're looking lovely today." He headed off toward Ladies Handkerchiefs.

"Mr. Cooper," Becky called out.

"Yes?"

"I've got—" Becky took a deep breath—"an idea."

There was no hint of mockery in Cooper's smile. "Go on." His blue eyes sparkled behind his tortoise-shell glasses. "I'm always ready to listen to my troops on the front line."

"It's about those goods in the warehouse. I've figured out a way to sell that merchandise and still keep us gung-ho with the war effort."

"What?" Cooper's normally pink, baby-smooth cheeks were turning a mottled, angry-looking red. "What?"

Becky felt sick at her stomach. Why was he glaring at her like that? "The washing machines and Scotch and stuff," she babbled, forgetting her carefully memorized lines in her nervousness at Cooper's reaction. "I've got an idea for a newspaper ad to—"

Cooper was muttering unintelligibly. He began to say something to her, but then he noticed a few curious stares and changed his mind. He hurried away.

Becky commanded herself not to faint no matter how awful she felt. She entered into a numb, heartsick daze, waiting on customers pleasantly and politely even as her humiliation festered.

How could she ever again face Mr. Cooper? As it turned out, she didn't have to wait very long to find out the answer to that question.

"You've been summoned upstairs," Winston Kelly stonily informed her at the midmorning lull. The merchandise manager was a soberly dressed, fat little fussbudget of an Irishman. When he stood in his favorite pose—pudgy manicured hands on wide hips—he looked exactly like a sugar bowl.

"Sixth floor," Kelly fumed. "I'll cover for you down

here. Whatever did you do? I hear Mr. Cooper is acting positively stricken.''

Becky wanted to journey to the sixth floor, but not like this, not in disgrace. She glumly made her way upstairs and through the warrens of the accounting department to present herself before Millie Kirby, who only shrugged off her questions, pressing a switch on her desk intercom. ''She's here.''

Cooper's voice came faint and tinny. ''Send her in.''

Millie jerked her thumb over her shoulder. ''To the lions.''

''Am I going to be fired?''

''Through the glass doors, then the door on your right—''

''Come on, Mil.''

Millie shrugged. ''I'll tell you one thing, you made one hell of an impression.'' She smiled. ''I had a talk with him and put in a good word for you. He knows you want the job. What he thinks about it I can't say. Now scoot. Keeping him waiting isn't going to help matters. Make sure you knock on the right-hand door. The ones on the left go to Mr. Pickman's office.''

The glass doors swung shut behind her. The clicking and clacking of the accounting department just beyond Millie's station did not reach this lush carpeted corridor. She glanced at the oaken double doors on the left.

Pickman was a tall, angular grey-haired man in his late fifties. He was a renowned philanthropist, and Becky remembered reading somewhere that in Pickman's youth he'd been a champion equestrian.

Whatever his activities, Carl Pickman left the stewardship of his family's store to his subordinate, Philip Cooper. In her two years at Pickman's Becky had glimpsed the store's owner on the sales floor a mere half a dozen times. Never had she seen stern Mr. Pickman so much as nod in the direction of an employee.

She turned away from Pickman's office and timidly knocked on Philip Cooper's far more modest door.

Cooper was coming around the side of his desk to shake hands with her. He offered her a chair and perched himself on the edge of his desk, crossing his arms as he regarded her.

"First of all, I want to apologize for my rudeness. You caught me by surprise, Miss Herodetsky."

"I should apologize—"

"Nonsense. Now then, let me begin by saying that you are not in any danger whatsoever of being fired. You're in no trouble at all." Cooper paused to remove his glasses and polish them on his crisp-looking pocket handkerchief. "It's just that I'm curious to know how you found out about the merchandise in our warehouse. I mean, it's all aboveboard, but it wasn't common knowledge by any means."

"A friend of mine in Shipping told me about it."

Cooper's baby-face lit up. "I see, your boyfriend."

"Oh, no," Becky said, aghast. "He's sort of a business acquaintance. You see, when I was working in my father's store—um, that's a grocery; I mean a supermarket on the Lower—um, it's downtown."

The appalled look on Cooper's face made Becky wish his carpeted floor would open up and swallow her, that she could just tumble back down to her nice, safe handbag counter. She stared at his wingtips and plowed ahead.

"What I learned from working in the supermarket was that if you knew your suppliers, they'd be more inclined to see to it that your deliveries arrived on time. So I figured it would work the same way here. I took some doughnuts down to the men in Shipping and Receiving and got to be friends with them. Now, when a customer wants a certain color handbag and it's in stock but downstairs, Joey will bring it right up for me, and I—we—Pickman's—doesn't lose the sale."

Cooper was laughing. "How extraordinary." He walked back around his desk and seated himself in his big leather chair. He opened a box on his desk and took a cigarette. Becky craved one, but of course she didn't ask and would have refused one if he'd offered. "And the warehouse merchandise? What was that all about?"

"Mr. Cooper, I want the job as Millie—Miss Kirby's—assistant."

Cooper smoked his cigarette and looked at her. "How much do you make?"

"As a senior sales clerk, thirty-seven dollars a week," she said proudly.

Cooper shrugged. "This job pays only thirty-two fifty. You'd be taking a substantial salary cut."

"Yes, sir." She waited, perched demurely on the edge of her chair, knees together, hands clasped in her lap, heart thudding, holding her breath.

"Millie has spoken quite enthusiastically about you."

"I know," Becky said nervously, without thinking.

"Yes," Cooper's blue eyes sparkled. "I suppose you would." He was quiet, making up his mind. "All right, we'll give it a try."

"Oh, thank you so much."

Cooper pressed down on his intercom and said, "Millie, we're going to take Miss Herodetsky on."

He got to his feet and Becky followed his lead. He shook hands with her and said, "Millie will work out the details."

Nodding so hard her neck made creaking noises, Becky backed out of the office.

"You're not by any chance a member of Phi Beta Kappa?" Cooper asked her as she got to the door.

"No, sir, not that one."

"Hmmm." Cooper nodded to her in dismissal. "We'll give it a try."

Outside Millie collared her. "Earlier, when Mr. Cooper

asked me if you could type, I lied and said yes. I'm a liar now, but I don't intend to be for long," she warned. "Get it?"

"I'll borrow a book from the library and come in early and practice every day."

"Come in very early." Millie grinned. "Congratulations."

Becky skipped out. She felt elated—no, exhilarated. She hadn't felt this way since the good times with Benny. She felt in love, not with some fickle man, but with this store.

She had to find Grace and tell her the news. Oh, what a fuss Grace would make! Tonight the two of them would go out and drink more champagne and talk forever about their tomorrows.

She'd have to call her father, of course, but only to tell him she'd be out late tonight. There was absolutely no point in telling him about her new job, she thought bitterly. He'd take no pleasure in her success. Her father had long ago ceased to be able to take pleasure in anything.

Chapter 38

"Big deal," said Abe Herodetzky to his daughter's news. "Big deal. So you're an assistant. For this you left our store? You told me you wanted to be a big-shot buyer. First you spend two years selling handbags, and what now? You're just the girl they have to shuffle the papers for them. Believe me, if an important job opens up, you'll never get it. And for this you took a cut in salary? Believe me, when they take away the money it's no promotion. You see how poorly our store is doing? You see how with the war rationing I got hardly nothing to sell? We needed the extra you were making as a sales clerk. We have to put away for your brother's education. You had no business taking a job that paid less. Selfish, that's what you are. You're a selfish girl."

Becky, quite indifferent, said, "I knew you wouldn't understand," like he was a stranger or an imbecile, and then she went to her bedroom.

That was six months ago, and since then she'd evidently not thought it was important enough to tell him how the job was going, so why should he give her the satisfaction of asking?

Abe knew why she was giving him the cold shoulder.

It was her guilt. He hadn't been lying when he warned her that the store was going under. The neighborhood was changing; his old, loyal customers were dying or moving away. Even Leah's sister Sadie and Joseph had moved to Chicago at the invitation of their oldest boy, a successful attorney.

What was left of his business was being choked off by the war and those coupon books with their goddamned blue points for canned goods and red points for meat and dairy products. Everything had to be labeled correctly, never mind the fact that the government was constantly issuing new guidelines on point values.

His meat case had been dark for months. He couldn't get it now that he lacked Stefano de Fazio's clout. What little meat there was went to the large supermarkets, who could pay the wholesalers' under-the-counter premiums. It was bitterly ironic that after all of those years of servitude to Stefano, now that he needed a black market connection, none was available to him.

One packer had the gall to offer Abe a shipment of horsemeat—horsemeat! After thirty years in business he should be reduced to such an indignity?

Maybe it was for the better that he had so little to sell. A succession of boys had worked for him, and every one of them was a lout, too stupid to succeed in school but too young to be swallowed up by the armed forces. Why did he need such louts when half the store was barren and dark?

These days Abe sat in his rocking chair behind the front counter, surrounded by his newspapers and the vodka bottles that he'd taken to bringing out whenever an old acquaintance happened by—but more usually when they didn't.

Becky began to issue empty threats about selling the building. She didn't like him being alone, she said. It was the solitude that was leading him back to the bottle.

Abe laughed in her face. He was sixty-six years old.
What should he do, go out and make new friends? Maybe
he should join the army? If she wanted to sell, that was
fine with him. He'd have himself another good laugh
watching her search for somebody who might want such a
property and who had the money to pay for it.

As for his drinking, well, he no longer had to answer
to anybody about his drinking.

July second, 1942, a Thursday, marked Daniel
Herodetzky's sixteenth birthday. He'd spent the better part
of that day, as he had every day since summer began, in a
sweltering remedial classroom, trying to raise his failing
grades so he would not be kept back for the next school
year.

How Danny hated school. Every day it was the same,
a mix of daydreaming, boredom and hot, sweaty humiliation when his teachers ridiculed him or his classmates
twittered at his stupid answers. As if nine months of that
each year weren't enough, come June, when the other kids
started their vacations, he'd been forced to attend summer
school—always the only Jew in summer school.

But no more, Danny thought as he walked along
Cherry Street on that smoldering July afternoon. Today
I'm sixteen. It's finished.

"So how did it go today?" his father asked over his
newspaper as Danny entered the store.

"It went swell. I quit."

Abe put down his newspaper. "What? What did you
say?" he squinted at Danny. "Quit what? I meant school,
how was school?"

"It's July second, Pop. Don't you know what day
that is?"

Abe nodded and went back to his paper. "It's the
anniversary of your mother's death."

Danny tore the newspaper out of his father's fingers

and threw it aside. "It's my birthday. I'm sixteen. I told my teachers they could go to hell, Pop, and now I'm telling you the same. I'm through with school."

"You'll apologize to your teachers," Abe said sternly, "and you'll go back to school—"

"No, Pop. It's a waste of time for me, and it always has been. The other kids laugh at me—"

"Fight them!"

"I can't," Danny shouted. "I can't fight! Look at me. For once in your life see your son as he is. I'm short and scrawny, plain-looking and a dunce. I'm not that guy Haim, Pop, I'm Danny, *your son*."

Abe turned away. "Some son."

"Thanks," Danny muttered. He began to weep. "I love you too. Thanks."

"Get control of yourself," Abe grumbled. "What are you crying for? Don't be a baby."

"I'll be what I want," Danny snapped. "I'm sixteen and you can't stop me. No more do I try to be what you want."

"You'll do what I say as long as you live here," Abe thundered.

"Don't make me laugh."

"You're under my roof."

"This slum belongs to my sister, not you."

"All right, I'll put you to work right here in the store."

"The hell with that. I ain't spending my life in this crummy place. I've been over to Lafayette Street, to the Norden bombsight factory. They've given up so many guys to the draft that I was able to finagle myself a spot as an apprentice machinist—"

"I order you to forget this nonsense, Danny. Go back to school and beg them to let you in. I've saved for your college so you can make something of yourself."

Danny ignored his father. He reached across the counter to help himself to a pack of cigarettes.

"Don't ruin your life," Abe roared, and then his tone abruptly shifted. "Stay in school for me. Your future is all I have left to look forward to and—"

"See you later, Pop."

"Danny, wait! You owe me, damnit. Remember how you fixed it so I can't even show myself at the synagogue? You fought with the rabbi. You wouldn't even study for your bar mitzvah."

Danny left the store and walked aimlessly around the neighborhood for a long while, smoking cigarettes, trying to regain his composure. He was old enough to leave school and take on a man's job. He was too old to let his father reduce him to tears. Anyway, he had set himself up to be knocked down. Imagine asking his old man, "Don't you know what day it is?"

"The anniversary of your mother's death"—why did I say that? Abe brooded. The bottle of vodka and the glass were on the counter before him. He poured himself a little more.

If only he could talk him into staying in school. He stopped, the glass halfway to his lips. "Like father, like son," he murmured.

Around goes the circle. My son is going to work in a factory just a few streets over from the sweatshop I struggled to escape. Like father, like son. I am weak and so is he.

He finished his drink and went around the counter to the front door to lock it. He drew the shades and made his way to the cot set up in a dark corner behind the empty meat counter. He stretched out and stared up at the ceiling. Closing his eyes, he willed himself into a private, far better world where he was young, a cobbler in Russia, embracing a strong, blond-haired, blue-eyed son, his real son.

Chapter 39

Degania

Herschel Kol returned to Degania directly from Habbaniyah and remained there for over a year. His mother welcomed him home and Herschel was content. His meandering journey from Iraq across the Transjordan had passed uneventfully, but Jerusalem Prison had taken its toll. Herschel was exhausted, his nerves worn ragged.

He did not fear being pursued by the police, who had their hands full attempting to block the steady stream of ships laden with illegal immigrants.

The Messerschmitt attack that claimed the life of David Raziel also dealt a death blow to the organization. With Raziel dead and its arms caches, money and printing presses lost, stolen by Arabs or confiscated, the Irgun was considered to be history by the authorities. A few scattered Irgunists like Herschel Kol, who had never harmed anyone British, were not considered worth chasing as long as they lay low. Accordingly, Herschel's quiet appearance in Degania attracted no police attention whatsoever.

The rigors of prison had cost Herschel twenty pounds of muscle. In the beginning of his Degania stay he would

be exhausted after an hour in the fields, but as the year
progressed his strength returned. His skin tanned to a
coppery hue as he labored beneath the strong sun clad only
in his khaki shorts and workshoes. Soon he was as dark as
when he ran about the kibbutz during his barefoot toddler
days, when he was a true child of Galilee. He cut his
thinning hair short and allowed his honey-colored beard to
grow. The beard, combined with the lines and furrows
etched into the weathered skin of his handsome face, made
him seem older than he was. His youth had been stolen
and no one would ever again mistake him for an English
gentleman. Happily, however, his physical transformation
meant that the authorities would have a hard time recognizing him.

When he returned to Degania he needed to rest and
replenish himself, but now that time was over. Once again
he felt strong enough to take an active role in the free
world's struggle against the Nazis and in the struggle for a
homeland. It was common knowledge that European Jewry
was being exterminated by the Nazis. The Jews of Palestine were also convinced that the Allies were aware of this,
but there the agreement between the various Jewish political factions ended. The old guard Zionist Socialists, the
Haganah lot, believed that the British were sympathetic.
Yol Popovich, for instance, tried to enlist in the embryonic British-sponsored Jewish brigade but was rejected
because of his advanced age and sent to Cairo by the labor
federation to be the Jewish soldiers' welfare officer. Jewish military units—an unofficial brigade of sorts—were
doing battle against Rommel in Libya.

There was no way for Herschel Kol, a fugitive, to
enlist. His Degania comrades sympathized and pointed out
that he was also serving by doing agricultural work. Many
able-bodied men had been kept back from soldiering in
order to increase food production.

In 1942 news reached Degania of a man who might

rebuild the Irgun. Menachem Begin had come to Palestine as a private in the Free Polish Army. He had been assigned to the staff of the Polish Town Major in Jerusalem. The call was going out among the revisionists: the little the British were doing for the refugees was an outrage and could no longer be met with indifference. The truce forged by the British and the late David Raziel was over. It was clear that military force was required to secure a homeland.

Frieda Litvinoff had reminisced about listening to a young Betar commander named Begin. It was Begin who had inspired her, just as she had inspired Herschel. In Frieda's memory Herschel would put himself in the service of Menachem Begin.

His mother tried to talk him out of it. Rosie Kolesnikoff was in her late sixties. She tended her garden and the preschool-age children of the kibbutz and still painted in her spare time.

Herschel knew his mother had been physically ailing and very depressed in the days following Yol's departure. His own return brought new hope and brightness into her life. When Rosie realized her son was free and the British were not much interested in recapturing him, she grew younger, more active, more interested in the world around her. This year-long reunion with her son was one of the happiest times of her life.

"If you return to Jerusalem, the police will arrest you and you'll end up back in prison."

"That's unlikely, Mother. First off, the police are far more concerned with the Stern gang's doings. Secondly, there are so many new arrivals in the coastal cities—Poles, refugees and so on—I doubt very much if one more will attract much attention. Third, I don't look like Herschel Kol any longer, and once I'm in Jerusalem, I'll arrange to get new papers."

Rosie looked hard at him. "You're proud of yourself, I see. Let me tell you one thing, and then you do as you want. This is the second war I've lived through. I've learned that despite all the flag waving and political noise, despite what the leaders trumpet, what persuades the average man to shoulder a gun and march off to battle is his home. Your father did not fight out of love of Palestine; he fought because he loved the dirt under our feet. The Arab who killed your father did that deed for the same reason. This last year you've spent with your old mother should live in your memory. When you go to Jerusalem and start to get caught up in all that dreadful, soul-killing nonsense about Socialist versus Haganah/Irgun/Stern, remember that you are not struggling to further ideology. You are all struggling to secure your home."

On his last evening at Degania Rosie sat him down at the table and placed a packet of papers before him.

"Like your father, you are a hard worker, and like your father, you are not at all interested in finances. However, despite my expectations I probably will not live forever. Since I have no idea when we'll meet again, it's important that you understand our financial affairs. These papers should explain everything."

Herschel spent several hours going through the documents. They were business letters and financial statements from the Glaser family's solicitors and the London bank.

He studied the long columns of pounds and dollars. The Depression had cut into the holdings, but the trustees had managed to recoup some of those losses by investing in shipping and munitions before the start of the war. The last communication from England was dated June 1939; since the war the mails to Palestine had been sporadic. That last statement put the Glaser estate on both sides of the Atlantic at twenty-five thousand pounds plus over a quarter of a million U.S. dollars.

"I issued instructions to begin shifting our holdings to America when you first got involved in your anti-British activities," Rosie explained. "I was afraid you'd end up on the wrong side of the law—"

"As I did, as it turned out," Herschel grinned, still dizzy over the realization of just how wealthy he and his mother were. The irony of it—he was a fugitive and his mother was a member of a socialist kibbutz, where she could not even lay claim to her clothing or the roof over her head, and yet they were rich.

"Don't worry, Mother. When the British are gone we will bring back our thousands to Palestine and invest them where they belong, in our homeland."

Rosie nodded. "I hope to live to see that day, Herschel."

"You will."

"But if I shouldn't, the money will pass to you on my death. That was arranged many years ago. If for some reason you are unable to claim it, our solicitors will continue as they have been."

"You're worried about my ending up in prison again," Herschel said. "Don't. When the British leave Palestine, there will be an amnesty."

"More ifs, more uncertainties. When you resume your fight, Herschel, remember what it is all about. Not amnesty or money or ideology, but the land and who shall own it."

In Jerusalem Herschel found the walls of the ancient city plastered over with tattered posters of Sir Harold MacMichael. WANTED FOR MURDER: THE HIGH COMMISSIONER OF PALESTINE. the posters read in both English and Hebrew, FOR DROWNING 800 REFUGEES ABOARD THE S.S. STRUMA.

The fate of the blockaded refugee ships inflamed the Jewish community, but they were nevertheless sullenly resigned to the restrictions of the British white paper, while Hitler was still a menace. Within Herschel's first week in Jerusalem he had managed to obtain identification in the name of Dov Katz. Finding and joining an active Irgun cell proved to be far more difficult.

Herschel had yet to meet Begin, but rumors had it that he was far from ready to wage an active battle against the British. Prior to his arrival in Palestine and his reunion with his wife Aliza, whom he hadn't seen for two years, Begin had been serving out a sentence as a Zionist anti-revolutionary in a Siberian labor camp. He was exhausted and needed to regain his health.

He was also a private in the Polish Army. He refused to serve the Irgun while sworn to the Polish flag, and he refused to desert for fear such an action would antagonize the Polish government, which was attempting to liberate the hundreds of thousands of Polish Jews still incarcerated in Soviet labor camps. All of this meant that the Irgun's interim leaders could only maintain the status quo while Begin rested and the lengthy negotiations to obtain his honorable release from the Polish army continued.

Toward the end of 1942 Rommel was driven back and the war's focus was moving toward Sicily and the rest of Italy. The Polish contingent, including Begin, was due to be transferred. Influential activists feverishly worked to obtain Begin's military discharge, claiming that he and others were needed for propaganda work in America to further the cause of the free Polish government in exile. In 1943 Begin was officially released. His health restored, he was ready to take command.

Herschel spent these months cautiously exploring what remained of his old network of Irgun contacts. He was living as a boarder with a family who owned a bookstore. Both the father and his son were Irgun followers and their shop functioned as a message drop. A trapdoor in the floor led to a basement printing press, one of the many that turned out Irgun propaganda. To earn his keep and help out as best he could Herschel ran the press, emerging from the dark basement at the end of each day pale and blinking, hopeful that the call to arms had been issued.

"We've been informed that Begin himself would like to meet you," the bookstore owner told Herschel one evening as the family sat down to supper. "He has a job for you. It's quite an honor, you should realize. My understanding is that he's been seeing nobody but his closest advisers. It must be quite some job if he feels he must offer it to you personally."

"When?" Herschel was eager. "Where?"

"You must go to Tel Aviv."

Chapter 40

New York, 1943

Becky spent most of her first year on the sixth floor typing and filing, but gradually she began to serve as Philip Cooper's personal assistant. Millie Kirby had more work than she was able to handle, so Cooper appreciated being able to lay claim to Becky's services.

At first Becky suffered an enormous crush on Cooper. How could she not swoon when he was so handsome and gentlemanly, when he had flowers delivered to her desk on her birthday? Grace Turner took delight in teasing Becky about him, but everyone knew he was happily married. Cooper's interest in her was strictly platonic.

Becky had plenty of work to do during normal working hours, so she arrived early and stayed late in order to go over the store's files on her own time. She had access to every report that crossed Millie's desk, and if she did not understand its contents, she worked at it until she did.

There was little distraction. Becky had no real friends except for Grace, who had quite a large crowd of her own to keep her occupied.

There was nothing for her at home. Her poor father—

she'd tried to keep him involved in what was happening in her life, but he only belittled her. Lately he'd latched onto her lack of a family. Never mind her accomplishments; why wasn't she married? Why didn't he have grandchildren? Danny's leaving school had embittered him. His two children had not done as he wished, so they could never do anything right. She would have moved out of Cherry Street, but she couldn't desert him no matter how awful he was.

By choice and by chance Pickman's became her world. Late at night, when she was cold, tired, discouraged, when she most felt her absolute loneliness, the dark corridors of the store seemed like a tomb and her inadequacies loomed before her, insurmountable.

She had no friends, family or lover, so she married the store. She came early and stayed late. Whenever she left the huge building, she felt diminished. On her days off she prowled the competition, taking notes, stealing ideas—a spy behind enemy lines.

She had talent and she learned fast. With Phil Cooper's blessings and encouragement she began to compile memos of her ideas and suggestions. These were circulated to Carl Pickman and always came back to Millie's desk initialed, signifying that Pickman had at least glanced at them.

Becky then had the odd chore of filing her own missives into what she had privately dubbed as the cabinet of no return.

But she knew that those nylons and refrigerators were still languishing in storage. Phil Cooper gave her the job without asking her about her idea, and Becky kept her mouth shut about it, figuring to leave well enough alone. The more she thought about it, however, the more incredible it seemed to her that such bounty should be kept away from the war-starved public and away from the profit side of the ledger.

The matter was far more complicated. She'd learned enough about the Pickman family to understand that they would rather lose profits than their reputation. The Pickmans were one of the foremost Jewish families in America. In these days of controversy concerning the nation's responsibilities to European Jews, she could understand reluctance to seem to be profiteering.

Becky believed she had the solution to the problem, but Phil Cooper made her revise her memo three times before he forwarded it to Carl Pickman. Becky was glad to have his advice. Pickman often nodded in her direction when he passed her desk, but she doubted that he thought about her at all. She'd heard his stentorian voice raging at buyers and floor managers who had somehow displeased him. Becky had no intention of being the object of such wrath.

Her memo, now a full-fledged advertising campaign proposal, went into Pickman's office bright and early on a Monday morning. The day crept along. At four o'clock Becky relaxed. Clearly Pickman had not had time to read it today.

At four-fifteen Millie's intercom buzzed and Becky thought she heard Pickman's voice mentioning her name.

"He wants to see you," Millie said.

Becky nodded. Then she was through the glass doors and floating down the hushed, carpeted corridor.

It was her first time in his office. Her first fleeting impression was of how large and bare it was, an enormous expanse of lamp-lit space, of carpet and closed draperies.

There was Pickman's oak desk, dominating the room from a slightly raised platform. Flanking the desk was a moss-green sofa upon which a fidgety Phil Cooper was seated. More or less in front of the desk were two armchairs.

"Come sit down," Pickman said.

He had yet to look up from his papers. As she crossed

the heathery carpet she had a chance to study his gleaming grey hair, long, thin face and broad shoulders. He was a fit-looking man, and except for his grey hair he looked far younger than his fifty-six years.

As she reached the armchairs she shot a questioning glance at Phil Cooper and jerked her head at the sofa.

Phil shook his head and indicated the chairs, so she seated herself before Pickman and waited.

There were closed draperies behind Pickman as well. It all seemed melodramatic—the shrouded windows and lamplight, the desk on its dais and Pickman himself, the pin-striped patrician, the lord and master of all he surveyed, including herself.

Despite the circumstances Becky found herself smiling, remembering that scene in *The Wizard of Oz* when Dorothy and her friends were finally brought before the ruler of the Emerald City.

Now she half expected to see a pair of shoes protruding from beneath the pulled draperies, to see a little man— perhaps her old boss from the handbag counter—busily pulling levers while Pickman himself chittered, "Pay no attention to the man behind the curtain! I am the great and powerful."

Carl Pickman looked up at her. He evidently noticed her smile, for he cocked his head and smiled back. Becky, meanwhile, was mesmerized by his eyes. They were bottle-green, clear and direct; they were youthful. Becky had never before had the opportunity to look at Pickman.

It was incredible and flustering, but she found herself liking him and wanting to show it. Oh, but she mustn't be foolish, this was business.

" 'In 1918 Pickman's announced that it would accept World War One Liberty Bonds presented by its patriotic customers in lieu of cash,' " Pickman read from the opening paragraph of her memo. He glanced at her. "Lieu is spelled wrong."

Out of the corner of her eye she could see Phil
Cooper flinching. Goddamned typos, she thought, turning
scarlet.

" 'That 1918 stroke of genius created an enormous
amount of favorable publicity for the store.' " Pickman
continued reading. " 'A picture is enclosed.' " He held
up a yellowed newspaper photograph showing the line of
customers extending out Pickman's door and down the
block.

"Last year, when I researched my idea, I came across
that photo," Becky offered, then shrugged. "I tore it out
of the paper when the librarian wasn't looking."

"Normally I do not approve of defacing public
property," Pickman said. "However, in this case . . ."

Again Becky was treated to his remarkable smile and
the way it seemed to set the light dancing in his eyes.

"I'd forgotten it ever happened," Pickman murmured.
"Thank you for reminding me, Miss Herodetsky, and for
the photograph."

"You're very welcome, sir."

The smile vanished and Pickman's green eyes cooled.
"Now then, I've read your proposal, but suppose you tell
it to me in your own words."

"It's simple, really. All we do is put one of the
warehoused items on sale as a loss leader every week."

"Sell it for less than the market can bear?" Pickman
asked, frowning slightly.

"Yes, sir. That way we get it moved and nobody can
claim we're profiteering. Shaving profits also ties in with
the theme of the ad campaign—A victory sale, as in
gardens and bicycles and scrap metal collections. We remind the public about Pickman's Liberty Bond sale during
the First World War and make the point that the tradition
of patriotism continues."

Pickman nodded. "I see that you propose our lead-off
be the nylons."

"Yes," Becky replied. "I've worked on that floor. We just don't get the right sort of customer for our ladies' apparel. If we could lure in the younger secretarial types, we might be able to get them to think Pickman's when it comes to fashion."

"I'm prepared to give it a try. Mr. Cooper will supervise, and as usual, I will personally approve all layouts, but you will act as the liaison between the advertising department and our offices."

"Thank you," Becky said.

Pickman smiled. "All right." He went back to the papers on his desk.

Phil Cooper stood up and Becky followed him out. In the corridor Cooper said, "You were first-rate in there, young lady. Congratulations."

"Thanks." Becky grinned. "Gee, it was exciting. He liked my idea."

Cooper had an odd look in his eyes. "I'd better start locking my office door. I might come in some morning to find you behind my desk."

"Oh, Mr. Cooper," Becky giggled, but something in his manner faded her smile.

Cooper evidently saw her concern. "That was supposed to be a compliment," he said weakly.

Becky headed back to her desk, uneasy. Her intuition suggested Mr. Cooper might not have been joking after all.

Chapter 41

Tel Aviv

In 1943 Tel Aviv was a carnival, a circus, a blaring, black-market urban nightmare, awake and kicking beneath the white-hot sun.

Herschel Kol, alias Dov Katz, knew his father had helped to build Tel Aviv, but upon his own arrival there he understood why his father had deserted it for Galilee. What Herschel did not understand was why God did not split asunder the flawless blue sky and sweep the entire tawdry mess into the sparkling Mediterranean. His puritan sensibility was offended by the black-market shops, cafes and whorehouses, by the dance halls trumpeting bad music over crackling loudspeakers, drowning out the roar and crash of the sea.

That the first Jewish city in Palestine was a Sodom horrified him, but he understood why Begin had chosen Tel Aviv as his headquarters. The myriad nationalities, the noise, confusion and color made Tel Aviv a marvelous place to hide.

Herschel only wanted to meet with Begin and quit the city before he began bashing in the smug, jowly faces of these unacceptable excuses for Zionists who called Tel Aviv their home.

Herschel's sole Irgun contact in this strange city was a waiter in a cafe off of Allenby Road. Joseph, a hulking ogre straight out of a dark Lithuanian forest, wore a waiter's soiled white jacket and found favor with the cafe owner, who undoubtedly saw some advantage in scaring away customers. Joseph had a horrendous mole sprouting hair on his chin and an ugly temper to match.

Herschel had been visiting the cafe every day in the hope of receiving an assignment, but each time he'd been disappointed by Joseph's curt, "Nothing." It had been going on far too long, and Herschel was discouraged. Today as he entered the cafe, he was contemplating his return to Degania. There at least he was growing food.

"Over there," Joseph hissed, "the corner table."

Herschel turned to look where the waiter was pointing. A little man with thinning dark hair and tortoise-shell glasses was sitting with his back to the wall, engrossed in the papers spilling out of a battered old briefcase on the table.

Herschel glanced around the cafe, noticing the intent, watchful men scattered at half a dozen tables. All of them were wearing jackets—to cover up their guns? There was no question that they were Menachem Begin's bodyguards.

"Mr. Katz, yes?" Begin smiled vaguely as Herschel approached. He stood up in order to shake hands.

Herschel took in Begin's baggy suit, fussy shirt and tie. Begin was just thirty, but he looked much older. His hair was dry as straw and his complexion was sallow. Herschel remembered the rumors of poor health—of a bad heart, bad lungs, weak eyes.

Begin's eyes behind the thick lenses glinted as he appraised Herschel. "I am Ben Zeev, yes? Come, sit down. Joseph, two coffees."

Herschel was not at all surprised to see how the surly waiter rushed to do Begin's bidding. "Ben Zeev, eh?"

"Zeev and Katz will do best for us," Begin agreed, packing away his papers into the old briefcase. "Ah, our coffee." He smiled at the waiter, who set down the cups and hurried away. "I'm sorry we made you wait so long, Mr. Katz, but we had to make sure you were not being followed by the British. I'm told your appearance has greatly changed, but still, you are an escaped convict."

"I'm surprised to see you out in the open like this," Herschel replied.

"Why should I hide? They make me sound much more inaccessible than I am." Again he showed that abstracted, quizzical smile. "Anyway, we had to meet somewhere, and though we've determined that you are not being tailed, we nevertheless decided it would be better for us not to meet at headquarters."

"Still, a cafe?"

"I have my bodyguards—"

"It's just that I know how easy it is to blow up a place like this and everyone in it," Herschel said, immediately feeling like an ass. Begin's reaction was a cross between amusement and annoyance.

"I'm sorry," Herschel muttered. "I'm trying to impress you and accomplishing exactly the opposite, I think."

"All right, no harm done," Begin said. "You should know that I am familiar with your record. I know you blew up that coffeehouse on instructions from the Irgun, and I know you kept your mouth shut in prison. This is all in your favor, Herschel—"

"Dov."

Begin laughed. "This sneaking and alias business is for children, yes? Still, we must be somewhat careful. The police have yet to search for me, but soon, when we get active, I'll be hunted. You recall what happened to Yair?"

Herschel nodded. Yair, or Abraham Stern, David

Raziel's old comrade, was leader of the radical Stern gang. The police had recently discovered him in hiding and shot him on the spot, claiming he was trying to escape.

"Yair is gone and so is Raziel," Begin mused. "I entertained hopes of serving under Raziel. There was the consummate military man, but he's dead. I understand that you were with him in Iraq?"

"Yes, sir." Herschel briefly told Begin about the air raid.

Begin listened soberly. "I met Raziel in Poland—this was perhaps 1939. How I idolized him, but he's gone and now I must take his place. You know his greatest accomplishment? His training manuals. Yes, the very ones on which he collaborated with Yair. As long as those manuals exist, they will both live forever. Do you agree, Mr. Katz?"

"I suppose." Herschel shrugged, wondering where Begin was leading.

"Training new volunteers will be all-important to us, you know. Oh, yes. Guns and explosives and supplies we can steal, but new followers—where do we get our new soldiers, eh?"

"They'll flock to you, sir, have no fear of that."

"That's not the question. I know they'll flock; what I'm asking is what use will flocks be? Our new strategy is very simple. We will harass the authorities at every turn. We will drive them to such repressive countermeasures that their own self-disgust plus world opinion will bring about a British crisis of will. They will not like our making them act like Nazis. They will withdraw and Palestine will be liberated."

Herschel said nothing. It could work, even if it was not very different from the system espoused in those old Irish Republican Army leaflets of Frieda Litvinoff's.

"There is one problem," Begin continued. "While British repression goes on there will be mass arrests, detention camps, perhaps executions. We will need a constant supply of trained soldiers if we are to keep up the pressure in the cities and towns all across Palestine.''

"What do you want me to do?"

Begin looked him in the eye. "Training camps are being set up all along the coast. I want you to revise our training manuals to take into account the new weapons we will be stealing from the British. I want you to head up one of these camps and to put together—under the supervision of my staff—a curriculum of training for the other camps. You'd be making a major contribution.''

"I think I'd be a laughingstock," Herschel objected. "They'd all laugh at me for teaching others how to fight but not doing so myself. I don't want to be left sitting on the sidelines of our great struggle.''

Begin waved him quiet. "You are a wanted man. Say we sent you out on a raid. There would always be the risk that you would compromise the operation if you were recognized, yes?''

Herschel was forced to agree. "But why think I'm capable of organizing your training program? What makes me a teacher?''

"You are capable because you have received university training—''

"That was in science, mathematics and engineering," Herschel protested. "I know nothing about teaching.''

Begin shrugged. "At least you have seen it done. You also know about guns and fighting. You grew up defending Degania, didn't you?''

"Guns I know," Herschel admitted, "but what about explosives, radios and so on?''

Begin glanced at his watch. "Please, this is time-wasting, you know? These are all details. Experts in various areas will be assigned to the training program, and you will be our headmaster.''

"There's no one else who could take on this job?" Herschel pleaded.

"Of course there are others. There are always others, but nobody so suitable. This assignment allows you to help the cause from behind the lines, where there will be little chance of exposure to the authorities. It also puts you where you can serve as an inspiration to our new recruits."

"I don't understand."

"You are a hero," Begin snapped. "You fought valiantly and escaped to return to the fold. You are also a Palestinian born and bred, one of the few the Irgun has managed to lure away from Ben-Gurion's Haganah. The would-be soldiers who enter our camps could do far worse than to emulate you." Begin regarded him. "Well, yes or no? Will you follow your commander's orders?"

"What choice do I have?"

Satisfied, Begin stood up, briefcase in hand. "Don't forget to pay for the coffee."

Chapter 42

New York, 1944

As Carl Pickman reviewed the sales reports stacked on his desk, a saying of his uncle Bernard's came to mind. "You have to know the dollars and cents side of the business, but if that's all you know, then get yourself over into accounting. You'll never be a good merchant."

It was amazing how sales had climbed since the store revamped its advertising. Gone was Pickman's Promise, which had been the staple of its advertising since the Thirty-fourth Street building first opened its doors. Gone as well was his own signature at the bottom of each ad. He had to give Miss Herodetsky credit for having the gumption to suggest that particular change.

The new campaign—Becky's series—was the talk of the business. The first one—the nylon stockings ad—had set the tone for the rest. The headline was a line from a popular song, "It decants on your pants." The leg makeup of the day had a tendency to rub off on a man's trouser leg. The ad went on to praise women's patriotism and then tie in Pickman's patriotic history, according to plan.

At first Pickman doubted that Miss Herodetsky would

succeed. Her ideas were sound, but experience had taught him that turning ideas into reality was an arduous process. He expected sabotage by the advertising and merchandising departments, enough to stop her in her tracks as soon as she tried to change the comfortable status quo of the last twenty years.

Pickman, who hated disturbance, was prepared to let them sabotage her. However, that did not happen. It turned out that Miss Herodetsky possessed the rarest of all attributes, the ability to persuade others to work for her. Her style was to lead them to think she needed and was eternally grateful for their help. True enough, too.

The rapid sellout of the nylons came as no surprise, but damned if Millinery and Better Dresses hadn't also both reported an increase in sales. For the second time in Pickman's history there was a line of customers down the block, and that line reappeared after each of her ads.

Miss Herodetsky was still at Millie Kirby's beck and call, still doing the typing and filing in addition to running a major retail advertising campaign. She was still earning less than when she sold handbags.

It seemed she couldn't be happier, as if the work alone was enough reward. These days she was popping into his office half a dozen times a day with proposals for approval, and she was always smiling and cheerful and in all lovely to behold.

Smiling, Pickman leaned back in his chair, savoring Miss Herodetsky's enthusiasm. To her it was always "we" and "us," as if she were a Pickman and had stock in the business. It seemed not to matter to her that only others were prospering by her efforts.

He suddenly remembered one other thing Bernard used to tell him. "Carl, wait until you discover how much fun it is to buy and sell." Uncle Bernard meant it as consolation to a heartsick young man.

*   *   *

Carl Pickman's grandfather, Wilhelm Licht, came to America from Austria in 1854. He traveled rural New England, peddling from a pack on his back. Eventually he changed his name to William Packman so his customers would remember him; then he went off to serve the Union in the Civil War. Just when "Packman" evolved into "Pickman" is unknown, but when William opened his dry-goods store in Salem, Massachusetts, after the war, the sign above the store read *Pickman's*.

By this time William had a wife and two sons as well as a solid reputation. His sons Leonard and Bernard entered the business young. When their father died the Pickman brothers decided it was time to expand. Boston briefly beckoned, but they were young and unmarried; they had an adventurous streak. They'd lived in Massachusetts their entire lives. It was time to try something new.

Leonard, the older, went to New York City, intending to smarten up by working for an established merchant while Bernard held the fort back in Salem.

Leonard went to work at Rowe's Emporium on Sixth Avenue near Fourteenth Street, where he met and married a young German-Jewish girl, Clara Hirsch, the daughter of a nearby optician.

Leonard saw the potential of Rowe's Emporium, but the owner, Wentworth Rowe, had lost his wife and son to diphtheria and no longer had the will to succeed. He was quick to sell out to the Pickman brothers, who bought the property with the proceeds from the sale of their Salem store. Bernard joined Leonard in New York and they changed the name to Pickman's Shoppers' House. They were successful and gradually bought up adjoining property into which to expand.

Leonard and Clara had three children. The eldest, Carl, was born in 1887, followed by Deborah in 1891 and Amy in 1898. Bernard never married. He was a painfully shy, kindly man ten years younger than Leonard. He lacked his older brother's cold pragmatism. As the Pickman brothers built up their reputation and wealth, Bernard devoted his free time to philanthropy. He also doted on his nephew Carl, who turned to his uncle for the love and attention he did not receive from his stern father.

The Pickman brothers had no trouble raising the capital to finance their Thirty-fourth Street store. By the time it was ready to open, Carl, just sixteen, was off to Amherst. He did exceedingly well in school and had hopes of going on to medical school; he had applied and been accepted to Harvard.

Bernard interceded with his brother on his nephew's behalf, but Leonard Pickman was adamant. Up until now he had humored his son. As a boy Carl spent his summers with his mother and sisters at Sea Bright, on the New Jersey shore. As a youth he was allowed his horseback riding, even if it was a waste of time; Leonard hated the idea that his son was caught up in that blue ribbon and trophy nonsense.

In any event, all that was over and the store was what mattered. The Pickman brothers, wisely concluding that the heyday of the carriage trade and the Ladies' Mile had come to an end, had chosen their Herald Square site to take advantage of the Sixth Avenue El and the crosstown trolley. Location told; the new store did an astounding amount of business. The loans would all be paid off in another couple of years.

Carl was the only male heir. He would go to work in the store. He began as general manager. He was twenty years old. That same year his mother died of cancer.

His father was a martinet in the office. He seemed to take grim satisfaction in belittling his son in front of outsiders. Bernard was the only bright spot in Carl's existence, and he spent as much time with his uncle as he could. Together they went to museums and the theater; they discussed literature, music and art; through Bernard

Carl savored all the finer things life had to offer a man of his station, which his father scornfully dismissed as womanly time-wasters.

Still, Leonard Pickman tolerated Carl's time with his uncle as long as he reported to the office bright and early every morning. Carl grew to believe his father was relieved not to have him around once the workday ended.

In 1917 Bernard Pickman drowned in a boating accident. "You see?" Leonard Pickman cautioned his son. "That's what comes of fun."

Carl's sisters were long since married, Amy to a surgeon and Deborah to a drone whom Leonard Pickman made comptroller and banished to the recesses of the accounting department.

With Bernard gone and his sisters in homes of their own, Carl had no one left. He withdrew into himself. He spent his nights reading and listening to his father's tapping cane echoing off of the polished marble floors of Pickman House, on Fifth Avenue across from Central Park.

In 1930 Carl's father sent him to Atlanta to see one of their furniture manufacturers about a shipment and to see the manufacturer's daughter.

"Joe Hoffer's girl is the right age, and she's our kind," Leonard declared. "You should have seen to this aspect of your life yourself, Carl. That's what a man would have done, but of course you haven't. You always have been more like Bernard. You've taken on all his charity work, haven't you? Well, that's all right; having the Pickman name prominent in philanthropy is good for the store. But you're forty-three years old. I won't have you ending up a bachelor. It's all been arranged between Joe Hoffer and me. All that remains is to inspect the goods for damage before you take delivery." He leered.

"You'll stay with the Hoffers for three weeks. They have a farm of sorts, I'm told. You'll like it there." Carl still remembered his father's sneer. "I understand they have horses."

Gertrude Hoffer was by no means a beauty, but at twenty she was certainly pretty, with reddish-blond hair, blue eyes and a scattering of freckles across her broad face. She had a southern belle's facility for putting a man at ease. She assured Carl that she found his shyness appealing, masculine. She filled the awkward silences in his halting conversation with her fetching drawl; she laughed at his feeble jokes; she introduced him to her friends.

The Hoffers did keep a stable. Riding was the one accomplishment Carl could claim. Trude squealed with delight and admiration when he took his mount over the hurdles. She understood when he confided to her that when he was riding, in control of a powerful steed, was the only time when he felt free and alive.

When the three weeks were up, Gertrude Hoffer sent him back with her touch stirring his memory and her lilting laughter still in his ears, back to his father's cool disdain and staid Pickman House. Carl's despair upon his return he took to be the pain that comes with departure from one's sweetheart.

He and his uncle had often discussed love over brandy after a night at the theater. Bernard knew romantic passion the way he knew poverty, through diligent study and profoundly developed empathy. Nevertheless, the naive nephew believed he could realize his celibate, spinsterish uncle's dreamy thoughts on love by marrying Gertrude Hoffer.

"I intend to propose marriage to Miss Hoffer, father."

"I'll take care of the details with Mr. Hoffer, Carl. There's no time to waste. I'm seventy-four and I intend to see my grandsons before I die."

As it turned out, he didn't. He died in his sleep a month after the wedding. Carl and his bride were still in Europe on their honeymoon. The new groom briefly entertained fantasies of causing a furor by not returning. He still mourned his uncle and his mother, but all he felt at his father's passing was relief. Nevertheless, he did return.

Carl Pickman put away his sales reports. He glanced at his desk clock. It was well after closing, but he knew Miss Herodetsky was still at her desk, and not only because staying late had become her habit.

Over the months he'd found himself preoccupied with her. He found himself encouraging her visits to his office and thinking up pretexts to see her.

You're lonely, just an old bachelor like Bernard.

He was still married, on paper at least. Whatever made him propose to Gertrude Hoffer was not love, he'd soon found out. Their thirteen years together had produced two daughters, now eleven and ten. There would be no other children. He and his wife had long since established separate bedrooms on separate floors. Carl couldn't fathom how he had ever made love to the stranger who was his wife; he certainly couldn't imagine ever doing so again.

He got up from his desk, stretched and went to the closet for his hat and coat. He left his office quietly. The corridor was dark. Through the glass doors he could see Miss Herodetsky at her desk. He watched her for several moments, taking in the way her dark hair shimmered in the lamplight.

Suddenly longing welled up in him. He was full of shame and guilt, but his infatuation, so long repressed, now refused to be denied. *She embodies everything I never had,* he thought, *that I never will have.*

He pushed open the glass doors. Rebecca looked up at him, smiling radiantly. *At least I can give her what she doesn't have but deserves,* Pickman decided. *It's in my power to help her, and I will.*

"Miss Herodetsky," he began, his tone quite businesslike, "tomorrow morning have Millie check my lunch calendar. Have her pencil you in."

"Sir?"

Her dark eyes were so large and round, so astounded, that he had to smile. "Lunch, if you please. It's time we discussed a promotion and salary increase for you."

"Why, thank you, Mr. Pickman."

Listen to the child, he lectured himself. She calls you "sir" and "Mr. Pickman." She's half your age and you're in rut for her.

He glanced at his watch. "Go home, Miss Herodetsky. Your family must be worried about you."

She shook her head. "My brother has been working an extra shift at his defense job, and my father—" she paused. "There's no one worrying about me, Mr. Pickman."

He nodded, thinking, there's no one worrying about me either. His daughters were away at school and his wife would be off to some dinner party or charity affair or else retired for the evening, as the servants put it. Last weekend was the last time he and Gertrude dined together, when they had people in for a musicale. Only the cook and maid waited tonight. He would be served in the dining room, alone at the massive table with nothing to break the silence but his knife and fork scraping against the plate and the dry rustle as he turned the pages of his newspaper.

He turned to go and caught his reflection in the glass doors. How exactly like his father he looked these days.

He asked her quickly, "Would you care to dine with me this evening?"

It took her a moment, but she smiled. "Yes, I would." She stood, bringing herself startlingly close. "Just give me a moment to freshen up."

He felt unsettled and suddenly miraculously young, enveloped in her perfume as she stepped around him. He made telephone reservations for dinner at a quiet restaurant he'd scouted long ago with this in mind.

                          *   *   *

They began to dine together once or twice a week. In the beginning it seemed to Becky to be strictly business. She'd been promoted to advertising manager. She had a staff of three—a copywriter, layout artist and a secretary— and a windowless cubbyhole of an office. Her salary had almost tripled to one hundred dollars a week. She did not mind the fact that her peers at the other stores around town were being paid salaries many times her own. Her loyalty was absolute.

The more she saw of Mr. Pickman, the less in awe she was. In many ways he reminded her of her own father; often he reminded her of herself. He always listened attentively when she answered his questions about herself and her family. He arranged for a real estate agent to talk to her about collecting rents and maintaining the Cherry Street building. Next he recommended an attorney and tax accountant.

One evening during dinner he asked her if she would mind accompanying him to a fund-raising luncheon on behalf of the Joint Distribution Committee. It was really more a business than social event, he confided, and besides, his wife considered daytime affairs dreary. She also did not favor the cause in this case, which was to fund a Jewish commonwealth in Palestine to absorb the refugees. Zionism had never been close to his own heart, Carl admitted, but he supported the JDC in memory of his uncle, who had been instrumental in its founding.

They left directly from the store on the day of the luncheon. Becky wore a cutaway suit and a shantung blouse Grace Turner had managed to find after scouring the city's most exclusive shops. The suit came from one of the fashion buyers; it was a sample from a manufacturer whose designs had recently been featured in *Vogue*. The seamstresses in the store's alterations department had worked late to make sure it fit properly.

Becky felt very much like Cinderella being readied for the prince's ball by an inordinate number of fairy godmothers. The store personnel were glad to do her these favors. Thanks to her ads business had increased, which in turn assured raises.

Becky's Cinderella aura was enhanced as she rode with Carl in his plush limousine and chain-smoked as she listened to him chat about the luminaries who would be attending.

The luncheon itself, at the Waldorf Astoria, was a sobering experience. Since the summer of 1942 reports that the Nazis had instituted what they were calling the "final solution" had been filtering across the Atlantic. To date millions of Jews were believed to have been destroyed. Despite these reports and the *Blueprint for Extermination*, a detailed account of the annihilation, President Roosevelt and the State Department still refused to admit Jewish refugees or endorse free immigration to Palestine. So awful was the situation that the American Jewish Committee reluctantly began a shift away from assimilation toward Zionism.

Mayor LaGuardia was the guest speaker. When he praised the name Pickman in the same breath as Schiff, Brandeis, and Marshall, Becky felt a thrill of pride.

There were other women in attendance, but they were generally there as wives or as board members of various Jewish philanthropies. Becky was the only working woman present. When Bernard Gimbel loudly complimented her on the job she was doing for Pickman's, Becky was ready to die and go to heaven.

The next day Grace Turner showed up in Becky's office with a newspaper clipping about the luncheon; Becky's name was mentioned. She immediately telephoned her father to make sure he read the article and sent out her secretary to buy half a dozen more copies of the paper.

The original clipping went on her bulletin board and Becky spent a large part of the rest of the day gazing at it.

She was very proud of herself. Not so long ago she had been a nobody on the Lower East Side, studying library books donated by some of the very people she had been hobnobbing with at yesterday's luncheon.

She wanted to do something that would show her appreciation to Carl for all that he had done for her. She decided to invite him out to dinner for a change.

They went by taxi to a West Side spaghetti house where Benny Talkin had taken her a couple of times. The place had red-checked tablecloths, drippy candles stuck in wine bottles and sawdust on the floor. Nobody recognized Pickman. When he asked for the wine list the waiter looked at Becky and asked, "Where'd you get this joker?"

Carl and Becky's eyes locked and they started to laugh, and that went on for so long that finally the waiter gave up and went away, disgusted.

Carl took one sip of the house Chianti and ordered a beer. While he was trying to eat his spaghetti, he got red sauce on his necktie.

Becky, her heart pounding, held her breath.

Carl took off his tie, shrugged and tossed it over his shoulder onto the floor.

"You brought up in a barn, bub?" the waiter sneered, plucking the tie from the sawdust.

At that the wine went right up Becky's nose as she surrendered to laughter. Carl, beaming, signaled for another beer.

Halfway through the evening he began to tell her about Bernard. He started by remarking how his uncle would have enjoyed a place like this, and that got him going about the good times they used to have and his own passion for horseback riding. Then he spoke of how he missed his little girls, away at boarding school by his wife's decree and of his favorite books, poetry, music.

Becky listened intently and made mental notes to search the library for the writers he mentioned.

When the check came, Becky paid it. Pickman confessed that it had been years since anyone took him out to dinner or he had so much fun.

Outside the restaurant he flagged down a taxi to take her home. He held the door for her, and as she moved sideways past him to get in, he kissed her.

Becky was caught off guard. It was a rather fatherly, chaste kiss, and he hadn't embraced her, but still, a kiss was a kiss.

"I've embarrassed you." He looked miserable. "I'm sorry."

"You embarrassed yourself, I think."

"I want us to be friends, but I went too far—"

Becky rose up on her toes to silence him with her lips. "There, now we've both gone too far. We're even. Good night, Mr. Pickman."

At work the next morning Becky agonized over what to do. She had an appointment with Pickman to go over an ad layout. She briefly considered sending the boards upstairs with her secretary, but avoiding him would only aggravate an already awkward situation.

Last night had to be put into manageable proportions if she was to go on working here. She found Mr. Pickman very attractive, but she'd never made love, and her first time would not be with a married man. Nor was she willing to trade her body for her job.

She wanted to trust him, but her experience with Benny Talkin had soured her. Mr. Pickman always treated her in a gentlemanly fashion, but so had Benny—until he didn't.

If he asks me to make love I'll quit, she resolved as she carried the boards upstairs. Outside his office she ran into Phil Cooper, who rolled his eyes and whispered, "Watch out. He's in a foul mood today."

"Oh great," Becky whispered back, trying to smile.

She placed boards on his desk and waited. He glanced at them, described some changes he wanted made and grumbled, "That's all." The light was flashing on his telephone, his in-box was heaped with papers, and Millie's voice was crackling over the intercom with messages from buyers and suppliers.

Becky started out of the office.

"Miss Herodetsky." He was standing. He leaned forward, resting his weight on his palms, as if he wanted to reach her, but his desk was in the way. "I've been mulling over last night. I want you to know that we are friends and that my definition of friendship goes beyond doing favors. It includes not asking for too much." His eyes bored into her. "I hope you understand what I'm saying and that it puts you at ease."

Becky nodded, smiled and took her leave. She tried to puzzle out her feelings on the way back to her own office. She could understand the relief, but not the vague but acute disappointment.

Chapter 43

While the newspapers were still full of D-Day, two weeks before his eighteenth birthday, Danny Herodetzky took advantage of the fact that his family had come together for a Sunday night supper to announce that he had enlisted in the Army Air Corps for aviation cadet training. There was a stunned silence at the table.

"Hey, everybody," Danny exclaimed, "I'm gonna be a fighter pilot."

"Um—congratulations," Becky said. "Danny, I thought a cadet had to have a college background."

"Not anymore," Danny replied. "They'll take any-one—"

"I'll bet," Abe interjected.

Danny scowled at his father. "I was going to say that they'll take anyone who can pass the written exam. I got the second highest score that day at the recruiting office. I didn't do so well on the history and logic parts, but I scored real high on the math and engineering sections. I've passed my physical as well. I've got good eyes, and guess what? Being a shrimp is a plus with the air corps. It seems the fighter cockpits aren't designed for bigger guys."

593

"But you had a defense job," Abe objected. "They can't draft you."

"Pop, you volunteer for the air corps."

"Danny, you don't know what war is—"

Danny rolled his eyes. "I knew it'd be too much to expect you to be enthusiastic—"

"For once in your life, Danny, please listen to me."

Danny nodded, intrigued by the lack of hectoring in his father's tone. "Okay," he said quietly. "Man to man. First you talk and then I will."

Abe nodded and smiled. "Man to man," he began, "I've been in war. Someday maybe I'll tell you my adventures and how I was able to escape to America. Now you must trust me. You must believe me when I tell you that war is something to avoid at all costs—"

"Pop, I understand what you're telling me, but damnit, didn't you ever have a dream? All my life I've wanted to be a flier. You remember those aviation adventure stories I used to read? It's what I want, Pop. Weren't you ever willing to sacrifice, to gamble, in order to get what you wanted?"

Abe thought back to when he was a young man, when he had his health and the intensity of his dreams to drive him on. He remembered sacrificing to save money; he remembered studying and working toward his goal of a business of his own. But a store was a sensible goal. He would never have dreamed of risking his life in some stupid flying contraption.

The words were on his lips: *You will do as I say. I am your father.* But saying that had never done any good in the past, so it wasn't likely it would instill obedience in his son this evening.

Abe said, "I'm going downstairs to read."

"To drink is what he means," Danny whispered after Abe had left the room.

Becky chose not to reply to that. "When do you leave?"

"Right after my birthday."

On Wednesday morning Abe was in his rocking chair behind the front counter discussing the headlines with Shumel Bloom and some of his other friends when he felt constriction in his chest. He managed to tell the others that he was having trouble breathing, and then he heard Shumel calling, "Abe? I don't think he's awake. Call an ambulance." Abe wanted to say he wouldn't go to a hospital, but he couldn't speak.

Becky was in a meeting with Cooper and Pickman when Millie rushed in to say her father had suffered a heart attack and been taken to Saint Vincent's Hospital.

"Millie, call them back," Pickman ordered. "See if he's well enough to be moved, and if he is, arrange for an ambulance to Mount Sinai."

Millie nodded. "I already did. He should be on his way uptown right now."

"Excellent. Go with Miss Herodetsky to the hospital. I'll call Sinai admissions." He glanced at Becky. "I'll also call a cardiologist."

"Thank you. You're all very kind," Becky said.

"Not at all," Pickman replied. "Our best wishes for your father."

Becky called Danny at the Norden factory while Millie summoned a taxi. The ride up to Fifth Avenue and One Hundredth Street lasted an eternity. When they arrived Abe had already been admitted to a private room.

"Thank God they had space for him," Becky told Millie as they hurried along the maze of corridors.

"Thank Pickman, you mean. Honey, Pickman money built this wing." Outside Abe's door Millie said, "You go in. I'll wait out here for Dr. Swerdlove."

"You know him?" Becky asked distractedly.

"Mr. Pickman has Swerdlove look after all his friends with heart trouble."

There was a nurse standing watch over her bedridden father. Abe looked pale, frightened and very old.

"That's my daughter." Abe tugged at the nurse's sleeve. "She works with Pickman, you know. Well, Becky, how do you figure this, eh?" His attempt at a laugh turned into a grimace of pain.

Becky's stomach lurched as she watched the tears spring to his eyes. She felt helpless and terrified; it was the parent who was supposed to comfort the child, not the other way around.

The door behind her opened and Jacob Swerdlove introduced himself. He was a middle-aged austere-looking man with a horseshoe fringe of dark hair, a bulbous nose and steel-rimmed bifocals.

"If you'll excuse us, Miss Herodetzky, we'll have a look at your father."

"Yes, of course. I'll just be outside."

"There's a smoking lounge at the far end of the hall," the nurse said. "You'll be more comfortable there."

Becky spent an anxious twenty minutes in the lounge, distractedly chatting with Millie. Danny appeared at the other end of the corridor, looking dazed and lost. She waved to him and he hurried toward her in his flapping overalls.

"I'm sorry it took me so long," he said as he reached her. "I came right from work, but the trains were slow."

"Danny, this is Miss Kirby."

"Nice to meet you," Millie said. "Becky, I'm going for a stroll. I'll be downstairs in the main lobby if you need me."

"How is he?" Danny asked.

Becky shrugged. "The doctor is with him now."

Danny sighed and his shoulders slumped. "Son of a bitch," he seethed. "I can't enlist now, can I?"

Becky shrugged. "As far as I'm concerned you can, but that's not really what you're asking me, is it?"

"I don't owe him. He was never any good when I needed him."

"That's true, but it's not really the issue." She stopped as Dr. Swerdlove entered the lounge.

"Your father has suffered a relatively mild coronary, and he seems to be bearing up reasonably well for a man of seventy-one."

"Holy cow," Danny blurted.

Swerdlove's dark eyes blinked owlishly behind his bifocals as he regarded him. "Excuse me. Is there some error? Mr. Herodetsky did tell me he was seventy-one."

"Yeah, sure." Danny nodded. "It's just that—well, I hadn't really thought about how old he's getting to be."

"I see. Are you Danny? Your father would like to see you."

"Okay." Danny glanced at Becky and left.

"Your father tells me he has a history of heart trouble," Swerdlove observed. "Also, I noticed that he's suffering from advanced alcoholism."

Becky turned away, ashamed. Swerdlove brusquely changed the subject.

"Surgery is not called for, and in any event would not be advisable at your father's age. We'll put him on medication, but frankly, there isn't much we can do except try to keep him calm, keep him from physical exertion and so on. To that end I can recommend some nursing homes."

"Oy." Becky dug into her purse for a cigarette. "You don't know my father," she said, shaking out her match.

"A nursing facility offers the care he's going to need and would also keep him away from alcohol. Of course there are other factors involved in what must be a family decision."

*   *   *

"I'd like to have a private conversation with my son," Abe told the nurse as Danny entered.

"Your son?" Danny smiled. "I don't think I've ever heard you call me that before."

"Danny, come sit beside me a minute. I want to talk with you about some things.

"You know, when they took me away in the ambulance I thought I was a goner. What went through my head was, 'Once again I've let my boy depart from me in anger, and once again I wish I could make up with him, but now it is too late.' "

"Pop—"

"That's what I thought, Danny, but I've got another chance."

"Don't make yourself excited. I'm not going, okay? I'm staying here—"

"Yes, you are going."

"Huh?"

"In the ambulance I passed out. I had a—I don't know—a dream or a memory of myself as a young man back in Russia. It was the eve of Haim's departure to Palestine and we were arguing. I didn't want him to go. I wanted him to come to America with me, but he wouldn't listen. How stubborn he was!"

"Haim? Stubborn?" Danny was incredulous. "I always thought that guy was perfect."

"In the dream, Danny, you were Haim, and our argument about Palestine became the argument about you becoming a flier. I realized then that Haim had insisted on living his own life, just as you have, but him I showered with love and understanding, so why not you?"

Danny, his voice trembling, said, "It was Mother dying, I guess. You sorta always held that against me, huh?"

Abe nodded. "But I had no right. Now that I almost

died I realize that. I can't go to my grave with that burden on my conscience."

"Cut out that talk," Danny scolded. "You're not dying so fast. You're too mean." He winked.

Abe smiled. "The war could go on a long time, Danny. Who knows when you'll come back?"

"I told you I'm not going."

"And in the ambulance I urged you to go. I'm telling you now. I wish you wouldn't because I'm afraid for you, but I want you to have your dream."

Danny was quiet for a moment, then said, "Okay, Pop. And thanks. I want you to know that I'd stay if it would make you happy."

"I know," Abe replied. "All your life you've been forgiving me my shortcomings, and all my life I've been wishing you were more like Haim." He paused. "Danny, you say you got the second highest score on the test? It must be difficult if it's for pilots."

"A lot of college men failed that test. I guess I'm not so dumb after all."

"Nobody thought you were dumb, only that you never applied yourself. Never mind that now. I'm trying to say I'm proud of you."

"Okay. I'm glad you are." Danny leaned over his father to kiss him on the forehead. "When I come back, I'll take you for a ride, Pop. We'll go high above the clouds and soar with the birds."

"Yeah," Abe chuckled weakly. "So everything's all right between us, yes?"

"Sure it is."

"Like a father and a son should be, right?" Abe's eyes fluttered closed and his voice faded away as he fell asleep.

While her father slept Becky sat by his bedside, watching him and thinking. She'd told her brother everything Dr. Swerdlove said and Danny agreed that their father could no longer spend his days alone.

Abe's eyes blinked open. "Huh? Danny?"

"He had to go back to work," Becky said, "but he told me what went on between you." She squeezed her father's hand. "I'm so happy."

"If he wants to be a flier, let him be a good one," Abe grunted. "You know, I'm proud of you too. We haven't gotten along too good lately. It's the drinking, I guess. I was impressed by how much Pickman must think of you for him to do so much for me. He got me a very fancy doctor, you know."

"I know."

"Well, please be sure to thank him."

"Father, they think you'll be out of here in a couple of weeks."

"Too long."

"A couple of weeks of observation," Becky declared. "But we've got to discuss what'll happen then."

"What do you mean? I'll go home is what'll happen then."

"You can't stay alone anymore. You must realize that."

"Yeah," Abe sighed. "I also know that Cherry Street is my home, where my friends are, what's left of them. I can't go somewhere new. You understand? Look, I'm old, I'm scared; I'm finished making trouble for my children—"

"You are mean," Becky laughed.

Abe grinned wolfishly. "That's what Danny said, that I was too mean to die." He shook his head. "Let me think things over, Becky. If I'm gonna be here awhile, we can take our time deciding what to do."

Her father regained his strength during the following week. Visiting hours lasted until eight o'clock, and Becky went to the hospital every evening directly from work. The family celebrated Danny's birthday in Abe's room. That morning Danny had been sworn into the Army. The next day he left by train for the Aviation Classification Center near San Antonio, Texas.

During the second week Becky and her father began to spend their visits strolling the corridors with Abe leaning on his daughter's arm.

"Shumel came to visit me today. Davy Kaplan brought him. Shumel don't see so good anymore. You know, Shumel's wife died last year. He's been living alone in that big railroad apartment on Ludlow Street, on the third floor. That's too many steps for an old man like him. So—" Abe waited.

"So what?"

"So I asked him to move into Cherry Street with me. He's nearly blind, but he's spry. The only thing is, you'll have to move out. Shumel ain't your brother. You get a nice, respectable place near your work. You're a good girl. You'll be okay."

"Thanks," Becky said dryly.

"Since that bastard Benny Talkin you haven't had a boyfriend. Am I right? I thought so. Well, if you ain't getting married you'll want a place of your own, and I know you're too dutiful to say so."

"I see. All this is for my benefit."

"For everybody's benefit—yours, Shumel's, mine. He and I can take care of one another and I can stay home. I know the store is too much for me now. I figure to sell off the meat and dairy cases and just keep a few things on the shelves. More like a candy store, you know? All I want is to keep it open with some chairs so I can sit with my friends. I know it's your building and I need your permission—"

"Oh, shut up."

Abe stared at her. "What are you crying for?"

"Maybe I'm homesick already." She wiped her eyes

with the back of her hand. "Enough walking. Back to your room."

"Homesick," Abe murmured in wonder. "I never figured about that."

"I'm willing to let you try it," Becky said, "but you've got to promise me no more drinking—"

"You don't have to tell me. I made a vow, you know. I won't take a drop while Danny's in the war, and never again if he comes back safe and sound."

Chapter 44

Carl Pickman liked a quiet morning. He awoke at six o'clock or a little after. He never overslept and he never relied upon an alarm clock. He bathed, shaved and dressed, then went downstairs to the dining room for breakfast. The morning papers kept him company. He spoke to no one, did not even say good morning to the maid. She understood; the first thing a new member of the house staff learned was that Carl Pickman enjoyed a quiet morning.

Gertrude slept late. A midmorning brunch would be brought to her in bed while she made her telephone calls, confirming her calendar for the afternoon and evening.

In their morning habits, as in so many things, Carl and Gertrude had very little in common, and their tacit understanding was that both preferred it that way. Accordingly, Carl was both surprised and displeased when his wife, puffy-eyed and wrapped in her morning robe, entered the dining room at seven on a suffocatingly humid August morning.

"Carl, I'd like to talk to you about a very important matter." Gertrude glanced at the maid. "That will be all," she said as her coffee appeared before her.

Carl sighed, folded away his newspaper and regarded

his wife over the rim of his cup. "They call for thunder-storms," he observed.

"I detest the city in the summer," Gertrude replied. "This horrid war has spoiled everything. I ask you, darling, what's the point of a summer residence if there's nothing going on in the country?" Behind her the maid was wheel-ing out the breakfast cart. Gertrude heard the glass doors quietly close behind her.

Carl watched his wife twist around to be sure they were alone. "She's gone, Gertrude. What's on your mind?"

"That popsy you're going around town with," Ger-trude spat. "It's got to stop."

"What?" Carl tried to laugh. "I don't know what you're talking about."

"Carl, you've been seen, don't you understand? Skulk-ing around those dark little hideaways has done you no good at all."

"Just a moment," he protested. "Are you speaking of Miss Herodetsky? We have dinner occasionally, it's true, but it's strictly business."

"I want it to stop, Carl."

"Be reasonable, Trude." He smiled. "She's done a wonderful job at the store and she's had some bad luck. Her father is an invalid and her brother is in the service—"

"You've helped her enough, Carl. I know about the apartment."

He shook his head ruefully. "Calm down, now. She needed a place to live. With the war there's a housing shortage. I merely phoned Charles and asked him if he had anything in any of his buildings, that's all. Rebecca's done so much for the store. Do you really mind that I used some pull to get her a modest walk-up on Riverside Drive?"

"Is that where you go to sleep with your slut? Did you furnish her nest for her or do you two just roll around on a mattress on the floor?"

Carl took a deep breath, trying to calm himself. He

wanted to smack Gertrude silly. "How odd," he said icily. "Jealousy on your part seems very peculiar after all these years. Nevertheless, I can assure you that Miss Herodetsky and I are not lovers." He looked at his watch. In precisely three minutes his driver would bring the car. He stood up. "Good morning, Gertrude."

"I'm warning you, Carl, I won't have it."

His fists clenched. "I don't care what you think or what you want." Carl stormed out of the dining room, shutting the glass doors behind him, cutting off his wife's tirade.

The car was waiting.

Damn Trude! He would think about Miss Herodetsky instead. He wanted to believe she was fond of him, but was her warmth solely due to his wealth and power? Obviously his position made some difference to her, as it did to everyone. It had to, but was that all there was to their relationship?

He knew very little about women. He'd always been shy, diffident; in his later years those traits had evolved into aloofness, and yet with Becky he had begun to feel more alive.

It was a long time since he'd felt anything for anyone. He loved his daughters, he supposed, but he saw them so rarely that they were alien to him. Between their boarding schools and summer camps he couldn't remember the last time the house rang with their laughter.

His marriage was a joke. Had it always been so? Had Trude always viewed their union as a business merger? Had she and his father laughed at his naivete behind his back?

I won't have it. Come to think of it, his father often used that expression. Yes, his wife and his father were two of a kind.

The sky darkened and there came a low rumble of thunder as the car cruised past the Plaza Hotel and its majestic fountain. A fat drop of rain splattered against the side window. A minute later it began to pour.

Along Fifth Avenue pedestrians popped open their umbrellas. Those caught unprepared held newspapers and briefcases above their heads as they ran for shelter, reminding Carl of his own undignified flight from his wife. Well, he was through backing down. It was time for him to take charge of his life.

He glanced out his window. Saks' awnings were crowded with passersby waiting for the worst of the storm to be over. From the ink-stained clouds Carl guessed it would rain for quite some time. When the department stores opened today, business would be brisk as the public, trapped inside by the rain, lingered over the merchandise.

Carl Pickman let the sound of the rain drumming on the roof wash away his anger. His wife had done him a favor. Not only had she crystallized his feelings about her, she had forced him to realize just how much Becky meant to him.

I wish she were here beside me now, he thought. I wish—

Well, there were many things he wished. This morning he had learned that there was really nothing standing in the way of those wishes coming true.

But first things first. A man had to start somewhere.

On that same humid August morning, as Carl Pickman's car was rolling down Fifth Avenue, Becky was readying herself for the day. Her apartment was on the fifth floor of a brownstone on the corner of Seventy-ninth and Riverside. It was a small place consisting of a tiny kitchen, a bath, a bedroom and a living room. Her apartment faced the rear, so she had no view of Riverside Park, but there was a skylight in the bathroom and a spacious balcony off the little living room, overlooking a garden courtyard. Thanks to Carl's influence the rent was reasonable, although the landlord could have charged what he wanted in the housing shortage brought on by the war.

During her first weeks of tenancy she was deliriously happy, but as the novelty wore off, she began to miss her father and the old neighborhood. Everybody on Cherry Street knew her name and had a smile for her in passing. Without realizing it until she moved, she had come to rely on the warmth of that close-knit community to replenish her strength after a grueling day's work. Now when she came home it was to a far posher neighborhood, but here she was just another New Yorker, a stranger to all, as all were strangers to her. She resigned herself to loneliness; it was just the way her life had turned out.

She grabbed her purse and hurried down the stairs and out the front door of her building, only to stop short as she caught a glimpse of the darkening sky over the Hudson River. It sure looked like rain; she hadn't bothered to listen to the radio weather report, and she'd left her umbrella four flights up.

She was already running late. She'd called a staff meeting for nine o'clock, and she had an enormous amount of paperwork to do before then.

The subway was two blocks east. She'd gamble on making it before the storm broke. She was just reaching West End Avenue when she heard a thunderous peal, saw morning turn to dusk and felt the first hard drops of rain.

A man wearing a trench coat and a fedora pulled low was approaching the corner. She impatiently waited for the traffic light to change so she could dash across the avenue. She was preoccupied with her soaked hair and clothing and how her whole stinking day was being ruined because she forgot to bring her stinking umbrella.

The man in the trench coat got his umbrella over her head just as the downpour began in earnest. She turned to look at him, startled, and her stomach churned and her knees weakened.

"Hi, Becky," Benny Talkin said. "Been a long time."

Four years, three months, one week, three days, she found herself effortlessly calculating. "Uh, yeah. It has been. Hi, Benny."

"Gee, you look great."

"You too," she said, and he did. He'd grown a handsome mustache. In his trench coat and fedora he looked like Humphrey Bogart in the movies—better. Humphrey Bogart probably wanted to look like Benny Talkin when he chose his costume. "What are you doing here?" she demanded. It came out like an accusation, not that Becky cared. It was all she could do to keep from crying, so great was the shock of seeing him. "You don't still live at the Dorilton?"

"Hell, no. I gave up that crib a long time ago."

" 'Crib?' " Becky smiled. "You still lurking around those Fifty-second Street swing clubs and picking up the musicians' slang?" There! The intervening years had taught her a thing or two about disdainful superiority!

Benny didn't seem to hear the sarcasm. "No more time for music, I'm afraid. I'm partners with my father-in-law and I've got three kids."

"Gee, that's great."

"Yeah," Benny grinned. "Twin boys and a girl. We live on West End and Ninety-fifth."

This handsome bastard still had the power to turn her into jelly. "I see that your eye healed up all right." She hated herself for digging up the past that way, but she'd forgotten Benny's ability to tune out what he didn't want to hear.

"You must live around here." She nodded and he said, "That makes us neighbors."

She smiled weakly. The traffic light had gone through three cycles. "I've got to go."

"Let me walk you down to Seventy-second," Benny

said. "You'll save time by catching the express to Pickman's."

He began to head along West End and Becky walked with him.

"How'd you know I work at Pickman's?"

He shrugged. "Word gets around, I guess. Anyway, I know you're doing real well. I'm proud of you, Becky. You know, I feel like I got you your start."

You almost finished me, as well. "What are you doing so far downtown if you live on Ninety-fifth?" she asked, taking his arm.

"I was heading for midtown. I got an appointment with a restaurant owner."

"No more maroon Cadillac convertible?"

"Oh, sure," Benny laughed, "a new one every year, up until the war, of course. Anyway, I like to walk. You remember that, don't you?"

Right then she was trying desperately not to remember things about him. "About the war—I see you didn't feel the need to enlist."

"That kinda thing is for chumps, honey. Anyhow, it isn't like I'm not doing my part. Stefano and I are engaged in some secret work for the Navy—"

"What?" Becky exclaimed, incredulous.

"It's true. These Navy guys came to Stefano to ask for his help . . ."

"Help for what?" Becky persisted.

Benny glanced around. "It isn't the kinda thing you're supposed to talk about on the street," he told her quietly. Then he brightened. "Say, why don't you and me get together for a drink? I could tell you all about it."

They were at Seventy-third and West End. Becky stopped walking. They were still a couple of blocks from the subway, but there were some things worse than getting wet. "I'm going to go on alone from here, Benny."

"Aw, why? Because I suggested a little drink? You know you want to."

She considered lying to him, but it hardly seemed necessary. "What I want and what I'm going to do are two different things, Benny. See you."

"Hold on."

"No, listen, Benny. It's nice to see you, sure, but you're a married man, with three kids, yet." She turned to go.

Benny grabbed her arm. She glared at him and he snatched his hand away. "I just wanted to give you my umbrella," he said in hurt tones.

Becky frowned and shook her head. "I don't need—"

"Go on and take it. It's just an umbrella, Becky. I got a coat, a hat—and you've got nothing." He smiled coolly.

She took the umbrella. There was no point in getting wet.

"Remember what I told you," he called after her. "You can call on me if you ever need help."

Becky heard him but didn't acknowledge it. She didn't even look back.

Benny stood on West End Avenue and watched until Becky disappeared around the corner. It occurred to him that they'd split up in the rain and now the rain had brought them together again, at least for a little while.

Maybe that line would have worked on her. Probably not. He continued walking downtown and realized he'd forgotten to ask about her father. He'd heard about Abe's heart attack. He doubted that his sympathies for her old man would have done much to get him on her right side, either. He could understand her anger, but that didn't give her the right to imply that he was always a liar.

For instance, it was true that he and Stefano were engaged in secret work for the military, and he for one was glad to do it. Getting drafted was a sucker's fate; it didn't happen to a guy with his connections. Anyway, he was too important to be just another Sad Sack, as the Navy would be the first to attest.

During the first years of the war the Allies lost hundreds of ships to the Germans. Washington must have gotten jittery when the S.S. *Lafayette* mysteriously burned in its berth on the Hudson. The Navy assumed the New York waterfront was riddled with spies and the Italian fishing fleet was running supplies and information out to the Kraut subs. The district attorney's office, acting as a buffer for Navy Intelligence, approached Stefano and asked him to cooperate in cleaning up the waterfront.

They began by sweet-talking Stefano, calling him master of the waterfront and stuff like that, all because of his warehouses, but it turned out that their sweet talk wasn't necessary. Stefano loved America, as did Benny, as did virtually all the Italians and Jews with whom they did business.

That was back in '42. They supplied union cards to Navy undercover agents so they could masquerade as longshoremen, fishermen, truck drivers and so on, and they passed the word to all their people to keep an eye out for Nazi rats. Their Navy contact, Captain Ronald Mac-Dougall, and Stefano got real chummy. Stefano was elated; Mac never ceased complimenting him on the great patriotic job he was doing.

Then the Navy wanted to expand operations, but that was too much for Stefano to handle alone. He didn't have the authority to issue orders to the unions that owned the Brooklyn docks. What Stefano needed was a mandate from on high if he was to whip the syndicate into line behind the Navy.

So Captain Mac, a bunch of lawyers and Meyer Lansky, who was still Luciano's second, journeyed to Great Meadow Prison near Albany, where Lucky was doing thirty to fifty for extortion. They met with Luciano, who agreed to help the Navy, since that would allow lots of unrecorded visits from Lansky and his people. How else could Luciano direct the antisabotage program? The Navy promised to keep his cooperation top secret, for Luciano was worried about what the angry Axis authorities would do to him if he ever got himself deported to Italy.

Since then everyone had been doing his part to keep the waterfronts clean. Lansky was proud to be getting an important job done with a minimum of violence. There were no wildcat strikes and no careless talk to supply enemy agents with information. The Navy was pleased and so was the syndicate, many of whom had been given unrestricted, unmonitored access to Luciano. He could now much more easily run his empire from his prison cell. The only dark spot was Stefano's furious jealousy when Meyer Lansky was issued an official Navy code number. These days Stefano's temper seemed to be shorter and shorter. It seemed Benny was his whipping boy.

Benny walked east, circling the slums west of Broadway, and continued downtown to Columbus Circle. Then he decided the hell with more walking and hailed a taxi. His cracked ribs were hurting.

Benny loved his kids with a passion, but unfortunately, he didn't feel the same about Dolores. Thanks to her father's power she'd long ago gained the upper hand on him. If he didn't toe the line Stefano heard about it, and Stefano de Fazio was not the kind of father-in-law a guy ought to antagonize. He and Stefano occasionally had sharp exchanges, and Stefano sometimes issued stern warnings, but Benny had never imagined that Stefano would have him physically harmed.

However, one day Tony called him out behind the warehouse on the pretext of discussing a cargo shipment. Suddenly three other guys came from nowhere to surround him. He had the time to ask, ''What's going on?'' and then he was on the ground and those four impassive faces were gazing down at him like circling moons as they kicked him.

When it was over Tony Bucci carried Benny into the office and taped up his ribs. "Don't let on to Dolores," he warned. "Tell her you fell down or something. And stay away from them hookers. That's what got Lucky thrown behind bars—"

"That's not true," Benny gasped. Luciano hadn't been lustful so much as greedy. He'd tried to skim too much profit off his bordellos, and the outraged madams went to Special Prosecutor Dewey.

"Don't matter. You'd better get the message, or next time it won't just be cracked ribs. Do as we tell you. You ain't a physical kind of guy, Benny. You don't wanna get hit on like this. It's too risky for a guy in partnership with Stefano de Fazio to sleep with a bunch of talkative whores. Find yourself some wised-up chippy who'll know better than to spill your business to the cops."

Benny kept quiet. He despised this four-eyed bald sadistic son of a bitch. He was also more than a little afraid.

How could he explain that it was exactly a whore's capacity to supply impersonal sex that he craved? He did not want to confide in a woman; he was sick of women. He was finding it increasingly difficult to make love to his wife; he'd begun to hate her the first time she ran to her daddy when they fought. He wasn't the man of his house; his father-in-law was. Sometimes he wondered why father and daughter didn't just sleep together and be done with it.

Damn, but his ribs ached. It was the rain, Benny guessed. He leaned back in the taxi and thought about Becky, trying to get his mind off of the pain. She looked good, really good, better than four years ago.

He wondered what it would have been like if he'd

married Becky instead of Dolores. Some nights he still found himself dreaming about Becky, a haunting, sexy ghost, making him strong and hard like Dolores never could and leaving him in turmoil when he awoke. If he'd married Becky he'd be poor, but the last four years as Stefano's partner had taught him that money wasn't everything. Without Stefano he probably would have ended up in the Army; well, he would have been a good soldier. He had guts and he could take care of himself; the fact that he hadn't the stomach for the de Fazio brand of violent retribution didn't make him a coward.

And when Benny came home from the war there would have been Becky waiting for him, ready to love him, to make him feel like a man.

Benny watched the rain slanting down on Central Park South and listened to the taxi's windshield wipers. He was trapped and he knew it. It was no longer the money; it was Stefano de Fazio's wrath that kept him caged.

Often he had thought of taking his kids and making a run for it, but it was a foolish, suicidal notion. He knew too much. Luciano, Lansky and the rest would all come after him; with or without his kids there was nowhere safe in the country.

Chapter 45

One of the night watchmen let Becky into Pickman's through the employees' entrance. "Still coming down, eh, miss?" he asked sorrowfully, eyeing Benny's dripping umbrella. "I didn't bring one."

"Take this one," Becky said, thrusting the umbrella into his hands.

She managed to brush past her secretary and lock her office door before she began to cry. How could she still be in thrall to that louse after all these years? What kind of sorcerer was Benny Talkin to have cast such a spell over her?

Like the storm, her crying was furiously intense if relatively brief. Unlike the storm, her tears did not leave the world washed fresh and clean.

Becky was repairing her makeup when her secretary timidly knocked on her door. "Millie's on the line."

Becky picked up the phone. Millie said, "He wants to talk to you," and put her through to Carl Pickman.

"Good morning, Mr. Pickman."

"Are you all right, Miss Herodetsky? Your voice sounds strained."

"Thanks for asking. I'm just feeling a little blue. I

ran into somebody on my way to work." She paused to chide herself. "I just had an upsetting morning. That's all."

"How extraordinary," Pickman said. "So did I. I was calling to ask if you'd take me to that spaghetti house again. I'm afraid they won't allow me in without you, my dear. Not after I threw my necktie into their nice clean sawdust."

Becky chuckled. "Oh, all right, Mr. Pickman, if you'll promise to behave. I do have a reputation to uphold—are you still there?"

"Yes, yes. I was just taken aback."

"I don't understand."

"Nor should you, my dear. As I said, it's been an extraordinary morning."

"Mr. Pickman, I have an idea. Why don't you come to my apartment after work and I'll fix us dinner?"

"Miss Herodetsky, I—"

"Please? Oh, please," she implored. "I'm sure it'll be a lovely, warm evening and we can eat on the balcony. You'll be my first guest. It'll be just the thing to cheer us both up. Please say you'll come."

Pickman laughed, trying to make a joke of her invitation. "Didn't you tell me you've got a fifth-floor walkup?"

"Well, yes, but I promise to make the climb worth your while."

"Hmmm—"

"Unless, of course, you think it would be improper."

There was an extended pause on the other end of the line. "Miss Herodetsky," he finally said, "Just who has the right to say what is proper or improper for us?"

"Well, I surely don't know," she replied, flustered.

"Would eight o'clock be convenient?"

"Yes, indeed."

"I'll bring some wine," he said, and hung up.

* * *

Becky left work early that afternoon. She stopped at several butchers along Broadway until she found one who would produce a pound of steak for a dollar. That was a third more than the ceiling price the government had imposed, but she paid it, and gladly. What a special, lovely night this was going to be. It would be her chance to show Mr. Pickman how much she appreciated all he'd done for her as well as her first chance to show off her new home.

There'd been nobody to visit her. Grace Turner kept promising she would, but she was too busy with her own work and social life. Danny wasn't around to visit, and her father had not left the Lower East Side for years. Anyway, she was not about to let her convalescent father climb four flights of stairs just to see two little rooms and a terrace.

As soon as she got home she turned on her radio to hear the news and weather. She was in luck. The forecast called for a clear, sultry night. Out on the balcony she unfolded the card table. After the war, when such things were available, she would buy a wrought-iron patio set, but for now the card table would have to do. She laid her best cloth and set out candles.

It was six o'clock. Two hours to go.

Becky began to sweep, dust, polish—more to rid herself of nervous energy than anything. She made the salad. She showered. She put on a light cotton skirt and a sleeveless blouse. She brushed her hair and did her makeup.

Seven o'clock.

She put the potatoes into the oven to bake. She stood at the door of the terrace and looked at the table she'd set. She told herself she absolutely would not burst into tears.

Why, oh why did she have to have run into Benny Talkin? Why couldn't she get over him? How demeaning to be just as heartbroken today as on the day he betrayed her, four long years ago. She couldn't help imagining that it was Benny she was waiting for and that there would be not merely polite, friendly conversation, but his strong arms around her as no man's had been before him and no man's had been since.

At eight on the dot Pickman arrived with four bottles of wine, two red and two white. "You didn't say what we were having, so I brought a selection."

He was still dressed for the office in a blue suit, white shirt, tie and wingtips. Becky smiled brightly, feeling sick to her stomach at the thick silence of unease. Pickman rather weakly smiled back.

He's used to formal meals that feature half a dozen forks, finger bowls and sherbet to clear the palate. She hadn't a thing to serve while they waited for dinner. There was nothing in her refrigerator but some Muenster cheese, yellow and dry as parchment. *Benny always enjoyed a steak and a baked potato.*

"Why don't you make yourself comfortable?" she told him. His look told her that it had come out sounding a trifle snappish. She felt her eyes filling up. Oh, that louse!

"Why don't I open the wine?" he suggested.

Becky nodded. "Oh, Mr. Pickman, I don't have a—"

"I figured. I brought a corkscrew along. Here. Put these whites in the icebox to cool. Perhaps we'll have some with dessert."

Dessert? She had no dessert. She felt feverish as she put away a fat dark green bottle and a tall light green one.

"I have a cellarful of wonderful German and Italian wines at home, but I have no palate for them now. The day the war ends I'll either serve them up at a victory party or smash them all with a hammer—not that I think there's much doubt now which way the war's going. Anyway, tonight it's all French, though I'm told it makes sense to look into some of the Californias."

"I forgot to get dessert."

"Never mind. I brought sauterne and champagne. You can pick one for dessert." He pulled the cork and asked for glasses.

Becky went to the cupboard. "I probably don't have the right kind."

Carl took her in his arms and kissed her lightly on the lips. He kissed her again and her lips parted in response to his lightly thrusting tongue. She caught the peppery scent of his shaving lotion and felt the corded muscles of his arms and back, surprisingly thick and strong beneath his blue jacket.

"I thought this would help to pass the time while the wine breathes," he murmured, his emerald green eyes intently watching her. Then he blushed. "Oh, that was a stupid thing to say, wasn't it, Miss Herodetsky—blast! May I call you Rebécca?" She nodded, eyes like saucers. "I rehearsed it and rehearsed it in the taxi—I thought a man had to have something clever to say to a woman—"

"Mr. Pickman, you don't have to say clever things. There's nothing to be sorry about." She hugged him. "I'm glad you're holding me. Tonight I think I'd like to be held."

"Rebecca, I'd like to make love to you."

She began to tremble. Why not? she thought. Look at him, feel his touch. He's as frightened as you are. This isn't just another conquest for him. And it's time.

"I've—I've never been with a man before." She spoke so softly, with her face pressed against his chest, that he might not have heard. She took him by the hand and led him toward the bedroom. They undressed silently. He resolutely turned his back, so she covertly watched him. Finally he turned and stood naked before her in the twilight. She saw that he was flaccid; should he be? When exactly did it change? Her heart was thumping and she was finding it difficult to breathe. She was naked in front of a

man. Her breasts felt huge, ungainly. Was she pretty
enough for him? Was he disappointed?

He stepped toward her. He was so tall, so handsome,
an aristocrat. Who was she to please such a man with her
dark features and peasant hips?

Carl held out his arms and they embraced. Both
moaned at the shock. Becky felt him beginning to swell
and harden as he rolled against her thighs. She began to
nibble kisses across the broad expanse of his chest, sprinkled with greying hairs. His hands, fluttering mothlike,
slid down her spine.

Still holding each other, they glided like dancers toward her wide, foolish bed, a grand four-poster with a
canopy that almost brushed her bedroom ceiling. It was the
sort of bed Becky had dreamed about since she was little.

Becky felt herself growing wet beneath his stroking
fingers and then surrendered herself to the wonderful sensation of his lips and tongue on her taut nipples. When she
heard him fumbling with something in a crinkly wrapping
she squeezed shut her eyes. The protection, she thought,
so there aren't babies. He was going to do it now . . . She
floated back against her pillows, tense and expectant in the
semidarkness.

He held her gently and lovingly. When he filled her
she cried out, not in pain but in wonder and apprehension.

He moved within her. She wondered, what next and
when? Carl rose up. His back arched and the cords strained
in his neck. He moaned and shuddered and Becky held
him as they exchanged roles. Now she was the protectress
and he the vulnerable one. He lightly collapsed on her,
sweat-damp and short of breath.

She thought sleepily, Is that all? Far less than when I
touch myself.

When she awoke the bedroom was dark and she was
alone in her bed. She could hear noise coming from the

kitchen. She took her robe from the closet and tiptoed out. She saw Pickman, barefoot, dressed only in his trousers and sleeveless undershirt, fussing at the counter, his back to her. She took the opportunity to gaze at him unawares. He was as strong and youthful-looking as a man half his age. Surely he was an accomplished lover, as he was accomplished in everything else. If she'd taken little pleasure, the fault was probably hers and not his.

He sensed her standing there, turned and smiled. "Hello."

"Hi." She smiled back, feeling bashful. "What time is it?"

"A little after ten. Have some wine." He winked at her. "It's breathed enough."

"I'm starving," Becky exclaimed, pouring herself a glass. "Oh, the potatoes!"

"They're fine. I checked. You can't overbake a potato. Now relax and drink your wine and I'll put the steak into the broiler."

"Mr. Pickman, it's my kitchen."

"But I never get a chance to cook," he complained.

"You know how?"

"The best chefs are men, Rebecca."

"Not on Cherry Street, they're not."

The candles had burned themselves down to stubs, so they ate by starlight, laughing and talking quietly. All around them the night was filled with city sounds and the feathery rustle of leaves in the summer breeze. After they were done Carl went back inside, to return with the sauterne and two fresh glasses. Becky dug out an old rug and the two sat with their arms around each other on the terrace floor, leaning against the wall, gazing at the heavens. Sipping the pale wine, Becky felt like a honey bee drunk on nectar in a field full of wild flowers. Carl's strong

fingers now and again gently tilted up her chin to lick the
sugary drops from her lips.

"I love you, Rebecca."

What could she say to him, that when they first met
she'd looked up to him as a sort of father figure and
teacher? That she was a good and dutiful Jewish girl in
search of a man to take over from her natural father? That
as Abe Herodetzky taught his child to transform onions
and potatoes into pennies, she looked to Carl Pickman to
initiate her into the wonders of business—and life—on a
far grander scale?

Or should she just tell him that when they were
making love, she desperately fought against her desire to
pretend he was a cheap, lying ganef who'd thrown her
over for a rich shiksa?

"You're crying," Pickman murmured. "Don't, Rebecca, my darling, you don't have to cry. It'll be all right.
You'll see."

"You don't understand."

"But I do." He squeezed her hand. "I'm leaving my
wife. No, don't say anything. Let me finish. It's not just
tonight, although I must tell you this is the first time in my
marriage I've been unfaithful. There's nothing between
Trude and me anymore. There certainly isn't any love, and
lately we've begun to hate each other."

"I'm sorry." Sorry, but I love another man.

"Don't be, my love. You've shown me what life is
all about. What a man has a right to aspire to, and if he's
lucky what he has a right to have. Becky, I know you
don't love me—yet. All I'm asking for is the chance to try
and win you. And while I'm trying, I want you to know
that I'll be in the process of freeing myself. I know you're
too fine a woman to be some man's mistress, my love. As
soon as it's possible, if you're willing, I intend to make
you my wife."

Chapter 46

Palestine, 1944–45

Soon after Herschel left Tel Aviv for one of the Irgun training camps strung along the coastline, the cities of Palestine became urban battle zones. British property was destroyed by Irgun bombs, and shootouts with the police became commonplace. The British, reacting as Begin predicted, instituted curfews and a firm policy of suppression, which included a possible death sentence for any Jews who possessed guns or explosives.

The Arab population was terrified. The observation, "There are no police," moved through the Arab quarters as the fellahin viewed the bombed-out remains of the Criminal Investigation Department and of the police stations.

The Zionist establishment condemned the Jewish terrorists as "fascist nihilists stabbing Zionism in the back." It reaffirmed the pledge of partnership with the British as well as official faith in diplomatic negotiation.

At the training camps the carefully screened volunteers studied Irgun ideology and the use and maintenance of weapons. The emphasis was on the British Bren submachine gun, stolen from armories. Those with the knack and

the nerve were taught how to make and use explosives.
Taking to heart his mandate from Begin, Herschel supervised the training programs and continually traveled from
camp to camp to institute revisions. Whenever he could,
Herschel passed through the cities, eager to get a sense
what was happening on the front line.

In the Jewish quarters all across Palestine the British
had taken to making mass arrests. The schism between the
Zionist establishment and the troublemakers widened.

Ben-Gurion informed Begin that a British-sponsored
partition plan for a Jewish state was being jeopardized by
the Irgun's operations and ordered Begin to submit his
own operational plans to Haganah for prior approval.

Begin refused, not trusting British promises but questioning the British right to carve up Palestine. He was
troubled by this animosity among Jews and attempted to
put together a coalition between the more militant members of Haganah, the Irgun and LEHI, a radical gang.
Unfortunately, LEHI's commander, a tough underground
fighter named Yitzhak Shamir, refused the offer. The Irgun
he trusted completely, but he would have nothing to do
with Haganah.

Things went from bad to worse. Every day new arrivals to Palestine offered eyewitness accounts of the Nazis'
atrocities, and each time the authorities brushed aside these
accounts as pro-immigration propaganda. And so the Irgun
training camps enjoyed an influx of volunteers.

In the fall of 1944 the British deported hundreds of
Irgun and LEHI prisoners to concentration camps in East
Africa. Remaining members began to draw up new battle
plans designed to force the British to return the exiles. The
Jewish Agency got wind of it and warned off Begin,
threatening to "step in and finish the Irgun" if it should
jeopardize the "fair deal" the British were promising the
Zionist establishment at the war's end.

On November 6 in Cairo two youths, acting on orders

from LEHI, assassinated Baron Moyne, Resident British Minister in the Middle East. Lord Moyne was Churchill's close friend. In London Chaim Weizmann issued a statement that Moyne's death shocked and numbed him more than the loss of his own son, missing in action over Germany. In Jerusalem the Jewish Agency expressed outraged horror at the crime, while the Hebrew press called it an abominable deed.

In settlements, towns and cities all across Palestine the Jewish community prepared for a rumored retaliatory massacre, and Kol and the other supervisors suspended training operations in preparation for the firestorm.

Herschel returned to Tel Aviv and remained there through January. The British were everywhere, and their manhunt was proving to be uncannily successful. As no place could be considered safe, Herschel decided his best chance to evade capture was to lose himself in the city's multitudes.

He did not know the whereabouts of Begin and his high command. The Irgun had split into two- and three-man cells and everything was on a need-to-know basis. Gradually it became known that Haganah was working with the British to track down Irgunists, who were being tortured and deported.

The urge to retaliate was strong, but Begin's edict went out. There shall be no civil war. Suffer and wait.

And the Irgun was losing the deadly game of hide and seek.

Herschel Kol, alias Dov Katz, mounted the stairs to his room in a dilapidated apartment house off Dizengoff Road. He was returning from a visit to Jaffa and the old Glaser inn. Herschel did not dare linger there very long; CID men and regular police were stationed on every corner in the old port city to calm the jittery Arab population.

Herschel unlocked his door and stepped inside his digs. A British policeman, lounging on Herschel's bed, a revolver in his hand, nodded affably. Herschel was about to bolt when he felt the chilly kiss of another revolver against his ear.

"CID," the man behind him said. "Herschel Kol, you are under arrest."

They handcuffed him and led him downstairs to a windowless van. As they took him away Herschel wondered what it was going to be, back to Jerusalem Prison to serve out the rest of his sentence or deportation to a concentration camp in East Africa.

Either way, first there would be the interrogation and the torture. He still vividly remembered what they'd done to him after his first arrest.

Chapter 47

Texas, 1945

The letter from home was postmarked December third, but it did not reach Danny Herodetzky until the second Monday morning in January. That kind of time lag for mail was usual for the military, Danny thought disgustedly as he huddled cross-legged on his bunk in the deserted barracks, his unopened letter on his lap and his extra blanket around his shoulders to ward off the morning chill. To be fair to the Army, however, his mail had been chasing him throughout his training. This latest letter from his father was addressed to him at the Army Air Corps Basic Flying School in Independence, Kansas. He'd graduated from there weeks ago and come to Eagle Pass, Texas, for advanced training.

The base was on the Rio Grande about a hundred miles north of Laredo. The grounds had long ago been cleared for airstrips, leaving the area nothing but a dark brown crust eternally baking beneath the Texas sun. In winter it was a pale ghost of itself but still one hell of a sun for a boy brought up in the canyons of New York City.

You didn't have to travel far to appreciate the rugged grandeur of the landscape, to marvel at the distant ocher buttes shimmering in the heat, at the yucca and mesquite and all their twisted prickly brother cacti.

This was a place tailor-made to satisfy the fantasy of the fellow who dreamed of mounting up and riding the range with Hopalong Cassidy, spurs on his heels and a six-gun on his hip.

The thing was, there was nobody like that around here. The men dreamed of flying single-engine fighters. They didn't want to ride; they wanted to soar through these flat gun-metal Texas skies with half a dozen fifty-cals spitting fire from beneath their eagles' wings.

It was just eleven. Danny was not scheduled for his training flight until the afternoon. He'd brought his letter back to the barracks because nobody was ever around here at this hour of the day. Danny liked to savor his mail from home; sometimes he even liked to read certain passages out loud to capture the inflections. A guy couldn't do something that screwy in front of the other cadets.

Dear Son,   12/2/44

Your letter of November tenth reached home safely and I read it out loud to all my friends. When I got to the part where you described the air maneuvers you are learning, those twists and turns and so forth, they all clapped for you and said how brave you were.

Here's a good laugh. I'm sure you remember Leo Gorfine. He was here that day, and when I read aloud about how hard you found it to do an Immelmann loop in your airplane, Leo, who don't hear so good anymore, says, "Immelmann? Tell Danny I knew a fellow named Immelmann. He was a rag-picker on Hester Street." Well, son, as you can imagine, we all had a good laugh on him here at the store.

About the store, you wouldn't recognize it these days. Gone are the meat case and the dairy cooler. We kept the little freezer so after the war we can maybe sell ice cream, and we kept the cooler for soda pop. But we tore out the old produce bins and the shelves are mostly cleared. I say good riddance. All that points stuff was giving me a headache. Now where the produce used to be, I got a card table and plenty of comfortable chairs bought second hand. Shumel and the others sit and read the papers or play a card game. I sit in my rocker behind the counter in case somebody should come in for some cigarettes or gum—recently I got plenty of gum and tobacco to sell. A good sign this terrible war is about over. Anyway, if you saw me you'd laugh. I got a pretty easy life, you'd say, and I'd have to agree. Oh well, your father has worked pretty hard in his day, I guess.

Your sister is doing well at her job. She tells me she has a boyfriend—imagine that. Thank God, I say. But she won't tell me who it is. Well, she is entitled to her privacy. In answer to your question, I have not seen her apartment. She invites me plenty and offers to take me and bring me home in a taxi, but what we can't figure is how to get me up those four flights of stairs. In my younger days it would have been no big deal, son, but now I can't do it, I'm sorry to say. Maybe when you come home you can fly me in an airplane up there! What do you say?

Speaking of my health, I am feeling strong. It seems my heart attack was so long ago. Shumel (he sents his best regards, by the way) keeps an eye on me, I keep an eye on him, and we manage. About the you-know-what, I tell you it is a thing of the past for your father. I'll never touch another drop of you-know-what except maybe a toast to my son when he comes home.

Well, I guess the big news is about the recent Presidential election. There was a little to-do about this being Roosevelt's fourth term, but all the kvetching came to nothing. Most voters felt like me, that FDR has done right, and you don't change horses in midstream. He's done all right against that bastard Hitler and those Japs so far. Mark my words, son, now that he's re-elected he will do something for the Jewish refugees, and all this tummel about how he is against us will vanish. He will act on the refugees' behalf. He must.

It wasn't until after you left us last summer that the newspapers began to let on about what the Russians discovered during their advance into Poland and that this horrible Majdanek extermination camp is only the beginning. They say to be prepared for what our own brave soldiers will discover as they push on into Germany.

It has taken me a long while to write about these things to you. I figured you had enough on your mind, but then I realized that you are probably reading the papers like everybody else. When I try to go to sleep at night I cannot because my mind dwells on the horror. During the day, in the store, I look at the old Coca-Cola clock on the wall, I straighten the stacks of Wrigley's Spearmint and I think my sane, familiar world is as unreal to the concentration camp victims as theirs is to me.

So I cheer on the Russians, and believe me, they are no saints either. I just wish the Stalin bastards and the Nazi bastards would kill each other off. Then at last the Jews could live in peace.

Anyway, FDR will fix things up for the poor refugees like he fixed up the Depression, just as soon

as he's done with our country's enemies. I'm praying
that maybe it'll end before more young men (not
mentioning any names) have to fight.

>   Your loving father,
>   Abe Herodetsky

Danny carefully refolded the letter, slipped it back
into its envelope and deposited it on top of the stack in a
corner of his foot locker.

He began to gather up his flying gear prior to heading
out to the airstrip. He put away his uniform and struggled
into his overalls, boots and leather jacket. He paused a
moment, as he always did, to ponder his goggles and snug
leather helmet. Vivid boyhood memories of Smilin' Jack
and Scorchy Smith reverberated within.

Then and now, Danny thought, I'm becoming what I
want to be. Goggles and a helmet were the pilot's symbols,
and they'd been issued to him by the United States Army.

Last summer Danny had reported to San Antonio
Aviation Cadet Center, an enormous and bewildering
complex. Right next door was the preflight school, but
there were obstacles to be overcome before a would-be
pilot could move over there.

Danny took a battery of physical and psychological
exams and along with the others waited nervously for the
results to be posted along with the dreaded G.D.O.—ground
duty only—list. There were plenty of washouts. During this
period of tests and endless marching drills the candidates
were asked to list on a scale of one to ten their preferences
for assignments: bombardier, navigator, pilot. Danny crossed
out the first two categories and boldly underlined the last.
He intended to be a fighter pilot, and he didn't figure he'd
get there by being reticent about his intentions.

The first round of tests was over and the considerably

thinned ranks of recruits could officially call themselves
aviation cadets. They were moved across the field to tackle
nine weeks of preflight instruction.

Danny discovered that preflight was very much like
boot camp, only worse. In addition to the physical drills,
surprise inspections, guard duty and KP there was classroom work in science, math, and physics and on military
protocol.

Danny worked hard, and when the numbers and facts
began to blur together and failure tried to close in, he
thought about himself in his fighter, skimming the tops
right off the clouds, and redoubled his efforts. He was
smart. He could do it if he tried. His only real fear was
that he would fail the physical tests—the high-altitude
chamber, for instance. His brain would not betray him, but
what about his body?

When the day for the altitude test came, Danny was
shaking with nervousness. One of the technicians noticed
and almost pulled him from the line, but he talked his way
into the chamber, which very much resembled a huge steel
oil drum turned on its side. He took his place on the hard
wooden bench. His oxygen mask muffled his prayers.

Danny made it through the altitude test and a week
later squeaked by on Morse code. Those two tests alone
wiped out a fifth of his class.

The next stop was primary flying school, Girder Field
near Pine Bluff, Arkansas. Danny arrived there in October
and was issued his flying gear, sheepskin-lined leather
pants, a jacket and a special helmet that would allow his
flight instructor to communicate with him when they went
up.

The Fairchild PT-19 was a big, beautiful brute with
sleek, low laminated wooden wings, a fabric-covered
fuselage, two open cockpits and a two-hundred horse-
power six-cylinder Ranger engine. The cadets were given

a parachute procedure briefing and then a familiarization ride.

Danny would never forget his first time. The instructor took in the rear cockpit and the cadet sat up front. The plane had no electrical system; it started up by hand cranking—the cadet's job. As soon as the engine caught, Danny stowed the crank and climbed aboard.

He plugged in to the communication system and heard his instructor say, "Sit back and enjoy the ride."

The PT-19 began to taxi, and then speedballed down the runway, wheels rumbling, engine screaming, and took off.

The wind tore at his goggles and pulled back the corners of his mouth into a mad dog's grin. Danny was mewling with fearful exhilaration as they banked and rolled through thin air. He found himself hanging from his seat straps. Earth was the sky, and the clouds were at his feet. He found himself pressed down into the cockpit as the plane clawed its way toward the sun, and suddenly the laws of physics and aeronautics made sense to him in a way they never had as equations on a blackboard.

After they landed Danny didn't want to leave the plane. How could he endure being earthbound after that?

"Well, what do you think?" his instructor asked slyly.

Danny's goggles were tear-streaked and his lips were dry, stretched, cracked. "I love it."

"Tomorrow you fly," the instructor drawled, and strode away.

"By the numbers. Brakes?"

"Set."

"Control?"

"Free."

"Gas on fuller tank and pressure up. Crank her up until that prop begins to roll.

"Taxi by making s-turns, and don't hit those brakes

too hard or you'll put her right on her nose. Check the sky
and then take her up.

"By the numbers. Fly straight and level. Make those
turns without slipping and sliding. Watch your turn and
bank indicator, cadet. The little black ball in the glass tube
stays right in the middle if you do it right."

By the numbers. Stalls, both with power on and
power off. The instructor would throttle back until the
engine was idling and haul the control stick right into his
crotch to get the nose up. Meanwhile, he'd be tap-dancing
on his rudder pedals to keep her from swinging right to
left. As the aircraft slows and its nose rises, there is no
longer sufficient lift to keep it airborne. The control stick
and rudders begin to float, and the aircraft trembles as if in
anticipation—and then the stall. Push the stick forward
into a nose dive, and once air speed is reattained, level off.

And then the instructor drawled, "It's your turn."

Every man got eight to twelve hours of dual instruction,
and after that if you didn't wash out the day would come
when you demonstrated everything you'd learned to your
instructor. Then he'd mutter something like, "I could use
a cup of joe, so if you want to take a little spin around on
your own, you might as well."

And then you did, and most made it, though somebody always didn't. If that unfortunate managed to parachute out, if he managed to walk away from it, if he didn't
crash and burn, he'd be a washout. Everyone would shrug
and pretend they weren't all pale and stricken and thankful
it wasn't them and echo what the instructors always said.
"He wasn't flying the plane; the plane was flying him . . ."

Following that solo was training in flying by instruments and the aerobatic maneuvers that are a fighter pilot's
stock in trade. A lot of cadets decided to be bomber and
transport pilots at that point, and there were more crashes
and burns.

By then it was November and the sky was grey

cotton-wool, the cold awesome. Danny liked it that way. Nobody wanted to go up in weather like that, which meant there was always a plane available for anyone who wanted to rack up double flight hours—guys like him, the crazy ones, the would-be fighter pilots.

In November, after seventy hours in PT-19s, Danny and his class moved on to Independence, Kansas, and basic flying school. Here they would log more hours in the air, this time in North American BT-14s, bigger than the PT-19 and twice as powerful. There was more aerobatics, far more satisfying in the heavier, more powerful BT-14. There were long cross-country solos and more classes in protocol.

At the end of basic came the final cut. There were hundreds more volunteers for single-engine advanced training than the army needed, and most cadets would be assigned to multi-engine training. Danny crossed his fingers, he prayed and he triumphed.

His orders read Eagle Pass, Texas, single-engine training. When he left there it would be in a box, as a washed-out former cadet—a new buck private in the Army—or as a fighter pilot with gold bars on his shoulders and silver wings pinned to his chest.

Danny wandered on down the airstrip, looking for his instructor and the plane he'd be taking up. As usual it was an AT-6, but with one vital difference. Today Danny drew one with a forward-firing machine gun in its nose. He was going to get his first opportunity to practice aerial gunnery.

There would be five other cadets taking turns blasting away at the banner target towed by airplane above an empty field. Scores could be sorted out because the bullet tips of each cadet's belt of ammo were painted an individual color. The paint ring on a bullet hole would later identify the shooter.

"How's your eye doing?" Danny's instructor said by way of greeting.

"It's just a shiner." Danny shrugged. "I can see okay." He got it in a fight last week with some Georgia cracker who cornered him in the latrine and demanded to see his Jew's horns. The guy got in his lucky punch to Danny's eye and Danny managed to land a right jab on the cracker's nose before they went into a clinch. The guy lost his footing, slipped on the wet floor and knocked himself out against the rim of a sink. That ended the fight and Danny's most recent experience of anti-Semitism. There'd not been as much of it as he'd feared, but then, he was coming into the military at a relatively late date.

Since the fight he and the cracker had stayed out of each other's way. Danny guessed all that noble stuff about guys having it out with their fists and then becoming the best of friends only happened in the movies.

"Well, you just remember to keep that shiner of yours on the turn and bank indicator. I don't want you forgetting everything you've learned just because you've got yourself a gunsight to look through."

"Yes, sir."

"And don't forget that you've only got a few seconds to make your approach, squeeze off a volley and get under the target."

"Yes, sir," Danny repeated a bit more impatiently.

The instructor scowled. "It's just that this here airplane cost Uncle Sam a pretty penny and I don't want some damn cadet cracking her up."

Danny grinned. His instructor was a real tiger in the air and a good teacher, even if he was something of a mother hen at times. The two men shook hands, and then Danny climbed into the cockpit and took off.

He had done as much ground training as possible in preparation for this day. They all became expert skeet-shooters, the theory being that shooting clay pigeons would hone their ability to hit fast-moving enemy fighters.

Danny took his position in the spread rectangular

flight formation a thousand feet above the target and waited for it to be his turn to attack, thinking back on what his father had written.

It seemed ironic that his father was praying for the war to end before his son got a taste of it. Danny was praying for exactly the opposite.

He was following the news and worrying himself sick over the possibility that he would never get to see action. The papers were full of stories about the thousand bomber armadas escorted by long-range fighters that had pounded Germany. General Eisenhower proclaimed to his ground forces, "If you see fighting aircraft over you, they will be ours." A GI might cheer such words, but they were not the sort of thing a fledging pilot with dreams of being an ace wanted to hear.

The Luftwaffe was far from being broken, Danny knew; on New Year's Day hundreds of German fighter-bombers had hurled themselves at the Allied airfields of Holland, Belgium and northern France in an attempt to shore up the crumbling German ground forces battling in the Ardennes. Since last summer they'd been sending up a new kind of plane, a jet, which flew without a propeller.

Nevertheless, Danny was in a race against time and time was winning out. If the war in Europe ended, he'd be out of it for good. There was no chance of his going to the Pacific. The Navy had retaken the Philippines and the sky was clear of Jap Zeros. There were still kamikazes to worry the aircraft carriers closing in on Japan, but with a British carrier force expected to lend a hand, there'd be no call for green pilots.

He peeled out of the flight formation and began his firing pass, steepening his bank to move his gunsight ahead of the target. He squeezed the trigger, felt the recoil tremor as the gun chattered, and then he was slipping beneath the towline before climbing back up to the formation.

He made ten passes that afternoon, and each time he wondered if this was as close to aerial combat as he was going to get.

They had a lot more gunnery practice and night flying and flying blind. The instructor would ride in the front cockpit to line up the craft on the strip's center line. The cadet would be in the rear under a hood. The lesson to be learned was how to take off using only your instruments.

On Sunday, January fourteenth, the Eighth Air Force resumed large-scale operations after a month-long interval during the Battle of the Bulge. Oil targets in Germany were attacked and heavy enemy fighter forces were encountered.

Solo cross-country night flights with nothing but the radium dials of the instruments and the dragon roar of the engine to keep you company against the endless velvety darkness lorded over by a leering sliver of moon. Then more ground school, more classes in protocol.

On January twenty-sixth the Russians isolated German forces in Prussia only a hundred sixty-one kilometers from Berlin.

On January thirty-first elements of the United States First Army crossed the German border.

Six-turn spins, slow rolls and flying upside down; more gunnery practice and at last graduation time drew near.

On February fourth Churchill, Roosevelt and Stalin met at Yalta in the Crimea. Germany, it was decided, would be divided into four zones of occupation.

It was traditional for instructors to take a final ride with their students just before graduation. As Danny expertly flew through the crisp February sky, his instructor spoke to him over the intercom.

"You're one hell of a flier, Dan."

"Thanks."

"You might have been one hell of an ace—"

Might have been? No! Oh, no! Danny pressed the button on his mike. "I'm gonna graduate, aren't I?"

"Of course you are, kid. You're gonna get your gold bars and your wings, and we'll even give you guys some P-40 training for old time's sake. But none of you are going to war, kid. We just got the word. Chances are you'll be mustered out before those wings even get tarnished."

On graduation day Danny and the rest exchanged their cadet's uniforms for officer's garb. They pinned their new second-lieutenant's bars onto their epaulets and stood at attention as they were presented with their silver wings.

Daniel Herodetzky, not yet nineteen years old, was a rated pilot and an officer in the Army Air Corps. He was saluted by enlisted men. He moved from the cadets' barracks to bachelor officers' quarters. He ate in the officers' mess and drank in the officers' club. As his instructor had promised, he received some flight time with a P-40, the shark-nosed fighter made famous by the exploits of Chennault's Flying Tigers, a volunteer group in China.

And it was ashes to Danny because now it was just play. He could continue to read about the winding down of the war in the newspapers; they didn't need him. Thanks anyway, kid.

He would not be going home like Smilin' Jack, or good old Scorchy, but untested, untried, a cherry.

He'd never know if he could have been a hero, if he had what it took. He'd missed his chance to find out and there wasn't a damned thing he could do to get that chance back again.

Chapter 48

Tel Aviv

After his arrest Herschel Kol found himself in a shuttered room with a mattress on the floor and a guard always at the locked door. Different guards brought him his meals and escorted him to the outhouse in the back yard of the house he was held in. He couldn't be sure of his whereabouts, but from the glimpse of an open field beyond the yard's fence and the scent of citrus in the air, Herschel guessed that he was somewhere in northern Tel Aviv, a rural part of the city known for its orange groves.

His guards were Jews, which could only mean that he was a prisoner of Haganah and that this was one of their safe houses. Two guards came for him late one night. Waking him up, they dragged him from his mattress and downstairs to the basement.

He steeled himself for the worst. The fact that he was a prisoner of Jews did not mean that he would be gently treated, and a Jewish hand holding a club would not make the blow any less painful. He was determined not to talk. The fact that his captors were Jews only deepened his resolve. No quarrel was as bitter as a family quarrel.

The basement was well lit and very clean, with white-washed cinder-block walls. Herschel allowed himself a spark of hope when he saw that there was no interrogation equipment there. The only furnishings were a plain wooden table and two chairs.

"Sit," one of the guards ordered in Hebrew. He sat under his escort's eyes, his back to the stairs, and waited. He rested his hands on the table and found that it was wobbly. He idly shook it a few times.

He heard the steps creaking as somebody came down. He did not turn around, but kept wobbling the table. His jailbird habits had come right back to him, he realized. Prisoners usually turned childish, and here he was.

"You two can go," the newcomer told the guards in Hebrew.

A sabra, Herschel thought, listening to the accent.

The guards left. Herschel glanced up at the man taking the chair across the table. The newcomer was heavy-set with broad shoulders and close-cropped thinning hair. He had high cheekbones that lent an almost Oriental cast to his features and a parrot's beak of a nose. He wore a black patch over his left eye.

"Herschel," the man said brightly, "I apologize for how you've been treated. I've been very busy, else I would have gotten to you before now. I say, it has been a long time, yes?"

Herschel rubbed his sleepy eyes. "Do I know you?"

"We were quite good boyhood friends, but my family moved from Degania in 1922. I'm Moshe Dayan."

Dayan! Herschel was only ten at the time, but he well remembered his old friendship.

"Moshe, of course I remember you now," Herschel said truthfully, thinking fast. "For old time's sake, can you get me out of here?"

Dayan laughed. "You're certainly an Irgunist, I see. There's nothing you won't exploit."

"You have no reason to act superior," Herschel said harshly. "Not when Haganah seems to be arm in arm with the CID. The British arrested me, and yet here I am in one of your safehouses. Tell me, do you really think it prudent to let the CID know your hideouts?"

"They don't know where our hideouts are, Herschel. This place and others like it are being used specifically for this operation. The British have no idea where Haganah goes to ground."

"You going to let me go or not?"

Dayan nodded. "You are free to go," he began, but when Herschel stood up, he added, "after you hear me out."

"Either I'm free or I'm not."

"Please don't make me summon the guards."

Herschel shrugged and sat back down.

Dayan's one eye sparkled with amusement. He looks more like a parrot than I first thought, Herschel mused, watching the way Dayan cocked and turned his head to focus upon him.

Kol indicated the eyepatch. "What happened?"

"In '39, when the political winds changed and the British began to worry about the Axis influence on the Arabs, they decided to prove how evenhanded they were by arresting some Haganah men. I got five years. In '41 they let me out the same as you, because I volunteered for a commando mission. We were in Syria and I was looking through a pair of binoculars." He shrugged. "Some sniper got in a lucky shot and my eye was gone."

"You made out better than Raziel at any rate," Herschel said. "What is it you want to talk to me about? Make it quick, please. I'd like to get out of here."

"And you will, Herschel, that I promise. Whether you agree to what I ask or not, you'll be free to go. We need your help, my old friend."

Herschel began to laugh. "Haganah—Ben-Gurion—

needs my help? What for, Moshe? You've got the British, yes? They will hand Haganah a little piece of Palestine because you have behaved and asked politely. So why should you need the help of a—what have you called us?—a maniac, a gangster, a terrorist?''

"The British will give us nothing. They will not make good on any promises. We all know that.''

"We do?''

"The British have told us what is expedient. Once the war is over they refuse to antagonize the Arabs and risk driving them into the Russian fold.''

"Then why have you helped them?''

"Because terrorism will rob us of sympathy. Herschel, what's happened between our organizations is ugly, I don't deny it, but it has been necessary. If we give the world an excuse to hate Jews, they will gladly take it. It's far more convenient for the powers that be to focus on Moyne's assassination than on the plight of the refugees in internment camps.'' Dayan frowned.

"You see, Irgun ideas are right, but the timing is all wrong. We must bide our time until the British reveal themselves as liars. Then we can begin to drive them out. Given a couple of years the British will withdraw from Palestine, confident that the Arabs will accomplish what has so far proved to be beyond Hitler's reach. The white paper's goal of an Arab Palestine will have been realized. Nobody will blame the British, and the world will go on merrily enjoying the region's output of petroleum.''

"It sounds to me like Ben-Gurion owes Begin an apology.''

"What's befallen the Irgun is its own fault,'' Dayan insisted. "Begin was given every opportunity to fall into line behind the establishment. He had his chance—''

"Like I'm having mine?''

Dayan regarded him. "I told you you'd be released no matter what, and I meant it. I am offering you a chance

to aid your organization by helping us. So far we've been
able to hold our own against the Arabs, but Jewish boys
repelling a Bedouin raid on an agricultural settlement is
one thing; the Jewish people defending themselves against
tens of thousands of British-trained soldiers of the Arab
Legion is quite something else. We—Haganah, Irgun and
LEHI—can train the manpower, but we don't have the
guns.''

It was all true, of course. Herschel had just spent a
year at various Irgun training camps and had helped write
a manual on the Bren gun, but not enough of these weapons were available. Fewer than one in ten had been issued
a weapon, and most of those were revolvers.

''You said that by helping you, I can also help the
Irgun. How so?''

''The three resistance organizations will all be in the
same boat when the British break their word. They—we—
will form the core of the army that will win the homeland.
Don't you agree?''

''I suppose,'' Herschel replied, ''but where do I fit
in?''

''You've become something of a weapons-expert in
the last year. You know not only how to use existing
weapons but how to make rudimentary arms. Isn't that
correct?''

Herschel shrugged. ''Pipe bombs, very primitive single-
shot pistols, a crude mortar—I tell you, Moshe, it was
more for morale than anything. You give a man a weapon—
any weapon—and he doesn't feel so powerless.''

Dayan nodded, smiling. ''Yes.'' His fingertips nervously tapped the tabletop. ''Before I tell you what it is we
want from you, I'll tell you what we can do for you. Our
relationship with the British is such that we could get you
a pardon. Your record would be clean. There'd be no more
threat of prison.''

"That would be very nice for me. Now suppose you tell me what it is you want."

"We are establishing a network all across the world to search for weapons. We will import all we can. Some of our people are finding guns and others are finding the money to pay for them. The arms we acquire will be distributed equally."

"So you want me to act as the Haganah's arms buyer?" Herschel asked.

"As one of them, yes. As I've said, there will be a network and you would be a part of it."

"Why are you doing this? For me, I mean. Here you are offering me what amounts to a full pardon to join in a cooperative effort that could proceed very well without me."

"We have no shortage of volunteers, but not so many are technically knowledgeable. We will come across many arms brokers who want to sell us junk, so men like you, who can tell what's good from what isn't, are very valuable." Dayan looked down at the table. "But it's more than that, Herschel. You see, I remember a conversation we had when we were boys. I was bragging about being named after a hero. You shamed me by telling me about your father. 'He's the real hero,' you maintained."

"I remember that very well," Herschel said. "I was still mourning him, I suppose."

"I'm offering you an opportunity to be just as much of a hero as your father. He did not shirk his duty and you must not. You speak English and you have the technical expertise to do the job, and so you must do it. The old generation were giants, and now we must be giants if the dream is to endure."

"Enough." Herschel smiled. "I'll do it. After all, my father did not hesitate to go to the rescue of his Moshe."

"Good." They shook hands, but when Dayan mentioned that Herschel should join Haganah, he refused.

"No more oaths. What use are they? Is it kiss the Bible and touch the pistol or the other way around, comrade?"

"You needn't join if you don't want it," Dayan said neutrally.

"You mentioned speaking English as a qualification for the job. I take it you're sending me to London?"

Dayan shook his head. "America."

PART IV

DREAMS REALIZED

Chapter 49

New York, 1945

Carl left the lobby of the East Side apartment building and after a moment's indecision decided to walk home. He had given his driver the weekend off and taken a taxi to Sonneborn's brunch. The temperature was in the nineties on this Sunday afternoon in July, but he was dressed for the weather in a white linen suit Becky had coerced onto his back. Well, he guessed man could not live in dark blue tropical worsted alone, and his suit did tie in with the festive mood of the city since V-E Day. Besides, linen was rather comfortable if one was intent on strolling Manhattan during a heat wave.

He did his second-best thinking on his feet. He did his best thinking on horseback, but it was late in the afternoon, too late to squeeze in a ride and still be on time at Becky's.

As he walked up Fifth Avenue, his mind went back over the extraordinary events of the morning. He had only a nodding acquaintance with Rudolf Sonneborn. He knew the family had made its money in oil and chemicals and that Sonneborn had an interest in Palestine. Carl doubted he would have thought to invite him if it hadn't been for their mutual friend Wendell Pearlmutter.

Wendell had a chain of tanneries and had supplied shoe leather to the government during the war. Yes, it was Wendell who got him the invitation to the brunch, although at this point Carl wasn't at all sure he appreciated it.

There were twenty or so others there. Some of the men Carl more or less knew from around town or at Jewish affairs. Others from out of town he knew by reputation only. The guest of honor was an elfin, white-haired little Palestinian who would have made a good Santa Claus for Pickman's Christmas season—If Ben-Gurion consented to grow a white beard and exchange his open-necked shirt and baggy pants for a red suit and cap.

Carl and the others listened to the spokesman for the Jews of Palestine. His speech was one part history lesson and one part predictions for Zionism.

"As the Jews have been betrayed before, they will be betrayed again. The Jews of Palestine can no longer beg the world's permission to survive. The world in which we all live is a barbaric place, and we Jews must make our own way and fend for ourselves if the homeland is to exist. The refugees will be brought to Palestine in defiance of the British, and a Jewish army will be formed to defend its people when the British turn loose the Arabs to do their dirty work."

Carl and the others listened, leaning forward in their chairs and straining to make out what the fast-talking, emotional Ben-Gurion was saying in his thick English as he restlessly paced the parquet floor of Sonneborn's crowded penthouse apartment. A cloud of smoke hovered in the still, sweltering air although the windows were thrown open in the hope of catching a breeze.

From where Carl was seated he could see a barge

peacefully making its way along the East River. He watched it and was mesmerized by its wake as the talk of DP camps and duplicitous British officials and fairytale armies marching under the Star of David swirled around him. Finally he lost himself in thoughts of Becky.

How exquisite it was to make love to her. How delicious it would be to make love tonight. He'd been bedding her at her little aerie overlooking the Hudson twice or thrice weekly. He was a silver-haired stallion perhaps, but a stallion nevertheless. He almost always used precautions, but occasionally not. Those were the warmest, sweetest, best times, when Becky said it was safe for her. Carl secretly hoped she was wrong and would get pregnant. He fully intended to ask her to marry him when his divorce was final. Perhaps if she was pregnant she'd accept.

When he was with her he hadn't a care in the world, but as soon as they parted the most awful ruminations entered his mind: that she would succumb to the charms of a damnable young war hero with a brawny chest full of medals.

If such adolescent heartsick pangs were unseemly for a man of his age and stature, so be it. Carl was marking his sixtieth year, and so he welcomed this second adolescence as a gift.

It was Becky who persuaded him to accept Sonneborn's invitation. He didn't want to come, but the plight of the refugees and Palestine in general was very close to Becky's heart. She said he should go to the meeting, and so he had. He could refuse her nothing, even if his instincts had warned him that something more than his money was going to be asked of him.

Wendell, seated nearby, jolted Carl out of his fantasies by loudly questioning Ben-Gurion. Carl blushed as if his romantic reveries were revealed to the room at large. At that point he brought his attention back to the present.

"All this talk about fighting the Arabs." Pearlmutter looked both angry and disgusted. "With all due respect, we *Americans* have just fought a war, and it looks as if we still have a nasty time ahead of us in the Pacific. When that's over we'd like to forget about fighting."

"You must not," Ben-Gurion said. "It was the Jews' tendency to avoid violence, to abhor fighting, that led them to the extermination camps."

"Very well," Pearlmutter allowed grudgingly. "We all mourned the loss of our President in April, but since Truman was inaugurated there's been some flexibility on the United States' position concerning the refugees. Truman has ordered Eisenhower to alleviate conditions in the European DP camps, and he's pressuring London to reopen Palestine—"

"Listen to me," Ben-Gurion broke in. "In February, when Roosevelt—may he rest in peace—was returning from Yalta, he stopped to pay a visit in Saudi Arabia, where he told the king that the United States supported an Arab Palestine. Your State Department is not so much in love with Jews, I think, and they wish America to have its share of Arab oil. Roosevelt was a nice man. Truman is a nice man as well, I suppose, but his good intentions will not bring about the homeland. That we must do for ourselves."

Ben-Gurion paused then; to Carl Pickman the little man looked very haggard indeed. "I know that what I'm asking is very difficult," he admitted. "You are all important men, highly visible in American Jewish society. You probably endorse assimilation, for look how well America has done by you. But will America embrace the refugees? No. Will England or France or any of the Allied nations? No. Can we send them back to Germany or Poland? Of course not. There is, however, one country that calls out in welcome to these Jews without a home. That country is Palestine. We will put the healthy to work and heal the sick. We will train them all to defend themselves so that what has just happened to the Jewish people will never happen again.''

"What is it you want?'' Carl Pickman heard himself asking. ''Is it money?''

''Money is always necessary,'' Ben-Gurion admitted, ''but I want none from any of you just now. I do ask that you keep in mind what we have discussed, that you talk among yourselves about these issues during the coming months. When the time is right, we will be in contact with you. Until then I ask that you keep our discussion confidential. The more enthusiastic among you may want to keep a list of potential recruits, but approach no one until things can be spelled out to you.''

At that point the meeting broke up into small clusters. Ben-Gurion circulated while Sonneborn's servants began to set out a cold buffet. Carl had always hated that point when the time for business had passed and he was expected to make small talk. Anyway, he had no appetite for cold cuts and cheeses after listening to Ben-Gurion's unsettling speech. He sought out his host and thanked him; Pearlmutter approached and offered to show Carl to the door.

''What do you think?'' Pearlmutter asked him once they were alone in Sonneborn's hallway.

''I think we've been involved in some kind of conspiracy, and I don't like it one bit,'' Carl muttered. ''Old Henry Ford—damn him and his miserable Protocols of Zion—would have the last laugh if this meeting ever got to the newspapers.'' He shivered.

''I think it's worse than that,'' Wendell replied as they reached the door. ''A little tame conspiracy is one thing.'' He sighed morosely. ''You know what? I think he's expecting us to break the law.''

*   *   *

On Becky's terrace that night she begged him to tell her everything. Carl tried to explain that it was confidential, but he did admit that Ben-Gurion had been there. Becky's lovely dark eyes went wide at that tidbit. She pestered him, and the night was sultry, and her perfume and silken dressing gown so intoxicating, and of course he could never deny her anything, so why even try?

After he told her, she led him to her bed and unwound her silky wrap, and there was nothing she denied him.

Chapter 50

New York

"Rebecca, you haven't heard a word I said," Carl scolded.

"Of course I have," Becky lied, then exploded with embarrassed laughter. "I'm sorry, darling." She squeezed his arm as they strolled through Central Park. "My mind is still on this morning's headlines about the new Labour government in England. Oh, how I despise that man Bevin. He gets to be prime minister, and then he breaks his word and upholds the white paper. He has the gall to say that if the Jews get too pushy it'll lead to anti-Semitism—"

"My dear, I'm afraid you're obsessed with this Palestine refugee situation."

"I am not." She paused. "Sonneborn hasn't been in touch yet, I suppose?"

"Becky!" Carl led her toward a park bench. "I don't disapprove of your interest in the matter, but you are obsessed."

"I'm sorry." She leaned against him, resting her head on the velvet collar of his overcoat. "I appreciate how much the Pickmans have done for the needy all over the world, but to you personally the plight of the refugees is impossibly remote. You've got to understand, Carl, that where I grew up, the goings-on in Palestine and the pros and cons of the various forms of Zionism were discussed as if the Mideast were part of the neighborhood. As a kid I walked past the Palestine Relief Collection Agency storefronts on East Broadway. I've moved away from there, but the old neighborhood is still a part of me."

"I don't see how that can be more important to you than our relationship."

"You don't understand." She dug into her purse for a cigarette.

It was a fine fall afternoon, a Thursday. They'd left the store a little early in order to enjoy the foliage gone crimson and gold beneath autumn's cool caress. All of the hoopla of V-J Day—of Japan's will to fight being broken by America's secret weapon, the A-bomb—had begun to fade with summer. The soldiers had come home and the nation was gearing down for peacetime.

Not far from where they were sitting a few boys were playing catch. The blustery weather had fanned the youngsters' cheeks to a rosy glow. They laughed and shouted, and Becky and Carl sat stolidly on their park bench and pretended to watch. They always felt uncomfortable with each other when the differences in their upbringings and outlooks sprang up between them, when they realized that more separated them than the few miles between upper Fifth Avenue and the Lower East Side.

One of the boys playing ball threw wild and the eraser-pink spauldeen went off-course toward their bench. Carl caught it and pegged it back.

"Not bad," Becky ventured.

"My dear girl," Carl began, his green eyes glittering in the frosty sunshine, "the mere fact that I've never enjoyed the dubious pleasure of playing stickball in the slimy gutters of your nasty neighborhood—"

Becky, hugging him, threw back her head and laughed

richly. A cavorting Dalmatian, attracted by the sound, veered toward them. Its coal-black nose was wet and shiny and its breath puffed clouds. The dog rested its head momentarily in each of their laps and then bounded off. Its master tipped his hat to them as he ambled along the path.

"We've got a brace of Irish setters at the house," Carl observed mildly, flicking doghairs off his coat.

"The house?"

"What I was asking you while you were off battling Mr. Bevin in Parliament was whether you'd care to spend this weekend in the country."

"At your house?"

"Yes, of course. I would have asked you long before this, but my wife and daughters were there for most of the season. Now my children are back at school and my wife is in Atlanta."

How odd, Becky thought. There was still so much about Carl and his world that she didn't know and never thought to ask about. He must think her terribly naive, but maybe it was her way of keeping him at arm's length. And isn't that an odd way to think about the man you take to bed, she chided herself. She was certainly very fond of him. He was physically attractive; he was a masterful, powerful man, and yet sometimes ingenuous.

Nonetheless, what she felt for him wasn't love. When she and Carl made love she felt warm and motherly toward him, and that was all she felt. She didn't know if that was her fault or his; maybe fault was the wrong word. She couldn't bring herself to ask advice on the matter; she would rather die than suffer the humiliation of discussing such private things with someone else.

Their relationship was common knowledge at work by now, but nobody dared to say anything. Anyway, nobody could snicker at her for being a kept woman; she was still more than earning her salary as Pickman's advertising manager. Last summer the women's magazines had been running such articles as "Welcoming Home the Returning Veteran" and "How to Redecorate the Boudoir" and "Recipes to Convince Your Man that He's Not in the Army Now." It was on the basis of those magazines Becky had scheduled her promotions for the store's restocked cookware assortments and the new, frilly decorating fabrics in Domestics. Her best idea, which had gotten Pickman's some newspaper publicity, was her ad offering a free pair of argyle socks to any serviceman who wore his uniform into Pickman's and bought a set of civvies. Their stock of suits was snatched off the racks in three days.

"Never underestimate the power of the word 'free,' " Becky said when the business reporter for the *Times* interviewed her for the article. The next day there she was, quoted in black and white, just like a VIP.

She was making more money, although not nearly as much as if she'd accepted any of several job offers from Pickman's competition. She'd turned those offers down out of loyalty to the store and to Carl, who had given her the opportunity to prove herself. Her own staff and all the employees of Pickman's were like family to her, and she didn't need more money. She had enough for fine clothes and to buy a car as soon as they were available again.

"It would be fun to spend the weekend out of the city," Becky said brightly, then laughed. "I don't know if it would, actually. I've never been."

"Splendid. We'll leave tomorrow night after dinner. I'll telephone the housekeeper and have our rooms prepared." He smiled excitedly. "We'll have great fun. We'll go riding."

"You'll go riding," Becky firmly corrected him. "I'll be waiting for you with the liniment."

Carl smiled and patted her hand. "I'll drive. We'll take the roadster."

*　　*　　*

Before the Depression there were hundreds of mansions along the Gold Coast, Long Island's north shore, Carl told Becky that Friday night as they drove along the Northern State Parkway. The more modest had been built by film stars, but the true castles belonged to the men who ruled the oil and railroads, the banks and the stock market.

The Vanderbilts and Morgans and Schiffs and Lehmans had built their estates and villas and chateaus out here and put up high, thick walls.

These men controlled the money, which meant they controlled the elected officials in Albany. They used their influence to get permission to incorporate their estates as villages, which allowed them to set their own rules regarding what constituted loitering and trespassing. The only police in the area were private guards.

Most important, there were no roads. Henry Ford might have put America on wheels, but without decent highways, what use was a car? The rabble could not penetrate Long Island.

"Robert Moses changed that," Carl explained, his eyes on the road as they sped along through the night. Becky could not tell from his neutral inflection how he felt about that change.

"In the late twenties Moses solidified his political base," Carl said. "In the thirties it was his shrewdness, determination and vision—and his ability to control public opinion—that crumbled those high thick walls and thrust public highways through the hearts of the grand estates."

"It's a good thing, too," Becky said.

"Is it? Or should I ask, was it? After all, it's pretty much over and done with now. The beginning of the end, as they say."

"But Carl, there are so many people. I mean, the few can't shut out the many forever."

Carl glanced at her. "You say that now, but what will you say when you're rich?"

"Oh, don't be a tease."

"Well, never mind the future. It's the weekend we've got, and it'll be beautiful. Most everyone prefers the summer, but the fall in the country is my favorite time."

"Mine, too," Becky said, then very shyly added, "I'm glad we're doing this, Carl."

He took his hand from the steering wheel long enough to caress her cheek. Becky leaned back against the leather seat and watched the markers along the parkway blur past.

Carl's roadster turned out to be a Cadillac convertible. It was black but otherwise identical to the one Benny Talkin used to drive. Seeing this onyx incarnation made Becky's heart falter. She prepared to welcome back her old friend, the blues, but this time the torch she'd been carrying for Benny all this while never flamed.

To her surprise she had to admit that her fling with Benny really was ancient history. She hadn't seen him since that rainy day a year ago.

Sure, it was ancient history, and now she found that the hurt had healed over, though there would always be a scar.

"It's not much farther," Carl announced. He slowed the Cadillac and turned off the parkway onto a two-lane macadamized road. He was an excellent driver, and he handled this road's dark turns and twists as easily as the parkway's straightaways.

The Cadillac's high beams picked up a pair of stone posts flanking a turnoff. Becky managed to read a carved wooden sign proclaiming the place to be Salem Farm.

"After the town north of Boston," Carl volunteered, "the site of the first Pickman's."

Becky also noticed far more prosaic signs proclaiming No Trespassing, Private Property. Every day, it seemed, such warnings were applying less and less to her.

They came around a bend and caught their first glimpse of the house. Even in the dark the lines of the whitewashed brick house were easily discernible, for every one of its tall, slender casement windows was ablaze with light.

"Oh, Carl—oh, my God."

He chuckled at the catch in her voice as he brought the car to a stop in the cobblestoned front court. "It is rather impressive, lit up that way. I'm almost—" He winked, "—*almost* embarrassed to say it's our tradition to have all the lights on when the head of the family arrives. Those lights once burned for my father, and someday I hope they'll burn for my son." He was looking at her so intently that Becky felt a shiver up her spine. Then he laughed. "Unless, of course, your great Robert Moses turns Salem Farm into a parkway rest stop. Come along, my dear. We've already kept Mr. and Mrs. Cody up past their bedtime."

He came around to her side of the car and opened the door. As they walked up the flagstones, the massive oak front door swung open, spilling out bright, warm light.

"Welcome, sir," Mrs. Cody cried out. She was a short, stout grey-haired woman in her sixties, dressed in a high-necked, long-sleeved dress, a cardigan and an immaculate white apron. Her husband, tall and thin, looked very much like a rough-hewn Franklin Roosevelt. He was wearing tan corduroy trousers, work boots and a black turtleneck sweater. He shook hands with Carl in a grave and dignified manner.

"Good to have you back, sir. You've been too long away."

"Thank you, Cody. It has been almost a year, hasn't it? Miss Herodetzky, may I introduce Ed and Emily Cody. They take care of things around here."

"I'll get the bags, sir," Ed Cody said. "Excuse me, Miss Herodetzky."

"I've got a snack for you in the pantry," Emily Cody chirped, "and I opened the wine to breathe, just as you instructed." She hurried off with their coats over her arm.

"It seems like such a huge place for just the two of them to maintain."

Carl laughed. "I'd say so. Twenty rooms downstairs, and on the second floor six bedroom suites and the nursery. Of course there's another fellow who looks after the stables, and in the summer we bring along some of the servants from town, but Ed Cody has authority over the grounds. I don't interfere with him. He hires on people for specific jobs as he needs them. In winter the house is shut down and the Codys retire to a snug little cottage on the edge of the woods."

He led her from the front hall into the heart of the house. To her left was a sunken ballroom with a wall of French doors and a massive oak serving bar. Directly before her was the sweep of the main staircase. Carl showed her the music room with its twenty-foot cathedral-beamed ceiling and the solarium, dark now, but Becky could imagine its glory when the potted palms, hanging plants and white wicker furniture were bathed in sunlight.

Becky felt overwhelmed, as lost as in a maze. She was relieved when they ended up in the library. Its warmth came from the intricate carved oak paneling as well as the merrily crackling fire and soothed her, and the relatively modest scale was a relief after the grandeur elsewhere.

She and Carl sat side by side in wing chairs, nibbling at snacks and wine. Becky tried to relax, but it wasn't easy. The house was just too big, its shadowy corners too remote to afford her a sense of shelter. She felt as vulnerable as if she were outside before a campfire.

She was also uneasy about the night ahead. Carl had never stayed the night at her apartment; he considered such behavior improper, especially for a married man, even in the process of divorce.

That was Carl's opinion about staying the night at her place. Becky assumed things would be different here at his own house. She wondered what it would be like to wake up together in the morning.

She was not to find out. Mrs. Cody was summoned to escort her upstairs to a guest suite. Her bath took up more space than her entire West Side apartment. Twin doors with lion's-head doorknobs led to the sitting room; the bedroom had intricate chinoiserie panels, wide-board pegged oak floors, hooked area rugs and a blazing fireplace. A pair of weeping stone angels supported the fireplace mantel. Once Becky was in bed with the lamp off and the flickering flames casting ominous shadows on the wall, she found that she was overtired and overexcited. Every time she closed her eyes she imagined those two brooding angels creeping toward her.

That took care of sleep. She lay stiff as a board, eyes wide, staring up at the ceiling, wishing she were home. Eventually she must have dozed off, because the next thing she knew the fire had died down to glowing embers and a hand, cold as stone, was brushing back her hair.

She almost screamed, but then she realized it was Carl, and his hands were freezing, so after he'd gotten into bed with her she took his hands and warmed them between her thighs. They made gentle love for a long time, which culminated when Carl cried out and she did not.

No matter, no matter.

Afterward they rested, limbs intertwined. Becky pleaded for him to stay the night, but he said he could not. It simply was not appropriate. There were appearances to uphold, but he promised to remain until she fell asleep.

She woke at seven-thirty. The fire was out. By day the brooding angels of stone seemed far less disquieting but just as sad.

Downstairs she found Mrs. Cody in the dining room. Mr. Pickman was riding and had asked that Miss Herodetzky meet him at the stables at noon. After breakfast Becky asked to see the kitchen. Mrs. Cody chuckled when Becky

went on to say she considered the kitchen to be the heart
and soul of a house. After her tour Becky went upstairs for
a sweater and outside to explore the grounds.

She spent two hours wandering through the gardens,
past the swimming pool, the lily ponds, the Victorian
wrought-iron gazebos and even a child-sized wishing well
surrounded by bronze statues of fairytale characters. Of
course the pool had been drained and the gardens were
straw-colored and lifeless now that it was fall, but the
landscaped grounds were still quite lovely in a melancholy
way. She came across Cody puttering at some task near
the garden wall. He answered her questions about the
estate, explaining that it ran seventy acres, mostly woods
and bridal paths.

One of the Irish setters needed only the slightest
coaxing to detach itself from Cody and come play. The
setter never tired of retrieving the stick Becky kept throwing.
Eventually she and her new friend headed over to the
stables, which were of brick and had a red-shingled curbed
roof crowned with a cupola and a weather vane.

She walked around the stables with the dog until she
happened past the window of a wood-paneled trophy room.
She tried the door, found it unlocked and went inside. The
walls bloomed with red, yellow and blue ribbons. Once
the satin had been fresh and bright, but now the ribbons
were dusty, fly-specked and mildewed. There were framed
photographs of Carl as he grew up, astride different horses
but always beaming triumphantly or being awarded his
ribbons. Carl had turned out ruggedly handsome, but what
a beautiful youth he had been. In some of the photographs
a dreamy-eyed older man was shaking hands with him in
an exaggerated display of congratulations. Becky recognized Bernard Pickman from the portraits in the store's
executive suite. There were no photographs of Carl with
his father.

The Irish setter, which had been lying across the

threshold, barked excitedly. A moment later Becky heard thudding hooves and ran outside in time to see Carl gallop through the stately stone arches that led from the beginnings of the bridal path to the main doors of the stables. He was dressed in boots, jodhpurs and a wool shirt; it was the first time Becky had ever seen him in anything but a business suit. His cheeks were ruddy and his emerald eyes exuberant. His grey hair, which he'd taken to wearing longer, was wind-tousled and curved in a roguish forelock across his brow.

"Becky, what a marvelous morning it's been," he cried, his voice deep and vibrant. He wheeled his horse—a big handsome roan, glistening from its run—and made it prance. Becky laughed and applauded; the setter went into a paroxysm of spinning, yipping excitement.

Watching Carl, Becky couldn't help thinking how much he still resembled that proud, happy boy in the trophy room photographs. He reined the horse to a stop and lithely dismounted before her. He smelled of sweat and leather and horse; he smelled altogether wonderful. Feverish with desire, Becky threw her arms around his neck and passionately kissed him.

Carl was trembling. "I love you so," he murmured, his voice husky with emotion.

I'll lure him into the stables, Becky thought. We'll fall back upon the piles of straw and he'll make love to me, and there'll be no holding back.

But then the stable doors creaked open and out shuffled the horse trainer, old Mr. McKay, eighty years old if a day. Carl stepped out of Becky's embrace and the rogue on horseback was once more the aloof, dignified lord of the manor.

McKay led away the roan and they walked back to the house, not touching. The dog did not follow. Carl went upstairs and Becky to the solarium. His scent was still upon her but fading fast.

*   *   *

Later Carl asked if she would mind having dinner in the kitchen with the Codys and McKay. Becky thought it would be far preferable to another self-conscious meal in the huge dining room. The kitchen was cavernous but homey.

That night they sat around one of the kitchen tables, ate roast beef and drank red wine while McKay told anecdotes about Carl's boyhood. Clearly the trainer's advanced age afforded him a privileged position, for Carl gracefully endured it. He seemed more relaxed than Becky had ever seen him, except perhaps for one raucous evening in a West Side spaghetti house.

Carl's good mood slipped a bit when Mrs. Cody rose to bring in dessert and Becky offered to get the coffee. She saw McKay's startled glance at her and sensed Carl's displeasure. At first she was embarrassed, then angry. To hell with knowing how to behave with servants. She'd grown up doing housework when she wasn't breaking her back in her father's store. She'd probably washed as many dishes and plucked as many chickens as Emily Cody, and she knew how to make borscht and do laundry, and she wasn't going to make a fool of herself by pretending anything else.

"I'll get the coffee," she repeated, feeling ornery and glaring at Carl.

He smiled thinly and looked away.

When she and Carl retired to the library he began at once. "Really, Becky, you were quite out of line at dinner."

"Oh, stop it. You're making it sound as if I'd begun emptying ashtrays at a ball. I thought these people were your friends."

"It is because I maintain proper discipline with the domestic staff that I can afford to be cordial."

"I don't want to discuss it," Becky said. "It's too absurd."

"You're going to have to learn how to deal with servants, my dear."

"Why?" she snapped. "I don't have any."

"But you will."

"I think the whole thing is—" Becky stopped short. "What? What are you talking about?"

"My divorce was granted last week. Becky, I want you to marry me." He took a small velvet box from his pocket and opened it. The diamond caught the firelight and hurled it into Becky's astounded eyes.

"Carl—I—"

"Wait. Before you answer or say anything, hear me out. You knew this day was coming. I've been courting you—trying to get you to love me as much as I love you. I'm not quite sure if I've succeeded, but more than a lover I'm a businessman, and you, my dear, are a businesswoman, if ever there was one. Accordingly, in exchange for your companionship and affection, I give you—"

"Carl, all this luxury is wonderful, but—"

"But it doesn't enchant you. I know that, Becky. That's why I'm offering you management of the store."

"What?"

"It's what you want, isn't it?" he asked affectionately. "I could buy you anything in the world, but nothing makes you happier than the store. As my wife you'd be in control. I would be merely a figurehead." He chuckled. "In a way I am that already. You and Philip Cooper make all the decisions. I just rubber-stamp your good judgments. Now that the war is over, think of what could be done with Pickman's. Think of all the marvelous changes you could make."

Becky shook her head. "I don't know whether to laugh or cry. You're trying to bribe me."

"No. Not at all a bribe." He took the ring from its

box and held it up. "A man wants to do all he can to make the woman he loves happy. If it is in my power to do so by giving you the store to run, how is that any different from any husband providing his wife with jewelry or a home or anything else? You have made me happy, Becky, happier than I ever thought I could be. Now I want to do the same for you."

She went over and sat on his lap. She hugged and kissed him and then said, "Carl, I won't live in that mausoleum."

He laughed. "Yes, that's exactly what it is, a mausoleum. We'll live anywhere you'd like, my love."

Becky nodded. "On Central Park West. And even if we have a servant, I warn you, nobody is going to make me a guest in my home or a stranger in my kitchen."

"Then your answer is yes?"

She ran her fingers through his hair. "Think carefully, Carl Pickman," she murmured. "This time you're not merely taking on another bauble. This time you're taking a wife."

She allowed him to slide the ring onto her finger, thinking, why not? Why shouldn't I marry him? He loves me, and I'll be a good wife and a good partner. I don't know if I love him, or even what love is. I know I loved Benny Talkin, and what good did that do?

Late that night he came to her bedroom. As they made love Becky desperately tried to recapture the spirit of that afternoon at the stables, but her tumultuous yearning and the intensity that had emanated from Carl now seemed impossibly remote, as ephemeral as vivid. She might just as well chase a dream.

Oh well, no matter. She would be good to Carl and he would be good to her.

As he bucked within her, the brooding stone-cold angels looked on with blind, impassive eyes.

Chapter 51

New York

"Philip, Rebecca and I are going to be married."

It was eight o'clock Monday morning, and Carl Pickman, who did not approve of procrastination, had summoned Philip Cooper to his office. Becky, having been warned during last night's drive back, was hiding out in her office. Millie had been given strict orders from Carl not to put through any calls. Carl was uncomfortable in any matter that called for warmth or a personal touch, whatever that was supposed to be. Nevertheless, he wanted very much to retain Cooper's good will during and after this interview.

Phil Cooper grinned. "That's wonderful news, Carl. When I walked in here and saw the grim look on your face, I thought you were going to tell me bad news."

Cooper had taken a seat on the sofa. Carl left his chair and came around his desk to sit beside his employee. He and Cooper had been together for many years, even socially sometimes, and yet Carl was reluctant to assume they were friends.

"Phil, you're vice president and general manager of

the store. Rebecca, as my wife, will be general manager and change your title to executive vice president.''

Cooper removed his horn-rimmed glasses to massage the bridge of his nose. ''I'll have my resignation on your desk by noon.''

''Absolutely not. I won't hear of it. We need you.''

''I suppose she'll be taking over my office. I wonder if she will remember the little joke I made to her some years ago. I said I had better be careful, else I'd come in some morning to find her behind my desk.'' He nodded and added brightly, ''Really, Carl, I offer my best wishes with my resignation.''

''Now listen to me,'' Carl said. ''First of all, your office belongs to you. I wouldn't think of having you anywhere but across the hall from me. Becky's office downstairs will be enlarged, as she'll continue to oversee our advertising. You're like family to me, my boy; we've always been a managerial partnership. That partnership has merely been strengthened by adding Becky to it.''

''Carl, I've enjoyed working here as your second in command, but you're asking me to accept a demotion. I've earned better than third place, Carl, and I intend to have what I deserve. The postwar expansion should be an exciting time in retailing, and I intend to be part of it—a vital part—even if it means working for our—I suppose I should say *your* competition.''

Carl looked away from Philip to hide his dismay. The young fellow did not hesitate to lay his cards on the table, and he held a strong hand. The one piece of advice from his father that Carl had taken to heart was to keep secrets about how the business was run. He was not his father and didn't possess the elder Pickman's talent for management. Carl needed help, and he'd found it in the talented young Philip Cooper. Now that he had Becky, he likely didn't need Cooper any longer, but he was terrified of letting

Cooper go off to work for a rival with all Pickman's secrets under his bonnet.

"Philip, I've said I consider you family, and I intend to prove it to you. As you know, Pickman's is a privately held company. Bernard never married. When he died his half went to my father, and when my father died, he bequeathed seventy percent to me and the rest to my sisters. As a token of appreciation for your years with us, I'm giving you ten percent of Pickman's to go along with your new title."

Cooper was quiet.

"There are only two stipulations—that you never vote your shares against me and that if you should leave Pickman's you'll sell back your shares."

"Can I think about it?"

"Of course," Carl said benevolently, patting Cooper's shoulder. "Take your time." He knew the young man was stalling merely to save face; he'd already accepted the offer. He ushered Cooper out of his office and went back to work. Within an hour his telephone rang. It was Cooper, officially accepting.

"Very good," Carl boomed. Macy's never told Gimbels, as the saying went, and now that Philip Cooper had agreed to remain, it looked as though Pickman's wouldn't be telling anybody.

"Carl, I was thinking," Cooper began. "Are you planning a large wedding?"

Carl hesitated before replying. Cooper's question caught him off guard, but the ceremony had been on his mind. His sisters were as much against this marriage as his former spouse, and for the same reason, that marriage into a poor Russian Jewish family was beneath him. His sisters had announced that they would not attend the ceremony, and his wife Gertrude had made it one of the conditions of her not contesting the divorce that their daughters, who would remain in her custody, not be humiliated by having to go.

Where to hold the ceremony troubled him as much as his family's boycott. He'd contemplated arranging for the rabbi's study at Temple Emanu-El, but there was Becky's family to consider. It would spoil the day if they proved to be an embarrassment in such grand surroundings. He intended to speak to Becky on this matter as soon as he managed to figure a way to broach the subject in an inoffensive manner.

"Actually, I imagine the wedding will be private, Philip."

"You've made a wonderful gesture to me, and I'd like to reciprocate. You know my apartment. Would you do me the honor of having your wedding there?

"How very kind of you, Philip." Carl thought it presumptuous. Oh well, he supposed he had better get used to it; Cooper was now family, after all, and the more he thought about Cooper's idea, the more he liked it. No matter how private the ceremony, a wedding at Temple Emanu-El would be grist for the congregation's gossip mill in no time at all. There would still be the potential for embarrassment in having the bride's clan traipsing into Cooper's elegant home, but that potential would be minimized. Carl had always known Becky's origins did not do her justice, but he was prepared to accept the inevitable scoffing as the price he had to pay for his love. "I'm agreeable, but let me talk it over with Rebecca."

"Tell Becky that this is my last act as her supervisor and I won't take no for an answer," Cooper said. They hung up, leaving Carl happy with his morning. Everything was falling into place, and he could look forward to a bright future with his bride-to-be.

Chapter 52

Becky's wedding was at ten o'clock in the morning on Sunday, December ninth. Danny thought his sister was kind of rushing things, but he figured it was Carl's fault. Hell, a guy turning sixty hooking up with a twenty-eight-year-old woman had every reason to be in a hurry.

Danny was in charge of getting their father there. At seven-fifteen he left his boarding house in the West Village and began the walk downtown. He was wearing his one and only suit, luckily a dark blue. He had only his unlined uniform trench coat, so he walked briskly, both to keep warm and to be early enough to play valet if Abe needed a hand with his tie or shave. Once he'd collected his father, they'd grab a cab on East Broadway, but for now Danny didn't mind walking. He liked the exercise and it was cheap.

He wasn't exactly hurting for money. He fell under the government program that paid unemployed discharged servicemen twenty bucks a week for up to a year. A double sawbuck didn't go all that far anymore, of course, but it covered his tab at the boarding house. Becky had lent him some money as well, explaining that as far as she was concerned the Cherry Street building was half his. She was going to arrange for his name to be put on the ownership papers, but he asked her to hold off. The rents didn't amount to much, and he didn't want to lose his stipend from Uncle Sam.

No apartments in the building had changed hands for as long as he could remember, and Becky steadfastly refused to raise the rents to what the tight housing market could bear. After all expenses were paid and the management company took its cut, there wasn't much left, but Becky had promised that Danny could always come to her for extra money.

I guess I can, Danny decided as he crossed Delancey Street. She's been making a good salary, and as of today she's going to be rolling in it.

He had his own key to the storefront. He relocked the door behind him and climbed the back staircase.

"You look real sharp, Pop," Danny grinned. His father was shaved and wearing a light brown pin-striped suit, a clean white shirt and a dark maroon tie.

"Where's your coat?"

"I'm wearing a coat."

"Shumel, feel how thin this so-called coat is." Abe rubbed the khaki between his fingers. As Shumel dutifully shuffled over in his backless slippers, his weak eyes swimming, Abe assured his son, "I'll get you a nice coat."

"Don't need one, Pop. I've bought myself a lot of nice clothes—slacks, shirts, sweaters. I never wear a suit so I never invested in a topcoat. My leather flight jacket usually does me fine." Government regulations had given all servicemen thirty days to switch from their uniforms to civvies, but the regs didn't apply to stuff like flight jackets or trench coats shorn of military insignia. That was fine with Danny. His gold bars and silver pilot's wings were packed away. He wouldn't have displayed them even if he'd been allowed.

"I bet it's cold in that slum you're living in," Abe went on. "Shumel, give him a hot glass tea."

"That's just like you, Pop. You've never even seen where I live."

"Well, isn't it a slum? You could live here with us. There's plenty room and you'd save a few bucks."

Oh, that'd be just great, Danny thought. Stay here and watch you order poor old Shumel around the way you used to order me. He smiled. "I appreciate it, Pop, but I've kind of gotten used to living alone. No offense."

Abe looked disgusted. "Drink your tea. Then we'll go."

"We've got plenty of time."

"I don't want to be late."

Danny just nodded. They took their time going down the stairs and walking to East Broadway, where they had no trouble flagging a taxi.

They rode quietly, Abe sitting straight and tall, his hands in his coat pockets and his collar turned up. "I still think a wedding should be in a shul," he suddenly said.

"Pop, when was the last time you were in shul?"

"That is not the point."

"I thought you told me you didn't even get married in a shul."

"Yeah, I did . . . didn't I?" Abe mused out loud. He turned to look at his son, his eyes suddenly frightened, beseeching.

Oh shit, I can't handle this, Danny thought. "Pop? Remember, you got married in Joseph and Sadie's apartment, on Montgomery Street."

"What a beautiful bride your mother was. Leah was so frightened to be married." He chuckled and nudged his son's ribs. "Not as much as I was. You know, I got a letter from Sadie and Joseph. They got a lot of snow in Chicago."

Relieved that his father's mind had cleared, Danny

absently listened to the family gossip. It was funny, or maybe more upsetting than funny, how somebody could seem not to age at all for a long time, and then suddenly get older in shocking jolts. That his father's memory was going was understandable if disturbing. Danny frowned. How is Carl Pickman's memory? he wondered. My sister's marrying a guy who's just turned sixty.

At Cooper's address Danny paid the driver and helped his father out of the taxi. He told the clerk, "Philip Cooper," and was waved on through to the elevators, where the attendant gave them both the onceover, unable to suppress a smirk at Danny's trench coat.

"Something strike you funny, pal?" Danny growled.

After a while the guy said, "Twentieth floor, sir."

"Happy landings," Danny shrugged off his trench coat and folded it over his arm before ringing Cooper's bell.

An old gent in formal attire let them in. Must be Pickman, Danny thought, and stuck out his hand. The old guy pretended not to see it, asking if he could take their coats, and Danny felt like kicking himself for not being able to tell the difference between the bridegroom and the butler.

Cooper had a pretty swanky place. The furniture was modern and there wasn't much of it, but that just seemed to add to the effect. The walls were pale violet; the floors were dark and highly polished. There were Oriental rugs, dramatically positioned paintings and so on. Danny got the feeling Cooper had done up his place with stuff that was the right color rather than with stuff he necessarily liked. Well, he didn't know much about decorating, but he did know this place was swanky.

Especially the view. One whole wall of the living room was windows, and the drapes had been pulled back. They were pretty high up, and the skyline view was in Danny's estimation as good as the one from the Empire

State Building's observation deck, better when you figured Cooper just had to roll out of bed to check it out.

One thing about the apartment, it sure didn't look set up for a wedding. Oh, there were vases filled with fresh flowers, but where was the wedding canopy? Danny glanced at his father, thinking, He ain't going to like this . . .

"Danny, Father," Becky called to them. She was wearing a blue textured silk suit and had a tall, grey-haired guy in dark blue pinstripes in tow.

"Danny, what? No wedding dress?" Abe whispered shakily.

"Don't say anything, Pop," Danny said out of the side of his mouth.

"Father, this is Carl Pickman," Becky said. "Carl, my father, Abraham Herodetzky, and my brother, Danny."

Sixty or not, this guy is in good shape, Danny concluded. If Pickman's hair weren't grey he could have passed for late forties. Danny was amused to see the relieved look on Pickman's face as they shook hands. He probably imagined his bride's kin showing up with long smelly beards and prayer shawls, Danny mused.

Becky introduced them to the other guests, but that didn't take very long. There was an older chubby lady named Millie, a blonde dish called Grace Turner who set Danny's heart thumping; a white-haired guy in double-breasted grey flannel who turned out to be a rabbi, and Philip Cooper, whom you really couldn't call a guest, since he lived here. Pickman had invited none of his family.

"Your sister is like a princess with these wealthy people," Abe boasted to Danny as they stood along the sidelines. "She has done well for herself. First she makes a fine career, and now she is marrying a rich man."

The ceremony took fifteen minutes. The bride's father was not asked to take part. Nobody, including the rabbi, wore a yarmulke, except for Abe, who'd brought his own.

When it was over there was a champagne toast to the new couple. The rabbi left and Becky came over to them.

"Father, how did you like the ceremony?"

Abe shrugged. "You shouldn't ask me. You already know how I stand on such matters. When you were younger I took you to shul. Maybe not enough, but I took you. On the other hand, Carl Pickman is well known in the community for kindness to those less fortunate, so who am I to say he is a bad Jew?"

"Oh, he's not, Father. It's just that he's not comfortable with—" She shook her head. "He tends toward understatement."

Abe looked at her blankly.

"Where you going for a honeymoon?" Danny interjected.

"Palm Beach, Florida."

"It must be nice there." Abe nodded shrewdly.

Becky giggled in a way that made Danny think she'd had too much of that champagne for so early in the day. Then he scolded himself. It's her wedding, after all.

"I'm surprised your husband would leave the store during the holiday season," Abe said.

Becky burst out laughing. "What do you think, we stand by the cash registers all day?"

Abe wilted like a scolded child and Danny was overwhelmed with resentment. Who is she to patronize us? Then he remembered all the times his sister had comforted him during his childhood estrangement from their father.

"Danny, speaking of the store," Becky said, turning to him, "I've talked to Carl about a position for you—"

"What?" Danny was appalled.

"Well, I know you're kind of at a loss for what to do with your life. I thought that if there was a job for you at Pickman's—"

"Becky," he replied evenly, struggling to keep his

voice under control, "I think I'm hearing that champagne talking." He smiled, trying to make a joke.

"I'm not talking about some menial position, Danny . . . . ."

"We'll discuss it when you get back from Florida."

"All right." Becky eyed him reluctantly. "That would be better, I guess. Right now I've got to talk to Philip. I love you both very much." She embraced her father and then turned to Danny, who pointed over her shoulder.

"I think your husband's getting jealous."

Becky giggled. "Jealous of a runt like you? Not a chance." She kissed him and whispered, "Think about what I've said."

"Danny, you saw? He didn't even break a wineglass at the end." Abe shook his head.

"That's understatement for you, Pop."

There was food and a wedding cake, but nobody seemed very hungry, including Danny, who had skipped breakfast with thoughts of stuffing himself. He realized that nothing, not even a wedding, was powerful enough to make this group of people feel even slightly easy together.

At noon that dish Grace Turner, who'd not deigned to notice him, and not for his lack of trying, took her leave. Danny went to fetch his father. He didn't want to be here any longer, and God forbid they should be the last to go. The few seconds he'd spent chatting with Pickman about his future had been excruciating enough.

His father was standing with his nose pressed up against the glass of Cooper's floor-to-ceiling windows. He was gazing in rapturous wonder at the skyline.

"Come on, Pop."

"Yeah, Danny," his father murmured. "Look how beautiful the view is."

Danny realized his father had never been in a sky-scraper before. "You know what, Pop? Next week I'll

take you to the Empire State Building. It makes this view
look like peanuts.''

"Yeah, son," Abe nodded, too mesmerized to listen.
"Look how tiny the cars are." He shook his head, amazed,
and the sudden sweep of his arms seemed to encompass all
of Philip Cooper's abode. "This must be like what flying
is, yeah, Danny?"

"For some people it is."

It was just a bit after one o'clock in the afternoon
when their taxi pulled up in front of Cherry Street. Danny
paid the driver and let the cab go, thinking to walk home.

"You want to come up for some tea?" Abe asked.

"Thanks, Pop, but I've got things to do," Danny
lied. He felt like being alone.

"All right. Thanks for taking me, Danny."

He kissed his father's cheek. "I'll see you in a couple
of days."

"Yeah." Abe looked at his son. "It was a nice
wedding, huh?"

"Sure."

"I see now why we couldn't invite Shumel and my
other friends," Abe said to himself. "Go, then!" he told
Danny. "I can climb the stairs myself."

"Okay," Danny said, but he still watched through
the window until his father disappeared up the back stairs.
He made sure the door was locked and walked off, smiling
to himself. He could imagine the fanciful tale his father
would tell Shumel: there would be yarmulkes, chupas,
keening cantors and shattered wineglasses galore.

The day had warmed up some, so Danny decided to
take a walk around the old neighborhood. He turned the
corner onto Jackson, passed a couple of storefront businesses and stopped. The Palestine Relief Agency had taken
the space that once housed the Eagle Pawn Shop. Today
only Leo was inside working. Danny had known Leo

Haskell since he was a kid. He tapped on the window and Leo beckoned him in.

The office contained several battered desks and typewriters, boxes of Zionist literature and an ancient black candlestick telephone. Leo was maybe sixty-five. He had a bushy grey beard and was wearing a tattered sweater and a battered fedora. In hot weather the sweater would come off, but Danny had never seen him without his hat.

Leo did not stand up as Danny entered. His spine had been injured in a fall down a sweatshop freight elevator's shaft forty years ago. As Leo told it, they hadn't thought he would ever walk again, but he did, although with a pair of canes. He went to work for the relief agency and was still at it.

"Danny! Our flier is home, I see. Push aside all that crap and sit down and talk to me."

Danny moved the stacks of newspapers and Zionist leaflets and took a seat. "How are you, Leo?"

"How should I be?"

These guys, Danny thought. "How come you moved from East Broadway?"

"Here the rent is cheaper. Also, we thought it would be better not to be so visible. Things are moving quickly over there, Danny. The great day is almost at hand."

"That's good, Leo." The old guy had been saying that for as long as he'd known him.

"So what are your plans?"

Danny shrugged. "I don't really know, Leo." He unbuttoned his coat and took out a cigarette, then offered the pack to the older man.

"Don't mind if I do," Leo said. "How old are you, Danny?" He found a match in his desk drawer and lit their smokes.

"I'll be twenty in July."

"Twenty," Leo chuckled, shaking his head. "And

you don't know what to do with your life in this glorious world? Didn't you train as a machinist?''

"Yeah.'' Danny blew a smoke ring. "But that's not for me.'' He watched Leo watching him, his hat brim pulled low so that just his two dark eyes and the smoldering Pall Mall were visible in that great expanse of beard. "What I really want to do,'' Danny heard himself confessing, "is make a living as an aviator.''

"Nu?''

"It's not so easy, Leo,'' Danny frowned. "After the First World War the returned pilots did okay barnstorming and giving people rides, but airplanes aren't that sort of novelty anymore. Sure, the big airlines are coming into their own, but all they're interested in are the multi-engine pilots, the guys who flew the bombers. A fighter-jock—that's me, Leo—hasn't got the training to fly a big plane. Oh, I could do it okay, but that doesn't do me much good.''

"I bet there's no kind of plane you couldn't fly.'' Leo stoutly declared.

Danny grinned. "It's not like going to a Ford from a Chevy,'' he cautioned. "It takes some getting used to, but sure, given a bit of time, there's no plane I can't fly.''

"You know, Danny, since you ain't got a job, maybe I got something for you.''

"I'm obliged to you, but I haven't got the patience to collect for charity.''

"I'm thinking maybe more of flying than collecting.''

Danny laughed out loud. "Flying! For you, Leo?''

"For Palestine.'' The old man seemed not to mind in the least that Danny had laughed in his face. "If—I'm saying if—it turned out you were the pilot you claim to be, would you be willing to do it? It might mean leaving the country.''

Danny lit another cigarette and leaned back in his chair. What did he have to lose? The newspapers were full of the renewed violence in Palestine despite the best efforts of the new United Nations. He'd missed the war, but maybe he could get a taste of combat there.

He had to chuckle at that. It sounded too farfetched even to make it between the covers of a *Tailspin Tommy*.

But what did he have to lose? He'd been spending his days sleeping late and smoking cigarettes, collecting his dole and borrowing from Becky—Becky! How it galled him that she would imagine he might consider working for her and that parody of a Jew, Carl Pickman.

"Leo, would this—job—pay something?"

"Maybe a little. Mainly you'd be paid in your own satisfaction at helping."

Danny nodded. Wouldn't that be something? How their father would look up to him if he was instrumental in establishing a Jewish state. "My daughter, she's very wealthy," Abe would tell people, "but my son—oy, there's a boy to make a father proud." Even if that was a pipe dream, there was still the real possibility that Danny would once again get to fly.

"Leo, for old time's sake level with me. I really might get to be a pilot again?"

"If you want, I can arrange that you meet someone in a better position to say."

Danny, chewing nervously on his bottom lip, nodded. "What have I got to lose? Okay, Leo."

"How about Wednesday afternoon? Come at three o'clock."

"It's okay by me, but what about the other guy? How can you be sure he's free?"

"Danny, you're a machinist and a trained pilot. He'll be free, don't worry." Leo paused, looking troubled. "Boychic, I've known you ever since you were born. I even watched you one day right after your mother died. I ask you now not to mention this meeting we've planned to anyone, including your father. I also ask that you use a different last name—"

"What? an alias?" Danny was enthralled. "How come?"

"I know you think I am just an old man spouting nonsense, but humor me. I will not tell this man your name, and neither should you. You'll understand better after the meeting, but until then, trust that I have your dear sister and your father in mind. We mustn't make them suffer for our activities."

"Well, okay, sure."

"I hope I haven't frightened you off."

"Are you kidding, Leo?" Danny glowed. "I get an alias? That's great! Let's see, who should I be?"

"You'll be Danny Hill," Leo said dryly.

"Swell. See you Wednesday."

Chapter 53

Abe Herodetzky was in the middle of retelling his story about Becky's wedding when the stranger came into the store. Abe was shocked. On a Wednesday afternoon around a quarter to three he rarely had a customer, and besides, he couldn't remember the last time he'd had a customer he didn't know.

"Excuse me for disturbing you, gentlemen," the stranger said in precise, clipped English. "I'm looking for Jackson Street."

Abe heaved himself up out of his rocking chair to squint at the man. There was nothing all that unusual about him. He was wearing a nondescript blue suit and knitted wool tie; he had on a dark grey overcoat and no hat. He had blue eyes and dirty blond curly hair getting kind of thin on top. The premature baldness made him seem older than he was. Abe guessed that the man was in his early thirties. His accent combined with his diffident, ill-at-ease manner made him seem like a foreigner.

But he seemed familiar to Abe, pit-of-the-stomach familiar, and yet he was sure they had never met.

"You go out the door and make a left. Jackson is at

the corner. The street sign fell down. You'll see Blaustein's shoe repair, and next to that a laundry. That's Jackson.''

"Thank you," the stranger said, and Abe nodded vaguely. He was so sure this was somebody from his past, but how could that be? This fellow was such a young man.

"Gentlemen," the stranger addressed them all, and took his leave.

Abe was on the verge of saying something to the man, asking his name, but then he decided against it. What point? he thought. I'm getting old. Plenty of times my mind has played tricks on me already. Why should I make a fool of myself in front of everyone?

"So what else, Abe?" one of his friends asked. "What else?"

"Well." Abe sat back down and began to rock. "You should have seen the splendid tallis my daughter gave her husband. From Jerusalem it came—"

"Abe?" Shumel asked. "You all right? You look funny."

From Jerusalem—Abe felt confused and unsettled. Did the stranger and Palestine have some connection?

He cleared his throat. "From Jerusalem the tallis came, and it was silk, and its fringe was made of real gold."

Herschel Kol stood on the sidewalk outside the little store and wondered why the man behind the counter seemed familiar. They'd certainly never met before, but there was something about him that struck a chord in his memory. He glanced at the window—Cherry Street Market. That wasn't much help. Below it A. something-or-other, & Son had once been painted in, but most of the lettering had worn away.

Herschel could have gone back and asked, but it was almost three o'clock and he didn't want to be late. He'd ordered his taxi driver to let him off several blocks away from Jackson Street as a precaution; there was no need to advertise that he had business at the Palestine Agency. He'd been to the Jackson Street address before, but he'd been many places in and out of New York since his arrival months ago, and he still found himself getting lost.

Immediately on Herschel's arrival in America he got in touch with Rudolf Sonneborn, who had put together a network of sympathetic Jewish Americans. This network, the Institute, arranged for him to rent a rambling seven-room apartment on the Upper West Side near Columbia University. He was supplied with a staff of student volunteers to research what Palestine would need to set up an arms industry of its own. The information was all there; one could get it from magazines and library books and by writing to the Patent Office. The youngsters were hard workers, but they still needed to be supervised by someone with more experience in technical matters.

In addition to supervising his armament research staff, Herschel had traveled to many cities across the United States, using his Institute-supplied guise of a scrap-metal dealer to buy up drill presses, lathes, grinders and so on. The Second World War was over and machines that had been worth millions when they were running full tilt to supply the war effort were now lying idle and being sold as scrap.

Even more valuable to Herschel were machines specifically designed to manufacture munitions. American law prohibited their sale, but they could be broken down by their owners and their parts sold as junk. Herschel as well as other Zionist agents, both American and Palestinian, visited junkyards nationwide. Thanks to the research of the Upper West Side staff, they knew what parts they wanted, and they bought them with funds from overseas and from the Institute.

Herschel regained his sense of direction once he found

Jackson Street. The old man in the store was correct; the
street sign had fallen down. Herschel would never have
found his way if he hadn't asked for directions.

The old man—there was something familiar about
him that was still gnawing at Herschel, but he put it out of
his mind as he entered the Palestine Relief Agency office,
nodded to Leo and looked over the potential new recruit.

The boy, for that's what he was, didn't look like
much. He was very short and thin to the point of
undernourishment, if such a thing was possible in America.
He was wearing pleated slacks, a turtleneck sweater and a
battered leather jacket. He had a hatchet face with a high,
bony forehead emphasized by his dark, wavy hair worn
slicked back. He was smoking a cigarette. His eyes were
narrow and he adopted a leering, sneering expression at
Herschel's entrance.

Herschel ignored the pose. It was irrelevant; such
swagger told one nothing about a man except that he'd
never been tested.

"Hi. I'm Danny—"

"Hill," Leo put in.

Herschel shrugged. "I'm Herschel Kol." He thought
about what Leo had told him. The boy was bright, trained
as a machinist. He was a military pilot but had never seen
action. He expected to be paid for his services. Well, that
was no problem. The Institute allowed him a personnel
budget, which he supplemented with his own funds.

Once his criminal record was expunged there was
nothing to stop Herschel from making contact with the
American representatives of his investment firm. He was
pleasantly surprised to find that his trust had grown to half
a million U.S. dollars. Arrangements were made with his
mother's approval for Herschel to draw on the income as
need be. He had already done so on behalf of his staff of
student researchers. They were not being paid, but Herschel knew of their money problems: tuition, rent, elderly

parents and so on. Herschel gave them money from his own pocket as they needed it, and not one of his staff had abused his generosity. He insisted that his older operatives submit detailed expense accounts. He himself took no Institute money beyond what he spent on machinery. He was also paying the rent on the Upper West Side apartment.

No, the fact that Danny wanted a salary was no problem. Institute funds were available, and Herschel could always sweeten the pot. He remembered what Leo had told him: more than anything young Danny wanted to fly. Herschel guessed that the chance to be an aviator was the best bait for this useful American.

"Leo," Herschel said, "would you mind awfully if Danny and I went for a walk?"

"It's cold out there," Danny complained.

"So after we've talked I'll buy you a cup of coffee."

Once they were outside, Danny asked, "Where do you want to walk?"

"Take me around Green-witch Village—why are you laughing?

"It's Grennitch, like in England, you know?"

"All right, but I don't know England."

Danny glanced at him. "You sound English."

"Let's walk."

Danny led him along Grand Street to the Bowery and then up to Spring Street, which they walked all the way to West Broadway. As they strolled Danny told Herschel about the history of the area, bringing to life the cast-iron factory buildings with tales of the countless Jewish men and women—including Danny's own father—who had slaved in the sweatshops.

"My pop was a big deal in the 1910 strike," Danny boasted.

"Oh, yes?" Herschel replied politely, not at all certain what they were talking about. "Is he still in the union?"

"No, he's—" Danny hesitated, rehashing Leo's cautions about involving his family in this mysterious business. "Look, Herschel, I don't know what you want from me, but whatever I decide to do, maybe we'd better keep my family out of it."

"Sure. I won't ask again about your family."

They had reached the corners of Bleecker and Macdougal streets, the heart of the village. Herschel pointed out a basement-level coffeehouse. They went inside and took a corner table in the nearly empty cafe but did not get down to brass tacks until the waitress had brought them their order and gone.

"How come you didn't want to talk in front of Leo?" Danny asked.

Herschel sipped at his coffee. It was called espresso and came in a familiar tiny cup, but despite his expectations the brew was far weaker than the Turkish coffee of his homeland. "There is such a thing as 'need to know,' Danny. What Leo doesn't hear he can't repeat."

"Come off it, pal. Leo's been devoted to Zionism for—"

"Danny, right now you should understand the dangers. Leo runs a relief office, and it's been planned that he sit there, vulnerable to the authorities, to divert attention from the important part of the operation. The less Leo knows, the less likely it is that he'll go to jail, or for that matter, that I'll go to jail . . ."

"Wow."

Herschel sipped his espresso, satisfied with Danny's reaction. Leo had suggested that he play up the melodramatic aspects of their operation, and it seemed to be working.

"Are you saying I might end up in prison if I go along with you?"

Careful—entice him, but don't scare him off. "I'm

saying that it is a possibility if you aren't careful." Herschel eyed his quarry. "Does that frighten you?"

Danny licked his lips. "I can play any hand I'm dealt."

"Listen to me. This will require you to be very clever if we are to succeed. Slang from your gangster cinema will not do."

Herschel quickly, quietly filled him in, first on the strife-torn history of the Zionist paramilitary organizations and then on how they'd come to band together to begin preparations for the day when the British withdrew from Palestine and the Jews would have to defend themselves against the Arab onslaught. "Others like me are gathering weapons and ammunition, but the best we can hope for is a bare trickle. We must set up within Palestine's borders a munitions industry." He then went on to detail his own part in the mission and what he wanted from Danny.

Danny's enthralled look was a scowl by the time Herschel was finished. "Sounds like you expect me to babysit a bunch of college kids whenever they aren't researching at the library—"

"Danny, it's an important job—"

"Bullshit. An old lady could do it if she happened to be a machinist." Danny's eyes widened. "That's it, isn't it, Kol? You and Leo were just making the flying stuff up, weren't you? It's my machinist's background that interests you."

"Flying comes later," Herschel said weakly.

"Bullshit."

"And there is much more to do. What we have so far purchased is in temporary storage all over the country. We must consolidate our purchases here in New York and figure out a way to get them to Palestine without alerting the authorities. There is much more to be bought, but some of it is so clearly designed for making munitions that I, as a foreigner, don't dare approach the owners. I need somebody who is American and has the technical ability to judge the merchandise. That's you. In New York I can fit in, but in most of your country I would attract too much attention. It is I who will be the babysitter, waiting here for your telephone calls."

Danny toyed with his coffee cup. "You know, I think I got an angle on that warehouse problem."

"Wonderful."

"I'm not saying I'll do it."

"There is so much you could take care of for me." Herschel paused. "I'm going to tell you a great secret. You must tell no one, even if you don't wish to help. What we've so far purchased will help make Palestine secure in the future, but what is needed is an innovative approach to a light automatic weapon, one that can be manufactured in existing factories. We need a gun every man can keep with him in his home so that when the alarm goes out he can take it from beneath the bed and stand ready to defend his homeland."

"Sure," Danny nodded. "Like the Bren and Sten guns and the MA31 submachine gun."

"Yes, but how did you know?"

"Hey, I was in the army, remember? I got some training with the MA31—we called it the grease gun because that's what it looked like. It was really cruddy—cast and stamped out with a minimum of machined parts. It worked, though. I think they got the inspiration from the Sten."

"That's what I always thought," Herschel replied. "You see, Danny, we are almost like brothers. We share the same thoughts and have the same interests."

Danny did not reply for a moment, and then he said, "All this talk about sneaking around, smuggling guns, and prison. I guess we really would be breaking the law?"

Herschel had been waiting for this last hurdle. "Danny, technically we are breaking the law. Morally I think we are justified, but you know the arguments for Zionism as well as I. You will never be asked to do your country harm. You must decide if it is worth the risk.''

Danny thought about his options, joining the machinists' union and shuffling papers for his big siser. He shook hands with Herschel and said, ''Okay, I'll get started on our warehousing problem.''

Within two weeks Danny had a clear picture of their storage needs. He telephoned Benny Talkin. As a kid Danny had suffered a case of hero worship for the popular, brawny young gang leader. Benny had always been cordial to Danny, but the great difference in their ages kept them from making friends. During his teens, Danny hoped that his sister and Danny would resume their romance so he might someday work for the trucking king with his glamorous rumored connections to the mob.

Danny spent an hour with Benny in his warehouse office on the Manhattan side of the Hudson, exchanging reminiscences about growing up in the old neighborhood, about Danny's military experience, about how prosperous Benny was looking. They even talked about Becky.

''Lucky girl,'' Benny observed. ''Marrying Carl Pickman put her right up on top.''

Sort of like marrying Stefano De Fazio's daughter, Danny thought, but all he said was, ''I guess she's made her own luck.''

Benny's smile was blinding. ''I can go along with that. Now what can I do for you, Danny boy?'' He shot his cuffs, planted his elbows on his desk and rested his jaw on his clasped hands. ''If I'm in luck you're here for a job, because I could do with a sharp guy like you.''

Danny blushed and tried not to stare at Benny's cuff links. They were glittering gold and the size of buffalo nickels. ''I'm not here for a job, but thanks anyway. I'm here to talk business. Have you been following the action in Palestine?''

"Who hasn't? The news is full of it.''

"Here's the story, Benny. I'm working for Zionists, but I don't want to go into detail. We need a warehouse. It's got to be the kind of place where people have learned not to be too nosey. It's got to have concrete floors and a loading dock strong enough to support heavy machinery. It's got to have good access to the piers—''

"You're talking to me, kid, but you're not saying much.''

"You know what I'm talking about.''

"Something shady for sure. Look, Danny, when it comes to Palestine, I've done my part and I'll do more if I can. A few months ago I got a call from a guy who's working with Ben Hecht, the big Hollywood writer. He's fund-raising for the Irgun, and me and a lot of my associates anted up. Everything those Irgun guys can dish out to the British they deserve. I say we've negotiated long enough. Negotiate is just another word for begging. The Jews have begged enough. Those poor saps in Germany probably begged all the way into the gas chambers, and what did it get them?''

He shook his head. "That's how I feel and I don't mind saying so, but I still want you to level with me about what you and your friends are planning to do with the warehouse. I've got to know what I'm getting myself—which means Stefano—involved in.''

Danny leveled with him. When he was done Benny said, "Renting you warehouse space would be just the beginning of it. Stefano owns the docks, and that means you're going to need us to get this stuff of yours out of the country.''

Danny tried Herschel's argument. "Nothing we've bought so far is technically against the law.''

Benny scoffed. "Take it from me, there's plenty of

guys in jail on technicalities. You on the War Assets Administration's mailing lists?''

Danny nodded. ''We have people going to all the auctions—''

Benny's smile turned hard. ''Tell me, kid, you think the Feds aren't there as well, watching to see who buys what and for how much? Sooner or later you guys are going to get a nice visit from the FBI.'' He shook his head. ''What I told you before about being contacted by some Hollywood guys to contribute to the Irgun—well, maybe those movie moguls have been watching their own gangster pictures too long. Maybe they expected us to ship our old tommy guns over there or something. Now, that's been done on a small scale, but maybe I looked into the profitability of a privately arranged large-scale arms shipment to Palestine. You know, make a few bucks and help our people out at the same time.''

''What happened?'' Danny smiled at the thought of how Herschel would drool over such a bonanza.

''That kind of deal, there's no way to do it without spreading the bribes all the way to the top. There are just too many officials involved. Anyway, I put some feelers out to a contact in Navy Intelligence—we did them some favors during the war—and the word came back. No way. No one would touch a bribe for that; the official word is that our country is neutral.''

''Which means screw the Jews,'' Danny remarked, ''just like always.''

''Truman wants to keep things nice and cozy with England while they try and put Europe back together. My contact in Navy Intelligence said that when the limeys finally pull out''—Benny pointed his finger—''and that's when, not *if*—Truman is going to slap an arms embargo on the Middle East.''

''Yeah, that's neutral all right,'' Danny growled, ''except that the Arabs already have guns.''

"And ve vas only neutral too." Benny mocked. "Ve only put dem in der gas chambers, ve didn't tell dem to breathe." He looked at Danny as he made up his mind. "Sorry, kid. It's too risky."

Danny imagined how it would be to tell Herschel he'd failed. "Listen, Benny. The machinery I told you about is a lot less obvious than tommy guns. Your plan called for officials to pretend they didn't see weapons. All we need is for them not to look too hard. We've got plenty of perfectly legal stuff for camouflage."

"I still think that as soon as the Feds suspect you intend to ship your stuff to Palestine they'll be all over you."

"Then I won't let them find out. Now, you want to talk business or no?"

Danny called Herschel from a pay telephone around the corner from Benny's office. "We've got ourselves a warehouse in the Bronx."

"How much?"

"It's perfect for us. It's got everything we need."

"*How much?*"

"Five thousand."

"Oy! Danny, go back and see if we can lease instead of buy—"

Danny closed his eyes. "That is to lease."

"Impossible! You told me this so-called friend of yours was a Jew."

"Look." Danny struggled to control his temper. "This isn't Palestine and the Jews here aren't Socialists—not the ones we need to do business with at least. Here people want to make a profit when they do business, and that means we have to pay them to take this big a risk. It's only fair, and besides, if we hurt feelings and make enemies, somebody will inform on us and we'll be washed up before we even get started. In this particular case I believe my friend is in a position to do a lot more for us than just lease us a warehouse. Maybe some of that five thousand is going for that, okay?''

Herschel sighed; in the past two weeks Danny had come to be amazed at just how eloquent the Palestinian's exhalations could be.

''I think Leo knew what he was saying when he told me that I needed you. Thanks.''

''Hey, somebody's got to look out for a greenhorn like you,'' Danny replied. When they hung up his heart was racing. Somebody needed him. It was weird, wonderful, and it made him feel ten feet tall.

Chapter 54

As the months passed and Herschel and Danny's working relationship deepened, the Palestinian's respect and admiration for his assistant increased. The two seemed to compensate for each other's shortcomings. When Herschel lost his temper over some petty mishap, Danny was quick to calm him down and restore his perspective. When Danny's pessimism flared and he began complaining that something couldn't be done, Herschel's enthusiasm restored the younger man's spirit.

It was strange to feel so close to the boy and yet know so little about him, but the less they knew about any of their associates the better. Herschel had even encouraged Danny to use phony identification when he attended the war surplus auctions, open only to U.S. citizens.

The majority of their purchases were from private dealers. If the seller was Jewish, an Institute phone call would smooth the way for Herschel and his assistant buyers. Meanwhile, his staff of student researchers continued to compile the technical information to manufacture munitions.

As their warehouse filled up Danny turned his attention to smuggling. A great deal of what they were shipping was innocuous and could go out as agricultural or textile

698

machinery. This would not do, however, for the more specialized items. There was no way to make a cartridge-loading machine look like a lathe. A method of camouflage had to be devised.

They came up with two ideas. The first was Danny's and stemmed from his childhood. He explained to Herschel about his youthful passion for assembling model airplanes. They went and bought a kit. Each numbered part, considered by itself, could have been a component of anything at all, and the kit came with an exploded schematic diagram as well as step-by-step instructions for its assembly.

The Institute supplied them with more student volunteers, who began the laborious process of dismantling the machinery and code-numbering the parts. Others looked over their shoulders and compiled instructions for reassembling it, after which they randomly scattered the pieces into harmless-looking crates.

The second idea was Herschel's. It was to use a technique perfected by Ehud Avriel, owner of a machine shop in Warsaw. Over the last decade Avriel had shipped thousands of weapons to kibbutzim by stripping down tractors, filling them with contraband, and then welding the bodies back together. In the same manner Herschel and Danny bought boilers, transformers and other large industrial machines that could be hollowed out and filled with contraband.

Their Institute connections came up with sympathetic export companies to furnish them their licenses, and Danny cajoled Benny Talkin into supplying his trucks and his father-in-law's influence to move the cargo through the labyrinthine bureaucracy of the Port of New York.

Neither system would have been sufficient on its own, but together the two served to transport tons of clandestine cargo into Palestine.

* * *

In June the Anglo-American Committee, formed at President Truman's suggestion to resolve the deadlock on immigration between the British government and the Jews, issued its report. On one hand it called for the repeal of all immigration restrictions to Palestine; on the other it called for the immediate dissolution of all private armies; in other words, Haganah and the Irgun. The British government rejected the committee's findings and announced its intention to use Palestine as a military base.

The "private armies" responded by blowing up bridges and railroad tracks, by raiding British arms caches, by doing everything in their power to obstruct the British in Palestine. The British struck back with massive sweeps, carting off thousands of Jews to detention camps.

In July Herschel's contacts warned him to prepare for trouble. On July twenty-second Irgun forces blew up Jerusalem's King David Hotel, the social center for the British. More than ninety people were killed and the explosion razed the hotel.

Moderate Jews all over the world denounced the attack. Ben-Gurion, safely in Paris, specifically denounced the Irgun as the enemy of the Jewish people, although the Irgun had executed the attack with Haganah's approval. Now Begin's force was ordered to bear the blame; it was hoped that the British could then find their way to a politically acceptable compromise with Haganah.

Instead the British invaded. An additional twenty thousand troops joined the established ten thousand. A white paper was released; it detailed Haganah's involvement in terrorism. A curfew for Jews was instituted; violators were to be shot on sight. When Irgun prisoners were flogged, British officers were kidnapped and whipped. In America Jews began to boycott British businesses, and in England Winston Churchill himself accused Bevin's government of acting dishonorably.

The British government, stung by worldwide disapproval, announced the death penalty for terrorists. The Irgun attacks continued, the curfew was maintained and the British retreated into highly guarded security zones. They rarely traveled without large armed escorts. Palestine was their prison.

The increased violence worked against Herschel and Danny in two ways. First, the bloodshed frightened off many of the more moderate members of Sonneborn's Institute.

Second, the increased British activity in Palestine caused the Haganah to modify its original plan. It had been thought the military supplies would be reassembled and put into operation at once in order to begin a stockpile of home-grown weaponry for the day the British left and the Jews would have to defend themselves against the Arabs.

That was now too risky. The British had increased their anti-terrorist activities, which meant there was an increased risk of the machinery being discovered and confiscated. Accordingly, Zionist leadership's attention turned to its operatives in Europe, who had been concentrating on ready-made arms, reasoning that a cache was easier to hide than a factory.

Herschel Kol found himself feeling unaccountably slighted and jealous now that his sphere of operations had been nudged out of the limelight. He, Danny and many others had been working to give Palestine an arms industry. Now they would not know if they had succeeded until the British were gone, which meant that there would be no time to get the machinery unpacked, assembled and running before the Arabs were upon them.

As far as Herschel was concerned, that just made his own pet project—an easily and cheaply manufactured submachine gun—all the more important.

As soon as he decided he could delegate authority to Danny, Herschel turned his attention to his gun. In February an Institute contact informed Herschel that he'd found the man for the job.

Wilbur Burns was a sixty-five-year-old semi-retired gunsmith who lived with his wife in Providence, Rhode Island. In his youth Burns worked for a local company on light machine guns.

The go-between, a Rhode Island businessman who had been in the arms business during the war, intimated to Burns that he would be interested in sponsoring an effort to design a new kind of submachine gun. Burns, who'd come to think his gunmaking days were over, leaped at the opportunity. A few days later Herschel took the train to Providence to meet him.

Burns met Herschel's train and drove him in his battered, rusting Ford to his two-family clapboard house on a modest side street.

Herschel concentrated on his host's personality and character. This was New England, and Burns, with his pale blue eyes, long, thin face and grey crew-cut, with his flannel shirt and corncob pipe, was a WASP. Herschel wondered whether the man would be so friendly when he found out what the gun was for. Herschel would have to tell Burns everything. He wanted the gunsmith to design not only the weapon, but the machines that would be needed to manufacture it. For that Burns would have to take into account the workplace.

Mrs. Burns was a stout, cheery woman with grey hair tinted blue and horn-rimmed eyeglasses studded with rhinestones. She made tea, set out cookies and retired to the parlor so the two men could talk business over her oilcloth-covered kitchen table.

They almost immediately agreed on design principles. Burns would attempt to design a sheet-metal stamped gun so cheap to make that when it broke, it would be thrown away rather than repaired. They discussed fitting a magazine-loading tool into the collapsible wire shoulder stock, an oil can into the hand grip and an optional flash hider to be used at night. They decided on a price of seventeen thousand dollars and a deadline of six months for the design.

Finally the time came for Herschel to reveal just who would be employing Burns. The gunsmith listened intently, puffing on his corncob pipe.

He thought a minute after Herschel finished and then said, ''I can trace my family back to the days when they followed Roger Williams out of the Massachusetts Bay Colony and came here for religious freedom. Roger Williams didn't take this land from the Indians, he bought it from them fair and square, and then he made Providence a homeland for folks who wanted to do things their own way. It seems to me that you folks are in the same boat as old Roger and my people, and if my ancestors helped him, I guess I can help you.''

That was in February. The six months were almost up. Now Herschel Kol was preoccupied as he went about his business, checking in with the students and hoping Wilbur Burns had called and his blueprints were ready.

Chapter 55

Carl Pickman slammed down the telephone. He sat statue-still, trying to calm himself, trying to will away the angry throbbing in his temples.

It was no use. His sister Deborah's complaining voice was still droning in his mind.

"When Daddy stuck Robert in accounting I didn't say a word, Carl. I didn't expect him to start at the top just because he's my husband. He's been comptroller for almost ten years now. I think it's time for him to take a more active role in running the store. You're not in your office very much anymore. Robert deserves his chance. Rebecca is very sweet, but she's not the family's choice to run the store. Amy agrees with me, Carl, and between us we control thirty percent of the stock."

Carl rose from his chair and left his study. He wandered down the long corridor of the apartment into the living room. It was a high-ceilinged, lavish room with gilded mirrors, old brocades and two magnificent chandeliers. The decorators had been closely supervised by Becky; the entire apartment had been done to her taste.

"I want fine old things, Carl," she said. "Nothing new. The only way to judge the quality of what's new is by its price tag. What's old, what endures is what's valuable.''

Carl loved what she'd done with their apartment, perhaps because he loved her. Being surrounded by her taste and personality made him feel relaxed and secure.

He moved to the great picture window that over-looked Central Park. From this high vantage at the very peak of summer the verdant landscape resembled a jungle carpet and the lake glittered like quicksilver in the fire-cracker July sun.

It was warm in the apartment. He threw open the casement windows, and along with a refreshing breeze came the faint honk and huff of the traffic, eternally crawling along Central Park West.

However, he could not still the echo of his sister's voice. ''Daddy never meant . . . Amy agrees with me. Rebecca's very sweet, but she's hardly—''

How dare his sisters question his judgment?

''You're not in your office very much anymore.''

Well, that much was true. Since their return from their honeymoon he'd been going to the store less and less frequently. Now he just stopped in for a few hours in the afternoon once or twice a week, and that was mostly to keep up his correspondence and to pretend to ponder the decisions already made by Becky and Philip. Really, he was only justifying his name on his office door.

He was very much like his uncle Bernard, a dabbler in the arts. He was painting these days; Becky had turned one room into a studio for him.

He had also taken up philanthropy. He was, however, not personally involved in any of that Palestine matter. The whole thing was just too unpleasant. Becky pestered him and pestered him about it until finally he told her to pick up the telephone and tell Sonneborn that she was interested in lending her support to his cause. He asked only two favors, that she keep him out of it and that she always bear in mind that she had the Pickman reputation to consider.

His own pet project was his campaign to turn Pickman House into a museum celebrating the cultural contributions of Jews in America. It was an outlook out of fashion just now, as American Jewry was preoccupied with the nightmare of the extermination camps, but he was convinced that the day would come when American Jews would be ready to turn away from their dark brooding and appreciate what they'd achieved.

It'd been a bit dicey at first, getting Pickman House out of his ex-wife's clutches. She received the property in their divorce settlement, but she'd never really wanted it, only demanded it out of spite. When he informed her that Becky had no intention of living there, Gertrude began to soften, and when he explained that he wanted to donate the property to the city of New York and name it the Gertrude Hoffer Pickman Museum, she quickly relented.

His painting, his reading and his charity work were more than enough to occupy him, especially in the summer. Odd—he used to enjoy outdoor sports in the summer, but lately he had developed an antipathy to warm weather. It first showed up during their honeymoon. He was swimming laps at their hotel; the water was quite warm, he remembered. The glass roof acted like a greenhouse, concentrating the winter-weakened sun and heating the pool area.

He'd only done a few laps when he felt a throbbing in his temples and his vision darkened. He had a panicky moment as he floundered in the deep end, swallowing some water, but he got his wits back and managed to get to the side and clutch on until the bad spell passed. Then he staggered out of the pool. After that he began to experiment and found that he could easily bring on the worrisome symptoms by overexerting himself, by standing up suddenly and by abruptly changing his mood, particularly losing his temper.

Upon their return to New York he saw his physician, who found nothing wrong on initial examination, but who strongly advised Carl to check into the hospital for a battery of tests. Ridiculous, Carl replied. He was a bridegroom. He wanted to be with his wife in their new apartment, not languishing in a hospital. Couldn't his symptoms be attributed to simple overheating?

The doctor allowed that they could.

Well then, Carl scoffed, the answer was to take it easy in the summertime.

It was the right decision, Carl reflected as he gazed out the window at Central Park. It would not do to let on that he was feeling ill; today's telephone exchange with his sister had convinced him of that. His sisters would seize on any excuse to rob Becky of her authority. He could hardly hold to his claim that she was working under his supervision if he was in a hospital.

Besides, it would be humiliating when it got around that he'd checked himself in for tests. He could hear the laughter now. What did the old goat expect, taking a bride half his age?

I got what I wanted and Becky got what she wanted. Now we can get on with being happy if only the world will see fit to leave us alone.

He sighed in resignation and left the living room for his studio. It was a glorious afternoon and the apartment was positively ticking with blessed quiet. Their housekeeper—Becky would not stand for more than one servant—was out shopping. He looked forward to getting at that watercolor still life before the light changed.

"I just think you should have consulted me, that's all." Cooper glowered, palms flat on Becky's desk, leaning over her. She rolled back her swivel chair as he loomed. "You've made your point, Phil. I understand that you don't agree. However, my decision stands. I appointed Grace Turner chief fashion buyer because I want somebody I can trust in Europe. I need to know exactly what Dior is doing in Paris, for example."

"My people have been buying for years, damnit. Are you saying you can't trust them?"

"Phil, you know me. I can sell anything, but I haven't got the clothes sense Grace was born with. I've known her a long time. We understand each other. I know what she means when she says something—"

"Authority over the buyers falls within the province of the vice president, not the general manager," Phil blurted, then blushed scarlet.

She lit a cigarette to blanket their embarrassment. "I've got an appointment in a few minutes," she said quietly, finding it hard to look him in the eye.

He nodded and turned to go, but at the door he stopped and stared at her. "You remember how you got here?" His voice was thick with bitterness.

"Yes, Phil, I remember. I'll never forget what you've done for me."

With a feral grin he shook his head. "I didn't bring up the past to draw lip service, but to make a point. You've changed a great deal, Rebecca, my dear. I doubt very much if you take the time these days to cozy up to your employees. When was the last time you strolled down to the shipping department to pick up some hot tips about what was in inventory? Go ahead and make Grace Turner your head fashion buyer. She knows you so well, after all. She knows just what you want to hear. If you weren't so unsure of yourself you wouldn't need that sort of obsequious—"

You're fired. It was on the tip of her tongue, but Becky knew better than to test her authority that far. She stabbed her cigarette into the ashtray and took a deep breath. "Phil," she began, her voice even despite her rage and hurt, "don't fight me. Cooperate with me. We're a team. Phil, I owe you—"

"You don't owe me a thing, Rebecca," he said coldly. "I was just a convenient rung in the ladder. You would have gotten exactly where you are now, one way or the other."

Becky's intercom buzzed. Her secretary said, "Mr. Kol to see you."

Before she could reply Cooper said, "I'll have her send him in on my way out. Becky, I apologize for my tone just now. I lost my temper."

"It's all right." She fought savagely against crying.

"For what it's worth to you, Becky, I meant what I said about your lack of self-confidence. It made you work harder when you were at the bottom, but now you're isolating yourself. I still make my daily rounds. When was the last time you were on the sales floor?" He turned and left.

She would never have fired Phil, even if she had that authority. She adored him for the kindnesses he'd shown, although she also resented the way he seemed to blame her for being successful. She'd worked hard, her marriage to Carl notwithstanding. How dare Philip reprimand her?

There was a knock at her door. "Come in."

"Mrs. Pickman." Herschel Kol nodded politely on his way into her office, briefcase in hand.

"Mr. Kol," she said cordially, "it's always a pleasure."

He sat down in one of the brass-studded green leather wing chairs in front of her desk and began to extract files from his briefcase.

She'd met Herschel Kol several months before at one of the Institute's hotel luncheons, and she remembered how charmed she'd been by his manner and his British accent, so improbable for a Palestinian. He was the grandson of a renowned artist named Glaser. Carl had an art collection that included Cezanne, Renoir and Degas, bought for him by Bernard when he was just a boy. She asked her husband about Glaser's work. Carl was not very enthusiastic, and Becky nodded sagely in response, although the truth was that she knew very little about such matters.

Her Institute work involved what she did know— merchandise. Becky was heading a new committee, the Palestine Supplies Association. It would raise not cash but materials, everything from construction supplies to canned food, shoes, pots and pans. Becky's connections with goods manufacturers and wholesalers made her the perfect one to supervise the work.

Herschel had begun to visit her at the store to query her on Pickman's contacts in Canada, of which there were quite a few. During each interview Herschel sat with his notes scattered on her desk and his pad on his knee, conscientiously jotting down her advice about wage levels and influential Jews in Canada. Becky told him what she could without prying into his reasons for asking. The little she knew about him—that a substantial portion of the Institute's cash was going into a special fund to pay for Herschel's machinery—had convinced her that this rakish, intense man had better be discreet.

Becky enjoyed Herschel's visits. She liked his aura of danger and adventure, of course, but there was something more. Herschel Kol seemed to have a special way of paying attention to a woman. When she spoke he listened closely, his eyes locked on her face; when he replied to her there was no hint of condescension. He was always polite as well as straightforward, and in fact devastatingly charming.

"What can I do for you, today, Herschel?" she asked, smiling.

Herschel shook his head. "I have no more questions. The time has come for me to ask your help in another important matter.'' He told her about the submachine gun being designed. He expected the blueprints for both the weapon and the manufacturing equipment any day.

''Prototypes must be delivered intact to Palestine. Machine shops are needed. Just now I think New York is a bad location for this phase. There are too many men like me working your country; the Zionist leadership has put all its eggs in one basket. I'd like to set up in Canada, both to protect the operation from the FBI and because I believe the work can be done more cheaply there. You see, although I consider this project important, the leadership is more concerned with collecting arms than with inventing new ones. My own opinion is that a new kind of army—a civilian militia—will require a new kind of weapon.''

''I don't know a thing about guns, so how can I help?''

''You have connections in Canada. Perhaps you can open the right doors for me or introduce me to someone who will.''

''I'll do my best.'' Becky smiled. ''I must confess, I find all this cloak-and-dagger stuff very exciting.''

''Mrs. Pickman—'' Herschel's clear, penetrating gaze thrilled and troubled her. ''Rebecca, if I may—I must ask you to think twice before you join us.''

''I already am involved.''

''Excuse me, but raising legitimate donations is one thing and conspiring to smuggle weapons is another. We would have to meet outside your office, for instance. You must understand the dangers.''

Becky nodded. What had she been thinking? She couldn't slink off to shadowy rendezvous with this attractive foreign agent. Perhaps her marriage wasn't all she'd hoped since Carl lost his robust vitality. Their relationship had regressed to a platonic level and they seemed more father and daughter than husband and wife.

"I'm not sure I can help you after all. I do have my reputation to protect." Hearing herself made Becky cringe.

"You are an important woman, already doing a great deal for the cause," Herschel said as he repacked his briefcase. He stood up. "Good-bye and thank you for your help."

She watched him turn to go. Philip Cooper's words came back to her. She felt uncertain, old and tired. "Mr. Kol, can I really help you? You need me?"

He nodded, his expression composed. "Time and money are running out. I don't know where else to turn."

"I see. If we meet, will we be alone?" She found it difficult to meet his quizzical stare. "I mean, could I take a chaperone? Well, never mind. I've changed my mind. I'll help. My father has always shown the greatest interest in Palestine. I suppose that interest has rubbed off on me." Did she see or imagine the flicker of uncertainty in his eyes? "I'm not usually so indecisive," she said ruefully.

Herschel grinned and Becky decided he had quite a wonderful grin.

After leaving Pickman's Herschel Kol took the subway downtown to Canal Street. From there he walked west to Benny Talkin's warehouse office. Danny had reported a slight mishap on the loading docks. A hollow boiler filled with pistols, rifles and ammunition had slipped and crashed to the dock while being craned aboard a freighter. A welded seam split and some of the longshoremen must have seen what was inside. Danny said not to worry; none of the witnesses would talk. Herschel was not so sure. He trusted Danny but kept in mind his assistant's extreme youth. Herschel had once been as cocksure, but a spell in prison had cured him. It was an experience he wished to avoid repeating and one he wanted to spare Danny if possible.

The first time he met Benny Talkin he'd disliked him,

but gradually Benny came to remind Herschel of Yol Popovich. Like Yol, beneath Benny's veneer of brash cynicism was a good streak. Danny said Benny was "connected," a bit of American jargon that meant he had ties to organized crime. This concept of crime as big business, a fact of life, at first confounded Herschel, but really, it was just like the Turks and their baksheesh.

Today Benny assured Herschel that the witnesses to the boiler mishap knew better than to talk about it. "Those guys kept their mouths shut when three corpses fell out of a shipment," Benny laughed. "Believe me, Kol, you don't need to sweat them going to the cops about a couple of measly popguns."

Benny's desk was a clutter of papers, some of which he shoved aside to make room for Herschel's briefcase. Herschel noticed something carrying the Pickman letter-head—a note from Rebecca soliciting Benny's help raising donations of supplies.

"Yeah, how about that," Benny shrugged when Herschel made mention of the letter. "I get it from both sides of the family, huh?"

"What do you mean?" Herschel asked, puzzled.

Benny stared at him. "You mean to say you don't know that Danny and Becky are brother and sister?"

"No, I didn't." Herschel laughed, totally flabbergasted. "What a coincidence. Why, I just came from her office." He went on to explain in vague terms that Rebecca was helping him in his work. "Wait until I tell Danny."

"Danny doesn't know?"

"No, it's never come up."

"Take my advice, Kol, and don't tell him. Danny's a hotheaded sort, and he's always had to live in his sister's shadow. If he finds out Becky's one of the big shots, he's likely to walk out on you."

"That would be terrible. I really need his help right now. Thanks, Talkin. I won't say a word."

Benny nodded. "Okay. You know, she and I used to date. It was a long time ago, but we were pretty serious about one another for a year or so."

"Oh, really?" Herschel began to fidget, not wanting to hear about Benny's relationship with Rebecca. "Why don't we get back to work?"

"Sure—you know, I still got a soft spot right here." He patted his heart. "You can't blame me; she's a great-looking broad." He winked. "She knows how to treat a guy right, too."

"Talkin!"

Talkin reared back in his chair, blinking in surprise at Herschel's aggrieved tone. "What's eating you? I say something wrong?"

"No. I mean—well, yes," Herschel replied. "She is married, after all."

"Yeah, she's married all right." A light seemed to dawn in Benny's eyes. "Hey, I get it. You've been working with her a couple of months, eh, Kol? That's long enough; I should know. Tough break, huh?"

"I don't know what you're talking about."

"Have it your way, Kol. No shame in it, though. I'd say she's your type." He grinned like a cat. "I don't want no one thinking I'm crude, though, so let's drop it and get back to work."

Forty minutes later Herschel was at a pay telephone, dialing the number of the headquarters apartment in the hope that Wilbur Burns had called. He was still disturbed by his reaction to Benny's gossip about Rebecca Pickman. Why should he care if the two of them had dated seriously? Rebecca's past was no concern of his.

As the phone rang he mused on how odd it felt to be thinking about a woman at all. He had not done so since that day years ago when Yol Popovich came to visit him in prison with the news of Frieda's death.

How young he was when he shared Frieda's bed, how deep and intense his love. To find himself thinking about another woman was disloyal to Frieda's memory.

All thoughts of women and love were swept from his mind as somebody at last picked up the phone. "Herschel, your friend from out of town has called three times already." The youngster at the other end of the line sounded frightened. "It sounds like bad trouble."

Chapter 56

"The telephone calls started coming a few weeks ago," Wilbur Burns said. "At first I denied everything, but there was no point in doing that once the fellow mentioned you. He knew everything—that I was designing a weapon for the Jews; when it was supposed to be finished; how much you were going to pay me."

"And he said he was representing Syria?" Herschel repeated. "He freely admitted that?"

They were sitting in the Burnses' tidy front parlor. Herschel slumped in a worn armchair with a rust-colored corduroy slipcover.

After their telephone conversation earlier that day, Herschel went directly to Penn Station, where he caught the three o'clock train to Providence. He arrived at eight o'clock and took a taxi to the Burnses' home. Mrs. Burns was now in the kitchen, scrambling eggs and making coffee. Wilbur was leaning forward on his couch, his hands clasped and his elbows planted on his knees as he told his story.

"This Syrian fellow mentioned the names and addresses of my son and daughter—she was widowed by the attack on Pearl Harbor. Anyway, this guy on the phone warned me that something might happen to my kids and my grandchildren if I didn't sell him my designs. I told him to call late tonight. Then I started phoning you.''

"And he offered you fifty thousand dollars?"

"That's what he said," Burns replied. "He said he had it in cash. I give him my designs and he hands over a briefcase.''

Nodding glumly, Herschel looked around at the modest furnishings, the tattered wallpaper. Music began filtering through the party wall of the two-family house.

"That's just my neighbor—Portuguese, but a nice family, born here and all. The husband works at the Narragansett brewery, and he likes to let off a little steam at night. The music's a nuisance usually, but tonight we can at least be sure nobody can hear our conversation.''

"Burns, I tell you now what I told you over the telephone. You don't have to put up with your family being threatened. The Syrians are offering almost triple what I can pay. Sell them the plans; take their fifty thousand dollars. Provide for your family and find yourself a more comfortable home.''

Burns fussed with his corncob pipe. "Don't you be talking so hard. Seventeen thousand is all your group can come up with, eh?''

Herschel could match the Syrians' bid out of his own pocket, but what was to prevent them from raising the ante? They were most likely backed by the oil-rich Transjordan. As wealthy as he was, he couldn't hope to outbid a nation. Besides, he'd already planned to pay for manufacture of the gun, and he had a responsibility to his mother not to deplete their fortune.

"Seventeen thousand is all I can pay. I can give you all sorts of arguments, but Palestine is very far away. You are an American, not even a Jew. Take the fifty thousand. You don't owe me anything.''

Mrs. Burns was still fussing in the kitchen, but it suddenly got quiet in there and Herschel could tell she was listening to them. In matters like this a wife had great influence on her husband, Herschel knew. What did she want him to do?

''Kol, I asked you to take the train up here so that we could talk face to face. I don't have a thing against the Syrian people, but I don't subscribe to a bunch of foreigners coming here to push me around. I admit their money was tempting, but they made the wrong move when they threatened me. I wouldn't have taken such treatment from you, and I won't take it from them. You and I shook hands on the deal and that's that as far as I'm concerned.''

As Herschel gratefully murmured his thanks, Mrs. Burns appeared in the doorway. She had a wooden spoon in one hand and a smile on her round face.

''I'm glad that's settled,'' she said. ''Now Mr. Kol, come have something to eat.''

As they headed into the kitchen Wilbur Burns stopped him. ''Damn. With all the excitement I forgot to tell you. I finished this morning.''

It was decided that Herschel would spend the night in their son's bedroom. ''We've used it for storage, but it's the best we can do. My daughter took her bedroom furniture with her when she moved, and that living room sofa isn't fit to sleep on.''

Herschel and Wilbur spread the blueprints out on the parlor carpet to go over them while they waited for the Syrians to call.

''Are you sure you want to go through with this?'' Wilbur asked him. ''It seems to me you're hunting trouble if you confront these people.''

"They will not harm your family," Herschel assured him.

"Figured that out for myself," Wilbur admitted. "There'll be no point once I turn the plans over to you, and they'd have hell to pay, since I'd never keep my mouth shut about it, but why do you want to take them on? Those Arabs would probably enjoy roughing up the likes of you."

"I don't intend to let them rough me up, but I need to know who they are. Clearly there is a leak in my organization, and I've got to plug it if I can. The man they send to the exchange is most likely the one in contact with our traitor. If I can force him to tell me who that is—"

"How do you intend to force him?"

Herschel looked away. "It's war between the Jews and the Arabs, my friend. Whatever happens, I promise that you will be in no way implicated."

Burns wanted to argue that point, but he never got the chance. The telephone rang.

The two men exchanged glances. "Could be my daughter. She and her mother do like to chat." He looked ready to bite clear through the stem of his pipe.

"Wilbur, it's for you," Mrs. Burns called from the kitchen.

"Shit," Burns sighed, reaching for the parlor extension.

Herschel listened as Burns arranged for a meeting at noon the next day. In accordance with his agreement with Herschel, Burns insisted that he did not want the Syrian to come to his house. They would meet in a public place; he suggested the carousel house in Roger Williams Park. It was a crowded spot, especially in summer, but just a few steps away were trees and shrubs for concealment.

Burns hung up the telephone. "It's all set. We'll drive over there, and—"

"We?" Herschel frowned. "You're not going."

"Don't be dumb, Kol. If I'm not at that damned merry-go-round tomorrow, they won't show themselves."

"How can I ever thank you?"

"By not getting me, yourself or anyone else killed. By waiting until you and the Syrians are back home before you have your damned war. Good night, Kol. I'm tired. It's been a long day, and tomorrow isn't going to be much shorter."

The son's bedroom was plastered with baseball pennants, and much of the floor was taken up with stacked cartons, old furniture and odds and ends. It made Herschel sad to be here, surrounded by the detritus of other people's lives. It made him desperately homesick.

He took his shaving kit from his overnight bag and rummaged through it for his toothbrush. Next to his safety razor and blades was a semiautomatic Beretta, small and square and deadly. It would go with him tomorrow for his day at the amusement park.

Much later he tossed and turned in the boy-sized bed, waiting for sleep that would not come. A cool breeze began to blow through the screened windows, ruffling the curtains and taking the worst out of the humid summer night.

Herschel kicked himself free of the tangled sheets, went to his bag to fetch the Beretta and put it under his pillow. He immediately relaxed. Sleeping with a gun at hand was a habit most Palestinians formed early. After he fell asleep he dreamed of Rebecca Pickman.

The next morning at eleven-fifteen they drove in Burns' rattly Ford to Roger Williams Park. Herschel's Beretta, a round in the chamber and the safety catch up, was in the pocket of his suit coat.

"Hope you're reluctant to use that piece of yours," Burns remarked as they drove into the park.

"You can see it?"

"Don't go getting upset, son. I've been around guns all my life. I can tell when a man's packing. I know how wound up you are, but do bear in mind that if you get nicked on a weapons charge—or for murder—it'll mean the end of your gun project and probably the end of your organization in America. Remember what I said about how the Syrians wouldn't dare harm a citizen of the United States? Think about the sort of press coverage you would get for starting a shoot-out near a merry-go-round full of kids on a sunny summer afternoon."

"I understand," Herschel sighed.

The area near the carousel was crowded, and both sides of the winding boulevard were lined with cars. Burns turned in to a cul-de-sac and slowed to let Herschel out.

"The carousel house is down that incline," he said. Herschel could hear the music. "I'll find a parking spot and have myself an ice cream, I guess," Burns continued. "I'll be here at noon." He checked his watch and nodded. "See you."

Herschel walked down the sloping lawn to the open-sided carousel house. It was chaotic. The paved area surrounding the building was mobbed with cart vendors selling balloons, peanuts, candied apples and frozen ices. Children dashed about, shrieking and laughing or tugging at their parents' hands to hurry their pace. People were shuffling and queuing to buy snacks or tickets for the carousel; fat yellow jackets swooped and darted above the trash barrels; and everywhere was the crashing nursery music of the carousel organ. Children were bouncing up and down on prancing candy-colored steeds while their parents or grandparents looked on.

Herschel noticed a fat policeman, his visored cap pushed back on his head, his belly straining his shirt buttons. The cop, casually twirling his nightstick, paused at a pushcart to help himself to a candied apple; the vendor looked resigned.

Somewhere on the other side of the park gates a factory siren blew noon. Herschel saw Burns walking toward the carousel. He had his hands in his pockets and his shoulders were hunched. He looked worried, Herschel thought as he stepped back to stand behind a tree. That was all right. He had ample reason to be worried.

Wilbur had promised to meet the Syrian and lead the man to his car; the designs were supposed to be in the trunk. Herschel had promised to intercept them before they got there, but it looked as though he'd have to follow them away from this place. It was too busy here, and the policeman was still lurking, munching his apple on a stick.

A child was throwing a tantrum nearby when Herschel saw the Arab coming around the far side of the carousel, heading directly for Wilbur Burns. He saw him, squeezed his eyes shut and opened them again, expecting the hallucination to vanish.

It didn't. It was he, looking exactly as he had the day Herschel watched him enter the coffeehouse in Jerusalem. Today, of course, he was not wearing his fez.

The Arab shook hands with Wilbur and said in faintly accented English, "I'm so glad you have accepted our offer."

"Well, you know how it is," Burns stammered, obviously stalling and most likely wondering where Herschel was. "Fifty thousand is a lot of money. You people must want my design something awful."

"Of course we value your work, Mr. Burns," the Arab replied diplomatically. "However, as I mentioned to you on the telephone, what is most important to us is your guarantee that the other interested party will not receive it."

"Hey—"

The Arab froze as Herschel stepped from behind the

tree. Glancing sorrowfully at Wilbur, he took several quick steps to separate himself from the gunsmith and then focused his attention on Herschel. "It is you and I once again, my old friend. Always, I suppose, it shall be you and I."

He's always known me, Herschel thought. He remembered how the Arab seemed to recognize him in the bazaar in Jerusalem. He scrutinized the Arab's features—low, dark hairline, thin nose, wide mouth and weak chin—but he had no idea who it was. His enemy seemed to sense Herschel's confusion and his black eyes sparkled with mirth.

As Herschel approached, the Arab transferred his briefcase to his left hand and unbuttoned his suit jacket, affording Herschel a glimpse of a gun butt in his waistband. Herschel slid his hand into his own pocket to thumb off the Beretta's safety.

The Arab's gaze flicked down. He looked philosophical. The two of them were no more than ten feet apart. A trio of children towing rainbow balloons ran between them. The balloons bobbed and swayed in the breeze and the Arab used his briefcase to deflect them from his face. Herschel looked for the cop and found him still there, still eating his candied apple, but in a slower, somewhat preoccupied manner. He was watching the tableau formed by Herschel, Wilbur Burns and the Arab; his policeman's intuition warned him that trouble was imminent. The cop was not going anywhere fast, Herschel knew.

The Arab looked over his shoulder at the policeman. "No, this isn't the place," he agreed, "unless, of course, it is your wish to languish in an American prison as you once did in a British one."

Herschel forced himself to let go of his gun and remove his hand from his pocket. "Who are you?"

"I identified you to the British. It was because of me that you went to prison. In those days the Irgun knew me as Eagle Owl, the slayer of Jews, and it was I you hoped to kill with your grenades.''

''But how do you know me?'' The carousel's sprightly bells and chimes formed an ironic counterpoint to Herschel's terror. ''How did you know my name?''

''Like father, like son,'' the Arab smiled.

Herschel began to sweat and shiver. *The gun was in his pocket—*

''Your resemblance to your father was once quite remarkable, but prison has aged you.'' Eagle Owl looked sympathetic. ''I too had a short childhood, Herschel.'' He switched from English to Hebrew. ''It was Yol who taught me your language. I used to practice my Hebrew with Yol and your father.''

''*Ma, leggo my balloon!*'' a three-year-old wailed.

Herschel made no sound as he stared beyond the pushcarts and balloons at his father's unmarked grave near Degania. Silently he began to weep.

''He used to tell me about you, Herschel. I probably spent more time with him than you did. He had his arm around me in a fatherly embrace when I sank my blade between his ribs.''

Herschel bit down on his lower lip to keep from screaming. His fingers itched to claw out his gun, but he kept his hand at his side, remembering Wilbur Burns' advice. Even if he managed to kill his father's murderer, the Arab would end up the winner, for Herschel's arrest and the subsequent publicity would destroy Zionism in America.

''Not here, not now, Jibarn Ahmed,'' Herschel announced in Arabic, ''but someday I will kill you.''

''Dry your eyes, Jew,'' Jibarn Ahmed replied in the same tongue. ''At a time and in a place that I deem appropriate, I shall reunite you with your father, though he deserved better than a dog for a son.''

He turned to Wilbur Burns. "Good-bye, Mr. Burns. I fear you have lost a great deal of money."

Wilbur Burns looked at him distastefully. "Money ain't everything, sonny."

Jibarn Ahmed backed away and in seconds had vanished into the throng.

Burns came over to Herschel. "What the hell just happened?"

Herschel tried to speak but couldn't. He shook his head.

"You got the safety on?" Burns whispered, keeping his eye on the munching policeman.

Herschel sighed. "Thanks." He reached into his pocket to secure the Beretta. "I do now."

"Been around guns all my life," Burns muttered knowingly. "A revolver's safe as home in bed, but you can't go neglecting those pocket autos." He peered at Herschel. "You look pale, son, and your lip is bleeding like a son of a bitch." He offered his handkerchief, which Herschel pressed to his bloody lower lip as they headed for the car.

"Figure you and that Arab don't much care for each other," Burns observed.

"No, we don't."

"Figure he did something bad to you."

"Yes, it was bad."

"Glad I didn't sell to him."

Chapter 57

After that Herschel Kol fretted about the security of the various operations sponsored by Sonneborn's Institute, but there was nothing he could do. His job was to amass weaponry, not engage in counterespionage, as he was repeatedly reminded by his superiors.

It was inevitable that a certain amount of sensitive information would leak. The several dozen wealthy Jews who formed the Institute's core, along with the many volunteers from all walks of life, could not be insulted with investigations or cross-examinations. Herschel was reminded that the Palestinians were in America as guests and supplicants. If on occasion a contributor committed an indiscretion, that was to be expected, even condoned. As many new connections had been made as secrets lost in such fashion. Herschel let the matter drop, resolving privately to keep a tighter rein on the security of his own group.

He did all he could on his own to try and ferret out Ahmed's whereabouts. He even asked Benny Talkin to lend a hand, but all efforts came to nothing. At last he forced himself to put the incident out of his mind. He and Jibarn Ahmed would one day meet again; it was inevitable. It was time to get back to work on the Canadian venture.

*   *   *

Throughout the fall of 1946 Herschel and Rebecca continued their meetings in coffee shops, hotel lobbies, cocktail lounges. Finally all the telephone calls had been made, all the groundwork laid. Rebecca scheduled a business trip to Toronto for the first week in November. Herschel would travel there separately and they would meet with some who were willing to help transform Wilbur Burns' designs into reality.

Pickman listened quietly as Becky told him the real reason behind her trip to Toronto. They were seated on the sofa in their living room overlooking Central Park. Carl took Becky's hand as she spoke excitedly of the progress she'd made on that fellow Kol's behalf. He had known before this Becky was working with Kol, but those meetings had lasted only an hour or so once or twice a week. Now she was asking his blessing on a week-long trip with him to another city. Carl trusted his wife; fidelity was not a concern. It was just that he felt excluded from this Palestine work; never mind that he wanted to be kept out of it. He was jealous of the way it monopolized Becky's time. It made him feel very lonely, very old. At the same time he knew he could not forbid the trip, much as he dreaded her being away.

"You and Herschel have gotten to be good friends, I imagine."

Becky looked thoughtful. "I suppose. For the time being, anyway," she said somewhat cynically. "I don't have any real friends."

Carl was troubled. "What about Grace Turner and Phil?"

For a moment Becky looked angry, but then she affectionately squeezed his hand. "I guess we're so busy we hardly listen to one another. Don't you remember what I've told you about my differences with Phil?"

"Have you?" Carl frowned.

Becky kissed him. "My absent-minded artist. Lucky for you I'm not the sort of wife who likes to chase her errant husband with a rolling pin."

"Yes." Carl nodded, not really listening. "What?"

"I said like *Jiggs and Maggie,* you know, the comics."

"Yes, of course, dear. It's just that someone the other day castigated me on my forgetting something." His brow furrowed. "Who was it?"

"If you came into the store more often you'd be more up on what's going on."

"Yes, I suppose," Carl mused. "Anyway, what about your friendship with Grace?"

Becky shrugged. "Grace and I haven't really been close for a long time," she sighed. "I thought my promoting her would draw us closer together, but the opposite has happened. She's always polite and respectful, always ready to chat, but she keeps her distance anymore. I'm afraid the only thing that I've accomplished by promoting Grace is antagonizing Phil."

"That's what comes from having power and authority, my dear," Carl said sympathetically. "The trappings of success afford one respect, but affection is another matter entirely."

"Carl, it would help if you came into the office more often. I know it would. Everyone misses you. I think sometimes they blame me for your absence. I know that's silly, but—"

"I understand. I—well, I haven't wanted to burden you, Becky, but I haven't been feeling well, I've been having bad headaches. It's annoying, really. I wake up and within an hour the pain is on me. It lessens toward evening, but I'm getting so little done . . ." He paused. "My dear, you're crying."

Becky rested her head on his shoulder. "I thought you were unhappy with me or— I didn't know what to think." She rubbed her wet eyes. "Why didn't you tell me you were ill? How long has it been going on?"

"Since last year, I'm afraid." He felt sheepish. "Perhaps you should be chasing me with that rolling pin. At first I just dismissed it as the result of warm weather. Then when the headaches began— Well, I suppose I've just been waiting and hoping that whatever it is would go away."

"Have you been to the doctor?"

"Yes, but he wanted me to check into the hospital for tests, and I didn't want to begin our marriage that way."

"Well, you must go now."

"Yes, but not while you're away, my dear—"

"Then I'll cancel the trip."

"You can't. It means too much to too many people. You simply have to go. I'll make arrangements to check into the hospital after you've come back. I just can't bear to be away from our home and you at the same time, my love. A few weeks now aren't going to make any difference. Most likely the tests will turn out inconclusive anyway. I suppose I'm just getting old. I know that I haven't been very much of a husband to you, Becky." He thought about the young, dynamic Palestinian. Did she regret it when she left that fellow to come home to him? "This last year has been one of the happiest in my life, but what about you? Are you sorry you married me?"

"No, Carl. I love you. Remember what I said before about not having friends? Well, we're friends, Carl, kindred souls. What we have is much more than I've seen in other marriages. When you're well, when you've regained your strength, we'll take some time off. We'll go back to Salem Farm. We'll go to the stables and make love in the hay—"

Carl, his heart pounding, pressed his face into her hair. "I love you so much."

*   *   *

Toronto in November was a grey and frigid city. To
Herschel it was just one more strange place he had to
endure. The winters in this part of the world were long and
debilitating. Herschel was both mentally and physically
exhausted. How he missed his mother and Yol, how he
missed Degania. There'd been letters during his twenty
months in America, but they could never substitute for a
loved one's embrace or the smell of cornflowers and the
look of Galilee's rugged hills beyond the fertile fields.

He and Rebecca stayed in different hotels. She was in
the luxurious Toronto Hilton. His own compulsion to spend
as little as possible on himself led him to a clean but
depressing little pension near the Yonge Street shopping
district.

Rebecca, it turned out, had business other than his to
conduct. Herschel spent two days waiting, lying on his bed
in his room, listening to the wind sweeping off Lake
Ontario.

On Wednesday evening Becky gave a dinner in a
steak house that overlooked the city's harbor. Her guests
were Horace Crown, who supplied wooden hangers to
department stores, and burly pockmarked Max Ross, the
former chief engineer at the John Inglis Company of Toronto,
which manufactured Browning automatic weapons.

It was a wonderful meal, and Herschel, who rarely
drank, ended up giddy from the wine. Thanks to Becky,
everything quickly and easily fell into place. Horace Crown
even volunteered to fund the project. Tomorrow Herschel
and Max Ross would get together to hammer out the
specifics.

After dinner Herschel was excited, unable to bear the
thought of returning to his dreary pension. He begged
Becky to join him for a drink in the restaurant's lounge.
She seemed reluctant, but he reminded her that they'd had
many such private meetings back in New York, so what
harm could there be in a drink tonight?

The lounge was a shadowy, candlelit place. They were shown to a secluded table with comfortable leather chairs and a majestic view of the harbor. When their drinks came, Herschel lifted his glass to Becky. "You were magnificent tonight. You managed everything. When Crown offered to pay, I nearly stood up and cheered."

Becky laughed, pleased. "I'm glad to see you so happy. I knew Horace would come up with the money. Believe me, he can afford it, and right now I don't think any Jew who is well off could say no."

"They say no to me, but nobody could refuse you," Herschel heard himself say. "You are far too lovely."

Becky looked away, obviously discomforted, and Herschel was embarrassed into chattering. "Yes, you are most definitely a heroine of Zionism. I thought my mother could command a meeting, but you, Becky—one-two-three, you could be the leader of a kibbutz."

Her laughter sounded grateful, Herschel thought, himself greatly relieved. When Becky lit a cigarette he asked if he could have one, reaching for the pack.

"I thought you didn't smoke."

"I haven't since prison," he blurted, and then it was his turn to look away. He toyed with the cigarettes and then put them down. "It was a British prison," he said weakly, wincing. "I'm talking like a fool. It's the alcohol going to my head, I suppose—that and being here with you in this strange city. I feel I'm dreaming. Anything is possible."

"I knew about prison," Becky said. "When we first began working together someone from the Institute approached me and told me you were a terrorist."

"I'm not. I'm not looking to terrorize anyone. I want only to return to my home and live in peace."

"I understand that. Tell me about Palestine. What's it like, living in a kibbutz? My husband claims people weren't meant to live like bees in a hive. He says once the necessities of life are provided, it's only natural to revert to capitalism." She paused.

"Carl's possessions mean a lot to him, but I don't think I'd mind not owning things very much as long as my work was interesting and everyone was friendly to me." She searched his face. "What I've read said that everyone on a kibbutz is very protective of one another, that there is no loneliness, no cause for shyness, that everyone takes care of one another."

"It is like that to a degree," Herschel replied, "but I wouldn't go so far as to say that there are never any spats. Despite what your husband may think, Socialists are individuals, not insects."

He began to tell her about his childhood at Degania, about what it was like to be the child of pioneers in a raw, unsettled land. He talked quietly and plainly of the beauty of Palestine and of the pride its people felt in building cities upon the shifting sands and turning swamps into gardens.

It had been so long since he'd let his guard down to speak of his past, his fears and his aspirations. As he spoke he watched Becky's reactions. She listened intently, nodding now and then, asking an occasional question, but mostly looking beautiful in the lambent candlelight, looking approving, looking admiring. Maybe she cared for him a little.

He downed his Scotch and ordered another. He talked of the adolescent, vulgar vitality of Tel Aviv and of the holy serenity of Jerusalem. He talked of orange groves and the Mediterranean, of hiding from the Turks during the First World War and of killing Arabs in defense of Degania later in the service of the Irgun. He talked about his mother and Yol.

If there'd been time, he probably would have found the courage to talk about his father and a certain unmarked grave close to Degania. If there'd been time, he might have told her that his family name was not Kol, but Kolesnikoff, that his father was able to reach the Holy Land thanks to the kindness of a guardian named Abe Herodetzky, that his father helped sire both Tel Aviv and Degania.

But long before he could bring himself to reveal so much, the waitress came to tell them that the cocktail lounge was closing. Herschel, his throat dry, realized he'd been talking for hours.

Becky let him pay for their drinks. He offered to escort her in a taxi back to her hotel, and she accepted. As they waited for the doorman to flag one he was acutely aware of her arm in his.

In the cab he told her, "Someday you must come to Palestine and see it with your own eyes. Perhaps my country would work its magic on you and you would stay."

"Oh, what could I do there?"

"You would live, thrive, and the country would thrive with you. In my country what one individual decides to do with life still makes a difference. Perhaps if we are fortunate it always shall."

"Perhaps some day you'll show me all this beauty first-hand." Her collar was turned up, framing her face. The cold had brought a blush to her cheeks and her lips looked delicious.

Thought and action became one. His fingers turned her head and tilted up her chin, and then his lips touched hers. She submitted to his kiss, or seemed to submit, but then she pushed him away and turned her head to the window.

"Y-you shouldn't have done that."

Her voice was hushed; was it a whisper or a sob?

"I love you," Herschel said, as surprised as she but sure it was the truth.

"No, you don't, Herschel. That's just the whiskey

and the night and your own loneliness talking. Believe me,
I know.'' She was still turned away.

"You must not be angry with me, Becky."

"I'm not." She turned to look at him and squeezed
his hand. "Listen to me. I'm married. I love my husband
very much. You are far away from your home. You've
grown fond of me because you're lonely. That's all right,
Herschel. I've grown fond of you as well."

"Then let me make love to you, Becky."

"Try and understand, Herschel. This isn't easy for
me to say." She stroked his cheek. "I want to too, but I
won't. All I have that matters besides my work is my
honor. If I betray my husband, my honor will be gone."

"We are so distant from New York. He would never
know—"

"I would know."

"Perhaps he cheats on you," Herschel said, frustrated and angry. If she wished to love him, why wouldn't
she?

"I don't think he does." Becky smiled. "But it
wouldn't matter if he did. If all the world cheated, I still
wouldn't. All I've got is my work and my honor."

The hotel loomed and the doorman was approaching.

"It doesn't matter, really," Herschel whispered. "In
our circumstances just saying you wished to is as important as doing it."

Then the doorman had the door open and Becky was
getting out. "Good night, Herschel," she said. Then she
was gone, leaving behind the lingering fragrance of her
perfume.

Herschel gave the driver the address of his pension
and the taxi pulled away. Now that Becky was gone and
the Scotch was wearing off, Herschel began to wonder if
he hadn't done something worse than act like a fool. He
wondered if he had done something dreadful to Becky.

He was mortified; he pressed his hot, flushed forehead to the cool glass of the taxi window. He had repaid her efforts to save his country by groping at her as if she were a whore.

He spent a fitful, sleepless night with his recriminations. The next day he scribbled a note of abject apology and sent it off with some flowers to Becky at her hotel. The flowers came back to the florist, who reported to Herschel that Mrs. Pickman had checked out of the hotel early that morning.

Herschel understood. She had left Toronto because she could not bring herself to see him again. He didn't blame her; he hated himself for his behavior.

During his appointment with Max Ross the engineer mentioned that it was a hell of a thing about Mrs. Pickman's husband.

"What do you mean?" Herschel asked.

"I guess you haven't heard." Ross shrugged. "I only found out because I talked to Horace Crown this morning. They found Carl Pickman dead last night."

"The housekeeper says Carl went out for his walk around six Wednesday night, and the doorman remembers warning him to mind the ice on the sidewalks." Norman Collins shook his head. "What I don't understand is why Carl would have wanted to go out for a stroll on a cold, dark November night."

"He'd been having bad headaches during the day." As Becky spoke she struggled to keep her tone emotionless and her grief and shock under control. "They went away toward evening. Wednesday night he'd probably been feeling better and wanted some air."

It was Friday morning and Becky was in Norman Collins' walnut-paneled study. The lawyer was in his sixties, a short, slender man with an abundance of snow-white, fluffy hair and a walrus mustache. He favored fancy walking sticks and tweedy country squire suits custom tailored in

England. For the past three decades he had been Carl's attorney and his closest friend.

"I'm sorry about the autopsy, Becky," Collins told her. "There was nothing I could do to prevent it. The authorities were adamant. It's not every day a man of Carl's stature is found lying dead in a city park. I'm just glad that I was able to keep most of this out of the newspapers."

Becky nodded. "I understand and I'm grateful for everything."

Collins called her in Toronto late Wednesday night with the terrible news and made reservations for her on the first flight home Thursday morning. He sent his limousine to meet her at the airport and all that day he dealt with the authorities while Becky made the funeral arrangements. The burial was at four, just before sunset.

"Don't forget that Carl was my friend," Collins said, waving aside her expressions of gratitude, "and don't forget that I'm your friend as well. It's been years since Carl introduced us so I could look after that building of yours downtown. I must admit that initially I concerned myself with it purely as a favor to Carl. Even then I could sense that you were quite special to him."

Becky nodded, swallowing hard, choking down her grief. All last night and the night before she had cried. Tonight she would wander the empty apartment on Central Park West and cry some more. Her tears were private, however.

"As best we can reconstruct it, Carl entered Central Park, slipped on some ice and rolled down an embankment. The fall broke his left hip. It was just bad luck that nobody came down that path in time to help him. The blood clot had been in his brain for quite some time, I'm told. Perhaps panic brought on the stroke. We'll never know. A gentleman out walking his dog about nine o'clock Wednesday evening discovered him and called the police."

*   *   *

The funeral was private. Phil Cooper was there. Becky spent a few tense moments with Gertrude Hoffer Pickman and her two young daughters and with Carl's sisters and their husbands. Then she moved away to sit with her father and brother.

Notes and telegrams of condolence were delivered to the apartment. In lieu of flowers, mourners were requested to make donations to the Gertrude Hoffer Pickman Museum fund, which Carl had chartered the previous summer. Carl was not religious, and neither was Becky. There would be no sitting shiva for a week. Carl's death had thrown Pickman's into disarray. She was needed at the store, and the best way she knew to honor his memory was to work night and day to make the store prosper.

On Tuesday morning she issued a staff memorandum thanking them for their expressions of sympathy and announcing that she would be assuming the post of president. That same day she began her move into Carl's office. By Friday she expected to be settled in. She had no plans to redecorate the office; she wanted it exactly the way Carl left it.

Thursday night Becky received a telephone call at home from Norman Collins; he asked her to come to his office on Friday morning. It seemed that there was some confusion as to whether Becky was the store's majority stockholder.

"I don't understand." Becky frowned at Collins across his paper-strewn desk. "I do inherit Carl's seventy percent of Pickman's, don't I? Is his ex-wife contesting that?"

Collins sighed. "Carl's divorce settlement was quite explicit about what Gertrude and the girls would receive. No, Becky, Gertrude isn't contesting anything. She doesn't have to."

"Norman, please, just explain. I don't care about anything but the store. As Carl's widow it seems to me—"

"Hold it," Collins said. "First of all, I loved Carl, but sometimes he was as stubborn as a mule, and this, unfortunately, was one of those times. Carl's sisters have fifteen percent each, and nineteen percent of the store is held in trust for his two daughters. Carl was to control those shares until they were twenty-one, a decade from now, but with his death those shares are now controlled by Gertrude."

"I see, but what's the problem? I still have Carl's fifty-one percent, which makes me the majority stockholder. Right, Norman?"

Collins stared at her, saying nothing. Becky lit a cigarette. "Norman, if you don't stop this sadistic teasing and tell me what's what I swear I'll scream."

The attorney nodded in satisfaction. "Then you don't know. I was hoping you didn't. I felt betrayed, you see. Becky, behind our backs Carl assigned ten percent to Philip Cooper. He went to another attorney to have their agreement drawn up. He probably figured that if I handled it, there would be a greater likelihood of your finding out about it."

Becky stood up and went to the windows. She stared down at the lanes of Park Avenue traffic disappearing into the mammoth portals carved into the base of the building. "I understand why he did it, Norman. You see, he lied to me about how happy Philip was that I was being made general manager. He was always so protective of me—he would have done anything to keep me from knowing he had to bribe Philip to accept me."

"Becky, come sit down. I'm afraid it gets worse." When Becky had returned to her chair he said, "The other attorney made a bad mistake. The agreement stated that Philip Cooper had to sell back all of his shares if he ever left Pickman's and that he could never vote against Carl, but no mention was made of what was to become of those shares if Carl should die."

"Oh, my God."

"Philip now has autonomy to vote his shares as he wishes. You have only forty-one percent in your control, Becky. If Gertrude and Carl's sisters vote together to oust you from the presidency, and there's every reason to think they shall, the vote will be their forty-nine percent to your forty-one."

"Then Phil Cooper's ten percent will be the deciding factor. If he votes with me I stay. If he votes against me or abstains . . ." she trailed off. "It just doesn't make sense. I love the store and I'm the best person to run it."

"That is so," Collins said. "However, to my constant sorrow we do not live in a logical world. Nevertheless, Becky, regardless of how this turns out, you remain a very rich woman—"

"Excuse me," she snapped, her voice dripping disdain. "I was already a rich woman. Now I'm a rich widow."

Collins winced and looked away.

"I'm sorry, Norman. I have no call to be angry with you."

"You loved Carl very much, didn't you?"

Becky nodded. "I know he meant for me to continue running the store. Without Pickman's I'm worthless."

"Now that's certainly not true."

"It is," Becky insisted. "The only time I'm really alive is when I'm working. Without the authority and power of the store behind me I'm useless, worthless, just as I said. It doesn't matter how much money I have."

"I understand how you feel," Collins replied. "If Carl had seen fit to trust me I could have protected you against this sad circumstance. Now it's too late. I can't help you maintain control, I'm sorry to say."

"Nobody can."

"Except Philip Cooper."

Chapter 58

Herschel Kol spent two weeks in Toronto establishing his operation. Max Ross was to be technical supervisor, and Horace Crown, true to his word, supplied financial backing. A loft in an industrial building on a Toronto back street was rented; Ross told the landlord that his business, Allied Machine Concepts, was developing a new machine for the textile industry.

Ross recruited machinists to work in house on the more sensitive projects. To save time it was agreed that the more innocent-looking components could be farmed out to other shops. Even so, Ross cautioned, the need for secrecy was going to slow them down. It would be at least six months before samples would be ready.

Herschel demanded that everything be finished in three months and returned to New York frantic over what he perceived as insurmountable deadlines. In a few weeks it would be 1947, and who could say what the new year would hold for Palestine? Every day the situation there was worsening, and the British stranglehold on immigration and imports kept tightening. The cleverest, simplest munitions factory in the world would do no good if the Jews of Palestine couldn't get their hands on it.

Herschel resolved to spend as much time as he could in Toronto, urging on his workers. Ross was a good man, but it wasn't his country that was in danger. The more time Herschel spent cracking the whip, the faster the guns and machines would be made.

He met with Danny to review the export side of their operation while he was away. Danny reported nothing out of the ordinary and then asked about Canada.

"Danny, you know it is better for everyone if we stick to what we need to know."

"Yeah, sure," Danny sneered, looking disgusted, "but everything went okay, right?"

"Right."

"Good. Then I quit."

"What? You can't quit now!"

"Sure I can," Danny shouted back. "I just did. Watch me do it again. I quit!"

"At least I should get an explanation."

"I don't owe you anything. Why didn't you tell me Becky was working with you, godamnit? I had a goddamned right to know."

"How did you find out?" Herschel asked calmly. "Was it Benny who told you?"

"It wasn't his fault. It slipped out while we were talking about Carl Pickman. You know Becky's husband died?"

Suddenly uneasy, Herschel nodded. His behavior on the night of his death still rankled. He had sent a note expressing his sympathies and begging forgiveness for what he had termed his rudeness. Even so, he dreaded the day he would face her.

"All my good work with you has been ruined," Danny complained. "I wanted to accomplish something important that nobody else could do, and what happens? My sister gets involved, and just like that she's the big shot and I'm small potatoes."

"She has the money to help us, Danny; I can't deny that. But it's your cleverness that allowed us to succeed. Money alone can't do it."

Danny looked unconvinced. "I appreciate what you said, but I'm still through. I got into this in the first place because I didn't want to work for my sister. I don't intend to work for her through you."

"Does Becky know how you feel?"

"Oh, so it's 'Becky,' is it?" Danny scowled. "You two must be closer than I thought. No, she doesn't know." He shrugged, his voice softening. "I'm not afraid of her or anything, but she is my sister, and with her husband just dying . . . well, I didn't have the heart to confront her."

Good, Herschel thought. That was one potential disaster out of the way. Becky was fully capable of disassociating herself from the cause so as not to antagonize her brother. If she backed out, who knew how long Horace Crown would continue to contribute?

"Danny, I need your help now more than ever. I must spend a lot of time in Canada, which means I need you here to watch over things in the States. I'm willing to make a deal with you." Herschel waited, watching, trying to fathom the depth of Danny's resolve to quit. If he wasn't interested in making deals, Herschel would have no choice but to let him go.

"What kind of deal?"

"You still want to fly?"

"Here we go again." Danny looked sour. "You must really think I'm stupid to fall for your tricks a second time."

"No tricks, Danny, I swear it."

"Herschel, there's nothing you wouldn't do or say to help Palestine."

"Absolutely true. However, in this case I am not lying. I can get you onto a list of pilots."

"Yeah? What's the catch?"

Herschel smiled grandly. "No catch." He put his arm around Danny's shoulders. "We are friends, yes? I help you; you help me."

"I swear to God, Herschel, if this is a trick—"

"Look, I'll telephone my contact that you are coming to see him. You'll go by yourself. He's an aviation expert and you are a pilot. You'll know soon enough if he is truthful."

Danny grudgingly nodded. "You knew about this guy all the time?"

"Yes."

"And you didn't tell me?"

"I wanted you to help me here first. I would have told you later, before I went home."

Lion Airlines turned out to be a hole in the wall in a building on far West Forty-second Street. It was mostly occupied by accountants, typewriter repair specialists and even a private detective. Danny identified himself to a fast-talking, chain-smoking man named Milty, stayed two hours and then went straight to headquarters.

"Well?" Herschel asked.

"He knows airplanes," Danny acknowledged. "I had to give him my real last name. I told him not even you know it, but—"

"He has to check on your flight training."

"That's what he said," Danny replied. "At first he wasn't too keen on the fact that I don't have a CAA license, but he perked up when I said I was a rated fighter jock. He said what he needed right away was guys able to fly cargo planes. I said that if he was in a real pinch I could always copilot. He wasn't too hot over that idea, but he said he'd check out my service record and keep me in mind. He said he could use me for sure later on, as a fighter pilot on one condition."

"And what was that?"

"Don't act so innocent. You know damn well what it was. I have to work with you until Milty sends for me."

"Danny, that only makes sense. This way he can keep tabs on you."

"I call it blackmail."

"Oh, is that what you call it? I'll tell you something. There are many men who would like to resume their aviation careers—many more than we'll need. These men have to pass through a number of preliminary interviews before they get to Lion Airlines. You may think what you like, but the fact is that without my help you wouldn't have made it. If Milty lets you fly, it will be as a favor to me. Understand?"

Danny nodded. He'd come to exactly that conclusion during his subway ride uptown. As much as he hated to admit it, at this point neither man could realize his goal without the help of the other.

Danny still desperately wanted to fly. It had been so long since he'd been able to talk knowledgeably with another aviator. His two-hour conversation with Milty had relit the fire. Toward the end of his interview he would have volunteered for any position on any flight crew. He would have kissed Milty's feet if the guy had offered him the chance to go along on a ride.

"I guess I got a little hot under the collar," Danny confessed. "I'm sorry. Calling you a blackmailer was unfair."

Herschel grinned. "Forget it. To show you that my heart's in the right place, when the time comes I swear I will allow you to risk your neck flying rickety airplanes on behalf of my country."

"Now that's fair and square," Danny laughed.

"But until then," Herschel admonished him, "you will continue to work with Benny Talkin."

Chapter 59

During the weeks following Carl's death Becky anxiously waited for his family to make a move to oust her from the presidency of Pickman's, but nothing happened. Philip Cooper was on vacation for all of December and the first week in January. Becky assumed that the coup would take place when he returned, but it didn't. Cooper was if anything friendlier and more cooperative than when Carl was alive.

The two of them went out to dinner to celebrate Pickman's banner holiday-season sales totals. Throughout the evening Becky itched to ask if he'd been approached by Carl's ex-wife and his sisters, but she didn't; it would not help matters to reveal her nervousness. After all, he was the fellow who had so accurately pointed out her insecurity in the first place.

Becky, deciding that it was up to the other side to attack, did her best to ignore the threat and turned her attention to her work. There was certainly a tremendous amount to do, both in the store and for Palestine.

In February the newspapers were full of the violence in Palestine and the British government's inability to control it. The English were still advancing their plan for a

745

"federated" Palestine. The country would be divided into three parts. The major portion would be Arab, the next in size would remain under the direct rule of England, and the smallest, approximately fifteen hundred square miles, was to be turned over to the Jews. The Jews were not to have control of immigration into their territory. A "super-government" made up of Arabs and British would retain authority over immigration policy.

The Zionist response to the English plan and to the current heightened restrictions on Jewish emigration to Palestine was to increase their attacks. In Parliament were cries to end this "squalid war" and for England either to govern Palestine or get out. At the end of the month the British announced the mandate was unworkable and turned the matter over to the United Nations.

Meanwhile, Institute branches all across the United States were increasing the frequency of their meetings. Large parts of Becky's days were taken up using Pickman's clout to coax other department stores, manufacturers and wholesalers to add to the inventories of her Palestine Supplies Association. Whenever she got word that some less innocent materials were available—ammunition from a sporting goods chain, perhaps, or several gross of hunting knives—she'd put the would-be contributor in touch with Benny Talkin. Talkin, along with an associate whom Becky had never met, had taken over most of the munitions operation in this country. Herschel was dividing his time between his Canadian operation and traveling to speak at fund-raisers.

Becky, all but overwhelmed with work, tried to get her brother Danny involved in PSA but he begged off, claiming that his job at a Brooklyn machine shop was keeping him too busy to get involved in charity work. Becky, trying to control her temper, offered to pay him a salary, but he still refused. Later she talked the matter over with her father, who said, "Leave the boy alone. He don't want to work for his sister. Who can blame him? He's a big boy now."

That spring the United Nations Special Commission on Palestine announced that it would issue a preliminary report in the fall. About that time Becky joined yet another project on Palestine's behalf.

The British, determined to staunch the flow of Jews into Palestine, were intercepting freighters packed with immigrants from Europe and escorting them to Cyprus and the displaced persons camps. Despite the British blockade there were many in Europe clamoring to make the journey, and more ships were needed.

An associate approached Becky with the information that a suitable ship—an old excursion steamer—was up for sale in Baltimore. Becky held a meeting to discuss the matter, excusing her housekeeper for the evening so that her guests could speak frankly. It was agreed that the group would raise the money to purchase and suitably refit the steamer to transport Jews to Palestine. They would meet weekly to plan and make reports.

Becky was glad to have an evening activity to pencil on her calendar. Loneliness had returned to her in the six months since Carl's death. Her days were busy, but her nights were agony, shuffling about the big apartment by herself once the housekeeper had retired to her own room for the night. When Carl was alive they had a busy social life, but nobody needed an extra woman.

With her brother Danny too busy for her, Becky had only her father. She asked him to move in with her, but Abe, stubborn as ever, refused to leave Cherry Street. His friends were there, he explained, and Becky, seeing how content he was surrounded by his old cronies, found herself envying him. Gradually she cut back her visits and replaced them with telephone calls. She felt awkward pull-

ing up in front of the store. She felt she was intruding on
an old men's club. She couldn't help remembering how
Stefano de Fazio used to visit her father in much the same
way; how pleased her father always was that Stefano
should come and how relieved he was when Stefano left.

Very late at night, when Becky sat up reading or
listening to music, her thoughts turned to Herschel Kol.
She'd seen him only a few times since last November. He
finally stopped apologizing for that pass in Toronto, but he
maintained propriety to the point of aloofness. If only he
would show that passion again, how she would welcome
his embrace.

Her incessant evening solitude and her yearnings began to work black magic on her, making her angry and
bitter. In the fall she would turn thirty, but she felt much
older.

Her father had always used her, as had her brother in
order to get his way with their father. Even Carl had used
her. Why should Herschel Kol be any different? He'd
gotten exactly what he wanted, hadn't he? Thanks to her
he now had his connections in Canada and the financing
for his precious project.

At other times, however, she found her thoughts turning to how guileless and radiant Herschel looked that night
as he told her about Palestine. She imagined how it would
be to turn away from this life and go with him to his
sun-drenched land, where by day they would work and
rejoice together with other Jews and by night retire to their
simple bed to make love.

One fine morning in May she arrived as usual, an
hour before the store was to open. Becky was in high
spirits. Tucked under her arm were the morning's newspapers, and in each were full-page Pickman's ads that
hadn't cost one cent. Becky had managed it by calling the
store's most popular brand-name appliance company and

offering to run a promotion on their entire line if they would agree to foot the bill for the ads. The grapevine had it that both Macy's and Gimbels—which also featured the appliance line—were furious.

On her way up to her office Becky stopped on floor three to see how the renovations were coming. She'd had the entire floor cleared for a tea room and to rearrange the outmoded counter displays of better women's apparel. The idea had been partly Grace Turner's—she had returned from Paris full of enthusiasm for the little shops called boutiques where a customer could choose from a complete line of merchandise from dresses to belts, scarves, shoes and so on. To Becky boutiques sounded very much like the storefronts on the Lower East Side, plus glamor.

However, soon one Pickman's salesperson would be able to walk a customer through the purchase of a complete new wardrobe. The new tea room, which Becky hoped would entice shoppers to the third floor, would be a convenient place for women to have lunch.

From the third floor Becky made her way to her office up on floor six. She had a morning's worth of dictation, an Institute luncheon and an afternoon of planning for Pickman's new public relations department.

She intended to have her new PR staff comb New York for amateur athletic teams, orchestras, flower clubs and churches that would benefit from Pickman's sponsorship. She wanted community classes in knitting, sewing, cooking, infant care—all the necessary supplies to be sold at discount to the students, who she hoped would form a lifelong attachment to Pickman's. That same staff was to see to it that the newspapers covered the store's goodwill campaign. It was the sort of advertising money couldn't buy.

As Becky entered the executive suite, she noticed that neither Millie nor the administrative assistant was at her desk. It was unusual for Millie to be late, Becky mused.

As she pushed through the glass doors and past Phil Cooper's office, she saw that his door was ajar and his office was empty. Where is everybody? Becky wondered.

And then she entered her own office and at once understood that everyone was hiding. Making herself comfortable on the moss-green sofa was Gertrude Hoffer Pickman.

"Rebecca, my dear." She did not stand. "I hope you don't mind my waiting for you in Carl's office."

"Your concern for my feelings is touching, Mrs. Pickman," Becky replied evenly as she took her place behind her desk. "However, since you're already in my office, what can I do for you?"

Gertrude's smile remained fixed in place, but she did not speak.

"Really, Mrs. Pickman, I'm quite busy," Becky said. "Can we get to the matter at hand?"

"No manners." Gertrude feigned a concerned sigh. "But then manners were always the least of your charms, I'd imagine. Well, we'll do it your way, Rebecca. There's no sense in mincing words, is there? Carl's sisters and I have decided there should be a change in management. We've waited what we consider a proper interval since Carl's passing so as to make it appear that we've always had confidence in Carl's most recent decisions."

She paused. "I suggest that you consider the next couple of months an interim in which to consider what you might like to do next. Retire or perhaps find a position in another store."

"You want me to resign?"

"My dear, it is not a question of what we'd like, but a declaration of what is going to happen. You are no longer the president of Pickman's. I'm merely offering you a way out without humiliation. You could issue a statement that you've decided to travel or that you've accepted another job because you enjoy the challenge of working your way up—''

''No.''

Gertrude Pickman looked pained. ''Well, of course it is up to you how you handle your leaving—''

Becky grinned. ''Mrs. Pickman, I meant no, I'm not leaving.''

''Perhaps you had better speak to your attorney, Rebecca,'' Gertrude said. ''I can only imagine that you don't understand your situation.''

''I understand it perfectly. You and yours control forty-nine percent to my forty-one. Tell me, who are you planning to put in my place?''

''We thought Deborah's husband Robert—''

Becky burst into delighted laughter. ''Oh, that's rich! Robert? You know what a schmo is?'' she asked, lighting a cigarette.

''Hardly,'' Gertrude sniffed. ''I don't care for that beastly Yiddish, and I'd prefer that you not smoke.''

''I do what I want in my own office.'' Becky puffed away. ''A schmo is a dolt, a lackey, a jerk. Get it? That's what good old Robert is. He couldn't run a sales counter, let alone Pickman's.''

''Nevertheless, he is going to be the next president of this store,'' Gertrude coldly replied.

''Why not Philip, for God's sake? At least he knows what he's doing.''

''Rebecca, you can't be that naive. Surely you would prefer to have the business remain under a Jewish individual?''

''I'd rather a goy make a success of it than a Jew know-nothing run it into the ground,'' Becky countered. ''You know, you amaze me. I always had the impression you were pretty fond of money, but I guess not. I am, though. You know what you're going to have to do? Get together with the unholy sisters and officially, formally, publicly vote me out, because the only way I'm going is kicking and screaming. Robert Meltzer is not going to fritter away my fortune.''

"As you wish, Rebecca," Gertrude said smugly, standing up. "This call was a courtesy to you, but of course your sort doesn't understand courtesy.''

"And just what is my sort?''

Gertrude looked amused. "I think you know." She turned and swept out.

Becky was vastly relieved when she had time to think about it. Phil would soon enough hear about Gertrude's plans, and it seemed highly unlikely that he would vote to move Robert Meltzer above him. The only thing she had to worry about now was whether Gertrude would take her advice and offer Phil the presidency, and that didn't seem likely.

She wondered idly what on earth made Gertrude think Phil would throw in with her. Maybe it was just arrogance, or maybe—her stomach felt a sudden chill—Gertrude had a lever to use on him. Lord, she'd better hope not.

Becky smoked another cigarette in silence, then went out to Millie's desk. "Is she gone?''

Millie seemed to have trouble looking her in the eye. "I'm sorry . . .''

"Goddamnit, Millie, in my own office!''

"She threatened to fire me—you know, after you're gone . . .'' Millie's voice trailed off. "I've worked here all my life. I can't let myself get fired. She told me she was going into your office to wait and that was that. She told me not to let on to you. I couldn't lie, so I just went away.''

"Where the hell is Phil?''

"He called and said he wouldn't be in this morning.''

"That figures.''

Millie finally looked up, her eyes huge and imploring. "You wouldn't fire me—?''

"Cut it out. Nobody is getting fired, okay? Everything is going to be all right." Becky trudged back to her office, where she shut and locked her door.

That afternoon's luncheon was held in the private room of a midtown restaurant. Benny Talkin arrived early. He was having a drink and talking baseball with the owner of a supermarket chain who got all his meat from de Fazio. He excused himself when he spotted Rebecca Pickman arriving just a few minutes before lunch was to begin.

Benny knew she was coming, but actually seeing her jolted him. They'd exchanged business correspondence and telephone calls since she recruited his help with PSA, but they'd not seen each other or spoken of personal matters for ages.

"Hi, Becky," he said tentatively, prepared for a cool reception but hoping for better.

"Hello, Benny. I never expected to see you at one of these." She smiled, extending her hand to him.

"I figured that considering all the work I've been doing, I might as well get a free meal out of it."

"Speaking of work, how are things going?"

"Not so good, I'm afraid." Benny looked around to make sure that they were not overheard. "We had some trouble on the Jersey side of the river. Some local cops showed up on what they claimed was an anonymous tip. They nosed around and discovered that some cargo marked fertilizer was really dynamite."

"Oh, no," Becky groaned. "What a day this is shaping up to be. Who could have done that to us—and why?"

Benny shrugged. "I'd like to know that myself. Obviously we've got a rat in our midst. The trouble is, I don't know if the informer was out to hurt us or Stefano."

"What does Stefano have to do with anything?"

"Well, now's not the time to talk about it, Becky.

Anyway, I was able to pay those cops off. The thing is, there's no way I can buy off the FBI if it gets wind of what's going on. I told your—'' Benny stopped abruptly. He had almost revealed that her brother Danny was involved in their work. "What I mean is, I'm telling people that we've got to lay off shipping contraband for a while, but when the time comes, your PSA stuff shouldn't be any problem." He smiled. "You look great, Becky. Hey, can I get you a drink?"

"Oh, no—" Becky looked thoughtful. "Well, yes. I would like a bloody mary. It's been one of the worst mornings for me—"

"Hold on, let me get you that drink." By the time he returned the meeting was being called to order. "We'll talk later," he promised.

The meeting ran until two o'clock. While it was breaking up Benny invited Becky out for a drink. "Come on, play hooky," he coaxed. "The store will be there when you get back."

"Maybe it will." Becky chuckled mysteriously. "Yes, let's play hooky. I don't want to go back just yet."

They walked around the block to a place Benny knew. He was surprised and gratified at how at ease Becky appeared to be with him and hoped it was her way of telling him that the acrimony between them was finally a thing of the past.

"Now, what does Stefano have to do with things?" Becky asked once they were comfortably settled at a table with their drinks in front of them.

"You know that I work for him," Benny explained. "If I get nabbed by the Feds for shipping contraband to Palestine, he's implicated, but what I don't know is which of us was supposed to be the target in this particular instance. You see, the New York D.A.'s office has been closing in on some of Stefano's operations. He suspects that the law has got something on one of his people and is using the threat of a long prison sentence to put pressure on the guy to turn state's evidence against him. Stefano's frantic. He doesn't know who in his organization is stabbing him in the back, and until he finds out he doesn't want to give the law more rope to hang him with. That's why he's ordered me to lay off on my Palestine work. As Stefano puts it, he isn't about to go to prison on behalf of a bunch of Jews.''

"I feel terrible," Becky mused, then laughed nervously. ''No offense to you, Benny, but I know Stefano is a gangster and that he's done some terrible things. Nevertheless, I can't forget his early friendship with my father and the way he used to bring flowers to my mother and candy to me when I was little.''

"Between us, Becky, my father-in-law doesn't bring little kids candy anymore,'' Benny said wryly. ''When he finds out who is double-crossing him, that guy is dead. Meanwhile, the D.A., in conjunction with the Feds, is on his heels like a pack of bloodhounds. And if they get Stefano, they get everybody, including me.''

"Oh, Benny, I'm sorry. It didn't occur to me how serious this could be to you personally.''

He nodded. ''Stefano is calling in every favor he can to get the law off our backs. A long time ago I told you we'd done some work for the Navy, keeping the docks safe for Allied transport. Well, all our Navy contacts have been transferred out of Intelligence or else ordered not to talk to us or to the law on our behalf. They're treating us the same way they treated Luciano. The government deported him to Italy last year after the Navy claimed that it never heard of him.'' He offered Becky a cigarette. ''Never mind,'' he said cheerfully, shaking out a match. ''Stefano's as tough as they come. He'll figure a way to get us out of this.'' He smiled. ''You know, talking like this seems like old times.''

"I think we can be friends again,'' Becky said, toying

with the book of matches he had set down on the table. "I still have your cigarette lighter."

"The Dunhill?" He laughed. "I always wondered what happened to it."

"Now you know. I suppose I should give it back to you."

"Forget it."

"I said I suppose I should. I didn't say I would."

They were quiet for a moment, and then Benny said, "Okay. I told you my troubles. Now why were you looking so glum this afternoon?"

Becky told him about the stock and the morning's confrontation with Gertrude Pickman.

"Gee, Becky, that's rough," Benny said quietly. "I had no idea you were in such trouble. I could have a couple of guys pay a visit to Phil Cooper—"

Becky broke up laughing. "Oh, please, stop."

"What's so funny?" Benny asked, stung by her reaction. "They wouldn't rough him up or nothing."

She was laughing so hard that tears were running down her cheeks. "I can just see a couple of your—whatchamacallits, *torpedoes*, with black shirts and white ties—showing up at Philip's apartment."

"They don't dress like that," Benny whined. "You've seen too many damned movies."

"So have you, Benny."

"Ain't that the truth," he agreed dolefully.

"Anyway, what I'd like is for your torpedoes to visit Mrs. Gertrude Hoffer Pickman and give her a cement overcoat."

"That's overshoes."

"In her case we'll spring for the whole outfit."

"What I can't figure is how Cark Pickman could've been so stupid—"

"Hey, that's my husband you're calling stupid."

Benny nodded. "You're one hell of a woman," he

said in admiration. "I must have been pretty stupid myself, to let you get away."

"Yes," Becky nodded seriously, "you were."

"Well . . ."

"Well what?"

"You're not married anymore, and my marriage stinks. Maybe we could make this our second chance."

"You know what I'd like for a second chance?" Becky said lazily. "A life like Herschel Kol's—before he came here, I mean."

"Come off it, Becky. You're a city kid. What would you do in a desert, or whatever they got over there? Anyway, you ignored my question. What about—"

"Benny, I never did properly thank you for arranging for me to own the Cherry Street property," she interrupted. "And I've never thanked you for contributing so much time and effort to Palestine."

"You don't have to thank me. I did it to kind of make up for that bad incident in my apartment that day."

"You don't have to say any more, Ben."

"Well, I want to. Back then you called what I did to you attempted rape. I didn't see it that way then, but I do now. I've played that whole scene over in my mind at least a thousand times, and there's no way I come out of it looking good. I can't tell you how much I regret what happened."

"I regret it, too, Benny."

"But you still hold it against me, don't you?"

She smiled at him and her radiant beauty thrilled him even as the look of pity in her eyes broke his heart. He saw everything in her look: compassion, forgiveness, empathy—everything but the slightest possibility that she would ever love him again.

"It's not something I have against you, like a grudge," she said kindly, "but what happened to me at your apartment is like a scar. It only hurts sometimes, but it'll never completely fade away. It won't keep us from being friends, but it will keep us from being anything more. Okay?"

"Damn. It was a goddamned tragedy."

During the next few weeks Becky made several brief trips to Canada. She fast-talked for cash to help pay for the refitting of the Baltimore excursion ship. Her contributors hinted that they expected Pickman's to throw some extra business their way in exchange. She told them they would do business with the store for as long as she was president, privately hoping that that would be for years to come.

In Canada she avoided Herschel Kol, not trusting herself to see him and not wanting to distract herself from her Palestine work in case she was ousted and lost the store's clout. There would be time enough in the near future to see Herschel—if he was still interested when she was no longer powerful, but merely a woman.

She relied heavily on Phil Cooper and gave him enough authority to run things smoothly, enough even to flatter him. She could hardly do less, and that was as likely to persuade him to back her as anything. Unless they offered him a fortune—or the presidency.

Norman Collins let her know the vote would take place in his office at ten o'clock Friday morning, May thirtieth. Becky, who had already arranged for Collins to have power of attorney to vote her shares, reiterated her decision not to attend.

On Friday morning, the last day in May and possibly the last day in her job, she arrived at her office an hour before opening, just as usual. She had already decided that she would simply not come in on Monday and that would be that. Carl had left her wealthy, but what she was going to do with her life was a question she hadn't yet addressed.

She tried to busy herself in paperwork but gave up. What was the point? The hands on the clock inched along towards ten and she waited for Norman's call.

It came at ten-fifteen.

"They're still sitting shell-shocked in my outer office," Collins chattered giddily. "Phil Cooper voted for you, Becky. He voted for you!"

"Norman? I'm still in? Why? Why did he do it?"

"Don't know." Collins laughed. "You ask him. He's on his way back."

He hung up and Becky asked Millie to let her know when Phil came in. Not much later Becky found herself in Phil's office, asking if she might sit down.

"Sure, help yourself."

"I want to thank you, Phil. I know you don't like working for me, and it must have been a temptation to get rid of me."

"My pleasure," he drawled, eyes glinting wickedly.

"Okey, Phil, what's the joke?"

He laughed. "Gertrude Pickman is. You'll never guess what she offered me. Notice how nice I've been lately? You'll see why in a minute." He laced his hands behind his head and leaned back luxuriously.

"Apparently you suggested she make me president if they ousted you. Thank you. That was very generous and unselfish of you. If she had taken your advice, I certainly would have voted against you.

"Apparently she recognized the merit of your counsel, but it's against her principles to do anything you say. She decided on a compromise."

Becky was leaning forward in her chair, entranced.

"She said Robert would be president and hold presidential powers but that he would allow me to run things without interference. In plain English, I would have all the responsibility and no authority. In return, they would sell me your stock."

"*My* stock! And just how, pray tell, were they going to get it in the first place?"

"Well, apparently you intimated to Gertrude that you

wouldn't trust Meltzer. She figured you'd sell out and I couldn't turn down your shares.''

"Why did you? You'd have controlling interest. You could kick Robert out and rule the roost.''

"Precisely what I was supposed to think. That's what tipped me off. The Pickmans were never going to give me controlling stock if they wouldn't trust me with the presidency. It was all pie in the sky. Besides, what if you decided to sell away from the family? I would, in your shoes.''

"She's got a nerve, all right.''

"Well, I had another reason, too. You know, Becky, you have no social graces, no clothes sense and no tact. On the other hand, you're the best retailer in the city and I'd be a fool to pass up the reputation and the education I'm getting under you.''

That weekend she received word that the refugee ship she had worked so hard to get overhauled and refitted had set sail at last, rechristened the *Exodus*.

Chapter 60

In July Danny Herodetzky, like most of the civilized world, was appalled by the newspaper accounts that serialized the sorry fate of the refugee ship *Exodus*. Upon its arrival in Palestine's waters its forty-three hundred passengers were taken off the ship by force and loaded onto three British transports.

The British announced that they were taking these people not to Cyprus but back to Germany. The voyage took forty-six days, during which the British endured attacks by the press for their "floating Auschwitzes" and more bombing by an enraged Irgun. Even the usually sanguine Haganah was sufficiently outraged to use limpet mines to send the British vessel *Empire Lifeguard* to the bottom of Haifa harbor. In all thirteen British lost their lives and scores were wounded in *Exodus*-related attacks.

To retaliate the British announced that three Irgunists who were imprisoned on unrelated charges would be hanged. This execution was so unjust as to impel the superintendent of Acre Prison to resign his office rather than comply. The hangings were carried out under the supervision of the new prison warden. Hours later the Irgun announced the executions by hanging of two British sergeants, and so the cycle of destruction and death continued unchecked.

It was during this time that the UN committee on Palestine was touring that country in preparation for issuing its recommendations. Danny read about the supposedly secret meeting between Ralph Bunche and Menachem Begin, during which the renowned black spokesman shook hands with the Irgun commander, declaring, "I understand you. I too am a member of a persecuted minority." In England there was a torrent of criticism against the meeting and against the Bevin government. How had Bunche found Begin so easily when the task seemed beyond the capability of the British authorities?

In the fall of 1947 the committee submitted to the General Assembly its report recommending the creation of independent Jewish and Arab states in the territory west of the Jordan and the internationalization of Jerusalem under UN trusteeship. In response Arab leaders such as Egypt's Mahmoud Fawzi and Prince Faisal of Saudi Arabia warned that they would not be bound by any partition proposal and threatened war if the General Assembly should vote to carry it out.

As debate proceeded, England announced that she would not cooperate with a multinational peacekeeping force in Palestine but would end her mandate on May 16, 1948. Russia made it known that she advocated the partition plan. Meanwhile everyone waited, wondering what position the United States would take.

Danny Herodetzky wondered if he'd ever be free of his waterfront duties and if Herschel Kol would ever make good on his promise to get Danny flying.

Once Danny's flight records had been checked out, Milty helped him apply for his passport, coaching him in what to say so that the State Department, which was fervently anti-Zionist and very suspicious of young Jewish men who wished to travel abroad, would not deny his application. Now that he had his passport, it was burning a hole in his pocket. When would he be allowed to fly? All Herschel would say was that Danny was needed in New York while he himself was occupied with the Canadian project.

His desire to quit his present duties and resume flying was not purely selfish. Newspaper editorialists pointed out that the United Nations had no armed force to impose peace on Palestine. The Jews would have only themselves to depend on if they were to survive the allied Arab attack to come in the wake of the British departure.

Danny had studied maps of the proposed partitioning. The Jews would be surrounded by hostile Arab nations on three sides and would have their backs to the Mediterranean. They would need air transport to move essential supplies over enemy lines and fighter planes if the Egyptians' strafing runs were not to cut the new nation into bloody ribbons.

Danny understood all this, but try as he might he could not turn Herschel's attention away from his gun project. "A little longer, a little longer," he would snap, then turn his back.

On Saturday evening, November twenty-ninth, the General Assembly approved the partition plan by a vote of thirty-three to thirteen. The historic event was broadcast on radio. Danny and his Upper West Side volunteers huddled around the old Philco with the cracked dial as the votes were tallied in Flushing Meadow.

As France, one of the last countries to vote, announced that it was for the partition plan, a cheer went up in the apartment. The students began hugging and kissing. They twisted the corks from several bottles of wine and began passing them around.

Danny watched quietly from the sidelines, feeling much older than these exuberant youngsters. He accepted some handshakes and a drink, wondering why these kids were congratulating him. He hadn't done anything special— yet.

On Saturday night Becky sat alone in her living room and listened to the live broadcast from the United Nations. She wanted to celebrate, but she didn't know how. There was no one with whom to rejoice, she was all alone.

A month ago she had dismissed the housekeeper. It made Becky nervous to have her around all the time. She preferred cooking her own meals to having somebody cook for her and then watch her eat. She'd begun to think about moving out of this apartment into a one- or two-bedroom place with less elegance and more real comfort.

Becky supposed she could call her father about the wonderful news. Yes, she would call her father. She was just about to pick up the telephone when it rang. "Hello?"

"It's me," Herschel Kol said. His voice was breathless, triumphant. "I'm in a telephone booth. I have turned all my money into Canadian silver in order to call you. You've heard the news, of course? I had to talk to you. There is no one else I wanted to share this moment with."

"I'm so glad you called. I can't tell you what it means to me. You must be so happy. Your whole life you've been waiting for this day."

"So I have, Becky, but it is only the beginning of a far more difficult struggle to come. You have seen the maps of the planned partition, yes? Tell me then, how can there be a Jewish state without Jerusalem? All of Palestine should be Jewish."

"Do you believe the Arabs will go to war?" Becky asked.

"It'll be a fight to the death. I am sorry for that, but there's no help for it. Let's not talk about death tonight, Becky, not when the homeland has at last been born. I have more good news. What you and I began here together is also practically finished. In another couple of weeks, I believe, my work in Canada will be done.''

"That's wonderful. I'll be in Canada on business in two weeks. Will I see you?''

"I'll be here. We'll celebrate together,'' Herschel said quietly. "Becky, I . . . I miss you very much. I have missed you these last few months.''

"We can talk about it when I see you.''

"No, it's easier for me to say these things on the telephone tonight. The grand news has given me courage. Do you believe me—will you, if I say now what I said that night? I love you.''

Becky gazed at her reflection in the gilded mirror above the mantel. Why didn't she feel anything? She wanted to, so why couldn't she? Why was she so frightened?

"I understand,'' Herschel said listlessly after an eternity of crackling silence over the wires. "Yes, I understand.''

"I'll see you there,'' Becky managed, her voice cracking. Don't be a fool, she thought. You mustn't let him think that you don't care.

He hung up.

Becky listened to the static for a moment, then set the receiver down in its cradle. She lit a cigarette and watched the blue smoke curl into nothingness. I'll see him in a few days' time, she told herself. It'll be different then.

The sad sound of Herschel's voice came back to her and she wondered why God had given her so much and yet seen fit to curse her. She wanted to surrender herself to the passion she felt for Herschel, but something about him made her hold back.

On Saturday night Benny Talkin listened to the UN proceedings over his car radio as he drove out to Stefano's home in Sheepshead Bay. He didn't want to make this trip—not that he ever wanted to go there—especially not tonight, just two days after a torturous Thanksgiving holiday there. Stefano had been impossible the entire time. He and Tony Bucci spent most of the day behind the closed door of Stefano's study, excluding Benny from their discussions. He knew how worried Stefano was about the D.A.'s vendetta against him, but his father-in-law still should have been more considerate of his feelings. How humiliating to have to sit with the women and children while Stefano and Tony discussed business. All of them, including Dolores, treated him like a second-class citizen.

He nosed the Caddy convertible along the driveway. Tony was at the open front door before Benny switched off his engine.

"Nice of you to come out on such short notice," Tony Bucci said, for all the world as if he were the host and this his house. He was wearing a dark business suit and a tie. Benny at once regretted showing up in casual clothes.

"What's going on, Tony? Trouble?"

"You could say that," Tony removed his glasses to polish them on his tie, squinting like a mole in sunlight. "Stefano's upstairs in his study. I gotta warn you, Benny, he's been acting a little crazy since he found out."

"Found out what?"

"Who the rat is. Who's been informing on us to the D.A."

"No shit!" Benny exclaimed. "Who?"

"I'll let him tell you. Just remember, don't act like you think anything is unusual with him, all right?"

Benny thought that he detected a note of pleading in Tony's voice. "Sure, Tony."

He followed Bucci into the house. The hallway was dark and there seemed to be no one else around, although Benny thought he could hear a radio faintly playing. He began to grow increasingly apprehensive as he followed Bucci upstairs. He didn't want to face a Stefano who was able to upset a stalwart like Gemstones.

The door to the study was closed. "Okay," Tony sighed, taking a deep breath. He opened the door.

The mahogany-paneled study was dimly lit. Stefano was sitting in a massive leather armchair drawn up to the wide picture window that looked out over the bay. He was funereally attired in a black double-breasted suit.

"Hello, Benny." It seemed an effort for Stefano to tear himself away from his view. He stood up, offering his hand. "Would you like a drink?"

"Maybe later," Benny said. He was intrigued by Stefano's sudden cordiality. It had been years since Stefano offered to shake hands with him.

"Make yourself comfortable, then." Stefano sat down in his armchair by the window. Benny took off his jacket and he and Tony took opposite ends of the long leather sofa.

"I've asked you to come here for a very important reason," Stefano began. As he spoke he continued to gaze out the window at the dark bay. His grey hair and mustache, along with the gold buckles on his black patent-leather loafers, gleamed in the faint light cast by the lamp on his desk. "Benny, you know that we've been plagued by traitors in our midst. They are a blight, like—like gangrenous flesh that must be ruthlessly carved away if the healthy part is to survive. Do you understand?"

"Yeah, I guess." Benny slowly nodded. "Anything I can do to help."

"Thank you, Benny. There is something you can do," Stefano said, at last turning away from the window to stare at Benny. "You must kill one of these traitors."

"It's Louie Carduello," Tony Bucci interjected.

"Louie?" Benny issued a short bark of nervous laughter. "This is a joke, right? You guys are kidding me."

Stefano shook his head.

"Louie's worked for you since—Jesus, 1925," Benny

insisted. "He's been running that meat packing plant on Washington since—"

"Louie has had it in for me all these years because of a trifling misunderstanding a long time ago," Stefano intoned. "I was going to put Abe Herodetzky in charge of that plant and make it up to Louie with cash payments. Louie *said* that would be all right, but he held a grudge." Stefano paused and nodded calmly. "Yes, a grudge. Even when my plans for Abe fell through, Louie didn't forgive me. He never has. It's Louie who has been betraying me."

"How could he?" Benny asked. "I mean, he's not in a position to know all that much about you."

"He knows certain things. But you're right. There are other traitors. They're jealous. They want to bring me down. It takes many to bring down a great man." Sweat appeared upon Stefano's forehead and drops of it glistened in his mustache. "Louie is one of the first who must die. I want you to kill him for me, Benny."

Benny stared back at his father-in-law. He's crazy, he thought. "Stefano, I can't. I never did anything like that—"

" 'I can't, I won't,' " Stefano mimicked crossly. "That's all I've ever heard from you, Benny. You're a weakling. Before all these betrayals your incompetence didn't matter to me. Now I can no longer afford incompetents."

"Not ever having shot a guy in the back of the head doesn't make me an incompetent," Benny snapped. "Right, Tony?" Bucci pretended not to hear him.

"Ever since you and Dolores got married you've been holding back on me," Stefano said accusingly. "I had big plans for you, but that's not the issue now. Loyalty is the issue. I got to know who is loyal and who isn't. I want you to kill Louie Carduello for me. Then I'll know that I can trust you. You want me to trust you, right?"

"Yeah, sure. Jesus, sure." He grinned uneasily. "I think I could use that drink now."

"Get it for him, Tony," Stefano instructed. As Bucci rose Stefano added, "Tony will help you with this if you'd like."

Benny repressed a shudder. "No. If I'm going to do this for you, let me do it myself—to prove myself, understand?" He tried his best to smile and then gulped the neat whiskey Bucci handed him.

"Yes," Stefano mused, "I like that." His gaze turned back to the picture window. "You take time to do this right, but you do it. Understand, Benny?"

"Yes."

"Tony will get you what you need. A gun, whatever . . . Oh, and don't forget what I told you about staying away from your Palestine friends. The FBI is already breathing down our necks. We don't need any more trouble than we already got."

"Yes."

"I'll see him to the door," Bucci volunteered.

Benny grabbed his coat and followed him out. Once they were in the upstairs hallway, out of earshot, Bucci started to complain. "He won't leave the house, not since late Thursday night. I had to sleep over these last two nights. He says he wants to be near the bay, near his wife. He says he'll be vulnerable if he comes away from the house."

"Jesus," Benny shook his head as they went downstairs. "Louie Carduello must be in his seventies."

"He's sixty-six, the same age as Stefano."

"He's no informer," Benny stated.

"No shit." Bucci looked pained. "But Stefano thinks he is, so Louie is history."

"This is nuts. Why do I have to do it?"

"Don't act the sap," Bucci snapped. "Up until now you've stayed clean. You could go to the cops with a song and dance about how you were just a front man and do a deal for yourself by testifying against Stefano. We intend to exterminate any rats who decide to desert this sinking ship.''

"Is it?" Benny asked, shocked. "Is it sinking?"

Bucci shrugged. "What can I tell you? Things are out of hand. Stefano's been greedy and cocky. He figured his good deeds during the war were enough to keep the government off his back. He was wrong. He knew that when the Navy double-crossed Luciano, but by then it was too late to buy protection. Now the law is after him and he's got nobody to turn to to get it called off.''

"What about the syndicate?"

"They'll let him go down," Bucci said. "It'll make the D.A. and the Feds look good in the papers, and that'll keep things quiet for a while. The other bosses will peacefully divvy up Stefano's holdings among themselves." He frowned. "Stefano is vulnerable at a thousand different points. We think his phones have been tapped since his days working with the Navy. The poor bastard thinks he can wipe out his betrayers, but it'll never happen. There's a whole bunch of little nobodies who'll beg to testify against Stefano to save their own asses.''

They were at the front door. Before Tony opened it he looked Benny straight in the eye and said, "Just so there's no misunderstanding, this talk of ours doesn't change anything, kid. You do have to do this; it's what Stefano wants. You never loved him like I did. You coulda, but you didn't. He's stood by you, kid, and now you'll stand by him. We're all going to go down together if that's the way it happens, or else you'll go down first. I'll see to that. Got it?"

"Yeah." Benny felt wretched. "Oh, God, how am I gonna get through this?"

"You will because your life depends on it." Bucci's tone became oddly comforting. "Buck up, kid. You had your share of the good time. Now you gotta pay up."

"He's gone crazy, you know."

Gemstones Bucci didn't deny it. "He's scared. He's thinking about what they did to Luciano. If he gets deported like that everything that he spent his life building will vanish. He's crazy, all right. He's scared out of his mind."

"So I'm to murder somebody on the orders of a crazy man?"

"Not just a crazy man," Bucci corrected him, "but Stefano de Fazio. Maybe he's been driven crazy. Maybe so am I, but that won't make us any less lethal if you cross us."

Chapter 61

There was nothing much left for Danny Herodetzky and the student volunteers to do. The instruction manuals had long since been cut and pasted; the contraband had been shipped. That was just as well, for Benny Talkin had made it clear that he could no longer help get the stuff out.

In Palestine the Zionist leadership's focus had long since switched from the trickle of arms and machinery coming out of America to the huge lots of ready-made munitions available in Europe. Here in the States activity was pretty much limited to fund-raising and managing legal shipments of nonmilitary goods.

Since the UN vote for partition and the resulting headline-grabbing violence that had erupted in Palestine, the public had developed a heightened awareness of what was going on in that part of the world. This made many influential Jews very wary.

Truman would be running for re-election in 1948. He had so far been generally sympathetic to Zionism and nobody wanted to stir up controversy over the administration's inability to crack down on the "dual loyalties" of America's Jews. This nasty dual loyalty business had come up before when Palestine-bound contraband was seized, and the Jewish establishment was sensitive to it.

Danny waited until the middle of December, when his sister would be in Canada with Herschel and they would be unable to stop him, to ask his contact at Lion Airways to give him a flying assignment. As it turned out, Milty needed very little persuasion; he had a cargo plane, a DC-3, parked at Teterboro Airport in New Jersey.

All over the world aircraft purchased with Institute funds were being shuffled about like chessmen in a desperate attempt to keep them from being impounded by local authorities. Right now in the States the prediction was that a storm was brewing. Rumor had it that the State Department was lobbying Truman to expand the munitions embargo to include commercial planes.

This meant Lion Airways had to get its planes out of the U.S. if they ever were to reach Palestine. The DC-3 at Teterboro was short a copilot. Danny was not rated to fly a big twin-engined craft, but as he himself pointed out to Milty, he was a pilot, his passport was in order and he was ready to go.

After a few moments of fidgety indecision Milty said he would make the arrangements. Danny was to report to the Lion office in New Jersey in forty-eight hours.

Danny went back to his boarding house in the Village and told his landlady he would be leaving. He packed his bag and settled down to write three letters.

The first two were short and to the point. They would go to Benny Talkin and Herschel Kol. The third letter was much longer. In it he expressed things he'd been yearning to say but had been keeping bottled up for a long while. This third letter would go to his sister Rebecca.

A few hours before his departure he grabbed his bag and visited his father. He and Abe went upstairs for privacy. Danny, sitting beside his father, held the old man's gnarled hands in his own, and explained where he was going.

Abe listened quietly. When Danny was finished, he said, "Thank God you missed the last war, but now you must go out of your way to fight in Palestine?"

He spoke without rancor, however; Danny was glad the strife between them had long ago been banished. "It's a chance for me to fly, Pop."

"Does your sister know you're going?"

"Yes," Danny lied. He felt bad about it, even though his letter would be waiting for Becky when she returned from Canada. "I told her, and while she is naturally worried about me, she gave me her blessing."

Abe nodded. "Well, your sister has been very active in Zionism."

"It's not that I want to leave you, Pop. I'll miss you . . ."

"I know. What do you think, I don't know my own son? The other day, cleaning out the closet, you know what I found? That big box of airplane comics you used to read. Your school books, your Bible, that's what they were to you. You know what else? I flipped through those books and began to read one. Yes, me! Maybe if you remember to write me when you can, we can discuss what's going on in them."

"*Tailspin Tommy* is the best one, Pop," Danny murmured, deeply touched.

"*Tailspin Tommy*. In my opinion the best is Tailspin Danny."

"I love you, Pop."

"This is the second time my heart has been broken by a dear son going away from me to Palestine," Abe sighed. "Someday I'll go just to see what is the big attraction."

The Lion Airways building at Teterboro was a mostly unheated shack furnished with a file cabinet and a rickety folding card table and four chairs. When Danny got there, the pilot was hopping up and down in place, trying to keep warm and the navigator was busy filling in the flight plan. They would be going via fuel stops in Canada, Greenland and Ireland to an airfield outside Paris. The French, embarrassed over the Vichy government's anti-Jewish policies, were disposed to let a few Palestine-bound planes at a time stop over for repairs and modifications.

In Paris Danny would make contact with a Haganah operative who would get him to Rome and eventually into Palestine. Danny had been told that a flying job awaited him there.

"You ever fly one of these Goonies?" the pilot asked when he and Danny were settled in the cockpit.

Danny looked around. There was rust all over the instrument panel. Half the throttle sticks were missing their knobs, and the cracked lens of the radio compass was stuck together with peeling cellophane tape. "No, sir."

The pilot shrugged. "No big deal. You'll catch on. And scratch that 'sir' stuff. Sam'll do."

He played the valves, selectors and taps with the deft touch of a musician, and eventually the big engines grudgingly coughed to life. As they began to taxi it sounded as if every rivet in the fuselage was squealing in protest. The pilot got airborne in much the same coaxing, gentle method that Danny had used some hours earlier to escort his father up the stairs to the apartment.

Once they were on their way, Sam began to explain how to work the flaps and what Danny would have to keep an eye on when Sam's nap time came around. "Hey, you listening to me, kid?"

"Sure, I am."

"Then wipe that shit-eating grin off your face. It's hard to talk to a guy who looks like he's getting laid."

Chapter 62

Toronto

The headlines of the Sunday newspaper told of the British refusal to supply escort protection to Jewish supply convoys trying to travel Palestine's main roads. The beleaguered Jewish quarter of Jerusalem was attempting to survive on the meager supplies that were making it past the Arab blockade lines.

The Arab strategy was simple: starve the Jews until they were forced to evacuate their holdings and the entire issue of partition would be moot. The British were also advising evacuation as the Jews' best protection, even as they denied the convoys the right to carry firearms or armor their trucks, as such actions might be taken as provocation by the Arabs. About fifty Jews a week were dying in Arab ambushes of the convoys. The newspaper carried photographs of the burnt-out trucks and buses littering the Jerusalem road to Tel Aviv.

Becky scanned the bottom half of the front page. A story there told of the street fighting going on along the Jaffa/Tel Aviv boundary.

Shuddering, she set aside the evidence of carnage.

Thank God her family was American, she thought, but what about Herschel? Last night during dinner he had told her he expected to return to Palestine as soon as this last phase of his gun project was completed.

She'd been in Canada for a week, fulfilling her commitments to expand Pickman's dealings with sympathetic Canadian manufacturers. They were robbing her blind, but Becky was in their debt for their support of Zionism. She stoically allowed them their due; these deals would not last forever, but still, she would have a hell of a time explaining to Phil Cooper why she was paying so much for Canadian goods.

She glanced at the time: eleven-thirty. She'd promised to call her father at noon. As she waited for it to be time she thought about how disappointing her meetings with Herschel had been during the past week. He was in a frenzied state over his project when she arrived and had not once brought up their telephone conversation, not that Becky blamed him. He'd tried twice to break the ice. He would not try again, she knew. This time it was up to her.

Once Herschel went home it was likely that she would never see him again. Against her will her eyes again strayed to the newspaper's gruesome headlines. *Face it,* she ordered herself. *Once he goes home, he'll probably get himself killed.*

The realization shocked her. She felt moved to tears and at once ridiculed herself. Soon Herschel would go, and while she wished him well, she also wished he would go soon, even today. With him would go her heart's longings and her hope. Then she might gain some measure of peace.

It was time to call her father.

"I'm very worried about Danny," her father said.

"What's wrong?"

"What kind of dumb question, eh, Rebecca? Don't play games. This is serious business."

"What are you talking about?"

"Becky? I thought—I mean, Danny said you knew."

The desk clerk rang up to say her visitor had arrived. When he got to her room he took one look at her and demanded, "So what's the big problem? I got your message. What emergency? What's going on?"

"Shut up," Becky snapped. It was three o'clock in the afternoon, and since her telephone conversation with her father Becky's fury had been building to fever pitch. "It was you who got my brother involved with Palestine, wasn't it? I just know it was you! How could you?"

"Hold it," Herschel implored. He took off his overcoat and dropped in onto a chair. "Please, start from the beginning."

"Don't take that goddamned patronizing tone with me, you double-crossing bastard. I spoke with my father earlier today. Danny has left for Palestine."

"I see." Herschel looked glum. "Listen, I didn't know about this. It is true that Danny and I have been working together for a long time, longer than you and I, as a matter of fact. I needed an American with technical training. It was Danny who masterminded the contraband past customs. It was Danny who introduced me to Benny Talkin—"

"And in payment for all Danny has done for you, for all I've done for you, you talked him into volunteering to be killed in Palestine."

"Becky, calm down." Herschel took a step toward her.

"You just stay away," she warned, maneuvering to put some furniture between them.

Herschel nodded. "Just listen one minute. I didn't entice Danny. It was exactly the opposite. I have consistently tried to talk him out of going."

"That's a laugh."

"It's true. Think a minute," Herschel said. "Why would I want him to go when I need his help so much? The truth is, Danny is obsessed with the desire to be a fighter pilot. From the beginning your brother has demanded that I wangle him a flying job. He wouldn't have helped me if I hadn't promised. I've been stalling him ever since. Don't you see, Becky? He's sneaked off when neither of us was around to stop him."

Becky turned away, still angry, though she had to admit that that was most probably what had happened. It was just like Danny.

"You should have told me, Herschel."

"I didn't know he was your brother for a long while," Herschel said, "not until Benny Talkin let it slip. You see, I didn't know—still don't know—Danny's real last name."

"Stop it, Herschel."

"It's true. We wanted to know as little as possible about each other. The work was extremely dangerous. Then, when Benny told me Danny was your brother, he immediately warned me to keep you two apart."

"Why?"

"You don't know?" Herschel searched her face as he slowly advanced toward her. "He's jealous of you, Becky. He wanted an accomplishment of his own to point to with pride."

"That's a lie," Becky said hotly. "You're just trying to change the subject." Herschel's calm only served to refuel her rage. "He's my little brother and I have a right to know what he's up to."

"He's a man, Becky, a man who has gone to fight for an important cause."

"Oh, that's a laugh." She fought against tears, furiously wiping her eyes. "I know the little creep. He'd fight for the goddamned Arabs if they'd let him fly."

Herschel smiled. "Lucky for me I met him first—and that I met his sister."

"Herschel, I'm so worried. It was enough for me to dread what you'd be confronting over there. Now I've got to worry about my brother as well." She had to turn away again to get control of herself.

"Becky, will you worry about me when I leave you?" The smug superiority was gone now. His tone was wavering and bashful. His hands touched her shoulders and seared her flesh through the fabric of her dress.

"Of course I'm going to worry about you, but it's different with Danny. He's not as capable as you."

"You don't know that, Becky." His lips were almost touching her ear. "It's true," she stammered, finding it difficult to speak. "He's just chasing a dream." She felt Herschel's lips against the nape of her neck.

He pulled her close, enfolding her in his arms. His lips were upon hers; he was devouring her. His hands were everywhere on her body. He found the zipper to her dress and tugged it down, his fingers dancing along her spine.

"I do love you, Becky," his voice was husky, overflowing with plaintive longing. "Let me love you."

He moved upon her hungrily. Her breasts swayed as he caressed them. Her nipples swelled. He lifted her easily to carry her to the bed.

She watched trance-like as he undressed them both, seeing only facets of him: his blue eyes, soft with love; the graceful arch of his broad, strong back as he searched out every part of her; his mouth as he nipped and licked at her tender inner thighs. A crimson flush of abandon spread from her breasts down her belly, reaching even to the juncture of her thighs, suddenly moist as she reached to stroke the rippled expanse of his stomach muscles, as she reached to draw him deep within her.

His long strokes spread an exquisite sensation that overwhelmed her.

Herschel rose up, back arched, and his hips bucked and twisted as he spent himself deep inside her. Becky cried out and her limbs clamped around him as wave after wave of shuddering feeling fountained. Somewhere far away she could hear a woman laughing triumphantly.

Eventually she floated back down upon the bed. Herschel was kissing her tenderly.

"I bet we made a baby," she said lazily.

He chuckled. "Typical overachiever. I love you, Becky."

"I love you," she said happily, and then, "Do you? Do you think we made a baby?"

"That would be wonderful," he smiled, gently brushing her hair off of her damp forehead. "But if not this time, certainly the next."

She nodded. "You're only the sécond man I've been with," she blurted.

"I have only been with one other woman," he murmured.

"Don't lie," she pleaded.

"Really, darling, it's true."

"What about all that free love that goes on in those kibbutzes?"

"Kibbutzim," he corrected her, affectionately patting her haunch. "It was not free love in my case."

She listened intently as he told her about Jerusalem and Hebrew University, and about Frieda. She felt a sudden flare of jealousy as he told her how they were to be married.

"We two are so much the same," Becky marveled. "Our hearts were locked in the past, but now we are free to belong to each other."

"Yes, that is so," Herschel agreed, but Becky heard and understood the doubt in his voice. Across the room lay the newspaper with its messages of the war that had prior claim upon her man.

*   *   *

During the next week's business appointments Becky's mind tended to wander from the matter at hand to Herschel. She would sit with her legs primly crossed, wearing sensible shoes, and nod sagely without hearing a word. She wondered if her colleagues could guess that an hour before she'd been a writhing, caterwauling creature in rut.

She would cancel an appointment at the spur of the moment if Herschel could get free for a while. She missed him desperately when he went off to work. She felt helpless when he unburdened himself.

The project had taken far too long. It was too late for it to do his people any good during the present conflict. Becky reminded him that what he had accomplished would benefit the Jews of Palestine in the future. Herschel grimly wondered if there would be a future; the news was worsening every day. It seemed as if every nation had an embargo against supplying arms to the Jews, while the British, claiming treaty obligations, were rushing to arm the Arabs.

At last the project was complete. Most of the machinery could be trucked across the Canadian border and shipped out of New York via PSA. The more specialized components and the prototypes of the gun itself were another matter. Getting them out of New York would be a problem, but before that they had to be gotten out of Canada.

"I can help you out with that," Becky told Herschel over dinner one night. "I'm shipping all sorts of samples back to New York. We'll disassemble the stuff and ship it to Pickman's."

"No, Becky, the risk for you would be too great. If the pieces are discovered customs will recognize them as munitions. You would be liable."

"My brother is risking his life in Palestine. Soon you will be as well. If I can't take this minor risk, how can I hold my head up around you two?"

Herschel was undecided. "If it goes wrong, you could end up in prison."

"It won't go wrong. Samples are shipped this way all the time. Customs will just wave the boxes right through. Anyway, if you could go to prison for Frieda, I can go to prison for you."

"God forbid." Herschel scowled and then his expression softened. "You love me that much?"

"I love you more, but until a better opportunity to prove it comes along, this one will do. Besides, I have an ulterior motive. We're going back home soon, but the samples won't reach New York for another week to ten days. That gives us all that extra time to spend together in bed."

Chapter 63

New York, 1948

"Becky, I gotta tell you what I told Herschel," Benny Talkin fumed. "There's no way I can arrange for that stuff of his to get past customs. Stefano would have a fit if he knew I was even discussing this with you."

"It's the last time we'll ask you to move contraband for us," Becky promised. "I swear it, Benny. Please, this project has been so important to Herschel. You're his only hope."

It was a Thursday morning midway through January, although the dingy coffee shop still had up its gaudy holiday tinsel.

"Herschel sent you here to talk me into this, didn't he?" Benny demanded, lighting a cigarette. "Hell of a thing."

"It'll be so simple," Becky coaxed. "I've pulled nine dozen disassembled bicycles out of PSA inventories. We'll scatter the gun parts and dies in the cartons—"

"The waterfront is crawling with G-men. What do you think, they're not going to check out a Palestine-bound shipment?"

"I'm talking nine dozen bikes' worth of gears, handlebars, cranks and whatever," Becky grinned. "Who is going to be able to make heads or tails of a mess like that?"

"They're checking everything going anywhere near the Mideast," Benny insisted. "They're dying to find something they can use to come down hard on your PSA program and to scare would-be contributors away from listening to that woman Golda Meir. Do you think the government is happy about millions of U.S. dollars going abroad? No, Becky, those customs agents are going to comb through anything on its way to Palestine."

"Then have your people—Stefano's people—bribe them not to comb this one time."

"If Stefano found out—"

"If he found out, so what? You could explain that you had to do it. How mad could he get?"

"Really mad," Benny grumbled. "It's more complicated than you know." He paused. How could he tell her what Stefano had ordered him to do to Louie Carduello?

He'd been stalling with nonsense about how he was staking out Carduello's daily routine in order to do the job right. He could tell Tony didn't believe a word of his excuses; he figured Bucci was content to let him stall. When Stefano got angry enough, Tony would be afforded the pleasure of being allowed to kill him.

Benny begged his wife to intercede with her father on his behalf, but she refused. Daddy could do no wrong. Benny's last hope was to mark time until the law caught up with Stefano. He himself had made some tentative overtures to an assistant district attorney, but he'd so far been unable to bring himself to turn state's evidence against Stefano. Meanwhile the pistol that Bucci had delivered to him weeks ago was gathering dust in the top drawer of his desk.

"I can't go into it," Benny shrugged uneasily. "Now is just a bad time for me to get Stefano upset."

"He'd never find out," Becky said. "Couldn't you do it one last time? Please?"

Benny eyed her suspiciously. "What the hell's gotten into you?"

"What? Why, nothing."

"Don't hand me that. You're acting crazy. This isn't like you. Jesus, you're flirting."

"I am not. Cut it out." Becky blushed scarlet. "You're the one being crazy." She looked away.

"Like hell, honey. I know flirting when I see it. You didn't even flirt when we were going together. You've changed. Yeah, I see it, now. You're acting different as well, coming around to plead Herschel's case—" He snapped his fingers as the truth dawned on him. "Goddamn! You and Herschel Kol!"

"Benny—" Becky looked around, clearly afraid someone would overhear.

"Calm down," Benny chuckled. "You're not exactly a well-known face on the waterfront." He gazed at her. "I'm right, aren't I?" he asked, and when she nodded, he shook his head. "Some guys have all the luck. I've been carrying a torch for you for years."

"Now you understand why this is so important to me."

"Yeah." He nodded glumly. "Now I understand."

"You once said that if I ever needed your help to call on you. Well, I need that help now."

Benny planted his elbows on the small table and rested his head in his hands. "Okay," he sighed. "I'll do it, but God help me if Stefano finds out." He laughed humorlessly. "Make that when he finds out."

"Oh, thank you, Benny," Becky gushed. "I'll never forget you for this."

"Becky, are you sure he's the one for you? He's not even American."

"I'm sure," Becky said gently. She reached across the table to squeeze his hand.

"I love you, you know. Just thought I'd say it for the record." He shrugged nonchalantly, throwing a bill on the table to cover their check.

Becky nodded and they stood up. "Just for the record," she murmured, coming around the table to kiss him, "I meant it. I'll never forget you."

"Yeah, sure," he said huskily. "You tell Herschel I'll get his junk outta New York. Have him come around to the office and we'll work out the details."

Tough break, he thought as he and Becky parted company and he watched her walk away. But then, tough breaks had been the only kind coming his way for a long time.

Two weeks later Benny got the shipment of guns and dies past customs and on its way to Palestine, nestled in those cartons packed with bicycle components. He hoped that the stuff would be worth the enormous trouble it had caused. The intermediaries who had so often followed his orders in the past this time rebelled against Benny's directives, rightly pointing out that Stefano had issued a hands-off policy for Palestine-bound contraband. Benny lied and bullied them into doing it, pretending that Stefano had given his okay for one last time, meanwhile nervously wondering when the shit was going to hit the fan.

It was a few days into February when Tony Bucci stormed into Benny's office. "Stand up," he demanded, a look of grim satisfaction on his sallow, homely face. "You're coming with me."

Benny swallowed hard and tried to smile. "What's doing?"

"We're going for a ride. Stefano wants to see you."

Benny gestured to the papers on his desk. "Tony, I'm busy here. Can't this wait?"

Bucci lunged across the desk to grab Benny's necktie. He used it like a lead to haul Benny up out of his chair and around to the front of the desk.

"What the hell you doing?" Benny exclaimed. "Let go, you four-eyed creep—"

Bucci shoved one foot behind Benny's heel and shouldered into him, knocking Benny off balance and sending him sprawling to the floor. "Jew trash," he muttered as he went around behind the desk to find the pistol he'd given Benny. He checked to see that it was loaded and then waved it in Benny's direction. "Get on your feet."

"Have you gone crazy?" Benny demanded, brushing himself off as he stood up. "You know how much this suit cost me?"

"A big shot, huh?" Bucci smiled thinly. "You've made a lot of mistakes, big shot." He held the gun loosely in his right hand as he spoke. "You should have done Louie and you shouldn't have sent out that Palestine shit."

"Ah, big deal," Benny said wearily. He wondered how Tony planned to kill him. The one thing in his favor was that Tony had come alone. "I'll explain everything to Stefano," Benny remarked. "Let me call him." He began to move toward the desk.

"Stand still," Bucci said icily.

"I'm just going to call Stefano—"

Bucci brought up the gun. "Don't touch the telephone."

Benny winced. "So I'm finished, huh? You plan to do it now?"

"You would have been all right," Bucci gloated. "Even without doing Louie in and with this Palestine business, you would've come through okay. Stefano has always liked you. You always knew how to charm him." He shook his head. "But you dug your own grave when you went to the cops."

His gun momentarily wagged from side to side in an admonishing gesture. Benny used the chance to sink his right fist deep into Bucci's soft belly. Tony jackknifed forward at the waist, and his glasses went flying to the floor. Benny slapped the gun out of his hand and delivered three short, sharp right jabs to Tony's face, rocking his skull, flattening his nose and bloodying his mouth.

Tony sank like a stone. Benny knelt beside him, taking pleasure in the crunch of Bucci's thick lenses beneath his knee.

"Like I've always said, I don't know shit about guns, but I've had my share of brawls in my time." He smiled down at Tony.

Bucci coughed, turning his head slightly to spit teeth. "Asshole," he managed weakly.

"How'd you know I went to the cops?"

Bucci's little eyes began to swim in his head. Benny lightly slapped his cheek. "Hey," he said, "I'm talking to you. How'd you know—"

"That junior D.A. you went to belongs to us, asshole. You hadn't hung up on him ten seconds before he called us." He offered Benny a bloody smile. "You got nothing, asshole. Your wife and kids are with Stefano right now. He's telling Dolores all about your whores. She didn't much care for you anyway. Don't expect her to shed any tears for you after today, Benny."

"I'm not dead yet."

"Yes, you are. You just don't know it. You can't go home. I put a couple of guys there just in case I missed you here. Your wife don't want anything to do with you. Who are you going to turn to, kid? Where are you going to go? You think you can outrun the contract Stefano will put on you?"

Benny shut him up with a hard right to the chin that bounced the back of Tony's skull against the floor. He stood up, glancing at the gun in the corner and forgetting it at once. He ran from the office.

Becky snapped awake. At the other end of the apartment the intercom was buzzing. She squinted at the radium dial of her alarm clock, glowing ghostly green: three o'clock. She fumbled for the lamp on the night stand and switched it on.

Beside her Herschel stirred sleepily. "Whatzit?"

"I dunno, but it better be good," Becky mumbled. Yawning and stretching, she fumbled out of bed and into her robe before shuffling to the kitchen.

"Shut up," she snarled, grabbing for the handset. "Hello?"

"I'm very sorry, Mrs. Pickman," the doorman said, "but there's someone here who insisted that I ring you."

Becky heard the doorman arguing, and then, "Becky? It's me—"

"Benny?"

"Becky, I need help."

They sat in the kitchen while Benny ate scrambled eggs and told his story. "So, I was thinking," Benny said haltingly, his anxious eyes upon them, "maybe I could go to Palestine. Maybe you two can help me get there."

Herschel whistled, running his fingers through his hair. "It's no holiday over there. It's war."

Benny rubbed at his weary eyes and lit a cigarette. "At least in a war I'd have a fighting chance. Here I'm a dead man for sure."

"Couldn't you go to the police?" Becky asked.

Benny laughed bitterly. "I tried."

"Not that awful, corrupt one you mentioned," she replied. "I mean, say, the FBI—authorities Stefano can't bribe."

"Like I said, I tried." Benny shrugged. "I didn't

want to mention this, but I guess I'd better. I called the FBI this afternoon, but nobody's buying what I have to sell. They already have enough on Stefano. They're going to let him stew for a while. Then the guy said that the only way that he'd help me is if I informed on the Jewish agents operating on the waterfront.''

"Oh, shit," Herschel muttered.

"Right." Benny scowled. "The Feds know something has been going on, and they figure that when I get desperate enough, I'll tell them all I know." He stared at Becky. "I wouldn't, of course."

"Of course not. Herschel?"

"Well, I suppose we can hardly say no. Talkin, do you have any money?"

"Only what's in my pocket."

"All right. Don't worry." Herschel said. "Everything will be taken care of. Tomorrow morning during rush hour you'll take the subway a few stops uptown to a safe house near Columbia. You'll be all right there. I know the people to get you your shots and a passport, though it'll have to be under an alias, I'm afraid. I'll arrange for money and a plane ticket to Paris. Toward the end of the month I'll join you there and we'll both go to Palestine.''

Benny nodded gratefully. "I don't know how to thank you.''

Herschel reached across the table to clasp his hand. "No thanks are necessary, comrade. You have done a great deal for the cause, and this trouble is partly our responsibility." His expression was grim. "Besides, in Palestine your work will be cut out for you. You will be a soldier. Do you understand that?''

"I'm no coward, Kol.''

"You will have ample opportunity to prove that.''

Becky settled Benny in a guest room and returned to her own bedroom, where Herschel was lying awake. "Is it going to be okay?" she asked.

Herschel shrugged. "I'll get him there, but then who can say? He'll have to adapt. We have many tailors in Palestine, but just now they are not concerned with haberdashery."

Becky giggled and pounced on him. "But you'll look out for him, right?"

"Becky, I will be very busy."

She silenced him with a kiss. "But you'll do it for me. Okay, Herschel? Benny's my friend. It's been one hell of a weird friendship, but we are friends. Please look out for him."

"And what about me?" Herschel teased, sliding his hands beneath Becky's robe to cup her bottom. "Should I look out for me?"

"Oh, yes."

Benny Talkin left the country without incident, and toward the end of the month, as promised, Herschel joined him in Paris and arranged for their passage to Palestine. The two men left from the same airfield where Danny had landed in December. They were granted space on a cargo plane loaded with gunny sacks of weapons and ammunition donated by ex-Resistance groups, many of which had been mainly Jewish. They would touch down in Rome to refuel and then fly over Greece to land at a makeshift secret landing strip south of Tel Aviv.

Herschel had newspapers with him to occupy himself and Benny during the uncomfortable flight. He began swearing as he read.

"What's wrong?"

Herschel showed him the article. "A couple of days ago the damned British expelled Palestine from the Sterling Block. That means nobody with savings in English institutions can get their money. It's robbery. Those bastards might as well have used a mask and a gun to rob us."

"Tough break," Benny said. "You lose anything?"

"About twenty thousand pounds."

"How much is that in real money?"

Herschel smiled. "Approximately a hundred thousand dollars."

"A hundred grand! Holy shit. How can you just sit there?"

"Thanks to my mother, what's been frozen in England is just a small portion of my family's assets. Most of our money is in America."

"You're saying that you're rich?"

"Somewhat."

"Don't hand me that limey understatement crap. You're rich, yes or no?"

"Yes."

"Does Becky know?"

"What an odd question. Well, no, I don't think she does." Herschel pondered him. "Benny, I hope you are not suggesting that Becky loves me for my money? That's absurd. She's wealthy in her own right."

"No, but it does mean you're not after hers." He winked. "It's a good thing I'm coming along, now that I think about it. I can take care of you for her."

"How thoughtful of you."

"And it's great about you being rich."

Herschel was amused. "I'm pleased that you're pleased."

"Hey, we're buddies, right?" Benny asked affectionately. "Once we get this war outa the way, you and me can go into business. We'll bring in some trucks."

Chapter 64

Palestine

Danny banked the droning Piper Cub in wide, lazy circles through the cloudless sky. It was March; spring had come early to Judaea tufting the rugged, rusty terrain with light green. As Danny circled, he kept his eye peeled for a sign of the ground party that was supposed to meet him.

The Piper Cub had had its two passenger seats pulled out and its doors removed to facilitate loading cargo. That was good for the ground crew but a little breezy for the pilot. Danny was wearing chino pants and a long-sleeved shirt, his leather jacket and goggles. The Cub was loaded with four hundred pounds—the maximum weight—of ammunition, food and medical supplies. When he received his signal he would set down on a nearby stretch of dirt road, unload and get the hell out of there before an Arab raiding party closed in.

He saw the dust cloud formed by two trucks coming out of a ravine. He waited for the signal that would identify the trucks as friendly, meanwhile noting how the hilly, arid country below reminded him of south Texas, where he had some flight training. Then a hand-held mirror began winking at him and he concentrated on the sequence in order to assure himself that it was the right signal.

There was no better plane than a Piper Cub for this sort of work, Danny knew. His initial flight out of Teterboro had unnerved him. The big DC-3 might as well have been an ocean liner; it just wasn't the sort of airplane a fighter jock could feel good in. He prayed to God that he wouldn't ever have to fly anything like that.

He wasn't in the Holy Land a week before they hurried him to a sideshow called the Palestine Flying Club in Tel Aviv. There Danny was interviewed by a former RAF pilot named Aaron Remez. He had been supplied with Danny's records by good old Milty of Lion Airways. He asked Danny a few questions, sympathized with his complaints about the DC-3 and promised him that an operation much to his liking was in the works. In the meantime they had something to keep a hotshot pilot occupied.

He was hustled to Lod Airport, where the embryonic air force of the soon-to-be Jewish state sheltered in a ramshackle hangar. That was where Danny and his Piper Cub fell in love at first sight. Flying the Cub was the perfect way to ease back into the air.

He began to bring her in for the landing. The road was two lanes wide and rutted in places. There was a much better landing strip not far away, at the Ezyon settlements in the Hebron hills. That was where the supplies in the Piper were going. The problem was that the settlements were surrounded by hostile Arabs trying to starve out the settlers. Two truck convoys had been massacred trying to reach the outpost. An airlift, meager as it might be, was the best that could be done for them.

Danny came in with full flaps and just a little power, keeping his air speed way down. As the tires kissed the earth he cut his engine, raised his flaps and stood on the brakes.

He was taxiing sedately as the trucks screeched to a halt. Two men hopped out of the cab of each truck. They were young and intense, dressed in baggy cotton clothes, sandals and wide-brimmed hats. They wore long sideburn locks as a sign of their orthodoxy and toted Sten guns.

Danny stepped out of his airplane and went to greet them, the old Webley revolver in its busted-up flap holster bouncing on his hip.

"Shalom," one of the settlers grinned.

Danny unzipped his leather jacket and pulled his goggles down so that they dangled from his neck. "How you doing?"

The settler smiled. "We'll do better now that you've come. That was a nice landing."

"Nice!" Danny exclaimed. "From touchdown to full stop less than two hundred feet. You won't ever see better."

"I'm sorry you could not use the strip we built."

"Yeah, well, maybe next time. It's a little unfriendly over there right now. Not even the Arabs could miss a Piper with massed machine guns and heavy-shot antiaircraft fire."

He helped the settlers load their trucks. When it was done he asked, "You guys will be okay getting back?"

The one who spoke English shrugged. "We got out okay. Go. We will stay to cover you until you are airborne. Shalom, comrade. God be with you."

"You too, pal." Danny climbed back into the Piper and took off. He waggled his wings in a good-bye salute and headed back to Lod, about fifty miles away. As he flew he found himself wondering how those settlers were going to make out. Since his arrival in Palestine he'd flown dozens of these pipsqueak airlifts to rural settlements. To him it was like the cavalry surrounded by Apaches in the old West. The problem was, this time it was the Indians who had the modern weapons and the good guys who were stuck with bows and arrows.

There was no way to supply all the settlements. There were only a handful of Pipers in the country to carry the precious supplies that could be spared from the cities. A lot of those settlements were stuck for water as well as food and weapons. Four hundred pounds of water was a spit in the bucket out in the desert, but carrying even that much meant Danny couldn't bring anything else.

He fingered the bullet hole in the windscreen. It had happened a few weeks ago, shocking the hell out of him, though he wasn't touched. It gave him pause. That was just one bullet. What must dog-fighting be like with an opponent's machine guns ripping after you? He knew the British were supplying the Arabs with the most modern of weapons but had taken solace in the notion that the enemy was untrained in their use.

Now he fingered the bullet hole, thinking that at least one guy down there had been practicing his target shooting.

Back at Lod he set down close to the Palestine Flying Club's hangar. The airport was still under British control, but the authorities either believed or were willing to pretend that the club's reason for existing was purely recreational.

The British Danny had met were a strange group. One thing about them was that you couldn't generalize. After listening to Herschel for so long, Danny arrived expecting to find a bunch of Nazis, and while it was true that some of the British had nothing to learn from Hitler, there were others who seemed deeply embarrassed about England's treatment of the Jews.

As Danny cut the engine he glimpsed Dov Gretz, the club's operations officer, waving at him from the office. He was chatting with a young man.

"What's up?" Danny asked, taking off his jacket and lighting a cigarette. "Everything went fine, if that's what you're—"

"You still want to fly a fighter?" Gretz asked.

"Yeah, sure."

"All right. I'm taking you off supply runs. Roy here will take your Cub. You two should get along. He also has no Hebrew."

"What happens to me?" Danny asked.

"You go for training—"

"Hey, I've had training."

"Not in these you haven't."

"What are they, Spitfires?"

"Nope. Messerschmitts."

Danny froze. "You're shitting me. Messerschmitts?"

"ME-109's."

"Kraut planes! All the fighters you guys coulda come up with—Spitfires, Mustangs—what was the matter, you couldn't find any Jap Zeros?"

"That's what we're getting," Gretz said. "You want in or not?"

"Sure, sure. Where am I taking training, the Black Forest?"

"Czechoslovakia. Pack your bag and you're out of here."

"You're not kidding, are you? I can't wait. Come on, Roy, I'll take you up. The Piper's a beauty, but there's a few things about her you oughta know."

They walked to the hangar where the Piper was parked. Roy stared at the cowling. "What is that painted on it," he asked, "an apple?"

"Nah, that's a cherry," Danny said proudly. "I did it myself." He smacked the black lettering beneath it.

CHERRY STREET MARKET

We deliver

"That's coming off," Roy warned.

"Suit yourself, pal," Danny said coolly. "I'm gonna paint it on my—Messerschmitt." He shuddered and made a face.

Chapter 65

It was May fourteenth, a Friday, and hot as hell in Tel Aviv. Benny Talkin had suffered through some pretty awful New York City summers, but this was hot. He felt he was suffocating, and moreover, being jammed into this stuffy meeting hall, busting his ass on a slat-backed folding chair, made it a lot worse.

The hall was part of Tel Aviv Museum. Hersch said that it was once the home of a guy named Meir Dizengoff, a big man in this burg. Evidently Hersch's old man and this Meir guy, once the mayor of Tel Aviv, had done a real estate deal here years ago. Anyway, that was the best Benny could figure it because Herschel had been too frazzled getting ready for this inaugural ceremony to explain more.

Benny had the sense to know that this was strictly a VIP affair. There were lots of Haganah cops out front checking everybody's credentials. It was a measure of Herschel's pull that he'd been able to get Benny in. Benny argued that as an American he was going to feel unwelcome, but Herschel insisted that Benny had done as much as anyone here and ought to share the moment of glory.

Since their arrival a couple of months ago they'd been

touring munitions factories. Sadly, Herschel's own gun
project was on the shelf for the time being. The leadership
considered that this was not the time to divert precious
manpower to developing a new, untried design.

Benny had taken a look at the prototypes, and while
he was no arms expert, he could tell it was a light automatic weapon, far less cumbersome than the Tommy gun
and far more reliable than the Sten. Benny's entrepreneur-
ial instincts told him Herschel's little submachine gun
would someday be a winner.

Hersch was a winner too, in Benny's opinion. Since
they got here he'd played big brother, warming as he never
had in New York. Benny figured he'd have gone crazy by
now if it hadn't been for Hersch. Everyone else here had
made a commitment to this new land, but Benny figured
he'd be going home eventually. Until then it was tough
trying to make out without speaking Hebrew. Benny had a
little Yiddish, but nobody here liked Yiddish at all. People
would speak English to him if they had to get some
information across, but when it came to pleasant conversation, they chose to leave him out rather than switch off
from their damned Hebrew.

But Herschel had been just grand to him. Right now
he was off speaking to some guy with an eye patch named
Dayan, so Benny was sitting by himself twiddling his
thumbs, but usually Hersch kept him company.

Benny glanced around the room. He recognized Golda
Meir from newspaper photos. Up on the dais were Ben-
Gurion and the other big shots of the provisional government.
Behind them on the wall was a huge and brooding portrait
of a bearded Theodor Herzl flanked by a brace of Mogen
Davids. A lot of men up there did not look all that happy,
and Benny, even if he was an out-of-towner, understood
why. They had tried to postpone their country's independence.

Back in December of '47 the representatives from the

seven Arab states issued a joint statement that they would support the Arabs of Palestine with arms and money and that their own armies would attack the Jews upon the British evacuation. In March, just a few days after he and Herschel arrived, the Arabs made good on their threat. Syrian regulars crossed the border, moving against the Jewish village of Magdiel in Galilee. The battle lasted ten days and ended in stalemate. Haganah then staged a series of retaliatory attacks against Arab villages in the Jordan valley, dynamiting the homes of suspected ringleaders. To Benny the policy of demolition seemed needlessly cruel; Herschel said it was a trick taught to the Jews by the British, who used dynamite to tame rioters during the thirties.

In April, while he and Hersch were smoothing out the glitches in the assembly lines of the underground munitions operations, the Haganah attacked the village of Castel, just west of Jerusalem. That same month combined Irgun and Stern group forces attacked the village of Deir Yassin, also near Jerusalem. Hundreds of Arabs, men, women and children were massacred. The provisional government was so shocked that it actually sent a cabled apology to Transjordan even as Palestine's Arabs began to flee in panic from the Haganah units advancing throughout Galilee. Haganah also turned its attention to punishing the rebellious Irgun. Grenades were tossed into the midst of Irgun rallies. In an attempt to halt what Benny viewed a gang war, the two rivals, Begin and Ben-Gurion, drafted a series of truces, none of which lasted long. It was a bad situation, Benny thought, and typically Jewish.

The British went beyond freezing Jewish assets in their attempt to stack the deck in favor of the Arabs. Benny had seen them act like spoiled children, causing as much chaos as they could during their departure. All equipment and property that could not be handed over to the Arabs was destroyed. A nasty unofficially sanctioned paramilitary group, the British League, had sprung up to terrorize Jewish civilians with grenade attacks and kidnappings, after which the victims were turned over to Arab mobs.

The British did their best to salt the earth as they left, but they did at last leave. The Jewish forces rushed to fill the vacuum. On the British withdrawal from Jaffa the Irgun, which had been massing just outside Tel Aviv, invaded the ancient Arab port city and drove out some ninety thousand Arabs. In Haifa days of street fighting culminated in a Haganah attack in the wake of the British departure. Seventy thousand Arabs were exiled, mostly to Lebanon. In the same manner Jewish forces grabbed all the rest of the territory granted to them by the UN. Of all the Jewish holdings, only the Ezyon Block—on Arab land according to the UN plan—had been lost. Jewish reinforcements had not been able to break through the Arab lines, while the airlifts had not been enough to keep the besieged settlements going.

As of today virtually all the territory granted under the partition plan, including Jerusalem with the exception of the Old City, was under Jewish control. It was Independence Eve, the British were gone and only a few thousand Arabs remained in Jewish territory.

And yet Benny could sympathize with those somber men on the dais who had begged Ben-Gurion to postpone independence and to accept Secretary of State George Marshall's recent offer to negotiate a truce with the Arabs. Their plan was to stall until the massive supplies of arms that had been purchased in Europe could be transported here, giving the new regular army a better chance when the Arab attacks did finally come. Marshall pointed out that President Truman was considering sending U.S. troops as a peacekeeping force but would do so only if the independence proclamation was delayed. If his offer was refused, Marshall warned, they would have themselves to blame for bringing upon the Jewish people a second holocaust.

All this last minute diplomatic maneuvering threw the provisional government into turmoil. Herschel had been busy the last few days using what limited influence he had to lobby for a forthright declaration of independence. Benny figured Ben-Gurion thought the same way, for that point of view had prevailed.

Now the seven Arab states would definitely attack, and despite the best efforts of men like Herschel, there were still only enough weapons in the country to arm one in three would-be soldiers. The Jews had so far done well in separate skirmishes, but could they manage against sustained attacks from all sides? Just as important, would the two feuding factions resist turning their guns on each other?

Benny watched as Herschel made his way down the aisle to take his seat beside him. He looked happy about something.

"It's arranged," Herschel whispered. "We're going with Moshe Dayan. It's not yet official, but he's been placed in command of the Jordan valley. The Syrians will invade there, and Dayan fought them during the Second World War."

"Good for him," Benny said. "Where are we going?"

"Remember I told you about Degania?"

"Sure, that's your home town."

"Something like that," Herschel chuckled. "Anyway, Degania is in the Jordan valley. My mother is there. It's where I wish to make my stand in the battle to come." He paused, his expression growing serious. "There's another reason, Benny, one nobody knows. I have a score to settle with someone. He will be fighting with the Syrians, and he will also come to Degania, looking for me the way I am looking for him."

"This guy's an Arab, huh? What did he do?"

"He killed my father."

Benny stared. "I see. Yeah, sure. Degania it is."

Herschel gripped Benny's arm. "Remember what I've told you. Now that the British are gone, the airfields are open and planes will be flying to transport arms. I can arrange for you to go to Europe if you'd like, Benny. You've no obligation to remain here."

Before Benny could reply Ben-Gurion's gavel rapped, signaling the start of the ceremony. It was four o'clock.

"Think about what I've said," Herschel whispered. "We must leave shortly."

The ceremony was in Hebrew, of course. To Benny the language was so much coughing and duck-quacks, but he felt his emotions stir in response to Ben-Gurion's majestic tones and the fervor in the upturned faces of his audience. Now and again Herschel, visibly moved, would lean toward him to whisper a translated phrase.

The whole thing took a little more than half an hour. Then Herschel was grabbing his elbow, bidding him rise with the rest of the assembly as Ben-Gurion's gavel sounded a second time.

Cheers erupted in the meeting hall. Weeping, Herschel embraced him. "Benny, it's done. The state of Israel has come into existence."

Radio transmitters carried the news of the ceremony to all parts of the infant nation and celebrations lined the streets of Tel Aviv. It reminded Benny, walking back to the quarters he and Herschel were sharing, of Times Square on New Year's Eve.

How he longed for New York, for home. Benny was walking alone. Herschel wanted to celebrate with some of the people at the ceremony, so Benny had excused himself in order to let Hersch enjoy the moment with his old friends.

Everywhere he looked people were laughing or crying

or linking hands to dance a joyous hora as if this were a goddamned wedding or something. He knew there were corners of Israel where the people were too busy fighting and bleeding to do much celebrating, and very soon the whole country was going to be in the same mess.

The Jews were outmanned and outgunned. The Syrians held the high ground in Galilee; Egyptian armored divisions were probably even now churning through the sands of the Negev; and the elite English-led five-thousand-man Arab Legion from Transjordan, was poised to storm Jerusalem.

The Jews had no artillery beyond a few handmade mortars and virtually no fighter aircraft. Until they received both, and shipments of small arms and ammo to supplement what Herschel's factories were churning out, the best the Jews could hope to do was to dig in and survive.

There would be women fighting in this war, and children. Herschel had shown him a classroom where the teacher was busy instructing the students on how to make Molotov cocktails. He could just see those kids pitching their little gasoline bombs at Egyptian tanks. He wondered how many of them would blow themselves up too.

Talk about long odds—if Benny had known the whereabouts of a bookie, and if he'd had any money, he would have put every dime on the opposing team.

As he paused on a street corner a girl in khaki shorts and a cotton blouse threw her arms about his neck, kissed him on the lips, said something in that damned Old Testament language and skipped away.

Benny watched her go, admiring her legs, although otherwise she wasn't his type. He preferred them with a future.

He dug the news clipping out of his pocket to look at it for what was possibly the hundredth time. It had come from none other but *The New York Times*.

Back in April the British cut off all mail and telegraph service to Palestine, and regular deliveries of anything, let alone periodicals, had not yet resumed. Herschel sensed how homesick Benny was, however, and had gotten him the rather dated but still complete copy of the *Times* from a pilot newly arrived from the States. Benny read the old paper from cover to cover and found the news item buried in the paper's second section. "Reputed Mobster Arraigned," the headline read. Stefano de Fazio, it seemed, had been arrested for racketeering, extortion and income tax evasion.

The paper was a month old when he got it. It meant that likely Benny was off the hook and could go home if that was what he chose to do.

He was through with Dolores, of course, and he doubted she'd let him get close to the kids, but he could be back on top in no time—if he returned, and why shouldn't he?

Okay, it would mean taking a powder on Herschel right when he could use some backup, going up against that guy who'd iced his old man. And it would mean deserting those kids, some no older than his own boys, who were filling bottles with gasoline and shoving in wicks torn from rags.

Kids against tanks—holy shit.

Maybe he would stick around, but just for a little while. As a kid he'd built up his own reputation leading a gang that defended against the roving Italian and Irish gangs who liked to bust Jewish heads.

That's what was going on here, Benny thought. Irish gangs or Hitler or these damned Arabs—what they all had in common was a desire to bust up Jews. He'd missed that scrape with Hitler, as Becky had once reminded him.

Getting killed in a war is a sucker's move, he told himself. Then he thought about the ceremony he'd just attended and how a tough guy like Herschel broke down to tears. He thought about this pipsqueak nation's chosen colors, blue and white. It was a nice flag, and it'd be a shame to let a bunch of camel drivers trample it into the mud before it had a chance to wave.

He crumpled up the newspaper clipping but hesitated to toss it away. What's the point in being a hero? he asked himself a final time. Where's the percentage?

There was none, but he knew that he was going to stick around anyway. Besides, being a war hero would likely impress Becky.

This time he did try to toss away the crumpled clipping, but it stuck to his sweaty fingers. It sure was hot.

Chapter 66

Czechoslovakia

Danny watched anxiously, his hands jammed into his pockets, biting his lower lip to keep from yelling out dumb advice that would only distract the ground crew. Slowly, gently, the dismantled fuselage of the Messerschmitt was lifted with a block and tackle and gingerly swung into the cavernous hold of the cargo plane. That was his fighter they were loading, and as soon as they were finished packing the wings, guns and ammo, he would board the big C-54 to return to Israel.

His training at the Czech fighter base had been an adventure more out of *Alice in Wonderland* than *Tailspin Tommy*—including last night's surprise ending.

He left Israel—Palestine then—with several other volunteers. He spent a restless night at the hotel that was to be his home during his training, and the next morning they took a bus to the fighter base. They were issued overalls embroidered with swastikas and introduced to their instructors, former RAF pilots. To Danny that just added to the madness. The British who were not leading the

Arabs of Transjordan against the Jews of Israel were training Jews wearing swastikas to shoot down Egyptians flying British-supplied Spitfires.

The Messerschmitt was unlike anything Danny had ever flown. The big Daimler-Benz engine was powerful and smooth. Danny had his plane nudging three-fifty at full throttle. The Messerschmitt had a nice tight turning radius. Unfortunately, his baby also had some severe drawbacks. It took real muscle to control her. After a flight his arms felt like rubber and his thigh ached from riding the rudder bar. Visibility was horrible, and in a dogfight the first guy to see his opponent usually ended up the winner.

There were other problems. It was the devil to handle on the ground due to its narrow-track landing gear. Taxiing was a symphony of rumbling engine and squealing brakes as Danny struggled not to dip a gull wing onto the grass. It had no artificial horizon and no cockpit armor to protect the pilot, who sat smack on top of the fuel tank. It carried only two machine guns, mounted on top of the engine cowling, as opposed to the Spitfire's eight. It was true that the ME-109 was also armed with a cannon in each wing, but their rate of fire was very slow, considering that on average a pilot had an enemy plane in his sights for only two seconds. Besides, cannon needed cannon shells and, as Danny knew, Herschel was busy churning out machine gun bullets, not cannon shells. Israel-bound cargo planes would airlift in shells as well as spare parts for the ten Messerschmitts that formed the core of the new nation's air force, but Danny knew those cannon were going to be empty more often than not.

Toward the end of his training Danny grew fond of the Messerschmitt. It wouldn't have been his first choice, but when he thought about it, he had to admit that the Nazis hadn't done so badly with it, so he figured the Jews could do okay as well. Anyway, any fighter at all was better than a Piper Cub with a hand-held submachine gun thrust out the side window, which was what his side had been using against the Spitfires.

He spent his days flying and his evenings flirting with bar girls, waitresses and maids. There was one big-busted maid who wore her long red hair in braids and had a wiggly behind that drove Danny crazy, but he didn't know how to do anything about it. His frantic efforts to communicate with the maid, who spoke no English, put his fellow pilots into hysterics.

As the training period wound down to its final days, Danny mercilessly began to badger his flight instructor, who spoke Czech, to jot down Danny's obvious desires so that he could pass the note to the luscious redhead. The instructor refused, adding insult to injury by also sternly lecturing Danny against fraternizing with the natives.

Danny seemed to be losing his mind. The redhead dominated his dreams and ruined his concentration during flight time. Czechoslovakia was his chance to lose his virginity; it was the best chance he would ever have, and poor old Danny, the world's biggest cherry, was going to miss out.

Last night, his final night in Czechoslovakia, desperation had finally overwhelmed bashfulness. He was on his way from his hotel room to the dining room on the main floor when he encountered the maid in the corridor. They exchanged smiles—she'd always seemed to like him—but then that fanny of hers was sashaying away and out of his life.

He looked around wildly and hurried after the maid. He spun her around and he grabbed her wrist to plant her fingers on his swelling groin.

Then Danny smiled in what he'd hoped was a beseeching manner. The redhead giggled, squeezing him tentatively. Then she took his wrist to lead him back to his room.

Beneath her maid's uniform was a black bra, black

panties and a black garter belt to hold up her stockings. The brassiere and panties came off, but through much mime and sign language, which also served to break the ice, Danny was able to persuade her to retain the garter belt and stockings.

She was a redhead all over. As he savored the maid's ruddy charms, he realized this was something that beat flying.

That was last night. Now Danny yawned and watched as the last of his guns and ammo canisters were packed aboard. Then, as the cargo pilot began to feather his engines, Danny got aboard as well.

He rode in the cargo bay, settling as comfortably as he could against the stacked wings, for the first leg of the flight back to Israel. Pretty soon the drone of the engines lulled him into a sort of half-sleep. He retasted some of last night's pleasures and then drifted back to his boyhood and the pleasure he took in assembling model airplanes.

His own laughter jolted him awake as he realized that he was now in charge of one of the biggest airplane kits in the world. Soon the Messerschmitt would be put together, and then he would be a combat pilot at last.

Chapter 67

First Danny went to Israel, and now Herschel and Benny were there as well. It was too much. Becky thought she would go insane with worrying.

She desperately tried to occupy herself organizing fund-raisers and making speeches. Her goal was to move a million dollars' worth of goods a month to Israel. Nothing less would do for those who were risking their lives for Israel.

March saw another attempt by the Pickman family to wrest away control of the store. Once again Phil Cooper stood by Becky.

It still riled Becky that Gertrude Hoffer Pickman excluded her from contributing her assistance to Carl's museum project. Becky had beaten Gertrude on two fronts. She'd kept control of the store and regained the social acceptance lost since Carl's death.

It was the beginning of April. To combat loneliness after Herschel's departure, she began to make an inventory of Carl's personal papers. She discovered a letter wedged into the back of a file drawer. It was still in its original envelope. Becky wondered whether Carl had misplaced it or hidden it. It was dated 1911. The stationery with the Harvard seal was yellowed and brittle.

It was Carl's acceptance letter. He'd wanted to be a doctor. It was so like him not to confide to her that his dream had been denied. She'd been his wife and lover, his protege, but she'd never known the truth about him. She thought back to how she felt as a girl, when her own father took her out of school. She and Carl had been more alike than they'd known.

She called Norman Collins and instructed him to deal with the paperwork. It had not taken long to establish a fund bearing Carl Pickman's name to award scholarships to worthy, financially needy medical students.

On May 17th Becky attended a luncheon during which the main speaker, a newspaper correspondent, lectured on the military situation in the Mideast. The speaker disclosed that the United States was calling for a truce resolution in the Security Council but that Great Britain was stalling, he suspected, in order to give the Arabs a chance to grab territory.

A large map had been erected to illustrate the speaker's talk. Red arrows signified enemy troop positions. There were a lot of red arrows. Someone asked about Galilee and the speaker predicted that it would fall to the Syrians.

Becky sat numb, staring at the map, which made it very clear that Degania was the gate through which the Syrians would have to pass if they wished to seize Galilee.

Chapter 68

Degania

The command meeting took place in the old dining hall late in the afternoon. The kibbutz membership attended; it was, after all, their home that had become the battlefield. The long tables had all been pushed to one side, the worn, backless benches arranged facing the front table, where Moshe Dayan and the leader of the three-hundred-man brigade assigned to protect the Jordan valley pondered their maps and quietly conferred.

For Herschel, sitting with Benny, his mother and old Yol Popovich, it was a long-awaited homecoming. How he had missed the land of his youth. Not even the hastily dug trenches, the barbed wire and the smell of death could mar this reunion. Benny Talkin had been unusually quiet since their arrival a few hours ago. It was as if the living, breathing history of the kibbtuz had instilled in him a sense of place, of history, of home, that the American had been sadly lacking since coming to this new country.

Degania was Israel, Herschel thought as he sat with one arm around his mother's thin shoulders and his other clasping Yol's gnarled, thick fingers. It would remain so despite the line of Syrian Renault tanks sitting motionless in the sun like basking black toads. It would remain so despite the neighboring villages that were overrun by the Syrians.

Dayan rapped the table top to bring the meeting to order. The brigade commander who until an hour ago had held the responsibility of protecting the area did not look pleased, and Herschel could understand why. Nobody liked to lose his authority at the last moment, as this poor fellow had when Dayan arrived, bringing along nothing but a platoon of frightened adolescents from the Youth Troops, a couple of rusty bazookas and of course Benny and himself.

Dayan cleared his throat. "From what I've been told, your few machine gun nests have served to keep away the Syrian infantry. They must cross the barley fields to get to us, and they will not do so as long as the guns have ammunition."

"What about those tanks?" the brigade commander demanded. "Machine guns won't stop tanks."

Dayan turned his head to glare at the officer. Herschel, as always, was struck by Dayan's birdlike mannerisms. The Haganah leader was dressed in the worn khakis that served as the uniform of the Israel. He and Benny had each been issued a set as well, along with Sten guns and an extra magazine of ammunition apiece. Herschel's pants were too short and his shirt had given way under his left arm. Becky would have to send them better uniforms. He smiled to himself. He could have daydreamed about her all day, but he pushed her from his mind to concentrate on what Dayan was saying.

"We'll need weapons far more effective than Molotov cocktails if we're to hold off the tanks. From what you people have reported and from what I've seen, we're up against a Syrian infantry brigade backed by tanks and armored cars. Deganias A and B must dig in far more effectively if they are to hold out. Things here are not so bad, but Degania B is practically undefended. I've also noticed that Bet Yerach, a stone's throw north of here, is unoccupied.''

"So what?" the brigade commander exploded. "It's nothing, merely an archaeological mound. I know you haven't been in combat for years, Moshe, and I am trying to make allowances for your inexperience, but diverting manpower and precious ammunition to protect a mound of dirt from the Syrians is going too far.''

"Commander, it is true that Bet Yerach is not a settlement, but if you look at the map, you'll see that it commands the road from Zemach, which the enemy has already taken. The Syrians must pass Bet Yerach if they wish to take Degania, the corridor between the Jordan River and the Sea of Galilee. If we can entrench ourselves on the mound's eastern slopes, we can fire on the Syrians as they pass. We will have flanked the enemy.'' Dayan shrugged. ''I can think of no better way to use what little we have.''

"Little is right," the commander scoffed. "What we need is artillery to blast those tanks.''

"Ben-Gurion has promised to send us artillery as soon as it can be spared from elsewhere.''

"It'll be too late then," the commander shouted in frustration. ''I say we should evacuate.''

"Never," Rosie murmured to her son. On her other side Yol was translating for Benny. Her hair was the color of slate, her face wrinkled by the years and made haggard by the violence of the last few days, but her deep brown eyes were as fiery as ever.

"They'll never make me leave Degania," Rosie went on. "How can he imagine that any of us would leave?''

"No one's leaving, Mama.''

"If we evacuate now, there's a chance we can all escape before they resume shelling,'' the commander was loudly announcing. "For the life of me, I don't know why they're not shelling us now."

"Perhaps they're just as short of ammunition as we are," Dayan suggested. "The Syrians were never the best-equipped of the Arab nations."

"What about my evacuation plan?" the commander insisted.

Dayan shook his head. "We must hold the Deganias. We cannot abandon the Jordan valley."

"I refuse to follow the orders of a novice."

"Hey, can I say something?" Benny got to his feet and glanced inquiringly at Yol. "Maybe you could translate for me."

"Everyone here speaks English," one of the old members shouted out.

Benny glanced at the brigade commander, who nodded. "Go ahead. Say what you've got on your mind."

"Well, maybe you won't like me too much when you hear what I got to say." Benny slipped his hands into his pockets and looked down at his shoes. "It seems to me that the big problem here, besides the Arabs, is who's in charge. When times are this bad, rank doesn't matter. Commander, you know you can't pull out and let those Syrian creeps just waltz in here. So that's that, right? What we can do is stall until those antitank guns get here. It seems to me that Moshe's idea of sending out a party of volunteers to flank the enemy is a good one." Benny shrugged. "So let's hop to it and cut the crap."

Yol nudged Herschel. "Your papa used to talk to the membership just that way." He beamed approvingly.

"I agree with Benny," Herschel said. "I also volunteer to lead the force to Bet Yerach."

"We have so many leaders," the brigade commander observed sarcastically.

"Hey." Benny pointed his finger in warning. "That's my friend you're talking to, wise guy. It just so happens that he grew up here. This is his turf. Get it? Who better to go running around out there in the dark?'' Benny winked at Herschel. ''I'll go with you.''

''I accept your offer, Herschel,'' Dayan said. ''It does make sense that somebody from Degania should be in charge at Bet Yerach. Let's get to it, then. This meeting is adjourned.''

As the others streamed out, Herschel noticed Yol staring at him suspiciously. ''I know why you volunteered,'' the old man hissed. ''Don't think I don't.''

''Quiet, you old monkey,'' Herschel whispered, cocking his thumb at his mother. ''We'll talk about it later.''

''No later,'' Rosie scolded. ''I'm old, not deaf. Anyway, I also know why you have volunteered, Herschel. It's because your father's grave is just behind Bet Yerach.''

''All right, then, I admit it,'' Herschel said soberly. ''Tell me, Yol, during the previous attacks did you see him?''

''See who?''

''You know who.'' Herschel clasped the old man's shoulder. ''Jibarn Ahmed.''

Benny asked, ''Hersch? Is that the guy who rubbed out your old man?''

Herschel nodded, and turned back to Yol. ''Tell me, have you seen him?''

''Leave me alone,'' Yol ordered, pulling away from Herschel. ''I'm an old man. I don't see so good anymore.''

''Yol, please. Don't you understand? He'll be waiting for me at my father's grave. I know it. I sense it. It's almost like he's my brother.''

Yol nodded in defeat. ''All right. Yes, I saw him. I was looking for him with binoculars. I knew he would come back to help destroy Degania. I saw him sitting in a command car with some other officers. I swear, it gave me a start—he suddenly turned and gazed right back at me.'' Yol seemed to cave in. He had aged considerably in the last few years. He had lost a great deal of weight, his beard had gone snow white and his scalp was totally bald and liver-spotted. "I know he could not see me, but I can't shake my gut feeling that he knew I was looking at him."

"The bond between the three of us is very strong, Yol," Herschel observed.

Yol suddenly embraced him. "Please, don't go to fight with him. I couldn't bear to know that I've been the cause of both the father and the son dying."

"Yol," Rosie interjected, "go with Benny for a walk, yes? I want to talk with my son."

When Benny and Yol had gone, she said, "He's a good man, Yol, but what he said about his eyes is true. He can't see so well anymore. The other day they took away his gun. He gets excited and everything is a blur to him." She paused, shrugging. "He almost shot one of our own boys, so now the two of us sit and load the magazines for the ones who can still shoot. I told him not to be ashamed. Most of the old people have chosen to evacuate along with the children."

"But you won't leave, and he'll never leave your side, right, Mama?" Herschel smiled.

"He's been a good friend, a good companion. Better than a cranky old lady like me deserves." She patted her son's cheek. "But now that you've brought that handsome young Benny here, well, Yol had better look out I don't two-time him."

Herschel laughed. "I'd better warn Benny. Mama, you understand that I have to meet Jibarn. I mean, maybe he won't even show himself, but if he does—"

"Quiet. He'll be there and you'll go to confront him no matter what I say, so I won't say a thing but this. Do not make the same mistake your father made. Yol has told me how Jibarn charmed your father. He played on the fact that they were both orphans, and Haim—" She paused, turning her head until she had regained her composure.

"Haim trusted people. Your father was a very brave, very strong man, but he was too good, too innocent. In this world that's dangerous for anybody, but for a Jew . . ." She shook her head.

"I'll be careful." Herschel hesitated. "You used to go to his grave; do you still?"

Rosie looked shocked that he had asked. "Every day. It's only this damned war that is keeping me away. Tomorrow when you go, tell him what's been keeping me."

"Come, Mama. I'll walk you back to the cottage."

Rosie smiled. "And I'll close my eyes so I don't see the guns or the barbed wire, and there will be just the smell of the cornflowers carried by the warm breeze . . . Yes, son. Just like we used to walk."

Herschel returned from his mother's cottage past tents filled with groaning wounded to find Moshe Dayan, Benny Talkin and the brigade commander standing in front of the dining hall, watching quietly as the sun went down.

"I think we'd better set up our Bet Yerach defenses tonight," Herschel said. All around him in the twilight were shadowy forms taking their posts for the night.

"I agree," Dayan said. "You'll take one of the bazookas and some Molotovs and every man in your party shall be issued a Sten gun and three magazines."

Herschel frowned. "That's less than a hundred rounds each."

"I'm sorry," the brigade commander said sincerely. "We have bullets, but there's a shortage of magazines."

"Then give me loose cartridges," Herschel said. "We can always load in quiet moments."

"When do we leave?" Benny interjected.

Herschel regarded him. "I'm sorry, but you can't come."

"What? Come on." Benny laughed nervously. "We're buddies, right?"

"Of course we are. Please understand, Benny. This is

a commando operation and you have no experience in such things.'' The look on Benny's face made him smile. ''For all that I would still take you, but you can't speak Hebrew, and the volunteers are all Haganah men. Most of them don't speak English. Quick, quiet communication will be essential. Do you understand?''

''Yeah, I guess.''

''Don't worry.'' The brigade commander clasped Benny's shoulder. ''You will find plenty of action here.'' He smiled. ''Wise guy.''

At dark Herschel and his thirty volunteers prepared their weapons and packed food and plenty of water. There would be no shade for them on Bet Yerach. Next to the Syrians the sun would be their worst enemy.

As they prepared to slip out of the compound, Yol called Herschel to one side. ''This is something you ought to have,'' the old man whispered, handing over an object wrapped in cloth.

Herschel unwound it. The seven-inch blade caught the starlight as he held it up to the night. ''Thank you, Yol, but I have a knife.'' The words died in his throat. His eyes locked with Yol's. ''Is this—?''

Yol nodded. ''It is the blade that killed your father.''

Herschel blinked back bitter tears. ''I shall see to it that this knife is returned to its rightful owner, Yol.''

''He'll want to afford you the chance.'' Yol embraced him a final time. ''Take care, boy. Take care.''

Chapter 69

Tel Aviv

The handful of Messerschmitts were hastily reassembled in the ramshackle hangars of a makeshift airstrip outside Tel Aviv. The airfield had once been an orange grove. The smell of the place reminded Danny of the time those goofs from the produce wholesalers had sent a delivery to the Cherry Street market with the fifty-pound sacks of potatoes piled on top of the cartons of Sunkist.

Spitfires equipped with bomb racks were making runs against Tel Aviv every day, and wandering enemy planes would often strafe the airfield where the Messerschmitts were being made ready. The sirens would sound and all work on the planes would cease as everyone ran for the trenches. More than once Danny watched with his heart in his mouth as the bombs came close to but never touched the hangar housing the precious Messerschmitts.

Reassembling the planes proved to be tougher than taking them apart. Landing gear would fail to function on one plane; unsynchronized machine guns splintered the propeller of another. The frustrated, exhausted mechanics ran about in circles, and when the sirens blew everyone ran for the trenches.

The combined Arab air forces were devastating the country, keeping the vulnerable Piper Cubs and other cargo planes from supplying the settlements and evacuating the wounded. The Messerschmitts had to get airborne before the bombs destroyed them on the ground.

The Syrian attack on Degania commenced with mortar fire shortly before dawn about thirty hours after Benny Talkin arrived at the settlement with Herschel and Dayan. Benny had been assigned a spot on the front line in support of a machine gun. He'd been issued a Lee-Enfield rifle, several clips of ammo and a Molotov cocktail. As the incoming rounds from the Syrian mortars streaked lightning across the paling sky and landed thunder within the confines of the kibbutz, Benny tightly gripped his rifle and hunkered down behind the sandbag barricade that also sheltered the two-man gun crew.

This can't last forever, Benny told himself. The shelling will have to end, and when it does, I'll be brave. I will be a hero very soon.

Between the thud of the mortars and the deafening explosions of the shells came the distant crackle of small-arms fire. "What's that?" he demanded, not at all liking the panic he heard in his voice.

"That would be the men on Bet Yerach, ambushing the advancing Syrians," the loader replied.

"Maybe they'll get them all," Benny said.

"Maybe." The loader shrugged. "And maybe God will send the Angel of Death to wipe them out like last time, but I wouldn't count on it."

"That was the Egyptians anyway," the gunner muttered as he peered over the water-cooled barrel of his weapon.

"Picky, picky," the loader complained. "An Arab is an Arab, right, Yank?"

Benny didn't answer; his attention was seized by the approaching rumble of engines and the creak and clank of tractor treads biting into the earth.

"Here they come," shouted the gunner as his loader clicked a belt into the breech.

Benny peeked over the sandbags. The Syrian tanks were rolling toward them flanked by infantry. "Good Lord, they're just marching over those fields like nothing can stop them."

From a few yards away on Benny's left came a whoosh as their lone bazooka fired. One of the Syrian tanks vanished in a blossom of orange fire amidst much cheering from Degania's line.

Then all hell broke loose. The Vickers gun began snarling and ejecting a shower of spent cartridge cases. One of them hit Benny and he screamed, thinking he'd been shot. Then he got hold of himself and aimed his rifle at a group of advancing Syrian troops. He squeezed off an entire clip of five rounds and not a man of the enemy went down. He might as well have been firing blanks.

The Vickers barrel veered toward his targets and spat flame; the Syrians fell. The bazooka fired again. Another tank blew up, but there were plenty more, and they were rolling closer to the fences all the time despite the Molotovs. The tanks' cannon began to bark. Their machine guns chewed away at the sandbag barricade. The Syrian infantry, which had been taking a drubbing from Degania's small-arms fire, took up defensive positions in the barley field, relying on their tanks to shatter the Jews' defenses.

Benny loaded another clip into his rifle and began to fire. After two shots his weapon jammed. He stared at it helplessly. Nobody had shown him what to do when it jammed. He looked to the Vickers crew for assistance, and as he did, the loader sprawled backward with the top of his head missing.

"Take over," the gunner shouted. "Smooth out those belts."

"Not how it's supposed to be," Benny mumbled, staring dazedly at the dead loader.

"Please, the belts," the gunner was begging.

This was crazy. Your gun wasn't supposed to jam, and what about the paralyzing fear that made him want to crawl into a hole somewhere safe and quiet? No, this was definitely all wrong, Benny thought.

The gunner screamed at him and the Vickers' point-blank rounds sprang off the armor plating of the tank just now crashing through the fence a few yards in front of their position.

Benny's eyes fell on the Molotov cocktail. Light the wick, make sure it catches and then throw it before it explodes in your hands.

He struck a match and held it to the torn cotton rag. When he had it flaming he grabbed hold of the top layer of sandbags and hoisted himself up over the barricade.

The tank was sixty feet away. Its turret began to swing in his direction, but slowly—too slowly. He would make it before they could shoot at him if he didn't louse up the throw.

You've done it a thousand times as a kid, he told himself. Any kid worth his salt could do it.

He lobbed the bottle and watched it arc, trailing greasy black smoke, to shatter against the turret and engulf the tank in a shower of burning gasoline. The hatches flew open and the three crewmen came scrambling out, one of them screaming, his arm and hair on fire. All three were knocked down by small-arms fire.

Benny was running like hell back to the relative safety of the sandbags when some dirty bastard planted something that felt like a sledgehammer between his shoulder blades, knocking him flat on his belly.

This is crazy, he thought as he lay with his face in the dust. All around him the noise of the battle seemed to recede. This is not how it is supposed to be at all.

Jibarn Ahmed set down his knapsack, gazing at Haim Kolesnikoff's grave. It seemed impossible that it had been close to thirty years since he avenged his grandfather's death. The surrounding countryside of this, his ancestors' land, still seemed the same—except, of course, for Degania, cursed Degania. The Jews had spoiled the stern grandeur of Allah's creation; the land had been painted with the Jews' settlements until it looked like a whore. How Jibarn wished his wife and son in Syria could see the land of his fathers as Allah had intended.

Soon they would, when the Jews had been swept away, when the cursed sons of death had been picked off like ticks from a sheep's belly and crushed under the righteous weight of the Arab holy war against them.

Jibarn retrieved his knapsack and moved back into the protection of the boulders. Herschel would be coming soon, he suspected, and it wouldn't do to let the Jew surprise him.

Soon, Jibarn thought, soon the son will be dead, like the father. Soon Degania will be dead if the Syrians showed mettle.

As he listened to the noise of the battle for Degania, he knew he had strong reasons to worry about the quality of the Syrian troops. What was needed to dislodge the tough kibbutz workers was a highly trained, highly motivated army like the British-led Arab League, the elite force just now clashing with the Jews in Jerusalem. Syrian soldiers were mostly ignorant fellahin rudely roused from their villages, given uniforms and weapons and told to march. These soldiers did not have the training to overcome a well-planned defense. Fortunately, the Jews had little artillery, but unfortunately, the Syrian tanks had little petrol and few shells for their cannon.

Well, that battle was in Allah's hands. His own war with Haim Kolesnikoff's heir was what personally concerned him.

It had been difficult to persuade Syrian President Shukri al-Kuwatly to let him serve as Colonel Wahab's scout in the area. The president was in a foul mood, afraid his peasant troops would humiliate him, and still angry at Jibarn for failing to get the Jews' gun designs from the American.

But he was here. Jibarn smiled to himself. Soon Herschel Kol would die. It was disquieting, but he had mixed emotions about killing his adversary. He felt hesitant about it. It seemed to him almost like killing a brother.

Herschel's soul was tempered by his father's death, Jibarn thought, and Haim Kolesnikoff's passing has formed my character as well. The father's ghost haunts his son and haunts me. Is Haim, then, any less my father? Have I not lived with his memory as intimately as any son?

He grew angry with himself for doubting at a crucial moment. It was like this after smoking hashish, as if there was poison in his blood stealing away his masculinity, making him weak, making him waver. Perhaps the blood feud was the poison in him. Perhaps it had possessed him, taken control of his soul, let in a demon that killed unrighteously, not in Allah's name but because it craved death and destruction.

No, such unseemly doubt must be banished. It was the Jews who were the poison sickening his spirit and the spirit of his people. Palestine was his country. The land had always sustained the Arabs with a proud dignity. Once the Jews were gone, the land would once again sustain his people's spirit.

And once Herschel Kol was dead, Jibarn's own spirit

would be cleansed. After today Jibarn could set aside the
role of warrior and begin his duties as a husband and a
father. He himself had grown to manhood without benefit
of masculine guidance—

He looked back toward Haim's grave. No guidance
but for the Jew's.

He must be hard and strong. The end of the blood
feud was within reach.

He began to unpack the knapsack. He would strip off
his Syrian officer's uniform for the simple robes of his
origin. Today he would kill the son dressed as on the day
he killed the father. When he was finished dressing, he
would see to his service revolver and await Herschel.

The smoldering wrecks of three burnt-out tanks clogged
the roadway past Bet Yerach. The bazooka had accounted
for one of the tanks before its firing mechanism broke.
Herschel, the only one of his volunteers with technical
training, hurriedly examined their single precious antitank
weapon, but with Syrian troops blasting away at him, he
had little time to tinker. His men destroyed the other two
tanks with Molotovs. The wrecks had blocked a second
wave of tanks from making it through the pass, but many
tanks had made it during the initial assault. Herschel and
his men could hear them attacking Degania as they traded
automatic-weapons fire with Syrian troops clustered around
an armored personnel carrier parked at the base of the
slope.

One of his men lobbed a Molotov at the carrier, and
as the Syrians scattered from the flaming petrol, Herschel
chased them with his Sten gun until the magazine was
empty. He loaded his last magazine and turned to his
second-in-command, a young sergeant who until recently
had been captain in Haganah. "Assign two men to begin
reloading magazines," Herschel said. "You're in com-

mand now. You and your men should have no trouble holding the high ground.''

Herschel scrambled up the side of the slope past his men firing down at the Syrians. He swung around over the summit of the mound and hurried down the peaceful back of the hill toward his father's grave.

The trip took less than five minutes, but as the sounds of battle faded, Herschel started to feel like that small, awe-struck boy who gazed up at his proud father in Bedouin garb.

As Herschel walked the quarter-mile to his father's grave, he thought about Jibarn Ahmed. He tried to see the blood feud from the Arab's point of view, but it was difficult to understand how Yol's accidental shooting of an old shepherd could lead a boy to murder Haim Kolesnikoff, who had shown Jibarn nothing but kindness.

There was no marker, but Herschel had no trouble finding the spot. A hundred thoughts ran through his brain as he stared at the grave. He supposed he ought to reconnoiter the immediate area, perhaps set up some kind of ambush. He did nothing but stare at his father's grave. Then he knelt to press his face against the grass that was now a part of Israel.

"Throw away your gun," Jibarn Ahmed called out in Hebrew from behind him. "Do not move."

Herschel tossed aside the Sten. Behind him he could hear Jibarn's approaching footsteps. "I knew you'd come," he said, still kneeling, not turning around. As Herschel spoke, he began unfastening the buttons of his shirt just above his belt buckle. The instrument of his father's death, loosely wrapped in cloth, was in his waistband.

"Being here was not as easy for me as you think, Herschel," Jibarn replied. "My star with the Syrians has fallen since you foiled me in Providence. I'll never understand why that Wilbur Burns turned down my money. I was willing to pay triple what you offered, and Burns a Christian—incomprehensible.''

"You Syrians will lose precisely because you can't understand such things,'' Herschel said, watching as Jibarn's shadow loomed across his father's grave.

"You are a romantic,'' Jibarn chuckled. "So was your father. It led to his undoing and it has led to yours. Besides, I am not Syrian; I am a Palestinian.''

Herschel was about to claim the same for himself, but then he realized it was no longer true. Since the fourteenth of May he had been an Israeli.

He watched Jibarn's shadow move, felt a gun barrel touch the back of his head. His fingers groped for the haft of the dagger. At least the Arab would die with him.

He sensed Jibarn's hesitation. Abruptly the gun barrel moved slightly away. Herschel felt the Arab's hand tentatively touch his shoulder. "My brother,'' Jibarn began, then faltered. "My brother, I—''

Don't be soft, his mother had warned. Herschel didn't wait to make his move. He threw himself sideways, using his strong legs to sweep Jibarn's feet out from under him. As the Arab fell, his revolver discharged and the bullet plowed a furrow across Haim's grave. Before Jibarn could aim and fire a second time, Herschel struck with the knife at Jibarn's chest.

The revolver fell from Jibarn's hand as he sagged across the grave. He rolled face down before settling into stillness. Herschel waited, tense and expectant; it had to be a trick.

But it wasn't. Jibarn Ahmed was dead. Herschel's father had been avenged. Why wasn't he glad? he wondered. Why was his triumph stained by regret?

He rested for several minutes and then turned over the body and began to go through the dead man's pockets for identification. One day it would be time for both sides to account for their dead. He found a small leather folder containing Jibarn's identification papers, some money and a photograph of a woman and a young boy.

Herschel knew that they had to be Jibarn's wife and son. He could hear the embittered, tearful wife now. ''The Jews killed your father. They are the children of death and have made you an orphan, me a widow. You must avenge your father's death, my son. You must kill the Jews.

And so it would go, Herschel thought as he pocketed the leather folder, retrieved his gun and began to make his way back to the position. So it would go.

Herschel returned to the battle.

The sun had been up only a few hours over the airstrip outside Tel Aviv when the air raid sirens began to sound. Danny glanced at the sky, but as yet there was no sign of Spitfires.

''Just a few more minutes,'' he muttered to himself. ''Just a few more—'' He watched as the only three Messerschmitts that could fly were wheeled out of the hangar. He and the other two pilots were in their flying overalls. They had their helmets under their arms. There were no intercoms in the helmets, but that didn't matter since none of the Messerschmitts had a radio.

''We gotta go,'' Danny yelled at the worried-looking crew chief.

''The cannon are malfunctioning,'' the chief argued.

''I knew that was going to happen,'' Danny spat disgustedly. He looked at his fellow pilots. ''I say there's no time to wait. If those Spitfires catch us on the ground—''

''Do the machine guns work?'' one of the pilots asked the chief.

''I hope so.''

''Me too.'' Danny scowled. ''All right, look. I say we go up and do the best we can.''

''I'll have another three ready to go, with cannon and bomb-racks, in an hour,'' the crew chief promised.

"Let's hope this fucking field is still here in an hour," Danny shouted over his shoulder as he ran to his plane.

His fighter was hurtling down the runway, the other two Messerschmitts behind him, when a wave of four Spitfires came in low, just skimming the treetops. They opened up, strafing the field. The Arabs must have spotted the Messerschmitts and panicked, because they immediately jettisoned their bombs in order to increase their agility for the coming dog-fight. The explosions tore up the vacant field bordering the airstrip, but the bombs didn't come close to the hangars sheltering the men and machinery.

Danny hauled back hard on the stick with his right hand and worked the throttle with his left, at last airborne. The second pilot, a Protestant ex-Marine flier named Charlie, made it into the sky as well, but the third was overtaken by a Spitfire while it was still barreling down the runway.

There was nothing anyone could do. Danny watched with a mixture of fascination and horror as the Spitfire peppered it, shattering its canopy. The hapless grounded fighter skidded off the runway over a grassy knoll and then nose-dived into a ditch just before disappearing in billowing flame and smoke.

Danny had the nose of his Messerschmitt tilted toward the heavens, climbing at three thousand feet per minute, desperate to gain the altitude he would need to come down hard on the enemy. Charlie was right beside him, and then on cue he dropped back a little to serve as Danny's wingman. There was no telling how many more enemy planes were in the vicinity, so they began to thatchweave, crossing each other's tail to protect against an ambush from behind as they went after the quartet of Spitfires.

The enemies banked around and tore back toward Tel Aviv and presumably easier pickings. Charlie broke away, wisely circling the air base to protect it against further attacks from other enemy planes.

Danny should stay behind as well, he knew, but he went after the Spitfires. This was, after all, his first chance for combat, and he just couldn't pass it up.

The Spitfires were flying in a ragged line abreast. The pilots on the ends saw him coming and peeled away to intercept him, while the other two went on toward Tel Aviv.

Danny put on throttle and climbed, then pushed his stick forward and dropped like an anvil toward the closest Spitfire. He knew the second was likely fastening on his tail at that very moment, but there was nothing he could do about it, so he decided to concentrate on the one in front of him. His altimeter unwound and speed indicator climbed as he power-dived for his target. He felt calm, completely in his element. He felt immortal and if he did die, it would be all right as long as he died up in the blue in a blaze of light.

The Spitfire floated into the Messerschmitt's gunsight. Danny squeezed the control-stick trigger of his machine guns, wishing he had the use of his wing cannon. The Messerschmitt's twin machine guns chattered away, their recoil slowing his attack dive. The Spitfire looked like it had been sprinkled with fairy dust as his rounds hit home, striking sparks off of its fuselage. White vapor—engine coolant, Danny guessed—began to stream from its cowling as the Spitfire banked steeply, trying to get away. Danny would have followed it, but at that instant his Messerschmitt began to shudder beneath the violent impact of the second enemy's machine guns. Danny hauled on the stick and worked his rudder, trying to slide away, but the bastard stayed on him. Danny glimpsed what looked like fireflies dancing along his wings toward his cockpit and then there were holes in his canopy and something was chewing hard on his left thigh.

His lap filled with blood. He felt faint and fought against a fatal blackout as he roared through the sky, desperately trying to get away from the Spitfire.

Suddenly it was swooping past him. He saw Charlie on its tail, hammering away with his twin guns.

"Get him, get him," Danny yelled, but Charlie peeled off and let the Spitfire escape. The last Danny saw of it, it was on its way back to Cairo, flying low and hard, looking for all the world like a whipped dog with its tail between its legs. Charlie zoomed by and Danny caught a glimpse of his anxious face peering at him. Danny waggled his wings to show that he was okay, sort of, and then brought his fighter around for landing. The Messerschmitt had taken a pummeling, but it landed beautifully. Danny managed to cut his engine before he passed out.

When he woke up they were cutting his trouser leg away. He was lying on a table in the infirmary. Charlie, the crew chief and some of the other pilots were anxiously crowding around as the doctor finished stitching up his leg. It turned out that the bullet had passed clear through his thigh muscle, causing a lot of blood and gore but no crippling damage. Danny would be walking with a cane, but considering the lack of pilots, he would be back on the active roster within the week.

"You should have clobbered that bastard, Charlie," Danny scolded.

"Another time," Charlie smiled. "You did okay, though."

"An unconfirmed kill." Danny wanted to be cool, but he couldn't contain himself. A smile broke through his studied indifference like the sun. "Yeah," he beamed. "I guess I did do okay."

His smile quickly faded as he remembered the third pilot, the one who'd never gotten off the ground. "Max?" he asked. Charlie shook his head.

Danny heard engines revving. "What's going on?"

"Three more fighters," the crew chief proudly announced, "fitted with cannon and bomb racks. They're on their way to Cairo to give the bastards a taste of their own medicine."

"Great."

Charlie said, "I can still hardly believe the two of us ran off four Spitfires."

"That's because they couldn't handle a fair fight," Danny responded. "They thought this war was going to be a turkey shoot. Now that we can shoot back, they'll fade. You'll see." Danny laced his hands behind his head, impatient for the doctor to finish bandaging his leg so he and Charlie could go have themselves a drink and rehash the dogfight. He was elated by his first taste of combat, secure in the knowledge that he had come through it okay. At long last he was a tried and true fighter jock.

"I still say it was a miracle," Charlie insisted.

Danny sighed happily. "This whole country's a miracle."

The battle for the Deganias lasted from dawn until mid-afternoon, when the promised artillery at last arrived at nearby Kinnereth and began to fire on the Syrians. The guns had no aiming devices, and most of the forty or so rounds went wild, but the Syrians were scared anyway. By four o'clock there was no sign of the enemy and the valley was completely quiet.

Herschel and his men held their position on Bet Yerach until the last retreating Syrian troops had passed by them. Then they returned to Degania.

Yol and his mother welcomed Herschel. The buildings and gardens of the kibbtuz had been damaged by the Syrian mortar barrage and there were bodies of fallen comrades still lying where they'd died, but overall the mood was joyous. Buildings could be repaired, and while life was precious, everyone had known there would be deaths if they stood and defended their home. Besides, there were many more Syrians dead than Jews, and the enemy's destroyed tanks were sending up black plumes of smoke that seemed to symbolize the Syrians' ignominious defeat.

"Well?" Yol demanded. "Did you return the dagger to its rightful owner?"

Herschel nodded. "I did." He looked at his mother. "You told me not to be soft, Mama, and I wasn't, but Jibarn Ahmed was. He could have killed me, but he hesitated. At the end, when I killed him, I felt I was killing a part of myself." He shook his head. "Thank God it's over and Degania is safe."

Herschel looked around. "Where's Benny?"

"He's in the infirmary," Yol said. "I'm sorry. It's bad."

"Oh, no." Herschel dropped his gun. "Oh, no."

There were two sections to the infirmary. In one the doctor and nurses worked feverishly to save the wounded. In the other section, toward the back of the building, the hopeless cases were lying on cots, made as comfortable as possible with the limited medical supplies available. This was where Herschel found Benny. His friend was lying with gauze wound around his naked torso. The bandages were soaked through with blood.

Benny smiled weakly as Herschel sat down beside him. "Hey, you get that guy who offed your old man?"

"I got him." Herschel took hold of Benny's hand. "They tell me you were a hero." He forced himself to smile. "You single-handedly took out a tank."

"Piece of cake," Benny said, and then he laughed. "Of course, I was scared shitless!" His laugh became a cough and blood bubbled out of his mouth.

Herschel tore a strip from his own shirttail—there

were no rags or bandages to spare—and wiped Benny's chin clean.

"Listen to me," Benny wheezed. "I'm lung-shot. I ain't got much time. You tell Becky this. Tell her to keep the Dunhill. Everything between us is all squared away." His eyes glowed intensely. "Tell her, Hersch. Promise you will. I know her; in some ways I know her better than you. She'll brood unless you tell her what I said."

Herschel nodded. "She can keep the Dunhill because everything between you two is all squared away. I'll tell her, Benny. I promise."

Benny relaxed. "That's okay, then. Hey, Hersch? I could sure use a smoke. They always go out with a smoke in the movies."

"I'm sorry, Benny. I have no cigarettes. I don't think there are any in Degania. The shortages—"

"Yeah, yeah." Benny squeezed Herschel's hand. "Don't you mind. It's just the story of my life."

A few minutes later he faded into unconsciousness. For the next four hours Herschel sat by him until he died.

That evening Herschel and a platoon of soldiers traveled by truck with Moshe Dayan to the nearby village of Zemkah, which had been the Syrians' stronghold in the area. They found abandoned vehicles and weapons but not one Syrian. The entire invading army had vanished.

Dayan threw back his head and roared with laughter. "Look! Look! We have had only to bang once on a tin plate, and the enemy has scattered like birds."

Epilogue

Israel, 1949

"Becky!" Herschel's voice reverberated against the walls of the hangar that was the main building of Lod Airport. As Becky turned, dimly aware of the boyish khaki-clad customs officer beaming at her, she thought she would not look at Herschel, that her eyes would tell her nothing about him. He had lived through too much.

"Becky!"

She ran to Herschel laughing and crying as he caught her up in his arms and spun her around. He kissed her and she knew at once that their love was as strong as ever.

"Hey, Becky." Danny was grinning at her. She hugged him, and then all three, arms entwined, walked to the front entrance of the airport, where Herschel's car was waiting.

There was much for her to learn and much she already knew from Herschel's letters. Herschel was an officer in the army, in charge of munitions development. Several modifications had been made in his gun design. It looked as if the weapon was going to fulfill its promise.

Danny worked for the air transport program. Herschel had lent him the money to purchase several old cargo planes, and now Danny and his partners—a group of the pilots who had flown some of the country's first fighters together—had a company of their own.

"You haven't heard the latest," Danny was saying. "Me and the guys are going to start building planes here." He winked. "Not bad for your little brother, huh?"

Becky laughed. "Now all you need is to find a girl and settle down."

"Well, maybe I'll just wait to see how marriage works out for you two."

Becky colored. "Nobody's asked me."

"If they did, would you say yes?" Herschel demanded.

She nodded, and Herschel beamed and kissed her again. She said, "I love you, and I'm so happy."

"You know we must live here?"

She nodded. "I thought about it on the plane. Philip Cooper has always stood by me. Together the two of us control the majority of stock in Pickman's. He's allowed me to be president, and now I intend to repay the favor by letting him have a chance at the job." She giggled. "Maybe I'll start a Pickman's branch here in Israel. You all can't wear khaki forever."

"First we'll start a family," Herschel insisted.

"First a family," she agreed.

"Hey," Danny cut in, "tell her about the portrait."

"Don't spoil the surprise," Herschel replied.

"What are you talking about?" Becky demanded. "What surprise?"

"You'll see it, but not until tomorrow, when we drive out to Degania," Herschel said. "There you'll meet my mother and Yol, and you'll see what we're talking about. It's a portrait of two men. My father brought it from Russia. Tell me, Becky—your own father, he's well?"

"Why, yes."

"Good." Danny chuckled. "Man, I can't wait to see Pop's face when he gets here."

"Oh, I don't think he'll make the trip, Danny."

"I think he will," Danny said, his eyes gleaming. "You'll understand later. When I visited Herschel at Degania and he showed it to me, I felt like I was dreaming. You'll understand everything when you see the portrait."

"I want your father to meet my mother. I want us all to have a most joyous reunion—"

"Hey," Danny complained, "now *you're* going to give it away."

"All right," Herschel laughed. "No more about it until tomorrow."

They went out to the car, Becky happier than she could ever have imagined possible. She'd promised her husband-to-be that there would be children, but once they were born—

She was, after all, her father's daughter, and this country would need a decent department store.